EVERYMAN'S LIBRARY

EVERYMAN,
I WILL GO WITH THEE,
AND BE THY GUIDE,
IN THY MOST NEED
TO GO BY THY SIDE

JOHN MILTON

The Complete English Poems

Edited and introduced by Gordon Campbell

EVERYMAN'S LIBRARY

97

This book is one of 250 volumes in Everyman's Library
which have been distributed to 4500 state schools
throughout the United Kingdom.
The project has been supported by a grant of £4 million
from the Millennium Commission.

First included in Everyman's Library, 1909
This edition first published 1980, revised 1990
Editing, Introduction, Bibliography and Chronology © David
Campbell Publishers Ltd., 1992
Typography by Peter B. Willberg

ISBN 1-85715-097-X

A CIP catalogue record for this book is available from the
British Library

Published by David Campbell Publishers Ltd.,
Gloucester Mansions, 140A Shaftesbury Avenue,
London WC2H 8HD

Distributed by Random House (UK) Ltd.,
20 Vauxhall Bridge Road, London SW1V 2SA

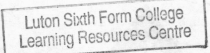

CONTENTS

JOHN MILTON

CONTENTS

TRANSLATIONS

vii

JOHN MILTON

INTRODUCTION

Milton is the most learned poet in the English literary tradition, and it is remarkable that the weight of his erudition did not crush his genius for writing poetry. In some of Milton's early Latin poems an excess of allusion leads one to suspect a rather self-conscious attitude to learning on the part of the poet, but by the time Milton had emerged from his years as a primarily Latin poet at the age of twenty-one, he was capable of writing poems in which his gifts as a poet are untrammelled by his learning. Milton was a learned poet, but he did not write learned poems. His poems contain very few allusions that would not be instantly understood by any seventeenth-century reader. Some of the minor poems of his youth are addressed to a university audience, but the poems of his maturity are not addressed to a highly educated audience. Anyone who had enjoyed a grammar school education would be able to read his Latin poems with ease and pleasure, and would be able to respond directly to the classical and Biblical allusions embodied in his English poems without recourse to learned footnotes.

Milton's earliest dated poems are his paraphrases of Psalms CXIV and CXXXVI. In a headnote to the poems in the 1645 collection Milton explains that they 'were done by the Author at fifteen years old'. Milton was fifteen in 1624, and was completing his final year as a pupil at St Paul's School in London. In that year he had begun his formal study of the Hebrew language and the Psalter, and he doubtless consulted the Hebrew text as well as the Greek and Latin versions of the psalms. The singing of psalms was an important part of Protestant congregational and domestic worship, and many Protestants published translations and paraphrases of the psalms in metres suitable for singing. Indeed, Milton's own father, who was a gifted amateur composer, had set some psalms to music for Ravenscroft's Psalter of 1621. The quality of Milton's paraphrases is not exceptional, but they are valuable in that they embody in a simple form some of the features that were later to characterize some of his greatest poems. Although he regarded every word of the original Hebrew texts as literally inspired by God, Milton felt free to elaborate many of the phrases of the Hebrew originals. The hand of Joshua Sylvester lies heavily on some of these embellishments, but one can none the less see in them something of Milton's own tastes. His use of the phrases 'Pharian fields' and 'Erythraean main' to refer to Egypt and the Red Sea, for example, indicates a nascent sense of the rhetorical advantages to be reaped from the use of classical place-names.

Most of the poems which Milton wrote while an undergraduate at Cambridge were composed in Latin. The choice of Latin as a literary medium was not at all unusual, for Latin composition formed part of the education of every school-boy and undergraduate. The fact that many of Milton's poems are written in Latin is not a mark of any exceptional learning on his part, but is symptomatic of the literary conventions of an age more learned than our own. Throughout Milton's years as a Latin poet he nourished ambitions to write in his native tongue. One of the earliest and most remarkable outpourings of this ambition occurs in *At a Vacation Exercise*, which Milton recited to the undergraduates of Christ's College in July 1628. The poem begins as a light-hearted address to Milton's native language, which was to be the medium of the satirical play which follows Milton's poem. In the course of this poem Milton digresses to announce that he aspires to use his native language for more exalted purposes:

> Yet I had rather, if I were to choose,
> Thy service in some graver subject use,
> Such as may make thee search thy coffers round,
> Before thou clothe my fancy in fit sound.

The tone of the ensuing description of Milton's poetical ambition is delicately poised, for it is at once a serious catalogue of ambitions and a nimble display of poetic virtuosity.

The first poem in which Milton achieved the greatness to which he aspired was his ode *On the Morning of Christ's Nativity*.

INTRODUCTION

At the end of *Elegia sexta* Milton explained to his friend Charles Diodati that he had written a poem as a birthday gift for Jesus. The context of this remark suggests that Milton may have seen the *Nativity Ode* as the first serious poem of a man who had dedicated his life to the composition of heroic poetry. The *Nativity Ode* was Milton's first English poem on a religious theme, and in order to indicate its importance in his spiritual and poetic development he placed it first in his 1645 and 1673 *Poems*.

The *Nativity Ode* partakes of a tradition that originates with Virgil's *Eclogue* IV, the 'Messianic' Eclogue, which associates the birth of a child with the return of the Golden Age in the reign of Augustus. The use of pastoral imagery in a poem which celebrates the birth of a child was congenial to Christian thought, in which Christ was the Good Shepherd. In Christian poetry Christ was commonly compared to Pan the guardian of sheep.

Milton refers to his poem as an ode (line 24), and it has long been known as the *Nativity Ode*, though this was not Milton's title. The term 'ode' would suggest to Milton the poems of Pindar, Anacreon and Horace. The canon of Pindar and Anacreon in Milton's time was slightly different from the modern canon, for new poems have been rediscovered and many others re-attributed, and the differences in structure, tone, and style that distinguish the works of these three poets would have seemed even sharper to Milton than they do to a modern reader. The form of Milton's poem does not descend from the odes of any of these three poets. On the contrary, Milton takes advantage of the diversity of the ancient tradition and creates a new form that suits his own poetic temperament.

Much of the power of the poem derives from Milton's concern to transcend the details of the nativity in order to assert the significance of the event. The image of the smiling baby in stanza XVI, for example, dissolves into a reminder of his destiny, for the baby is the Christ

That on the bitter cross
Must redeem our loss.

For Milton the importance of the nativity was that it consti-tuted the essential prerequisite to the redemption of our loss. Milton's imagination seemed to respond more easily to an event highly charged with future significance than to the future event itself. When in *The Passion* he tried to contemplate the redemptive act directly, he was unable to complete the poem. In the *Nativity Ode* Milton succeeds because he concen-trates on an event distanced from the redemption. He was to repeat this success in a modest way in *Upon the Circumcision*, for he was able to seize on the theological significance of the circumcision: the shedding of the blood of the infant Christ was the first act in the passion, and prefigured the day when

> Huge pangs and strong
> Will pierce more near his heart.

The companion poems *L'Allegro* and *Il Penseroso* must be counted among the finest poems of Milton's youth. Com-panion poems were popular in the late sixteenth and early seventeenth centuries. It should be remembered that the second poem in the pair was not always written at the same time, or even by the same person, as the first poem. Marlowe's *Passionate Shepherd to his Love*, for example, was written as an autonomous poem, and later Ralegh wrote a companion poem, *The Nymph's Reply to the Shepherd*. Marlowe's poem concludes with the couplet

> If these delights thy mind may move,
> Then live with me and be my love

and Ralegh's with a similar couplet. These invitations are clearly the originals of the couplets which conclude Milton's poems.

L'Allegro, or a portion of it, may have been written as an independent poem, though attempts to argue this hypothesis on prosodic grounds have proved inconclusive. If, however, *Il Penseroso* does represent a later stage in Milton's poetic development, then it would seem fitting to view the thought in the poems as progressing from *L'Allegro* to *Il Penseroso* rather than to see the points of view as two carefully-balanced alternatives. There are many exact parallels between the poems: the metre of *Il Penseroso* imitates that of *L'Allegro*, the preludes are similar, and the catalogues of pleasures contain many exact oppositions. On the other hand there are some indications that *Il Penseroso* has the upper hand. In the ten-line preludes to the poems, for example, one notes that whilst the deluding joys banished by *Il Penseroso* bear some resemblance to the joys celebrated in *L'Allegro*, the melancholy banished by *L'Allegro* is of a different kind from that celebrated by *Il Penseroso*. *Il Penseroso* welcomes the melancholy of Aristotle and Ficino, who associated it with an artistic or philosophical temperament, but *L'Allegro* condemns the melancholy of Galen and Burton, who associated it with a medical imbalance causing torpor, madness, and fear. A similar weighting of the scales in favour of *Il Penseroso* is evident in the final movements of the poems, for not only is *Il Penseroso* longer, but it also concludes with a religious experience that has no parallel in the earlier poem.

A Masque Presented at Ludlow Castle, which since the late seventeenth century has been known as *Comus*, was performed before the Earl of Bridgewater and his guests on 29 September 1634. Although both Milton and Lawes termed *Comus* a masque, it is not a representative Stuart masque, as a comparison with Jonson's masques or the masques incorporated in Shakespeare's plays makes readily apparent. *Comus* is not alone among masques in absorbing into its fabric elements from related forms such as the moral interlude and the pastoral play, but the dominance of dramatic dialogue over the music and spectacle is unusual in a play that retains so many of the traditional features of the masque. The journey to Ludlow in *Comus* reflects the processional element in traditional masques. The element of compliment in court masques is presented indirectly in *Comus* through a portrayal of the virtue of Lord Bridgewater's children, who at the dramatic climax of the masque are presented to the Earl and Countess as 'three fair branches of your own'; the virtue of the children is a compliment to their parents.

The subject of *Comus* is virtue. As virtue in women was thought to manifest itself in chastity, which for an unmarried woman meant virginity, and as the central character in the play is the Lady, Milton's exposition of virtue is couched in terms of chastity and virginity. While Comus is on the stage virtue is tested; this portion of the play constitutes Milton's first dramatic exposition of the theme of temptation, a theme to which he was to return in *Paradise Lost*, *Paradise Regained*, and *Samson Agonistes*. When Comus is replaced by Sabrina – the parts may have been played by the same actor – chastity is celebrated rather than tested, and becomes a positive virtue rather than an inhibiting one. The dramatic realization of this aspect of virtue is reserved until the end of the masque, but Milton had allowed the Lady to articulate the positive aspect of chastity in her first speech:

> O welcome pure-eyed Faith, white-handed Hope,
> Thou hovering angel girt with golden wings,
> And thou unblemished form of Chastity!

The mention of faith and hope in line 213 naturally leads Milton's readers or listeners to expect a description of charity. Milton skilfully prolongs the expectation by spending his next line on a visual image of hope, and at the end of line 215 suddenly fulfils the anticipation of charity with a presentation of chastity. The effect of this paranomasia is an alteration in the meaning of chastity. The word normally carries the suggestion of a withholding or suppressing of natural desires in the interests of a lofty ideal, and later in the poem Comus exploits this negative idea of chastity. The Lady's speech anticipates these arguments by forcefully conjoining charity and chastity, and so removes the stigma of withholding from chastity, which becomes an image of love. The Lady has transformed chastity into a positive virtue which represents the giving of love rather than its denial.

The greatest of Milton's minor poems is *Lycidas*, which is justly regarded as one of the finest poems in the English language. *Lycidas* was first published in a collection of poems commemorating the death of Edward King, a Fellow of Christ's College. Milton had probably not known King well, but was none the less deeply moved by his premature death. Milton's poem originated in a desire to lament this specific death, but in the act of composition Milton transcended his ostensible subject to produce a meditation on personal mortality that retains the power to move readers centuries after King and his mourners have turned to dust.

Lycidas is a pastoral elegy, a form that was absorbed into the literary tradition in the third century BC when Theocritus composed his lament for Daphnis (*Idyll* I). The authors of *Lament for Adonis* and *Lament for Bion* (traditionally attributed to Bion and Moschus respectively) sustained the tradition in Greek poetry, and Virgil imitated Theocritus' *Idyll* I in his *Eclogue* X. The pastoral elegy was a popular form in the late Middle Ages and the Renaissance, and even in the nineteenth century the pastoral elegy was chosen by Shelley for *Adonais* and by Arnold for *Thyrsis*, their laments for Keats and Clough.

In pastoral elegy the poet and his subject are described as shepherds or goatherds. As the form evolved it became increasingly distanced from shepherd life in ancient Sicily. Virgil elevated the style of pastoral elegy and included in it personal and public comments unrelated to the death of the person represented as a shepherd. Christian writers of the late Middle Ages and the Renaissance seized on the joyous conclusion of Virgil's *Eclogue* V as a model for the Christian consolation at the end of their elegies. In the Renaissance pastoral these innovations were combined with traditional features such as the procession of mourners and the lament of nature, and with features that had appeared in other pastoral poems, such as the ecclesiastical satire in the eclogues of Petrarch (VI and VII) and Mantuan (IX). The pastoral elegy was established in England by Spenser in the November eclogue of the *Shepherd's Calendar* and in *Astrophel*, his lament for Sidney. *Lycidas* is firmly rooted in the tradition of pastoral elegy and displays many of its characteristic features. Milton was not bound by the tradition – he omitted, for example, the refrain which was a prominent feature of ancient pastoral elegies – but drew on it to shape and temper his emotions and poetical impulses.

The composition of a lament for Edward King prompted Milton to reflect on the meaning and purpose of human life. King was a young man who had shared with Milton the experience of the same tutor in the same college, who had shared Milton's commitment to the Protestant faith, and who, like Milton, had published a few poems. King's premature death called into question Milton's ambition to become a great Christian poet:

> Alas! What boots it with uncessant care
> To tend the homely slighted shepherd's trade,
> And strictly meditate the thankless muse?

Lycidas is a quest for an answer to that question. At the beginning of the poem Milton's imagination is constrained by the thought of his own death:

> So may some gentle muse
> With lucky words favour my destined urn,
> And as he passes turn,
> And bid fair peace be to my sable shroud.

At this moment the poem is saved from what seems an inevitable plunge into self-pity by the impersonality of the pastoral mode. Milton gradually transcends not only the death of King but also the brutal reminder of his own mortality that King's death afforded. At its most profound level the poem considers the purpose of human existence and effort in a world in which evil is allowed to flourish and virtuous men like King are allowed to die. Milton's characteristic integrity of mind prevents him from accepting the platitudinous assurances of Phoebus, and from acquiescing in the consolation offered by the ceremony of throwing poetical flowers on the hearse of Lycidas. Consolation finally comes with the realization that Lycidas 'is not dead', for he is experiencing the inexpressible joy of heaven and as the 'genius of the shore' is continuing to minister to mankind as he did on earth. Milton's calm of mind is restored, and his detachment from his grief is marked by a change of poetic voice in the last stanza of the poem. Milton is reconciled to mortality, and has summoned up the strength to enter 'fresh woods, and pastures new'.

In 1641 and 1642 Milton published his five anti-episcopal pamphlets, and so began his career as a writer of prose. In 1644 he published the two prose tracts that continue to attract a readership beyond professional students of Milton: *Of Educa-tion and Areopagitica*. *Of Education* takes the form of a public letter to Milton's friend Samuel Hartlib, who had asked Milton to set out his views on the ways in which education should be reformed. Some educational reformers were addressing issues such as the education of women and the possibility of making education available to all; others were concerned with primary education and professional training. Milton chose to concentrate on the education desirable for young gentlemen who were destined to hold high public office. There was a long tradition of educational writing on this theme, and in the seventeenth century such books as James Cleland's *Hρωπαιδεία, or the Institution of a Young Nobleman* (1607) and Henry Peacham's *The Complete Gentleman* had explored the same issue. Milton's choice of subject constituted a muted repudiation of the views of John Amos Comenius, the Moravian educational reformer who had visited England in the winter of 1641-2. Comenius wanted to establish a system of state schools in order to educate all children, without respect to class or gender. Hartlib was the chief English disciple of Comenius, and had published at his own expense many of the tracts that he had commissioned from Milton's contemporaries. The fact that Milton's tract was not pub-lished by Hartlib may indicate that Hartlib was not pleased with Milton's studied dismissal of Comenius in *Of Education*: Milton was unashamedly concerned with the education of the governing class. To the modern reader the strenuous demands that Milton proposes to make on these adolescent boys may seem unrealistic. In fact his programme of reading derives from his practical experience as a teacher responsible for the education of his two young nephews. In 1694 the elder nephew, Edward Phillips, published a biography of his uncle that included an account (here printed as an appendix) of the programme of education to which he and his brother had been subjected. Phillips names twenty-one authors, fourteen of whom reappear as recommended authors in Milton's tract.

Later in 1644 Milton published *Areopagitica*, a belated response to the Licensing Order of June 1643 (here printed as an appendix) according to which all books had to be examined by a censor before publication. Milton sought to oppose this Order by associating its principles and procedures with censorship in Catholic countries (especially Spain) and with the Star Chamber Decree of July 1637, to which the Order bears many resemblances. The Star Chamber was detested by Puritans because it had been used extensively by Charles I to maintain his royal authority during the years of his personal rule, and in July 1641 it had been dissolved by the Long Parliament. In *Areopagitica* Milton accused Parliament of reviving the oppressive measures of the Star Chamber Decree. In the short term Milton ws unsuccessful, in that Parliament ignored his plea; in later centuries, however, *Areopagitica* came to be regarded as the most eloquent defence in English of religious toleration and the right to publish without prior censorship.

In the course of the next three years Milton published four tracts in defence of divorce; in 1649 he was appointed Secretary for Foreign Tongues to the Council of State, and his formidable abilities as a pamphleteer were turned to the defence of the Commonwealth, and in particular to the defence of the execution of Charles I. Milton continued to defend his republican principles until the eve of the Restoration in 1660. During these two decades of pamphleteering Milton continually reminded his readers of his plans to write a national epic. But his only finished English poems composed during this period are his sonnets.

Milton's sonnets constitute an important contribution to the English sonnet tradition. Sometimes his subject so inflamed his imagination that his sonnets achieved greatness. In *Sonnet* XVIII his horror at the barbarity of the recent massacre in Piedmont is condensed into an explosive sonnet; in *Sonnet* XIX, on the other hand, quiet reflection on his blindness has impelled him to write a sonnet that begins in despair and frustration and rises to a sense of spiritual calmness that recalls the ending of *Lycidas*.

Milton's English predecessors in the art of the sonnet had developed conventions that had originated in Petrarch's sonnets and then been modified by poets adapting the form to their own purposes. Shakespeare, for example, turned the

Petrarchan sestet into a third quatrain and an independently rhymed couplet. Milton continued this tradition of innovation, but experimented with one eye on Italian poets (particularly Giovanni Della Casa) who had attempted similar variations. Like these Italian poets, Milton sometimes chose to blur the distinction between octave and sestet by making both sense and syntax continuous between the eighth and ninth lines. The fluidity and continuity of thought which Milton is able to achieve by allowing his sentences to come to a natural conclusion remind one of the style of Shakespeare's last plays, in which the sense flows from line to line with scarcely any end-stopping. Milton's poetry similarly flourished when he over-rode the constraints of form. The exploration of this freedom is an important element in the poetic accomplishment of *Paradise Lost*, in which, as Milton explains in his prefatory note on the verse (p. 148), 'the sense [is] variously drawn out from one verse into another'.

Paradise Lost represented for Milton the fulfilment of two aspirations. He had for several decades wanted to write an epic, and for a similar length of time had wanted to re-create the story of the fall of man. Originally these were separate projects; the epic was to be an Arthuriad, and the exposition of the fall of man was to be a tragedy. Disenchantment about the historicity of Arthur gradually led to the abandonment of the plan to write an Arthurian epic, and the two projects merged into the composition of an epic which dealt with the tragedy of the fall of man. The decision to explore his chosen theme in an epic rather than a tragedy gave Milton licence to range over vast tracts of human experience. Thus the poem extends chronologically from the exaltation of the Son (V 575 ff.) before the creation of the universe through human history to the second coming of the Son (XII 458–65) Geographically the poem ranges over the entire world, and Milton delights in cataloguing place-names culled from contemporary atlases, the Bible and Biblical commentaries, and the works of classical antiquity. Two of the competing cosmologies of the seventeenth century are incorporated into the poem, and Milton has also invented splendid prelapsarian versions of both the Ptolemaic and Copernican cosmologies.

The presence of these two competing theories of the universe is suggestive of the public nature of the poem. Milton did not use the poem as a vehicle for his own opinions, but allowed it to voice the range of opinions represented in Protestant England. Thus when the poem approaches controversial issues of theology, Milton set aside his own theological opinions (which he expresses elsewhere in his systematic theology, *De Doctrina Christiana*) in favour of a public statement phrased in the language of the Bible. In Book III, for example, God the Father explains his position regarding election to salvation and damnation (ll. 173–90). Some critics have claimed that the passage is wholly Calvinistic, others have found it to be uncompromisingly Arminian, and still others have seen it as an attempt to tread a middle way between these extremes. This ambiguity suggests that God's words were not meant to endorse any particular doctrine. On the contrary, the fact that Milton has grounded virtually every phrase on the Scriptures would enable every seventeenth-century reader to respond to the passage in accordance with the doctrinal interpretation he gave to the Biblical passages which underlie it. The freedom of interpretation which the Biblical texture of the language allows the reader recalls the insistence of Milton and his contemporaries on the freedom of the individual to interpret the Bible under the guidance of the Spirit. In the invocations to *Paradise Lost* Milton makes it clear that he thinks of his poem as divinely inspired, and it is therefore fitting that he encourage in his readers the Protestant virtue of individual interpretation.

The Bible and Biblical commentaries account for much of the substance of the poem; the form of the poem, however, is that of classical epic. The ten books of the first edition of *Paradise Lost* recall Milton's original intention to present the story as a tragedy, for the ten books comprise five acts of two books each. In the second edition Milton divided the poem into twelve books in imitation of classical epic, particularly Virgil's *Aeneid*. The debt to classical epic extends far beyond this structural imitation, for *Paradise Lost* almost continuously alludes to incidents in the epics of Homer and Virgil. Milton attempts to renovate the epic tradition, and he does so by

setting his own poem firmly within that tradition, and then
distinguishing it from its predecessors. At the beginning of
Book IX Milton announces that his subject will be the tragedy
of the fall, and asserts that this theme is 'not less but more
heroic' than the subjects of the epics of Homer and Virgil.

In *Paradise Lost* Milton attempts to

> assert eternal providence,
> And justify the ways of God to men.   (I 25–6).

A reading of the narrative of the fall in Books IX and X might
lead one to conclude that Milton's actual purpose was the
opposite of his stated purpose, for in those books Milton's
exquisite portrayal of the motives and reactions of Adam and
Eve seems to constitute an attempt to justify the ways of men
to God. In the first eight books, however, Milton educates the
reader in the values which must be brought to bear on the
tragedy of Adam and Eve. The clearest statement of these
values occurs in Book III, in which Milton boldly presents
God the Father and God the Son as dramatic characters. The
Son volunteers to redeem mankind, and at the conclusion of
his speech the narrator says

> His words here ended; but his meek aspéct
> Silent yet spake, and breathed immortal love
> To mortal men, above which only shone
> Filial obedience: as a sacrifice
> Glad to be offered, he attends the will
> Of his great Father.   (III 266–71)

In this passage Milton asserts the pre-eminence of obedience
over love, and so establishes a priority of values which informs
the action of Book IX, where the fallen Eve presents Adam's
temptation as a 'glorious trial of exceeding love' (961). There
is an apparent similarity between the Son's willingness to die
for mankind, and Adam's willingness to die for Eve, but the
values of Book III make it clear that the similarity is an
illusion. The Son's act entailed obedience; Adam's, disobe-
dience. The Son's act was heroic; Adam's had only the illusion

xxi

of heroism. The Son's sacrifice has shown the reader a truly heroic act.

The reader has also been prepared for Adam's falsely heroic pose, for in the first two books of the poem Milton presents Satan, the master of illusory heroism. The seventeenth-century reader shared with Milton an unshakeable conviction of the total and irredeemable depravity of Satan. This conviction underlies Milton's description of Satan in heroic terms in the opening books of the poem. The falseness of his heroism becomes more apparent as the poem progresses, and the last illusions are shattered in Book IV, where the imagery deployed to describe Satan is bestial, and he is variously compared to such animals as a wolf (183), a cormorant (196), a lion (402), a tiger (403), and a toad (800). Although the first four animals are capable of heroic representation, in the pastoral world of Eden they are animals of rapine; and it is difficult to imagine an heroic toad.

The justification of God's ways must of course extend beyond an account of the fall of man to an affirmation of his redemption. In the first sentence of the poem Milton had linked the fall with man's eventual restoration by 'one greater man', and as the narrative progresses the Son's presence is increasingly felt in the poem. At the earliest point in the poem the Son is exalted, and this exaltation initiates the action of the poem, for Satan reacts with envy and malice (V 662-6). In Book VI Milton organizes his account of the war in heaven so that its climax is the heroic intervention of the Son. Similarly, the account of creation in Book VII culminates in a celebration of the Son as creator. The centrality of the Son in the poem is the reason that it does not end with the description of the immediate consequences of the fall in Book X. Books XI and XII show how the fall leads to the redemptive act of the Son by presenting a series of visions which demonstrate to Adam and the reader the historical effects of the fall and prefigure man's eventual restoration. In Book XII Adam learns that the ultimate effect of the fall will be the triumph of the Son, and suddenly realizes that God will turn the evil of the fall into an instrument of his greater glory. Adam's impulse to repent of his sin is now mingled with an urge to

                    rejoice
          Much more that much more good thereof shall spring –
          To God more glory, more good-will to men
          From God – and over wrath grace shall abound.

                                                    (XII 475–8)

The loss of Paradise is the cause of 'all our woe', but it also
prompts God's exercise of grace and leads to his greater
glorification, which is the ultimate justification of his myster-
ious ways.

   The texture of *Paradise Lost* is remarkable for its suppleness,
which derives from its syntactical range and the nature of its
vocabulary. One of the most remarkable aspects of its syntacti-
cal flexibility is the recurrent use of double syntax. Thus in the
first line of the poem – 'Of man's first disobedience, and the
fruit' – the word 'fruit' seems at first to be connected with
'disobedience', and to mean 'result', but as one reads on it
becomes apparent that 'fruit' is grammatically connected to
'Of that forbidden tree'. The last word in a line often acts as a
syntactical pivot, completing one grammatical sequence and
initiating another. The vocabulary of the poem is similarly
fluid, for although the contemporary English meaning of a
word is almost inevitably the primary meaning, the etymolo-
gical sense of a word – usually Latin but sometimes Greek or
Hebrew – often contributes a secondary meaning. Thus in
Book IX 'sapience' means 'wisdom', but retains an etymologi-
cal connection with 'taste' (IX 442, 797, 1018).

   Paradise Lose portrays the disobedience of Adam in yielding
to temptation; *Paradise Regained* portrays the obedience of the
Son, the second Adam, in resisting temptation. This exact
correspondence in subject is not matched by a similarity in
style or scope. Some indication of the nature of the differences
between the poems may be gleaned from the preface to the
second book of *Reason of Church-Government* (1641), in which
Milton mentions his ambition to write an epic, and dis-
tinguishes 'diffuse' epics such as Homer's *Iliad* and *Odyssey*,
Virgil's *Aeneid*, and Tasso's *Gerusalemme Liberata*, from 'brief'
epics such as 'the book of *Job*'. Milton was not predicting the
composition of *Paradise Lost* and *Paradise Regained*, but was

simply elaborating Aristotle's distinction between a brief epic with an abrupt ending and a lengthier epic in which the subject is diffuse, or 'watery' (*Poetics* xxvi). In the event Milton's epic did conform to this distinction, and *Paradise Regained* became Milton's brief epic. The structure of *Paradise Regained* is carefully shaped to provide a dramatic climax to the poem. Medieval and Renaissance artistic and theological presentations of the temptation had traditionally followed the order of temptation as presented in Matthew iv, in which Jesus' first temptation is to turn stones into bread, his second to cast himself down from the pinnacle of the temple, and his third to worship Satan in exchange for the kingdoms of the world. Milton chose to follow instead the order outlined in Luke iv, in which the second and third temptations are reversed, thus enabling him to finish his poem with the climactic episode of the pinnacle. Milton chose to follow Matthew, however, in placing all the temptations after the forty days of fasting, and thus transformed brevity into intensity. He also interpolated two temptations of his own devising into the series – the banquet and the storm – and greatly elaborated the temptation of the kingdoms.

Milton divides the temptation of the kingdoms into a series of related temptations, and the Son's responses to two of these may seem puzzling to the modern reader. At the beginning of Book III Satan tempts the Son with glory. Jesus replies that glory is merely the people's praise, and then remarks

And what the people but a herd confused,
A miscellaneous rabble, who extol
Things vulgar, and well weighed, scarce worth the praise?

Milton's Jesus has little in common with the sentimentalized figure of more recent centuries, and he here reflects an attitude that has since gone out of fashion. Milton's political radicalism did not extend to an enthusiasm for popular democracy, and he shared with many of his contemporaries a disdain for the multitude. The undemocratic remarks of Milton's Jesus would have seemed quite unexceptionable to Milton's seventeenth-century readers.

The second puzzling response is the Son's reply to the

temptation of wisdom, which Satan illustrates by reference to Athens (IV 221-84). Jesus replies with a breath-taking denunciation of the accomplishments of ancient Greece (ll. 285-364). One of the central civilizing forces in Milton's life had been his close study of the literature and philosophy of classical antiquity, and it does seem odd that his Jesus should articulate barbarian sentiments with such ferocity. Milton was aware, however, that the historical Jesus had good reason to be anti-Hellenic, and his fictional Jesus compares Roman violations of the Temple and the Law to the earlier abominations of Antiochus IV (III 160-3). The forced Hellenization of Judea which Antiochus had inaugurated was still government policy at the time of Jesus. The fact that the historical element in Milton's portrayal of Jesus probably lies behind Jesus' remarks does not, however, entitle one to drive a wedge between Milton's own attitudes and those of his fictional Jesus, for Milton would not allow his Jesus to articulate ideas which Milton thought perverse. The judgement that the literature of Greece is 'unworthy to compare/With Zion's songs, to all true tastes excelling' (IV 346-7) does seem perverse to a modern reader, but it should be remembered that for Milton and his contemporaries 'true tastes' were those tempered by the conviction that Hebrew literature was 'from God inspired'. One must also respect the fact that the judgement of Milton's generation was based on a reading of both literatures in the original languages.

Samson Agonistes was Milton's third dramatic poem. In his youth he had written *Arcades* and *Comus*, both of which are indebted to the masque tradition and accordingly partake of the masque convention of the delayed journey. When Milton returned to poetic drama to write *Samson* (at an unknown date) he again incorporated an interrupted journey into the fabric of his poem, but transformed the outward journey of the masque into an interior journey, Samson's progress towards spiritual regeneration.

Samson Agonistes is a play about an episode in Hebrew history written by a Christian in the style of Greek drama. The extraordinary result of this blend of Hellenism, Hebraism, and Christianity is a play in which these elements coalesce with a minimum of compromise. Of the three elements Christianity is probably the most difficult for the modern reader to recognize, but an encounter with the tough-minded Jesus of *Paradise Regained* (which appeared in the same volume as *Samson Agonistes*) helps one to appreciate the nature of the Christian elements in Milton's play. Milton's Jesus was not a pacifist: he 'came not to send peace, but a sword'. The Jesus of *Paradise Regained* would have viewed the death of the Philistines at the end of *Samson Agonistes* with satisfaction. The fact that some Philistine lords could be described by Manoa as generous, civil, and magnanimous (ll. 1467–70) would not have muddied the moral water for a seventeenth-century Christian reader: worshippers of Dagon must die. If the ending of the play now seems to be a celebration of primitive savagery, that is because our sensibility has changed in the three centuries since Milton wrote the play.

In the seventeenth century the Old Testament was thought to be not only a record of historical events, but also a foreshadowing of New Testament events. The tradition which represented Samson as a type of Jesus originated with Ambrose in the fourth century, and by Milton's time was highly diffuse. Milton draws no specific parallels between Samson and Jesus, so it would be incautious to argue that Milton has shaped details of specific episodes, such as the death of Samson, to remind us of parallels in the life of Jesus. On the other hand one must remember that Milton shared with his contemporaries the belief that in some sense the life of Samson prefigured that of Jesus, and that Milton's contemporaries would read the poem with this parallel in mind. To the modern reader the Hebraic element seems irreconcilable with Christianity; Milton's seventeenth-century readers would not have sensed a gulf between the Hebraic and Christian elements.

Milton's play is modelled on the tragedies of ancient Greece. But like Racine, who was at the height of his powers when Milton published *Samson Agonistes*, Milton used the traditional form of Greek drama to create highly original art. Racine and Milton both made their characters more self-conscious than the characters of antiquity, though Milton checked this modernizing tendency to some extent by limiting Samson's intelligence (ll. 52, 207), and both authors concentrate their attention on the debilitating effects of passion in a way that recalls the intellectual temper of the authors' backgrounds more readily than the attitudes implied in ancient Greek drama.

For a reader accustomed to Shakespearian tragedy, Samson's absence in the last scene of the play may seem strange. In English Renaissance tragedy the hero dies on stage, often amidst a litter of bodies. In Greek tragedy the hero leaves the stage before the final scene and is replaced by a messenger (often played by the same actor) who reports the fate of the hero. The description of Samson's death in the Book of Judges does not readily lend itself to presentation on the stage, but it is easily accommodated to the convention of Greek tragedy.

The conventions of Greek drama were admirably suited to Milton's purposes. The fate that dominates Greek tragedy becomes for Samson the promise that he will deliver 'Israel from Philistian yoke' (39). Greek fate would have been readily translated into Christian providence by Milton's contemporary readers, and his Puritan readers would have believed, with Milton, that they had a sacred obligation to search themselves for indications of God's plan for their lives. Samson's cast of mind would not have seemed remote. Because the audience of a Greek play knew at the outset how fate was going to direct the course of a play, the playwrights of antiquity could make full use of dramatic irony. Milton's readers were similarly familiar with God's plan for the life of Samson, and Milton follows the ancients by imbuing his play with dramatic irony. In Milton's case this irony does not entirely replace narrative suspense, for his interpolation of imagined incidents into the story creates local uncertainties about the resolution of individual scenes. We do not know if Samson will forgive Dalila, and the knowledge that violence was not permitted on the Greek stage does not abate the feeling that the scene with Harapha could erupt into a brawl at any moment.

In the preface to *Samson Agonistes* Milton discusses the idea of catharsis, and the details of his account show that he has drawn not only on Aristotle but also on recent Italian criticism. His view that tragedy has the power 'to purge the mind' is illustrated by analogy to 'physic', and so reflects the Italian idea that cartharsis is a medical metaphor (though his use on the title-page of *lustratio* rather than *purgatio* to translate *catharsis* suggests resistance to the Italian theory in favour of a more ancient interpretation). Aristotle had outlined a theory of catharsis in the *Poetics* and had discussed the notion of an ideal state of mind – the 'Aristotelian mean' – in the *Politics*. Italian theorists had linked these two ideas, and Milton's assertion that tragedy has the power to temper and reduce the passions 'to just measure' reflects the Italian idea that catharsis should lead to the ideal of emotional harmony. Milton concludes the play with an expression of the connection between catharsis and inner harmony that articulates his hope for the effect of the play on the sympathetic reader: 'And calm of mind, all passion spent'.

The theme that unites Milton's greatest poems is temptation. In *Comus* and the epics temptation is central to the plot, and in those poems Milton exalts the virtue of resisting temptation. His fondness for this theme is related to the moral and intellectual integrity that is such a prominent feature of Milton's own character, and that shapes the character of his poems. This integrity was tested in Milton's youth by the death of Edward King, and he responded to the questions raised by his death with a poem that steadfastly resists easy consolations. The question of how a just God could permit an unjust event to occur was raised again when God permitted the restoration of the monarchy in 1660. There is a sense in which *Paradise Lost*, *Paradise Regained*, and *Samson Agonistes* represent Milton's attempt to understand the moral issues raised by the Restoration, and the integrity with which Milton responded to these complex questions contributes substantially to the greatness of these poems.

Gordon Campbell

SELECT BIBLIOGRAPHY

MANUSCRIPTS

The Trinity MS (Trinity College Cambridge MS R.3.4.) contains holographs of many of the poems (including early drafts) published in 1645, including *Comus* and 'Lycidas'; it also contains many of the sonnets first published in 1673, but those from about 1652 are in the hands of amanuenses. A facsimile edition was published by Scolar Press in 1970 (corrected edition 1972). A scribal MS of 'An Epitaph on the Marchioness of Winchester', apparently earlier than the printed text, is in the British Library (Sloane MS 1446); the scribal MS of 'On Time' in the Bodleian Library, Oxford (Ashmole MS 36, 37) also precedes the printed version. There is a scribal MS of 'On the University Carrier' in the Folger Shakespeare Library, Washington (recently re-catalogued as MS V.a.96); scribal MSS of Milton's second 'Hobson' poem ('Another on the Same') are in the Bodleian (Corpus Christi College MS E.309 and Malone MS 21) and in the Huntingdon Library, California (MS H.M. 116). The holograph of 'Fix here' is on the back of a letter to Milton (from Henry Lawes) attached to Milton's 'Commonplace Book' (British Library Add MS 36354). Several transcriptions almost certainly derive from Milton's 1645 text, including a partial transcription (in the hand of Peter Sterry) of 'At a Solemn Music' in Emmanuel College, Cambridge (Sterry MS 289), and transcriptions of 'Psalm cxxxvi' and the 'Nativity Ode' (in the hand of William Sancroft in the Bodleian, Tanner MS 466).

The presentation copy of *Comus* (in a scribal hand) known as the Bridgewater MS has been deposited (on terms that restrict access) in the British Library ('Loan 76'); for a facsimile see Harris Fletcher, *John Milton's Complete Poetical Works, Reproduced in Photographic Facsimile* (4 vols., 1943–8); see also S. E. Sprott, *John Milton, A Maske: the Earlier Versions* (1973). The five songs of *Comus* (with music) exist in a scribal MS in the British Library (Add MS 11518, facsimile in Fletcher) and in a MS in the hand of Henry Lawes, also in the British Library (Add MS 52723), published in facsimile by Pamela Willetts as *The Henry Lawes Manuscript* (1969). The transcription of *Comus* in a commonplace book in the Yale University Library (James Osborn b.63) is dated 1658, and derives from the printed 1645 text.

The MS of Book I of *Paradise Lost*, now in the Pierpont Morgan Library, New York, seems to be part of the copy text for the 1667 edition. A facsimile was published by Helen Darbishire in *The Manuscript of Milton's 'Paradise Lost' Book I* (1931).

FIRST EDITIONS

'On Shakespeare', in the Second Folio of Shakespeare (1632).

A Masque (Comus), 1637; published by Henry Lawes.

'Lycidas', in *Justa Eduardo King* (1638).

'Upon Old Hobson the Carrier of Cambridge' (Milton's second Hobson poem) in *A Banquet of Jests* (1640).

Of Education. To Master Samuel Hartlib (1644).

Areopagitica (1644).

Poems of Mr John Milton, both Latin and English (1645); second edition, *Poems etc upon Several Occasions*, 1673.

Sonnet XIII ('To Mr H. Lawes') in *Choice Psalms put into Music* (1648).

Sonnet XVII ('To Sir Henry Vane') in *The Life and Death of Sir Henry Vane* (1662).

Sonnets XV (to Fairfax), XVI (to Cromwell), and XXII ('Cyriack, this three years' day'), in *Letters of State* (1694), edited by Milton's nephew Edward Phillips.

Paradise Lost 1667; revised edition, 1674.

Paradise Regained and *Samson Agonistes*, 1671.

'Fix here', in A. J. Horwood, *A Commonplace Book of John Milton* (1876).

LATER EDITIONS

Poetical Works, with Patrick Hume's commentary on *Paradise Lost*, published by Jacob Tonson, 1695.

Paradise Lost, ed. Richard Bentley, 1732.

 Zachary Pearce: *Review of the text of ... 'Paradise Lost'* (viz. Bentley's), 1733.

 Jonathan Richardson: *Explanatory Notes and Remarks on 'Paradise Lost'*, 1734.

Poetical Works, ed. Thomas Newton, 1749–52.

Poems upon Several Occasions, ed. Thomas Warton, 2nd edition, 1791.

Poems, ed. William Cowper, 4 vols., 1810.

Poetical Works, variorum edition, ed. H. J. Todd, 1826.

Poems, ed. T Keightley, 1859.

Poetical Works, ed. D. Masson, 1874.

The Cambridge Milton for Schools, ed. A. W. Verity, 1891–6.

IMPORTANT MODERN EDITIONS

The Works of John Milton, gen. ed. F. A. Patterson, 18 vols., Columbia University Press, New York; Oxford University Press, London, 1931–8.

JOHN MILTON

Complete Prose Works, gen. ed. D. M. Wolfe, 8 vols., Yale University Press, Connecticut; Oxford University Press, London.
Sonnets, gen. ed. J. S. Smart, 1921, ed. E. A. J. Honigmann, Maclehose, Glasgow, 1966.
Shorter Poems, ed. B. A. Wright, Macmillan, London, 1938.
Complete Poems and Major Prose, ed. M. Y. Hughes, Odyssey, New York, 1957.
Poetical Works, ed. H. Darbishire, 2 vols., Clarendon Press, London, 1952 5.
Poetical Works, ed. D. Bush, Longman, London, 1966.
Poems, ed. J. Carey and A. D. S. Fowler, Longman, London, 1968.
Complete Poetry, ed. J. T. Shawcross (revised edition, 1971), Anchor Books, New York.

BIOGRAPHY

Milton's autobiographical remarks have been assembled by J. S. Dickhoff, *Milton on Himself*, Oxford University Press, London, 1939. The six early accounts have been collected by H. Darbishire in *Early Lives of Milton*, Constable, London, 1932; her attribution of the anonymous *Life* to John Phillips has not been received uncritically. Of later biographies, Dr Johnson's version in *Lives of the Poets*, Clarendon Press, London, (Definitive Edition 1905), is remarkable for its insights and prejudices. The great Victorian biography, D. Masson's *Life of John Milton* (7 vols., Macmillan, London, 1859 94) remains indispensable. *The Life Records of John Milton* have been collected by J. M. French (5 vols., Rutgers University Press, New Jersey; Cambridge University Press, London, 1949–58). The authoritative modern biography is W. R. Parker's *Milton: A Biography* (2 vols., Clarendon Press, London, 1968).

BIBLIOGRAPHICAL GUIDES

D. H. STEVENS, *A Reference Guide to Milton from 1800 to the Present Day*, Chicago University Press, Chicago; Cambridge University Press, Cambridge, 1930.
H. F. FLETCHER, *Contributions to a Milton Bibliography, 1800–1930*, University of Illinois, Illinois, 1931.
C. HUCKABAY, *John Milton, An Annotated Bibliography 1929 1968*, Duquesne University Press, Pittsburgh, 1969.
J. H. HANFORD, *Milton* (Goldentree Bibliographies), second edition (revised by W. A. McQueen), AHM Publishing Corporation, Illinois, Illinois, 1979.
C. A. PATRIDES, *An Annotated Critical Bibliography of Milton*, 1979.

SELECT BIBLIOGRAPHY

Bibliographies of books and articles on Milton are published annually in the Modern Humanities Research Association's *Annual Bibliography of English Language and Literature* and in *PMLA*.

REFERENCE BOOKS

C. G. OSGOOD, *The Classical Mythology of Milton's English Poems*, Henry Holt, New York, 1900 (published as *The Classical Mythology of Milton's English Poems*, Gordian Press, New York, 1964).

L. E. LOCKWOOD, *Lexicon to the English Poetical Works of John Milton*, Macmillan, London, 1907.

A. H. GILBERT, *A Geographical Dictionary of Milton*, Yale University Press, Connecticut; Oxford University Press, London, 1919.

E. S. LECOMTE, *A Milton Dictionary*, Peter Owen, London, 1961.

W. INGRAM and K. SWAIN, *A Concordance to Milton's English Poetry*, Oxford University Press, London, 1972.

J. C. BOSWELL, *Milton's Library*, Garland Publishers, New York; George Prior, London, 1975.

Milton Encyclopedia, gen. ed. W. B. Hunter, 9 vols., Bucknell University Press, Pennsylvania; Associated University Presses, London, 1978–83.

J. T. SHAWCROSS, *Milton: A Bibliography for the Years 1624–1700*, Center for Medieval and Early Renaissance Studies, New York, 1984.

CRITICISM

The Variorum Commentary on the Poems of John Milton (8 vols., Routledge & Kegan Paul, London, 1970–) contains summaries of criticism and line-by-line commentaries. Early criticism has been collected by J. T. Shawcross in *Milton: The Critical Heritage* (2 vols., Routledge & Kegan Paul, London, 1970, 1972) and J. A. Wittreich Jr in *The Romantics on Milton*, Press of Case Western Reserve University, Ohio. Many journals publish articles on Milton, and three are wholly devoted to Milton: *Milton Studies* is an annual volume of essays, *Milton Quarterly* is a friendly compilation of articles and reviews, and *MCJ News* (in English and Japanese versions) is an annual report on the publications and conference papers of members of the Milton Center of Japan. The English Association's *Year's Work in English Studies* contains an annual review of all books and articles on Milton.

CHRONOLOGY

DATE	AUTHOR'S LIFE	LITERARY CONTEXT
1608	Born in Cheapside, London, (9 December), the second of three children of John Milton and his wife Sarah. Milton's	Joseph Hall: *The Characters of Virtue and Vice* (first English collection of 'characters').
1609	birthplace and childhood home was the Spread Eagle, in Bread Street, where his father conducted his business as a	William Shakespeare: *Sonnets.* Francis Bacon: *De Sapienta Verterum.*
1610	scrivener (by the 17th century this profession had diversified to include the functions of notary, moneylender and investment broker). John Milton the elder, disinherited by his family for converting from	Ben Jonson: *The Alchemist.* Shakespeare: *The Winter's Tale.* Beaumont and Fletcher: *The Maid's Tragedy.* William Camden's *Britannia* translated into English by Philemon Holland.
1611	Roman Catholicism, was Puritan in sympathy, but a lover of literature and music (he was also an amateur composer) and his son enjoyed all the	Shakespeare: *Cymbeline; The Tempest.* Cyril Tourneur: *The Atheist's Tragedy.* Donne's first *Anniversary.*
1612	advantages of a cultivated home. In 'Ad Patrem' Milton thanks his father for the gift of five languages – Latin, Greek,	John Webster: *The White Devil.* Michael Drayton: *The Poly-Olbion* (part 1).
1614	Hebrew, French and Italian. His early education is entrusted to private tutors.	Webster: *The Duchess of Malfi.* Walter Raleigh: *History of the World.* Jonson: *Bartholomew Fair.*
1615	Brother, Christopher, born (24 November).	Cervantes: *Don Quixote* (part 2).
1616		Death of Shakespeare. George Chapman completes his translation of Homer. Ben Jonson: *Epigrams* and *The Frost* published.
1618	Portrait painted by Cornelius Janssen.	Jonson: *Pleasure Reconciled to Virtue* (gives Milton the idea of *Comus*) – one of Jonson's many court masques 1605–31 in collaboration with Inigo Jones.

Plantation of Ulster by Protestant English and Scots begins, sowing seeds of future religious and territorial conflict. First English Baptist congregation (under John Smyth in Amsterdam; first in London 1612). Champlain founds Quebec.

Henry Hudson discovers river named after him. Viriginia Company formed. English colony in Guiana. English settlements of the Bermudas, Leeward Islands and Barbados (to 1632). Kepler: *Astronomia Nova* (demonstrates orbit of Mars elliptical).

Parliament presents Petition of Grievances; rejects Salisbury's Great Contract whereby they would vote the monarchy a regular income in perpetuity. Murder of Henri IV of France; regency of Marie de'Medici. Galileo's telescope: discovers the rings of Saturn and the four satellites of Jupiter. Sir Thomas Roe sails up the Amazon. John Florio's Italian/English dictionary; John Cotgrave's French/English dictionary. Monteverdi: *Vespers.*

The King James 'Authorized' Version of the Bible published. (The Bible, with Foxe's *Book of Martyrs*, the most widely owned book amongst lower classes in the 17th century.) Gustavus Adolphus king of Sweden. William Byrd: *Psalmes, Songs and Sonnets* (madrigals).

Death of Henry, Prince of Wales and of Robert Cecil, Earl of Salisbury. Orlando Gibbons' *Madrigals and Mottets, apt for Viols and Voyces* includes settings of Raleigh and Donne. Dowland's collection of songs, *A Pilgrimes Solace.*

The 'Addled' Parliament proves as recalcitrant as its predecessor on the question of supply; dissolved without passing a single Act. French States-General dissolved (does not meet again until 1789). Spilbergen sails round the world. Napier of Merchiston discovers logarithms. El Greco: *The Assumption of the Virgin.*

George Villiers, afterwards Duke of Buckingham, becomes the latest in a line of unpopular royal favourites.

James I dismisses Edward Coke, Chief Justice of the king's bench, and champion of the common law versus the prerogative. Ben Jonson, granted a pension by James I, effectively becomes first poet laureate.

Dispatch of English trading mission to Persia.

Execution of Sir Walter Raleigh. Sir Francis Bacon appointed Chancellor. 'Defenestration of Prague': beginning of Thirty Years War, primarily a contest between Protestantism and Catholicism within the Holy Roman Empire but complicated by the intervention of non-German powers for both religious and political reasons.

DATE	AUTHOR'S LIFE	LITERARY CONTEXT
1619		Giovanni Battista Manso: *Life of Tasso*.
1620	Enters St Paul's School, under Alexander Gill. Friendship with Charles Diodati begins.	Francis Quarles: *A Feast for Worms*. English translation of the *Decameron* (to 1625). Middleton and Rowley: *Women Beware Women* (1620s). Birth of Andrew Marvell.
1621	John Donne appointed Dean of St Paul's Cathedral and Milton probably heard him preach on a number of occasions between 1621–4.	Donne writes most of his *Holy Sonnets* and many *Divine Poems* (to 1631). Robert Burton: *The Anatomy of Melancholy*.
1622	Milton's private tuition continues under, amongst others, Thomas Young (the 'ty' of the 1641 anti-episcopal 'Smectymnuus' pamphlet). In *Defensio Secunda* he asserts that from the age of 12 he habitually studied until midnight. His schoolday began at 7.00 am.	Bacon: *History of the Reign of Henry VII*. First performance of *The Changeling* by Middleton and Rowley. George Wither: *Fair Virtue*.
1623		Shakespeare First Folio. William Drummond: *A Cypresse Grove*. Giambattista Marino: *Adone*.
1624	His paraphrases of psalms cxiv and cxxxvi.	Henry King: *The Exequy*. Lord Herbert of Cherbury: *De Veritate* (advocating religious toleration). Hugo Grotius: *De jure belli ac pacis* (treatise on international law). Third, expanded, edition of Bacon's *Essays*.
1625	Admitted to Christ's College, Cambridge (February) where his first tutor is William Chappell. He acquires the nickname 'The lady of Christ's.'	
1626	Falls out with Chappell for unknown reasons (according to John Aubrey, Chappell whipped Milton). He is temporarily rusticated. After re-admission to the university, he is assigned to a new tutor, Nathaniel Tovey.	Philip Massinger: *A New Way to Pay Old Debts*. Jonson: *The Staple of News*. Death of Sir Francis Bacon. George Sandys' verse translation of Ovid's *Metamorphosis*. Birth of John Aubrey.

CHRONOLOGY

Ferdinand II elected Holy Roman Emperor; rejected by predominantly Protestant Bohemia which offers crown to the Calvinist Frederick, Elector Palatine, husband of James I's daughter Elizabeth.

Ferdinand defeats Frederick at the Battle of the White Mountain. Spanish army invades the Palatinate. James I, reluctant to take on Spain, incenses public opinion by failing to intervene on behalf of his son-in-law and the Protestant cause. Massacre of Protestants in the Valtalline. Pilgrim Fathers set sail in the *Mayflower* and found the first New England colony. Inigo Jones begins the Whitehall Banqueting House (to 1622).

England in depth of economic slump, blamed on the king for his interference in the wool trade and use of monopolies. Bacon and Mompesson impeached by Commons. First English news-sheets published (in Holland). Edinburgh University founded. Death of Philip III and accession of Philip IV of Spain; ascendancy of Olivarez begins.

Growth of Arminianism within Church of England. James I's *Direction to Preachers* aims to suppress contentious (Calvinist) preaching; arouses fears of crypto-Catholicism, exacerbated by Arminian adherence to High Church ritual, emphasis on the authority of bishops and off the sermon. Invention of sliderule by William Oughtred.

To relief of Presbyterians, James's Spanish Marriage project collapses: abortive expedition of Prince Charles and Buckingham to Spain to win hand of Infanta. Statute of Monopolies forbids royal granting of monopoly rights; allows 14-year exclusive rights for new inventions, the beginning of patent laws.

Cardinal Richelieu becomes chief minister in France. Henry Wotton's *Elements of Architecture*. Bernini's sculpture of *Apollo and Daphne*. Poussin: *Echo and Narcissus*. Rubens: *Massacre of the Innocents*.

Outbreak of plague in England. Death of James I; accession of Charles I. Marriage of Charles and Henrietta Maria. Buckingham's naval raid on Cadiz, designed to renew the glories of Elizabeth's reign, an expensive fiasco. Nicholas Ferrar establishes Anglican community at Little Gidding (broken up by Puritans in 1647).

In series of campaigns (1625–30) Wallenstein, new general-in-chief of Imperial armies, defeats Protestant armies under Count Mansfeld, brings Bethlen Gabor of Transylvania to terms and, in conjunction with Count John Tzerklaes von Tilly, overwhelms Denmark which had intervened in the Thirty Years War as champion of Protestant cause.

DATE	AUTHOR'S LIFE	LITERARY CONTEXT
1627	In Milton's words, 'a certain niceness of nature, an honest haughtiness', may have led to his unpopularity amongst fellow-students. Also dissatisfied with Cambridge syllabus. Begins to write poetry in Latin and Hebrew on both sacred and secular themes.	Bacon: *New Atlantis*. Thomas May's translation of Lucan's *Pharsalia*. Phineas Fletcher's anti-Catholic *The Locusts, or The Apollyonists*. Drayton: *The Battle of Agincourt*; *Nimphidia*.
1628	His first known English verse, *On the Death of a Fair Infant* thought to date from this time, coinciding with the death of his niece, Anne Phillips. Also probably writes *At a Vacation Exercise*.	John Earle: *Microcosmographie*, a collection of character sketches. William Harvey publishes his theories on the circulation of the blood: *De Motu Cordis et Sanguinis*.
1629	Takes BA degree (26 March). Milton is placed fourth in the honours list of the 24 undergraduates deemed to be the most distinguished of the 259 graduating that year. Writes *On the Morning of Christ's Nativity* (December).	Lancelot Andrewes: *Ninety-Six Sermons*. Hobbes: *The Peloponnesian War of Thucydides* (transl.). Chapman: *The Justification of a Strange Action of Nero: The Fifth Satire of Juvenal* (transl.)
1630	'Arcades, Part of an entertainment presented to the Countess Dowager of Darby at Harefield, by som Nooble persons of her Family', probably devised by Milton this year, with songs by his friend the composer Henry Lawes.	1630s: Lord Falkland's Great Tew home becomes centre for liberal thinkers – poets (Jonson, Carew, Waller); philosophers and theologians (John Earle, William Chillingworth, John Hales, Edward Hyde) – whose Christian humanism wholly out of sympathy with recent bitter denominational controversy.
1631	Writes *On Shakespeare*; two epitaphs on the university carrier; 'An Epitaph on the Marchioness of Winchester'. Christopher Milton admitted to the Inner Temple.	Chapman: *Caesar and Pompey*. Death of John Donne.

CHRONOLOGY

England at war with France. Buckingham leads unsuccessful naval expedition for the relief of French Huguenots besieged at La Rochelle – regarded as deep humiliation by English. Charles I, with the backing of Arminian divines, Sibthorpe and Manwaring, raises money by forced loans. Case of the Five Knights who unsuccessfully test the legality of confinement for those who refuse to contribute. Charles buys great art collection of the Gonzaga Dukes of Mantua. Inigo Jones completes Queen's Chapel at St James's Palace. Kepler compiles *Rudolphine Tables* for calculating astronomical positions.

Laud is made Bishop of London; Manwaring, impeached for his Divine Right sermon, receives royal pardon: Arminianism and support of the prerogative become inextricably linked in the minds of Presbyterians. New Parliament passes Petition of Right, masterminded by Sir Edward Coke and John Eliot, in protest against arbitrary taxation and church reform: chief targets are Buckingham and Laud. King counters with Declaration to promote religious conformity, referring any disputes over interpretation of the 39 Articles to Convocation. Assassination of Buckingham.

Opposition, led by Eliot and Holles, forcibly delay dissolution of Parliament to pass three further resolutions attacking Court policy. Ringleaders imprisoned (quickly released, apart from the unrepentant Eliot, who dies in prison in 1632, regarded by many as a martyr). Charles rules for 11 years without Parliament. Great 'Puritan migration' to New England begins. Massachusetts charter granted. Rubens presents *Peace and War* to Charles I. Vermuyden contracted to drain Great Fens (to 1652).

Birth of the future Charles II. Peace made with France. Gustavus Adolphus of Sweden lands in Pomerania to take over as Protestant leader in the Thirty Years War. Providence Company founded (to establish settlements on the Connecticut) by, amongst other leading Puritans, Lord Warwick and John Pym.

Peace between England and Spain. Magdeberg sacked with hideous savagery by Imperial troops under Tilly. Gustavus Adolphus embarks on brief but brilliant career of victory, overthrowing Tilly at Breitenfeld. Henry Lawes becomes one of Charles I's court composers. His 430 odd songs include settings of Carew, Waller, Herrick, Suckling, Lovelace as well as Milton.

DATE	AUTHOR'S LIFE	LITERARY CONTEXT
1632	*On Shakespeare* published in the Second Folio of Shakespeare's plays. Takes MA degree (3 July). (The award of university degrees being subject to the candidate's subscribing in writing to the doctrines of the Church of England and acknowledging the supremacy of the King, it would appear that Milton's republican views and unorthodox religious principles were not yet strongly developed.) Joins his family in Hammersmith (where his father had retired) and devotes himself to classical studies.	John Ford: *'Tis Pity She's a Whore*; *Love's Sacrifice*. William Prynne: *Historio-Mastix* (an extremist Puritan attack on stage plays, allegedly containing aspersions on Charles I and Henrietta Maria, for which in 1634 Prynne is sentenced by Star Chamber to imprisonment and loss of his ears); meanwhile Roman Catholic John Braidshaigh's *Virginalia*, comprising sonnets in honour of the Virgin, is licensed for publication without problem.
1633	Writes *L'Allegro* and *Il Penseroso*.	Death of George Herbert. Poems of Donne and Herbert (*The Temple*) published. Abraham Cowley: *Poetical Blossoms*. William D'Avenant: *The Wits* first performed. Phineas Fletcher: *The Purple Island*.
1634	*A Masque [Comus]* performed at Ludlow (29 September), with music by Henry Lawes. 'Ad Patrem' probably written in an attempt to persuade his father that to be a poet and a clergyman need not be incompatible.	*Coelum Britannicum*, a masque by Thomas Carew and Inigo Jones, performed by the King. James Shirley: *The Triumph of Peace*, a masque with music by William Lawes, one of the earliest English composers to experiment with recitative style of Italian opera.
1635	Moves with his family to Horton, Buckinghamshire. Continues his reading in Greek, Latin and Italian and amuses himself with mathematics and music.	John Selden: *Mare Clausum*. Shirley: *The Lady of Pleasure*. Death of Felix Lope de Vega.
1637	*Comus* published. Mother dies (3 April). Milton considers entering one of the Inns of Court.	Death of Jonson. Chillingworth: *The Religion of the Protestants a Safe Way to Salvation*. Corneille: *Le Cid*. Descartes: *Discourse on Method*.

CHRONOLOGY

Charles issues proclamation banishing gentry and nobility to their country estates; increasing isolation of the court, which under Henrietta Maria also begins to take on a Roman Catholic aura. Laud, now effectively chief minister, relying on hated Tudor prerogative courts of the Star Chamber and High Commission to enforce policy. Van Dyck becomes court painter to Charles I and sets style of the grand portrait for the next two centuries. Charles builds up royal art collection – Titian, Mantegna, Raphael, Tintoretto, Correggio, Giorgione, etc. Death of Tilly and victory of Gustavus Adolphus at Lech. Ferdinand compelled to call Wallenstein from retirement. Swedes win battle of Lützen but Gustavus Adolphus is killed. Accession of Queen Christina in Sweden, with Oxenstierna as regent. Henceforward, most of the religious idealism inspiring the protagonists in the Thirty Years War gives way to aspirations of personal aggrandisement. Thomas Wentworth (later Earl of Strafford) Lord Deputy in Ireland. Birth of philosophers John Locke and Spinoza and of architect Christopher Wren.

William Laud becomes Archbishop of Canterbury. Wentworth's policy of 'Thorough' in Ireland brings in revenue for the Crown but also antagonizes Presbyterian settlers and opposition at home. Condemnation of Galileo by Inquisition for upholding the Copernican system. In France, the Abbé de St Cyran is appointed director of Port-Royal which becomes a centre for Jansenism. Port-Royal circle included Angélique and Antoine Arnauld, Pascal and Quesnel.

King follows a mercantilist, interventionist economic policy, winning the support of merchants and financiers. Cycle of good harvests during the 1630s contributes to enhanced prosperity. First writs for ship money on coastal counties, for naval defence of country. Settlement in Maryland (established by Roman Catholic George Calvert). Laud's religious policy further antagonizes Puritans: conventicles are suppressed and King James's Declaration of Sports revised and read in churches, implying condemnation of the Puritan sabbath. Assassination of Wallenstein.

Ship money extended to inland counties – in fact a highly efficient tax, in spite of its unpopularity. Rubens' Banqueting House ceiling depicts blessings of monarchical rule and apotheosis of James I. War between France and Spain. French settlement of Martinique and Guadeloupe. Claude Lorraine: *Rest on the Flight to Egypt*. Richelieu founds *L'Académie française*.
Prynne and Puritan pamphleteers Bastwick, Burton and Lilburne are mutilated, branded and imprisoned for seditious libel. Laud attempts to impose Book of Common Prayer on the Presbyterian Kirk, leading to riots in St Giles' Cathedral. Van Dyck paints triple portrait of Charles I to help Bernini execute a bust. Bernini said to remark that he had never seen a 'countenance so unfortunate'.

DATE	AUTHOR'S LIFE	LITERARY CONTEXT
1638	*Lycidas* – in which Milton for the first time proclaims his adherence to the Puritan cause – printed in a memorial volume to Milton's college friend, Edward King. Embarks on a Continental tour. In France (May) calls on Grotius (whose Latin play, *Adamus Exul*, 1601, dealt with a theme Milton would take up in *Paradise Lost*). In Florence (August) he is befriended by leading intellectuals – Gaddi, Dati, Frescobaldi, Cultellino, etc., evidently unperturbed by their Roman Catholicism. Visits Galileo. At Rome dines at the English Jesuit College, meets Lucas Holstein, one of the Vatican librarians, and enters the circle of Cardinal Barberini, Prime Minister, and chief counsellor to his uncle Pope Urban VIII, by whose 'submissive loftiness of mind' he is much impressed. Attends concerts in the Barberini palace. Meets Manso in Naples (December).	Abraham Cowley: *Loves Riddle* and *Naufragium Joculaire*. John Suckling: *Aglaura*. Thomas Randolph's *Poems*; and *Amyntas, The Muse's Looking Glass* (plays) printed. Robert Filmer's *Patriarcha, or the Natural Power of Kings*, in defence of Divine Right. Francis Quarles: *Hieroglyphikes of the Life of Man*. Kenelm Digby: *Conference with a Lady about Choice of Religion*. John Lilburne: *The Work of the Beast*. Antonio Malatesti, a friend from Milton's Florence trip, dedicates to him his cycle of 50 obscene sonnets in the Baroque idiom – *La Tina* – to which Milton seems to have had no objection.
1639	Receives news of Charles Diodati's death. Gives up plan of crossing to Sicily and Greece, not wishing to be 'peacefully travelling for culture' while his countrymen are 'fighting for their liberty at home'. In Rome hears Leona Baroni sing; in Florence reads from his work at the Svogliati Academy. Returns to London (July). Takes lodgings near Fleet Street; begins to tutor his two nephews, John and Edward Phillips, aged 8 and 9. Probably writes his Latin address, 'Mansus'.	Thomas Fuller: *The History of the Holy War*. Richard Brome: *The Lovesick Court; A Mad Couple Well Matched*. D'Avenant: *The Spanish Lovers*. Suckling: *Brennoralt, or The Discontented Colonel*. James Shirley and the Earl of Newcastle collaborate on a play, *The Country Captain*. Rotrou: *Iphigénie*. Birth of Racine. Death of Ford.

CHRONOLOGY

D'Avenant succeeds Jonson as official poet laureate.

Following celebrated 'Rex v Hampden' case John Hampden fined for refusing to pay ship money. The decision that ship money is legal taken by many to imply that non-Parliamentary government had come to stay. Tax becomes increasingly difficult to collect, because of the fear that it might be used to finance a standing army.

General Assembly of Church of Scotland assumes leadership of national revolt, organizing Covenant against episcopacy, popular subscription to which being almost unanimous. Scots protest they are merely acting to protect Charles from 'popish' councillors but loyalty to church and king prove impossible to reconcile: Charles I mobilizes army.

Pope Urban VIII at time of Milton's visit preserving formal neutrality in Thirty Years War (to the benefit of Richelieu, since his policy of allying with Protestant German princes against the Habsburgs thereby escaped censure). Later, in 1642-4, Urban attempts to take advantage of the situation to increase his own power and territory in Italy, which ends badly for the Papal states and marks another step in the decline of the influence of the Papacy in international diplomacy. Urban VIII notorious for huge military expenditure and shameless nepotism. His Barberini nephews amassed vast fortunes.

This was the period of Rome's transformation by Bernini and Borromini. The Barberini's own magnificent Baroque palace (1632) was built from stones wrenched from the Coliseum; bronze was also torn from the Pantheon to make the baldachinum at St Peter's, eliciting Pasquino's bitter gibe 'What the barbarians left undone the Barberini did'.

Guido Reni: *The Purification of the Virgin*; Rembrandt: *The Marriage of Samson*.

First Bishops' War. Ill-equipped English army repelled by Scots under Alexander Leslie. Truce (Treaty of Berwick) in June. General Assembly sweeps away episcopacy; Scotland's political dissociation from England demonstrated by introduction of reconstructed Lords of the Articles, free from royal control. Charles, determined to renew war, recalls Strafford from Ireland. Strafford advises calling new Parliament to vote the necessary supply.

English found Madras. Battle of the Downs: Dutch Admiral Tromp destroys the Spanish fleet.

Poussin: *A Dance to the Music of Time* and *The Gathering of the Manna*. Cavalli: *Le Nozzedi Teti e di Peleo* (opera).

DATE	AUTHOR'S LIFE	LITERARY CONTEXT
1640	Continues tutoring, taking on other pupils. Within a year his nephews are able to read Latin authors with comparative ease. Poem on Hobson published in *A Banquet of Jests*. The enthusiasm with which his Latin poems were received in Italy had encouraged Milton in his resolve to become a great national poet. In his *Epitaphium Damonis* (epitaph for Charles Diodati) he makes reference to a poem on an Arthurian theme he was contemplating writing, but which never materialized. Starts compiling *De Doctrina Christiana* (published 1825).	First volume of Donne's Sermons, prefaced by Izaak Walton's *Life of Donne*. Carew: *Poems*. Suckling: *Ballad upon a Wedding*. Jonson's *The Underwood*, a translation of Horace's *Ars Poetica*, and his two prose works *The English Grammar* and *Timber, or Discoveries*. Thomas Killigrew: *The Parson's Wedding*. *Wit's Recreations* (collection of epigrams and epitaphs).
1641	Milton's poetry interrupted by his political activities and defence of religious, civil and domestic liberties. Takes on Joseph Hall, Bishop of Exeter, and James Ussher, Archbishop of Armagh, in extended controversy. His three anti-episcopal pamphlets, *Of Reformation touching Church Discipline in England*, *Of Prelatical Episcopacy*, and *Animadversions upon the Remonstrant's Defence* published in July.	John Evelyn begins his *Diary*. Wither: *Heleluiah* (hymns). John Denham: *Sophy*. Richard Overton: *Lambeth Fayre* (a Leveller attack on bishops). Brome: *The Joviall Crew*. Shirley: *The Cardinal*. Samuel Hartlib's vision of Utopian society: *A Description of the Famous Kingdom of Macaria*. First publication of *Diurnal Occurrences in Parliament*. Descartes: *Meditationes de prima philosophia*. Corneille: *Polyeucte*.
1642	Publishes two further anti-episcopal pamphlets, *The Reason of Church Government* and *An Apology against a Pamphlet ... against Smectymnuus*. Marries Mary Powell, aged 17 (May), who returns home to her Royalist family at Forest Hill, near Oxford, a few months afterwards, presumably for reasons connected with the Civil	Denham's *Cooper's Hill* pays tribute to Charles I. Death of Cavalier poets William Cartwright (of a fever) and Sidney Godolphin (in battle). Richard Lovelace (imprisoned by Parliament for supporting the 'Kentish Petition'): writes 'To Althea'. Thomas Fuller: *The Holy State*

CHRONOLOGY

Strafford wins Irish Parliament's support to raise army to be used against Scots in Ulster and Scotland (March). Short Parliament (April–May), refuses to vote supply until grievances settled. Pym emerges as opposition leader. When opposition found to be negotiating with Scots, Charles dissolves Parliament, ending all hope of conciliation. Strafford argues king free of 'all restraint'. Convocation passes provocative series of legal canons asserting divine right dogma. Scots defeat English at Newburn and take Newcastle (29 August). Subsidy of £25,000 a month payable to Scots by Treaty of Ripon effectively shackles Charles to Long Parliament (meets 3 November; dissolved 16 March 1660). New Parliament hostile to king; he is supported by only a third of MPs in 1640, even moderates such as Edward Hyde opposing him. Initially reform, not revolution is their aim, though Pym's 'keynote speech' (7 November) demonstrates that a core of members existed convinced of a conspiracy to introduce despotism and papacy into the country – a fear fuelled by apocalyptic preaching of Puritan divines. Root and Branch petition (11 December) signed by 15,000 Londoners, calls for abolition of episcopacy. Laud imprisoned.

Riots in London (January). Triennial Act (February). Impeachment of Strafford, whose execution (May) Charles is obliged to sanction, but never forgives. Protestation (3 May) of Commons to the country. Earl of Bristol's son, George Digby, emerges as Royalist spokesman in the Lords. Betrothal of Princess Mary to William, son of Frederick Henry, Dutch Stadholder. First Army plot (May) – Henrietta Maria found to be soliciting aid from Louis XIII. Abolition of prerogative courts. Root and Branch bill. Pym's Ten Propositions (24 June). Charles leaves for Scotland (August). Rebellion of Irish Catholics in Ulster (October) which Parliament cannot trust Charles with an army to suppress. Commons pass Grand Remonstrance (22 November) – by majority of only 159 to 148, the radical restructuring of the Church being repellant to moderate Anglicans led by Falkland, Hyde and Colpepper. Charles returns to London and is welcomed by the city (1 December); Parliamentary opposition sweeps board in London Common Council elections. Riots against bishops; 12 bishops sent to the Tower. Death of Van Dyck. Monteverdi: *The Return of Ulysses*.

King moves to impeach the Five Members – Pym, Hampden, Holles, Haslerigg, Strode – and Viscount Mandeville. Takes unprecedented step of entering Commons to arrest them, but they had already fled. Public opinion swings against king. Parliament pass Militia Bill and bill excluding bishops from House of Lords. Social order breaking down. Hunger riots and riots against enclosure throughout country by June. Parliament sends Charles, in the north, Nineteen Propositions, terms of unconditional surrender so harsh that Charles begins to look quite moderate in comparison. Edward Hyde (later Earl of Clarendon) becomes king's chief adviser and instrumental in building up a Royalist party. King's supporters rally to him at York (July). Parliament mobilizes army under Earl of Essex.

xlv

DATE	AUTHOR'S LIFE	LITERARY CONTEXT
1642 *cont*	War. Though he had originally given dispensation for absence until Michaelmas, Milton sends for her without success. Christopher Milton's name appears on the Reading Muster-roll, supporting the Royalist cause (November). Milton's sonnet 'Captain or colonel or knight at arms whose chance on these defenceless doors may seize' probably written during height of the panic in London at Royalist advance.	*and the Profane State.* Edward Coke: *Second Institutes.* Henry More: *Psychodia Platonica* (poems). Cowley: *The Guardian.* Shirley: *The Sisters.* Corneille: *Cinna.* Cornelius Jansen: *Augustinus.*
1643	Publishes *The Doctrine and Discipline of Divorce* (August). His liberal thesis that divorce is justifiable on grounds of mental incompatability – as opposed to adultery only – deeply shocked his contemporaries, not least Prynne and the Presbyterians. Milton's brother-in-law, Richard Powell, engaged in intelligence work for the Royalists.	Prynne: *The Sovereign Power of Parliament.* Thomas Browne: *Religio Medici.* Kenelm Digby: *Observations* (on the above); *Of Bodies.* Cowley: *The Puritan and the Papist*; *The Civil War.* William Walwyn: *Power of Love*, a Leveller's arguments for religious toleration. Marchamont Nedham's *Mercurius Britannicus*, a Parliamentary newsbook, established as a rival to Sir John Berkenhead's Royalist *Mercurius Aulicus.*
1644	Publishes *On Education*, an exposition of his theories of education in the Renaissance Humanist tradition (June), which he dedicates to his friend Hartlib. Second edition of Milton's divorce pamphlet; he also translates a Judgement of Martin Bucer concerning divorce, attacked by Herbert Palmer (13 August) in a sermon before Parliament. London stationers petition against the divorce books (24–26 August). Plans to marry the daughter of	Overton: *Man's Mortality.* Henry Hammond: *Practical Catechism.* [First half of seventeenth century saw vast amount of pious and devotional literature. Arthur Dent's *Plaine Mans Path-Way to Heaven* went through 25 editions 1601–40; Thomas Egerton's *Brief Method of Catechizing* reached its 39th edition in 1631. John Norden's *Pensive Mans Practise* reached its 40th impression

CHRONOLOGY

King raises standard at Nottingham (21 August). Royalists win battle of Edgehill (October). Prince Rupert, the king's nephew, wins his reputation as brilliant cavalry general but prevented from taking London; royalist army turned back by City trained bands at Turnham Green. Parliament orders all theatres to be closed (September). The ban on plays which lasts until the Restoration, is never wholly successfully enforced.

Death of Richelieu. Conspiracy of Cinq-Mars. Abel Tasman discovers Tasmania and South Island of New Zealand. Monteverdi: *The Coronation of Poppaea*. Rembrandt: *The Night Watch*. Educationalist Comenius organizing schools in Sweden (to 1646); then Hungary (1650-4).

Growing agitation for peace. King rejects 'Propositions of Oxford'. Royalist military successes – Ralph Hopton at Roundaway Down; Prince Rupert at Bristol, Lord Newcastle at Adwalton Moor. Siege of Gloucester. Charles unsuccessfully urging Ormonde to negotiate a truce in Ireland to release troops. Pym gains support of Scots whose terms involve import of Solemn League and Covenant into England church – far too extreme for most English Presbyterians. Westminster Assembly of Divines (to 1648) set up to oversee this. Parliament proves more efficient at raising money than Royalists, with Pym's county tax assessment, excise on popular commodities and Sequestration Ordinance. King relies on voluntary contributions. Death of Pym (December).

Fall of Olivarez (Spain). Death of Louis XIII and regency of Anne of Austria. Mazarin chief minister in France. Condé's defeat of Spanish at Rocroi; Condé and Turenne win series of victories throughout remainder of the Thirty Years War, ensuring France's supremacy. Invention of the barometer by Torricelli.

Sir Henry Vane, the Younger, emerges as Pym's successor, though his party, the Independents, are not a majority in the Commons. Unlike the Presbyterians, they favour religious toleration. Vane, who has republican leanings, becomes closely allied with Oliver Cromwell, rising star of the Army. Other Parliamentary generals – Manchester, Essex, Waller – still hope for negotiated settlement with king. Scots invade England. Join Parliamentary armies to defeat Royalists at Marston Moor, near York (2 July), Rupert's cavalry, for the first time, being beaten by Cromwell's Ironsides. Parliamentary armies do not follow up advantage gained. After battle of Newbury Cromwell accuses Manchester of not wanting to defeat the king conclusively. Henrietta Maria, having given birth to Princess Henriette, escapes to France. The Directory is substituted for the Book of Common Prayer. Ejection of Royalist or 'unsuitable' clergy from their livings begins (over a third by the end of the Interregnum). Ordinance ordering removal from churches and destruction of all organs – not strictly enforced.

DATE	AUTHOR'S LIFE	LITERARY CONTEXT
1644 *cont*	one Dr Davis. He begins to notice failure of sight (September). *Areopagitica* published (November), a plea to Parliament to end censorship before publication. Now a leading spokesman for the Independents, Milton again incurring the hostility of the Presbyterians.	in 1644. Such books, popular amongst lower classes, encouraged independent thought and separatism in religion.] Arnauld: *Apologie pour Jansénius*.
1645	Publishes two more pamphlets on the divorce question – *Tetrarchordon* and *Colasterion*. His wife returns now the Royalist cause appears lost. First edition of *The Poems of Mr John Milton* registered for publication (December). Moves to a larger house at the Barbican.	Marvell: *Flecknoe, an English Priest at Rome.* Edmund Waller: *Poems.* Fuller: *Good Thoughts in Bad Times.* Digby: *Of the Immortality of Man's Soul.* Ussher: *A Body of Divinitie.* Wither: *Vox Pacifica.*
1646	Poems published (January). Daughter Anne born (29 July). Takes in his wife's family. Writes sonnet to his friend the composer and royalist Henry Lawes (published in 1648 in a volume commemorating William Lawes, and dedicated to Charles I, then in prison).	Henry Vaughan: *Poems.* Richard Crashaw: *Steps to the Temple* and *The Delights of the Muses.* Thomas Browne: *Pseudodoxia Epidemica* (*Vulgar Errors*). Suckling: *Fragmenta Aurea*; *The Goblins.* Clarendon begins his *History of the Rebellion* and writes most of the character studies of Falkland, Charles I, John Hampden, etc.
1647	Father-in-Law, Richard Powell, dies (1 Jan). Milton's father dies, leaving him the house in Bread Street. Also takes possession of Powell property at Wheatley. Moves to a smaller house in High Holborn.	Cowley: *The Mistress.* Richard Corbett: *Certain Elegant Poems.* Fuller: *Good Thoughts in Worse Times.* First of 25 editions of poems of hugely popular Cavalier poet, Nicholas Cleveland. Jeremy Taylor: *The Liberty of Prophesying* (an Anglican argument for religious toleration).

Execution of Laud (January). Cromwell and Independents obtain Self-
Denying Ordinance (April) whereby all MPs obliged to resign their
military commands. New Model Army formed under Sir Thomas Fairfax.
Cromwell reappointed as second in command; does not resign his seat.
Charles rejects Uxbridge peace proposals. New Model Army wins decisive
victories at Naseby (June) and Langport (July). Rupert surrenders Bristol,
and, having quarrelled with the king, goes abroad. Montrose defeated at
Philiphaugh (September). Matthew Hopkins' crusade against witches in
the eastern counties results in over two hundred executions.

King surrenders to Scots at Newark (May). Oxford capitulates (June).
Intensifying of Presbyterian-Independent conflict. Propositions put to the
king in June still stipulate acceptance of the Solemn League and Covenant.
Independents open separate negotiations with king. Levellers argue for the
abolition of monarchy and the sovereignty of the people in *Remonstrance of
Many Thousand Citizens.* John Lilburne, their leader, derives his theories
from Sir Edward's Coke's proposition that the monarchy was a Norman
device unconstitutionally imposed on the free and equal society of Anglo-
Saxon England. Abolition of bishops (October).

Birth of German philosopher and mathematician, Leibniz. David Teniers
the Younger paints *The Village Fête.*

Parliament pays Scots £400,000 to hand over Charles I (February). New
Model Army 'agitators' demand arrears of pay. Religious sectaries in Army
regard success as a sign of God's favour; their radical political views lie behind
The Case of the Army Truly Stated (October). Levellers, also influential in army,
put forward the *Agreement of the People*, recommending, amongst other things,
universal suffrage. Army Council (including Cromwell and Ireton) debate
constitutional issues with army agitators (led by Sexby) at Putney. Mob
violence in London provokes group of Independents to flee capital, begging
army to restore order – which it does. Cromwell negotiating directly with the
king, produces the Heads of Proposals, less extreme than Parliament's
Newcastle Propositions. Charles flees from Holmby to Carrisbrooke
(November). Signs Engagement with Scots (December) accepting their
support in subduing England in return for a three-year trial of Presbyterian
Church government. Lely paints *The Children of Charles I.*

JOHN MILTON

DATE	AUTHOR'S LIFE	LITERARY CONTEXT
1648	Daughter Mary born (25 October). Completely loses sight in his left eye. Writes sonnet on Lord General Fairfax at the Siege of Colchester.	Robert Herrick, ejected from his living by Parliament in 1647, publishes *Hesperides* and religious poems, *Noble Numbers*. Richard Lovelace, imprisoned (1648–9) as a Royalist, writes *Lucasta, Odes* and *Sonnets*.
1649	In *The Tenure of Kings and Magistrates*, argues that a free people have a right to depose tyrants but attacks Presbyterians, who, having exercised this right, are themselves becoming tyrannical. Appointed Secretary for Foreign Tongues to the Council of State (March) at £288 p.a. Instructed to answer *Eikon Basilike* ('The Royal Image'). Replies with *Eikonoklastes* ('The Image Breaker'). Milton sees Providence leading to King's execution, and the success of the Opposition a sign of God's approval. Given lodgings for official work in Scotland Yard.	Poems on the death of Lord Hastings by Marvell, Dryden, Herrick and Denham. Gerrard Winstanley: *The True Levellers' Standard Advanced*. Overton, and other Levellers: *England's New Chains Discovered*, for which they are sent to the Tower. Madeleine de Scudéry: *Artamène, ou le Grand Cyrus* (10 vols. to 1653). Bossuet: *Méditations sur la brièveté de la vie*. Descartes: *Le Traité des passions de l'âme*.
1650	His eyesight deteriorates rapidly. Ordered to reply to Salmasius' *Defensio Regia*.	Marvell: *An Horatian Ode on Cromwell's Return from Ireland*; *Tom May's Death*. Marvell tutoring Mary Fairfax, daughter of the Parliamentary general, at Nun Appleton in Yorkshire, where it is assumed that he writes 'Upon Appleton House' and lyrics such as 'The Garden' and the Mower poems. Thomas Hobbes: *Treatise of Human Nature; De Corpore Politico*. Henry Vaughan: *Silex scintillans; Magia adamica*. Anne Bradstreet's poems: *The Tenth Muse Lately Sprung up in America*.

CHRONOLOGY

Second Civil War. Army passes Vote of No Address (January). Cromwell defeats Scots at Preston (August). More serious reprisals against Royalists, as at Colchester, show mood of Opposition has changed. Army press for trial of king, referred to in Ireton's Remonstrance as 'that man of blood'; Parliament continues to negotiate with him. In 'Pride's Purge' Army forcibly reduces membership of Parliament to 150, known as 'The Rump'. The Rump and the army become centre of power in the country.

Fronde of the Parlement begins in France (May). Peace of Westphalia (October) ends Thirty Years War. France, Saxony and Bavaria chief territorial gainers; Habsburg power is contained.

Trial and execution of Charles I (January). Publication of the anonymous *Eikon Basilike*, an immediate bestseller (unlike Milton's reply), presenting the late king as a martyr and a moderate peace-loving ruler. Does much to turn tide against Puritan revolution. Monarchy and House of Lords abolished (February). New republic essentially oligarchic with no concessions to 'the people's rights' as pressed by Levellers. Economic depression and unemployment. Winstanley and the Diggers occupy common land on St George's Hill, Surrey (April), denouncing property as a Norman invention. Proliferation of disaffected sectaries – Anabaptists, Ranters, Familists, Adamites, Brownists, Fifth Monarchists, etc.; many lay preachers (including women). Cromwell and Fairfax crush Levellers as political force and Lilburne spends most of 1650s in prison. Cromwell brutally suppresses Irish Catholics at Drogheda. Charles II proclaimed in Scotland. Fairfax, who had opposed the execution of the late king, retires from public life.

End of Fronde of the parlement and beginning of Princes' Fronde, with Condé opposing Mazarin.

Execution of Montrose. Cromwell defeats Scots at Dunbar. Ordinance repealing penalties for non-attendance at Church, provided one attended an alternative public place of worship, favours Independents, but also Roman Catholics. Society of Friends ('Quakers') founded by George Foxe.

Velasquez paints *Pope Innocent X*; Claude Lorraine *The Flight into Egypt*. Giacomo Carissimi: *Jephtha* – one of the earliest oratorios. Couperin: *Livre d'Orgue*. John Playford, probably the first regular music publisher in England, publishes *The English Dancing Master*. Von Guericke invents the air pump and initiates experiments with vacuums.

JOHN MILTON

DATE	AUTHOR'S LIFE	LITERARY CONTEXT
1651	In *Defensio pro populo Anglicano* (24 February) Milton argues that the authority of kings is committed to them 'in trust from the People, to the Common good of all' – anathema to supporters of the theory of Divine Right. The book causes considerable alarm on the Continent and is publicly burnt in Paris and Toulouse. Milton's only son, John, born (16 March). Moves, for the sake of his health, to Petty France, near St James's Park.	Hobbes: *Leviathan*. Vaughan: *Olor Iscanus*. Donne's *Essays in Divinity* published. D'Avenant: *Gondibert*. Cartwright: *Comedies, Tragedies, with other poems*. Taylor: *The Rule and Exercise of Holy Living* (1650) and ... *of Holy Dying* (1651), for which he is charged with atheism. Henry Wotton's collection of poems *Reliquiae Wottonianae*. Corneille: *Andromède*.
1652	Right eye collapses and he becomes totally blind. Daughter Deborah born (2 May). Wife dies (5 May) and Milton is left to cope with four young children. Six weeks later, son John dies. Pierre du Moulin's *Regii Sanguinis Clamor* – attributed by Milton to Alexander More – published (August) in reply to Milton's *Defensio*, and he is ordered to reply by the Council of State. William D'Avenant, a prisoner in the Tower since 1650, is said to have been saved by Milton. Writes sonnet to the Lord General Cromwell and sonnet 'On his blindness'.	Gerrard Winstanley: *Law of Freedom*. Crashaw's posthumous poems, *Carmen Deo Nostro*. Vaughan: *The Mount of Olives, or Solitary Devotions*. English translation by Richard Loveday and others of La Calprenède's *Cléopâtre* (12 vols., to 1659). Edward Benlowes: *Theophila, or Love's Sacrifice*. Letters of Dorothy Osborne to William Temple (to 1654).
1653	Milton's translations of the Psalms. First evidence of Milton's acquaintance with Marvell (in a letter dated 21 February he recommends Marvell to John Bradshaw). Though Milton entertains no higher view of the Irish than most of his contemporaries, he does intervene with Cromwell to have confiscated lands restored to Spenser's grandson.	Marvell: *The Character of Holland*; *The Bermudas*. Begins work on *The First Anniversary of the Government under His Highness the Lord Protector*. Izaak Walton: *The Compleat Angler*. Shirley: *Cupid and Death* with music by Matthew Locke.

CHRONOLOGY

Charles II invades England; defeated by Cromwell at Worcester – 'God's "crowning mercy"'. Scotland and England forcibly united. English naval superiority over Dutch and French confirmed. First English Navigation Acts (October) to break hold of Dutch carrying trade between Europe and America. Cape Colony founded by Dutch. Lely's portrait of Oliver Cromwell. Riccioli and Grimaldi's lunar map (Grimaldi also first to discover diffraction of light and evolve wave theory of light.)

End of war in Ireland. Settlement of demobilized English troops on lands of former Catholic rebels. First Anglo-Dutch war (to 1654). Blake's victory off the Kentish Knock; his defeat off Dungeness. Parliament resolve tithe system should continue until Committee of Propagation of the Gospel comes up with alternative system of providing for clergy (Milton and Independents oppose any form of state support for clergy; hence his sonnet to Cromwell). Parliament passes Act of Pardon and Oblivion to reconcile Royalists. Condé, with Spanish support, marches on France and occupies Paris. Dutch create colony at Cape of Good Hope. John Hilton's collection of catches, *Catch as Catch Can*. First coffee house in London in Cornhill.

Naval victories against Dutch by Blake and Monck. The Rump, finally on the point of introducing a Bill of Elections, is dissolved by Cromwell. Shortlived 'Barebones' Parliament, composed of 140 delegates handpicked from lists provided by separatist Puritan congregations. Cromwell becomes Lord Protector (December) under Lambert's 'Instrument of Government'. Ruysdael: *Two Water Mills and an Open Sluice*.

DATE	AUTHOR'S LIFE	LITERARY CONTEXT
1654	*Defensio Secunda* publilshed (30 May). In this Milton makes clear that though he supported the revolution he is not in favour of extending the franchise, asking what would have happened if the mob had demanded that the king be restored. Probably writes the two sonnets to his friend Cyriack Skinner.	Richard Flecknoe's *Ariadne*, probably the first English opera. Madeleine de Scudéry: *Clélie, histoire romaine* (10 vols. to 1660). Roger Boyle: *Parthenissa* (in imitation of French heroic romances). John Playford: *A Breif Introduction to the Skill of Musick*.
1655	By this time Milton is assisted in his secretarial duties by G. R. Weckherlin and Philip Meadows, which gives him time to resume his private studies. He starts compiling a Latin dictionary and Greek lexicon. Works on *De Doctrina* and, possibly, on *Paradise Lost*. His salary is reduced from £288 to £150 p.a. but is made a pension for life. *Defensio Pro se* (8 August). Writes sonnet 'Avenge, O Lord, Thy slaughter'd saints', on the expulsion and massacre of the Protestant Vaudois by orders of the Prince of Savoy.	Thomas Fuller: *Church History*. Edmund Waller: *Ayres and Dialogues*, including 'Go Lovely Rose'. Thomas Stanley: *A History of Philosophy* (to 1662). Mme de Sévigné begins to write her *Letters*. 1650s: Cambridge Platonists – Benjamin Whichcote, John Smith, Henry More, Ralph Cudworth, etc., try to combat the sort of materialism preached by Hobbes and to free religion from fanaticism and controversy.
1656	Marries Katherine Woodcock, aged 28. Begins to part company with Cromwell's government which appears to him to be shedding its revolutionary ideals.	James Harrington: *The Commonwealth of Oceana* in opposition to *Leviathan*. Cowley: *Poems*. D'Avenant's *The Siege of Rhodes*, one of the earliest Engish operas, evades ban on stage-plays.
1657	Daughter Katherine born (19 October). Andrew Marvell appointed his assistant in the Secretaryship.	John Bunyan: *A Vindication* (anti-Quaker). Unauthorized edition of poems of Henry King. Richard Baxter: *Call to the Unconverted*.

CHRONOLOGY

Expedition of Penn and Venables to Hispaniola (part of Cromwell's grand 'Western Design' to secure settlements in West Indies). England makes commercial treaties with Sweden, Denmark and Portugal. Successful revolt of Brazil against Dutch dominion. John de Witt becomes Pensionary of Holland. End of Frondes in France. Mazarin's authority confirmed. Abdication of Queen Christina of Sweden. New interest, during Commonwealth, in Elizabethan diplomacy; publication of *The Compleat Ambassador* (7 vols.) by Sir Dudley Digges, Elizabeth I's Master of the Rolls. At Oxford, Bible translated into Irish, Welsh, Turkish and Malay (to 1658).

Cromwell divides country into districts and appoints a major general to undertake the policing of each. Encourages Jews to return to England (expelled by Edward I), partly for mercantile reasons. Jamaica seized. As centre of slave trade it was to become central to English imperial policy. Trade boom. Cromwell living at Whitehall, assumes many of the external trappings of royalty. Secretary Thurloe has complete control of all printed material. Free discussion and pamphleteering ends. Nedham's *Mercurius Politicus* and *The Public Intelligencer* remain. John Wallis' *Arithmetica Infinitorum* contains the principles of differential calculus; becomes a standard work. Isaac Newton becomes professor of mathematics at Cambridge. Rembrandt: *Woman Bathing*. Murillo: *Birth of the Virgin*.

Alliance of England and France against Spain; Spain blockaded throughout winter. War against England's traditional enemy, regarded as war against anti-Christ, at first popular, but trade rather than religion influences Cromwell's foreign policy. That Mazarin is willing to ally with England demonstrates English government no longer regarded as revolutionary, but as a conservative national government. Birth of Edmund Hallé.

In 'The Humble Petition and Advice' Parliament invites Cromwell to assume hereditary kingship, which he refuses. Republicans led by Lambert oppose any move towards a monarchy. Royalists intriguing with disaffected Levellers (eg. Edward Sexby, whose *Killing No Murder* calls for Cromwell's assassination). Blake's destruction of Spanish silver fleet at Santa-Cruz. Clearing up of privateers protects English merchants. Republic confirmed as major maritime power and gains increased prestige in Europe. Invention of pendulum clock. Tea and drinking chocolate first sold in London.

DATE	AUTHOR'S LIFE	LITERARY CONTEXT
1658	Wife dies (3 February), followed by daughter Katherine (17 March). Milton edits and publishes his ms. of Sir Walter Raleigh's *Cabinet Council*. Begins work in earnest on *Paradise Lost*.	Marvell: *A Poem upon the Death of His Late Highness the Lord Protector*. Thomas Browne: *Urne Burial*. Edward Phillips: *The New World of English Words*.
1659	Milton publishes *A Treatise of Civil Power* (pro religious toleration though acknowledging that reasons of state might justify exclusion of Catholics) and *Considerations touching the Likeliest means to remove Hirelings out of the Church*, and writes *A Letter to a Friend, Concerning the Ruptures of the Commonwealth* (published 1698).	Edward Stillingfleet: *Irenicum*. John Hales: *Golden Remains*. Henry Vane: *A Needful Corrective or Ballance in Popular Government*. Molière: *Les Précieuses ridicules*. One-volume publication of the 18 *Provinciales* of Pascal.
1660	*The Readie and Easie Way to Establish a Free Commonwealth* (March) and *Brief Notes Upon a Late Sermon* (April) – 'The last words', as he put it, 'of expiring liberty' – courageously published on the eve of the Restoration. Goes into hiding in a friend's house to escape retaliation (May). Parliament takes steps to have him arrested (June). Copies of *Defensio pro populo Anglicano* and *Eikonoklastes* burnt by public hangman in London (August). Milton, excluded from Act of Indemnity, is arrested and imprisoned (October). Released on 15 December. Marvell defends Milton at his prosecution and protests to Parliament about his excessive gaol fees of £150. May also have been defended by D'Avenant whom he had earlier protected. Prynne, now a Royalist, and always opposed to Milton's views on toleration, presses for his execution as a	Samuel Pepys begins his *Diary*. Birth of Daniel Defoe. Harrington: *Political Discourses tending to the introduction of a free Commonwealth in England* (he is imprisoned in the Tower in 1661). Bunyan arrested for preaching without a licence and spends next 12 years in Bedford gaol. Cowley: *Ode, upon the Blessed Restoration*. Falkland: *Discourses of Infallibility* and a *Reply*. Fuller: *Mixed Contemplations in Better Times*. Dryden celebrates the Restoration in *Astraea Redux*. Tatham: *The Rump, or The Mirror of the Late Times* (a play). Charles Hoole: *New Discovery of the Old Art of Teaching Schoole*. Hobbes: *Behemoth*. Spinoza: *Short Treatise on God, Man and his Faith*.

CHRONOLOGY

HISTORICAL EVENTS

Anglo-French siege of Dunkirk; Battle of the Dunes. Death of Cromwell. Protectorate passes to his son, Richard (3 September), a tool of army chiefs Fleetwood and Disbrowe. Birth of Purcell. First bank note (in Sweden). Velasquez: *The Rokeby Venus*; Rembrandt: *Self-Portrait with a Stick*.

Richard deposed by army coup. Rump of 1653 recalled. Derby Petition. Lambert's rising. Second forcible dissolution of the Rump (of which Milton greatly disapproves – 'illegal and scandalous ... barbarous ... that a paid army should ... thus subdue the supream power that set them up'.) Lambert rules through the Committee of Safety. Rump reconvenes in December on news that George Monck had mobilized army of occupation in Scotland. John Rushworth's first great collection of State Papers (for years 1618-29). Treaty of the Pyrenees between France and Spain.

Monck marches south, raising another regiment en route (named after border town of Coldstream), invading England 1 January. Fairfax, rallying in support, takes York. Lambert's army offers no opposition. Monck reaches London 3 February, pragmatically not having announced any intention other than to establish a free and full Parliament to replace the discredited Rump. Members of Long Parliament expelled by Pride are allowed to return and Parliament thereupon votes for its own dissolution. New Parliament, including restored House of Lords, meets (25 April) and is presented with letter from Charles II and conciliatory Declaration of Breda, in which, subject to Parliament's approval, he promises a free pardon for his former enemies, payment of arrears to army and navy, confirmation of titles to land and limited religious toleration. Terms accepted with enthusiasm. Charles returns to England, reaching London 29 May. Act of Indemnity and Oblivion. Theatres re-open. D'Avenant and Killigrew granted monopoly of acting in London.

Marriage of Louis XIV and Maria Teresa of Spain. Robert Boyle: *New Experiments Physio-mechanical, Touching the Spring of the Air and Its Effects*.

DATE	AUTHOR'S LIFE	LITERARY CONTEXT
1660 *cont*	regicide; but it is generally considered that his blindness is God's punishment and therefore sufficient.	
1661	Milton's time no longer being taken up by political writings, he is free to turn to his abandoned vocation to be a major national poet and produce something 'for aftertimes as they should not willingly let it die'. Works in earnest on *Paradise Lost* which is finished, accordingly to Aubrey, by 1663.	Waller: *St James's Park*; *To My Lady Morton*. Glanvill: *The Vanity of Dogmatizing*. Charles II attracts to his court aristocratic coterie of writers – 'the Merry Gang' – including George Villiers, Duke of Buckingham, Charles Sackville, and Sir Charles Sedley. Evelyn: *Fumifugium, or The Inconvenience of the Air and Smoke of London Dissipated*. Molière: *L'Ecole des maris*.
1662	Meets the Quaker Thomas Ellwood and begins tutoring him. Sonnet to Sir Henry Vane published (probably written in 1652. Vane, a prominent member of the Council of State until 1653 when he broke with Cromwell over dissolution of the Rump, is executed as a regicide in January 1662).	Samuel Butler: *Hudibras* (part 1). Fuller: *History of the Worthies of England*. Molière: *L'Ecole des femmes*. Mme de La Fayette: *La Princesse de Montpensier*. La Rochefoucauld: *Mémoires*. Bossuet: *Sermons*.
1663	Marries Elizabeth Minshull, aged 24 (24 February), who is allegedly severe to Milton's daughters 'the two eldest of which she bound prentices to Workers in Gold Lace without his knowledge; and forc'd the youngest to leave his Family'. Moves house to what is now Bunhill Fields where he spends the remainder of his life.	Shakespeare Third Folio. Cowley: *Verses on Several Occasions*. Herbert of Cherbury: *De religione Gentilium*. Thomas Stanley's edition of Aeschylus. John Wilmot, Earl of Rochester, joins the 'Merry Gang'.
1664		Collected plays of Thomas Killigrew published. George Etherege: *The Comical Revenge, or Love in a Tub*. Molière: *Tartuffe*. Lucy Hutchinson begins her Memoirs of the Life of Colonel John Hutchinson.

CHRONOLOGY

Of the 59 who signed Charles I's death warrant, 29 are sentenced to death, of which 10 are executed. On anniversary of king's execution, bodies of Cromwell, Ireton, and Bradshaw are dug up from Westminster Abbey and reburied at Tyburn. Convention parliament's failure to secure accommodation for their predominantly Presbyterian views signals beginning of collapse of Puritanism as a political force. Fifth Monarchist revolt under Venner does not help cause of toleration. New 'Cavalier' Parliament with Anglican majority obliterates most of constitutional reforms of previous twenty years, orders burning of the Solemn League and Covenant and repeals 1642 statute excluding bishops from the House of Lords. Militia Act places armed forces under command of king. Corporation Act: all local government officers obliged to take an oath of non-resistance, abjure the Covenant and take Anglican communion. Louis XIV assumes full powers in France; Colbert put in control of finance and economy.

Charles marries the Roman Catholic Catherine of Braganza. Secret marriage of James, Duke of York to Clarendon's daughter, Anne Hyde. Parliament now defines parameters of national religion, enforcing the Clarendon Code in defiance of the king's Declaration of Indulgence. Act of Uniformity imposes oaths of non-resistance, etc., on clergy, who are obliged to accept Book of Common Prayer and the 39 Articles in their entirety. Nearly 2,000 (out of 9,000) Presbyterian clergy give up their livings in the greatest purge since the Reformation. Lambert is imprisoned for life. Wren's Sheldonian Theatre at Oxford. Robert Boyle: *The Sceptical Chymist*, sweeps away alchemical theories and insists on the importance of experiment and sound deduction. Death of naturalist John Tradescant whose natural history collection later forms nucleus of Ashmolean Museum in Oxford.

The Royal Society gains its charter. Founders and early members include Boyle, Hooke, Petty, Ray, Wilkins, Wren, Ashmole, Aubrey, Cowley, Dryden, Evelyn and Waller. Staple Act confirms 1651 Navigation Acts, closing off colonial trade to foreign shipping. America and West Indian colonies rapidly emerge as staple suppliers of tobacco, raw cotton and rice to Europe – all transhipped through England. Drury Lane Theatre opens. First Turnpike Act. John Webb, Inigo Jones' pupil, begins the King Charles Building at Greenwich Palace, in Baroque style. Palladio's *First Book of Architecture*.

English capture Niew Amsterdam from Dutch and rename it New York after James, Duke of York. Triennial Act made non-compulsory. Conventicle Act to suppress Dissenting congregations; sporadically enforced but religious non-conformity too widespread now to be stamped out. Work starts on Versailles under Le Vaux and Le Nôtre. Evelyn's *Sylva*, an influential book on practical arboriculture, followed up by *Kalendarium Hortense, or the Gardener's Almanack*. Hals: *Men . . . and Women Governors of the Haarlem Almshouse.*

DATE	AUTHOR'S LIFE	LITERARY CONTEXT
1665	Thomas Ellwood takes a house for Milton in Chalfont St Giles to avoid plague.	John Bunyan: *The Holy City, or the New Jerusalem.* John Dryden: *The Indian Emperor* (stars Nell Gwyn). La Rochefoucauld: *Maximes.* La Fontaine: *Contes et nouvelles en vers.*
1666	House in Bread Street destroyed by fire (2–6 September). No longer in office, and having already lost £2,000 which he had lent to the Republican government and a considerable sum through malversation, Milton does not appear to be discontented.	Bunyan: *Grace Abounding.* Waller: *Instructions to a Painter* (on the battle of Sole Bay). Molière: *Le Misanthrope; Le Médicin malgré lui.* Glanvill: *Philosophical Considerations Concerning Witches and Witchcraft.*
1667	*Paradise Lost* published. (When Dryden asks permission to adapt this for the stage (*The State of Innocence and the Fall of Man*, 1677), Milton receives him civilly and gives him 'leave to tagge his Verses'.)	Dryden: *Annus mirabilis.* Marvell writes *Last Instructions to a Painter* attacking financial and sexual corruption at Court and in Parliament. Also writes satires against Clarendon and takes part in his impeachment. Birth of Jonathan Swift. Racine: *Andromaque.*
1668	There are numerous stories about Milton's authoritarian attitude to his family, though his daughter Deborah, who acted as his amenuensis, reported that he was excellent company, especially for young people. He is said, in his later years to have enjoyed gardening and playing the organ; he received many visitors from home and abroad and remained on excellent terms with Catholic and Royalist relations.	Dryden: *Of Dramatick Poesy.* Thomas Traherne: *Centuries of Meditations.* Etherege: *She Would if she Could.* Thomas Shadwell: *The Sullen Lovers.* Cowley: *Essays in Verse and Prose.* Peter Heylen: *Cyprianus Anglicus, or The History of the Life and Death of Archbishop Laud.* Boileau: *Satires VIII–IX.*
1669	*Accedence Commenced Grammar* published.	Dryden: *Tyrannic Love.* William Penn (from the Tower of London): *No Cross, No Crown.* Burnet: *Conference between a Conformist and a Non-Conformist.*

CHRONOLOGY

Outbreak of bubonic plague kills 70,000 Londoners and paralyses port for three months. Five Miles Act further restricts activities of Dissenting ministers, though half-heartedly enforced. Second Dutch War (to 1667) appeases public clamour though does not resolve trade issue. James defeats Dutch off Lowestoft. Newton's theory of the use of fluxions. *Philosophical Transactions*, published by the Royal Society, the first permanent scientific journal. Robert Hooke's *Micrographia* (studies crystal structure of snowflakes). Hooke's studies of microscopic fossils lead him to become one of the first proponents of a theory of evolution.

Great Fire of London. *London Gazette* founded as organ of Government. Scottish Covenanters defeated at the battle of Pentland Hills. Newton's theory of gravitation. Wenceslaus Hollar, draughtsman to the king since 1660 makes the last of his famous engravings of London pre-Fire. Leibniz: *De Arte Combinatoria* in which he argues that all reasoning is reducible to an ordered combination of elements such as words, sounds and colours (anticipating some modern computers). Vermeer: *Allegory on the Art of Painting*.

While peace negotiations being held at Breda, Dutch raiding force sails up the Medway, sinks three ships and tows away the flagship, *The Royal Charles*. Dismissal and exile of Clarendon, unfairly charged with embezzlement and unpopular owing to lack of tangible war successes. Replaced by no less unpopular 'Cabal' (formed from the initials of their names – Clifford, Arlington, Buckingham, Ashley Cooper and Lauderdale). Reforms of Treasury; exchequer certificates circulate as embryonic paper currency. Lauderdale begins to impose autocratic rule on Scotland. Newton's optical discoveries begin. Naturalist John Ray, founder of modern biological science, begins his classification of species.

Triple alliance of England, Holland and Sweden to protect the Netherlands against France, organized by Temple and Arlington, a rather too advanced diplomatic coup for Parliament who still regard the Dutch as England's principal enemy. Increasing distrust of the Cabal. Sir William Coventry resigns from Government and becomes focus of what for the first time is a regular Opposition or 'Country' Party, convinced of corruption in high places, suspicious of Charles' foreign policy and beginning to suspect his loyalty to Protestantism. Claude Lorraine: *Landscape with the Angel Appearing to Hagar*. Dryden becomes poet laureate.

James, Duke of York, publicly acknowledges his conversion to Roman Catholicism the previous year; Charles insists his daughters are brought up as Anglicans. Sir Christopher Wren becomes Surveyor of Works and responsible for the rebuilding of London following the Great Fire. His work includes St Paul's Cathedral and 51 other London churches.

DATE	AUTHOR'S LIFE	LITERARY CONTEXT
1670	*History of Britain* published (from legendary times to Norman Conquest). Portrait by William Faithorne.	Dryden: *The Conquest of Granada.* Aphra Behn's first play, *The Forced Marriage.* Birth of William Congreve. Izaak Walton: *Life of George Herbert.* Heylen: *Aerius Redivivus, or The History of Presbyterianism.* Pascal: *Pensées.* Spinoza: *Tractatus Theologico-Politicus.*
1671	*Paradise Regained* and *Samson Agonistes* published jointly. Milton's three great post-Restoration works all to some extent express the bitterness he feels at the reinstatement of the episcopacy, and his attempt to understand the failure of the Puritan revolution which had seemed to its supporters to have been ordained by God.	Traherne: majority of *Thanksgivings* and probably collected and arranged 'Dobell' sequence of poems. George Villiers, Second Duke of Buckingham: *The Rehearsal* (attrib.). Bunyan writing his *Pilgrim's Progress* (published 1678). William Wycherley: *Love in a Wood.*
1672	Publishes *Artis logicae plenior institutio* ('A Fuller Institution of the Art of Logic').	Anonymous publication of Marvell's *The Rehearsal Transposed,* advocating toleration for Dissenters. Bunyan: *A Confession of my Faith and a Reason of my Practice.* Dryden: *Marriage à-la-Mode; Of Heroik Plays.* Births of Joseph Addison and Richard Steele.
1673	*Of True religion, Heresy, Schism and Toleration.* Second edition of the minor poems, originally published in 1645.	Wycherley: *The Gentleman Dancing-Master.* Shadwell: *Epsom Wells.* Behn: *The Dutch Lover.* William Temple: *Essay on the Origin and Nature of Government.* Racine: *Mithradate.*

HISTORICAL EVENTS

Rumours re. King's possible divorce. Treaty of Dover, whereby Charles
agrees to support Louis' annexation of the Netherlands with naval help, for
which he receives a subsidy of 3 million *livres* p.a. By a secret clause Charles
agrees to declare his Catholicism at an appropriate time (which never
occurs), whereupon the subsidy would be increased, together with military
aid if necessary. Death of Charles' favourite sister, Henriette, Duchess of
Orleans. Hudson's Bay Trading Company established.

English buccaneers destroy Panama. French Senegal Company founded.
Colonel Blood attempts to steal the Crown Jewels and is pardoned.
Grinling Gibbons' carving of Tintoretto's *Crucifixion* leads to Wren's
patronage and his employment at St Paul's, Blenheim, Chatsworth, etc.

Charles II's Declaration of Indulgence suspends penal laws against
Protestant Nonconformists and Catholics alike. Viewed by some as part of
a pro-French, Roman Catholic conspiracy. Third Dutch War. Louis
invades Holland (June); halted by William of Orange who is elected
Stadtholder after popular uprising overthrows republic. The Stop of the
Exchequer – repayment of Government debts suspended with the promise
of an extra 6% interest to creditors as compensation – a radical step but the
only one Charles can find to finance war. Pepys appointed Secretary to the
Admiralty. Ashley Cooper made Earl of Shaftesbury and Lord Chancellor.
The two Van de Velde brothers, maritime painters, enter royal service.

Parliament makes supply dependent upon withdrawal of Declaration of
Indulgence; Charles humiliatingly concedes. Parliamentary opinion begins
to swing in favour of William of Orange, encouraged by Dutch propaganda
and bribery. Outrage at news of James's impending marriage to the
Catholic Mary of Modena; Shaftesbury dismissed for his opposition. Test
Act passed whereby office holders are obliged to make declaration denying
transubstantiation and produce a certificate that they have recently taken
Anglican communion. Clifford and the Duke of York resign, confirming
public's worst fears. Lully's *Tragédies-lyriques*. First public concerts held in
London. Christian Huygen's *Horlogium Oscillatorum* contains earliest attempt
to apply dynamics to bodies of finite size.

DATE	AUTHOR'S LIFE	LITERARY CONTEXT
1674	Publishes *Epistolae familiares et prolusiones* ('Letters and Prolusions'). Marvell writes commendatory poem for the second, revised edition of *Paradise Lost*. Milton dies at home of 'gout struck in' between 8 and 10 November. Buried (12 November) at St Giles, Cripplegate. Wife survives him until 1727.	Wycherley: *The Plain Dealer*. Shadwell's opera *The Enchanted Island* (adaptation of *The Tempest*). Hobbes' translation of Homer's *Odyssey*. Racine: *Iphigénie*. Boileau: *L'Art poétique*.

CHRONOLOGY

Fall of the Cabal (except Lauderdale). Treaty of Westminster; Charles pulls out of the war. First moves by Parliament towards the Exclusion of James, as a Roman Catholic, from the throne, and to reduce royal power over the judiciary, Parliament, tax and religion, leads to prorogation. Shaftesbury, espousing cause of popular Protestantism, emerging as leader of Whig opposition. Way clear for rise of Thomas Osborne, later Earl of Danby, as chief minister.

Organist and composer John Blow becomes Master of the Children of the Chapel Royal where he later becomes Henry Purcell's teacher.

THE EVERYMAN MILTON

This is the fourth Everyman Milton, and the second with which I have been associated. The changes in editorial practice that have made new editions desirable reflect the history of scholarly editing in this century. The first Everyman Milton appeared in 1909, edited by W. H. D. Rouse. At the time Rouse was headmaster of the Perse School in Cambridge, university lecturer in Sanscrit, and editor of *Classical Review*. Rouse was a pioneer of the direct method of teaching, and insisted that his conversations with the boys of the Perse be conducted in Greek or Latin. His edition of Milton assumes a familiarity and sympathy with this classical culture. Milton's Greek, Latin and Italian poems are included without translations, and assistance to the reader consists of a boldly modernized text of the English poems and a short glossary.

The second Everyman Milton appeared in 1956, with a new text by B. A. Wright, Professor of English at the University of Southampton. Editing in the 1950s was characterized by an attempt to reconstruct original texts, which were usually printed in old spelling. In the case of Milton the process of reconstruction was shaped by the publication in 1931 of the manuscript of Book I of *Paradise Lost*. Study of this manuscript had convinced scholars that Milton had taken advantage of the lack of uniformity in seventeenth-century spelling by using spelling variants to mark differences in pronunciation and meaning and to control prosody. Milton's nephew Edward Phillips had described how he had assisted his uncle with the revision of passages that 'might possibly want correction as to the orthography and pointing', and so it was assumed that the spelling and punctuation in the printed editions had the authority of the author. The fourth issue of the first edition of *Paradise Lost* contained an erratum in which the reader was asked to substitute 'wee' for 'we' in II 414, and this erratum led scholars to believe that Milton distinguished between emphatic forms of personal pronouns (*hee, mee, wee, yee, you,*

their) and unemphatic forms (*he, me, we, ye, thir*). Two import-
ant editions were based on principles of spelling extrapolated
from the manuscript and printed versions of *Paradise Lost*: one
was Helen Darbishire's Oxford edition (2 vols, 1952 and
1955), and the other was B. A. Wright's Everyman edition.
The fact that these two editions differed so radically was the
first indication of the perils of any attempt to reconstruct
Milton's text on the basis of these newly-discovered principles.
The debate on Milton's spelling continued throughout the
1950s, but was eventually quelled by a lethal attack on
theories of special spelling mounted by J. T. Shawcross in 'One
Aspect of Milton's Spelling: Idle Final "E"' (*PMLA* 78, 1963,
501–10).

Miltonic spelling seemed to be a dead issue, but Miltonic
punctuation remained an article of faith, the best exposition of
which was Mindele Treip's *Milton's Punctuation* (1970). The
assumption that the spelling of Milton's poems could safely be
modernized, but that his punctuation should be retained
became the guiding principle of the edition published in 1968
by John Carey and Alastair Fowler; the quality of the
annotation of Milton's poems in this edition rightly estab-
lished it as the finest scholarly edition of the century, and the
authority of its commentary remains undiminished. Wright's
Everyman text was still favoured by a rearguard, however,
but the lack of annotation and translation had hampered its
effectiveness as a student text. I accordingly undertook to
prepare a third Everyman. Milton, which was published in
1980 with Wright's text supplemented by translations of the
Latin, Greek and Italian poems, and by notes on all the
poems.

In the 1980s the issues of spelling and punctuation con-
tinued to be debated, and the assumptions of Carey and
Fowler as well of those of Darbishire and Wright came under
scrutiny, most notably by John Creaser ('Editorial Problems
in Milton', in *RES* 34 (1983), 279–303 and 35 (1984), 45–60)
and R. G. Moyles (*The Text of 'Paradise Lost': A Study in
Editorial Procedure*, 1985). Wright's text is now beyond all
possibility of defence, and can no longer be used in good
conscience by an editor. I have therefore prepared a fresh

edition, the fourth Everyman Milton. All of Milton's English poems (and his translations into English from other languages) have been included in this edition. I have also included a few poems in other languages: the Italian sonnets, which are an integral part of Milton's development as a sonneteer; the translation of Psalm CXIV into Greek, which is a useful companion to Milton's translation of the same psalm into English; the Latin poem that prefaces *Paradise Lost*, because it constitutes part of the experience of a seventeenth-century reader in encountering Milton's epic; and the Hebrew annotations to the psalms, because they are related to Milton's choice of vocabulary in his translations. In all cases I have provided translations that aim to be literal cribs rather than imitations of poetic effects that are only accessible in the original languages. I have also included Milton's two most famous prose tracts, *Areopagitica* and *Of Education*. The cost of this additional material has been the omission of Milton's Latin poems. The classical culture that kept these poems in the canon has disappeared, and there seems little point in retaining poems that will not be read. *Amissum quod nescitur non amittitur*.

I am convinced by Professor Creaser's argument that there is little sense in preserving the typographical features of the early texts, and have therefore modernized the spelling and capitalization, and dispensed with italics. Spurred on by Stanley Wells's *Modernizing Shakespeare's Spelling* (1979), I have ejected such much-loved archaisms as 'highth' and 'sovran'. As clarity is more important than consistency, I have sometimes printed proper names in seventeenth-century spelling, either because the old form referred to something different from that of its successor ('Marocco', for example, refers to Marrakech, one of the sultanates in what is now Morocco) or because a modernized form would disrupt the metre; the only exceptions in the case of italics are the psalms in which Milton used italics to signal (not always accurately) departures from the original texts. I have extended the principle of modernizing spelling to the Italian sonnets, but not to the Hebrew annotations of the psalms, where I have limited myself to the correction of three obvious misprints.

Punctuation remains a controversial issue, especially in the case of *Paradise Lost*. I have some sympathy with the view that the manuscript of Book I of *Paradise Lost* enjoys a measure of authority denied to the printed text, which seems in many places both inaccurate and inconsistent in its pointing, but I have nonetheless concluded that the punctuation should be modernized. My experience of teaching Milton's poems over many years has convinced me that reproduction of the sparse (and sometimes inaccurate) punctuation of the early editions merely compounds the difficulties experienced by students attempting to understand Milton's syntax. I have therefore decided that the punctuation of the seventeenth-century texts and manuscripts should be supplemented and amended in the interests of communicating the syntax to readers who merely want to know what the lines mean. Dr Rouse simply replaced the seventeenth-century punctuation with stately Edwardian punctuation; I have been more cautious, in that I retain the original punctuation whenever it does not limit understanding, and I do not break up the sentences of the early texts, except in a few cases where a question mark is needed. In altering the original punctuation I have been aware that such alteration constitutes an act of interpretation, but I take that to be the proper task of an editor who is attempting to present seventeenth-century poetry to a twentieth-century audience. I have also added quotation marks to indicate direct speech, and have sometimes added accents in order to indicate stress.

This edition has been prepared primarily for students rather than for professional scholars, so the texts of the poems are eclectic, in that I sometimes silently incorporate variants from manuscripts and early editions and occasionally accept emendations that originate in the eighteenth century. In the notes I try to distinguish between allusions (usually to the Bible or classical literature), which I try to explain, and sources, for which I only give a reference. I have not documented allusions to Gensis i–iii in my notes on *Paradise Lost*; similarly, the notes to *Paradise Regained* and *Samson Agonistes* do not record allusions to the accounts in Matthew, Luke and Judges. If, however, Milton's text reflects readings embodied in the Hebrew,

Greek, Latin or Syriac traditions that do not appear in English Bibles, I do comment in the notes. Such comments should not be construed as identifications of sources, but rather as indications of alternative traditions. Milton's usual Bible was the Protestant Latin translation known as Junius-Tremellius, and he also consulted Hebrew, Greek and Syriac texts. In an edition designed for scholars one would refer primarily to Junius-Tremellius, but in a student edition it seems more sensible to refer to accessible editions. I therefore commonly cite the Authorized Version and the Vulgate, neither of which would have been read by someone of Milton's theological convictions, but both of which contain readings that can facilitate understanding of Milton's allusions. The Authorized (or 'King James') Version is abbreviated as A.V., the Revised Version as R.V., the Old and New Testaments as O.T. and N.T., and the Septuagint (the Greek version of the O.T.). as LXX; *Paradise Lost*, *Paradise Regained* and *Samson Agonistes* appear as *PL*, *PR* and *SA*. In the case of references to classical authors I have sought to avoid confusion and achieve brevity by adopting an inconsistent system. If an author is associated with only one book, I sometimes append the precise reference to the author's name without referring to the title. In the case of Greek or Latin books known by a single English title, I have used that title; in the case of Greek works known by Latin titles, I have given the Latin title, and if its meaning is not obvious, have translated it; in the case of minor Greek works with no agreed English or Latin title, I have printed the title in Greek and then translated it.

ACKNOWLEDGEMENTS

The process of editing Milton is inevitably collaborative, because recourse to the scholarly tradition of serious annotation that began in 1695 with the publication of Patrick Hume's commentary on *Paradise Lost* enables the editor to transcend the limitations of a modern education by drawing on the learning of those educated in the centuries that preceded our own. Our dependence on eighteenth- and nineteenth-century commentators has meant that when they nodded, we have tended to nod with them, and so some errors in modern editions, such as the idea that the Spanish historian Juan de Mariana described a massacre at Fuenterrabia (*Paradise Lost* I 587), can be traced back (through the occasional protests of Victorian editors) to the eighteenth century. In struggling to avoid the occasional perils of dependence on earlier editors I have doubtless made mistakes of my own invention; scope for independent error is particularly capacious in the annotation of the prose tracts included in this volume, because there is no tradition of learned commentary on Milton's prose. On occasions when I have known my knowledge to be defective, I have turned to friends for advice, and so have received the generous assistance of Neil Harris, Roy Flannagan, Alastair Fowler and Leo Miller. Other friends have assisted unwittingly through their published work, particularly Cedric Brown, John Carey and John Creaser. I am also grateful to Gavin Campbell for helping to prepare the text of this edition.

I assumed responsibility for the Everyman Milton at the suggestion of C. A. Patrides, who had earlier inducted me into the scholarly tradition that he represented with such distinction. I should like to dedicate this edition to his memory.

1990   G.C.

POEMS

OF

MR. *John Milton,*

BOTH

ENGLISH and LATIN,

Compos'd at several times.

Printed by his true Copies.

The SONGS were set in Musick by
MR. HENRY LAWES Gentleman of
the KINGS Chappel, and one
of His MAIESTIES
Private Musick.

———*Baccare frontem*
Cingite, ne vati noceat mala lingua futuro,
Virgil, Eclog. 7.

The quotation from Virgil means 'Wreathe my forehead with bacchar, and let not an
evil tongue injure the destined poet.'

PREFACE TO THE FIRST EDITION

1645

THE STATIONER TO THE READER

It is not any private respect of gain, gentle reader – for the slightest pamphlet is nowadays more vendible than the works of learnedest men – but it is the love I have to our own language that hath made me diligent to collect and set forth such pieces, both in prose and verse, as may renew the wonted honour and esteem of our English tongue; and it's the worth of these both English and Latin poems, not the flourish of any prefixed encomions, that can invite thee to buy them – though these are not without the highest commendations and applause of the learnedest academics, both domestic and foreign, and, amongst those of our own country, the unparalleled attestation of that renowned Provost of Eton, Sir Henry Wotton.[1] I know not thy palate, how it relishes such dainties, nor how harmonious thy soul is: perhaps more trivial airs may please thee better. But howsoever thy opinion is spent upon these, that encouragement I have already received from the most ingenious men, in their clear and courteous entertainment of Mr Waller's[2] late choice pieces, hath once more made me adventure into the world, presenting it with these ever-green and not to be blasted laurels. The author's more peculiar excellency in these studies was too well known to conceal his papers, or to keep me from attempting to solicit them from him. Let the event guide itself which way it will, I shall deserve of the age by bringing into the light as true a birth as the Muses have brought forth since our famous Spenser wrote; whose poems in these English ones are as rarely imitated as sweetly excelled. Reader, if thou art eagle-eyed to censure their worth, I am not fearful to expose them to thy exactest perusal.

Thine to command,

HUMPH. MOSELEY[3]

The Stationer to the Reader

1 Wotton] See Wotton's letter, p. 59.
2 Mr Waller] Edmund Waller's *Poems* had been published by Moseley earlier in 1645.
3 Moseley] Humphrey Moseley (d. 1661), the principal literary publisher of the mid-seventeenth century, also published editions of Beaumont and Fletcher, Crashaw, Fanshawe, D'Avenant, Denham, Donne and Vaughan.

ON THE MORNING OF CHRIST'S NATIVITY

Composed 1629

I

This is the month, and this the happy morn,
Wherein the Son of heaven's eternal King,
Of wedded maid and virgin mother born,
Our great redemption from above did bring;
For so the holy sages once did sing,   5
    That he our deadly forfeit should release,
And with his Father work us a perpetual peace.

II

That glorious form, that light unsufferable,
And that far-beaming blaze of majesty,
Wherewith he wont at heaven's high council-table   10
To sit the midst of trinal unity,
He laid aside, and here with us to be,
    Forsook the courts of everlasting day,
And chose with us a darksome house of mortal clay.

III

Say, heavenly Muse, shall not thy sacred vein   15
Afford a present to the infant God?
Hast thou no verse, no hymn, or solemn strain,
To welcome him to this his new abode,
Now while the heaven, by the sun's team untrod,
    Hath took no print of the approaching light,   20
And all the spangled host keep watch in squadrons bright?

IV

See how from far upon the eastern road
The star-led wizards haste with odours sweet!
O run, prevent them with thy humble ode,

On the Morning of Christ's Nativity. Milton describes the 'Nativity Ode' in his Latin
poem *Elegia* VI, noting that it was composed early on Christmas Day (1629).
5 holy sages] Hebrew prophets.
15 heavenly Muse] Urania; see *PL* VII In.
24 prevent] anticipate.

And lay it lowly at his blessed feet;   25
Have thou the honour first, thy Lord to greet,
   And join thy voice unto the angel choir,
From out his secret altar touched with hallowed fire.

THE HYMN

I

    It was the winter wild,
    While the heaven-born child   30
All meanly wrapped in the rude manger lies;
    Nature, in awe to him,
    Had doffed her gaudy trim,
With her great master so to sympathise;
It was no season then for her   35
To wanton with the sun, her lusty paramour.

II

    Only with speeches fair
    She woos the gentle air
To hide her guilty front with innocent snow,
    And on her naked shame,   40
    Pollute with sinful blame,
The saintly veil of maiden white to throw,
Confounded, that her maker's eyes
Should look so near upon her foul deformities.

III

    But he, her fears to cease,   45
    Sent down the meek-eyed Peace:
She, crowned with olive green, came softly sliding
    Down through the turning sphere,
    His ready harbinger,
With turtle wing the amorous clouds dividing,   50
And waving wide her myrtle wand,
She strikes a universal peace through sea and land.

28] Isa. vi. 6–7; 'secret' means 'set apart'.
48 sphere] the firmament of the Mosaic cosmology (*PL* VII 261–75, Gen. i. 6–8)
    and the spheres of the Ptolemaic cosmology.
50 turtle] turtle dove.
    amorous] fond of peace.

IV

No war, or battle's sound
Was heard the world around,
The idle spear and shield were high uphung;   55
The hookèd chariot stood
Unstained with hostile blood;
The trumpet spake not to the armèd throng;
And kings sat still with awful eye,
As if they surely knew their sovereign Lord was by.   60

V

But peaceful was the night
Wherein the Prince of Light
His reign of peace upon the earth began.
The winds, with wonder whist,
Smoothly the waters kissed,   65
Whispering new joys to the mild oceán,
Who now hath quite forgot to rave,
While birds of calm sit brooding on the charmèd wave.

VI

The stars with deep amaze
Stand fixed in steadfast gaze,   70
Bending one way their precious influence,
And will not take their flight,
For all the morning light,
Or Lucifer that often warned them thence;
But in their glimmering orbs did glow,   75
Until their Lord himself bespake, and bid them go.

VII

And though the shady gloom
Had given day her room,

56 hookèd] equipped with scythes.
64 whist] hushed.
68 birds of calm] halcyons. The line recalls the classical belief that the sea
    remained calm during the days preceding and following the winter solstice
    to enable the birds to brood on their floating nests, and also echoes the
    image of Gen. i. 2 and *PL* VII 234-5.
71 one way] i.e. towards Bethlehem.
74 Lucifer] the morning star, Venus.
75 orbs] in the Ptolemaic cosmology, orbs are the concentric hollow spheres
    which carry the planets and fixed stars around the earth.

The sun himself withheld his wonted speed,
   And hid his head for shame,   80
   As his inferior flame
The new enlightened world no more should need;
He saw a greater sun appear
Than his bright throne or burning axletree could bear.

VIII

The shepherds on the lawn,   85
   Or ere the point of dawn,
Sat simply chatting in a rustic row;
   Full little thought they then
   That the mighty Pan
Was kindly come to live with them below;   90
Perhaps their loves, or else their sheep,
Was all that did their silly thoughts so busy keep.

IX

When such music sweet
   Their hearts and ears did greet,
As never was by mortal finger strook,   95
   Divinely-warbled voice
   Answering the stringèd noise,
As all their souls in blissful rapture took:
The air, such pleasure loath to lose,
With thousand echoes still prolongs each heavenly
   close.   100

X

Nature, that heard such sound
   Beneath the hollow round
Of Cynthia's seat the airy region thrilling,
   Now was almost won
   To think her part was done,   105

81 as] as if.
89 Pan] The Greek god was a guardian of sheep, and in the Renaissance he was
   commonly compared to Christ as the good shepherd. The name Pan was
   associated with *pan* (all) in antiquity (though the words are etymologically
   distinct), and he became a universal god in late Greek theology. Cf. *PL* IV
   266.
92 silly] simple and innocent.
98 took] bewitched.
100 close] the end of a musical phrase.
102-3 hollow ... seat] the sphere of the moon. Diana, the moon-goddess, is here
   named after her birthplace, Mount Cynthus, on Delos.

And that her reign had here its last fulfilling;
She knew such harmony alone
Could hold all heaven and earth in happier union.

XI

At last surround their sight
A globe of circular light,   110
That with long beams the shamefaced night arrayed;
The helmèd cherubim
And sworded seraphim
Are seen in glittering ranks with wings displayed,
Harping in loud and solemn choir,   115
With unexpressive notes to heaven's new-born heir.

XII

Such music (as 'tis said)
Before was never made,
But when of old the sons of morning sung,
While the creator great   120
His constellations set,
And the well-balanced world on hinges hung,
And cast the dark foundations deep,
And bid the weltering waves their oozy channel keep.

XIII

Ring out, ye crystal spheres,   125
Once bless our human ears,
(If ye have power to touch our senses so)
And let your silver chime
Move in melodious time;
And let the bass of heaven's deep organ blow;   130
And with your ninefold harmony
Make up full consort to the angelic symphony.

XIV

For, if such holy song
Enwrap our fancy long,

115 choir] refers to musical choirs and to each of the nine orders of angels.
116 unexpressive] inexpressible.
122 hinges] the earth's axis.
125-32] According to a tradition deriving from Pythagoras each of the spheres
    surrounding the earth was said to produce a note as it revolved. Cf. *Arcades*
    62-73, *Solemn Music* 19-24, *Comus* 1020-21, *PL* V 178.

Time will run back and fetch the age of gold; 135
   And speckled vanity
   Will sicken soon and die,
And leprous sin will melt from earthly mould,
And hell itself will pass away,
And leave her dolorous mansions to the peering day. 140

XV

   Yea, Truth and Justice then
   Will down return to men,
Orbed in a rainbow; and, like glories wearing,
   Mercy will sit between,
   Throned in celestial sheen, 145
With radiant feet the tissued clouds down steering;
And heaven, as at some festival,
Will open wide the gates of her high palace-hall.

XVI

   But wisest fate says no,
   This must not yet be so; 150
The Babe yet lies in smiling infancy
   That on the bitter cross
   Must redeem our loss,
So both himself and us to glorify:
Yet first, to those ychained in sleep, 155
The wakeful trump of doom must thunder through
   the deep,

XVII

   With such a horrid clang
   As on Mount Sinai rang,

140 peering] may mean 'appearing' or 'prying'.
141 Justice] Astrea, who lived on earth during the Golden Age, and was later stellified as the constellation Virgo (cf. *Fair Infant* 50-2, *PL* IV 998). Milton conflates her return with that of Truth and Mercy as recorded in Psalm lxxxv. 10-11, where the 'righteousness' of the A.V. is *justitia* in the Vulgate. Peace (introduced in stanza III), Truth, Justice, and Mercy were the four daughters of God in a prominent medieval allegorical tradition which survived into the Renaissance.
149 wisest fate] the will of God (see *PL* VII 173).
151 infancy] may retain the Latin sense of 'inability to speak'.
155 ychaind] The 'y' is an archaism which derives from the Anglo-Saxon 'ge', the prefix for past participles. As 'chain' derives from Old French rather than Anglo-Saxon, the archaism is a false one. The prosthesis is occasioned by the demands of metre. Cf. 'ypointing' in *Shakespeare* 4 and 'yclept' in *Allegro* 12.
158-9] Exod. xix. 16-18; cf. *PL* VI 56-60.

While the red fire and smouldering clouds out brake:
   The aged earth, aghast,   160
   With terror of that blast,
Shall from the surface to the centre shake,
When, at the world's last session,
The dreadful judge in middle air shall spread his throne.

XVIII

And then at last our bliss   165
   Full and perfect is,
But now begins; for from this happy day
   The old dragon under ground,
   In straiter limits bound,
Not half so far casts his usurpèd sway,   170
And, wroth to see his kingdom fail,
Swinges the scaly horror of his folded tail.

XIX

The oracles are dumb;
   No voice or hideous hum
Runs through the archèd roof in words deceiving.   175
   Apollo from his shrine
   Can no more divine,
With hollow shriek the steep of Delphos leaving.
No nightly trance, or breathèd spell,
Inspires the pale-eyed priest from the prophetic cell.   180

XX

The lonely mountains o'er,
   And the resounding shore,
A voice of weeping heard and loud lament;
   From haunted spring, and dale
   Edged with poplar pale,   185
The parting genius is with sighing sent;

159 smouldering] stifling (not, as now, 'burning slowly').
160–2] Psalm cxiv. 7 (l. 15 of Milton's English version.)
164 middle air] the 'clouds of heaven' of Matt. xxiv. 30; see I Thess. iv. 17.
168 dragon] Rev. xii, xx; cf. *PL* IV 3.
172 Swinges] lashes.
173] Milton is drawing on the ancient tradition that the pagan oracles ceased
   when Jesus was born. Cf. *PR* I 456.
179 nightly] nocturnal.
186 genius] local god, the Roman *genius loci*. Cf. *Arcades* 25–6, *Lycidas* 183–5,
   Penseroso 154.

With flower-inwoven tresses torn
The nymphs in twilight shade of tangled thickets mourn.

XXI

In consecrated earth,
And on the holy hearth,   190
The lars and lemures moan with midnight plaint;
In urns, and altars round,
A drear and dying sound
Affrights the flamens at their service quaint;
And the chill marble seems to sweat,   195
While each peculiar power forgoes his wonted seat.

XXII

Peor and Baälim
Forsake their temples dim,
With that twice-battered god of Palestine;
And moonèd Ashtaroth,   200
Heaven's queen and mother both,
Now sits not girt with tapers' holy shine:
The Libyc Hammon shrinks his horn;
In vain the Tyrian maids their wounded Thammuz mourn.

XXIII

And sullen Moloch, fled,   205

191 lars, lemures] lemures: spirits of the dead – may be good (lares) or evil (larvae), but Milton's identification of lemures with larvae is not uncommon.

194 flamens] an order of Roman priests.

197 Peor and Baälim] Peor is the name of a mountain, the god of which was Baal-Peor (see Psalm cvi. 28). Cf *PL* I 412. Baälim is the plural of Baal (see Judges ii. II), and alludes to other forms of the god, such as Baäl-zebub (*SA* 1231).

199 twice-battered god] Dagon. See I Sam. v. 2-4, and cf. *PL* I 457-66 and *SA* 13.

200 Ashtaroth] the collective name for the manifestations of Ashtoreth, the Syrian goddess. Cf. *PL* I 438-9, *PR* III 417, and *SA* 1242. Baälim and Ashtaroth are contrasted in *PL* I 421-3. Ashtoreth entered Greek mythology (through Cyprus) as Aphrodite.

203 Hammon] An Egyptian god whose oracle in Libya was well known to the Greeks. Cf. *PL* IV 277.

204 Tyrian ... Thammuz] Thammuz, who was identified by Jerome with Adonis, was worshipped in Phoenicia, of which Tyre was an important city. Cf. Ezek. viii. 14 and *PL* I 446-57.

205 Moloch] Ammonite fire-god, associated in the O.T. with the sacrifice of children. See Lev. xviii. 21, II Kings xxiii. 10, Psalm cvi. 37-8. In *PL* he is a fallen angel (I 392. ff.).

Hath left in shadows dread
His burning idol all of blackest hue;
   In vain with cymbals' ring
   They call the grisly king,
In dismal dance about the furnace blue;   210
The brutish gods of Nile as fast,
Isis, and Orus, and the dog Anubis, haste.

XXIV

Nor is Osiris seen
In Memphian grove or green,
Trampling the unshowered grass with lowings loud; 215
   Nor can he be at rest
   Within his sacred chest,
Nought but profoundest hell can be his shroud;
In vain, with timbrelled anthems dark,
The sable-stolèd sorcerers bear his worshipped ark.   220

XXV

He feels from Juda's land
The dreaded infant's hand;
The rays of Bethlehem blind his dusky eyn;
   Nor all the gods beside
   Longer dare abide,   225
Not Typhon huge ending in snaky twine:
Our babe, to show his Godhead true,
Can in his swaddling bands control the damnèd crew.

XXVI

So, when the sun in bed,
Curtained with cloudy red,   230
Pillows his chin upon an orient wave,
   The flocking shadows pale
   Troop to the infernal jail,

212-13] Isis, the Egyptian goddess of the moon, is the wife and sister of Osiris
the sun-god, and the mother of Orus (usually Horus). All three appear as
rebel angels in *PL* I 478. Anubis is a son of Osiris and Nephthys, reared by
Isis.

223 eyn] archaic plural of 'eye'.

226 Typhon] A conflation of the Egyptian Typhon, who killed Osiris, and the
Greek monster, half serpent, who was killed by Zeus.

227-8] Milton is comparing Jesus to the infant Hercules, who strangled
serpents in his cradle. Cf. *Passion* 13-14.

Each fettered ghost slips to his several grave,
And the yellow-skirted fays   235
Fly after the night-steeds, leaving their moon-loved maze.

XXVII

But see the virgin blest
Hath laid her babe to rest.
Time is our tedious song should here have ending:
Heaven's youngest-teemèd star   240
Hath fixed her polished car,
Her sleeping Lord with handmaid lamp attending;
And all about the courtly stable
Bright-harnessed angels sit in order serviceable.

ON THE DEATH OF A FAIR
INFANT DYING OF A COUGH

Anno aetatis 17

I

O fairest flower, no sooner blown but blasted,
Soft silken primrose fading timelessly,
Summer's chief honour, if thou hadst outlasted
Bleak winter's force that made thy blossom dry;
For he, being amorous on that lovely dye   5
    That did thy cheek envermeil, thought to kiss,
But killed, alas, and then bewailed his fatal bliss.

II

For since grim Aquilo, his charioteer,
By boisterous rape the Athenian damsel got,
He thought it touched his deity full near,   10
If likewise he some fair one wedded not,
Thereby to wipe away the infámous blot
    Of long uncoupled bed and childless eld,
Which 'mongst the wanton gods a foul reproach was held.

III

So, mounting up in icy-pearlèd car,   15
Through middle empire of the freezing air
He wandered long, till thee he spied from far;
There ended was his quest, there ceased his care:
Down he descended from his snow-soft chair,

On the Death of a Fair Infant. The date of composition is debatable. Edward
Phillips, Milton's nephew, wrote in 1694 that the poem was occasioned by 'the
Death of one of his Sister's Children (a daughter), who died in her infancy'.
Should this be true, then Milton's 'Anno aetatis 17' (i.e. 9 December 1625–8
December 1626) may be an error, for Milton's eldest niece, Anne Phillips, died
on 22 January 1628. On the other hand, the plague to which Milton refers in
stanza X is almost certainly the great plague of 1625.
2 timelessly] unseasonably.
8 Aquilo] Boreas, the north wind, who abducted Orithyia, the 'Athenian
damsel'.
13 eld] old age.
16 middle . . . air] the middle of the three layers of air above the earth, and the
    one in which inclement weather was generated.

But, all unwares, with his cold-kind embrace,   20
Unhoused thy virgin soul from her fair biding-place.

IV

Yet art thou not inglorious in thy fate;
For so Apollo, with unweeting hand,
Whilom did slay his dearly-lovèd mate,
Young Hyacinth, born on Eurotas' strand,   25
Young Hyacinth, the pride of Spartan land;
    But then transformed him to a purple flower:
Alack, that so to change thee winter had no power.

V

Yet can I not persuade me thou art dead,
Or that thy corse corrupts in earth's dark womb,   30
Or that thy beauties lie in wormy bed,
Hid from the world in a low-delvèd tomb;
Could heaven, for pity, thee so strictly doom?
    Oh no, for something in thy face did shine
Above mortality, that showed thou wast divine.   35

VI

Resolve me, then, O soul most surely blest
(If so it be that thou these plaints dost hear);
Tell me, bright spirit, where'er thou hoverest,
Whether above that high first-moving sphere,
Or in the Elysian fields (if such there were),   40
    Oh, say me true if thou wert mortal wight,
And why from us so quickly thou didst take thy flight.

VII

Wert thou some star, which from the ruined roof
Of shaked Olympus by mischance didst fall;
Which careful Jove in nature's true behoof   45
Took up, and in fit place did reinstall?
Or did of late Earth's sons besiege the wall

23-6] Hyacinth was accidentally killed by the discus of his lover Apollo, who
    transformed the blood of Hyacinth into a flower (*Metamorphoses* x
    162-219; cf. *Lycidas* 106, *PL* IV 310). Eurotas is a river in Laconia, and
    flows by Sparta.
39 first-moving sphere] the *primum mobile* of Ptolemaic cosmology was the
    outermost sphere, where motion originated. Cf. *PL* III 482-3, VIII 133-6.
40 Elysian fields] Not the paradise of Homer, which was at the extremity of the
    earth, but that of Plato, which was in the highest heaven. Cf. *PL* III 472.

Of sheeny heaven, and thou some goddess fled
Amongst us here below to hide thy nectared head?

VIII

Or wert thou that just maid who once before   50
Forsook the hated earth, O tell me sooth,
And camest again to visit us once more?
Or wert thou [Mercy], that sweet smiling Youth?
Or that crowned Matron, sage white-robèd Truth?
    Or any other of that heavenly brood   55
Let down in cloudy throne to do the world some good?

IX

Or wert thou of the golden-wingèd host,
Who, having clad thyself in human weed,
To earth from thy prefixèd seat didst post,
And after short abode fly back with speed,   60
As if to show what creatures heaven doth breed;
    Thereby to set the hearts of men on fire
To scorn the sordid world, and unto heaven aspire?

X

But O why didst thou not stay here below
To bless us with thy heaven-loved innocence,   65
To slake his wrath whom sin hath made our foe,
To turn swift-rushing black perdition hence,
Or drive away the slaughtering pestilence,
    To stand 'twixt us and our deservèd smart?
But thou canst best perform that office where thou art. 70

XI

Then thou, the mother of so sweet a child,
Her false-imagined loss cease to lament,
And wisely learn to curb thy sorrows wild;
Think what a present thou to God hast sent,
And render him with patience what he lent: 75
    This if thou do, he will an offspring give
That till the world's last end shall make thy name to live.

50-2] See *Nativity* 141n.
53 Mercy] A traditional editorial conjecture. Two syllables are clearly missing
    in the original version. Other suggestions for the missing disyllable are
    'Virtue', 'Peace, in', 'Honour', and 'Temperance' (pronounced as a
    disyllable).
77] Isa. lvi. 5.

AT A VACATION EXERCISE IN
THE COLLEGE, PART LATIN,
PART ENGLISH

Anno aetatis 19

The Latin Speeches ended, the English thus began:–

Hail, native language, that by sinews weak
Didst move my first endeavouring tongue to speak,
And mad'st imperfect words with childish trips,
Half unpronounced, slide through my infant lips,
Driving dumb silence from the portal door,   5
Where he had mutely sat two years before:
Here I salute thee, and thy pardon ask
That now I use thee in my latter task;
Small loss it is that thence can come unto thee,
I know my tongue but little grace can do thee.   10
Thou need'st not be ambitious to be first;
Believe me, I have thither packed the worst:
And, if it happen as I did forecast,
The daintiest dishes shall be served up last.
I pray thee then deny me not thy aid,   15
For this same small neglect that I have made;
But haste thee straight to do me once a pleasure,
And from thy wardrobe bring thy chiefest treasure;
Not those new-fangled toys, and trimming slight
Which takes our late fantastics with delight,   20
But cull those richest robes and gayest attire,
Which deepest spirits and choicest wits desire.
I have some naked thoughts that rove about,
And loudly knock to have their passage out,
And, weary of their place, do only stay   25
Till thou hast decked them in thy best array;
That so they may, without suspect or fears,
Fly swiftly to this fair assembly's ears.
Yet I had rather, if I were to choose,
Thy service in some graver subject use,   30
Such as may make thee search thy coffers round,

At a Vacation Exercise. The poem was written in 1628. The Latin speeches to
which Milton alludes consist of an oration and a prolusion which Milton
delivered at Christ's College in July 1628. The prolusion ends with the
announcement that Milton is adding a section in English to the Latin discourse.

Before thou clothe my fancy in fit sound:
Such where the deep transported mind may soar
Above the wheeling poles, and at heaven's door
Look in, and see each blissful deity   35
How he before the thunderous throne doth lie,
Listening to what unshorn Apollo sings
To the touch of golden wires, while Hebe brings
Immortal nectar to her kingly sire;
Then, passing through the spheres of watchful fire,   40
And misty regions of wide air next under,
And hills of snow and lofts of pilèd thunder,
May tell at length how green-eyed Neptune raves,
In heaven's defiance mustering all his waves;
Then sing of secret things that came to pass   45
When beldam Nature in her cradle was;
And last of kings and queens and heroes old,
Such as the wise Demodocus once told
In solemn songs at king Alcinous' feast,
While sad Ulysses' soul and all the rest   50
Are held, with his melodious harmony,
In willing chains and sweet captivity.
But fie, my wandering Muse, how thou dost stray!
Expectance calls thee now another way;
Thou know'st it must be now thy only bent   55
To keep in compass of thy predicament.
Then quick about thy purposed business come,
That to the next I may resign my room.

34 wheeling poles] The poles are the extremities of the axis around which the
    spheres revolve.
36 thunderous throne] of Jove, the thunderer.
37 unshorn] a common classical epithet for Apollo.
38 Hebe] daughter of Zeus and Hera; she frequently personifies youth. Cf.
    Allegro 29, *Comus* 290.
40 spheres of watchful fire] The exact reference of the phrase is difficult to
    determine. Milton may be referring to the spheres of the Ptolemaic system,
    the heavenly bodies of which were located in the region of fire, and were
    according to Plato created to watch over the numbers of time. Alterna-
    tively, he may be referring to a layer of fire directly under the sphere of the
    moon; this layer could be said to be 'watchful' in that it protects the
    supralunar vault from contamination.
41-2] See *Fair Infant* 16n.
46 beldam] may mean grandmother, or nurse.
48-52] In *Odyssey* viii 487-543 the minstrel Demodocus sings of the fall of Troy
    while Odysseus is being entertained by Alcinous, king of the Phaeacians;
    the song moves Odysseus to tears.
56 predicament] Milton plays on the common meaning of the word and the
    technical meaning (an Aristotelian category).

Then ENS *is represented as Father of the Predicaments, his ten
    sons; whereof the eldest stood for* SUBSTANCE *with his
    Canons; which* ENS, *thus speaking, explains:*

Good luck befriend thee, son; for at thy birth
The fairy ladies danced upon the hearth;   60
Thy drowsy nurse hath sworn she did them spy
Come tripping to the room where thou didst lie,
And, sweetly singing round about thy bed,
Strew all their blessings on thy sleeping head.
She heard them give thee this, that thou should'st still 65
From eyes of mortals walk invisible.
Yet there is something that doth force my fear,
For once it was my dismal hap to hear
A sibyl old, bow-bent with crooked age,
That far events full wisely could presage,   70
And, in time's long and dark prospective glass,
Foresaw what future days should bring to pass.
'Your son,' said she, '(nor can you it prevent)
Shall subject be to many an accident.
O'er all his brethren he shall reign as king,   75
Yet every one shall make him underling,
And those that cannot live from him asunder
Ungratefully shall strive to keep him under;
In worth and excellence he shall outgo them,
Yet, being above them, he shall be below them;   80
From others he shall stand in need of nothing,
Yet on his brothers shall depend for clothing.
To find a foe it shall not be his hap,
And peace shall lull him in her flowery lap;
Yet shall he live in strife, and at his door   85
Devouring war shall never cease to roar;
Yet, it shall be his natural property
To harbour those that are at enmity.'
What power, what force, what mighty spell, if not
Your learned hands, can loose this Gordian knot?   90

The next, QUANTITY *and* QUALITY, *spake in prose: then*
    RELATION *was called by his name.*

Stage Direction] In the satirical entertainment which Milton is introducing, he
    acts the part of Ens, or 'Being', himself, and ten of his fellow undergrad-
    uates act the parts of the 'Sons', Aristotle's ten categories, of which four –
    Substance, Quantity, Quality, and Relation – are represented in the
    portion of the play which Milton has preserved.
69 sibyl] a prophetic hag.

Rivers, arise: whether thou be the son
Of utmost Tweed, or Ouse, or gulfy Dun,
Or Trent, who, like some earth-born giant, spreads
His thirty arms along the indented meads,
Or sullen Mole, that runneth underneath,   95
Or Severn swift, guilty of maiden's death,
Or rocky Avon, or of sedgy Lea,
Or coaly Tyne, or ancient hallowed Dee,
Or Humber loud, that keeps the Scythian's name,
Or Medway smooth, or royal-towered Thame.   100

The rest was prose.

91 Rivers arise] The part of Relation was evidently played by one of the two
    Rivers brothers who had been admitted to Christ's College on 28 May 1628.
    The catalogue of rivers that follows is a parody of the catalogues of rivers
    composed by Spenser and Drayton.
92 utmost] i.e. outermost, as the Tweed formed the border between England
    and Scotland.
    gulfy] i.e. full of eddies; the river is the Don, in Yorkshire.
96 maiden's death] The maiden is Sabrina; see *Comus* 824 ff.
98 hallowed] The changes in the course of the Dee were said to be prophetic. Cf.
    Lycidas 55.

THE PASSION

I

Erewhile of music, and ethereal mirth,
Wherewith the stage of air and earth did ring,
And joyous news of heavenly infant's birth,
My muse with angels did divide to sing;
But headlong joy is ever on the wing,   5
   In wintry solstice like the shortened light
Soon swallowed up in dark and long outliving night.

II

For now to sorrow must I tune my song,
And set my harp to notes of saddest woe,
Which on our dearest Lord did seize ere long,   10
Dangers, and snares, and wrongs, and worse than so,
Which he for us did freely undergo;
   Most perfect hero, tried in heaviest plight
Of labours huge and hard, too hard for human wight.

III

He, sovereign priest, stooping his regal head,   15
That dropped with odorous oil down his fair eyes,
Poor fleshly tabernacle enterèd,
His starry front low-roofed beneath the skies;
Oh, what a mask was there, what a disguise!
   Yet more: the stroke of death he must abide,   20
Then lies him meekly down fast by his brethren's side.

IV

These latest scenes confine my roving verse:
To this horizon is my Phoebus bound.
His godlike acts, and his temptations fierce,
And former sufferings, otherwise are found;   25

The Passion. As the first four lines of the poem clearly allude to the 'Nativity Ode' it seems likely that this poem was written the following Easter; in 1630 Good Friday fell on 26 March.

4 divide] Milton conflates the primary meaning ('to join') with the technical meaning in music ('to execute a florid melodic variation').

13–14] The hero is Jesus, whose trials Milton compares to the labours of Hercules. Cf. *Nativity* 227–8.

17 fleshly tabernacle] See Heb. ix. 11–12, and cf. *PR* IV 599.

21] See Heb. ii. 17.

23 Phoebus] Apollo, god of the sun, was often identified with poetic inspiration.

Loud o'er the rest Cremona's trump doth sound:
  Me softer airs befit, and softer strings
Of lute, or viol still, more apt for mournful things.

V

Befriend me, night, best patroness of grief,
Over the pole thy thickest mantle throw,   30
And work my flattered fancy to belief
That heaven and earth are coloured with my woe;
My sorrows are too dark for day to know:
  The leaves should all be black whereon I write,
And letters, where my tears have washed, a wannish
    white.   35

VI

See, see the chariot, and those rushing wheels,
That whirled the prophet up at Chebar flood;
My spirit some transporting cherub feels
To bear me where the towers of Salem stood,
Once glorious towers, now sunk in guiltless blood;   40
  There doth my soul in holy vision sit,
In pensive trance, and anguish, and ecstatic fit.

VII

Mine eye hath found that sad sepulchral rock
That was the casket of heaven's richest store,
And here, though grief my feeble hands uplock,   45
Yet on the softened quarry would I score
My plaining verse as lively as before;
  For sure so well instructed are my tears
That they would fitly fall in ordered characters.

26 o'er] over.
  Cremona's trump] The *Christiad*, a Latin poem by Marco Girolamo Vida,
    published in Cremona in 1535.
28 still] quiet.
30 pole] the sky. Cf. *Vacation Exercise* 34n.
36–40] Milton's account of Ezekiel's vision is based on Ezek. i and x. The vision
    occurred by the river of Chebar; Salem was the ancient name for Jerusalem.
    Cf. *Penseroso* 53 and *PL* VI 750–3.

VIII

Or, should I thence, hurried on viewless wing,   50
Take up a weeping on the mountains wild,
The gentle neighbourhood of grove and spring
Would soon unbosom all their echoes mild;
And I (for grief is easily beguiled)
    Might think the infection of my sorrows loud   55
Had got a race of mourners on some pregnant cloud.

*This Subject the Author finding to be above the years he had
when he wrote it, and nothing satisfied with what was begun,
left it unfinished.*

ON TIME

Fly, envious Time, till thou run out thy race;
Call on the lazy leaden-stepping Hours,
Whose speed is but the heavy plummet's pace;
And glut thyself with what thy womb devours,
Which is no more than what is false and vain,   5
And merely mortal dross;
So little is our loss,
So little is thy gain.
For, when as each thing bad thou hast entombed,
And, last of all, thy greedy self consumed,   10
Then long Eternity shall greet our bliss
With an individual kiss,

50 viewless] invisible.
51] Jer. ix. 10.
56] Probably an allusion to the story of Ixion, who begot Centaurus on a cloud
    shaped like Hera. Cf. *PR* IV 318-21.
On Time. The date of the poem is not known. In the manuscript Milton wrote
    (and afterwards deleted) the phrase 'to be set on a clock case' under the
    title. This phrase explains the appropriateness of the metaphor of the lead
    plummet in ll. 1-3.
3 plummet] the weight (not the pendulum) of a clock.
4 womb] stomach; Milton glances at the traditional identification of Chronos
    (Time) with Cronos (Saturn), who devoured his own children.
9 when as] when.
12 individual] probably means inseparable (cf. *PL* V 610), but may also
    encompass the modern meaning, which existed in Milton's time, in which
    case the word affirms personal immortality.

And Joy shall overtake us as a flood;
When every thing that is sincerely good,
And perfectly divine,   15
With Truth, and Peace, and Love, shall ever shine
About the supreme throne
Of him, to whose happy-making sight alone
When once our heavenly-guided soul shall climb,
Then, all this earthly grossness quit,   20
Attired with stars we shall for ever sit,
    Triumphing over Death, and Chance, and thee, O Time!

UPON THE CIRCUMCISION

Ye flaming powers, and wingèd warriors bright,
That erst with music, and triumphant song
First heard by happy watchful shepherds' ear,
So sweetly sung your joy the clouds along,
Through the soft silence of the listening night;   5
Now mourn, and if sad share with us to bear
Your fiery essence can distil no tear,
Burn in your sighs, and borrow
Seas wept from our deep sorrow,
He who with all heaven's heraldry whilere   10
Entered the world now bleeds to give us ease;
Alas, how soon our sin
    Sore doth begin
        His infancy to seize!

O more exceeding love, or law more just?   15
Just law, indeed, but more exceeding love!
For we, by rightful doom remediless,
Were lost in death, till he that dwelt above
High-throned in secret bliss, for us frail dust

14 sincerely] purely, wholly.
18 happy-making sight] an Anglicized form of the term 'beatific vision'. See *PL*
    I 684n.
Upon the Circumcision. The poem was probably written on the Feast of the
Circumcision, which falls on 1 January. The year of composition is not known,
though 1633 is not improbable. In the poem Milton regards the circumcision as
the first act of the passion, and a foreshadowing of the crucifixion.
1 powers] one of the nine orders of angels.
10 heraldry] heraldic pomp.

Emptied his glory, even to nakedness; 20
And that great covenant which we still transgress
Entirely satisfied,
And the full wrath beside
Of vengeful justice bore for our excess,
And seals obedience first with wounding smart 25
This day; but O ere long,
   Huge pangs and strong
      Will pierce more near his heart.

AT A SOLEMN MUSIC

Blest pair of sirens, pledges of heaven's joy,
Sphere-born harmonious sisters, Voice and Verse,
Wed your divine sounds, and mixed power employ,
Dead things with inbreathed sense able to pierce,
And to our high-raised fantasy present 5
That undisturbèd song of pure concent,
Aye sung before the sapphire-coloured throne
To him that sits thereon,
With saintly shout and solemn jubilee;
Where the bright seraphim in burning row 10
Their loud uplifted angel-trumpets blow,

20 Emptied his glory]. In the Greek of Phil. ii. 7 Christ is said to have emptied (ἐκένωσε) himself.

21 that great covenant] of works.

24 excess] extravagant violation of law and morality. Cf. *PL* XI 111.

At a Solemn Music. The date is uncertain, but the poem was probably written sometime between 1631 and 1637. The 'solemn music' of the title would nowadays be called a 'sacred concert'.

1-2 sirens ... Sphere-born] In the manuscript versions of the poem Milton uses 'borne', but in the two printed versions 'born'. He may have distinguished the two words. If 'borne' is intended, then these are the sirens of *Arcades* 63-4, for the sirens 'sit upon the ... spheres'; if 'born' is intended then the sirens should be compared with Echo in *Comus* 241, for she is 'daughter of the sphere'.

4] alludes to the myth of Orpheus. See *Allegro* 145-50n.

6 concent] harmony.

7 sapphire-coloured throne] the throne of God in Ezekiel's vision. See Ezek. i. 26, x. 1.

10 seraphim] one of the nine orders of angels. Cherubim, in l. 12, are another order.

And the cherubic host in thousand choirs
Touch their immortal harps of golden wires,
With those just spirits that wear victorious palms,
Hymns devout and holy psalms   15
Singing everlastingly;
That we on earth, with undiscording voice,
May rightly answer that melodious noise;
As once we did, till disproportioned sin
Jarred against nature's chime, and with harsh din   20
Broke the fair music that all creatures made
To their great Lord, whose love their motion swayed
In perfect diapason, whilst they stood
In first obedience, and their state of good.
O may we soon again renew that song,   25
And keep in tune with heaven, till God ere long
To his celestial consort us unite,
To live with him, and sing in endless morn of light.

23 diapason] harmony.

AN EPITAPH ON THE
MARCHIONESS OF WINCHESTER

This rich marble doth inter
The honoured wife of Winchester,
A viscount's daughter, an earl's heir,
Besides what her virtues fair
Added to her noble birth,   5
More than she could own from earth.
Summers three times eight save one
She had told, alas too soon,
After so short time of breath,
To house with darkness and with death.   10
Yet had the number of her days
Been as complete as was her praise,
Nature and fate had had no strife
In giving limit to her life.
Her high birth and her graces sweet   15
Quickly found a lover meet;
The virgin choir for her request
The god that sits at marriage feast;
He at their invoking came,
But with a scarce-well-lighted flame;   20
And in his garland, as he stood,
Ye might discern a cypress-bud.
Once had the early matrons run
To greet her of a lovely son,
And now with second hope she goes,   25
And calls Lucina to her throes;
But, whether by mischance or blame,
Atropos for Lucina came,

An Epitaph on the Marchioness of Winchester. Jane Savage, Marchioness of
Winchester, died on 15 April 1631. She was a Catholic (though one seventeenth-
century source says that 'she was inclining to become a protestant') and a
Royalist. No connection between Milton and the family of the Marchioness is
known, so the poem may have been composed as a contribution to a collection
of memorial verses by Cambridge poets.
18 The god] Hymen.
20 scarce-well-lighted flame] At the marriage of Orpheus and Eurydice the
    torch of Hymen is smoky. Contrast *Allegro* 125–6, where Hymen's taper is
    'clear'.
24 son] Charles, born 1629, later the sixth Marquis.
26 Lucina] Roman goddess of childbirth.
28 Atropos] One of the three Parcae, Roman goddesses of birth and fate.
    Atropos cut the thread of life (cf. *Lycidas* 76) which Clotho spun and
    Lachesis measured.

And with remorseless cruelty
Spoiled at once both fruit and tree;   30
The hapless babe before his birth
Had burial, not yet laid in earth,
And the languished mother's womb
Was not long a living tomb.
So have I seen some tender slip,   35
Saved with care from winter's nip,
The pride of her carnation train,
Plucked up by some unheedy swain,
Who only thought to crop the flower
New shot up from vernal shower;   40
But the fair blossom hangs the head
Sideways as on a dying bed,
And those pearls of dew she wears
Prove to be presaging tears
Which the sad morn had let fall   45
On her hastening funeral.
Gentle Lady, may thy grave
Peace and quiet ever have;
After this thy travail sore,
Sweet rest seize thee evermore,   50
That, to give the world increase,
Shortened hast thy own life's lease;
Here, besides the sorrowing
That thy noble house doth bring,
Here be tears of perfect moan   55
Wept for thee in Helicon;
And some flowers and some bays
For thy hearse, to strew the ways,
Sent thee from the banks of Came,
Devoted to thy virtuous name;   60
Whilst thou, bright saint, high sitt'st in glory,
Next her, much like to thee in story,
That fair Syrian shepherdess,
Who, after years of barrenness,
The highy-favoured Joseph bore   65
To him that served for her before,

43–6] Alludes to Aurora, goddess of the dawn, who weeps tears of dew because
     her son Memnon has been killed by Achilles.
56 Helicon] A mountain in Boeotia, sacred to Apollo and muses.
59 Came] The river Cam, in Cambridge.
63 Syrian shepherdess] Rachel. See Gen. xxix and xxx.
66 him] Jacob.

And at her next birth, much like thee,
Through pangs fled to felicity,
Far within the bosom bright
Of blazing majesty and light: 70
There with thee, new-welcome saint,
Like fortunes may her soul acquaint,
With thee there clad in radiant sheen,
No marchioness, but now a queen.

67 her next birth] Benjamin, whose mother Rachel died giving birth to him
    (Gen. xxxv. 18).

SONG ON MAY MORNING

Now the bright morning star, Day's harbinger,
Comes dancing from the east, and leads with her
The flowery May, who from her green lap throws
The yellow cowslip and the pale primrose.
    Hail, bounteous May, that dost inspire   5
    Mirth, and youth, and warm desire!
    Woods and groves are of thy dressing;
    Hill and dale doth boast thy blessing.
Thus we salute thee with our early song,
And welcome thee, and wish thee long.   10

ON SHAKESPEARE. 1630

What needs my Shakespeare for his honoured bones
The labour of an age in pilèd stones?
Or that his hallowed relics should be hid
Under a star-ypointing pyramid?
Dear son of memory, great heir of fame,   5
What need'st thou such weak witness of thy name?
Thou in our wonder and astonishment
Has built thyself a livelong monument.
For whilst, to the shame of slow-endeavouring art,
Thy easy numbers flow, and that each heart   10
Hath from the leaves of thy unvalued book
Those Delphic lines with deep impression took,
Then thou, our fancy of itself bereaving,
Dost make us marble with too much conceiving,
And so sepúlchred in such pomp dost lie   15
That kings for such a tomb would wish to die.

Song on May Morning. The many similarities to Milton's Latin poem *Elegia* V, which was composed in the spring of 1629, suggest that the poem may have been written on 1 May 1629, or possibly the same date in 1630 or 1631.
On Shakespeare. 1630 The poem was first published in the Second Folio of Shakespeare (1632).
4 star-ypointing] a present participle. See *Nativity* 155n.
11 unvalued] invaluable.
12 Delphic lines] Apollo, the patron of poetry, had his oracle at Delphi.

ON THE UNIVERSITY CARRIER

*Who sickened in the time of his Vacancy, being forbid
to go to London by reason of the Plague*

Here lies old Hobson; Death hath broke his girt,
And here, alas, hath laid him in the dirt;
Or else, the way being foul, twenty to one
He's here stuck in a slough, and overthrown.
'Twas such a shifter that, if truth were known,   5
Death was half glad when he had got him down;
For he had any time this ten years full
Dodged with him betwixt Cambridge and the Bull.
And surely Death could never have prevailed,
Had not his weekly course of carriage failed;   10
But lately, finding him so long at home,
And thinking now his journey's end was come,
And that he had ta'en up his latest inn,
In the kind office of a chamberlain
Showed him his room where he must lodge that night,   15
Pulled off his boots, and took away the light.
If any ask for him, it shall be said,
'Hobson has supped, and's newly gone to bed.'

On the University Carrier. Thomas Hobson died, aged 86, on 1 January 1631. He
had been well known in Cambridge for over 60 years. He drove a weekly coach
to London, and also hired out horses. His insistence that each customer take the
horse nearest the door is the origin of the proverbial phrase 'Hobson's choice'.
His death prompted the composition of many light-hearted commemorative
poems by Cambridge students.
1 girt] saddle girth.
5 shifter] trickster, evader.
8 Bull] the Bull Inn, Bishopsgate, London.
14 chamberlain] an attendant in charge of the bed-chambers in an inn.

ANOTHER ON THE SAME

Here lieth one who did most truly prove
That he could never die while he could move;
So hung his destiny, never to rot
While he might still jog on and keep his trot;
Made of sphere-metal, never to decay   5
Until his revolution was at stay.
Time numbers motion, yet (without a crime
'Gainst old truth) motion numbered out his time;
And, like an engine moved with wheel and weight,
His principles being ceased, he ended straight.   10
Rest, that gives all men life, gave him his death,
And too much breathing put him out of breath;
Nor were it contradiction to affirm
Too long vacation hastened on his term.
Merely to drive the time away he sickened,   15
Fainted, and died, nor would with ale be quickened.
'Nay,' quoth he, on his swooning bed out-stretched,
'If I may not carry, sure I'll ne'er be fetched,
But vow, though the cross doctors all stood hearers,
For one carrier put down to make six bearers.'   20
Ease was his chief disease; and, to judge right,
He died for heaviness that his cart went light;
His leisure told him that his time was come,

Another on the Same. See previous headnote.

5 sphere-metal] Aristotle argued that the material of which the celestial spheres
    were composed was indestructible.
7 Time numbers motion] Aristotle described time as the measure of motion. Cf.
    PL V 580-2.
9 engine] a machine, here a clock.
10 principles] source of motion.
12 breathing] time for rest.
14-34] The lines contain a series of puns. 'Vacation' and 'term' (14) have a
    special university sense, but also mean 'freedom from business' and 'end'
    respectively. 'Drive . . . away' (15) contains an obvious pun. In l. 18 Milton
    plays on the phrase 'fetch and carry', and 'fetched' also means 'restored to
    consciousness'. 'Put down' (20) means 'dismissed from office' or 'killed'.
    'Bearers' (20) refers to porters and pall bearers. 'Heaviness' (22) refers to
    sadness and weight. 'Weight' (26) plays on 'wait'. 'Wain' (32) means both
    'waggon' and 'decrease'. 'Superscription' (34) refers to the addresses on the
    letters which Hobson carried, and to the epitaph on his gravestone.

And lack of load made his life burdensome,
That even to his last breath (there be that say't)   25
As he were pressed to death, he cried, 'More weight!'
But, had his doings lasted as they were,
He had been an immortal carrier.
Obedient to the moon he spent his date
In course reciprocal, and had his fate   30

Linked to the mutual flowing of the seas;
Yet (strange to think) his wain was his increase
His letters are delivered all and gone;
Only remains this superscription.

---

30 In course reciprocal] i.e. like the tides.

L'ALLEGRO

Hence, loathed Melancholy,
　Of Cerberus and blackest Midnight born
In Stygian cave forlorn
　'Mongst horrid shapes, and shrieks, and sights unholy;
Find out some uncouth cell,　　　　　　　　　　　　　5
　Where brooding Darkness spreads his jealous wings,
And the night-raven sings;
　There, under ebon shades and low-browed rocks,
As ragged as thy locks,
　In dark Cimmerian desert ever dwell.　　　　　　　10
But come, thou Goddess fair and free,
In heaven yclept Euphrosyne,
And by men, heart-easing Mirth;
Whom lovely Venus, at a birth,
With two sister Graces more,　　　　　　　　　　　　15
To ivy-crownèd Bacchus bore;
Or whether (as some sager sing)
The frolic wind that breathes the spring,
Zephyr, with Aurora playing,
As he met her once a-Maying,　　　　　　　　　　.　20
There, on beds of violets blue,
And fresh-blown roses washed in dew,

L'Allegro. L'Allegro and *Il Penseroso* cannot be dated precisely, but they may
have been written while Milton was in Hammersmith (1632-5) or Horton
(1635-8).

title] The phrase is Italian, and means 'the cheerful man'.

1-2] Melancholy was not a personage in classical myth; Milton has invented her
　parentage. In classical myth Erebus was the brother and husband of Night,
　but Milton has substituted Cerberus, the hound of Hades, for Erebus,
　possibly in view of the usual derivation of Cerebus from Κὴρ Βορόσ,
　heart-devouring.

3 Stygian cave] Cerberus had a cave on the bank of the Styx.

5 uncouth cell] desolate cave.

8 shades] trees.

10 Cimmerian] The land of the Cimmerians, which Odysseus visited (*Odyssey* xi
　13-22) was proverbially dark.

12 yclept] called. See *Nativity* 155n.

12-16] The three Graces were Euphrosyne (Mirth), Aglaia (Brilliance), and
　Thalia (Bloom). According to one tradition they were the daughters of
　Venus and Bacchus.

19] Zephyr is the west wind, Aurora the dawn.

Filled her with thee, a daughter fair,
So buxom, blithe, and debonair.
Haste thee, Nymph, and bring with thee   25
Jest, and youthful Jollity,
Quips and cranks and wanton wiles,
Nods and becks and wreathèd smiles,
Such as hang on Hebe's cheek,
And love to live in dimple sleek;   30
Sport that wrinkled Care derides,
And Laughter holding both his sides.
Come, and trip it, as you go,
On the light fantastic toe;
And in thy right hand lead with thee   35
The mountain-nymph, sweet Liberty;
And, if I give thee honour due,
Mirth, admit me of thy crew,
To live with her, and live with thee,
In unreprovèd pleasures free;   40
To hear the lark begin his flight,
And, singing, startle the dull night,
From his watch-tower in the skies,
Till the dappled dawn doth rise;
Then to come, in spite of sorrow,   45
And at my window bid good-morrow,
Through the sweet-briar or the vine,
Or the twisted eglantine;
While the cock, with lively din,
Scatters the rear of darkness thin;   50
And to the stack, or the barn-door,
Stoutly struts his dames before,
Oft listening how the hounds and horn
Cheerly rouse the slumbering morn,
From the side of some hoar hill,   55
Through the high wood echoing shrill.
Sometime walking, not unseen,
By hedgerow elms, on hillocks green,
Right against the eastern gate
Where the great sun begins his state,   60

24 buxom] yielding.
27 cranks] jokes dependent on verbal twists.
28 becks] upward nods corresponding to a beckoning by hand.
29 Hebe] see *Vacation Exercise* 38n.
33 trip] move lightly.
55 hoar] i.e. grey with mist.
60 state] the stately progress of the sun, as described in *PL* VI 12-15.

Robed in flames and amber light,
The clouds in thousand liveries dight;
While the ploughman, near at hand,
Whistles o'er the furrowed land,
And the milkmaid singeth blithe,   65
And the mower whets his scythe,
And every shepherd tells his tale
Under the hawthorn in the dale.
Straight mine eye hath caught new pleasures,
Whilst the landscape round it measures: 70
Russet lawns, and fallows grey,
Where the nibbling flocks do stray;
Mountains on whose barren breast
The labouring clouds do often rest;
Meadows trim, with daisies pied,   75
Shallow brooks, and rivers wide.
Towers and battlements it sees
Bosomed high in tufted trees,
Where perhaps some beauty lies,
The cynosure of neighbouring eyes.   80
Hard by a cottage chimney smokes
From betwixt two aged oaks,
Where Corydon and Thyrsis met
Are at their savoury dinner set
Of herbs and other country messes,   85
Which the neat-handed Phyllis dresses;
And then in haste her bower she leaves,
With Thestylis to bind the sheaves;
Or, if the earlier season lead,
To the tanned haycock in the mead.   90
Sometimes, with secure delight,
The upland hamlets will invite,
When the merry bells ring round,
And the jocund rebecks sound
To many a youth and many a maid   95
Dancing in the chequered shade,

---

62 dight] clothed.
67 tells his tale] either 'counts his sheep' or 'tells his story'.
74 labouring clouds] echoes the story of Ixion. Cf. *Passion* 56n.
75 pied] variegated.
80 cynosure] See *Comus* 342n.
83–8] The names of Milton's rustics occur commonly in classical and Renais-
sance pastoral poetry.
91 secure] here used in the Latin sense of 'carefree'.
94 rebecks] early bowed instruments.

And young and old come forth to play
On a sunshine holiday,
Till the livelong daylight fail,
Then to a spicy nut-brown ale,   100
With stories told of many a feat,
How Fairy Mab the junkets eat;
She was pinched and pulled, she said,
And by the friar's lantern led,
Tells how the drudging goblin sweat   105
To earn his cream-bowl duly set,
When in one night, ere glimpse of morn,
His shadowy flail hath threshed the corn
That ten day-labourers could not end;
Then lies him down, the lubber fiend,   110
And, stretched out all the chimney's length
Basks at the fire his hairy strength,
And crop-full out of doors he flings,
Ere the first cock his matin rings.
Thus done the tales, to bed they creep,   115
By whispering winds soon lulled asleep.
Towered cities please us then,
And the busy hum of men,
Where throngs of knights and barons hold,
In weeds of peace, high triumphs hold,   120
With store of ladies, whose bright eyes
Rain influence, and judge the prize
Of wit or arms, while both contend
To win her grace whom all commend.
There let Hymen oft appear   125
In saffron robe, with taper clear,
And pomp, and feast, and revelry,
With mask and antique pageantry;
Such sights as youthful poets dream
On summer eves by haunted stream.   130
Then to the well-trod stage anon,
If Jonson's learned sock be on,

102 Mab] queen of the fairies.
104 friar's lantern] the will-o'-the-wisp.
110 lubber] drudging.
111 chimney] fireplace.
20 weeds] clothes.
   triumphs] pageants or spectacles.
121-2] The bright eyes are compared to stars, the ethereal fluid of which rains
   on mankind, thus controlling character and destiny.
125-6] See *Winchester* 20n.
132 sock] low-heeled slipper worn by Greek comic actors.

Or sweetest Shakespeare, Fancy's child,
Warble his native wood-notes wild.
And ever, against eating cares,   135
Lap me in soft Lydian airs,
Married to immortal verse,
Such as the meeting soul may pierce,
In notes with many a winding bout
Of linkèd sweetness long drawn out   140
With wanton heed and giddy cunning,
The melting voice through mazes running,
Untwisting all the chains that tie
The hidden soul of harmony.
That Orpheus' self may heave his head   145
From golden slumber on a bed
Of heaped Elysian flowers, and hear
Such strains as would have won the ear
Of Pluto to have quite set free
His half-regained Eurydice.   150
These delights if thou canst give,
Mirth, with thee I mean to live.

136 Lydian] a musical mode usually thought to be morally enervating. In a
    minority tradition which can be traced to Cassiodorus the Lydian mode
    was deemed to be relaxing and delightful.
145-50] Orpheus sang so beautifully that human beings, beasts, and even
    inanimate nature responded. He went to Hades in order to recover his dead
    wife Eurydice, and so moved Pluto and Proserpina with his music that
    they consented to Eurydice's return, on condition that Orpheus should not
    look back upon her until he emerged into the upper air. Near the end of the
    journey he looked back, and Eurydice, 'half-regained', vanished.

IL PENSEROSO

Hence, vain deluding Joys,
    The brood of Folly without father bred,
How little you bestead,
    Or fill the fixèd mind with all your toys;
Dwell in some idle brain,   5
    And fancies fond with gaudy shapes possess,
As thick and numberless
    As the gay motes that people the sunbeams,
Or likest hovering dreams,
    The fickle pensioners of Morpheus' train.   10
But, hail thou goddess, sage and holy,
Hail, divinest Melancholy,
Whose saintly visage is too bright
To hit the sense of human sight,
And therefore to our weaker view   15
O'erlaid with black, staid wisdom's hue.
Black, but such as in esteem
Prince Memnon's sister might beseem,
Or that starred Ethiop queen that strove
To set her beauty's praise above   20
The sea-nymphs, and their powers offended;
Yet thou art higher far descended,
Thee bright-haired Vesta long of yore
To solitary Saturn bore;
His daughter she (in Saturn's reign   25

Il Penseroso.
title] The phrase is Italian, and means 'the contemplative man'.
3 bestead] help.
10 pensioners] attendants.
    Morpheus] the god of dreams, one of the sons of Somnus (sleep).
18 Prince Memnon's sister] In late antiquity the mythical Ethiopian Prince
    Memnon, the son of the goddess Aurora and the mortal Tithonus, was
    given a beautiful sister called Hemera.
19–21] Cassiopeia, wife of Ethiopean King Cephalus, boasted that she was more
    beautiful than the nereids ('sea-nymphs'), and after her death was trans-
    lated into a constellation ('starred').
23–30] Melancholy's parentage is Milton's invention. Vesta was the virgin
    goddess of the hearth, born to Saturn before Saturn was overthrown by
    Jove (hence l. 30). Ida is the name of a mountain near Troy, and of another
    mountain on Crete.

Such mixture was not held a stain),
Oft in glimmering bowers and glades
He met her, and in secret shades
Of woody Ida's inmost grove,
Whilst yet there was no fear of Jove.   30
Come, pensive nun, devout and pure,
Sober, steadfast, and demure,
All in a robe of darkest grain,
Flowing with majestic train,
And sable stole of cypress lawn   35
Over thy decent shoulders drawn.
Come, but keep thy wonted state,
With even step, and musing gait,
And looks commercing with the skies,
Thy rapt soul sitting in thine eyes: 40
There, held in holy passion still,
Forget thyself to marble, till
With a sad leaden downward cast
Thou fix them on the earth as fast.
And join with thee calm Peace and Quiet,   45
Spare Fast, that oft with gods doth diet,
And hears the Muses in a ring
Aye round about Jove's altar sing.
And add to these retired Leisure,
That in trim gardens takes his pleasure;   50
But, first and chiefest, with thee bring
Him that yon soars on golden wing,
Guiding the fiery-wheelèd throne,
The cherub Contemplation;
And the mute Silence hist along,   55
'Less Philomel will deign a song,
In her sweetest saddest plight,
Smoothing the rugged brow of Night,
While Cynthia checks her dragon yoke
Gently o'er the accustomed oak.   60
Sweet bird, that shunn'st the noise of folly,
Most musical, most melancholy!

---

31 nun] The primary meaning is that of a pagan priestess, but a suggestion of
   the modern meaning is evident in Milton's association of the nun with
   contemplation.
33 grain] colour.
35 cypress lawn] fine black linen.
43 sad] serious.
53] see *Passion* 36-40n.
55 hist] to call with the exclamation 'hist'.
59 Cynthia] see *Nativity Ode* 102-3n.

Thee, chauntress, oft the woods among
I woo, to hear thy even-song;
And, missing thee, I walk unseen   65
On the dry smooth-shaven green
To behold the wandering moon,
Riding near her highest noon,
Like one that had been led astray
Through the heaven's wide pathless way,   70
And oft, as if her head she bowed,
Stooping through a fleecy cloud,
Oft, on a plat of rising ground,
I hear the far-off curfew sound,
Over some wide-watered shore,   75
Swinging slow with sullen roar;
Or, if the air will not permit,
Some still removèd place will fit,
Where glowing embers through the room
Teach light to counterfeit a gloom,   80
Far from all resort of mirth,
Save the cricket on the hearth,
Or the bellman's drowsy charm
To bless the doors from nightly harm;
Or let my lamp, at midnight hour,   85
Be seen in some high lonely tower,
Where I may oft outwatch the Bear,
With thrice great Hermes, or unsphere
The spirit of Plato, to unfold
What worlds or what past regions hold   90
The immortal mind that hath forsook
Her mansion in this fleshly nook;
And of those demons that are found
In fire, air, flood, or underground,
Whose power hath a true consent   95
With planet or with element.
Sometimes let gorgeous Tragedy
In sceptered pall come sweeping by,

73 plat] plot.
77 air] weather.
83 bellman's drowsy charm] night-watchman's drowsy chant.
87 outwatch the Bear] stay up all night. The Bear (Ursa Major) never sets.
88 Hermes] Hermes Trismegistus ('thrice great'), the Greek name for Thoth,
    the Egyptian god of letters, to whom were attributed many occult works
    written by Alexandrian Greeks in the second and third centuries AD.
    unsphere] call back.

Presenting Thebes, or Pelops' line,
Or the tale of Troy divine,   100
Or what (though rare) of later age
Ennobled hath the buskined stage.
But, O sad Virgin, that thy power
Might raise Musaeus from his bower;
Or bid the soul of Orpheus sing   105
Such notes as, warbled to the string,
Drew iron tears down Pluto's cheek,
And made hell grant what love did seek;
Or call up him that left half-told
The story of Cambuscan bold,   110
Of Camball, and of Algarsife,
And who had Canace to wife,
That owned the virtuous ring and glass,
And of the wondrous horse of brass
On which the Tartar king did ride;   115
And if aught else great bards beside
In sage and solemn tunes have sung,
Of tourneys, and of trophies hung,
Of forests, and enchantments drear,
Where more is meant than meets the ear;   120
Thus, Night, oft see me in thy pale career,
Till civil-suited Morn appear,
Not tricked and frounced, as she was wont
With the Attic boy to hunt,
But kerchiefed in a comely cloud,   125
While rocking winds are piping loud,
Or ushered with a shower still,
When the gust hath blown his fill,
Ending on the rustling leaves,

---

99 Thebes] the scene of tragedies about Oedipus and his family.
      Pelops' line] plays about Agamemnon, Orestes, Electra, and Iphigenia.
100 *Troy*] the setting of such plays as Euripides' *Trojan Women* and Sophocles'
      Ajax.
102 buskined] the buskin was a high boot worn by Greek tragic actors.
104 Musaeus] a mythical Greek singer.
105-8] See *Allegro* 145-50n.
109-15] refers to Chaucer's unfinished *Squire's Tale*.
116-20] refers principally to Spenser, but also to Tasso and Ariosto, whose epics
      had been allegorized.
122-4] The 'Attic boy' is Cephalus, who replaced the aged Tithonus as the lover
      of Aurora the dawn. 'Civil-suited' means soberly dressed; 'tricked and
      frounced' means adorned and curly-haired.
127 still] quiet.

With minute-drops from off the eaves.   130
And, when the sun begins to fling
His flaring beams, me, goddess, bring
To archèd walks of twilight groves,
And shadows brown, that Sylvan loves,
Of pine, or monumental oak,   135
Where the rude axe with heavèd stroke
Was never heard the nymphs to daunt,
Or fright them from their hallowed haunt.
There, in close covert, by some brook,
Where no profaner eye may look,   140
Hide me from day's garish eye,
While the bee with honeyed thigh,
That at her flowery work doth sing,
And the waters murmuring,
With such consort as they keep,   145
Entice the dewy-feathered Sleep;
And let some strange mysterious dream
Wave at his wings, in airy stream
Of lively portraiture displayed,
Softly on my eyelids laid;   150
And, as I wake, sweet music breathe
Above, about, or underneath,
Sent by some spirit to mortals good,
Or the unseen genius of the wood.
But let my due feet never fail   155
To walk the studious cloister's pale,
And love the high embowèd roof,
With antique pillars' massy-proof,
And storied windows richly dight,
Casting a dim religious light.   160
There let the pealing organ blow,
To the full-voiced choir below,
In service high and anthems clear,

130 minute] falling at intervals of one minute.
134 Sylvan] Roman god of fields and forests.
145 consort] musical harmony.
154 genius of the wood] See *Nativity* 186n.
156 pale] enclosure.
157 embowèd] vaulted.
158 antique] may mean 'old' or 'fantastic, grotesque'.
    massy-proof] massive, and proof against the weight of the roof.
159 storied] depicting Biblical stories.
163 service, anthems] The terms are both Protestant. A service is a setting of
    the canticles, and an anthem is the vernacular Protestant equivalent of the
    Latin motet, from which it derives.

As may with sweetness, through mine ear,
Dissolve me into ecstasies,　　　　　　　　165
And bring all heaven before mine eyes.
And may at last my weary age
Find out the peaceful hermitage,
The hairy gown and mossy cell,
Where I may sit and rightly spell　　　　　170
Of every star that heaven doth show,
And every herb that sips the dew,
Till old experience do attain
To something like prophetic strain.
These pleasures, Melancholy, give;　　　　175
And I with thee will choose to live.

170-1 spell/Of] interpret.

ARCADES

*Part of an Entertainment presented to the Countess
Dowager of Derby at Harefield by some Noble
Persons of her family, who appear on the scene in
pastoral habit, moving towards the seat of state, with
this song:*

I. SONG

Look, nymphs and shepherds, look,
What sudden blaze of majesty
Is that which we from hence descry,
Too divine to be mistook?
   This, this is she   5
To whom our vows and wishes bend,
Here our solemn search hath end.

Fame, that her high worth to raise
Seemed erst so lavish and profuse,
We may justly now accuse   10
Of detraction from her praise,
   Less than half we find expressed;
   Envy bid conceal the rest.

Mark what radiant state she spreads,
In circle round her shining throne   15
Shooting her beams like silver threads,
This, this is she alone,
   Sitting like a goddess bright
   In the centre of her light.

Arcades. This short pastoral was performed at an unknown date early in the
1630s for Alice, Dowager Countess of Derby. The performance was held in the
garden of Harefield, her estate near Uxbridge. The elderly Countess (b. 1559)
had long been a notable patroness of literature; in her youth her virtues had
been celebrated by Spenser. One of her daughters (Lady Frances) by her first
husband (Lord Derby) married John Egerton, the son by a previous marriage of
Lady Alice's second husband, Sir Thomas Egerton. The children of Frances and
John Egerton (to whom Lady Alice was both maternal grandmother and
stepmother of their father) were later to act in Milton's *Comus*, and one or more
of them was probably included in the 'Noble Persons of her family' who acted in
Arcades.
title] refers to the inhabitants of ancient Arcadia, a mountainous area in central
    Peloponnesus which was often used as the setting of Renaissance pastoral
    fictions.
12 less than half] I Kings x. 7.

Might she the wise Latona be,   20
Or the towered Cybele,
Mother of a hundred gods?
Juno dares not give her odds;
   Who had thought this clime had held
   A deity so unparalleled?   25

*As they come forward, the Genius of the Wood appears, and
turning toward them, speaks.*

   Gen. Stay, gentle swains, for though in this disguise,
I see bright honour sparkle through your eyes;
Of famous Arcady ye are, and sprung
Of that renownèd flood, so often sung,
Divine Alpheus, who, by secret sluice,   30
Stole under seas to meet his Arethuse;
And ye, the breathing roses of the wood,
Fair silver-buskined nymphs, as great and good.
I know this quest of yours and free intent
Was all in honour and devotion meant   35
To the great mistress of yon princely shrine,
Whom with low reverence I adore as mine,
And with all helpful service will comply
To further this night's glad solemnity,
And lead ye where ye may more near behold   40
What shallow-searching Fame hath left untold;
Which I full oft, amidst these shades alone,
Have sat to wonder at, and gaze upon.
For know, by lot from Jove, I am the power
Of this fair wood, and live in oaken bower,   45
To nurse the saplings tall, and curl the grove
With ringlets quaint and wanton windings wove.
And all my plants I save from nightly ill
Of noisome winds and blasting vapours chill;
And from the boughs brush off the evil dew,   50
And heal the harms of thwarting thunder blue,

---

20 Latona] See *Sonnet* XII 5–7n.
21 Cybele] mother of the gods, often portrayed with a crown of towers.
23 Juno] wife of Jove, queen of the gods.
25–6 Genius of the Wood] See *Nativity* 186n.
30–1 Alpheus is a river in Arcadia. The youth Alpheus loved the nymph
    Arethusa. She fled to Sicily, and became a fountain, and he, changed to a
    river, flowed to her by a hidden channel under the sea. Cf. *Lycidas* 85n and
    132.
48 nightly] nocturnal.

Or what the cross dire-looking planet smites,
Or hurtful worm with cankered venom bites.
When evening grey doth rise, I fetch my round
Over the mount, and all this hallowed ground,   55
And early, ere the odorous breath of morn
Awakes the slumbering leaves, or tasselled horn
Shakes the high thicket, haste I all about,
Number my ranks, and visit every sprout
With puissant words and murmurs made to bless;   60
But else, in deep of night, when drowsiness
Hath locked up mortal sense, then listen I
To the celestial sirens' harmony,
That sit upon the nine enfolded spheres,
And sing to those that hold the vital shears,   65
And turn the adamantine spindle round
On which the fate of gods and men is wound.
Such sweet compulsion doth in music lie,
To lull the daughters of Necessity,
And keep unsteady Nature to her law,   70
And the low world in measured motion draw
After the heavenly tune, which none can hear
Of human mould with gross unpurgèd ear;
And yet such music worthiest were to blaze
The peerless height of her immortal praise   75
Whose lustre leads us, and for her most fit,
If my inferior hand or voice could hit
Inimitable sounds; yet, as we go,
Whate'er the skill of lesser gods can show
I will assay, her worth to celebrate,   80
And so attend ye toward her glittering state;
Where ye may all, that are of noble stem,
Approach, and kiss her sacred vesture's hem.

II. SONG

O'er the smooth enamelled green,
Where no print of step hath been,   85

---

52 planet] Saturn, the malign planet.
63–73] Not Homer's sirens, but Plato's (*Republic* x 616–17). In Plato's account
  a spindle of adamant rests on the knees of Necessity, whose three
  daughters, the Fates (see *Winchester* 28n.) turn the spindle upon which are
  threaded the eight concentric whorls of the universe; a siren stood on the
  rim of each circle. In accordance with Renaissance Ptolemaic thought
  Milton has nine spheres rather than Plato's eight. Cf. *Solemn Music* 1–2.
82 stem] descent.
84 enamelled] beautified with various colours.

Follow me, as I sing
And touch the warbled string;
Under the shady roof
Of branching elm star-proof
　　Follow me;   90
I will bring you where she sits,
Clad in splendour as befits
　　Her deity.
Such a rural Queen
All Arcadia hath not seen.   95

III. SONG

Nymphs and shepherds, dance no more
　By sandy Ladon's lilied banks;
On old Lycaeus, or Cyllene hoar,
　Trip no more in twilight ranks;
Though Erymanth your loss deplore,   100
　A better soil shall give ye thanks.
From the stony Maenalus
Bring your flocks, and live with us;
Here ye shall have greater grace,
To serve the Lady of this place.   105
Though Syrinx your Pan's mistress were,
Yet Syrinx well might wait on her.
　　Such a rural Queen
　　All Arcadia hath not seen.

97] The Ladon was a river in Arcadia.
98-102] names of Arcadian mountains associated with Pan.
105　Syrinx] a nymph beloved of Pan.

LYCIDAS

*In this monody the author bewails a learned friend,
unfortunately drowned in his passage from Chester on
the Irish Seas, 1637; and, by occasion, foretells the
ruin of our corrupted clergy, then in their height.*

Yet once more, O ye laurels, and once more
Ye myrtles brown, with ivy never sere,
I come to pluck your berries harsh and crude,
And with forced fingers rude
Shatter your leaves before the mellowing year.   5
Bitter constraint and sad occasion dear
Compels me to disturb your season due;
For Lycidas is dead, dead ere his prime,
Young Lycidas, and hath not left his peer.
Who would not sing for Lycidas? He knew   10
Himself to sing, and build the lofty rhyme.
He must not float upon his watery bier
Unwept, and welter to the parching wind,
Without the meed of some melodious tear.
    Begin, then, sisters of the sacred well   15
That from beneath the seat of Jove doth spring;
Begin, and somewhat loudly sweep the string.
Hence with denial vain and coy excuse;

Lycidas. On 10 August 1637 Edward King, a Fellow of Christ's College
Cambridge, was drowned. Milton dated his pastoral elegy 'November, 1637' in
the Trinity MS, and published it the following year in a commemorative volume
entitled *Justa Eduardo King*, a collection of poems in Latin, Greek, and English
written by King's Cambridge contemporaries.

title] Lycidas is a common name in pastoral verse.

epigraph] The first line appears in the MS, but the second does not. Neither is
    printed in the 1638 version, but the complete epigraph is printed in
    Milton's 1645 *Poems*.

1 Yet once more] see Heb. xii. 26–7.

2 sere] dry, withered.

3 crude] used in the Latin sense of 'unripe'.

4 rude] used in the Latin sense of 'unskilled'.

8 ere his prime] King was twenty-five.

13 welter] writhe. Cf. *PL* 1 78.

14 meed] reward.

    tear] Collections of elegies issued by the universities were often entitled
    Lacrymae, so 'tear' means 'elegy'.

15–16] The sisters are the muses, the sacred well is Aganippe, on Mount
    Helicon, and the seat of Jove is the altar to Zeus on the same mountain.

So may some gentle muse
With lucky words favour my destined urn,   20
And as he passes turn,
And bid fair peace be to my sable shroud.
    For we were nursed upon the self-same hill,
Fed the same flock, by fountain, shade, and rill;
Together both, ere the high lawns appeared   25
Under the opening eyelids of the morn,
We drove a-field, and both together heard
What time the grey-fly winds her sultry horn,
Battening our flocks with the fresh dews of night,
Oft till the star that rose, at evening, bright,   30
Toward heaven's descent had sloped his westering wheel.
Meanwhile the rural ditties were not mute;
Tempered to the oaten flute,
Rough satyrs danced, and fauns with cloven heel
From the glad sound would not be absent long;   35
And old Damaetus loved to hear our song.
    But O the heavy change, now thou art gone,
Now thou art gone and never must return!
Thee, shepherd, thee the woods and desert caves,
With wild thyme and the gadding vine o'ergrown,   40
And all their echoes, mourn.
The willows, and the hazel copses green,
Shall now no more be seen
Fanning their joyous leaves to thy soft lays.
As killing as the canker to the rose,   45
Or taint-worm to the weanling herds that graze,
Or frost to flowers, that their gay wardrobe wear,
When first the white-thorn blows;
Such, Lycidas, thy loss to shepherd's ear.
    Where were ye, nymphs, when the remorseless deep   50
Closed o'er the head of your loved Lycidas?
For neither were ye playing on the steep
Where your old bards, the famous Druids, lie,
Nor on the shaggy top of Mona high,
Nor yet where Deva spreads her wizard stream.   55
Ay me! I fondly dream

22 sable] black.
36 Damaetus] a pastoral name, here probably used as an allusion to a tutor at
    Christ's.
48 blows] blooms.
52 steep] refers to the Welsh island of Bardsey, which Milton (erroneously)
    thought was adjacent to Anglesey.
54 Mona] Anglesey.
55 Deva] The Dee. See *Vacation Exercise* 98n.

'Had ye been there,' . . . for what could that have done?
What could the muse herself that Orpheus bore,
The muse herself, for her enchanting son,
Whom universal nature did lament,   60
When, by the rout that made the hideous roar,
His gory visage down the stream was sent,
Down the swift Hebrus to the Lesbian shore?
    Alas! What boots it with uncessant care
To tend the homely slighted shepherd's trade,   65
And strictly meditate the thankless muse?
Were it not better done, as others use,
To sport with Amaryllis in the shade,
Or with the tangles of Neaera's hair?
Fame is the spur that the clear spirit doth raise   70
(That last infirmity of noble mind)
To scorn delights and live laborious days;
But the fair guerdon when we hope to find,
And think to burst out into sudden blaze,
Comes the blind Fury with the abhorrèd shears,   75
And slits the thin-spun life. 'But not the praise,'
Phoebus replied, and touched my trembling ears:
'Fame is no plant that grows on mortal soil,
Nor in the glistening foil
Set off to the world, nor in broad rumour lies,   80
But lives and spreads aloft by those pure eyes
And perfect witness of all-judging Jove;
As he pronounces lastly on each deed,
Of so much fame in heaven expect thy meed.'
    O fountain Arethuse, and thou honoured flood,   85
Smooth-sliding Mincius, crowned with vocal reeds,
That strain I heard was of a higher mood;

58-63] The muse is Calliope; in the course of the orgies of Bacchus, her son
    Orpheus was dismembered by the Maenads, who threw his head (and his
    lyre) into the Hebrus River, from which both floated to the island of
    Lesbos. Cf. *PL* VII 32-8.
64 boots] avails, profits.
68-9] Both names are common in pastoral verse. Nearea's tangled hair often
    appears in Renaissance verse.
75 Fury] Atropos is a Fate (see *Winchester* 28n.), but Milton endows her with
    the menacing and repulsive character of a Fury.
77 Phoebus] See *Passion* 23n.
79 foil] the setting of a jewel.
85 Arethuse] represents the Greek pastoral poetry of Sicily; see *Arcades* 30-1n.
86 Mincius] represents Roman pastoral poetry, especially that of Virgil, who
    was born near Mantua, which is situated on two islands in the Mincio.
87 mood] musical mode.

But now my oat proceeds,
And listens to the herald of the sea,
That came in Neptune's plea.   90
He asked the waves, and asked the felon winds,
What hard mishap hath doomed this gentle swain?
And questioned every gust of rugged wings
That blows from off each beakèd promontory:
They knew not of his story;   95
And sage Hippotades their answer brings,
That not a blast was from his dungeon strayed;
The air was calm, and on the level brine
Sleek Panope with all her sisters played.
It was that fatal and perfidious bark,   100
Built in the eclipse, and rigged with curses dark,
That sunk so low that sacred head of thine.
     Next, Camus, reverend sire, went footing slow,
His mantle hairy, and his bonnet sedge,
Inwrought with figures dim, and on the edge   105
Like to that sanguine flower inscribed with woe.
'Ah! who hath reft,' quoth he, 'my dearest pledge?'
Last came, and last did go,
The pilot of the Galilean lake;
Two massy keys he bore of metals twain   110
(The golden opes, the iron shuts amain).
He shook his mitred locks, and stern bespake:
'How well could I have spared for thee, young swain,
Enow of such as, for their bellies' sake,
Creep, and intrude, and climb into the fold!   115
Of other care they little reckoning make
Than how to scramble at the shearers' feast,
And shove away the worthy bidden guest;

---

89 herald] Triton. See *Comus* 873n.
91 felon] means 'savage, wild' (the primary meaning), and 'felonious'.
96 Hippotades] means son of Hippotes, and refers to Aeolus, god of the winds.
97 dungeon] the cave of Aeolus, in which Jove imprisoned the winds.
99 Panope] one of the fifty sea-nymphs (nereids).
103 Camus] the river Cam represents the University of Cambridge.
106 flower] the hyacinth; see *Fair Infant* 23-6n.
107 pledge] child.
109 pilot] St Peter, who was a Galilean fisherman when Jesus called him. (Luke
     v. 3-11).
110] Matt. xvi. 19.
111 amain] with full force.
112 mitred] St Peter was the first bishop of the church, and so wears a mitre.
113-21] See the parable in John x. 1-28.
114 Enow] plural of 'enough'.

Blind mouths! That scarce themselves know how to hold
A sheep-hook, or have learned aught else the least   120
That to the faithful herdman's art belongs!
What recks it them? What need they? They are sped;
And, when they list, their lean and flashy songs
Grate on their scrannel pipes of wretched straw;
The hungry sheep look up, and are not fed,   125
But, swoll'n with wind and the rank mist they draw,
Rot inwardly, and foul contagion spread;
Besides what the grim wolf with privy paw
Daily devours apace, and nothing said.
But that two-handed engine at the door   130
Stands ready to smite once, and smite no more.'
   Return, Alpheus; the dread voice is past
That shrunk thy streams; return Sicilian muse,
And call the vales, and bid them hither cast
Their bells and flowerets of a thousand hues.   135
Ye valleys low, where the mild whispers use
Of shades, and wanton winds, and gushing brooks,
On whose fresh lap the swart star sparely looks,
Throw hither all your quaint enamelled eyes,
That on the green turf suck the honeyed showers,   140
And purple all the ground with vernal flowers.
Bring the rathe primrose that forsaken dies,
The tufted crow-toe, and pale jessamine,
The white pink, and the pansy freaked with jet,
The glowing violet,   145
The musk rose, and the well-attired woodbine,
With cowslips wan that hang the pensive head,
And every flower that sad embroidery wears;
Bid amaranthus all his beauty shed,

---

122 sped] satisfied.
123 list] choose, desire.
    flashy] trifling, destitute of solidity or purpose.
124 scrannel] thin, weak.
130 two-handed engine] the most famous crux in Milton's poetry; scores of interpretations have been advanced. The engine is evidently an instrument of retribution or reform. The second line of Milton's headnote seems to refer to ll. 130-1.
132 Alpheus] see *Arcades* 30-1n.
136 use] go habitually.
138 swart star] probably refers to Sirius, the Dog Star, the heliacal rising of which occurs in mid-summer. 'Swart' (blackened by heat) has been transferred from effect to cause.
142 rathe] early.
149 amaranthus] see *PL* III 352-61n.

And daffadillies fill their cups with tears, 150
To strew the laureate hearse where Lycid lies.
For so, to interpose a little ease,
Let our frail thoughts dally with false surmise.
Ay me! Whilst thee the shores and sounding seas
Wash far away, where'er thy bones are hurled; 155
Whether beyond the stormy Hebrides,
Where thou perhaps under the whelming tide
Visit'st the bottom of the monstrous world;
Or whether thou, to our moist vows denied,
Sleep'st by the fable of Bellerus old, 160
Where the great vision of the guarded mount
Looks toward Namancos and Bayona's hold.
Look homeward, angel, now, and melt with ruth;
And, O ye dolphins, waft the hapless youth.
Weep no more, woeful shepherds, weep no more, 165
For Lycidas, your sorrow, is not dead,
Sunk though he be beneath the watery floor.
So sinks the day-star in the ocean bed,
And yet anon repairs his drooping head,
And tricks his beams, and with new-spangled ore 170
Flames in the forehead of the morning sky:
So Lycidas sunk low, but mounted high,
Through the dear might of him that walked the waves,
Where, other groves and other streams along,
With nectar pure his oozy locks he laves, 175
And hears the unexpressive nuptial song,
In the blest kingdoms meek of joy and love.
There entertain him all the saints above,

158 monstrous world] the world of sea-monsters.
160 Bellerus] Milton's invention, by analogy to Bellerium, the Latin name for
    Land's End.
161] According to a Cornish legend, in the year 495 St Michael appeared to
    some fishermen who saw him standing on the Mount that now bears his
    name.
162] Namancos and Bayona represent Spain, the Catholicism of which St
    Michael guards against.
163 ruth] pity.
164] alludes to the ancient and Renaissance belief that the dolphin, which was
    known as a lover of mankind ('philanthropos'), often carried humans (both
    alive and dead) towards land.
168 day-star] the sun.
170 tricks] adorns.
173 him] Jesus. See Math. xiv. 25-31.
174] See Rev. xxii. 1-2, vii. 17.
176 unexpressive] inexpressible.
    nuptial song] Rev. xix. 6-9.

In solemn troops, and sweet societies,
That sing, and singing in their glory move,   180
And wipe the tears for ever from his eyes.
Now, Lycidas, the shepherds weep no more;
Henceforth thou art the genius of the shore,
In thy large recompense, and shalt be good
To all that wander in that perilous flood.   185

    Thus sang the uncouth swain to the oaks and rills,
While the still morn went out with sandals grey;
He touched the tender stops of various quills;
With eager thought warbling his Doric lay:
And now the sun had stretched out all the hills,   190
And now was dropped into the western bay
At last he rose, and twitched his mantle blue:
To-morrow to fresh woods, and pastures new.

'FIX HERE'

Fix here ye overdated spheres
That wing the restless foot of time.

181] See Isa. xxv. 8, Rev. vii. 17, xxi. 4.
183] See *Nativity* 186n.
186 uncouth] may mean 'unknown' or 'rustic'.
189 Doric lay] pastoral song. Theocritus, Moschus, and Bion wrote in the Doric
    dialect.
'Fix here'. Milton wrote these lines on the back of a letter to him from Henry
    Lawes; the letter contained Milton's passport, and was therefore probably
    written c. April 1638, just before Milton travelled abroad.

A MASKE

PRESENTED
At Ludlow Castle,
1634:

On Michaelmaſſe night, before the
RIGHT HONORABLE,

IOHN *Earle of Bridgewater, Viscount* BRACKLY,
Lord Præſident of WALES, And one of
His MAIESTIES most honorable
Privie Counsell.

Eheu quid volui miſero mihi! floribus auſtrum
Perditus ———

A Masque Presented at Ludlow Castle, which since the late seventeenth century has been popularly known as *Comus* (the name of the tempter in the play), was first performed on 29 September 1634 at the Shropshire home of the Earl of Bridgewater as part of the festivities celebrating his appointment as Lord President of Wales. The parts of the Lady and the two Brothers were acted by the Earl's children, and the part of the Attendant Spirit was acted by Henry Lawes, the children's music tutor. Lawes wrote the music for the songs, and was probably responsible for the commission to Milton to compose the text. In 1637 Lawes published the text.

Title page] The Latin epigraph is taken from Virgil's Second Eclogue (ll. 58–9), and means 'Alas, what have I wished on my miserable self! Destroyed, I have let the south wind blow on my flowers.'

COMUS

A Masque presented at Ludlow Castle

To the Right Honourable John, Lord Brackley, son and heir-apparent to the Earl of Bridgewater, etc.

My Lord, – This Poem, which received its first occasion of birth from yourself and others of your noble family, and much honour from your own person in the performance, now returns again to make a final dedication of itself to you. Although not openly acknowledged by the author, yet it is a legitimate offspring, so lovely and so much desired that the often copying of it hath tired my pen to give my several friends satisfaction, and brought me to a necessity of producing it to the public view, and now to offer it up, in all rightful devotion, to those fair hopes and rare endowments of your much-promising youth, which give a full assurance to all that know you of a future excellence. Live, sweet Lord, to be the honour of your name; and receive this as your own from the hands of him who hath by many favours been long obliged to your most honoured parents, and, as in this representation your attendant Thyrsis, so now in all real expression – Your faithful and most humble servant,

H. LAWES.

The Copy of a Letter written by Sir Henry Wotton to the Author upon the following Poem[1]

From the College, this 13 of April, 1638.

Sir, – It was a special favour when you lately bestowed upon me here the first taste of your acquaintance, though no longer than to make me know that I wanted more time to value it and to enjoy it rightly; and, in truth, if I could then have imagined your farther stay in these parts, which I understood afterwards by Mr H.,[2] I would have been bold, in our vulgar phrase, to mend my draught (for you left me

---

A Masque (Comus).

1 The Copy of a Letter] Sir Henry Wotton (1568-1639) had served as an ambassador to various countries in Europe for 20 years, and in 1624 had returned to England to become Provost of Eton. On 6 April 1638 Milton wrote to Wotton, enclosing a copy of *Comus* and mentioning his plans to travel to Italy in the next few weeks. This letter is Wotton's reply.
2 Mr H.] traditionally identified as the 'ever-memorable' John Hales, a Fellow of Eton.

with an extreme thirst), and to have begged your conversation again, jointly with your said learned friend, over a poor meal or two, that we might have banded together some good authors of the ancient time; among which I observed you to have been familiar.

Since your going, you have charged me with new obligations, both for a very kind letter from you dated the 6th of this month, and for a dainty piece of entertainment which came therewith. Wherein I should much commend the tragical part, if the lyrical did not ravish me with a certain Doric delicacy in your songs and odes, whereunto I must plainly confess to have seen yet nothing parallel in our language: *Ipsa mollities*.[1] But I must not omit to tell you that I now only owe you thanks for intimating unto me (how modestly soever) the true artificer. For the work itself I had viewed some good while before with singular delight; having received it from our common friend Mr R.,[2] in the very close of the late R.'s Poems,[3] printed at Oxford: whereunto it was added (as I now suppose) that the accessory might help out the principal, according to the art of the stationers, and to leave the reader *con la bocca dolce*.[4]

Now, Sir, concerning your travels; wherein I may challenge a little more privilege of discourse with you. I suppose you will not blanch[5] Paris in your way: therefore I have been bold to trouble you with a few lines to Mr M. B.,[6] whom you shall easily find attending the young Lord S.[7] as his governor; and you may surely receive from him good directions for the shaping of your farther journey into Italy, where he did reside, by my choice, some time for the King, after mine own recess from Venice.

I should think that your best line will be through the whole length of France to Marseilles, and thence by sea to Genoa; whence the passage into Tuscany is as diurnal as a Gravesend barge. I hasten, as you do, to Florence or Siena, the rather to tell you a short story, from the interest you have given me in your safety.

---

1 *Ipsa mollities*] delicacy itself.
2 Mr R.] has not been identified with certainty.
3 late R's Poems] refers to Thomas Randolph's *Poems* (Oxford, 1638).
4 *con la bocca dolce*] i.e. with a sweet taste in his mouth.
5 blanch] avoid.
6 Mr M. B.] Michael Branthwaite, who had served with Wotton in Venice.
7 Lord S.] James Scudamore, son of Viscount Scudamore, the ambassador in Paris.

At Siena I was tabled in the house of one Alberto Scipioni, an old Roman courtier in dangerous times; having been steward to the Duca di Pagliano, who with all his family were strangled, save this only man that escaped by foresight of the tempest. With him I had often much chat of those affairs, into which he took pleasure to look back from his native harbour; and, at my departure toward Rome (which had been the centre of his experience), I had won his confidence enough to beg his advice how I might carry myself there without offence of others or of mine conscience. '*Signor Arrigo mio*,' says he, '*I pensieri stretti ed il viso sciolto*[1] will go safely over the whole world.' Of which Delphian oracle (for so I have found it) your judgement doth need no commentary; and therefore, Sir, I will commit you, with it, to the best of all securities, God's dear love, remaining – Your friend, as much to command as any of longer date,

HENRY WOTTON.

Postscript

Sir: I have expressly sent this my footboy to prevent your departure without some acknowledgement from me of the receipt of your obliging letter; having myself through some business, I know not how, neglected the ordinary conveyance. In any part where I shall understand you fixed, I shall be glad and diligent to entertain you with home novelties,[2] even for some fomentation of our friendship, too soon interrupted in the cradle.

---

1 *Signor ... sciolto*] translated by Wotton as 'My Signor Harry, your thoughts close and your countenance loose'.
2 home novelties] newsletters.

COMUS

THE PERSONS

The ATTENDANT SPIRIT,	THE LADY.
afterwards in the habit	FIRST BROTHER.
of THYRSIS.	SECOND BROTHER.
COMUS, with his Crew.	SABRINA, the Nymph.

The Chief Persons which presented were:-

The Lord Brackley;
Mr Thomas Egerton, his Brother;
The Lady Alice Egerton.

The first Scene discovers a wild wood.

The ATTENDANT SPIRIT *descends or enters.*

Before the starry threshold of Jove's court
My mansion is, where those immortal shapes
Of bright aerial spirits live enspher'd
In regions mild of calm and serene air,
Above the smoke and stir of this dim spot   5
Which men call earth, and, with low-thoughted care,
Confined and pester'd in this pinfold here,
Strive to keep up a frail and feverish being
Unmindful of the crown that virtue gives,
After this mortal change, to her true servants   10
Amongst the enthronèd gods on sainted seats.
Yet some there be that by due steps aspire
To lay their just hands on that golden key

Lord Brackley] In September 1634 John Egerton, Viscount Brackley, was 11
  years old; he acted the part of the elder brother. In 1638 Lawes dedicated
  his edition of *Comus* to Lord Brackley. Milton printed the dedication and
  the letter from Wotton in his 1645 *Poems*, but not in 1673.
Thomas Egerton] 9 years old in September 1634; he acted the part of the second
  brother.
Lady Alice Egerton] 15 years old in September 1634; she played the part of the
  Lady.
4 serene] used in the Latin sense of 'clear, bright'.
7 pestered] crowded.
  pinfold] animal pound.
11] See Rev. iv. 4.
13 golden key] cf. *Lycidas* 111.

That opes the palace of eternity:
To such my errand is; and but for such, 15
I would not soil these pure ambrosial weeds
With the rank vapours of this sin-worn mould.
    But to my task. Neptune, besides the sway
Of every salt flood and each ebbing stream,
Took in by lot, 'twixt high and nether Jove, 20
Imperial rule of all the sea-girt isles
That, like to rich and various gems, inlay
The unadornèd bosom of the deep;
Which he, to grace his tributary gods,
By course commits to several government, 25
And gives them leave to wear their sapphire crowns
And wield their little tridents; but this isle,
The greatest and the best of all the main,
He quarters to his blue-haired deities;
And all this tract that fronts the falling sun 30
A noble peer of mickle trust and power
Has in his charge, with tempered awe to guide
An old and haughty nation, proud in arms:
Where his fair offspring, nursed in princely lore,
Are coming to attend their father's state, 35
And new-entrusted sceptre; but their way
Lies through the perplexed paths of this drear wood,
The nodding horror of whose shady brows
Threats the forlorn and wandering passenger;
And here their tender age might suffer peril, 4
But that, by quick command from sovereign Jove,
I was despatched for their defence and guard:
And listen why; for I will tell you now
What never yet was heard in tale or song,
From old or modern bard, in hall or bower. 45
    Bacchus, that first from out the purple grape
Crushed the sweet poison of misusèd wine,
After the Tuscan mariners transformed,
Coasting the Tyrrhene shore, as the winds listed,

---

16 ambrosial weeds] immortal clothes.
18-20] Jove ruled the heavens, Neptune the sea, and Pluto ('nether Jove') the
    underworld.
24 grace] honour.
31 peer] The Earl of Bridgewater.
37 perplexed] used in the Latin sense of 'entangled'.
48 transformed] i.e. were transformed (a Latinism). Bacchus transformed the
    sailors who had kidnapped him into dolphins.

On Circe's island fell. (Who knows not Circe,   50
The daughter of the Sun, whose charmèd cup
Whoever tasted lost his upright shape,
And downward fell into a grovelling swine?)
This Nymph, that gazed upon his clustering locks,
With ivy berries wreathed, and his blithe youth,   55
Had by him, ere he parted thence, a son
Much like his father, but his mother more,
Whom therefore she brought up, and Comus named:
Who, ripe and frolic of his full-grown age,
Roving the Celtic and Iberian fields,   60
At last betakes him to this ominous wood,
And, in thick shelter of black shades embowered,
Excels his mother at her mighty art,
Offering to every weary traveller
His orient liquor in a crystal glass,   65
To quench the drought of Phoebus; which as they taste
(For most do taste through fond intemperate thirst),
Soon as the potion works, their human countenance,
The express resemblance of the gods, is changed
Into some brutish form of wolf or bear,   70
Or ounce or tiger, hog, or bearded goat,
All other parts remaining as they were,
And they, so perfect in their misery,
Not once perceive their foul disfigurement,
But boast themselves more comely than before,   75
And all their friends and native home forget,
To roll with pleasure in a sensual sty.
Therefore, when any favoured of high Jove
Chances to pass through this adventurous glade,
Swift as the sparkle of a glancing star   80
I shoot from heaven, to give him safe convoy,
As now I do; but first I must put off
These my sky-robes, spun out of Iris' woof,

50 Circe's island] Aeaea, in the Tyrrhenian Sea. Circe, the daughter of the sun
    (Helios), was visited by Odysseus, and according to one tradition bore him
    a son, Telegonus. She turned his sailors into swine by means of a magic
    potion (*Odyssey* x 135ff.).
58 Comus] The name means 'revelry' in Greek. His parentage is Milton's
    invention.
60 Celtic and Iberian] French and Spanish.
65 orient] bright, like pearls from the east.
66 drought of Phoebus] thirst caused by the sun.
71 ounce] name used of various small feline beasts, vaguely identified.
83 Iris' woof] the woven fabric of the rainbow, of which Iris was the goddess.

And take the weeds and likeness of a swain
That to the service of this house belongs,   85
Who, with his soft pipe and smooth-dittied song,
Well knows to still the wild winds when they roar,
And hush the waving woods; nor of less faith,
And in this office of his mountain watch
Likeliest, and nearest to the present aid   90
Of this occasion. But I hear the tread
Of hateful steps; I must be viewless now.

COMUS *enters, with a charming rod in one hand, his glass in the
other; with him a rout of monsters, headed like sundry sorts of
wild beasts, but otherwise like men and women, their apparel
glistering; they come in, making a riotous and unruly noise,
with torches in their hands.*

   Comus. The star that bids the shepherd fold
Now the top of heaven doth hold;
And the gilded car of day   95
His glowing axle doth allay
In the steep Atlantic stream;
And the slope sun his upward beam
Shoots against the dusky pole,
Pacing toward the other goal   100
Of his chamber in the east.
Meanwhile, welcome joy and feast,
Midnight shout and revelry,
Tipsy dance and jollity.
Braid your locks with rosy twine,   105
Dropping odours, dropping wine.
Rigour now is gone to bed;
And Advice with scrupulous head,
Strict Age, and sour Severity,
With their grave saws, in slumber lie.   110
We, that are of purer fire,
Imitate the starry choir,
Who, in their nightly watchful spheres,
Lead in swift round the months and years.
The sounds and seas, with all their finny drove,   115
Now to the moon in wavering morris move;

92 viewless] invisible.
93 star] Hesperus, the evening star.
95 car of day] the chariot of the sun.
97 stream] the ancients believed that the earth was encircled by a river,
    Oceanus.
110 saws] sententious sayings.
113 watchful spheres] see *Vacation Exercise* 40n.
116 morris] morris dance.

And on the tawny sands and shelves
Trip the pert fairies and the dapper elves;
By dimpled brook and fountain-brim,
The wood-nymphs, decked with daisies trim,   120
Their merry wakes and pastimes keep:
Wha hath night to do with sleep?
Night hath better sweets to prove;
Venus now wakes, and wakens Love.
Come, let us our rites begin;   125
'Tis only daylight that makes sin,
Which these dun shades will ne'er report.
Hail, goddess of nocturnal sport,
Dark-veiled Cotytto, to whom the secret flame
Of midnight torches burns; mysterious dame,   130
That ne'er art called but when the dragon womb
Of Stygian darkness spits her thickest gloom,
And makes one blot of all the air;
Stay thy cloudy ebon chair,
Wherein thou ridest with Hecat', and befriend   135
Us thy vowed priests, till utmost end
Of all thy dues be done, and none left out;
Ere the blabbing eastern scout,
The nice Morn on the Indian steep,
From her cabined loop-hole peep,   140
And to the tell-tale Sun descry
Our concealed solemnity.
Come, knit hands, and beat the ground
In a light fantastic round.

The Measure.

Break off, break off! I feel the different pace   145
Of some chaste footing near about this ground.
Run to your shrouds within these brakes and trees;
Our number may affright: some virgin sure
(For so I can distinguish by mine art)
Benighted in these woods! Now to my charms,   150
And to my wily trains; I shall ere long
Be well stocked with as fair a herd as grazed
About my mother Circe. Thus I hurl

117 shelves] sandbanks or shallows.
126ff.] John iii. 19-20.
129 Cotytto] Thracian goddess celebrated in nocturnal orgies.
135 Hecat'] goddess of witchcraft.
151 trains] deceits.

My dazzling spells into the spongy air,
Of power to cheat the eye with blear illusion,   155
And give it false presentments, lest the place,
And my quaint habits breed astonishment,
And put the damsel to suspicious flight;
Which must not be, for that's against my course.
I, under fair pretence of friendly ends,   160
And well-placed words of glozing courtesy,
Baited with reasons not unplausible,
Wind me into the easy-hearted man,
And hug him into snares. When once her eye
Hath met the virtue of this magic dust,   165
I shall appear some harmless villager
Whom thrift keeps up about his country gear.
But here she comes; I fairly step aside,
And hearken, if I may her business hear.

THE LADY *enters*.

Lady. This way the noise was, if mine ear be true,   170
My best guide now; methought it was the sound
Of riot and ill-managed merriment,
Such as the jocund flute or gamesome pipe
Stirs up among the loose unlettered hinds,
When, for their teeming flocks and granges full,   175
In wanton dance they praise the bounteous Pan,
And thank the gods amiss. I should be loath
To meet the rudeness and swilled insolence
Of such late wassailers; yet O where else
Shall I inform my unacquainted feet   180
In the blind mazes of this tangled wood?
My brothers, when they saw me wearied out
With this long way, resolving here to lodge
Under the spreading favour of these pines,
Stepped, as they said, to the next thicket-side   185
To bring me berries, or such cooling fruit
As the kind hospitable woods provide.

154 spongy] absorbent.
161 glozing] flattering.
165 virtue] power, efficacy.
167 The 1673 edition omits this line ('Whom . . . gear') and reverses lines 168
    and 169.
168 fairly] quietly.
174 loose unlettered hinds] dissolute and illiterate rustics.
176 Pan] Greek god of woods, fields, and shepherds.
179 wassailers] revellers.

They left me then when the grey-hooded Even,
Like a sad votarist in palmer's weed,
Rose from the hindmost wheels of Phoebus' wain.   190
But where they are, and why they came not back,
Is now the labour of my thoughts; 'tis likeliest
They had engaged their wandering steps too far;
And envious darkness, ere they could return,
Had stole them from me: else, O thievish Night,   195
Why shouldst thou, but for some felonious end,
In thy dark lantern thus close up the stars
That Nature hung in heaven, and filled their lamps
With everlasting oil to give due light
To the misled and lonely traveller?   200
This is the place, as well as I may guess,
Whence even now the tumult of loud mirth
Was rife, and perfect in my listening ear;
Yet nought but single darkness do I find.
What might this be? A thousand fantasies   205
Begin to throng into my memory,
Of calling shapes, and beckoning shadows dire,
And airy tongues that syllable men's names
On sands and shores and desert wildernesses.
These thoughts may startle well, but not astound   210
The virtuous mind, that ever walks attended
By a strong siding champion, Conscience. . . .
O welcome pure-eyed Faith, white-handed Hope,
Thou hovering angel girt with golden wings,
And thou unblemished form of Chastity!   215
I see ye visibly, and now believe
That he, the Supreme Good, to whom all things ill
Are but as slavish officers of vengeance,
Would send a glistering guardian, if need were,
To keep my life and honour unassailed.   220
Was I deceived, or did a sable cloud
Turn forth her silver lining on the night?
I did not err: there does a sable cloud
Turn forth her silver lining on the night,
And casts a gleam over this tufted grove.   225
I cannot hallo to my brothers, but
Such noise as I can make to be heard farthest

189] 'Sad' means both 'serious' and 'darkly dressed'. A 'votarist' is one bound
   by a vow. 'Palmer' is not used in the strict sense of 'one who has been to the
   Holy Land', but simply means 'pilgrim'.
197 dark lantern] a lantern, the light from which can be darkened with a
   shutter.
212 siding] supporting.

I'll venture, for my new-enlivened spirits
Prompt me; and they perhaps are not far off.

SONG

Sweet Echo, sweetest nymph, that liv'st unseen   230
  Within thy airy shell
 By slow Meander's margent green,
And in the violet-embroidered vale
 Where the love-lorn nightingale
Nightly to thee her sad song mourneth well.   235
Canst thou not tell me of a gentle pair
  That likest thy Narcissus are?
   O, if thou have
  Hid them in some flowery cave,
   Tell me but where,   240
 Sweet queen of parley, daughter of the sphere!
 So may'st thou be translated to the skies,
And give resounding grace to all heaven's harmonies.

Comus. Can any mortal mixture of earth's mould
Breathe such divine enchanting ravishment?   245
Sure something holy lodges in that breast,
And with these raptures moves the vocal air
To testify his hidden residence;
How sweetly did they float upon the wings
Of silence, through the empty-vaulted night,   250
At every fall smoothing the raven down
Of darkness till it smiled; I have oft heard
My mother Circe with the Sirens three,
Amidst the flowery-kirtled Naiades,
Culling their potent herbs and baleful drugs,   255
Who, as they sung, would take the prisoned soul,

230 Echo] a Greek nymph who loved Narcissus, a beautiful youth. Narcissus
  spurned her love, and was punished by Aphrodite, who made him fall in
  love with his own reflection in the water; he pined away, and was
  transformed into a flower (*Metamorphoses* iii 402–510).
232 Meander] a winding river in Asia Minor.
241 parley] speech.
  daughter of the sphere] See *Solemn Music* 1–2n.
251 fall] cadence.
253 Sirens] In Homer two Sirens (named by Milton in ll. 876 and 878) lure
  sailors to their deaths (*Odyssey* xii 166–200); later authors speak of three or
  four Sirens.
254 Naiades] river and fountain nymphs.

And lap it in Elysium; Scylla wept,
And chid her barking waves into attention,
And fell Charybdis murmured soft applause;
Yet they in pleasing slumber lulled the sense,   260
And in sweet madness robbed it of itself;
But such a sacred and home-felt delight,
Such sober certainty of waking bliss,
I never heard till now. I'll speak to her,
And she shall be my queen. – Hail, foreign wonder!   265
Whom certain these rough shades did never breed,
Unless the goddess that in rural shrine
Dwell'st here with Pan or Sylvan, by blest song,
Forbidding every bleak unkindly fog
To touch the prosperous growth of this tall wood.   270
    Lady. Nay gentle shepherd, ill is lost that praise
That is addressed to unattending ears;
Not any boast of skill, but extreme shift
How to regain my severed company,
Compelled me to awake the courteous Echo   275
To give me answer from her mossy couch.
    Comus. What chance, good Lady, hath bereft you thus?
    Lady. Dim darkness and this leafy labyrinth.
    Comus. Could that divide you from near-ushering
        guides?
    Lady. They left me weary on a grassy turf.   280
    Comus. By falsehood, or discourtesy, or why?
    Lady. To seek i' the valley some cool friendly spring.
    Comus. And left your fair side all unguarded, Lady?
    Lady. They were but twain, and purposed quick return.
    Comus. Perhaps forestalling night prevented them.   285
    Lady. How easy my misfortune is to hit!
    Comus. Imports their loss, beside the present need?
    Lady. No less than if I should my brothers lose.
    Comus. Were they of manly prime, or youthful bloom?
    Lady. As smooth as Hebe's their unrazored lips.   290
    Comus. Two such I saw, what time the laboured ox

257–9] Monsters associated with the rocks of Scylla and the whirlpool of
    Charybdis were the twin hazards of the Straits of Messina (*Odyssey* xii
    73–100; cf. *PL* II 1019–20).
262 home-felt] intimately felt.
267 Unless the goddess] Unless you are the goddess.
268 Sylvan] Sylvanus, the Roman forest-god.
277–90] This dialogue in alternate single lines imitates the stichomythia of
    Greek drama.
290 *Hebe*] see *Vacation Exercise* 38n.

In his loose traces from the furrow came,
And the swinked hedger at his supper sat.
I saw them under a green mantling vine,
That crawls along the side of yon small hill,   295
Plucking ripe clusters from the tender shoots;
Their port was more than human, as they stood.
I took it for a fairy vision
Of some gay creatures of the element,
That in the colours of the rainbow live,   300
And play i' the plighted clouds. I was awe-struck,
And, as I passed, I worshipped; if those you seek,
It were a journey like the path to heaven
To help you find them.
    Lady.   Gentle villager,   305
What readiest way would bring me to that place?
    Comus. Due west it rises from this shrubby point.
    Lady. To find out that, good shepherd, I suppose,
In such a scant allowance of star-light,
Would overtask the best land-pilot's art,
Without the sure guess of well-practised feet.   310
    Comus. I know each lane, and every alley green,
Dingle, or bushy dell, of this wild wood,
And every bosky bourn from side to side,
My daily walks and ancient neighbourhood;
And, if your stray attendance be yet lodged,   315
Or shroud within these limits, I shall know
Ere morrow wake, or the low-roosted lark
From her thatched pallet rouse. If otherwise,
I can conduct you, Lady, to a low
But loyal cottage, where you may be safe   320
Till further quest.
    Lady.   Shepherd, I take thy word,
And trust the honest-offered courtesy,
Which oft is sooner found in lowly sheds,
With smoky rafters, than in tapestry halls   325
And courts of princes, where it first was named,
And yet is most pretended: in a place
Less warranted than this, or less secure,

293 swinked] tired.
297 port] deportment, bearing.
301 plighted] plaited, interwoven.
312 Dingle] wooded hollow.
313 bosky bourn] small stream overhung with bushes.
315 attendance] attendants.
318 thatched pallet] straw bed.

I cannot be, that I should fear to change it.
Eye me, blest Providence, and square my trial
To my proportioned strength! Shepherd, lead on. . . .   330

The TWO BROTHERS.

Eld. Bro. Unmuffle, ye faint stars; and thou, fair moon,
That wont'st to love the traveller's benison,
Stoop thy pale visage through an amber cloud,
And disinherit Chaos, that reigns here
In double night of darkness and of shades;   335
Or, if your influence be quite dammed up
With black usurping mists, some gentle taper,
Though a rush-candle from the wicker hole
Or some clay habitation, visit us
With thy long levelled rule of streaming light,   340
And thou shalt be our Star of Arcady,
Or Tyrian Cynosure.
    Sec. Bro.   Or, if our eyes
Be barred that happiness, might we but hear
The folded flocks, penned in their wattled cotes,   345
Or sound of pastoral reed with oaten stops,
Or whistle from the lodge, or village cock
Count the night-watches to his feathery dames,
'Twould be some solace yet, some little cheering,
In this close dungeon of innumerous boughs.
But, O, that hapless virgin, our lost sister!   350
Where may she wander now, whither betake her
From the chill dew, amongst rude burs and thistles?
Perhaps some cold bank is her bolster now,
Or 'gainst the rugged bark of some broad elm
Leans her unpillowed head, fraught with sad fears.   355
What if in wild amazement and affright,
Or, while we speak, within the direful grasp
Of savage hunger, or of savage heat!
    Eld. Bro. Peace, brother: be not over-exquisite
To cast the fashion of uncertain evils;   360

---

332 benison] blessing.
341 Star of Arcady] Arcturus, in the constellation Boötes, was the pole star of
    the ancient Greeks. Arcturus was thought by the Greeks to be a stellifica-
    tion of Arcas, the son of Callisto, an Arcadian princess (hence 'of Arcady')
    who was stellified as Ursa Major.
342 Tyrian Cynosure] The Phoenician (or Tyrian) pole star, which is also the
    modern pole star, is in Ursa Minor, which the Greeks called Cynosura (dog's
    tail).
359 over-exquisite] too precise.
360 cast] forecast.

For, grant they be so, while they rest unknown,
What need a man forestall his date of grief,
And run to meet what he would most avoid?
Or, if they be but false alarms of fear,
How bitter is such self-delusion!   365
I do not think my sister so to seek,
Or so unprincipled in virtue's book,
And the sweet peace that goodness bosoms ever,
As that the single want of light and noise
(Not being in danger, as I trust she is not)   370
Could stir the constant mood of her calm thoughts,
And put them into misbecoming plight.
Virtue could see to do what Virtue would
By her own radiant light, though sun and moon
Were in the flat sea sunk. And Wisdom's self   375
Oft seeks to sweet retired solitude,
Where, with her best nurse, Contemplation,
She plumes her feathers, and lets grow her wings,
That, in the various bustle of resort,
Were all to-ruffled, and sometimes impaired.   380
He that has light within his own clear breast
May sit i' the centre, and enjoy bright day;
But he that hides a dark soul and foul thoughts
Benighted walks under the mid-day sun;
Himself is his own dungeon.
    Sec. Bro.   'Tis most true   385
That musing Meditation most affects
The pensive secrecy of desert cell,
Far from the cheerful haunt of men and herds,
And sits as safe as in a senate-house;
For who would rob a hermit of his weeds,   390
His few books, or his beads, or maple dish,
Or do his grey hairs any violence?
But Beauty, like the fair Hesperian tree
Laden with blooming gold, had need the guard
Of dragon-watch with unenchanted eye   395
To save her blossoms, and defend her fruit,
From the rash hand of bold Incontinence.

366 to seek] deficient.
380 to] an archaic intensive prefix.
382 centre] of the earth.
386 affects] loves.
393-5] In the garden of the Hesperides a tree bearing golden apples was
    guarded by the beautiful daughters of Hesperus (the Hesperides) and by a
    sleepless dragon. Cf. ii. 981-3.

You may as well spread out the unsunned heaps
Of miser's treasure by an outlaw's den,   400
And tell me it is safe, as bid me hope
Danger will wink on Opportunity,
And let a single helpless maiden pass
Uninjured in this wild surrounding waste.
Of night or loneliness it recks me not;
I fear the dread events that dog them both,   405
Lest some ill-greeting touch attempt the person
Of our unownèd sister.
    Eld. Bro.   I do not, brother,
Infer as if I thought my sister's state
Secure without all doubt or controversy;
Yet, where an equal poise of hope and fear   410
Does arbitrate the event, my nature is
That I incline to hope rather than fear,
And gladly banish squint suspicion.
My sister is not so defenceless left
As you imagine; she has a hidden strength,   415
Which you remember not.
    Sec. Bro.   What hidden strength,
Unless the strength of heaven, if you mean that?
    Eld. Bro. I mean that too, but yet a hidden strength,
Which, if heaven gave it, may be termed her own.
'Tis chastity, my brother, chastity: 420
She that has that is clad in complete steel,
And, like a quivered nymph with arrows keen,
May trace huge forests, and unharboured heaths,
Infámous hills, and sandy perilous wilds;
Where, through the sacred rays of chastity,   425
No savage fierce, bandit, or mountaineer,
Will dare to soil her virgin purity.
Yea, there where very desolation dwells,
By grots and caverns shagged with horrid shades,
She may pass on with unblenched majesty,   430
Be it not done in pride, or in presumption.
Some say no evil thing that walks by night,
In fog or fire, by lake or moorish fen,
Blue meagre hag, or stubborn unlaid ghost,
That breaks his magic chains at curfew time,   435

404 it recks me not] I am not concerned.
407 unownèd] lost.
411 arbitrate the event] decide the outcome.
423 unharboured] offering no shelter.
433 fire] will-o'-the-wisp.

No goblin or swart fairy of the mine,
Hath hurtful power o'er true virginity.
Do ye believe me yet, or shall I call
Antiquity from the old schools of Greece
To testify the arms of chastity?   440
Hence had the huntress Dian her dread bow,
Fair silver-shafted queen for ever chaste,
Wherewith she tamed the brinded lioness
And spotted mountain-pard, but set at nought
The frivolous bow of Cupid; gods and men   445
Feared her stern frown, and she was queen o' the woods.
What was the snaky-headed Gorgon shield
That wise Minerva wore, unconquered virgin,
Wherewith she freezed her foes to congealed stone,
But rigid looks of chaste austerity,   450
And noble grace that dashed brute violence
With sudden adoration and blank awe?
So dear to heaven is saintly chastity
That, when a soul is found sincerely so,
A thousand liveried angels lackey her,   455
Driving far off each thing of sin and guilt,
And in clear dream and solemn vision
Tell her of things that no gross ear can hear;
Till oft converse with heavenly habitants
Begin to cast a beam on the outward shape,   460
The unpolluted temple of the mind,
And turns it by degrees to the soul's essence,
Till all be made immortal. But when lust,
By unchaste looks, loose gestures, and foul talk,
But most by lewd and lavish act of sin,   465
Lets in defilement to the inward parts,
The soul grows clotted by contagion,
Embodies, and imbrutes, till she quite lose
The divine property of her first being.
Such are those thick and gloomy shadows damp   470

441-2] Diana, the virgin goddess and huntress, was also a moon-goddess, and
    the shafts may be moonbeams (hence 'silver') as well as arrows.
444 pard] panther or leopard.
447-52] Minerva, the virgin goddess of the arts, of war, and of healing, wore on
    her shield the head of Medusa (one of the three Gorgons), whose hair
    Minerva had transformed into snakes. The gaze of a Gorgon turned the
    beholder into stone.
463-75] An adaptation of Plato, *Phaedo* 81.
465 lavish] licentious.
468 Embodies, and imbrutes] becomes corporeal and bestial.

Oft seen in charnel-vaults and sepulchres,
Lingering and sitting by a new-made grave,
As loath to leave the body that it loved,
And linked itself by carnal sensualty
To a degenerate and degraded state.   475
  Sec. Bro. How charming is divine philosophy!
Not harsh and crabbed, as dull fools suppose,
But musical as is Apollo's lute,
And a perpetual feast of nectared sweets,
Where no crude surfeit reigns.
  Eld. Bro.   List! list! I hear   480
Some far-off hallo break the silent air.
  Sec. Bro. Methought so too; what should it be?
  Eld. Bro.   For certain,
Either some one, like us, night-foundered here,
Or else some neighbour woodman, or, at worst,
Some roving robber calling to his fellows.   485
  Sec. Bro. Heaven keep my sister! Again, again, and
    near!
Best draw, and stand upon our guard.
  Eld. Bro.   I'll hallo.
If he be friendly, he comes well; if not,
Defence is a good cause, and heaven be for us!

  The ATTENDANT SPIRIT, *habited like a shepherd.*

That hallo I should know. What are you? Speak.   490
Come not too near; you fall on iron stakes else.
  Spir. What voice is that? My young Lord? Speak again.
  Sec. Bro. O brother, 'tis my father's shepherd, sure.
  Eld. Bro. Thyrsis? Whose artful strains have oft delayed
The huddling brook to hear his madrigal,   495
And sweetened every musk-rose of the dale,
How camest thou here, good swain? Hath any ram
Slipped from the fold, or young kid lost his dam,
Or straggling wether the pent flock forsook?
How couldst thou find this dark sequestered nook?   500
  Spir. O my loved master's heir, and his next joy,
I came not here on such a trivial toy
As a strayed ewe, or to pursue the stealth
Of pilfering wolf; not all the fleecy wealth

497 crude] indigestible.
483 night-foundered] engulfed in night.
491 stakes] swords.
494 Thyrsis] common name in pastoral poetry, sometimes used for shepherd
     singers.

That doth enrich these downs is worth a thought   505
To this my errand, and the care it brought.
But O my virgin Lady, where is she?
How chance she is not in your company?
    Eld. Bro. To tell thee sadly, shepherd, without blame
Or our neglect, we lost her as we came.   510
    Spir. Ay me unhappy! Then my fears are true.
    Eld. Bro. What fears, good Thyrsis? Prithee briefly
        show.
    Spir. I'll tell ye; 'tis not vain or fabulous
(Though so esteemed by shallow ignorance)
What the sage poets, taught by the heavenly Muse,   515
Storied of old in high immortal verse
Of dire chimeras and enchanted isles,
And rifted rocks whose entrance leads to hell;
For such there be, but unbelief is blind.
    Within the navel of this hideous wood,   520
Immured in cypress shades, a sorcerer dwells,
Of Bacchus and of Circe born, great Comus,
Deep skilled in all his mother's witcheries,
And here to every thirsty wanderer
By sly enticement gives his baneful cup,   525
With many murmurs mixed, whose pleasing poison
The visage quite transforms of him that drinks,
And the inglorious likeness of a beast
Fixes instead, unmoulding reason's mintage
Charactered in the face; this have I learnt   530
Tending my flocks hard by i' the hilly crofts
That brow this bottom glade, whence night by night
He and his monstrous rout are heard to howl
Like stabled wolves, or tigers at their prey,
Doing abhorred rites to Hecate   535
In their obscurèd haunts of inmost bowers;
Yet have they many baits and guileful spells
To inveigle and invite the unwary sense
Of them that pass unweeting by the way.
This evening late, by then the chewing flocks   540
Had ta'en their supper on the savoury herb
Of knot-grass dew-besprent, and were in fold,
I sat me down to watch upon a bank

---

509 sadly] seriously.
517 chimera] a fire-breathing monster with the head of a lion, the body of a
    female goat, and the tail of a dragon.
533 monstrous rout] rout of monsters.
542 dew-besprent] sprinkled with dew.

With ivy canopied, and interwove
With flaunting honeysuckle, and began,   545
Wrapped in a pleasing fit of melancholy,
To meditate my rural minstrelsy,
Till fancy had her fill; but ere a close
The wonted roar was up amidst the woods,
And filled the air with barbarous dissonance   550
At which I ceased, and listened them a while,
Till an unusual stop of sudden silence
Gave respite to the drowsy-flighted steeds
That draw the litter of close-curtained sleep.
At last a soft and solemn-breathing sound   555
Rose like a steam of rich distilled perfumes,
And stole upon the air, that even Silence
Was took ere she was ware, and wished she might
Deny her nature, and be never more,
Still to be so displaced. I was all ear,   560
And took in strains that might create a soul
Under the ribs of Death. But O ere long
Too well I did perceive it was the voice
Of my most honoured Lady, your dear sister.
Amazed I stood, harrowed with grief and fear;   565
And 'O poor hapless nightingale,' thought I,
'How sweet thou sing'st, how near the deadly snare!'
Then down the lawns I ran with headlong haste,
Through paths and turnings often trod by day,
Till, guided by mine ear, I found the place   570
Where that damned wizard, hid in sly disguise
(For so by certain signs I knew), had met
Already, ere my best speed could prevent,
The aidless innocent Lady, his wished prey,
Who gently asked if he had seen such two,   575
Supposing him some neighbour villager;
Longer I durst not stay, but soon I guessed
Ye were the two she meant; with that I sprung
Into swift flight, till I had found you here;
But further know I not.

    Sec. Bro.   O night and shades,   580
How are ye joined with hell in triple knot
Against the unarmed weakness of one virgin,
Alone and helpless! Is this the confidence
You gave me, brother?

    Eld. Bro.   Yes, and keep it still;

547 meditate] practise.

Lean on it safely; not a period   585
Shall be unsaid for me. Against the threats
Of malice or of sorcery, or that power
Which erring men call chance, this I hold firm:
Virtue may be assailed, but never hurt,
Surprised by unjust force, but not enthralled;   590
Yea, even that which mischief meant most harm
Shall in the happy trial prove most glory.
But evil on itself shall back recoil,
And mix no more with goodness, when at last,
Gathered like scum, and settled to itself,   595
It shall be in eternal restless change
Self-fed and self-consumed. If this fail,
The pillared firmament is rottenness,
And earth's base built on stubble. But come, let's on!
Against the opposing will and arm of heaven   600
May never this just sword be lifted up;
But, for that damned magician, let him be girt
With all the grisly legions that troop
Under the sooty flag of Acheron,
Harpies and Hydras, or all the monstrous forms   605
'Twixt Africa and Ind, I'll find him out,
And force him to return his purchase back,
Or drag him by the curls to a foul death,
Cursed as his life.
    Spir.   Alas, good venturous youth,
I love thy courage yet, and bold emprise;   610
But here thy sword can do thee little stead;
Far other arms and other weapons must
Be those that quell the might of hellish charms;
He with his bare wand can unthread thy joints,
And crumble all thy sinews.
    Eld. Bro.   Why, prithee, shepherd,   615
How durst thou then thyself approach so near
As to make this relation?
    Spir.   Care and utmost shifts

---

585 period] sentence.
586 for me] for my part.
598 pillared firmament] the dome of the sky supported by pillars. Cf. *PR* IV 455 and Job xxvi. 11.
604 Acheron] one of the rivers of the underworld; see *PL* II 578.
605 Harpies] long-clawed birds with the faces of hags who lived at the entrance to the underworld.
    Hydras] here refers to a fifty-headed monster, a guardian in the underworld.
610 emprise] chivalric prowess.

How to secure the lady from surprisal
Brought to mind a certain shepherd lad
Of small regard to see to, yet well skilled   620
In every virtuous plant and healing herb
That spreads her verdant leaf to the morning ray;
He loved me well, and oft would beg me sing,
Which when I did, he on the tender grass
Would sit, and hearken even to ecstasy,   625
And in requital ope his leathern scrip,
And show me simples of a thousand names,
Telling their strange and vigorous faculties;
Amongst the rest a small unsightly root,
But of divine effect, he culled me out;   630
The leaf was darkish, and had prickles on it,
But in another country, as he said,
Bore a bright golden flower, but not in this soil:
Unknown, and like esteemed, and the dull swain
Treads on it daily with his clouted shoon;   635
And yet more med'cinal is it than that moly
That Hermes once to wise Ulysses gave.
He called it haemony, and gave it me,
And bade me keep it as of sovereign use
'Gainst all enchantments, mildew blast, or damp,   640
Or ghastly Furies' apparition;
I pursed it up, but little reckoning made,
Till now that this extremity compelled,
But now I find it true; for by this means
I knew the foul enchanter, though disguised,   645
Entered the very lime-twigs of his spells,
And yet came off. If you have this about you
(As I will give you when we go) you may
Boldly assault the necromancer's hall;
Where if he be, with dauntless hardihood   650

620 to see to] to look at.
621 virtuous] efficacious.
626 scrip] bag.
627 simples] medicinal herbs.
628 faculties] properties.
635 clouted shoon] shoes protected with iron plates, or studded with large-
     headed nails.
636 moly] Plant given to Ulysses to protect him from Circe (*Odyssey* x 305).
637 Hermes] Hermes (Mercury), the messenger of Zeus and God of good
     fortune.
638 haemony] Milton probably derived the name from Haemonia (Thessaly),
     the land of magic, but other etymologies are possible.
646 lime-twigs] twigs smeared with bird-lime for trapping birds.

And brandished blade rush on him, break his glass,
And shed the luscious liquid on the ground,
But seize his wand; though he and his cursed crew
Fierce sign of battle make, and menace high,
Or like the sons of Vulcan, vomit smoke,   655
Yet will they soon retire, if he but shrink.
    Eld. Bro. Thyrsis, lead on apace; I'll follow thee,
And some good angel bear a shield before us!

*The scene changes to a stately palace, set out with all manner of
deliciousness: soft music, tables spread with all dainties.*
COMUS *appears with his rabble, and* THE LADY *set in an
enchanted chair: to whom he offers his glass, which she puts by,
and goes about to rise.*

    Comus. Nay, Lady, sit. If I but wave this wand,
Your nerves are all chained up in alabaster,   660
And you a statue, or as Daphne was,
Root-bound, that fled Apollo.
    Lady.   Fool, do not boast;
Thou canst not touch the freedom of my mind
With all thy charms, although this corporal rind
Thou hast immanacled while heaven sees good.   665
    Comus. Why are you vexed, Lady? Why do you frown?
Here dwell no frowns, nor anger; from these gates
Sorrow flies far. See, here be all the pleasures
That fancy can beget on youthful thoughts,
When the fresh blood grows lively, and returns   670
Brisk as the April buds in primrose season.
And first behold this cordial julep here,
That flames and dances in his crystal bounds,
With spirits of balm and fragrant syrups mixed.
Not that Nepenthes which the wife of Thone   675
In Egypt gave to Jove-born Helena
Is of such power to stir up joy as this,
To life so friendly, or so cool to thirst.
Why should you be so cruel to yourself,
And to those dainty limbs, which Nature lent   680
For gentle usage and soft delicacy?

655 Vulcan] god of fire and volcanoes; one of his sons, Cacus, belched out smoke
    in an unsuccessful attempt to protect himself from Hercules.
661-2] *See PL* IV 272-4n.
672 julep] literally a sweet drink, but the word carries a secondary sense of a
    drink to cool the heat of passion.
675-6] Nepenthes means in Greek 'banishing pain and sorrow'. *Pharmakon
    Nepenthes* was a drug, possibly opium, given to Helen on her way home
    from Troy by Polydamna, the wife of the Egyptian Thon.

But you invert the covenants of her trust,
And harshly deal, like an ill borrower,
With that which you received on other terms,
Scorning the unexempt condition   685
By which all mortal frailty must subsist,
Refreshment after toil, ease after pain,
That have been tired all day without repast,
And timely rest have wanted. But, fair virgin,
This will restore all soon.
    Lady.   'Twill not, false traitor!   690
'Twill not restore the truth and honesty
That thou hast banished from thy tongue with lies;
Was this the cottage and the safe abode
Thou told'st me of? What grim aspects are these,
These ugly-headed monsters? Mercy guard me!   695
Hence with thy brewed enchantments, foul deceiver!
Hast thou betrayed my credulous innocence
With vizored falsehood and base forgery?
And would'st thou seek again to trap me here
With liquorish baits, fit to ensnare a brute?   700
Were it a draught for Juno when she banquets,
I would not taste thy treasonous offer; none
But such as are good men can give good things,
And that which is not good is not delicious
To a well-governed and wise appetite.   705
    Comus. O foolishness of men! That lend their ears
To those budge doctors of the Stoic fur,
And fetch their precepts from the Cynic tub,
Praising the lean and sallow Abstinence!
Wherefore did Nature pour her bounties forth   710
With such a full and unwithdrawing hand,
Covering the earth with odours, fruits, and flocks,
Thronging the seas with spawn innumerable,
But all to please and sate the curious taste?
And set to work millions of spinning worms,   715

---

700 liquorish] 'pleasant to the palate', but the word carries a secondary sense of
    'lecherous, lustful'.
707–8] Stoics and Cynics were ancient groups of philosophers who abjured all
    luxury. The Stoic school was founded by Zeno, and by the 'Doctors' of the
    school Milton might mean ancients such as Seneca, Epictetus, and Marcus
    Aurelius. The Cynic school was founded by Antisthenes, and one of its
    leaders, Diogenes, lived in a tub; see *Areopagitica* p. 579, note on 'Cynic'.
    'Budge' means 'solemn' or 'pompous', but the word 'fur' at the end of the
    line brings out the secondary meaning of 'budge', 'the fur used to trim
    academic robes'.

That in their green shops weave the smooth-haired silk,
To deck her sons; and, that no corner might
Be vacant of her plenty, in her own loins
She hutched the all-worshipped ore and precious gems,
To store her children with; if all the world   720
Should, in a pet of temperance, feed on pulse,
Drink the clear stream, and nothing wear but frieze,
The all-giver would be unthanked, would be unpraised,
Not half his riches known, and yet despised;
And we should serve him as a grudging master,   725
As a penurious niggard of his wealth,
And live like Nature's bastards, not her sons,
Who would be quite surcharged with her own weight,
And strangled with her waste fertility:
The earth cumbered, and the winged air darked with
      plumes,   730
The herds would over-multitude their lords,
The sea o'erfraught would swell, and the unsought
      diamonds
Would so emblaze the forehead of the deep,
And so bestud with stars, that they below
Would grow inured to light, and come at last   735
To gaze upon the sun with shameless brows.
List, Lady; be not coy, and be not cozened
With that same vaunted name, Virginity.
Beauty is Nature's coin; must not be hoarded,
But must be current; and the good thereof   740
Consists in mutual and partaken bliss,
Unsavoury in the enjoyment of itself.
If you let slip time, like a neglected rose
It withers on the stalk with languished head.
Beauty is Nature's brag, and must be shown   745
In courts, at feasts, and high solemnities,
Where most may wonder at the workmanship.
It is for homely features to keep home;
They had their name thence: coarse complexions
And cheeks of sorry grain will serve to ply   750
The sampler, and to tease the housewife's wool.
What need a vermeil-tinctured lip for that,
Love-darting eyes, or tresses like the morn?

721-2] See Dan. i. 8–16. Frieze is a coarse woollen cloth.
733 deep] centre of the earth, the 'forehead' of which is the roof of the inside of
      the earth.
734 they below] the spirits of the underworld.
750 grain] hue.

There was another meaning in these gifts;
Think what, and be advised; you are but young yet.   755
   Lady. I had not thought to have unlocked my lips
In this unhallowed air, but that this juggler
Would think to charm my judgement, as mine eyes,
Obtruding false rules pranked in reason's garb.
I hate when vice can bolt her arguments   760
And virtue has no tongue to check her pride.
Impostor! Do not charge most innocent Nature,
As if she would her children should be riotous
With her abundance. She, good cateress,
Means her provision only to the good,   765
That live according to her sober laws,
And holy dictate of spare Temperance.
If every just man that now pines with want
Had but a moderate and beseeming share
Of that which lewdly-pampered Luxury   770
Now heaps upon some few with vast excess,
Nature's full blessings would be well-dispensed
In unsuperfluous even proportion,
And she no whit encumbered with her store;
And then the giver would be better thanked   775
His praise due paid: for swinish gluttony
Ne'er looks to heaven amidst his gorgeous feast,
But with besotted base ingratitude
Crams, and blasphemes his feeder. Shall I go on?
Or have I said enough? To him that dares   780
Arm his profane tongue with contemptuous words
Against the sun-clad power of chastity
Fain would I something say – yet to what end?
Thou hast nor ear, nor soul, to apprehend
The sublime notion and high mystery   785
That must be uttered to unfold the sage
And serious doctrine of Virginity;
And thou art worthy that thou shouldst not know
More happiness than this thy present lot.
Enjoy your dear wit, and gay rhetoric,   790
That hath so well been taught her dazzling fence;
Thou art not fit to hear thyself convinced.

757 juggler] 'sorcerer', with a secondary suggestion of 'trickster'.
759 pranked] showily dressed.
760 bolt] may mean 'refine', or 'utter hastily'.
778 besotted] intellectually or morally stupefied or blinded.
782 sun-clad] see Rev. xii. 1.
791 fence] the art of fencing.

Yet, should I try, the uncontrollèd worth
Of this pure cause would kindle my rapt spirits
To such a flame of sacred vehemence   795
That dumb things would be moved to sympathise,
And the brute Earth would lend her nerves, and shake,
Till all thy magic structures, reared so high,
Were shattered into heaps o'er thy false head.

Comus. She fables not. I feel that I do fear   800
Her words set off by some superior power;
And, though not mortal, yet a cold shuddering dew
Dips me all o'er, as when the wrath of Jove
Speaks thunder and the chains of Erebus
To some of Saturn's crew. I must dissemble,   805
And try her yet more strongly. Come, no more!
This is mere moral babble, and direct
Against the canon laws of our foundation.
I must not suffer this; yet 'tis but the lees
And settlings of a melancholy blood.   810
But this will cure all straight; one sip of this
Will bathe the drooping spirits in delight
Beyond the bliss of dreams. Be wise, and taste. . . .

The BROTHERS *rush in with swords drawn, wrest his glass out
of his hand, and break it against the ground; his rout make sign
of resistance, but are all driven in. The* ATTENDANT SPIRIT
comes in.

Spir. What! Have you let the false enchanter scape?
O ye mistook; ye should have snatched his wand,   815
And bound him fast. Without his rod reversed,
And backward mutters of disservering power,
We cannot free the Lady that sits here
In stony fetters fixed and motionless.
Yet stay: be not disturbed; now I bethink me,   820
Some other means I have which may be used,
Which once of Meliboeus old I learnt,
The soothest shepherd that e'er piped on plains.
    There is a gentle Nymph not far from hence,

793 uncontrollèd] indisputable.
797 nerves] sinews.
803-5] Jove used thunderbolts to depose his father Saturn, and then chained
    Saturn and his supporters ('crew'), the Titans, in Erebus, the underworld.
809 lees] sediment.
822 Meliboeus] commonly identified with Spenser, who told the story of
    Sabrina in *Faerie Queene* II. x. 14-19.
823 soothest] most truthful.

That with moist curb sways the smooth Severn
    stream: 825
Sabrina is her name, a virgin pure;
Whilom she was the daughter of Locrine,
That had the sceptre from his father Brute.
She, guileless damsel, flying the mad pursuit
Of her enragèd stepdame, Guendolen,   830
Commended her fair innocence to the flood
That stayed her flight with his cross-flowing course;
The water-nymphs, that in the bottom played,
Held up their pearlèd wrists, and took her in,
Bearing her straight to aged Nereus' hall,   835
Who, piteous of her woes, reared her lank head,
And gave her to his daughters to imbathe
In nectared lavers strewed with asphodel,
And through the porch and inlet of each sense
Dropped in ambrosial oils, till she revived,   840
And underwent a quick immortal change,
Made goddess of the river; still she retains
Her maiden gentleness, and oft at eve
Visits the herds along the twilight meadows,
Helping all urchin blasts, and ill-luck signs   845
That the shrewd meddling elf delights to make,
Which she with precious vialed liquors heals.
For which the shepherds at their festivals
Carol her goodness loud in rustic lays,
And throw sweet garland wreaths into her stream   850
Of pansies, pinks, and gaudy daffodils.
And, as the old swain said, she can unlock
The clasping charm, and thaw the numbing spell,
If she be right invoked in warbled song;
For maidenhood she loves, and will be swift   855
To aid a virgin, such as was herself,
In hard-besetting need; this will I try,
And add the power of some adjuring verse.

826ff.] Milton's version of the legend of Sabrina, goddess of the Severn, differs
    from the multitude of earlier versions in emphasizing her virginity and in
    obscuring the fact that she was born of the adulterous union of Locrine and
    Estrildis.
828 Brute] great-grandson of Aeneas, legendary founder of Britain.
835 Nereus] father of the fifty nereids (sea-nymphs).
836 lank] drooping.
838 lavers] basins.
    asphodel] the immortal flower of the Elysian fields.
845 urchin blasts] infections breathed by mischievous fairies.
852 swain] Meliboeus.

SONG

Sabrina fair,
   Listen where thou art sitting   860
Under the glassy, cool, translucent wave,
   In twisted braids of lilies knitting
The loose train of thy amber-dropping hair;
    Listen for dear honour's sake,
    Goddess of the silver lake,   865
      Listen and save.

Listen, and appear to us,
In name of great Oceanus.
By the earth-shaking Neptune's mace,
And Tethys' grave majestic pace;   870
By hoary Nereus' wrinkled look,
And the Carpathian wizard's hook;
By scaly Triton's winding shell,
And old soothsaying Glaucus' spell;
By Leucothea's lovely hands,   875
And her son that rules the strands;
By Thetis' tinsel-slippered feet,
And the songs of Sirens sweet;
By dead Parthenope's dear tomb,
And fair Ligea's golden comb,   880
Wherewith she sits on diamond rocks
Sleeking her soft alluring locks;
By all the Nymphs that nightly dance
Upon thy streams with wily glance;

868 Oceanus] see l. 97n.
869 earth-shaking] the Homeric epithet for Poseidon (Neptune), who carries a
    trident ('mace').
870 Tethys] wife of Oceanus.
872 Carpathian wizard] Proteus, who according to one tradition lived in the sea
    near the island of Carpathos (between Rhodes and Crete), was a seer
    ('wizard'), and was the shepherd (hence 'hook') of Poseidon's seals.
873 Triton] son of Poseidon (Neptune) who blew on his conch-shell to calm the
    seas. Cf. *Lycidas* 89.
874 Glaucus] a Greek fisherman who ate a magic herb and was changed into a
    sea-god with prophetic powers.
875 Leucothea] a sea-goddess, whose name in Greek means 'white goddess'.
876 her son] Melicertes, god of harbours.
877 Thetis] One of the nereids (sea-nymphs); her Homeric epithet was 'silver
    footed'.
879 Parthenope] one of the Sirens; her tomb was near Naples, the ancient name
    of which was Parthenope.
880 Ligea] the other Homeric Siren (according to a late tradition).

Rise, rise, and heave thy rosy head   885
From thy coral-paven bed,
And bridle in thy headlong wave,
Till thou our summons answered have.
                    Listen and save.

SABRINA *rises, attended by water-nymphs, and sings.*

By the rushy-fringèd bank,   890
Where grows the willow and the osier dank,
    My sliding chariot stays,
Thick set with agate, and the azurn sheen
Of turkis blue, and emerald green,
    That in the channel strays;   895
Whilst from off the waters fleet
Thus I set my printless feet
O'er the cowslip's velvet head,
    That bends not as I tread.
Gentle swain, at thy request   900
    I am here.
    Spir.   Goddess dear,
We implore thy powerful hand
To undo the charmèd band
Of true virgin here distressed   905
Through the force and through the wile
Of unblessed enchanter vile.
    Sabr. Shepherd, 'tis my office best
To help ensnarèd chastity.
Brightest Lady, look on me.   910
Thus I sprinkle on thy breast
Drops that from my fountain pure
I have kept of precious cure;
Thrice upon thy finger's tip,
Thrice upon thy rubied lip: 915
Next this marble venomed seat,
Smeared with gums of glutinous heat,
I touch with chaste palms moist and cold.
Now the spell hath lost his hold;
And I must haste ere morning hour   920
To wait in Amphitrite's bower.

SABRINA *descends, and* THE LADY *rises out of her seat.*

    Spir. Virgin, daughter of Locrine,
Sprung of old Anchises' line,

921 Amphitrite] Neptune's wife.
923 Anchises] father of Aeneas. See 828n.

May thy brimmèd waves for this
Their full tribute never miss   925
From a thousand petty rills,
That tumble down the snowy hills;
Summer drought or singèd air
Never scorch thy tresses fair,
Nor wet October's torrent flood   930
Thy molten crystal fill with mud;
May thy billows roll ashore
The beryl and the golden ore;
May thy lofty head be crowned
With many a tower and terrace round,   935
And here and there thy banks upon
With groves of myrrh and cinnamon.
Come, Lady; while heaven lends us grace,
Let us fly this cursèd place,
Lest the sorcerer us entice   940
With some other new device.
Not a waste or needless sound
Till we come to holier ground.
I shall be your faithful guide
Through this gloomy covert wide;   945
And not many furlongs thence
Is your father's residence,
Where this night are met in state
Many a friend to gratulate
His wished presence, and beside   950
All the swains that there abide
With jigs and rural dance resort;
We shall catch them at their sport,
And our sudden coming there
Will double all their mirth and cheer.   955
Come, let us haste; the stars grow high,
But Night sits monarch yet in the mid sky.

*The Scene changes, presenting Ludlow Town, and the Presi-
dent's Castle: then come in country dancers; after them the*
ATTENDANT SPIRIT, *with the two* BROTHERS *and* THE LADY.

SONG

Spir. Back, shepherds, back! Enough your play
Till next sun-shine holiday.
Here be, without duck or nod,   960
Other trippings to be trod
Of lighter toes, and such court guise
As Mercury did first devise

With the mincing Dryades
On the lawns and on the leas.   965

This second Song presents them to their Father and Mother.

Noble Lord and Lady bright,
I have brought ye new delight.
Here behold so goodly grown
Three fair branches of your own;
Heaven hath timely tried their youth,   970
Their faith, their patience, and their truth,
And sent them here through hard assays
With a crown of deathless praise,
To triumph in victorious dance
O'er sensual folly and intemperance.   975

The dances ended, the SPIRIT *epiloguizes.*

Spir. To the ocean now I fly,
And those happy climes that lie
Where day never shuts his eye,
Up in the broad fields of the sky;
There I suck the liquid air,   980
All amidst the gardens fair
Of Hesperus, and his daughters three
That sing about the golden tree.
Along the crispèd shades and bowers
Revels the spruce and jocund Spring;   985
The Graces and the rosy-bosomed Hours
Thither all their bounties bring.
There eternal summer dwells,
And west winds with musky wing
About the cedarn alleys fling   990
Nard and cassia's balmy smells.

---

964 Dryades] woodland nymphs.
970 timely] early.
972 assays] tests and tribulations.
980 liquid] clear, bright.
981-3] see 393-5n.
984 crispèd] the precise meaning is not clear, but the word may mean 'curled' or 'ruffled'.
986 Graces] See *Allegro* 12-16n.
     Hours] Greek goddesses who presided over the changing seasons and protected the rural order.
989 west winds] the Zephyrs, harbingers of spring.
990 cedarn] composed of cedars.
991 Nard and cassia] aromatic plants.

Iris there with humid bow
Waters the odorous banks, that blow
Flowers of more mingled hue
Than her purfled scarf can show,   995
And drenches with Elysian dew
(List, mortals, if your ears be true)
Beds of hyacinth and roses,
Where young Adonis oft reposes,
Waxing well of his deep wound,   1000
In slumber soft, and on the ground
Sadly sits the Assyrian queen;
But far above, in spangled sheen,
Celestial Cupid, her famed son, advanced,
Holds his dear Psyche, sweet entranced   1005
After her wandering labours long,
Till free consent the gods among
Make her his eternal bride,
And from her fair unspotted side
Two blissful twins are to be born,   1010
Youth and Joy; so Jove hath sworn.
        But now my task is smoothly done;
I can fly, or I can run
Quickly to the green earth's end,
Where the bowed welkin slow doth bend,   1015
And from thence can soar as soon
To the corners of the moon.
Mortals, that would follow me,
Love Virtue; she alone is free;
She can teach ye how to climb   1020
Higher than the sphery chime;
Or, if Virtue feeble were,
Heaven itself would stoop to her.

992 Iris] goddess of the rainbow.
995 purfled] variegated.
996-1011] Milton intended his readers to recall Spenser's Garden of Adonis,
    Faerie Queene III. vi. 43-50.
999-1002] Adonis, a youthful hunter beloved of Venus (the 'Assyrian queen'),
    was slain by a boar.
1003-11] In the fable of Apuleius Cupid fell in love with Psyche (whose name
    means 'breath' or 'soul'), and visited her in darkness. When she discovered
    her lover's identity, he fled. She roamed the world in search of him
    ('wandering labours') and after they were reconciled bore him a son,
    Voluptas. In Spenser's version the child is called Pleasure. Milton gives
    them twins.
1004 advanced] elevated.
1015 bowed welkin] the curved vault of the sky.
1017 corners] may be a Latinism meaning 'horns' (from cornu).
1021 sphery chime] the music of the spheres.

SONNETS

I

O nightingale that on yon bloomy spray
  Warblest at eve, when all the woods are still,
  Thou with fresh hope the lover's heart dost fill,
  While the jolly hours lead on propitious May.
Thy liquid notes that close the eye of day,   5
  First heard before the shallow cuckoo's bill,
  Portend success in love. O, if Jove's will
  Have linked that amorous power to thy soft lay,
Now timely sing, ere the rude bird of hate
  Foretell my hopeless doom, in some grove nigh;   10
  As thou from year to year hast sung too late
For my relief, yet hadst no reason why.
  Whether the Muse or Love call thee his mate,
  Both them I serve, and of their train am I.

II

Donna leggiadra, il cui bel nome onora

Sonnet I. The date of composition is not known. It is a poem of spring, like 'May Morning', and may have been composed at the same time (between 1629 and 1631) as a Petrarchan variation on the theme.
4 hours] See *Comus* 986n.
9 bird of hate] the cuckoo.
The Italian Sonnets. Milton's six Italian sonnets are love poems written for a lady called Emilia, who may have been real or imaginary. They were written in 1629 or 1630, long before Milton went to Italy in 1638.
Sonnet II. Lovely lady, whose beautiful name honours[1] the grassy valley of Reno and the glorious ford,[2] truly is he destitute of all value who is not charmed by your gentle spirit, which sweetly shows itself, never sparing its gracious gestures, and by the gifts which are the bows and arrows of Love there[8] where your lofty virtue flowers.
  When you speak beautifully, or sing joyfully, which can move hard mountainous trees,[10] let whoever is unworthy of you[12] guard the entrance of his eyes and ears.[11] Only grace from above can help him, before amorous desire becomes inveterate in his heart.
1-2] The Reno is a river in the province of Emilia, and the glorious ford is the
    Rubicon, which is also in Emilia. Milton is explaining the name of the lady
    in a form that had precedent in Italian sonnets.

L'erbosa val di Reno e il nobil varco,
    Ben è colui d' ogni valore scarco
    Qual tuo spirto gentil non innamora,
Che dolcemente mostrasi di fuora,   5
    De' suoi atti soavi giammai parco,
    E i don', che son d' amor saette ed arco,
    Là onde l' alta tua virtù s' infiora.
Quando tu vaga parli, o lieta canti,
    Che mover possa duro alpestre legno,   10
    Guardi ciascun a gli occhi ed a gli orecchi
L'entrata chi di te si truova indegno;
    Grazia sola di sù gli vaglia, innanti
    Che 'l disio amoroso al cuor s' invecchi.

III

Qual in colle aspro, a l' imbrunir di sera,
    L' avvezza giovinetta pastorella
    Va bagnando l' erbetta strana e bella
    Che mal si spande a disusata spera
Fuor di sua natía alma primavera,   5
    Così Amor meco insù la lingua snella
    Desta il fior novo di strania favella,
    Mentre io di te, vezzosamente altera,
Canto, dal mio buon popol non inteso,
    E 'l bel Tamigi cangio col bel Arno.   10
    Amor lo volse, ed io a l' altrui peso
Seppi ch' Amor cosa mai volse indarno.
    Deh! foss' il mio cuor lento e 'l duro seno
    A chi pianta dal ciel si buon terreno.

8 Là] i.e. in her eyes.
10] a comparison to Orpheus.
10–12] a comparison of the Lady to Homer's Sirens, the sweetness of whose
    song Milton affirmed in *Comus* 878. Cf. *Sonnet IV* 14.
Sonnet III. As on a steep hill, at the twilight of evening, a youthful shepherdess,
at home there, waters a strange and beautiful plant which scarcely spreads its
leaves in the unfamiliar air, parted from its life-giving native springtime, so
Love in me upon my nimble tongue awakens the strange flower of a foreign
speech, as I sing to you, charmingly proud lady, not understood by my own
good countrymen, and I exchange the beautiful Thames for the beautiful
Arno.[10] Love willed it, and I have learned from the burden of others that Love
never willed anything in vain. Ah, would that my slow heart and hard breast
were as good a soil to Him who plants from heaven.
10] The Thames represents the English language, and the Arno, which flows
    through Tuscany, represents the Tuscan dialect of Italian, i.e. the classic
    literary form.

CANZONE

Ridonsi donne e giovani amorosi
M' accostandosi attorno, e 'Perché scrivi,
Perché tu scrivi in lingua ignota e strana
lingua ignota e strana
Verseggiando d' amor, e come t'osi?
Dinne, se la tua speme sia mai vana,   5
E de' pensieri lo miglior t' arrivi;'
Così mi van burlando: 'altri rivi,
Altri lidi t' aspettan, ed altre onde,
Nelle cui verdi sponde
Spuntati ad or ad or a la tua chioma   10
L'immortal guiderdon d' eterne frondi,
Perché alle spalle tue soverchia soma?'
   Canzon dirotti, e tu per me rispondi:
Dice mia Donna, e 'l suo dir è il mio cuore
'Questa è lingua di cui si vanta Amore.'   15

IV

Diodati, e te 'l dirò con maraviglia,
   Quel ritroso io, ch' amor spreggiar soléa

Canzone. A *canzone* is an Italian (or Provençal) lyric consisting of several long
stanzas with lines of irregular length and concluding with a short stanza called
the *commiato* (dismissal). Milton's *canzone* would more commonly be termed a
stanza di canzone, since it consists of only one stanza and an envoy.

Young men and women, of an age for love, laugh, and gathering about me, ask
'Why do you write, why do you write in a strange and unknown language,
versifying about love? How dare you? Tell us, so that your hope may never be
vain, and your best wishes may be fulfilled.' Thus they make fun of me: 'Other
streams, others shores await you, and other waters on whose green banks are
now sprouting the immortal guerdon of undying fronds for your hair: why add
an excessive burden to your shoulders?'
   Canzone. I shall tell you, and you will answer for me: my lady says, and her
word is my heart, 'This is the language in which Love prides himself.'
Sonnet IV. Diodati,[1] I shall say it to you with astonishment, I, that reluctant
one who used to despise Love, and frequently laughed at his snares, have now
fallen where a good man sometimes entangles himself. Neither tresses of gold
nor rosy cheeks have dazzled me so, but a foreign beauty modelled on a rare idea
delights my heart, a bearing proud and modest, a clear blaze of lovely darkness
in her eyes, speech adorned by more than one language, and singing which
might well lead the labouring moon[12] astray in the middle of the sky. And from
her eyes there shoots such fierce flame that to stop my ears with wax would be of
little use.[14]

1 *Diodati*] Charles Diodati was the most intimate friend of Milton's early life.
   His family home was near Milton's, and he was a fellow pupil with Milton at
   St Paul's School before going up to Oxford.

E de' suoi lacci spesso mi ridéa,
  Gia caddi, ov' uom dabben talor s' impiglia.
Nè treccie d' oro, nè guancia vermiglia   5
  M' abbaglian sì, ma sotto nova idea
  Pellegrina bellezza che 'l cuor bea,
  Portamenti alti onesti, e nelle ciglia
Quel sereno fulgor d'amabil nero,
  Parole adorne di lingua piu d'una,   10
  E 'l cantar che di mezzo l'emisfero
Traviar ben può la faticosa Luna;
  E degli occhi suoi avventa sì gran fuoco
  Che l' incerar gli orecchi mi fia poco.

V

Per certo i bei vostr' occhi, Donna mia,
  Esser non può che non sian lo mio sole;
  Sì mi percuoton forte, come ei suole
  Per l' arene di Libia chi s' invia,
Mentre un caldo vapor (nè sentì pria)   5
  Da quel lato si spinge ove mi duole,
  Che forse amanti nelle lor parole
  Chiaman sospir; io non so che si sia.
Parte rinchiusa e turbida si cela
  Scosso mi il petto, e poi n' uscendo poco   10
  Quivi d' attorno o s' agghiaccia o s' ingela;
Ma quanto a gli occhi giunge a trovar loco
  Tutte le notti a me suol far piovose,
  Finchè mia Alba rivien colma di rose.

---

12 *faticosa Luna*] Cf. *PL* II 665.
14] Odysseus put wax in the ears of his crew so that they would not be able to hear the song of the Sirens. Cf. *Sonnet* II 11-12.
Sonnet V. In truth, my lady, your beautiful eyes can be for me nothing other than the sun. They strike me as powerfully as does the sun on one who makes his way across the sands of Libya; meanwhile a hot vapour (which I have not felt before) presses up from the side where I am aching. Perhaps lovers in their language call it a sigh; I do not know what it may be. Part of it, confined and agitated, hides itself, and having shaken my breast, a little escapes, and all around here it is either chilled or frozen. But that part of it which finds a place in my eyes makes every night a rainy one for me, until my Dawn returns, brimming with roses.

VI

Giovane piano, e semplicetto amante,
　　Poichè fuggir me stesso in dubbio sono,
　　Madonna, a voi del mio cuor l' umil dono
　　Farò divoto; io certo a prove tante
L' ebbi fedele, intrepido, costante,　　　　　　　　　5
　　Di pensieri leggiadro, accorto, e buono.
　　Quando rugge il gran mondo, e scocca il tuono,
　　S' arma di se, e d' intero diamante,
Tanto del forse e d'invidia sicuro,
　　Di timori, e speranze al popol use,　　　　　　　10
　　Quanto d' ingegno e d' alto valor vago,
E di cetra sonora, e delle Muse.
　　Sol troverete in tal parte men duro
　　Ove Amor mise l' insanabil ago.

VII

How soon hath Time, the subtle thief of youth,
　　Stolen on his wing my three-and-twentieth year!
　　My hasting days fly on with full career,
　　But my late spring no bud or blossom sheweth.
Perhaps my semblance might deceive the truth,　　5
　　That I to manhood am arrived so near;
　　And inward ripeness doth much less appear,
　　That some more timely-happy spirits endueth.
Yet, be it less or more, or soon or slow,
　　It shall be still in strictest measure even　　　10
　　To that same lot, however mean or high,

Sonnet VI. Youthful, gentle, and artless lover that I am, since I am in doubt about how to escape from myself, I shall devoutly make a humble gift of my heart to you, my lady. I have tested it many times, and found it loyal, fearless, constant, and in its thoughts gracious, gentle, and kind. When the great world roars and the thunder claps, my heart arms itself with itself and with complete adamant, as safe from chance and envy, from the fears and hopes of common people, as it is eager for distinction of mind and high worth, for the resounding lyre and the Muses. You will find it less hard only in the place where Love has put his incurable sting.

Sonnet VII. Line 2 suggests a date of composition on or near 9 December 1631, Milton's twenty-third birthday.

5 semblance] appearance.

8 timely] 'seasonable', with a secondary sense of 'early'.
　　endueth] is inherent in.

10 still] forever.

10–11 even/To] appropriate to, equal to.

Toward which Time leads me, and the will of heaven,
  All is, if I have grace to use it so,
  As ever in my great task-master's eye.

VIII

WHEN THE ASSAULT WAS INTENDED TO THE CITY

Captain or colonel, or knight in arms,
  Whose chance on these defenceless doors may seize,
  If deed of honour did thee ever please,
  Guard them, and him within protect from harms.
He can requite thee; for he knows the charms   5
  That call fame on such gentle acts as these,
  And he can spread thy name o'er lands and seas,
  Whatever clime the sun's bright circle warms.
Lift not thy spear against the Muses' bower:
  The great Emathian conqueror bid spare   10
  The house of Pindarus, when temple and tower
Went to the ground; and the repeated air
  Of sad Electra's poet had the power
  To save the Athenian walls from ruin bare.

IX

Lady, that in the prime of earliest youth
  Wisely hast shunned the broad way and the green,
  And with those few art eminently seen
  That labour up the hill of heavenly truth,

Sonnet VIII. The poem is dated 1642 in the Trinity MS. After the Battle of
Edgehill on 23 October 1642 the Parliamentary army retreated to Warwick,
thus leaving the road to London open to the army of Charles, who advanced as
far as Turnham Green, which was only a few miles from Milton's house on
Aldersgate Street. The prospect of the fall of London may have occasioned the
poem.

10–12] When the army of Alexander (who is here called 'Emathian', Emathia
    being a district of Macedon) was destroying Thebes, Alexander spared the
    house in which Pindar had lived, and also spared the descendants of the
    poet.

12–14] The Spartans defeated Athens in 404 BC, and were allegedly restrained
    from destroying the city by a Phocian who sang the first chorus of
    Euripides' *Electra*, and thus persuaded the conquerors to spare the city
    that had produced such a great poet.

Sonnet IX. As the identity of the lady is not known, the date of composition is
uncertain. In the Trinity MS it follows *Sonnet VIII*, which suggests that it was
written after 1642.

2 broad way] Matt. vii. 13–14.

The better part with Mary and with Ruth,   5
    Chosen thou hast; and they that overween,
    And at thy growing virtues fret their spleen,
    No anger find in thee, but pity and ruth.
Thy care is fixed, and zealously attends
    To fill thy odorous lamp with deeds of light,   10
    And hope that reaps not shame. Therefore be sure
Thou, when the bridegroom with his feastful friends
    Passes to bliss at the mid-hour of night,
    Hast gained thy entrance, virgin wise and pure.

X

TO THE LADY MARGARET LEY

Daughter to that good Earl, once President
    Of England's Council and her Treasury,
    Who lived in both unstained with gold or fee,
    And left them both, more in himself content,
Till the sad breaking of that Parliament   5
    Broke him, as that dishonest victory

5 Mary] Mary, the sister of Martha and Lazarus, chose to sit at the feet of Jesus
    while Martha served; Jesus said that Mary had 'chosen the good part'.
    Ruth] Ruth chose to stay with her mother-in-law Naomi rather than return
    with Orpah to Moab to find a new husband.
9-14] based on the parable of the virgins, Matt. xxv. 1-13.
11 hope ... shame] cf. Rom. v. 5.
Sonnet X. The daughter is identified by the title of the poem in the Trinity MS as
Lady Margaret Ley, who, according to Edward Phillips, Milton's nephew, 'took
much delight in [Milton's] company, as likewise her husband Captain Hobson'.
Captain Hobson (who fought on the side of Parliament) and his wife lived in
Aldersgate Street, and were therefore Milton's neighbours. The poem cannot be
dated exactly, but was probably written between 1642 and 1645.
1-2] The 'good Earl' was James Ley, who in 1624 became Lord High Treasurer,
    in 1628 was created Earl of Marlborough, and in 1628 became for a short
    time Lord President of the Council.
4] Ley retired as Lord President of the Council on 14 December 1628.
    According to Clarendon he 'was removed under pretence of his age and
    disability for the work'.
5] On 2 March 1629 Charles ordered the dissolution of Parliament. The
    Parliamentarians rebelled, and forcibly held the Speaker in his chair while
    passing Sir John Eliot's three resolutions condemning the King's administra-
    tration. Parliament was finally dissolved on 10 March 1629.
6 broke him] Ley died on 14 March 1629.

At Chaeronea, fatal to liberty,
   Killed with report that old man eloquent,
Though later born than to have known the days
   Wherein your father flourished, yet by you,   10
   Madam, methinks I see him living yet;
So well your words his noble virtues praise
   That all both judge you to relate them true
   And to possess them, honoured Margaret.

XI

THE DETRACTION WHICH FOLLOWED UPON MY
WRITING CERTAIN TREATISES

A book was writ of late called *Tetrachordon*,
   And woven close, both matter, form, and style;
   The subject new: it walked the town a while,
   Numbering good intellects; now seldom pored on.
Cries the stall-reader, 'Bless us! what a word on   5
   A title-page is this!'; and some in file
   Stand spelling false, while one might walk to Mile-
   End Green. Why, is it harder, sirs, than Gordon,
Colkitto, or Macdonnel, or Galasp?
   Those rugged names to our like mouths grow sleek,   10
   That would have made Quintilian stare and gasp.
Thy age, like ours, O soul of Sir John Cheke,

6–8] The 'old man' is the Athenian orator Isocrates, who was so distressed by
   Philip of Macedon's victory over the Athenian and Theban forces at
   Chaeronea in 338 BC that he starved himself to death. 'Dishonest' means
   'shameful'.
Sonnet XI. The 'certain treatises' of the MS title are Milton's four divorce tracts:
Doctrine and Discipline of Divorce, The Judgement of Martin Bucer, Tetrachordon,
and *Colasterion*. Milton's *Tetrachordon* was published on 4 March 1645. The
phrases 'it walked the town a while' (line 3) and 'now seldom pored on' (line 4)
suggest that the sonnet was written after an interval of several months.
1 *Tetrachordon*] The Greek word *tetrachordon* means 'four-stringed', and refers
   to a scale of four notes. Milton applied the word to the four texts of
   Scripture which he wished to compare and explain.
6–7 Mile-/End Green] a common at the eastern limit of London.
7–8] The Scottish names were doubtless chosen for their harsh sounds, but they
   may refer to individuals, presumably followers of Montrose.
11 Quintilian] In his *Institutes* Quintilian, the Roman rhetorician, censures
   foreign words as a threat to the purity of Latin.
12–14] Sir John Cheke (1514–57), tutor to Edward VI, was Professor of Greek
   at Cambridge.

Hated not learning worse than toad or asp,
When thou taught'st Cambridge and King Edward
   Greek.

XII

ON THE SAME

I did but prompt the age to quit their clogs
   By the known rules of ancient liberty,
   When straight a barbarous noise environs me
   Of owls and cuckoos, asses, apes, and dogs;
As when those hinds that were transformed to frogs   5
   Railed at Latona's twin-born progeny,
   Which after held the sun and moon in fee.
   But this is got by casting pearl to hogs,
That bawl for freedom in their senseless mood,
   And still revolt when truth would set them free.   10
   Licence they mean when they cry liberty;
For who loves that must first be wise and good;
   But from that mark how far they rove we see,
   For all this waste of wealth and loss of blood.

XIII

TO MR H. LAWES, ON HIS AIRS

Harry, whose tuneful and well-measured song
   First taught our English music how to span
   Words with just note and accent, not to scan

Sonnet XII. The title 'On the Same' refers to Milton's four divorce tracts rather
than to *Tetrachordon* in particular. The poem was probably written in the second
half of 1645.

1 quit their clogs] throw off their shackles.

5–7] Latona was the mother of Apollo and Diana, who were later to possess
   (hold 'in fee') the sun and moon. Latona stopped at a pool to drink, and
   when prevented from doing so by some peasants ('hinds') who stirred up
   the water to make it muddy, turned them into frogs (*Metamorphoses* vi
   317–81; cf. *Arcades* 20).

8] Matt. vii. 6.

10] John viii. 32.

13] a metaphor from archery: they shoot ('rove') away from the target ('mark').
Sonnet XIII. To Mr H. Lawes, on his Airs. The sonnet is dated in MS 9 February
1645 (i.e. 1646), and was first published by Henry Lawes (the court musician
with whom Milton had collaborated in *Comus*) in *Choice Psalmes* (1648), which
was dedicated to Charles I, who was then a prisoner.

With Midas' ears, committing short and long,
Thy worth and skill exempts thee from the throng,   5
    With praise enough for envy to look wan;
    To after age thou shalt be writ the man
    That with smooth air couldst humour best our tongue.
Thou honour'st verse, and verse must lend her wing
    To honour thee, the priest of Phoebus' choir,   10
    That tunest their happiest lines in hymn or story.
Dante shall give fame leave to set thee higher
    Than his Casella, whom he wooed to sing,
    Met in the milder shades of Purgatory.

XIV

ON THE RELIGIOUS MEMORY OF MRS CATHERINE
THOMASON, MY CHRISTIAN FRIEND,
DECEASED DECEMBER 1646

When Faith and Love, which parted from thee never,
    Had ripened thy just soul to dwell with God,
    Meekly thou didst resign this earthly load
    Of death, called life, which us from life doth sever.
Thy works, and alms, and all thy good endeavour,   5
    Stayed not behind, nor in the grave were trod;
    But, as Faith pointed with her golden rod,
    Followed thee up to joy and bliss for ever.
Love led them on; and Faith, who knew them best
    Thy handmaids, clad them o'er with purple beams   10
    And azure wings, that up they flew so dressed,
And spake the truth of thee on glorious themes
    Before the judge; who thenceforth bid thee rest,
    And drink thy fill of pure immortal streams.

4 Midas] King of Phrygia who preferred the music of Pan to that of Apollo,
    whereupon Apollo changed his ears to those of an ass.
10 Phoebus] see *Passion* 23n.
12–14] In *Purgatorio* ii Dante meets his friend Casella the musician, and asks
    him to sing. Casella sings Dante's own *canzone* 'Amor che ne la mente mi
    ragiona'.
Sonnet XIV. The MS title indicates that the sonnet was written in memory of
Mrs Catharine Thomason, who died in December 1646. Mrs Thomason was the
wife of Milton's friend, George Thomason, the bookseller and collector of civil
war pamphlets.

XV

ON THE LORD GENERAL FAIRFAX AT THE SIEGE
OF COLCHESTER

Fairfax, whose name in arms through Europe rings,
    Filling each mouth with envy or with praise,
    And all her jealous monarchs with amaze,
    And rumours loud that daunt remotest kings,
Thy firm unshaken virtue ever brings   5
    Victory home, though new rebellions raise
    Their hydra heads, and the false North displays
    Her broken league to imp their serpent wings.
O yet a nobler task awaits thy hand
    For what can war but endless war still breed   10
    Till truth and right from violence be freed,
And public faith cleared from the shameful brand
    Of public fraud. In vain doth Valour bleed,
    While Avarice and Rapine share the land.

Sonnet XV. On the Lord General Fairfax at the Siege of Colchester. Sir Thomas Fairfax was commander-in-chief of the New Model Army. He was a military genius of immense personal courage, and led the Parliamentary army to a series of victories. He besieged Colchester on 13 June 1647, and the city fell on 27 August. Milton's hopes for Fairfax, as expressed in the sestet, never came to fruition, for Fairfax withdrew from public life after the execution of Charles, to which he objected.

5 virtue] means both 'valour' and 'moral worth'.

6 new rebellions] the Royalist rebellions of 1648, i.e. the Second Civil War.

7 hydra] mythical water serpent with seven or more heads, killed by Hercules.

7-8 false ... league] The 'false North' is Scotland, and the 'broken league' is the Solemn League and Covenant (on which see *Sonnet* XVI 4n), which the Scots violated by invading England on 8 July 1648.

8 imp ... wings] to strengthen or improve the flight of a bird by engrafting new feathers in the wing.

12-14] Milton often denounced the well-attested corruption of the Long Parliament.

XVI

TO THE LORD GENERAL CROMWELL, MAY 1652, ON THE
PROPOSALS OF CERTAIN MINISTERS AT THE COMMITTEE
FOR PROPAGATION OF THE GOSPEL

Cromwell, our chief of men, who through a cloud
   Not of war only, but detractions rude,
   Guided by faith and matchless fortitude,
   To peace and truth thy glorious way hast ploughed,
And on the neck of crownèd Fortune proud   5
   Hast reared God's trophies, and his work pursued,
   While Darwen stream, with blood of Scots imbrued,
   And Dunbar field resounds thy praises loud,
And Worcester's laureate wreath; yet much remains
   To conquer still; Peace hath her victories   10
   No less renowned than War: new foes arise,
Threatening to bind our souls with secular chains:
   Help us to save free conscience from the paw
   Of hireling wolves, whose gospel is their maw.

Sonnet XVI. To the Lord General Cromwell, 1 May 1652. In February 1652
Parliament appointed a Committee for the Propagation of the Gospel to
consider the proposals of fifteen ministers, whose number included John Owen,
formerly Cromwell's chaplain, and Philip Nye, one of the original Dissenting
Brethren. The ministers proposed, *inter alia*, limited toleration and a stipendi-
ary clergy. In this sonnet Milton addresses Cromwell as a member of the
committee.

4 peace and truth] a popular catch-phrase, Biblical in origin (Isa. xxxxix. 8),
    here quite possibly used as an allusion to the Solemn League and Covenant
    (the league between England and Scotland on the basis of the establish-
    ment of Presbyterianism in both countries, signed in 1643), of which these
    were the closing words.
5 crownèd Fortune] Fortuna, the pagan goddess, here represents Charles I, who
    had been executed on 30 January 1649. See l. 9n.
7 Darwen stream] refers to the Battle of Preston, which was fought near the
    river Darwen in Lancashire from 17–19 August 1648, and at which
    Cromwell defeated the Covenanters under the Duke of Hamilton, half of
    whose army was destroyed in the engagement.
8 Dunbar field] refers to the Battle of Dunbar on 3 September 1650 at which
    Cromwell defeated the Covenanters under Leslie and went on to occupy
    Scotland.
9 Worcester's laureate wreath] On 3 September 1651, the anniversary of
    Dunbar, Cromwell crushed the Covenanters under Charles II (who had
    been crowned king in Scotland on 1 January 1651, and may therefore be
    included in the phrase 'crownèd Fortune' in l. 5).
12 secular chains] alludes to the proposal that the state should enforce the
    limits of toleration.
14 hireling wolves] stipendiary clergy.

XVII

TO SIR HENRY VANE THE YOUNGER

Vane, young in years, but in sage counsel old,
    Than whom a better senator ne'er held
    The helm of Rome, when gowns, not arms, repelled
    The fierce Epirot, and the African bold;
Whether to settle peace, or to unfold   5
    The drift of hollow states hard to be spelled;
    Then to advise how war may best, upheld,
    Move by her two main nerves, iron and gold,
In all her equipage; besides, to know
    Both spiritual power and civil, what each means,   10
    What severs each, thou hast learned, which few have
        done.
The bounds of either sword to thee we owe;
    Therefore on thy firm hand Religion leans
    In peace, and reckons thee her eldest son.

Sonnet XVII. To Sir Henry Vane the Younger. Sir Henry Vane the Younger (so called to distinguish him from his eminent father), 1613–62, was an important figure in the Puritan cause. Unlike Milton, he advocated toleration for all religious opinions. Though not a regicide, he was executed after the Restoration. Milton sent the sonnet to Vane on 3 July 1652.

3 gowns] civil power. The phrase 'gowns, not arms' alludes to the ancient dictum *Cedant arma togae* (let arms yield to the gown).

3–4] alludes to accounts of the firmness of the Roman senate in the face of invasions by Pyrrhus, king of Epirus, and the African Hannibal.

6 hollow states] 'hollow' puns on Holland, and retains the secondary meanings of 'insincere' and 'low-lying', while 'states' puns on States-General, the Dutch legislative assembly. Vane had attempted to negotiate a union between the Commonwealth and the Dutch Republic. The attempt failed, and shortly before Milton wrote his sonnet the First Anglo-Dutch War began.

spelled] comprehended.

12 either sword] the spiritual sword and the civil sword. See *On the New Forcers*, 5.

XVIII

ON THE LATE MASSACRE IN PIEDMONT

Avenge, O Lord, thy slaughtered saints, whose bones
  Lie scattered on the Alpine mountains cold;
  Even them who kept thy truth so pure of old,
When all our fathers worshipped stocks and stones,
Forget not: in thy book record their groans   5
  Who were thy sheep, and in their ancient fold
  Slain by the bloody Piedmontese, that rolled
Mother with infant down the rocks. Their moans
The vales redoubled to the hills, and they
  To heaven. Their martyred blood and ashes sow   10
  O'er all the Italian fields, where still doth sway
The triple Tyrant; that from these may grow
  A hundredfold, who, having learnt thy way,
  Early may fly the Babylonian woe.

Sonnet XVIII. On the Late Massacre in Piedmont. The sect known as the
Vaudois or Waldenses were believed by seventeenth-century Protestants to
represent the continuity of Protestantism from earliest times to the Reforma-
tion. The Vaudois sect had been persecuted since its foundation in the twelfth
century, and the frequency and intensity of the persecution increased as the sect
became absorbed into the Protestant movement. The massacre to which
Milton's sonnet seems to be an immediate response was perpetrated by French
and Irish troops sent to the Vaudois valleys by the Duke of Savoy. On 24 April
1655 this army began the mutilation, torture and slaughter of the members of
the sect, and a few days later over 1700 Vaudois were dead. Protestant Europe
was outraged and Cromwell protested to the Duke of Savoy with a letter written
by Milton.

1] See Luke xviii. 7, Rev. vi. 9–10.
2] See Psalm cxli. 7.
4 stocks and stones] see Jer. ii. 27.
5 book] Rev. xx. 12.
10 martyred ... sow] Alludes to Tertullian's famous maxim 'The blood of the
    martyrs is the seed of the church' (*Plures efficimur, quoties metimur a vobis:*
    semen est sanguis Christianorum). The phrase also introduces an extended
    allusion to the parable of the sower (Matt. xiii. 3–9).
12 triple Tyrant] the pope, whose crown has three tiers.
14 Babylonian] The Protestants commonly identified the Babylon of Revela-
    tion with papal Rome.

XIX

When I consider how my light is spent
  Ere half my days in this dark world and wide,
  And that one talent which is death to hide
  Lodged with me useless, though my soul more bent
To serve therewith my maker, and present   5
  My true account, lest he returning chide,
  'Doth God exact day-labour, light denied?'
  I fondly ask. But Patience, to prevent
That murmur, soon replies, 'God doth not need
  Either man's work or his own gifts; who best   10
  Bear his mild yoke, they serve him best: his state
Is kingly. Thousands at his bidding speed,
  And post o'er land and ocean without rest;
  They also serve who only stand and wait.'

XX

Lawrence, of virtuous father virtuous son,
  Now that the fields are dank, and ways are mire,
  Where shall we sometimes meet, and by the fire
  Help waste a sullen day, what may be won
From the hard season gaining? Time will run   5
  On smoother, till Favonius reinspire
  The frozen earth, and clothe in fresh attire
  The lily and rose, that neither sowed nor spun.
What neat repast shall feast us, light and choice,

Sonnet XIX. The date of composition is not known, but it may have been written shortly after Milton went blind early in 1652. The fact that the poem follows the Piedmont massacre in Milton's 1673 *Poems* may, on the other hand, indicate a date of 1655.

3-6] The lines are based on the parable of the talents, Matt. xxv. 14-30.
11 mild yoke] Matt. xi. 29-30.

Sonnet XX. According to Edward Phillips, Milton's nephew, Milton was often visited by 'young Laurence (the Son of him that was President of Oliver's Council)'. 'Young Laurence' is probably Edward Lawrence (1633-57), who may have been a pupil of Milton. Lawrence became an MP in 1656 and died, aged 24, in the second half of 1657.

The poem could have been written at any time from the winter of 1651-2, when Milton moved to Westminster and began to be visited by Lawrence, to the winter of 1656-7.

1 father] Edward Lawrence was the eldest son of Henry Lawrence, a prominent figure in Cromwell's Council of State and the author of several theological treatises.

6 Favonius] Roman personification of the west wind, and the messenger of spring.

8] Matt. vi. 28.

Of Attic taste, with wine, whence we may rise, 10
To hear the lute well touched, or artful voice
Warble immortal notes and Tuscan air?
He who of those delights can judge, and spare
To interpose them oft, is not unwise.

XXI

Cyriack, whose grandsire on the Royal Bench
Of British Themis, with no mean applause,
Pronounced, and in his volumes taught, our laws,
Which others at their bar so often wrench,
To-day deep thoughts resolve with me to drench 5
In mirth that after no repenting draws;
Let Euclid rest, and Archimedes pause,
And what the Swede intend, and what the French.
To measure life learn thou betimes, and know
Towards solid good what leads the nearest way; 10
For other things mild heaven a time ordains,
And disapproves that care, though wise in show,
That with superfluous burden loads the day,
And, when God sends a cheerful hour, refrains.

10 Attic taste] taste characterized by the simple and refined elegance of Athens.
13–14 spare/To interpose] The phrase is ambiguous, and may mean 'refrain
    from interposing', or may signify the opposite, 'spare time for interposing'.
Sonnet XXI. Cyriack Skinner (1627–1700) was a pupil of Milton in the 1640s,
and a regular visitor at his house in the 1650s. The sonnet was probably written
in 1655.
1 grandsire] Skinner's maternal grandfather was Sir Edward Coke, the most
    distinguished lawyer of his generation, famed as the defender of law and
    Parliament against archbishops and kings.
    Royal Bench] Coke became Chief Justice of the King's Bench in 1613.
2 Themis] Greek goddess of law, called Justitia by the Romans.
3 volumes] Coke was the author of *Reports, Booke of Entries,* and *Institutes of the
    Laws of England.*
7] Euclid and Archimedes represent Skinner's interest in mathematics and
    physics.
8] 'The Swede' is probably Charles X, who in 1655 was commanding his army
    in Poland. 'The French' alludes to the war between France and Spain, and
    to Cardinal Mazarin (the chief minister of France) in particular. Together
    the allusions constitute a reference to Skinner's interest in politics.

XXII

Cyriack, this three years' day these eyes, though clear,
    To outward view, of blemish or of spot,
    Bereft of light, their seeing have forgot;
    Nor to their idle orbs doth sight appear
Of sun, or moon, or star, throughout the year,   5
    Or man, or woman. Yet I argue not
    Against heaven's hand or will, nor bate a jot
    Of heart or hope, but still bear up and steer
Right onward. What supports me, dost thou ask?
    The conscience, friend, to have lost them overplied   10
    In liberty's defence, my noble task,
Of which all Europe talks from side to side.
    This thought might lead me through the world's vain
        mask
    Content, though blind, had I no better guide.

XXIII

Methought I saw my late espousèd saint
    Brought to me like Alcestis from the grave,
    Whom Jove's great son to her glad husband gave,
    Rescued from Death by force, though pale and faint.
Mine, as whom washed from spot of child-bed taint   5
    Purification in the old Law did save,
    And such as yet once more I trust to have
    Full sight of her in heaven without restraint,
Came vested all in white, pure as her mind.

Sonnet XXII. To Mr Cyriack Skinner upon his Blindness. On Skinner see
headnote to previous poem. The phrase 'three years' day' suggests a date of
composition in 1655.
10 conscience] inward knowledge.
Sonnet XXIII. The date of composition is not known, as it is not clear whether
the subject of the poem is Milton's first wife, Mary Powell, who died in May
1652, three days after the birth of their daughter Deborah, or his second wife,
Katherine Woodcock, who died in February 1658 after giving birth in October
1657 to their daughter Katherine, who died six weeks after her mother.
2-3] In Euripides' *Alcestis* Hercules ('Jove's great son') rescues Alcestis from
    Death and returns her, veiled, to Admetus, her husband. In antiquity
    Alcestis represented conjugal fidelity and devotion.
6 old Law] a woman was deemed to be unclean for 80 days after the birth of a
    daughter (Lev. xii. 4-8).
9 vested all in white] See Rev. vii. 13-14.

Her face was veiled; yet to my fancied sight   10
  Love, sweetness, goodness, in her person shined
So clear as in no face with more delight.
  But O as to embrace me she inclined,
  I waked, she fled, and day brought back my night.

ON THE NEW FORCERS OF CONSCIENCE UNDER THE
LONG PARLIAMENT

Because you have thrown off your prelate lord,
  And with stiff vows renounced his liturgy,
  To seize the widowed whore Plurality
From them whose sin ye envied, not abhorred,
Dare ye for this adjure the civil sword   5
  To force our consciences that Christ set free,
  And ride us with a classic hierarchy,

On the New Forcers of Conscience under the Long Parliament. The latest event to which Milton alludes in the poem is the decree of 28 August 1646, when Parliament established the ordination of ministers by 'the Classical Presbyteries'. The phrase 'just fears' in line 18 may mean that the poem was written in horrified anticipation of this decree shortly before it was passed.

The sonnet is unique among Milton's poems in that it is a *sonetto caudato*, a sonnet with a *coda* (tail). Milton's sonnet has two *code*, each consisting of a half-line and a couplet.

title] The new forcers of conscience are the Presbyterians, who had led the Puritan attack on Laudian episcopacy and since 1643 had gradually established a Presbyterian system. The phrase 'under the Long Parliament' does not appear in the Trinity MS, but was added in 1673, by which time the phrase 'Long Parliament' was understood to refer to the Parliament which extended (with interruptions) from 1640 to 1660.

1] Although the Act abolishing archbishops and bishops was not passed until 9 October 1646, episcopacy had been effectively abolished since January 1643.

2] refers to the abolition of the *Book of Common Prayer* and the adoption of the *Directory for Public Worship* on 4 January 1645.

3 widowed whore Plurality] Milton's personification of the practice of securing the income from more than one benefice at a time. She is 'widowed' because the Anglican clergymen who had indulged in the practice had been replaced by Presbyterians.

4 abhorred] plays on 'whore' (line 3).

5 civil sword] the authority of the state. See *Sonnet XVII* 12n.

7 classic] refers to the *classis*, or presbytery, a body of elders acting as an ecclesiastical court.

hierarchy] refers to the hierarchy of four courts under the Presbytery system: consistory, *classis*, synod, and national assembly. Milton intended the word to recall the Anglican hierarchy.

Taught ye by mere A. S. and Rutherford?
Men whose life, learning, faith, and pure intent,
   Would have been held in high esteem with Paul   10
   Must now be named and printed heretics
By shallow Edwards and Scotch what-d'ye-call!
   But we do hope to find out all your tricks,
   Your plots and packing, worse than those of Trent,
      That so the Parliament   15
May with their wholesome and preventive shears
Clip your phylacteries, though baulk your ears,
      And succour our just fears,
When they shall read this clearly in your charge:
New *Presbyter* is but old *Priest* writ large.   20

8 A. S.] Adam Stewart, a Scottish Presbyterian living in London in the 1640s. Pamphlets, including Stewart's anti-Independent pamphlets, were often signed by initials rather than names, and Milton's use of initials alludes to Stewart's pamphleteering activities.
Rutherford] Samuel Rutherford, one of the four Commissioners sent by the Church of Scotland to the Westminster Assembly.
12 Edwards] Thomas Edwards, English Presbyterian apologist, and the author of *Gangrena* (1646), which included an attack on Milton's divorce tracts. Scotch what-d'ye-call] Usually identified (without proof) as Robert Baillie, one of the Scottish Commissioners, and the author of *Dissuasive from the Errors of the Time* (1645), which included an attack on Milton's divorce tracts.
14] A comparison of the Westminster Assembly to the Council of Trent (1545–63), at which the Protestant delegates were a minority in a council 'packed' in the Catholic interest.
17 phylacteries] here used metaphorically to mean an ostentatious display of piety. See Matt. xxiii. 5.
baulk your ears] 'baulk' means 'ignore'. The phrase glances at the fate of William Prynne, whose ears had been clipped in 1634 as a punishment for alleged defamation of the King and Queen in his *Histriomastix*; in 1637 his ears were removed completely for another offence. The MS version of the line makes the allusion clearer: 'Cropp yee as close as marginall P-s eares'.
20] Etymologically 'priest' is an abbreviated form of 'presbyter'.

TRANSLATIONS

THE FIFTH ODE OF HORACE,
LIB. I

Quis multâ gracilis te puer in rosâ.

Rendered almost word for word, without rhyme, according to the
Latin measure, as near as the language will permit.

What slender youth, bedewed with liquid odours,
Courts thee on roses in some pleasant cave,
  Pyrrha? For whom bind'st thou
  In wreaths thy golden hair,
Plain in thy neatness? O how oft shall he   5
On faith and changèd gods complain, and seas
  Rough with black winds and storms
  Unwonted shall admire,
Who now enjoys thee credulous, all gold;
Who always vacant, always amiable,   10
  Hopes thee, of flattering gales
  Unmindful. Hapless they
To whom thou untried seem'st fair. Me, in my vowed
Picture, the sacred wall declares to have hung
  My dank and dropping weeds   15
  To the stern god of sea.

AD PYRRHAM. ODE V.

*Horatius ex Phyrrhoe illecebris tanquam e naufragio
enataverat cujus amore irretitos affirmat esse miseros.*

Quis multâ gracilis te puer in rosâ
Perfusus liquidis urget odoribus
  Grato, Pyrrha, sub antro?
   Cui flavam religas comam

The Fifth Ode of Horace
The date of the translation is unknown, but its absence from the Trinity MS
may suggest a date before 1632. The text of 'Ad Pyrrham' which Milton used is
printed below his translation.

Simplex munditie? Heu, quoties fidem   5
Mutatosque deos flebit, et aspera
    Nigris aequora ventis
        Emirabitur insolens,
Qui nunc te fruitur credulus aureâ;
Qui semper vacuam, semper amabilem,   10
    Sperat, nescius aurae
        Fallacis. Miseri quibus
Intentata nites. Me tabulâ sacer
Votivâ paries indicat uvida
    Suspendisse potenti   15
        Vestimenta maris deo.

PSALMS

A PARAPHRASE ON PSALM CXIV

*This and the following Psalm were done by the Author at
fifteen years old*

When the blessed seed of Terah's faithful son
After long toil their liberty had won,
And passed from Pharian fields to Canaan land,
Led by the strength of the Almighty's hand,
Jehovah's wonders were in Israel shown,   5
His praise and glory was in Israel known.
That saw the troubled sea, and shivering fled,
And sought to hide his froth-becurlèd head
Low in the earth; Jordan's clear streams recoil,
As a faint host that hath received the foil.   10
The high huge-bellied mountains skip like rams
Amongst their ewes, the little hills like lambs.
Why fled the ocean? And why skipped the mountains?
Why turnèd Jordan toward his crystal fountains?
Shake, earth, and at the presence be aghast   15
Of him that ever was and aye shall last,
That glassy floods from rugged rocks can crush,
And make soft rills from fiery flint-stones gush.

PSALM CXXXVI

Let us with a gladsome mind
Praise the Lord, for he is kind;
    For his mercies aye endure,
    Ever faithful, ever sure.

Let us blaze his name abroad,   5
For of gods he is the God;
    For his, etc.

Psalm CXIV

fifteen years old] i.e. 1624. This and the following psalm may have been school
exercises based primarily on Latin and Greek versions of the Bible. Milton may
also have consulted the Hebrew version, for he began his study of Hebrew in
1624. He later composed a Greek version of the same psalm.
1 Terah's faithful Son] Abraham.
3 Pharian fields] Pharos, a small island near Alexandria, here represents Egypt.

O let us his praises tell,
Who doth the wrathful tyrants quell;   10
    For his, etc.

Who with his miracles doth make
Amazèd heaven and earth to shake;
    For his, etc.   15

Who by his wisdom did create
The painted heavens so full of state;
    For his, etc.   19

Who did the solid earth ordain
To rise above the watery plain;
    For his, etc.

Who, by his all-commanding might,   25
Did fill the new-made world with light;
    For his, etc.

And caused the golden-tressèd sun
All the day long his course to run;   30
    For his, etc.

The hornèd moon to shine by night
Amongst her spangled sisters bright;
    For his, etc.   35

He, with his thunder-clasping hand,
Smote the first-born of Egypt land;
    For his, etc.   39

And, in despite of Pharaoh fell,
He brought from thence his Israel;
    For his, etc.

The ruddy waves he cleft in twain   45
Of the Erythraean main;
    For his, etc.

The floods stood still, like walls of glass,
While the Hebrew bands did pass;   50
    For his, etc.

46 Erythraean main] The Red Sea.

But full soon they did devour
The tawny king with all his power;
    For his, etc.
         55

His chosen people he did bless
In the wasteful wilderness;
    For his, etc.
         59

In bloody battle he brought down
Kings of prowess and renown;
    For his, etc.

He foiled bold Seon and his host,
That ruled the Amorean coast;
    For his, etc.
         65

And large-limbed Og he did subdue,
With all his over-hardy crew;
    For his, etc.
         70

And to his servant Israël
He gave their land, therein to dwell;
    For his, etc.
         75

He hath, with a piteous eye,
Beheld us in our misery;
    For his, etc.
         79

And freed us from the slavery
Of the invading enemy;
    For his, etc.

All living creatures he doth feed,
And with full hand supplies their need;
    For his, etc.
         85

Let us, therefore, warble forth
His mighty majesty and worth;
    For his, etc.
         90

65 Seon] Sihon, king of the Amonites (Num. xxi. 21-32).
69 Og] king of Bashan (Num. xxi. 33-5. Deut. iii. 1-5). On his huge limbs see
    Deut. iii. 11. Cf. *SA* 1080.
73 servant Israël] Jacob.

That his mansion hath on high,
above the reach of mortal eye;
  For his mercies aye endure,   95
  Ever faithful, ever sure.

PSALM CXIV

Ἰσραὴλ ὅτε παῖδες, ὅτ᾿ ἀγλαὰ φῦλ᾿ Ἰακώβου
Αἰγύπτιον λίπε δῆμον, ἀπεχθέα, βαρβαρόφωνον,
Δὴ τότε μοῦνον ἔην ὅσιον γένος υἷες᾿ Ἰούδα.
Ἐν δὲ θεὸς λαοίσι μέγα κρείων βασίλευεν.
Εἶδε καὶ ἐντροπάδην φύγαδ᾿ ἐρρώησε θάασσα   5
Κύματι ἐιλυμένη ῥοθίῳ, ὁ δ᾿ ἄρ ἐστυφελίχθη
Ἱρὸς᾿ Ἰορδάνης ποτὶ ἀργυροειδέα πηγήν.
Ἐκ δ᾿ ὄρεα σκαρθμοῖσιν ἀπειρέσια κλονέοντο,
Ὡς κριοὶ σφριγόωντες ἐϋτραφερῷ ἐν ἀλωῇ.
Βαιότεραι δ᾿ ἅμα πᾶσαι ἀνασκίρτησαν ἐρίπναι,   10
Οἷα παραὶ σύριγγι φίλῃ ὑπὸ μητέρι ἄρνες.
Τίπτε σύ γ᾿ αἰνὰ θάλασσα πέλωρ φύγαδ᾿ ἐρρώησας,
Κύματι ἐιλυμένη ῥοθίῳ; τί δ᾿ ἄρ ἐστυφελίχθης
Ἱρὸς᾿ Ἰορδάνη ποτὶ ἀργυροειδέα πηγήν;
Τίπτ᾿ ὄρεα σκαρθμοῖσιν ἀπειρέσια κλονέεσθε   15
Ὡς κριοὶ σφριγόωντες ἐϋτραφερῷ ἐν ἀλωῇ;
Βαιότεραι τί δ᾿ ἄρ ὑμμὲς ἀνασκιρτήσατ᾿ ἐρίπναι,
Οἷα παραὶ σύριγγι φίλῃ ὑπὸ μητέρι ἄρνες;
Σείεο γαῖα τρέουσα θεὸν μεγάλ᾿ ἐκκτυπέοντα

Psalm CXIV (Greek)

When the children of Israel, when the glorious tribes of Jacob left the land of
Egypt, a hateful place of barbarous speech, then indeed were the sons of Judah
the only holy race, and among these peoples the mighty God was king. Sacred
Jordan was thrust back towards its silvery source. The immense mountains
rushed wildly about, leaping like lusty rams in a rich meadow. All the smaller
crags skipped like lambs about their dear mother to the sound of the syrinx.
Why, grim and monstrous sea, did you, coiled in roaring waves, rush in
headlong flight? Why, sacred Jordan, were you thrust back towards your silvery
source? Why, immense mountains, did you rush wildly about, leaping like lusty
rams in a rich meadow? Why, smaller crags, did you skip like lambs about their
dear mother to the sound of the syrinx? Shake, earth, in fear of God who
thunders out his greatness. Earth, fear God, the highest majesty revered by the
seed of Isaac, God who pours roaring rivers out of the crags, and an eternal
spring from a weeping rock.

Milton enclosed his translation with a letter to Alexander Gill dated 4 December
1634, explaining that he had written it the previous week. Cf. Milton's English
version of the same psalm, p. 113.

Γαῖα θεὸν τρείους' ὕπατον σέβας' Ἰσσακίδαο   20
Ὅς τε καὶ ἐκ σπιλάδων ποταμοὺς χέε μορμύροντας
Κρήνην τ' ἀεναὸν πέρης ἀπὸ δακρυοέσσης.

April, 1648. – J. M.

*Nine of the Psalms done into metre; wherein all, but what is
in a different character, are the very words of the Text,
translated from the original.*

PSALM LXXX

1 Thou shepherd that dost Israel *keep*,
    Give ear *in time of need*,
  Who leadest like a flock of sheep
    Thy loved Joseph's seed,
  That sitt'st between the cherubs bright,   5
    Between their wings outspread;
    Shine forth, *and from thy cloud give light*,
      And on our foes thy dread.

2 In Ephraim's view and Benjamin's,
    And in Manasseh's sight,   10
  Awake* thy strength, come, and *be seen*   *Gnorera
    To save us *by thy might*.

3 Turn us again; *thy grace divine*
    To us, O God, *vouchsafe*;
  Cause thou thy face on us to shine,   15
    And then we shall be safe.

4 Lord God of Hosts, how long wilt thou,
    How long wilt thou declare
  Thy *smoking wrath, *and angry brow*   *Gnashanta
    Against thy people's prayer?   20

5 Thou feed'st them with the bread of tears;
    Their bread with tears they eat;
  And mak'st them *largely drink the tears   *Shalish
    Wherewith their cheeks are wet.

6 A strife thou mak'st us *and a prey*   25
    To every neighbour foe,

Psalms lxxx-lxxxviii were translated in April 1647, at a time when there was
considerable controversy over the metrical psalter. This controversy may
have occasioned Milton's translations.

Psalm LXXX

11 Awake thy strength] *Gnorera* means 'rouse'.
18-19 declare/Thy smoking wrath] *Gnashanta* means 'you are smoking'.
23 largely] *Shalish* is probably the name of a measure, one third of a unit; cf.
    Isa. xl. 12 (and A. V. marginal note), its only other occurrence.

Among themselves they *laugh, they *play,   *Jilgnagu
  And *flouts at us they throw.
7 Return us, *and thy grace divine,*
    O God of Hosts, *vouchsafe;*   30
  Cause thou thy face on us to shine,
    And then we shall be safe.
8 A vine from Egypt thou hast brought,
    Thy free love made it thine,
  And drov'st out nations *proud and haught,*   35
    To plant this *lovely* vine.
9 Thou didst prepare for it a place,
    And root it deep and fast,
  That it *began to grow apace,*
    And filled the land *at last.*   40
10 With her *green* shade that covered *all*
    The hills were *overspread;*
  Her boughs as *high* as cedars tall
    Advanced their lofty head.
11 Her branches *on the western side*   45
    Down to the sea she sent,
  And *upward* to that river *wide*
    Her other branches *went.*
12 Why hast thou laid her hedges low,
    And broken down her fence,
  That all may pluck her, as they go,   50
    With rudest violence?
13 The *tuskèd* boar out of the wood
    Upturns it by the roots;
  Wild beasts there browse, and make their food   55
    Her grapes and tender shoots.
14 Return now, God of Hosts; look down
    From Heaven, thy seat divine;
  Behold *us, but without a frown,*
    And visit this *thy* vine.   60
15 Visit this vine, which thy right hand
    Hath set, and planted *long,*
  And the young branch, that for thyself
    Thou hast made firm and strong.
16 But now it is consumed with fire,   65
    And cut *with axes* down;
  They perish at thy dreadful ire,
    At thy rebuke and frown.
17 Upon the man of thy right hand
    Let thy *good* hand be *laid;*   70

27-8 laugh ... throw] The verb *Jilgnagu* means 'scorn'.

Upon the Son of Man, whom thou
    Strong for thyself hast made.
18 So shall we not go back from thee
    To ways of sin and shame:
Quicken us thou, then *gladly* we   75
    Shall call upon thy name.
19 Return us, *and thy grace divine*,
    Lord God of Hosts, *vouchsafe*;
Cause thou thy face on us to shine,
    And then we shall be safe.   80

PSALM LXXXI

1 To God our strength sing loud *and clear*;
    Sing loud to God *our King*;
To Jacob's God, *that all may hear*,
    Loud acclamations ring.
2 Prepare a hymn, prepare a song,   5
    The timbrel hither bring;
The *cheerful* psaltery bring along,
    And harp *with* pleasant *string*.
3 Blow, *as is wont*, in the new moon,
    With trumpets' *lofty sound*,   10
The appointed time, the day whereon
    Our solemn feast *comes round*.
4 This was a statute *given of old*
    For Israel *to observe*,
A law of Jacob's God *to hold*,   15
    From whence they might not swerve.
5 This he a testimony ordained
    In Joseph, *not to change*,
When as he passed through Egypt-land;
    The tongue I heard was strange.   20
6 From burden, *and from slavish toil*,
    I set his shoulder free;
His hands from pots, *and miry soil*,
    Delivered were *by me*.
7 When trouble did thee sore assail,   25
    On me then didst thou call,
And I to free thee *did not fail*,
    And led thee out of thrall.
I answered thee in *thunder deep   *Besether ragnam*
    With clouds encompassed round;
I tried thee at the water *steep*

29 in thunder deep] *Besether ragnam* means 'in the secret place of thunder'.

Of Meriba *renowned*.

8 Hear, O my people, *hearken well*:
    I testify to thee,
    Thou ancient stock of Israel,   35
    If thou wilt list to me:

9 Throughout the land of thy abode
    No alien god shall be,
    Nor shalt thou to a foreign god
    In honour bend thy knee.   40

10 I am the Lord thy God, which brought
    Thee out of Egypt-land;
    Ask large enough, and I, *besought*,
    Will grant thy full demand.

11 And yet my people would not *hear*,   45
    Nor hearken to my voice;
    And Israel, *whom I loved so dear*,
    Misliked me for his choice.

12 Then did I leave them to their will,
    And to their wandering mind;   50
    Their own conceits they followed still,
    Their own devices blind.

13 O that my people would *be wise*,
    To serve me *all their days*,
    And O that Israel would *advise*   55
    To walk my *righteous* ways

14 Then would I soon bring down their foes,
    That now so proudly rise,
    And turn my hand against *all those*
    That are their enemies.   60

15 Who hate the Lord should *then be fain*
    To bow to him and bend;
    But *they, his people, should remain*;
    Their time should have no end.

16 And he would feed them *from the shock*   65
    With flour of finest wheat,
    And satisfy them from the rock
    With honey *for their meat*.

PSALM LXXXII

1 God in the *great *assembly stands   *Bagnadath-el*
    Of kings and lordly states,

Psalm LXXXII
1 great assembly] *Bagnadath-el* may mean 'assembly of the might one' or 'assembly of God'.

Among the gods † on both his hands   †*Bekerev*
  He judges and debates.
2 How long will ye *pervert the right   **Tishpetu gnavel* 5
    With *judgement false and wrong
  Favouring the wicked *by your might,*
    Who thence grow bold and strong?
3 *Regard the *weak and fatherless   **Shiphtu-dal*
    *Dispatch the *poor man's cause,   10
  And † raise the man in deep distress
    By † just and equal laws.   †*Hatzdiku*
4 Defend the poor and desolate,
    And rescue from the hands
  Of wicked men the low estate   15
    Of him *that help demands.*
5 They know not nor will understand,
    In darkness they walk on,
  The earth's foundations all are *moved   **Jimmotu*
    And *out of order gone.   20
6 I said that ye were gods, yea all
    The sons of God most high,
7 But ye shall die like men, and fall
    As other princes *die.*
8 Rise God, *judge thou the earth *in might,*   25
    This *wicked* earth *redress,   **Shophta*
  For thou art he who shalt by right
    The nations all possess.

PSALM LXXXIII

1 Be not thou silent, *now at length*
    O God hold not thy peace,
  Sit not thou still O God of *strength*;
    We cry, and do not cease.
2 For lo thy *furious* foes now *swell   5
    And *storm outrageously,   **Jehemajun*

---

3 Among . . . on both his hands] *Bekerev* means 'in the midst of'.
5-6 pervert . . . wrong] *Tishpetu gnavel* means 'judge perversely'.
9-10 Regard . . . cause] *Shiphtu-dal* means 'judge the poor' or 'judge the weak'.
11-12 raise . . . laws] *Hatzdiku* means 'declare right or just'.
19-20 are moved . . . gone] *Jimmotu* means 'moved'.
25-6 judge . . . redress] The verb *Shophta* means 'judge'.
                    Psalm LXXXIII
5-6 swell . . . outrageously] *Jehemajun* means 'are in turmoil'.

And they that hate thee *proud and fell*
  Exalt their heads full high.
3 Against thy people they †contrive   *†Jagnarimu*
  †Their plots and counsels deep   †*Sod* 10
  *Them to ensnare they chiefly strive   *Jithjagnatsu gnal*
  *Whom thou dost hide and keep.   *Tsephumeca*
4 'Come, let us cut them off,' say they,
  'Till they no nation be;
  That Israel's name for ever may   15
  Be lost in memory.'
5 For they consult †with all their might,   †*Lev jachdau*
  And all as one in mind
  Themselves against thee they unite,
  And in firm union bind.   20
6 The tents of Edom, and the brood
  Of *scornful* Ishmael,
  Moab, with them of Hagar's blood,
  That in the desert dwell,
7 Gebal and Ammon *there conspire*,   25
  And *hateful* Amalec,
  The Philistines, and they of Tyre,
  Whose bounds the sea doth check.
8 With them *great* Ashur also bands,
  And doth confirm the knot;   30
  All these have have lent their armed hands
  To aid the sons of Lot.
9 Do to them as to Midian *bold*,
  That wasted all the coast;
  To Sisera, and as *is told*   35
  Thou didst to Jabin's *host*,
  When at the brook of Kishon *old*
  They were repulsed and slain,
10 At Endor quite cut off, and rolled
  As dung upon the plain.   40
11 As Zeb and Oreb evil sped,
  So let their princes speed;
  As Zeba and Zalmunna *bled*,
  So let their princes *bleed*.
12 *For they amidst their pride* have said,   45
  'By right now shall we seize

9-10 contrive ... deep] *Jagnarimu Sod* means 'deliberate cunningly'.
11 to ensnare ... strive] *Jithjagnatsu gnal* means 'conspire against'.
11-12 Them ... Whom ... keep] *Tsephuneca* means 'your hidden things'.
17 with all their might] *Lev jachdau* means 'together with one heart'.

God's houses, and *will now invade*
　†Their stately palaces.'　　　　　　　†*Neoth Elohim bears both*

13 My God, O make them as a wheel,
　　No quiet let them find;　　　　　　　　　　　　　50
　Giddy and *restless* let *them reel*,
　　Like stubble from the wind.

14 As, *when* an *aged* wood takes fire
　　Which on a sudden strays,
　The *greedy* flame runs higher and higher,　　　　55
　　Till all the mountains blaze;

15 So with thy whirlwind them pursue,
　　And with thy tempest chase;

16 And till they *yield thee honour due,　　　*They seek thy
　　Lord, fill with shame their face.　　　　　　*Name*. Heb.

17 Ashamed and troubled let them be,　　　　　　61
　　Troubled and shamed for ever,
　Ever confounded, and so die
　　With shame, *and scape it never*.

18 Then shall they know that thou whose name　　65
　　Jehovah is, alone
　Art the Most High, *and thou the same*
　　O'er all the earth *art One*.

PSALM LXXXIV

1 How lovely are thy dwellings fair!
　　O Lord of Hosts, how dear
　The *pleasant* tabernacles are
　　Where thou dost dwell so near!

2 My soul doth long and almost die　　　　　　　5
　　Thy courts O Lord to see;
　My heart and flesh aloud do cry,
　　O living God, for thee.

3 There even the sparrow, *freed from wrong*,
　　Hath found a house of *rest*;　　　　　　　　10
　The swallow there, to lay her young,
　　Hath built her *brooding* nest;
　Even *by* thy altars, Lord of Hosts,
　　They find their safe abode;

47-8 God's houses ... Their stately palaces] In the phrase *Neoth Elohim bears both* Milton asserts (correctly) that the Hebrew phrase is ambiguous, and can be translated by either English phrase. *Elohim* means 'God', but can also be used as a superlative; *Neoth* is really 'pastures' (as in Psalm xxiii. 2), thence 'dwelling places', but hardly 'palaces'.

And home they fly from round the coasts   15
    Toward thee, my King, my God.
4 Happy who in thy house reside,
    Where thee they ever praise,
5 Happy whose strength in thee doth bide,
    And in their hearts thy ways.   20
6 They pass through Baca's *thirsty* vale,
    That dry and barren ground,
As through a fruitful watery dale
    Where springs and showers abound.
7 They journey on from strength to strength   25
    With joy and gladsome cheer,
Till all before *our* God *at length*
    In Zion do appear.
8 Lord God of Hosts, hear *now* my prayer,
    O Jacob's God, give ear: 30
9 Thou, God, our shield, look on the face
    Of thy anointed *dear*.
10 For one day in thy courts *to be*
    Is better *and more blest*
Than *in the joys of vanity*   35
    A thousand days *at best*.
I in the temple of my God
    Had rather keep a door
Than dwell in tents *and rich abode*
    With sin *for evermore*.   40
11 For God, the Lord, both sun and shield,
    Gives grace and glory *bright*;
No good from them shall be withheld
    Whose ways are just and right.
12 Lord *God* of Hosts *that reign'st on high*,   45
    That man is *truly* blest
Who *only* on thee doth rely,
    And in thee only rest.

PSALM LXXXV

1 Thy land to favour graciously
    Thou hast not, Lord, been slack;
Thou hast from *hard* captivity
    Returned Jacob back.
2 The iniquity thou didst forgive   5
    That wrought thy people woe,
And all their sin *that did thee grieve*
    Hast did *where none shall know*.

3 Thine anger all thou hadst removed,
    And *calmly* didst return
  From thy †fierce wrath which we had proved
    Far worse than fire to burn.

†Heb.
*the burning
heat of thy
wrath*

4 God of our saving health and peace,
    Turn us, and us restore;
  Thine indignation cause to cease
    Toward us, *and chide no more*.

5 Wilt thou be angry without end,
    For ever angry thus?
  Wilt thou thy frowning ire extend
    From age to age on us?

6 Wilt thou not *turn, and *hear our voice*
    And us again *revive,
  That so thy people may rejoice,
    By thee preserved alive?

*Heb. *Turn
to quicken us*

7 Cause us to see thy goodness, Lord;
    To us thy mercy show;
  Thy saving health to us afford,
    And life in us renew.

8 *And now* what God the Lord will speak
    I will *go straight and* hear,
  For to his people he speaks peace,
    And to his saints *full dear*;
  To his dear saints he will speak peace,
    But let them never more
  Return to folly, *but surcease
    To trespass as before*.

9 Surely to such as do him fear
    Salvation is at hand,
  And glory shall *ere long appear
    To* dwell within our land.

10 Mercy and Truth, *that long were missed*,
    Now *joyfully* are met;
  Sweet Peace and Righteousness have kissed,
    And hand in hand are set.

11 Truth from the earth *like to a flower*
    Shall bud and blossom *then*:
  And Justice from her heavenly bower
    Look down *on mortal men*.

12 The Lord will also then bestow
    Whatever thing is good;
  Our land shall forth in plenty throw
    Her fruits *to be our food*.

13 Before him Righteousness shall go,

His royal harbinger: 54
Then *will he come, and not be slow,   *Heb. *He will*
His footsteps cannot err.   *set his steps*
                                                               to the way

PSALM LXXXVI

1 Thy *gracious* ear, O Lord, incline,
    O hear me *I thee pray*,
  For I am poor, and almost pine
    With need, *and sad decay*.   4
2 Preserve my soul, for †I have trod   †Heb. *I am good,*
    Thy ways, and love the just,   *loving, a doer of*
  Save thou thy servant O my God   *good and holy*
    Who *still* in thee doth trust.   *things*
3 Pity me, Lord, for daily thee
    I call; 4 O make rejoice   10
  Thy servant's soul; for Lord to thee
    I lift my soul *and voice*;
5 For thou art good; thou, Lord, art prone
    To pardon; thou to all
  Art full of mercy, thou *alone*,   15
    To them that on thee call.
6 Unto my supplication, Lord,
    Give ear, and to the cry
  Of my *incessant* prayers afford
    Thy hearing graciously.   20
7 I in the day of my distress
    Will call on thee *for aid*;
  For thou wilt *grant* me *free access*,
    And answer *what I prayed*.
8 Like thee among the gods is none,   25
    O Lord; nor any works
  Of all that other gods have done
    Like to thy *glorious* works.
9 The nations all whom thou hast made
    Shall come, *and all shall frame*   30
  To bow them low before thee, Lord,
    And glorify thy name.
10 For great thou art, and wonders great
    By thy strong hand are done;
  Thou *in thy everlasting seat*   35
    Remainest God alone.
11 Teach me, O Lord, thy way *most right*,

I in thy truth will bide;
To fear thy name my heart unite,
So shall it never slide.

12 Thee will I praise, O Lord my God,
Thee honour and adore
With my whole heart, and blaze abroad
Thy name for evermore.

13 For great thy mercy is toward me,
And thou hast freed my soul,
Ev'n from the lowest hell set free,
From deepest darkness foul.

14 O God, the proud against me rise,
And violent men are met
To seek my life, and in their eyes
No fear of thee have set.

15 But thou, Lord, art the God most mild,
Readiest thy grace to shew,
Slow to angry, and *art styled*
Most merciful, most true.

16 O turn to me *thy face at length*,
And me have mercy on;
Unto thy servant give thy strength,
And save thy handmaid's son.

17 Some sign of good to me afford,
And let my foes *then* see,
And be ashamed, because thou, Lord,
Dost help and comfort me.

PSALM LXXXVII

1 Among the holy mountains *high*
Is his foundation fast;
There seated in his sanctuary,
His temple there is placed.

2 Zion's *fair* gates the Lord loves more
Than all the dwellings *fair*
Of Jacob's *land, though there be store,*
And all within his care.

3 City of God, most glorious things
Of thee *abroad* are spoke;
I mention Egypt, *where proud kings*
Did our forefathers yoke;

4 I mention Babel to my friends,
Philistia *full of scorn*,
And Tyre, with Ethiop's *utmost ends*:

40

45

50

55

60

5

10

15

Lo this man there was born.
5 But *twice that praise shall in our ear*
    Be said of Zion *last*:
This and this man was born in her;
    High God shall fix her fast.   20
6 The Lord shall write it in a scroll,
    That ne'er shall be out-worn,
When he the nations doth enrol,
    That this man there was born.
7 Both they who sing and they who dance   25
    With sacred songs are there;
In thee *fresh brooks and soft streams glance,*
    And all my fountains *clear*.

PSALM LXXXVIII

1 Lord God, that dost me save and keep,
    All day to thee I cry,
And all night long before thee *weep*,
    Before thee *prostrate lie*.
2 Into thy presence let my prayer,   5
    With sighs devout, ascend;
And to my cries, that *ceaseless are*,
    Thine ear with favour bend.
3 For, cloyed with woes and trouble store,
    Surcharged my soul doth lie;   10
My life, *at death's uncheerful door*,
    Unto the grave draws nigh.
4 Reckoned I am with them that pass
    Down to the *dismal* pit;   14
I am a *man, but weak alas   *Heb. *A man*
    And for that name unfit.   *without manly*
5 From life discharged and parted quite   *strength*
    Among the dead *to sleep*,
And like the slain *in bloody fight*
    That in the grave lie *deep*;   20
Whom thou rememberest no more,
    Dost never more regard:
Them from thy hand delivered o'er,
    Death's hideous house hath barred.
6 Thou, in the lowest pit *profound*,   25
    Hast set me *all forlorn*,
Where thickest darkness *hovers round*,
    In horrid deeps *to mourn*.

7 *Thy wrath, from which no shelter saves,*
  Full sore doth press on me;   30
  *Thou break'st upon me all thy waves,   *The Heb.
  *And all thy waves break me.   bears both
8 Thou dost my friends from me estrange,
  And mak'st me odious,
  Me to them odious, *for they change,*   35
  And I here pent up thus.
9 Through sorrow and affliction great
  Mine eye grows dim and dead;
  Lord, all the day I thee entreat,
  My hands to thee I spread.   40
10 Wilt thou do wonders on the dead?
   Shall the deceased arise
   And praise thee *from their loathsome bed
   With pale and hollow eyes?*
11 Shall they thy loving-kindness tell   45
   On whom the grave *hath hold?*
   Or they *who* in perdition *dwell*
   Thy faithfulness *unfold?*
12 In darkness can thy mighty *hand*
   Or wondrous acts be known?   50
   Thy justice in the *gloomy* land
   Of *dark* oblivion?
13 But I to thee, O Lord, do cry
   Ere yet my life be spent;
   And *up to thee* my prayer *doth hie*   55
   Each morn, and thee prevent.
14 Why wilt thou, Lord, my soul forsake
   And hide thy face from me,
15 That am already bruised, and †shake   †Heb. *Prae
   With terror sent from thee;   *Concussione*
   Bruised and afflicted, and *so low*   60
   As ready to expire,
   While I thy terrors undergo,
   Astonished with thine ire?
16 Thy fierce wrath over me doth flow,   65

31-2] In the phrase '*The* Heb. *bears both*' Milton asserts (incorrectly) that the
  Hebrew phrase is ambiguous, and can be translated by either English
  phrase. In fact only line 31 is a correct translation.

59 shake] The phrase *Prae Concussione* is not a clarification of the Hebrew (it
  merely translates Milton's phrase), but rather an assertion of Milton's
  preference for the meaning 'shaking'. The Hebrew word means 'youth' (cf.
  A. V. 'from my youth up'), but Milton has enlisted an homonymous root
  that means 'to shake' to help him understand a difficult line.

Thy threatenings cut me through;
17 All day they round about me go,
Like waves they me pursue.
18 Lover and friend thou hast removed,
And severed from me far: 70
They *fly me now* whom I have loved,
And as in darkness are.

PSALM I

Done into verse 1653

Blest is the man who hath not walked astray
In counsel of the wicked, and i' the way
Of sinners hath not stood, and in the seat
Of scorners hath not sat; but in the great
Jehovah's law is ever his delight,   5
And in his law he studies day and night.
He shall be as a tree which planted grows
By watery streams, and in his season knows
To yield his fruit; and his leaf shall not fall,
And what he takes in hand shall prosper all.   10
Not so the wicked; but, as chaff which fanned
The wind drives, so the wicked shall not stand
In judgement, or abide their trial then,
Nor sinners in the assembly of just men.
For the Lord knows the upright way of the just,   15
And the way of bad men to ruin must.

PSALM II

Done August 8, 1653 – Terzetti

Why do the Gentiles tumult, and the nations
Muse a vain thing, the kings of the earth upstand
With power, and princes in their congregations
Lay deep their plots together through each land
Against the Lord and his Messiah dear?   5
'Let us break off,' say they, 'by strength of hand,
Their bonds, and cast from us, no more to wear,

Psalms i–viii were translated from the original Hebrew in 1653, when Milton
had been blind for a year and a half.
Ps. ii. *Terzetti*] the translation is written in the *terza rima* of Dante, i.e. as a
series of interlocking tercets in which the second line of each tercet rhymes
with the first and third lines of the succeeding tercet.

Their twisted cords'; he who in heaven doth dwell
  Shall laugh; the Lord shall scoff them, then severe
Speak to them in his wrath, and in his fell   10
  And fierce ire trouble them. 'But I,' saith he,
  'Anointed have my king (though ye rebel)
On Zion my holy hill.' A firm decree
  I will declare: the Lord to me hath said,
  'Thou art my Son; I have begotten thee   15
This day; ask of me, and the grant is made:
  As thy possession I on thee bestow
  The heathen, and as thy conquest to be swayed,
Earth's utmost bounds: them shalt thou bring full low
  With iron sceptre bruised, and them disperse   20
  Like to a potter's vessel shivered so.'
And now be wise at length, ye kings averse;
  Be taught, ye judges of the earth; with fear
  Jehovah serve, and let your joy converse
With trembling; kiss the Son, lest he appear   25
  In anger, and ye perish in the way,
  If once his wrath take fire, like fuel sere.
Happy all those who have in him their stay.

PSALM III

August 9, 1653

When he fled from Absalom

Lord, how many are my foes,
        How many those
    That in arms against me rise;
        Many are they
    That of my life distrustfully thus say,   5
'No help for him in God there lies.'
But thou Lord art my shield, my glory;
        Thee through my story
    The exalter of my head I count:
        Aloud I cried   10
Unto Jehovah; he full soon replied,
And heard me from his holy mount.
I lay and slept: I waked again:
        For my sustain
    Was the Lord. Of many millions   15
        The populous rout
    I fear not though encamping round about,
They pitch against me their pavilions.
Rise, Lord; save me my God, for thou

Hast smote ere now   20
On the cheek-bone all my foes,
    Of men abhorred
Hast broke the teeth. This help was from the Lord;
Thy blessing on thy people flows.

PSALM VI

August 10, 1653

Answer me when I call,
God of my righteousness;
    In straits and in distress
    Thou didst me disenthrall
And set at large: now spare,   5
Now pity me, and hear my earnest prayer.
    Great ones, how long will ye
    My glory have in scorn?
    How long be thus forborne
    Still to love vanity?   10
To love, to seek, to prize
Things false and vain, and nothing else but lies?
    Yet know the Lord hath chose,
    Chose to himself apart,
    The good and meek of heart   15
    (For whom to choose he knows);
    Jehovah from on high
Will hear my voice what time to him I cry.
    Be awed, and do not sin;
    Speak to your hearts alone   20
    Upon your beds, each one,
    And be at peace within.
    Offer the offerings just
Of righteousness, and in Jehovah trust.
    Many there be that say   25
    'Who yet will show us good?'
    Talking like this world's brood;
    But, Lord, thus let me pray:
    On us lift up the light,
Lift up the favour of thy count'nance bright.   30
    Into my heart more joy
    And gladness thou hast put
    Than when a year of glut
    Their stores doth over-cloy,
    And from their plenteous grounds   35
With vast increase their corn and wine abounds.

In peace at once will I
Both lay me down and sleep;
For thou alone dost keep
Me safe where'er I lie;   40
As in a rocky cell
Thou, Lord, alone in safety mak'st me dwell.

PSALM V

August 12, 1653

Jehovah, to my words give ear,
    My meditation weigh;
The voice of my complaining hear,
My King and God, for unto thee I pray.
    Jehovah, thou my early voice   5
        Shalt in the morning hear;
    I' the morning I to thee with choice
Will rank my prayers, and watch till thou appear.
    For thou art not a God that takes
        In wickedness delight;   10
    Evil with thee no biding makes;
Fools or mad men stand not within thy sight.
    All workers of iniquity
        Thou hat'st; and them unblest
    Thou wilt destroy that speak a lie;   15
The bloody and guileful man God doth detest.
    But I will in thy mercies dear,
        Thy numerous mercies, go
    Into thy house; I in thy fear,
Will towards thy holy temple worship low.   20
    Lord, lead me in thy righteousness,
        Lead me because of those
    That do observe if I transgress;
Set thy ways right before where my step goes.
    For in his faltering mouth unstable   25
        No word is firm or sooth;
    Their inside, troubles miserable;
An open grave their throat, their tongue they smooth.
    God, find them guilty, let them fall
        By their own counsels quelled;   30
    Push them in their rebellions all
Still on; for against thee they have rebelled;
    Then all who trust in thee shall bring
        Their joy, while thou from blame
Defend'st them: they shall ever sing,   35

And shall triumph in thee, who love thy name.
 For thou, Jehovah, wilt be found
  To bless the just man still:
 As with a shield thou wilt surround
Him with thy lasting favour and good will.   40

PSALM VI

August 13, 1643

Lord, in thy anger do not reprehend me,
 Nor in thy hot displeasure me correct;
 Pity me, Lord, for I am much deject,
And very weak and faint; heal and amend me:
For all my bones, that even with anguish ache, 5
 Are troubled; yea, my soul is troubled sore;
 And thou, O Lord, how long? Turn, Lord; restore
My soul; O save me, for thy goodness' sake;
For in death no remembrance is of thee;
 Who in the grave can celebrate thy praise? 10
 Wearied I am with sighing out my days:
Nightly my couch I make a kind of sea;
My bed I water with my tears; mine eye
 Through grief consumes, is waxen old and dark
 I' the midst of all mine enemies that mark. 15
Depart all ye that work iniquity,
Depart from me; for the voice of my weeping
 The Lord hath heard; the Lord hath heard my prayer;
 My supplication with acceptance fair
The Lord will own, and have me in his keeping. 20
Mine enemies shall all be blank, and dashed
 With much confusion; then grow red with shame,
 They shall return in haste the way they came,
And in a moment shall be quite abashed.

PSALM VII

August 14, 1653

Upon the words of Chush the Benjamite against him

Lord, my God, to thee I fly;
Save me, and secure me under
Thy protection while I cry;
Lest, as a lion (and no wonder),
He haste to tear my soul asunder, 5
Tearing and no rescue nigh.

Lord, my God, if I have thought
Or done this, if wickedness
Be in my hands, if I have wrought
Ill to him that meant me peace,
Or to him have rendered less,
And not freed my foe for nought:

Let the enemy pursue my soul,
And overtake it; let him tread
My life down to the earth, and roll
In the dust my glory dead,
In the dust, and there outspread
Lodge it with dishonour foul.

Rise, Jehovah, in thine ire;
Rouse thyself amidst the rage
Of my foes that urge like fire;
And wake for me, their fury assuage;
Judgement here thou didst engage
And command, which I desire.

So the assemblies of each nation
Will surround thee, seeking right:
Thence to thy glorious habitation
Return on high, and in their sight.
Jehovah judgeth most upright
All people from the world's foundation.

Judge me, Lord; be judge in this
According to my righteousness,
And the innocence which is
Upon me: cause at length to cease
Of evil men the wickedness,
And their power that do amiss.

But the just establish fast,
Since thou art the just God that tries
Hearts and reins. On God is cast
My defence, and in him lies;
In him who, both just and wise,
Saves the upright of heart at last.

God is a just judge and severe,
And God is every day offended;
If the unjust will not forbear,

10

15

20

25

30

35

40

45

His sword he whets; his bow hath bended
Already, and for him intended
The tools of death that waits him near.

(His arrows purposely made he
For them that persecute.) Behold,   50
He travails big with vanity;
Trouble he hath conceived of old
As in a womb, and from that mould
Hath at length brought forth a lie.

He digg'd a pit, and delved it deep,   55
And fell into the pit he made:
His mischief, that due course doth keep,
Turns on his head: and his ill trade
Of violence will undelayed
Fall on his crown with ruin steep.   60

Then will I Jehovah's praise
According to his justice raise,
And sing the name and deity
Of Jehovah the most high.

PSALM VIII

August 14, 1653

O Jehovah our Lord, how wondrous great
   And glorious is thy name through all the earth,
So as above the heavens thy praise to set!
   Out of the tender mouths of latest birth,
Out of the mouths of babes and sucklings thou   5
   Hast founded strength, because of all thy foes,
To stint the enemy, and slack the avenger's brow,
   That bends his rage thy providence to oppose.

When I behold thy heavens, thy fingers' art,
   The moon and stars, which thou so bright hast set   10
In the pure firmament, then saith my heart,
   O, what is man that thou rememberest yet
And think'st upon him, or of man begot
   That him thou visit'st, and of him art found?
Scarce to be less than gods thou mad'st his lot;   15
   With honour and with state thou hast him crowned.

O'er the works of thy hand thou mad'st him lord;
  Thou hast put all under his lordly feet,
All flocks and herds, by thy commanding word,
  All beasts that in the field or forest meet,   20
Fowl of the heavens, and fish that through the wet
  Sea-paths in shoals do slide, and know no dearth.
O Jehovah our Lord, how wondrous great
  And glorious is thy name through all the earth.

TRANSLATIONS FROM THE PROSE WRITINGS

From *Of Reformation* (1641)

1 Ah, Constantine, of how much ill was cause.
  Not thy conversion, but those rich domains
  That the first wealthy Pope received of thee.

2 Founded in chaste and humble poverty,
  'Gainst them that raised thee dost thou lift thy horn, 5
  Impudent whore? Where hast thou placed thy hope?
  In thy adulterers, or thy ill-got wealth?
  Another Constantine comes not in haste.

3 Then passed he to a flowery mountain green,
  Which once smelt sweet, now stinks as odiously: 10
  This was the gift (if you the truth will have)
  That Constantine to good Silvestro gave.

From *Reason of Church-Government* (1641)

4 When I die, let the earth be rolled in flames.

1] From Dante, *Inferno* xix 115-17:
  Ahi, Costantin, di quanto mal fu matre,
    non la tua conversion, ma quella dote
    che da te prese il primo ricco patre!

The three translations from *Of Reformation* allude to the medieval forgery
  known as the Donation of Constantine, in which the emperor Constantine
  was purported to confer on Pope Silvester I the primacy of Europe and the
  Near East.

2] From Petrarch, *Le Rime* cxxxviii 9-13:
  Fondata in casta et umil povertate,
    Contra tuoi fondatori alzi le corna,
    Putta sfacciata: e dove ài poste spene?
  Negli adulteri' tuoi, ne le mal nate
    Ricchezze tane? Or Costantin non torna.

3] From Ariosto, *Orlando Furioso* xxxiv 80:
  Di varii fiori ad un gran monte passa,
  ch'ebbe già buono odore, or putia forte.
  Questo era il dono (se però dir lece)
  che Constantino al buon Silvestro fece.

4] possibly from *Bellerophon*, a lost play by Euripides:
  Ἐμοῦ γαῖα θανόντος μιχθήτω πυρί
The line was sufficiently famous to be quoted (in Greek) by Jonson in *Sejanus*
  II. ii. 330.

From *An Apology for Smectymnuus* (1642)

5   Laughing to teach the truth
What hinders? As some teachers give to boys
Junkets and knacks, that they may learn apace.

6   Jesting decides great things
Stronglier and better oft than earnest can.   5

7 'Tis you that say it, not I; you do the deeds,
And your ungodly deeds find me the words.

From the title-page of *Areopagitica* (1644)

8 This is true liberty, when freeborn men
Having to advise the public may speak free,
Which he who can, and will, deserves his praise,
Who neither can nor will, may hold his peace;
What can be juster in a state than this?

From *Tetrachordon* (1645)

9 Whom do we count a good man, whom but he
Who keeps the laws and statutes of the senate,

5] From Horace, *Satire* I i 24-6:
      quamquam ridentem dicere verum
quid vetat? ut pueris olim dant crustula blandi
doctores, elementa velint ut discere prima.

6] From Horace, *Satire* I x 14-15:
         Ridiculum acri
fortius et melius magnas plerumque secat res.

7] From Sophocles, *Electra* 624-5:
  οὔ τοι λέγεις νυν, οὐχ ἐγώ σὺ γὰρ ποε
τοῦγον· τὰ δ' ἔργα τοὺς λόγους εὑρίσκεται.
The 'you' is Clytemnestra, the 'I' Electra.

8] From Euripides, *Supplices* 438-41. For the Greek text see the title-page of *Areopagitica*, p. 573.

9] From Horace, *Epistle* I xvi 40-5:
      Vir bonus est quis?
'qui consulta patrum, qui leges iuraque servat,
quo multae magnaeque secantur iudice lites,
quo res sponsore et quo causae teste tenentur.'
sed videt hunc omnis domus et vicinia tota
introrsum turpem, speciosum pelle decora.

Who judges in great suits and controversies,
Whose witness and opinion wins the cause?
But his own house, and the whole neighbourhood,
Sees his foul inside through his whited skin.

From *Tenure of Kings and Magistrates* (1649)

10   There can be slain
     No sacrifice to God more acceptable
     Than an unjust and wicked king.

From *The History of Britain* (written 1649, published 1670)

11 Goddess of shades, and huntress, who at will
    Walk'st on the rolling sphere, and through the deep,
    On thy third reign, the earth, look now and tell
    What land, what seat of rest thou bidd'st me seek,
    What certain seat, that I may worship thee
    For aye, with temples vowed, and virgin choirs.

12 Brutus, far to the west, in the ocean wide,
    Beyond the realm of Gaul, a land there lies,
    Sea-girt it lies, where giants dwelt of old;

10] From Seneca, *Hercules Furens* 922–4
                  victima haud ulla amplior
          potest magisque opima mactari Iovi
          quam rex iniquus.
Tenure of Kings and Magistrates was published on 13 February 1649; King
    Charles had been executed a fortnight earlier (30 January).

11 and 12] From Geoffrey of Monmouth, *Historia Regum Britanniae* I xi;
          (11) is Brutus' prayer to Diana, and (12) is her reply:
          Diva potens nemorum, terror silvestribus apris:
              Cui licet amfractus ire per aethereos,
          Infernasque domos: terrestria iura resolve,
              Et dic quas terras nos habitare velis?
          Dic certam sedem qua te venerator in aevum,
              Qua tibi virgineis templa dicabo choris?

          Brute sub occasum solis trans Gallica regna
              Insula in oceano est undique clausia mari:
          Insula in oceano est habitata gigantibus olim,
              Nunc deserta quidem: gentibus apta tuis.
          Hanc pete, namque tibi sedes erit illa perennis:
              Sic fiet natis altera Troia tuis:
          Sic de prole tua reges nascentur: et ipsis
              Totius terrae subditus orbis erit.

Now void, it fits thy people; thither bend
Thy course; there shalt thou find a lasting seat;
There to thy sons another Troy shall rise,
And kings be born of thee, whose dreaded might
Shall awe the world, and conquer nations bold.

13 Low in a mead of kine under a thorn,
Of head bereft lieth poor Kenelm king-born.

13] From *Flores Historiarum*, a medieval chronicle that extends from the creation to 1235; the murder of Kenelm is described in the account of AD 821. The location of Kenelm's body was revealed by a dove which carried to Rome the information (in Anglo-Saxon) that *In clento cou hathe Kenelm Kynebearn lith under thorne haenedes bereafed*, which the compiler of the *Flores* translated into Latin as *In pastura vaccarum Kenelmus regis filius iacet sub spina, capite privatus*; this in turn was transformed into the couplet (attributed to John de Cella, Abbot of St Albans) that Milton translates:

> In clent sub spina iacet in convalle bovina,
> Vertice privatus, Kenelmus rege creatus.

Paradise Lost.
A
POEM
IN
TWELVE BOOKS

The Author
John Milton.

COMMENDATORY POEMS

IN *PARADISUM AMISSAM*
SUMMI POETÆ
JOHANNIS MILTONI

Qui Legis *Amissam Paradisum*, grandia magni
    Carmina Miltoni, quid nisi cuncta legis?
Res cunctas, et cunctarum primordia rerum
    Et fata, et fines, continet iste liber.
Intima panduntur magni penetralia mundi,
    Scribitur et toto quicquid in orbe latet;
Terræque, tractusque maris, cœlumque profundum,
    Sulphureumque Erebi flammivomumque specus;
Quæque colunt terras, pontumque, et Tartara cæca,
    Quæque colunt summi lucida regna poli;
Et quodcunque ullis conclusum est finibus usquam;
    Et sine fine chaos, et sine fine Deus;
Et sine fine magis, si quid magis est sine fine,
    In Christo erga homines conciliatus amor.
Hæc qui speraret quis crederet esse futurum?
    Et tamen hæc hodie terra Britanna legit.
O quantos in bella duces, quæ protulit arma!
    Quæ canit, et quantâ prælia dira tubâ!
Cœlestes acies, atque in certamine coelum!
    Et quæ cœlestes pugna deceret agros!
Quantus in ætheriis tollis se Lucifer armis,
    Atque ipso graditur vix Michæle minor!
Quantis et quam funestis concurritur iris,
    Dum ferus hic stellas protegit, ille rapit!
Dum vulsos montes ceu tela reciproca torquent,
    Et non mortali desuper igne pluunt,
Stat dubius cui se parti concedat Olympus,
    Et metuit pugnæ non superesse suæ.
At simul in cœlis Messi ˀnsignis fulgent,
    Et currus animes, armaque digna Deo,
Horrendumque rotæ strident, et sæva rotarum
    Erumpunt torvis fulgura luminibus,
Et flammæ vibrant, et vera tonitrua rauco
    Admistis flammis insonuere polo,
Excidit attonitis mens omnis, et impetus omnis,

Et cassis dextris irrita tela cadunt;
Ad pœnas fugiunt, et, ceu foret Orcus asylum,
   Infernis certant condere se tenebris.
Cedite, Romani scriptores; cedite, Graii;
   Et quos fama recens vel celebravit anus:
Hæc quicunque leget tantum cecinisse putabit
   Mæonidem ranas, Virgilium culices.

                                        S.B., M.D.

In Paradisum Amissam
On Paradise Lost, by John Milton, the Greatest Poet.

You who read Paradise Lost, the sublime poem of the great Milton, what do you read except the whole poem? That book contains all things, the first beginnings of all things, their destinies and their final ends. The innermost chambers of the great world are thrown open and whatever in the world lies hidden is described: the lands and the stretches of sea, the depths of the heavens, and the sulphurous, flame-vomiting den of Erebus; all that dwell on earth, in the sea, and in dark Tartarus and in the bright kingdom of highest heaven; whatever is confined anywhere by any bounds, and also boundless chaos and boundless God, and more that is boundless, if anything be more without limits, love among men united in Christ. Who that had hoped for this would believe that it would ever be written? And yet the land of Britain reads these things today. O, what leaders in war, what arms, appear! What fearful battles he sings on the war-trumpet! Celestial armies and heaven in conflict! What a battle, fit for the celestial fields! What a Lucifer, bearing ethereal armour, and as he walks, hardly inferior to Michael himself! With what great and deadly anger do they join battle. While the latter fiercely defends the stars the former assaults. While they fling uprooted mountains at each other as darts, rain falls from above with immortal fire. Olympus stands doubtful to which side it will submit, and fears that it may not survive its own battle. But as soon as the standards of the Messiah glisten in the heavens with living chariots and armour worthy of God, the wheels creak horribly and fierce flashes burst forth from savage eyes, the flames threaten and real thunder mixed with flames resounds hoarsely in the heavens. All the boldness and fury of the amazed foe fails, and useless weapons fall from hands that have lost all strength. They flee to their punishments as if Orcus were a refuge and they struggle to hide themselves in the infernal darkness. Yield writers of Rome, yield writers of Greece and those whom fame, recent or ancient, has celebrated. Who reads this poem will think Maeonides sang of frogs, Virgil of gnats.

[The author of the poem was probably Milton's physician friend, Dr Samuel Barrow. The last line refers to the pseudo-Homeric *Batrachomyomachia* ('Battle of the Frogs and Mice') and to Virgil's *Culex* ('Gnat').]

ON PARADISE LOST

When I beheld the poet blind, yet bold,
In slender book his vast design unfold –
Messiah crowned, God's reconciled decree,
Rebelling angels, the forbidden tree,
Heaven, hell, earth, chaos, all – the argument   5
Held me a while misdoubting his intent,
That he would ruin (for I saw him strong)
The sacred truths to fable and old song
(So Samson groped the temple's posts in spite),
The world o'erwhelming to revenge his sight.   10

Yet, as I read, soon growing less severe,
I liked his project, the success did fear –
Through that wide field how he his way should find
O'er which lame faith leads understanding blind;
Lest he perplexed the things he would explain,   15
And what was easy he should render vain.

Or, if a work so infinite he spanned,
Jealous I was that some less skilful hand
(Such as disquiet always what is well,
And by ill-imitating would excel)   20
Might hence presume the whole creation's day
To change in scenes, and show it in a play.

Pardon me, mighty poet; nor despise
My causeless, yet not impious, surmise.
But I am now convinced, and none will dare   25
Within thy labours to pretend a share.
Thou hast not missed one thought that could be fit,
And all that was improper dost omit;
So that no room is here for writers left,
But to detect their ignorance or theft.   30

That majesty which through thy work doth reign
Draws the devout, deterring the profane.
And things divine thou treat'st of in such state
As them preserves, and thee, inviolate.
At once delight and horror on us seize;   35
Thou sing'st with so much gravity and ease,

9] Milton had published *SA* in 1671.
18-22] The lines allude to Dryden, to whom (according to John Aubrey) Milton
had granted permission to 'putt his Paradise Lost into a drama in rhymne'.

And above human flight dost soar aloft
With plume so strong, so equal, and so soft.
The bird named from the paradise you sing
So never flags, but always keeps on wing.   40
    Where could'st thou words of such a compass find?
Whence furnish such a vast expense of mind?
Just heaven, thee like Tiresias to requite,
Rewards with prophecy thy loss of sight.
    Well might'st thou scorn thy readers to allure   45
With tinkling rhyme, of thy own sense secure;
While the Town-Bayes writes all the while and spells,
And, like a pack-horse, tires without his bells.
Their fancies like our bushy points appear;
The poets tag them, we for fashion wear.   50
I too, transported by the mode, offend,
And, while I meant to praise thee, must commend.
Thy verse, created, like thy theme sublime,
In number, weight, and measure, needs not rhyme.

                                                       A.M.

39–40] Birds of Paradise were popularly believed to have no feet, and therefore
    to be perpetually in flight.
43 Tiresias] See *PL* III 36n.
47 Bayes] a popular nickname for Dryden, originating in the satire on Dryden
    in Buckingham's *The Rehearsal* (1672).
45–54] Rhyme was a much-debated subject at the time. Marvell alludes
    specifically to Milton's remarks on the subject in his note on 'The Verse'
    (p. 148).
49 bushy points] tasselled hose-fasteners.
    A.M.] Andrew Marvell.

THE PRINTER TO THE READER

Courteous reader, there was no argument at first intended to the book, but for the satisfaction of many that have desired it, I have procured it, and withal a reason of that which stumbled many others: why the poem rhymes not.

S. Simmons

THE VERSE

The measure is English heroic verse without rhyme, as that of Homer in Greek, and of Virgil in Latin – rhyme being no necessary adjunct or true ornament of poem or good verse, in longer works especially, but the invention of a barbarous age, to set off wretched matter and lame metre; graced indeed since by the use of some famous modern poets, carried away by custom, but much to their own vexation, hindrance, and constraint to express many things otherwise, and for the most part worse, than else they would have expressed them. Not without cause therefore some both Italian and Spanish poets[1] of prime note have rejected rhyme both in longer and shorter works, as have also long since our best English tragedies, as a thing of itself, to all judicious ears, trivial and of no true musical delight; which consists only in apt numbers, fit quantity of syllables, and the sense variously drawn out from one verse into another, not in the jingling sound of like endings – a fault avoided by the learned ancients both in poetry and all good oratory. This neglect then of rhyme so little is to be taken for a defect, though it may seem so perhaps to vulgar readers, that it rather is to be esteemed an example set, the first in English, of ancient liberty recovered to heroic poem from the troublesome and modern bondage of rhyming.

---

[1] Spanish poets] Spanish poetry was normally rhymed, but blank verse (*versos sueltos*) was introduced into Spain (at the invitation of the Venetian ambassador) by Joan Boscà Almugaver in *Leandro* (1543), and was subsequently used by Boscà's friend Garcilaso de la Vega; it was later popularised by Cervantes' friend Francisco de Figueroa. The form was never acclimatised, and was always seen as a conscious imitation of the Italian *versi sciolti*.

PARADISE LOST

BOOK I

THE ARGUMENT

This first book proposes, first in brief, the whole subject – man's disobedience, and the loss thereupon of Paradise, wherein he was placed: then touches the prime cause of his fall – the serpent, or rather Satan in the serpent; who, revolting from God, and drawing to his side many legions of angels, was, by the command of God, driven out of heaven, with all his crew, into the great deep. Which action passed over, the poem hastens into the midst of things; presenting Satan, with his angels, now fallen into hell – described here not in the centre (for heaven and earth may be supposed as yet not made, certainly not yet accursed) but in a place of utter darkness, fitliest called Chaos. Here Satan, with his angels lying on the burning lake, thunderstruck and astonished, after a certain space recovers, as from confusion; calls up him who, next in order and dignity, lay by him; they confer of their miserable fall. Satan awakens all his legions, who lay till then in the same manner confounded; they rise: their numbers; array of battle; their chief leaders named, according to the idols known afterwards in Canaan and the countries adjoining. To these Satan directs his speech; comforts them with hope yet of regaining heaven; but tells them, lastly, of a new world and new kind of creature to be created, according to an ancient prophecy, or report, in heaven – for that angels were long before this visible creation was the opinion of many ancient fathers. To find out the truth of this prophecy, and what to determine thereon, he refers to a full council. What his associates thence attempt. Pandemonium, the palace of Satan, rises, suddenly built out of the deep: the infernal peers there sit in council.

Of man's first disobedience, and the fruit
Of that forbidden tree whose mortal taste
Brought death into the world, and all our woe,
With loss of Eden, till one greater man
Restore us, and regain the blissful seat,   5
Sing, heavenly Muse, that, on the secret top
Of Oreb, or of Sinai, didst inspire

---

1 fruit] means 'fruit' and 'result'.
4 greater man] Jesus. See Rom. v. 12, 19.
6 heavenly Muse] Urania. See *PL* VII 1n.
7–8] Moses saw the burning bush on Mount Horeb (Exod. iii). There is some confusion in the Pentateuch about the mountain on which Moses received the tablets of the law, for the names Sinai and Horeb seem to be interchangeable. See Exod. xix. 16–25 and Deut. iv. 10–13. The 'chosen seed' is Israel, whom Moses taught about the creation in Genesis.

That shepherd who first taught the chosen seed
In the beginning how the heavens and earth
Rose out of chaos: or, if Zion hill   10
Delight thee more, and Siloa's brook that flowed
Fast by the oracle of God, I thence
Invoke thy aid to my adventurous song,
That with no middle flight intends to soar
Above the Aonian mount, while it pursues   15
Things unattempted yet in prose or rhyme.
And chiefly thou, O Spirit, that dost prefer
Before all temples the upright heart and pure,
Instruct me, for thou know'st; thou from the first
Wast present, and, with mighty wings outspread   20
Dove-like sat'st brooding on the vast abyss,
And mad'st it pregnant: what in me is dark
Illumine, what is low raise and support:
That, to the height of this great argument,
I may assert eternal providence,   25
And justify the ways of God to men.
    Say first – for heaven hides nothing from thy view,
Nor the deep tract of hell – say first what cause
Moved our grand parents, in that happy state,
Favoured of heaven so highly, to fall off   30
From their creator, and transgress his will
For one restraint, lords of the world besides.
Who first seduced them to that foul revolt?
    The infernal serpent; he it was whose guile,
Stirred up with envy and revenge, deceived   35
The mother of mankind, what time his pride
Had cast him out from heaven, with all his host
Of rebel angels, by whose aid, aspiring
To set himself in glory above his peers,
He trusted to have equalled the most high,   40
If he opposed, and, with ambitious aim
Against the throne and monarchy of God,
Raised impious war in heaven and battle proud,

---

10 Zion hill] one of the hills of Jerusalem, and the site of the temple.
11 Siloa] a pool near the temple in Jerusalem. See Isa. viii. 6, John ix. 7, 11.
15 Aonian mount] Helicon, home of the muses.
16] An ironic translation of a line in the second octave of Ariosto's *Orlando
    Furioso*: *'Cosa non detta in prosa mai, né in rima'*.
21] Gen. i. 2; Luke iii. 22.
34 infernal serpent] Satan. See Rev. xii. 9.
38–48] a tissue of Biblical phrases (e.g. Isa. xiv. 13–15, Luke x. 18, Rev. xvii. 8,
    II Pet. ii. 4, Jude 6).

With vain attempt. Him the almighty power
Hurled headlong flaming from the ethereal sky,   45
With hideous ruin and combustion, down
To bottomless perdition, there to dwell
In adamantine chains and penal fire,
Who durst defy the omnipotent to arms.
    Nine times the space that measures day and night   50
To mortal men, he with his horrid crew
Lay vanquished, rolling in the fiery gulf,
Confounded, though immortal: but his doom
Reserved him to more wrath; for now the thought
Both of lost happiness and lasting pain   55
Torments him; round he throws his baleful eyes,
That witnessed huge affliction and dismay,
Mixed with obdurate pride and steadfast hate;
At once, as far as angels ken, he views
The dismal situation waste and wild: 60
A dungeon horrible, on all sides round,
As one great furnace flamed, yet from those flames
No light, but rather darkness visible
Served only to discover sights of woe,
Regions of sorrow, doleful shades, where peace   65
And rest can never dwell, hope never comes
That comes to all, but torture without end
Still urges, and a fiery deluge, fed
With ever-burning sulphur unconsumed:
Such place eternal justice had prepared   70
For those rebellious; here their prison ordained
In utter darkness, and their portion set,
As far removed from God and light of heaven
As from the centre thrice to the utmost pole.
O how unlike the place from whence they fell!   75
There the companions of his fall, o'erwhelmed
With floods and whirlwinds of tempestuous fire,
He soon discerns; and weltering by his side,
One next himself in power, and next in crime,
Long after known in Palestine, and named   80

50] Recalls the fall of the Titans, who according to Hesiod fell nine days and
    nights into Tartarus (*Theogony* 664–735).
57 witnessed] bore witness to.
59 angels] May be a possessive, in the which case 'ken' would be a noun.
66] Alludes to the inscription over the gate of Hell in Dante's *Inferno* iii. 9,
    Lasciate ogni speranza voi ch'entrate ('Abandon all hope, you who enter
    here').
72 utter] outer.

Beëlzebub. To whom the arch-enemy,
And thence in heaven called Satan, with bold words
Breaking the horrid silence, thus began:
   'If thou beest he – but O how fallen! How changed
From him, who in the happy realms of light,   85
Clothed with transcendent brightness, didst outshine
Myriads, though bright – if he whom mutual league,
United thoughts and counsels, equal hope
And hazard in the glorious enterprise,
Joined with me once, now misery hath joined   90
In equal ruin; into what pit thou seest
From what height fallen: so much the stronger proved
He with his thunder: and till then who knew
The force of those dire arms? Yet not for those,
Nor what the potent victor in his rage   95
Can else inflict, do I repent, or change,
Though changed in outward lustre, that fixed mind,
And high disdain from sense of injured merit,
That with the mightiest raised me to contend,
And to the fierce contentions brought along   100
Innumerable force of spirits armed,
That durst dislike his reign, and, me preferring,
His utmost power with adverse power opposed
In dubious battle on the plains of heaven,
And shook his throne. What though the field be lost?   105
All is not lost – the unconquerable will,
And study of revenge, immortal hate,
And courage never to submit or yield:
And what is else not to be overcome?
That glory never shall his wrath or might   110
Extort from me. To bow and sue for grace
With suppliant knee, and deify his power
Who, from the terror of this arm, so late
Doubted his empire – that were low indeed;
That were an ignominy and shame beneath   115
This downfall; since, by fate, the strength of gods,
And this empyreal substance, cannot fail;
Since, through experience of this great event,

---

81 Beëlzebub] 'prince of devils' (Matt. xii. 24), and in the O.T. a Philistine god
    (see *SA* 1231 and II Kings i. 2) whose name means 'Lord of the Flies' in
    Hebrew.
82 Satan] the name means 'adversary', or 'one who plots against another' in
    Hebrew. See the A.V. marginal note to Job i. 6.
84–5] Isa. xiv. 12, *Aeneid* ii. 274–5.
114 Doubted] feared for.

In arms not worse, in foresight much advanced,
We may with more successful hope resolve   120
To wage by force or guile eternal war,
Irreconcilable to our grand foe,
Who now triumphs, and in the excess of joy
Sole reigning holds the tyranny of heaven.'
  So spake the apostate angel, though in pain,   125
Vaunting aloud, but racked with deep despair;
And him thus answered soon his bold compeer:
  'O Prince, O chief of many thronèd powers
That led the embattled seraphim to war
Under thy conduct, and in dreadful deeds   130
Fearless, endangered heaven's perpetual king,
And put to proof his high supremacy,
Whether upheld by strength, or chance, or fate,
Too well I see and rue the dire event
That, with sad overthrow and foul defeat,   135
Hath lost us heaven, and all this mighty host
In horrible destruction laid thus low,
As far as gods and heavenly essences
Can perish: for the mind and spirit remains
Invincible, and vigour soon returns,   140
Though all our glory extinct, and happy state
Here swallowed up in endless misery.
But what if he our conqueror (whom I now
Of force believe almighty, since no less
Than such could have o'erpowered such force as ours)   145
Have left us this our spirit and strength entire,
Strongly to suffer and support our pains,
That we may so suffice his vengeful ire,
Or do him mightier service as his thralls
By right of war, whate'er his business be,   150
Here in the heart of hell to work in fire,
Or do his errands in the gloomy deep?
What can it then avail though yet we feel
Strength undiminished, or eternal being
To undergo eternal punishment?'   155
  Whereto with speedy words the arch-fiend replied:
'Fallen cherub, to be weak is miserable,
Doing or suffering: but of this be sure –
To do aught good never will be our task,
But ever to do ill our sole delight,   160

---

128 powers] one of the orders of angels; seraphim (l.129) and cherubim (l. 157)
    are other orders.

As being the contrary to his high will
Whom we resist. If then his providence
Out of our evil seek to bring forth good,
Our labour must be to pervert that end,
And out of good still to find means of evil;   165
Which ofttimes may succeed so as perhaps
Shall grieve him, if I fail not, and disturb
His inmost counsels from their destined aim.
But see, the angry victor hath recalled
His ministers of vengeance and pursuit   170
Back to the gates of heaven: the sulphurous hail,
Shot after us in storm, o'erblown hath laid
The fiery surge that from the precipice
Of heaven received us falling; and the thunder,
Winged with red lightning and impetuous rage,   175
Perhaps hath spent his shafts, and ceases now
To bellow through the vast and boundless deep.
Let us not slip the occasion, whether scorn
Or satiate fury yield it from our foe.
Seest thou yon dreary plain, forlorn and wild,   180
The seat of desolation, void of light,
Save what the glimmering of these livid flames
Casts pale and dreadful? Thither let us tend
From off the tossing of these fiery waves;
There rest, if any rest can harbour there;   185
And, re-assembling our afflicted powers,
Consult how we may henceforth most offend
Our enemy, our own loss how repair,
How overcome this dire calamity,
What reinforcement we may gain from hope,   190
If not, what resolution from despair.'
   Thus Satan, talking to his nearest mate,
With head uplift above the wave, and eyes
That sparkling blazed; his other parts besides
Prone on the flood, extended long and large,   195
Lay floating many a rood, in bulk as huge
As whom the fables name of monstrous size,
Titanian or Earth-born, that warred on Jove,
Briareos or Typhon, whom the den

167 fail] err.
187 offend] injure.
197-200] Briareos was a Titan, Typhon, a Giant; both were sons of Gaea
   (Mother Earth). The Titans and the Giants (the two races were sometimes
   confused in antiquity) rebelled against Zeus. A later Christian tradition
   established the parallel between these rebellions and the rebellion of Satan.

By ancient Tarsus held, or that sea-beast   200
Leviathan, which God of all his works
Created hugest that swim the ocean stream;
Him, haply slumbering on the Norway foam,
The pilot of some small night-foundered skiff,
Deeming some island, oft, as seamen tell,   205
With fixèd anchor in his scaly rind,
Moors by his side under the lee, while night
Invests the sea, and wishèd morn delays;
So stretched out huge in length the arch-fiend lay,
Chained on the burning lake; nor ever thence   210
Had risen, or heaved his head, but that the will
And high permission of all-ruling heaven
Left him at large to his own dark designs,
That with reiterated crimes he might
Heap on himself damnation, while he sought   215
Evil to others, and enraged might see
How all his malice served but to bring forth
Infinite goodness, grace and mercy, shown
On man by him seduced, but on himself
Treble confusion, wrath, and vengeance poured.   220
  Forthwith upright he rears from off the pool
His mighty stature; on each hand the flames
Driven backward slope their pointing spires, and, rolled
In billows, leave i' the midst a horrid vale.
Then with expanded wings he steers his flight   225
Aloft, incumbent on the dusky air,
That felt unusual weight; till on dry land
He lights – if it were land that ever burned
With solid, as the lake with liquid fire,
And such appeared in hue as when the force   230

200–8] Leviathan, the sea-monster of Job xli, was often thought to be a whale.
    The story of the illusory island occurs in *Physiologus* ('The Naturalist'), the
    moralizing anecdotes of which were translated into the main languages of
    Europe and the Near East. Many versions of the story exist in medieval
    and Renaissance art and literature.
202 ocean stream] See *Comus* 97n.
208 Invests] covers, envelops.
224 horrid] The primary sense is 'bristling' (with 'pointing spires'), but the
    word probably carries the secondary sense of 'abominable'. The image
    ironically echoes Exod. xiv. 21–2.
230–7] The lines conflate Virgil's and Ovid's descriptions of Etna (*Aeneid* iii.
    570–7, *Metamorphoses* xv. 298–306). In antiquity and in the Renaissance
    volcanoes and earthquakes were attributed to the periodic escape of winds
    trapped in the earth. Pelorus is the promontory at the north-eastern corner
    of Sicily, near Etna. 'Sublimed' is an alchemical term meaning 'vaporized'.

Of subterranean wind transports a hill
Torn from Pelorus, or the shattered side
Of thundering Etna, whose combustible
And fuelled entrails, thence conceiving fire,
Sublimed with mineral fury, aid the winds,   235
And leave a singèd bottom all involved
With stench and smoke: such resting found the sole
Of unblessed feet. Him followed his next mate,
Both glorying to have scaped the Stygian flood
As gods, and by their own recovered strength,   240
Not by the sufferance of supernal power.
    'Is this the region, this the soil, the clime,'
Said then the lost archangel, 'this the seat
That we must change for heaven, this mournful
        gloom
For that celestial light? Be it so, since he   245
Who now is sovereign can dispose and bid
What shall be right: farthest from him is best,
Whom reason hath equalled, force hath made supreme
Above his equals. Farewell, happy fields,
Where joy for ever dwells; hail, horrors, hail,   250
Infernal world; and thou, profoundest hell,
Receive thy new possessor – one who brings
A mind not to be changed by place or time.
The mind is its own place, and in itself
Can make a heaven of hell, a hell of heaven.   255
What matter where, if I be still the same,
And what I should be, all, but less than he
Whom thunder hath made greater? Here at least
We shall be free; the almighty hath not built
Here for his envy, will not drive us hence: 260
Here we may reign secure; and, in my choice,
To reign is worth ambition, though in hell:
Better to reign in hell than serve in heaven.
But wherefore let we then our faithful friends,
The associates and co-partners of our loss,   265

239 Stygian] here means 'dark'. Cf. *Comus* l.132.
254-5] The heresy that heaven and hell are merely states of mind was devised
    by Amalric of Bena (near Chartres), a scholastic philosopher whose
    doctrines were condemned in 1204, and probably has its ultimate origins in
    Stoic doctrine.
263] Cf. Milton's translation of Psalm lxxxiv. 10 (ll 37-40). The sentiment is
    virtually proverbial in antiquity and the Renaissance.

Lie thus astonished on the oblivious pool,
And call them not to share with us their part
In this unhappy mansion, or once more
With rallied arms to try what may be yet
Regained in heaven, or what more lost in hell?'   270
    So Satan spake, and him Beëlzebub
Thus answered: 'Leader of those armies bright
Which, but the omnipotent, none could have foiled;
If once they hear that voice, their liveliest pledge
Of hope in fears and dangers – heard so oft   275
In worst extremes, and on the perilous edge
Of battle, when it raged, in all assaults
Their surest signal – they will soon resume
New courage and revive, though now they lie
Grovelling and prostrate on yon lake of fire,   280
As we erewhile, astounded and amazed;
No wonder, fallen such a pernicious height.'
    He scarce had ceased when the superior fiend
Was moving toward the shore; his ponderous shield,
Ethereal temper, massy, large, and round,   285
Behind him cast: the broad circumference
Hung on his shoulders like the moon, whose orb
Through optic glass the Tuscan artist views
At evening, from the top of Fesolè,
Or in Valdarno, to descry new lands,   290
Rivers, or mountains, in her spotty globe.
His spear – to equal which the tallest pine
Hewn on Norwegian hills, to be the mast
Of some great ammiral, were but a wand –
He walked with, to support uneasy steps   295
Over the burning marl, not like those steps
On heaven's azure; and the torrid clime
Smote on him sore besides, vaulted with fire;
Nathless he so endured, till on the beach

---

266 oblivious pool] Milton's 'forgetful lake' (II 74) is an adaptation of the river
    Lethe of the classical underworld, for the devil's loss of memory is
    temporary. Cf. the classic version of Lethe in *PL* II 582-6, 604-14.
276 edge] carries the Latin sense of 'front line'.
285 Ethereal temper] tempered by celestial fire.
288-91] The 'Tuscan artist' (i.e. scientist) is Galileo, whom Milton visited in
    1638 or 1639. Fiesole (Fesolè) overlooks the valley of Arno (Valdarno).
    Cf. III 588-90, V 261-3.
294 ammiral] flagship.
296 marl] a kind of soil.
299 Nathless] nevertheless.

Of that inflamèd sea he stood, and called   300
His legions – angel forms, who lay entranced
Thick as autumnal leaves that strew the brooks
In Vallombrosa, where the Etrurian shades
High over-arched embower; or scattered sedge
Afloat, when with fierce winds Orion armed   305
Hath vexed the Red Sea coast, whose waves o'erthrew
Busiris and his Memphian chivalry,
While with perfidious hatred they pursued
The sojourners of Goshen, who beheld
From the safe shore their floating carcasses   310
And broken chariot-wheels: so thick bestrewn,
Abject and lost, lay these, covering the flood,
Under amazement of their hideous change.
He called so loud that all the hollow deep
Of hell resounded: 'Princes, potentates,   315
Warriors, the flower of heaven – once yours; now lost,
If such astonishment as this can seize
Eternal spirits; or have ye chosen this place
After the toil of battle to repose
Your wearied virtue, for the ease you find   320
To slumber here, as in the vales of heaven?
Or in this abject posture have ye sworn
To adore the conqueror, who now beholds
Cherub and seraph rolling in the flood
With scattered arms and ensigns, till anon   325
His swift pursuers from heaven-gates discern
The advantage, and, descending, tread us down
Thus drooping, or with linkèd thunderbolts
Transfix us to the bottom of this gulf?
Awake, arise, or be for ever fallen.'   330
    They heard, and were abashed, and up they sprung
Upon the wing, as when men wont to watch,
On duty sleeping found by whom they dread,
Rouse and bestir themselves ere well awake.
Nor did they not perceive the evil plight   335
In which they were, or the fierce pains not feel;

303] Vallombrosa is a wooded valley in Tuscany (ancient Etruria); on the leaf
    simile cf. *Iliad* vi 146, *Aeneid* vi 309.
305] The late rising of Orion was anciently thought to portend stormy weather.
306-11] The Pharaoh of Exod. xiv was sometimes identified with the mythical
    king Busiris. Memphis was the ancient capital of Egypt; Goshen was the
    area east of the Nile where the Israelites lived. The connection between the
    destruction of Pharaoh's cavalry and Orion may have been suggested by
    Amos v. 8.

Yet to their general's voice they soon obeyed
Innumerable. As when the potent rod
Of Amram's son, in Egypt's evil day,
Waved round the coast, up called a pitchy cloud   340
Of locusts, warping on the eastern wind,
That o'er the realm of impious Pharaoh hung
Like night, and darkened all the land of Nile;
So numberless were those bad angels seen
Hovering on wing under the cope of hell,   345
'Twixt upper, nether, and surrounding fires;
Till, as a signal given, the uplifted spear
Of their great sultan waving to direct
Their course, in even balance down they light
On the firm brimstone, and fill all the plain: 350
A multitude like which the populous North
Poured never from her frozen loins to pass
Rhene or the Danaw, when her barbarous sons
Came like a deluge on the South, and spread
Beneath Gibraltar to the Libyan sands.   355
Forthwith, from every squadron and each band,
The heads and leaders thither haste where stood
Their great commander – godlike shapes, and forms
Excelling human, princely dignities,
And powers that erst in heaven sat on thrones;   360
Though of their names in heavenly records now
Be no memorial, blotted out and razed
By their rebellion from the Books of Life.
Nor had they yet among the sons of Eve
Got them new names, till wandering o'er the earth,   365
Through God's high sufferance for the trial of man,
By falsities and lies the greatest part
Of mankind they corrupted to forsake
God their creator, and the invisible
Glory of him that made them, to transform   370
Oft to the image of a brute, adorned
With gay religions full of pomp and gold,

338–43] Moses was the son of Amram. See Exod. x. 12–15, and cf. *PL* XII
    184–8.
351–5] refers to the barbarian invasions of late antiquity. Rhene is the Rhine,
    Danaw the Danube.
363 Books of Life] Rev. iii. 5, xx. 15, xxi. 27; Exod. xxxii. 32–3.
365 new names] an ironic contrast to Rev. iii. 12, for the new names of the fallen
    angels are those of the idols of l.375.
368–71] Rom. i. 23.
372 religions] religious rites.

And devils to adore for deities:
Then were they known to men by various names,
And various idols through the heathen world.   375
     Say, Muse, their names then known, who first, who
          last,
Roused from the slumber on that fiery couch,
At their great emperor's call, as next in worth
Came singly where he stood on the bare strand,
While the promiscuous crowd stood yet aloof.   380
     The chief were those who, from the pit of hell
Roaming to seek their prey on earth, durst fix
Their seats, long after, next the seat of God,
Their altars by his altar, gods adored
Among the nations round, and durst abide   385
Jehovah thundering out of Zion, throned
Between the cherubim; yea, often placed
Within his sanctuary itself their shrines,
Abominations; and with cursed things
His holy rites and solemn feasts profaned,   390
And with their darkness durst affront his light.
First, Moloch, horrid king, besmeared with blood
Of human sacrifice, and parents' tears;
Though for the noise of drums and timbrels loud,
Their children's cries unheard that passed through fire 395
To his grim idol. Him the Ammonite
Worshipped in Rabba and her watery plain,
In Argob and in Basan, to the stream
Of utmost Arnon. Nor content with such
Audacious neighbourhood, the wisest heart   400
Of Solomon he led by fraud to build
His temple right against the temple of God
On that opprobrious hill, and made his grove

376] The Homeric and Virgilian catalogues which Milton is about to imitate
     begin with appeals to the muse (*Iliad* ii 484, *Aeneid* vii 641).
386 Jehovah] see *Areopagitica*, p. 590, n.6.
387 Between the cherubim] Cf. Milton's translation of Psalm lxxx. 1.
392] Moloch means 'king' in Hebrew. See *Nativity* 205-12 and 205n.
396-7] Rabba, the royal city of the Ammonites, was conquered by David (II
     Sam. xii. 26-31).
398-9] The Israelites conquered the Ammonites of Argob and Basan, parts of
     the kingdom of Og, as far as the border with the Moabites, the stream of
     Arnon (Deut. iii. 1-13).
400-3] I Kings xi. 7. The 'opprobrious hill' is the Mount of Olives, the 'hill of
     scandal' of l.416, the 'offensive mountain' of 1.443, and the 'mount of
     corruption' of II Kings xxiii. 13.

The pleasant valley of Hinnom, Tophet thence
And black Gehenna called, the type of hell.   405
Next Chemos, the obscene dread of Moab's sons,
From Aroer to Nebo and the wild
Of southmost Abarim; in Hesebon
And Horonaim, Seon's realm, beyond
The flowery dale of Sibma clad with vines,   410
And Elealè to the Asphaltic Pool:
Peor his other name, when he enticed
Israel in Sittim, on their march from Nile,
To do him wanton rites, which cost them woe.
Yet thence his lustful orgies he enlarged   415
Even to that hill of scandal, by the grove
Of Moloch homicide, lust hard by hate,
Till good Josiah drove them thence to hell.
With these came they who, from the bordering flood
Of old Euphrates to the brook that parts   420
Egypt from Syrian ground, had general names
Of Baälim and Ashtaroth – those male,
These feminine. For spirits, when they please,
Can either sex assume, or both; so oft
And uncompounded is their essence pure,   425
Not tied or manacled with joint or limb,
Nor founded on the brittle strength of bones,
Like cumbrous flesh; but in what shape they choose,
Dilated or condensed, bright or obscure,
Can execute their airy purposes,   430
And works of love or enmity fulfil.
For those the race of Israel oft forsook

404-5] II Kings xxiii. 10. The Greek word *Gehenna* (Matt. v. 29) derives from the Hebrew phrase which means 'valley of the son of Hinnom'.
406] I Kings xi. 7.
407-8] I Chron. v. 8. On Aroer see Deut. ii. 36 and Jer. xlviii. 19. Milton's Nebo may be the town in Moab, or the mountain from which Moses viewed the promised land; the city was near the Abarim mountains.
408-11] Isa. xv. 4-5, xvi. 8-9. Seon was an Amorite king: see Numbers xxi. 21-30. The 'Asphaltic Pool' is the Dead Sea, called *Asphaltites* by Josephus because of its deposits of bitumen.
412 Peor] See *Nativity* 197n.
412-14] Numbers xxv. 1-9. On the 'woe' see also I Cor. x. 8.
418] On Josiah see II Kings xxii-xxiii.
420 brook] Besor. I Sam. xxx. 9, 10, 21.
422-3] See *Nativity* 197n., 200n.; 'im' is normally a masculine plural inflection, 'oth' a feminine plural inflection.
432-3] I Sam. xv. 29.

Their living strength, and unfrequented left
His righteous altar, bowing lowly down
To bestial gods; for which their heads, as low   435
Bowed down in battle, sunk before the spear
Of despicable foes. With these in troop
Came Ashtoreth, whom the Phoenicians called
Astarte, queen of heaven, with crescent horns;
To whose bright image nightly by the moon   440
Sidonian virgins paid their vows and songs;
In Zion also not unsung, where stood
Her temple on the offensive mountain, built
By that uxorious king whose heart, though large,
Beguiled by fair idolatresses, fell   445
To idols foul. Thammuz came next behind,
Whose annual wound in Lebanon allured
The Syrian damsels to lament his fate
In amorous ditties all a summer's day,
While smooth Adonis from his native rock   450
Ran purple to the sea, supposed with blood
Of Thammuz yearly wounded: the love-tale
Infected Zion's daughters with like heat,
Whose wanton passions in the sacred porch
Ezekiel saw, when by the vision led   455
His eye surveyed the dark idolatries
Of alienated Judah. Next came one
Who mourned in earnest, when the captive ark
Maimed his brute image, head and hands lopped off,
In his own temple, on the groundsel edge,   460
Where he fell flat and shamed his worshippers:
Dagon his name, sea-monster, upward man
And downward fish; yet had his temple high
Reared in Azotus, dreaded through the coast
Of Palestine, in Gath and Ascalon,   465
And Accaron and Gaza's frontier bounds.

438-9] See *Nativity* 200n.
441 Sidonian] of Sidon, the Phoenician city.
444 king] Solomon, whose wives 'turned away his heart after other gods' (I
    Kings xi. 1-8).
446-57] See *Nativity* 204n. and Ezek. viii. 14. It is appropriate for Thammuz to
    follow Ashtoreth because Adonis (Thammuz) was the lover of
    Astarte-Aphrodite.
457-66] See *Nativity* 199n. 'Groundsel' (460) means 'threshold'.
464-6] The five cities of Philistia were Azotus (or Asdod), Gath, Ascalon,
    Accaron (or Ecron) and Gaza (or Azza). The forms in parentheses appear in
    SA.

Him followed Rimmon, whose delightful seat
Was fair Damascus, on the fertile banks
Of Abbana and Pharphar, lucid streams.
He also against the house of God was bold: 470
A leper once he lost, and gained a king –
Ahaz, his sottish conqueror, whom he drew
God's altar to disparage and displace
For one of Syrian mode, whereon to burn
His odious offerings, and adore the gods   475
Whom he had vanquished. After these appeared
A crew who, under names of old renown –
Osiris, Isis, Orus, and their train –
With monstrous shapes and sorceries abused
Fanatic Egypt and her priests to seek   480
Their wandering gods disguised in brutish forms
Rather than human. Nor did Israel scape
The infection, when their borrowed gold composed
The calf in Oreb; and the rebel king
Doubled that sin in Bethel and in Dan,   485
Likening his maker to the grazèd ox –
Jehovah, who, in one night, when he passed
From Egypt marching, equalled with one stroke
Both her first-born and all her bleating gods.
Belial came last; than whom a spirit more lewd   490
Fell not from heaven, or more gross to love
Vice for itself: to him no temple stood
Or altar smoked; yet who more oft than he
In temples and at altars, when the priest

467 Rimmon] a Syrian god.
468–71] In II Kings v Elisha tells the Syrian leper Naaman to wash in the
   Jordan, and Naaman replies (v. 12) 'Are not Abbana and Pharpar ['Phar-
   phar' in LXX and Vulgate] rivers of Damascus, better than all the waters
   of Israel?'
471–6] The king is Ahaz; see II Kings xvi.
478] See *Nativity* 212–13n.
482–4] Exod. xxxii; Psalm cvi. 19. The connection with Egypt is the traditional
   identification of the golden calf with the Egyptian Apis. On the gold having
   been 'borrowed' see Exod. xii. 35.
484–5] The 'rebel king' is Jereboam, who 'doubled that sin' by making two
   calves of gold, one for Bethel and one for Dan (I Kings xii. 28–9).
486] Psalm cvi. 19–20.
487–9] Exod. xii. 12–30.
490 Belial] The word *Belial* in Hebrew is not a proper name, but an abstraction,
   and can mean either 'worthlessness' or 'destruction'; it is usually rendered
   in the Vulgate as a proper name. In II Cor. vi. 15 the word appears as a
   proper name.
494–6] I Sam. ii. 12–25; 'the sons of Eli were sons of Belial' (v. 12).

Turns atheist, as did Eli's sons, who filled   495
With lust and violence the house of God?
In courts and palaces he also reigns,
And in luxurious cities, where the noise
Of riot ascends above their loftiest towers,
And injury and outrage; and when night   500
Darkens the streets, then wander forth the sons
Of Belial, flown with insolence and wine.
Witness the streets of Sodom, and that night
In Gibeah, when the hospitable door
Exposed a matron, to avoid worse rape.   505
　　These were the prime in order and in might:
The rest were long to tell, though far renowned,
The Ionian gods – of Javan's issue held
Gods, yet confessed later than heaven and earth,
Their boasted parents – Titan, heaven's first-born,   510
With his enormous brood, and birthright seized
By younger Saturn: he from mightier Jove,
His own and Rhea's son, like measure found;
So Jove usurping reigned; these, first in Crete
And Ida known, thence on the snowy top   515
Of cold Olympus ruled the middle air,
Their highest heaven; or on the Delphian cliff,
Or in Dodona, and through all the bounds
Of Doric land; or who with Saturn old
Fled over Adria to the Hesperian fields,   520
And o'er the Celtic roamed the utmost isles.
　　All these and more came flocking; but with looks
Downcast and damp; yet such wherein appeared
Obscure some glimpse of joy to have found their chief

---

502 flown] This archaic past-participle of 'flow' (not 'fly') literally means 'swollen' or 'in flood'.

503-5] Gen. xix. 4-11; Judges xix. 12-30.

508] Javan, the grandson of Noah (Gen. x. 1-5) was thought to be the progenitor of the Ionians.

509-21] Uranus and Gaea ('heaven and earth') were the parents of the twelve Titans, two of whom were Saturn and Rhea, who became the parents of Jove. Jove, who was born in a cave on Mount Ida in Crete, overthrew his father. Jove lived on Mt Olympus (on 'middle air' see *Fair Infant* 16n.), and was venerated at Dodona (in northern Greece), and throughout Greece ('Doric land'); his son Apollo revealed the will of the gods at Delphi. Saturn was eventually banished by Jove, and fled across the Adriatic (Adria) to Italy ('Hesperian fields'). Later he fled to France ('Celtic' fields) and finally to the 'utmost isles' the *ultima Thule* of classical antiquity. The story of Titan to which Milton alludes (l.510) exists only in a late tradition transmitted by Lactantius.

Not in despair, to have found themselves not lost   525
In loss itself; which on his countenance cast
Like doubtful hue; but he, his wonted pride
Soon recollecting, with high words, that bore
Semblance of worth, not substance, gently raised
Their fainting courage, and dispelled their fears.   530
Then straight commands that, at the warlike sound
Of trumpets loud and clarions, be upreared
His mighty standard; that proud honour claimed
Azazel as his right, a cherub tall:
Who forthwith from the glittering staff unfurled   535
The imperial ensign, which, full high advanced,
Shone like a meteor streaming to the wind,
With gems and golden lustre rich emblazed,
Seraphic arms and trophies; all the while
Sonorous metal blowing martial sounds: 540
At which the universal host upsent
A shout that tore hell's concave, and beyond
Frighted the reign of Chaos and old Night.
All in a moment through the gloom were seen
Ten thousand banners rise into the air,   545
With orient colours waving: with them rose
A forest huge of spears; and thronging helms
Appeared, and serried shields in thick array
Of depth immeasurable; anon they move
In perfect phalanx to the Dorian mood   550
Of flutes and soft recorders – such as raised
To height of noblest temper heroes old
Arming to battle, and instead of rage
Deliberate valour breathed, firm and unmoved
With dread of death to flight or foul retreat;   555
Nor wanting power to mitigate and swage
With solemn touches troubled thoughts, and chase
Anguish and doubt and fear and sorrow and pain

533-4] The word translated as 'scapegoat' in Lev. xvi refers in Hebrew to the
goat 'for Azazel', Azazel being the name of the spirit living in the wilderness
to whom the goat was sent. In a cabbalistic tradition with which Milton
was familiar the spirit Azazel is represented as an angel who serves in
Satan's army as a standard-bearer.
543 reign] realm.
550 Dorian mood] one of the musical modes of ancient Greece, characterized by
simplicity and solemnity.
551] The Spartan army went into battle to the music of the flute (whereas the
Romans used trumpets).
556 swage] assuage.

From mortal or immortal minds. Thus they,
Breathing united force with fixèd thought,   560
Moved on in silence to soft pipes that charmed
Their painful steps o'er the burnt soil; and now
Advanced in view they stand – a horrid front
Of dreadful length and dazzling arms, in guise
Of warriors old, with ordered spear and shield,   565
Awaiting what command their mighty chief
Had to impose: he through the armèd files
Darts his experienced eye, and soon traverse
The whole battalion views – their order due,
Their visages and stature as of gods;   570
Their number last he sums. And now his heart
Distends with pride, and, hardening in his strength,
Glories: for never, since created man,
Met such embodied force as, named with these,
Could merit more than that small infantry   575
Warred on by cranes – though all the giant brood
Of Phlegra with the heroic race were joined
That fought at Thebes and Ilium, on each side
Mixed with auxiliar gods; and what resounds
In fable or romance of Uther's son,   580
Begirt with British and Armoric knights;
And all who since, baptized or infidel,
Jousted in Aspramont, or Montalban,
Damasco, or Marocco, or Trebizond,
Or whom Bizerta sent from Afric shore   585

563 horrid] means both 'bristling' (with spears) and 'abominable'.

571-3] Dan. v. 20; 'since created man' is a Latin construction meaning 'since
man was created'.

575 small infantry] pygmies. On the attack on the pygmies by cranes see *Iliad*
iii 3-6; 'infantry' may be a pun.

577 Phlegra] The war of the giants and the gods took place on the Phlegraean
plains in Macedonia, and on the Phlegraean Fields near Naples.

578] The fates of the Theban princes and the tale of Troy ('Ilium') were the
central themes of Greek tragedy and epic.

580-1] Uther's son is King Arthur, some of whose knights were Breton
('Armoric').

583-4] Aspramont, a mountain range in Calabria, was celebrated in romances
as the site of one of Charlemagne's victories over the Saracens. Montalban,
in Languedoc, was the home of Rinaldo, whose story was a popular
romance subject; Damascus ('Damasco') is the scene of a tournament in one
of these romances, *Orlando Furioso* (xvii); Marocco is Marrakesh, a sulta-
nate in what is now Morocco; Trebizond (now Trabzon), the Byzantine city
on the Black Sea, was associated with the romance tradition.

585 Bizerta] a Tunisian port at which, according to Boiardo, the Saracens
assembled for their invasion of Spain (*Orlando Innamorato* ii).

When Charlemagne with all his peerage fell
By Fontarabbia. Thus far these beyond
Compare of mortal prowess, yet observed
Their dread commander; he above the rest
In shape and gesture proudly eminent,   590
Stood like a tower; his form had yet not lost
All her original brightness, nor appeared
Less than archangel ruined, and the excess
Of glory obscured: as when the sun new risen
Looks through the horizontal misty air   595
Shorn of his beams, or from behind the moon
In dim eclipse, disastrous twilight sheds
On half the nations, and with fear of change
Perplexes monarchs. Darkened so, yet shone
Above them all the archangel: but his face   600
Deep scars of thunder had intrenched, and care
Sat on his faded cheek, but under brows
Of dauntless courage, and considerate pride
Waiting revenge; cruel his eye, but cast
Signs of remorse and passion, to behold   605
The fellows of his crime, the followers rather
(Far other once beheld in bliss), condemned
For ever now to have their lot in pain –
Millions of spirits for his fault amerced
Of heaven, and from eternal splendours flung   610
For his revolt – yet faithful how they stood,
Their glory withered; as, when heaven's fire
Hath scathed the forest oaks or mountain pines,
With singèd top their stately growth, though bare,
Stands on the blasted heath. He now prepared   615
To speak; whereat their doubled ranks they bend
From wing to wing, and half enclose him round
With all his peers: attention held them mute.
Thrice he assayed, and thrice, in spite of scorn,
Tears, such as angels weep, burst forth: at last   620

586-7] No extant version of the Charlemagne legend records the death of
  Charlemagne and his peers (see *PR* III 337-43n.) at 'Fontarabbia' (Fuen-
  terrabia, on the coast of Spain by the French border), though several late
  versions record the massacre of Roland (Orlando) and his rearguard at
  Roncesvalles, about 40 miles inland. Milton may be alluding to the abortive
  visit of Charles II to Fuenterrabia after the failure of the Royalist uprising
  in August 1659.
597 disastrous] foreboding disaster.
603 considerate] considered, deliberate.
609 amerced] deprived.

Words interwove with sighs found out their way:
  'O myriads of immortal spirits, O powers
Matchless, but with the Almighty – and that strife
Was not inglorious, though the event was dire,
As this place testifies, and this dire change,   625
Hateful to utter; but what power of mind,
Foreseeing or presaging, from the depth
Of knowledge past or present, could have feared
How such united force of gods, how such
As stood like these, could ever know repulse?   630
For who can yet believe, though after loss,
That all these puissant legions, whose exile
Hath emptied heaven, shall fail to re-ascend,
Self-raised, and repossess their native seat?
For me be witness all the host of heaven   635
If counsels different, or danger shunned
By me, have lost our hopes. But he who reigns
Monarch in heaven, till then as one secure
Sat on his throne, upheld by old repute,
Consent or custom, and his regal state   640
Put forth at full, but still his strength concealed –
Which tempted our attempt, and wrought our fall.
Henceforth his might we know, and know our own,
So as not either to provoke, or dread
New war provoked: our better part remains   645
To work in close design, by fraud or guile,
What force effected not; that he no less
At length from us may find, who overcomes
By force hath overcome but half his foe.
Space may produce new worlds; whereof so rife   650
There went a flame in heaven that he ere long
Intended to create, and therein plant
A generation whom his choice regard
Should favour equal to the sons of heaven.
Thither, if but to pry, shall be perhaps   655
Our first eruption – thither, or elsewhere;
For this infernal pit shall never hold
Celestial spirits in bondage, nor the abyss
Long under darkness cover. But these thoughts
Full counsel must mature; peace is despaired,   660
For who can think submission? War, then, war
Open or understood, must be resolved.'
  He spake; and to confirm his words, outflew

---

636 different] may mean 'differing' or 'procrastinating'.

Millions of flaming swords, drawn from the thighs
Of mighty cherubim; the sudden blaze   665
Far round illumined hell; highly they raged
Against the highest, and fierce with graspèd arms
Clashed on their sounding shields the din of war,
Hurling defiance toward the vault of heaven.
    There stood a hill not far, whose grisly top   670
Belched fire and rolling smoke; the rest entire
Shone with a glossy scurf – undoubted sign
That in his womb was hid metallic ore,
The work of sulphur. Thither, winged with speed,
A numerous brigade hastened: as when bands   675
Of pioneers with spade and pickaxe armed,
Forerun the royal camp, to trench a field,
Or cast a rampart. Mammon led them on –
Mammon, the least erected spirit that fell   679
From heaven; for even in heaven his looks and thoughts
Were always downward bent, admiring more
The riches of heaven's pavement, trodden gold,
Than aught divine or holy else enjoyed
In vision beatific; by him first
Men also, and by his suggestion taught,   685
Ransacked the centre, and with impious hands
Rifled the bowels of their mother earth
For treasures better hid. Soon had his crew
Opened into the hill a spacious wound,
And digged out ribs of gold. Let none admire   690
That riches grow in hell; that soil may best
Deserve the precious bane. And here let those
Who boast in mortal things, and wondering tell
Of Babel, and the works of Memphian kings,
Learn how their greatest monuments of fame   695
And strength, and art, are easily outdone

678] *Mammon*, the Aramaic word for 'riches', is personified in Matt. vi. 24 and
    Luke xvi. 13. In late traditions this personification became identified with
    Plutus, the Greek god of wealth, and with Pluto, the god of the under-
    world. Burton made him prince of the ninth order of devils (*Anatomy of
    Melancholy* I ii I 2).
679 erected] exalted.
682] Rev. xxi. 21.
684 vision beatific] the scholastic term for the 'sight of God' promised in Matt.
    v. 8. Cf. 'On Time' 18, *PL* V 613, and *Areopagitica* p. 607.
684–92] See *Metamorphoses* i 137–42.
694] Alludes to the tower of Babel (cf. *PL* XII 38–62) and the pyramids of
    Egypt.

By spirits reprobate, and in an hour
What in an age they, with incessant toil
And hands innumerable, scarce perform.
Nigh on the plain, in many cells prepared,   700
That underneath had veins of liquid fire
Sluiced from the lake, a second multitude
With wondrous art founded the massy ore,
Severing each kind, and scummed the bullion-dross.
A third as soon had formed within the ground   705
A various mould, and from the boiling cells
By strange conveyance filled each hollow nook;
As in an organ, from one blast of wind,
To many a row of pipes the sound-board breathes.
Anon out of the earth a fabric huge   710
Rose like an exhalation, with the sound
Of dulcet symphonies and voices sweet –
Built like a temple, where pilasters round
Were set, and Doric pillars overlaid
With golden architrave; nor did there want   715
Cornice or frieze, with bossy sculptures graven;
The roof was fretted gold. Not Babylon
Nor great Alcairo such magnificence
Equalled in all their glories, to enshrine
Belus or Serapis their gods, or seat   720
Their kings, when Egypt with Assyria strove
In wealth and luxury. The ascending pile
Stood fixed her stately height; and straight the doors,
Opening their brazen folds discover, wide
Within, her ample spaces o'er the smooth   725
And level pavement: from the archèd roof,
Pendent by subtle magic, many a row
Of starry lamps and blazing cressets, fed
With naphtha and asphaltus, yielded light
As from a sky. The hasty multitude   730
Admiring entered; and the work some praise,
And some the architect: his hand was known
In heaven by many a towered structure high,
Where sceptred angels held their residence,
And sat as princes, whom the supreme king   735
Exalted to such power, and gave to rule,
Each in his hierarchy, the orders bright.

---

718 Alcairo] Memphis, the ancient city near modern Cairo.
720 Belus] Babylonian Baal.
    Serapis] The state god of Ptolemaic Egypt, a combination of Apsis and
    Osiris.

Nor was his name unheard or unadored
In ancient Greece; and in Ausonian land
Men called him Mulciber; and how he fell   740
From heaven they fabled, thrown by angry Jove
Sheer o'er the crystal battlements: from morn
To noon he fell, from noon to dewy eve,
A summer's day, and with the setting sun
Dropped from the zenith, like a falling star,   745
On Lemnos, the Aegean isle: thus they relate,
Erring; for he with his rebellious rout
Fell long before; nor aught availed him now
To have built in heaven high towers; nor did he scape
By all his engines, but was headlong sent,   750
With his industrious crew, to build in hell.
    Meanwhile the wingèd heralds, by command
Of sovereign power, with awful ceremony
And trumpet's sound, throughout the host proclaim
A solemn council forthwith to be held   755
At Pandemonium, the high capital
Of Satan and his peers; their summons called
From every band and squarèd regiment
By place or choice the worthiest; they anon
With hundreds and with thousands trooping came   760
Attended; all access was thronged; the gates
And porches wide, but chief the spacious hall
(Though like a covered field, where champions bold
Wont ride in armed, and at the soldan's chair
Defied the best of paynim chivalry   765
To mortal combat, or career with lance),
Thick swarmed, both on the ground and in the air,
Brushed with the hiss of rustling wings. As bees
In spring-time, when the sun with Taurus rides,
Pour forth their populous youth about the hive   770
In clusters; they among fresh dews and flowers

738-46] Mulciber (Vulcan), the god of fire and of arts for which fire is needed,
    was known in Greece as Hephaestus; see *Iliad*, i 588-95. In Augustan
    poetry 'Ausonia' is a synonym for Italy.
756 Pandemonium] Milton's coinage, probably formed from πάν (all) + δαίμον
    ('demon, evil spirit', especially in New Testament Greek) + ιον, a suffix
    which here suggests 'place'.
765 paynim] pagan.
766 career] a charge or encounter at a tournament.
768-75] A common metaphor in antiquity. See *Iliad* ii 87-90. *Aeneid* i 430-6,
    and especially Virgil's *Georgics* iv 149-227.
769] The sun enters the zodiacal sign of Taurus in April.

Fly to and fro, or on the smoothèd plank,
The suburb of their straw-built citadel,
New rubbed with balm, expatiate, and confer
Their state-affairs: so thick the airy crowd   775
Swarmed and were straitened; till, the signal given
Behold a wonder! They but now who seemed
In bigness to surpass Earth's giant sons,
Now less than smallest dwarfs, in narrow room
Throng numberless – like that pygmean race   780
Beyond the Indian mount, or fairy elves,
Whose midnight revels, by a forest side
Or fountain, some belated peasant sees,
Or dreams he sees, while overhead the moon
Sits arbitress, and nearer to the earth   785
Wheels her pale course: they, on their mirth and dance
Intent, with jocund music charm his ear;
At once with joy and fear his heart rebounds.
Thus incorporeal spirits to smallest forms
Reduced their shapes immense, and were at large,   790
Though without number still amidst the hall
Of that infernal court. But far within,
And in their own dimensions like themselves,
The great seraphic lords and cherubim
In close recess and secret conclave sat,   795
A thousand demi-gods on golden seats,
Frequent and full. After short silence then,
And summons read, the great consult began.

THE END OF THE FIRST BOOK

774 expatiate] to walk about at large.
780-1] Since antiquity the land of the pygmies was thought to be in eastern
    Asia. See l.575n.
783-4] See *Aeneid* vi 451-4.
795 close recess] secret meeting-place.
    conclave] here used to refer to an assembly of cardinals who have met to
    elect a pope.
797 Frequent] crowded.

BOOK II

THE ARGUMENT

The consultation begun, Satan debates whether another battle be
to be hazarded for the recovery of heaven: some advise it, others
dissuade; a third proposal is preferred, mentioned before by Satan
– to search the truth of that prophecy or tradition in heaven
concerning another world, and another kind of creature, equal, or
not much inferior, to themselves, about this time to be created;
their doubt who shall be sent on this difficult search: Satan, their
chief, undertakes alone the voyage; is honoured and applauded.
The council thus ended, the rest betake them several ways and to
several employments, as their inclinations lead them, to entertain
the time till Satan return. He passes on his journey to hell gates,
finds them shut, and who sat there to guard them; by whom at
length they are opened, and discover to him the great gulf between
hell and heaven. With what difficulty he passes through, directed
by Chaos, the power of that place, to the sight of this new world
which he sought.

High on a throne of royal state, which far
Outshone the wealth of Ormus and of Ind,
Or where the gorgeous East with richest hand
Showers on her kings barbaric pearl and gold,
Satan exalted sat, by merit raised   5
To that bad eminence; and, from despair
Thus high uplifted beyond hope, aspires
Beyond thus high, insatiate to pursue
Vain war with heaven; and, by success untaught,
His proud imaginations thus displayed: 10
   'Powers and dominions, deities of heaven –
For since no deep within her gulf can hold
Immortal vigour, though oppressed and fallen,
I give not heaven for lost. From this descent
Celestial virtues rising will appear   15
More glorious and more dread than from no fall,
And trust themselves to fear no second fate –
Me though just right, and the fixed laws of heaven,

---

2 Ormus] Hormuz, a Portuguese trading city on an island at the mouth of the
    Persian Gulf; it had been attacked by an English expedition in 1622, and
    some of the booty had been paid to King James and the Duke of
    Buckingham: it was thus associated with corruption.
9 success] result.
11–15 powers, dominions, virtues] three of the orders of angels.

Did first create your leader – next, free choice,
With what besides in council or in fight   20
Hath been achieved of merit – yet this loss,
Thus far at least recovered, hath much more
Established in a safe unenvied throne,
Yielded with full consent. The happier state
In heaven, which follows dignity, might draw   25
Envy from each inferior; but who here
Will envy whom the highest place exposes
Foremost to stand against the thunderer's aim
Your bulwark, and condemns to greatest share
Of endless pain? Where there is, then, no good   30
For which to strive, no strife can grow up there
From faction: for none sure will claim in hell
Precedence; none whose portion is so small
Of present pain that with ambitious mind
Will covet more. With this advantage, then,   35
To union, and firm faith, and firm accord,
More than can be in heaven, we now return
To claim our just inheritance of old,
Surer to prosper than prosperity
Could have assured us; and by what best way,   40
Whether of open war or covert guile,
We now debate: who can advise may speak.'
   He ceased; and next him Moloch, sceptred king,
Stood up – the strongest and the fiercest spirit
That fought in heaven, now fiercer by despair   45
His trust was with the eternal to be deemed
Equal in strength, and rather than be less
Cared not to be at all; with that care lost
Went all his fear: of God, or hell, or worse,
He recked not, and these words thereafter spake: 50
   'My sentence is for open war; of wiles,
More unexpert, I boast not: them let those
Contrive who need, or when they need; not now.
For while they sit contriving, shall the rest –
Millions that stand in arms, and longing wait   55
The signal to ascend – sit lingering here,
Heaven's fugitives, and for their dwelling place
Accept this dark opprobrious den of shame,
The prison of his tyranny who reigns
By our delay? No, let us rather choose,   60
Armed with hell flames and fury all at once

28 thunderer] classical epithet for Jove.
51 sentence] judgement, opinion.

O'er heaven's high towers to force resistless way,
Turning our tortures into horrid arms
Against the torturer; when to meet the noise
Of his almighty engine, he shall hear   65
Infernal thunder, and for lightning see
Black fire and horror shot with equal rage
Among his angels, and his throne itself
Mixed with Tartarean sulphur and strange fire,
His own invented torments. But perhaps   70
The way seems difficult, and steep to scale
With upright wing against a higher foe.
Let such bethink them, if the sleepy drench
Of that forgetful lake benumb not still,
That in our proper motion we ascend   75
Up to our native seat; descent and fall
To us is adverse. Who but felt of late,
When the fierce foe hung on our broken rear
Insulting, and pursued us through the deep,
With what compulsion and laborious flight   80
We sunk thus low? The ascent is easy, then;
The event is feared; should we again provoke
Our stronger, some worse way his wrath may find
To our destruction, if there be in hell
Fear to be worse destroyed; what can be worse   85
Than to dwell here, driven out from bliss, condemned
In this abhorrèd deep to utter woe;
Where pain of unextinguishable fire
Must exercise us without hope of end
The vassals of his anger, when the scourge   90
Inexorably, and the torturing hour,
Calls us to penance? More destroyed than thus,
We should be quite abolished, and expire.
What fear we then? What doubt we to incense
His utmost ire? Which, to the height enraged,   95
Will either quite consume us, and reduce
To nothing this essential – happier far
Than miserable to have eternal being –
Or, if our substance be indeed divine,
And cannot cease to be, we are at worst   100

69] Tartarus was the place of the damned in the classical underworld.
73–4] See I 266n.
79 Insulting] means both 'contemptuously abusing' and 'assaulting'.
81] Milton asserts the falseness of the boast by the allusion to *Aeneid* vi 126–9.
87 utter] acts as both verb and adjective.
89 exercise] afflict.
97 essential] essence.

On this side nothing; and by proof we feel
Our power sufficient to disturb his heaven,
And with perpetual inroads to alarm,
Though inaccessible, his fatal throne:
Which, if not victory, is yet revenge.'   105
   He ended frowning, and his look denounced
Desperate revenge, and battle dangerous
To less than gods. On the other side up rose
Belial, in act more graceful and humane;
A fairer person lost not heaven; he seemed   110
For dignity composed, and high exploit:
But all was false and hollow; though his tongue
Dropped manna, and could make the worse appear
The better reason, to perplex and dash
Maturest counsels: for his thoughts were low –   115
To vice industrious, but to nobler deeds
Timorous and slothful; yet he pleased the ear,
And with persuasive accent thus began:
   'I should be much for open war, O peers,
As not behind in hate, if what was urged   120
Main reason to persuade immediate war
Did not dissuade me most, and seem to cast
Ominous conjecture on the whole success;
When he who most excels in fact of arms,
In what he counsels and in what excels   125
Mistrustful, grounds his courage on despair
And utter dissolution, as the scope
Of all his aim, after some dire revenge.
First, what revenge? The towers of heaven are filled
With armèd watch, that render all access   130
Impregnable: oft on the bordering deep
Encamp their legions, or with obscure wing
Scout far and wide into the realm of night,
Scorning surprise. Or could we break our way
By force, and at our heels all hell should rise   135
With blackest insurrection to confound
Heaven's purest light, yet our great enemy,
All incorruptible, would on his throne
Sit unpolluted, and the ethereal mould,
Incapable of stain, would soon expel   140
Her mischief, and purge off the baser fire,
Victorious. Thus repulsed, our final hope

104 fatal] means both 'destined' and 'ruinous'.
106 denounced] portended.
124 fact] feat of valour or skill.

Is flat despair: we must exasperate
The almighty victor to spend all his rage,
And that must end us, that must be our cure –   145
To be no more; sad cure; for who would lose,
Though full of pain, this intellectual being,
Those thoughts that wander through eternity,
To perish rather, swallowed up and lost
In the wide womb of uncreated night,   150
Devoid of sense and motion? And who knows,
Let this be good, whether our angry foe
Can give it, or will ever? How he can
Is doubtful; that he never will is sure.
Will he, so wise, let loose at once his ire,   155
Belike through impotence or unaware,
To give his enemies their wish, and end
Them in his anger whom his anger saves
To punish endless? "Wherefore cease we, then?"
Say they who counsel war; "we are decreed,   160
Reserved, and destined to eternal woe;
Whatever doing, what can we suffer more,
What can we suffer worse?" Is this, then, worst –
Thus sitting, thus consulting, thus in arms?
What when we fled amain, pursued and struck   165
With heaven's afflicting thunder, and besought
The deep to shelter us? This hell then seemed
A refuge from those wounds; or when we lay
Chained on the burning lake? That sure was worse.
What if the breath that kindled those grim fires,   170
Awaked, should blow them into sevenfold rage,
And plunge us in the flames? Or from above
Should intermitted vengeance arm again
His red right hand to plague us? What if all
Her stores were opened, and this firmament   175
Of hell should spout her cataracts of fire,
Impendent horrors, threatening hideous fall
One day upon our heads; while we perhaps,
Designing or exhorting glorious war,
Caught in a fiery tempest, shall be hurled,   180
Each on his rock transfixed, the sport and prey

156 Belike] in all likelihood.
165 What] what about the occasion.
     amain] in haste.
170] Isa. xxx. 33.
174] Horace, *Odes* I. ii. 2–3.
180–82] Cf. the punishment of Ajax (*Aeneid* i 44–5).

Of racking whirlwinds, or for ever sunk
Under yon boiling ocean, wrapped in chains,
There to converse with everlasting groans,
Unrespited, unpitied, unreprieved,   185
Ages of hopeless end? This would be worse.
War, therefore, open or concealed, alike
My voice dissuades; for what can force or guile
With him, or who deceive his mind, whose eye
Views all things at one view? He from heaven's
          height   190
All these our motions vain sees and derides,
Not more almighty to resist our might
Than wise to frustrate all our plots and wiles.
Shall we, then, live thus vile – the race of heaven
Thus trampled, thus expelled, to suffer here   195
Chains and these torments? Better these than worse,
By my advice; since fate inevitable
Subdues us, and omnipotent decree,
The victor's will. To suffer, as to do,
Our strength is equal, nor the law unjust   200
That so ordains; this was at first resolved,
If we were wise, against so great a foe
Contending, and so doubtful what might fall.
I laugh when those who at the spear are bold
And venturous, if that fail them, shrink, and fear   205
What yet they know must follow – to endure
Exile, or ignominy, or bonds, or pain,
The sentence of their conqueror: this is now
Our doom; which if we can sustain and bear,
Our supreme foe in time may much remit   210
His anger, and perhaps, thus far removed,
Not mind us not offending, satisfied
With what is punished; whence these raging fires
Will slacken, if his breath stir not their flames.
Our purer essence then will overcome   215
Their noxious vapour, or, inured, not feel,
Or, changed at length, and to the place conformed
In temper and in nature, will receive
Familiar the fierce heat; and, void of pain,
This horror will grow mild, this darkness light;   220
Besides what hope the never-ending flight
Of future days may bring, what chance, what change

190-1] Cf. Milton's translation of Psalm II. 4 (ll. 8-9).
218 temper] temperament (the balance of humours; see *Education* p. 562).
220 light] means both 'brighter' and 'easier to bear'.

Worth waiting – since our present lot appears
For happy though but ill, for ill not worst,
If we procure not to ourselves more woe.'   225
    Thus Belial, with words clothed in reason's garb,
Counselled ignoble ease and peaceful sloth,
Not peace; and after him thus Mammon spake:
    'Either to disenthrone the king of heaven
We war, if war be best, or to regain   230
Our own right lost; him to unthrone we then
May hope, when everlasting Fate shall yield
To fickle Chance, and Chaos judge the strife:
The former, vain to hope, argues as vain
The latter; for what place can be for us   235
Within heaven's bound, unless heaven's lord supreme
We overpower? Suppose he should relent,
And publish grace to all, on promise made
Of new subjection; with what eyes could we
Stand in his presence humble, and receive   240
Strict laws imposed, to celebrate his throne
With warbled hymns, and to his Godhead sing
Forced halleluiahs, while he lordly sits
Our envied sovereign, and his altar breathes
Ambrosial odours and ambrosial flowers,   245
Our servile offerings? This must be our task
In heaven, this our delight; how wearisome
Eternity so spent in worship paid
To whom we hate. Let us not then pursue,
By force impossible, by leave obtained   250
Unacceptable, though in heaven, our state
Of splendid vassalage; but rather seek
Our own good from ourselves, and from our own
Live to ourselves, though in this vast recess,
Free and to none accountable, preferring   255
Hard liberty before the easy yoke
Of servile pomp. Our greatness will appear
Then most conspicuous when great things of small,
Useful of hurtful, prosperous of adverse,
We can create, and in what place so e'er   260

224 For happy] in terms of happiness.
238 publish] announce.
243 halleluiahs] refers to the heavenly songs of Rev. xix. 1-7, and also recalls
    the origin of the word as a transliteration of the Hebrew injunction 'praise
    Jah' (Yahweh).
245] Ambrosia is the food of the gods.
249-51] The object of 'pursue' is 'state'.
256 easy yoke] Matt. xi. 30.

Thrive under evil, and work ease out of pain
Through labour and endurance. This deep world
Of darkness do we dread? How oft amidst
Thick clouds and dark doth heaven's all-ruling sire
Choose to reside, his glory unobscured,   265
And with the majesty of darkness round
Covers his throne, from whence deep thunders roar,
Mustering their rage, and heaven resembles hell?
As he our darkness, cannot we his light
Imitate when we please? This desert soil   270
Wants not her hidden lustre, gems and gold;
Nor want we skill or art from whence to raise
Magnificence; and what can heaven show more?
Our torments also may, in length of time,
Become our elements, these piercing fires   275
As soft as now severe, our temper changed
Into their temper; which must needs remove
The sensible of pain. All things invite
To peaceful counsels, and the settled state
Of order, how in safety best we may   280
Compose our present evils, with regard
Of what we are and where, dismissing quite
All thoughts of war; ye have what I advise.'
     He scarce had finished, when such murmur filled
The assembly as when hollow rocks retain   285
The sound of blustering winds, which all night long
Had roused the sea, now with hoarse cadence lull
Seafaring men o'erwatched, whose bark by chance,
Or pinnace anchors in a craggy bay
After the tempest; such applause was heard   290
As Mammon ended, and his sentence pleased,
Advising peace: for such another field
They dreaded worse than hell; so much the fear
Of thunder and the sword of Michaël
Wrought still within them; and no less desire   295
To found this nether empire, which might rise,
By policy and long process of time,
In emulation opposite to heaven.
Which when Beëlzebub perceived – than whom,
Satan except, none higher sat – with grave   300
Aspect he rose, and in his rising seemed

263-7] Exod. xix. 16-29, II Chron. v. 13-vi. 1.
278 sensible] perception through the senses.
297 policy] statesmanship. The word was often used pejoratively to refer to
   political cunning.

A pillar of state; deep on his front engraven
Deliberation sat, and public care;
And princely counsel in his face yet shone,
Majestic, though in ruin; sage he stood,   305
With Atlantean shoulders, fit to bear
The weight of mightiest monarchies; his look
Drew audience and attention still as night
Or summer's noontide air, while thus he spake:
    'Thrones and imperial powers, offspring of heaven,   310
Ethereal virtues; or these titles now
Must we renounce, and, changing style, be called
Princes of hell? For so the popular vote
Inclines — here to continue, and build up here
A growing empire; doubtless; while we dream,   315
And know not that the king of heaven hath doomed
This place our dungeon — not our safe retreat
Beyond his potent arm, to live exempt
From heaven's high jurisdiction, in new league
Banded against his throne, but to remain   320
In strictest bondage, though thus far removed,
Under the inevitable curb, reserved
His captive multitude; for he, be sure,
In height or depth, still first and last will reign
Sole king, and of his kingdom lose no part   325
By our revolt, but over hell extend
His empire, and with iron sceptre rule
Us here, as with his golden those in heaven.
What sit we then projecting peace and war?
War hath determined us, and foiled with loss   330
Irreparable; terms of peace yet none
Vouchsafed or sought; for what peace will be given
To us enslaved, but custody severe,
And stripes and arbitrary punishment
Inflicted? And what peace can we return,   335
But, to our power, hostility and hate,
Untamed reluctance, and revenge, though slow,
Yet ever plotting how the conqueror least
May reap his conquest, and may least rejoice
In doing what we most in suffering feel?   340

302 front] forehead or face.
306 Atlantean] Atlas, one of the Titans, was condemned to carry the heavens
     on his shoulders as a punishment for his part in the invasion of the heavens.
312 style] ceremonial designation.
324 first and last] Rev. i. 11.
327 iron sceptre] See Milton's translation of Psalm II. 9 (l.20).
336 to] to the limit of.

Nor will occasion want, nor shall we need
With dangerous expedition to invade
Heaven, whose high walls fear no assault or siege,
Or ambush from the deep. What if we find
Some easier enterprise? There is a place   345
(If ancient and prophetic fame in heaven
Err not) – another world, the happy seat
Of some new race called Man, about this time
To be created like to us, though less
In power and excellence, but favoured more   350
Of him who rules above; so was his will
Pronounced among the gods, and by an oath
That shook heaven's whole circumference, confirmed.
Thither let us bend all our thoughts, to learn
What creatures there inhabit, of what mould   355
Or substance, how endued, and what their power
And where their weakness; how attempted best
By force or subtlety; though heaven be shut,
And heaven's high arbitrator sit secure
In his own strength, this place may lie exposed,   360
The utmost border of his kingdom, left
To their defence who hold it: here perhaps
Some advantageous acts may be achieved
By sudden onset – either with hell-fire
To waste his whole creation, or possess   365
All as our own, and drive, as we are driven,
The puny habitants; or if not drive,
Seduce them to our party, that their God
May prove their foe, and with repenting hand
Abolish his own works. This would surpass   370
Common revenge, and interrupt his joy
In our confusion, and our joy upraise
In his disturbance; when his darling sons,
Hurled headlong to partake with us, shall curse
Their frail original, and faded bliss –   375
Faded so soon. Advise if this be worth
Attempting, or to sit in darkness here
Hatching vain empires.' Thus Beëlzebub
Pleaded his devilish counsel – first devised

352] Isa. xiii. 12–13; Heb. vi. 17; *Iliad* i 530; *Aeneid* ix 106.
367 puny] means 'born later' (*puis né*), 'inferior in rank' (cf. ll. 349–50, Psalm
    viii. 5) and 'weak'.
375 original] progenitor, i.e. Adam.
376 Advise] ponder.
377 sit in darkness] Psalm cvii. 10–11.

By Satan, and in part proposed: for whence,   380
But from the author of all ill, could spring
So deep a malice, to confound the race
Of mankind in one root, and earth with hell
To mingle and involve, done all to spite
The great creator? But their spite still serves   385
His glory to augment. The bold design
Pleased highly those infernal states, and joy
Sparkled in all their eyes; with full assent
They vote: whereat his speech he thus renews:
    'Well have ye judged, well ended long debate,   390
Synod of gods, and like to what ye are,
Great things resolved, which from the lowest deep
Will once more lift us up, in spite of fate,
Nearer our ancient seat – perhaps in view   394
Of those bright confines, whence, with neighbouring arms
And opportune excursion, we may chance
Re-enter heaven; or else in some mild zone
Dwell, not unvisited of heaven's fair light
Secure, and at the brightening orient beam
Purge off this gloom: the soft delicious air,   400
To heal the scar of these corrosive fires,
Shall breathe her balm. But, first, whom shall we send
In search of this new world, whom shall we find
Sufficient? Who shall tempt with wandering feet
The dark, unbottomed, infinite abyss,   405
And through the palpable obscure find out
His uncouth way, or spread his airy flight,
Upborne with indefatigable wings
Over the vast abrupt, ere he arrive
The happy isle? What strength, what art, can then   410
Suffice, or what evasion bear him safe,
Through the strict senteries and stations thick
Of angels watching round? Here he had need
All circumspection, and we now no less
Choice in our suffrage; for on whom we send   415
The weight of all, and our last hope, relies.'
    This said, he sat; and expectation held

387 states] the 'estates' of Parliament.
391 Synod] means 'assembly of clergy' and secondarily, 'conjunction of stars'.
402–4] Isa. vi. 8.
404 tempt] risk the perils of.
406 palpable obscure] See XII 184–8n.
407 uncouth] unknown.
409 abrupt] abyss.
412 senteries] sentries.

His look suspense, awaiting who appeared
To second, or oppose, or undertake
The perilous attempt; but all sat mute,   420
Pondering the danger with deep thoughts; and each
In other's countenance read his own dismay,
Astonished; none among the choice and prime
Of those heaven-warring champions could be found
So hardy as to proffer or accept,   425
Alone, the dreadful voyage; till at last
Satan, whom now transcendent glory raised
Above his fellows, with monarchal pride
Conscious of highest worth, unmoved thus spake:
    'O progeny of heaven, empyreal thrones;   430
With reason hath deep silence and demur
Seized us, though undismayed; long is the way
And hard, that out of hell leads up to light;
Our prison strong, this huge convex of fire,
Outrageous to devour, immures us round   435
Ninefold; and gates of burning adamant,
Barred over us, prohibit all egress.
These passed, if any pass, the void profound
Of unessential night receives him next,
Wide gaping, and with utter loss of being   440
Threatens him, plunged in that abortive gulf.
If thence he scape, into whatever world,
Or unknown region, what remains him less
Than unknown dangers, and as hard escape?
But I should ill become this throne, O peers,   445
And this imperial sovereignty, adorned
With splendour, armed with power, if aught proposed
And judged of public moment in the shape
Of difficulty or danger, could deter
Me from attempting. Wherefore do I assume   450
These royalties, and not refuse to reign,
Refusing to accept as great a share
Of hazard as of honour, due alike
To him who reigns, and so much to him due
Of hazard more as he above the rest   455
High honoured sits? Go therefore mighty powers,
Terror of heaven, though fallen; intend at home,

432-3] Cf.*Aeneid* vi 126-9, and Dante, *Inferno* xxxiv. 95.
434 convex] the vault of hell.
439 unessential] without being, uncreated (cf.l.150).
441 abortive] rendering fruitless.
452 Refusing] if I refuse.
457 intend] consider.

While here shall be our home, what best may ease
The present misery, and render hell
More tolerable; if there be cure or charm   460
To respite or deceive, or slack the pain
Of this ill mansion: intermit no watch
Against a wakeful foe, while I abroad
Through all the coasts of dark destruction seek
Deliverance for us all; this enterprise   465
None shall partake with me.' Thus saying, rose
The monarch, and prevented all reply;
Prudent lest, from his resolution raised,
Others among the chief might offer now
(Certain to be refused) what erst they feared,   470
And so refused might in opinion stand
His rivals, winning cheap the high repute
Which he through hazard huge must earn. But they
Dreaded not more the adventure than his voice
Forbidding; and at once with him they rose;   475
Their rising all at once was as the sound
Of thunder heard remote. Towards him they bend
With awful reverence prone, and as a god
Extol him equal to the highest in heaven.
Nor failed they to express how much they praised   480
That for the general safety he despised
His own: for neither do the spirits damned
Lose all their virtue; lest bad men should boast
Their specious deeds on earth, which glory excites,
Or close ambition varnished o'er with zeal.   485
    Thus they their doubtful consultations dark
Ended, rejoicing in their matchless chief:
As, when from mountain tops the dusky clouds
Ascending, while the north wind sleeps, o'erspread
Heaven's cheerful face, the louring element   490
Scowls o'er the darkened landscape snow or shower,
If chance the radiant sun, with farewell sweet,
Extend his evening beam, the fields revive,
The birds their notes renew, and bleating herds
Attest their joy, that hill and valley rings.   495
O shame to men! Devil with devil damned
Firm concord holds; men only disagree
Of creatures rational, though under hope
Of heavenly grace, and, God proclaiming peace,

461 deceive] beguile.
468 raised] inspired with courage.
478 awful] full of awe.

Yet live in hatred, enmity, and strife   500
Among themselves, and levy cruel wars
Wasting the earth, each other to destroy:
As if (which might induce us to accord)
Man had not hellish foes enow besides,
That day and night for his destruction wait.   505
   The Stygian council thus dissolved; and forth
In order came the grand infernal peers:
Midst came their mighty paramount, and seemed
Alone the antagonist of heaven, nor less
Than hell's dread emperor, with pomp supreme   510
And god-like imitated state; him round
A globe of fiery seraphim enclosed
With bright emblazonry, and horrent arms.
Then of their session ended they bid cry
With trumpets' regal sound the great result: 515
Toward the four winds four speedy cherubim
Put to their mouths the sounding alchemy,
By herald's voice explained; the hollow abyss
Heard far and wide, and all the host of hell
With deafening shout returned them loud acclaim.   520
Thence more at ease their minds, and somewhat raised
By false presumptuous hope, the rangèd powers
Disband; and, wandering, each his several way
Pursues, as inclination or sad choice
Leads him perplexed, where he may likeliest find   525
Truce to his restless thoughts, and entertain
The irksome hours, till his great chief return.
Part on the plain, or in the air sublime,
Upon the wing or in swift race contend,
As at the Olympian games or Pythian fields;   530
Part curb their fiery steeds, or shun the goal
With rapid wheels, or fronted brigades form:
As when, to warn proud cities, war appears
Waged in the troubled sky, and armies rush
To battle in the clouds; before each van   535
Prick forth the airy knights, and couch their spears,
Till thickest legions close; with feats of arms

504 enow] enough.
512 globe] used in the Latin sense of 'a throng of people'.
513 emblazonry] heraldic devices.
    horrent] bristling.
517 alchemy] brass (i.e. trumpets).
521–69] *Iliad* xxiii 287–897, *Aeneid* v 104–603, vi 642–59.
522 powers] here means 'armies'.
530 Pythian] The Pythian games were held at Delphi.

From either end of heaven the welkin burns.
Others, with vast Typhoean rage, more fell,
Rend up both rocks and hills, and ride the air   540
In whirlwind; hell scarce holds the wild uproar:
As when Alcides, from Oechalia crowned
With conquest, felt the envenomed robe, and tore
Through pain up by the roots Thessalian pines,
And Lichas from the top of Oeta threw   545
Into the Euboic sea. Others, more mild,
Retreated in a silent valley, sing
With notes angelical to many a harp
Their own heroic deeds, and hapless fall
By doom of battle, and complain that fate   550
Free virtue should enthral to force or chance.
Their song was partial; but the harmony
(What could it less when spirits immortal sing?)
Suspended hell, and took with ravishment
The thronging audience. In discourse more sweet   555
(For eloquence the soul, song charms the sense)
Others apart sat on a hill retired,
In thoughts more elevate, and reasoned high
Of providence, foreknowledge, will, and fate –
Fixed fate, free will, foreknowledge absolute,   560
And found no end, in wandering mazes lost.
Of good and evil much they argued then,
Of happiness and final misery,
Passion and apathy, and glory and shame:
Vain wisdom all, and false philosophy –   565
Yet with a pleasing sorcery could charm
Pain for a while or anguish, and excite
Fallacious hope, or arm the obdurèd breast
With stubborn patience as with triple steel.
Another part, in squadrons and gross bands,   570

539 Typhoean] See I 197–200n. The word 'Typhon' also meant 'whirlwind' (see l. 541).

542–6] Hercules ('Alcides') mortally wounded the Centaur Nessus, who took his revenge by telling Deianira (Hercules' wife) that she should soak a garment in Nessus' blood in order to revive Hercules' love for her. Hercules, returning from a victory on Oechalia, put on the poisoned robe, which corroded his flesh. Distracted with pain, Hercules blamed his attendant Lichas (who had brought the robe) and threw him from the top of Oeta, a mountain in southern Thessaly, into the Euboean (Euboic) sea. See *Metamorphoses* ix 134 ff.

552 partial] biased.

564 apathy] refers to the Stoic ideal of calmness, dispassionateness (ἀπάθεια); cf. *PR* IV 300–9.

On bold adventure to discover wide
That dismal world, if any clime perhaps
Might yield them easier habitation, bend
Four ways their flying march, along the banks
Of four infernal rivers, that disgorge   575
Into the burning lake their baleful streams –
Abhorrèd Styx, the flood of deadly hate;
Sad Acheron of sorrow, black and deep;
Cocytus, named of lamentation loud
Heard on the rueful stream; fierce Phlegeton,   580
Whose waves of torrent fire inflame with rage.
Far off from these, a slow and silent stream,
Lethe, the river of oblivion, rolls
Her watery labyrinth, whereof who drinks
Forthwith his former state and being forgets –   585
Forgets both joy and grief, pleasure and pain.
Beyond this flood a frozen continent
Lies dark and wild, beat with perpetual storms
Of whirlwind and dire hail, which on firm land
Thaws not, but gathers heap, and ruin seems   590
Of ancient pile; all else deep snow and ice,
A gulf profound as that Serbonian bog
Betwixt Damiata and Mount Casius old,
Where armies whole have sunk: the parching air
Burns frore, and cold performs the effect of fire.   595
Thither, by harpy-footed Furies haled,
At certain revolutions all the damned
Are brought; and feel by turns the bitter change
Of fierce extremes, extremes by change more fierce,
From beds of raging fire to starve in ice   600
Their soft ethereal warmth, and there to pine
Immovable, infixed, and frozen round
Periods of time – thence hurried back to fire.
They ferry over this Lethean sound
Both to and fro, their sorrow to augment,   605
And wish and struggle, as they pass, to reach
The tempting stream, with one small drop to lose
In sweet forgetfulness all pain and woe,

575-81] The epithet which Milton applies to each of the four rivers of Hades is a
translation of its Greek name.

592-4] According to an ancient tradition which survived into the Renaissance,
Lake Serbonis (near the Egyptian coast) had swallowed whole armies.
Damiata, modern Damietta, is a city at the eastern mouth of the Nile.

595 frore] cold, frosty.

596 Furies] The Roman name for the Erinyes, the avenging goddesses. On
harpies see *Comus* 605n.

All in one moment, and so near the brink;
But fate withstands, and, to oppose the attempt,   610
Medusa with Gorgonian terror guards
The ford, and of itself the water flies
All taste of living wight, as once it fled
The lip of Tantalus. Thus roving on
In confused march forlorn, the adventurous bands   615
With shuddering horror pale, and eyes aghast,
Viewed first their lamentable lot, and found
No rest; through many a dark and dreary vale
They passed, and many a region dolorous,
O'er many a frozen, many a fiery alp,   620
Rocks, caves, lakes, fens, bogs, dens, and shades of death –
A universe of death, which God by curse
Created evil, for evil only good;
Where all life dies, death lives, and nature breeds,
Perverse, all monstrous, all prodigious things,   625
Abominable, inutterable, and worse
Than fables yet have feigned or fear conceived,
Gorgons, and Hydras, and Chimeras dire.
    Meanwhile the adversary of God and man,
Satan, with thoughts inflamed of highest design,   630
Puts on swift wings, and toward the gates of hell
Explores his solitary flight; sometimes
He scours the right hand coast, sometimes the left;
Now shaves with level wing the deep, then soars
Up to the fiery concave towering high.   635
As when far off at sea a fleet descried
Hangs in the clouds, by equinoctial winds
Close sailing from Bengala, or the isles
Of Ternate and Tidore, whence merchants bring
Their spicy drugs; they on the trading flood,   640
Through the wide Ethiopian to the Cape,
Ply stemming nightly toward the pole: so seemed
Far off the flying fiend; at last appear

611 Medusa] See *Comus* 447–52n.
614] Tantalus was condemned to stand in a pool in Tartarus; the water in the
    pool receded when he tried to drink. (*Odyssey* xi 582–92).
628] See *Comus* 447–52n., and 517n.; *Aeneid* vi 287–9. The Hydras are sea-
    serpents, not the Hydras of *Comus* 605.
632 Explores] used in the Latin sense of 'tests'.
639 Ternate, Tidore] Two tiny islands of the Moluccas.
641 Ethiopian] Indian Ocean.
    Cape] Cape of Good Hope.
642 Ply stemming] make headway against the wind.
    Pole] South Pole.

Hell-bounds, high reaching to the horrid roof,
And thrice threefold the gates; three folds were brass, 645
Three iron, three of adamantine rock,
Impenetrable, impaled with circling fire,
Yet unconsumed. Before the gates there sat
On either side a formidable shape;
The one seemed woman to the waist, and fair,   650
But ended foul in many a scaly fold,
Voluminous and vast – a serpent armed
With mortal sting; about her middle round
A cry of hell hounds never ceasing barked
With wide Cerberean mouths full loud, and rung   655
A hideous peal; yet, when they list, would creep,
If aught disturbed their noise, into her womb,
And kennel there; yet there still barked and howled
Within unseen. Far less abhorred than these
Vexed Scylla, bathing in the sea that parts   660
Calabria from the hoarse Trinacrian shore;
Nor uglier follow the night-hag, when, called
In secret, riding through the air she comes,
Lured with the smell of infant blood, to dance
With Lapland witches, while the labouring moon   665
Eclipses at their charms. The other shape –
If shape it might be called that shape had none
Distinguishable in member, joint, or limb;
Or substance might be called that shadow seemed,
For each seemed either – black it stood as night,   670
Fierce as ten Furies, terrible as hell,
And shook a dreadful dart: what seemed his head
The likeness of a kingly crown had on.
Satan was now at hand, and from his seat
The monster moving onward came as fast   675
With horrid strides; hell trembled as he strode.

647 impaled] surrounded, fenced in.
648–889] The allegory of Sin and Death is based on James i. 15, and examples of
    expansions of the allegory exist in patristic, medieval, and Renaissance
    literature.
652 Voluminous] consisting of many coils.
654 cry] pack.
655] On Cerberus see *Allegro* 1–2n.
660 Scylla] See *Comus* 257–9n. According to an ancient Christian tradition
    Scylla was a symbol of sin.
661 Trinacrian] Sicilian.
662 night-hag] Hecate, goddess of witchcraft.
665 labouring] suffering eclipse. Cf. *faticosa Luna* (*Sonnet* IV 12).
673] Rev. vi. 2.

The undaunted fiend what this might be admired,
Admired, not feared – God and his Son except,
Created thing nought valued he nor shunned –
And with disdainful look thus first began: 680
  'Whence and what art thou, execrable shape,
That dar'st, though grim and terrible, advance
Thy miscreated front athwart my way
To yonder gates? Through them I mean to pass,
That be assured, without leave asked of thee: 685
Retire, or taste thy folly, and learn by proof,
Hell-born, not to contend with spirits of heaven.'
  To whom the goblin, full of wrath, replied:
'Art thou that traitor angel, art thou he,
Who first broke peace in heaven and faith, till then   690
Unbroken, and in proud rebellious arms
Drew after him the third part of heaven's sons,
Conjured against the highest – for which both thou
And they outcast from God, are here condemned
To waste eternal days in woe and pain?   695
And reckon'st thou thyself with spirits of heaven,
Hell-doomed, and breath'st defiance here and scorn,
Where I reign king, and to enrage thee more,
Thy king and lord? Back to thy punishment,
False fugitive, and to thy speed add wings,   700
Lest with a whip of scorpions I pursue
Thy lingering, or with one stroke of this dart
Strange horror seize thee, and pangs unfelt before.'
  So spake the grisly terror, and in shape,
So speaking and so threatening, grew tenfold   705
More dreadful and deform; on the other side,
Incensed with indignation, Satan stood
Unterrified, and like a comet burned,
That fires the length of Ophiucus huge
In the arctic sky, and from his horrid hair   710
Shakes pestilence and war. Each at the head
Levelled his deadly aim; their fatal hands
No second stroke intend; and such a frown
Each cast at the other as when two black clouds,
With heaven's artillery fraught, come rattling on   715

677 admired] wondered.
692] Rev. xii. 4. Cf. *PL* I 633.
693 Conjured] sworn together in a conspiracy.
701] I Kings xii. 11.
708–11] Comets were traditionally an ominous sign; see *Aeneid* x 272–5. The
    'hair' of l.710 alludes to the Greek phrase for a comet, 'long-haired
    (κομήτης) star'. Ophiucus is the constellation of the Serpent Bearer.

Over the Caspian – then stand front to front
Hovering a space, till winds the signal blow
To join their dark encounter in mid air;
So frowned the mighty combatants that hell
Grew darker at their frown; so matched they stood;   720
For never but once more was either like
To meet so great a foe; and now great deeds
Had been achieved, whereof all hell had rung,
Had not the snaky sorceress, that sat
Fast by hell gate and kept the fatal key,   725
Risen, and with hideous outcry rushed between.
    'O father, what intends thy hand,' she cried,
'Against thy only son? What fury, O son,
Possesses thee to bend that mortal dart
Against thy father's head? And know'st for whom?   730
For him who sits above, and laughs the while
At thee, ordained his drudge to execute
Whate'er his wrath, which he calls justice, bids –
His wrath, which one day will destroy ye both.'
    She spake, and at her words the hellish pest   735
Forbore; then these to her Satan returned;
    'So strange thy outcry, and thy words so strange
Thou interposest, that my sudden hand,
Prevented, spares to tell thee yet by deeds
What it intends, till first I know of thee   740
What thing thou art, thus double-formed, and why,
In this infernal vale first me, thou call'st
Me father, and that phantasm call'st my son.
I know thee not, nor ever saw till now
Sight more detestable than him and thee.'   745
    To whom thus the portress of hell gate replied:
'Hast thou forgot me, then; and do I seem
Now in thine eye so foul? – once deemed so fair
In heaven, when at the assembly, and in sight
Of all the seraphim with thee combined   750
In bold conspiracy against heaven's king,
All on a sudden miserable pain
Surprised thee, dim thine eyes and dizzy swum
In darkness, while thy head flames thick and fast
Threw forth, till on the left side opening wide,   755

718 mid air] see *Fair Infant* 16n.
752-9] The primary allusion is to the myth of Athena's birth from the head of
    Zeus, but as that myth was seen in the Renaissance as a pagan counterpart
    to the generation of God the Son, the passage can also be seen as a parody of
    that event.

Likest to thee in shape and countenance bright,
Then shining heavenly fair, a goddess armed,
Out of thy head I sprung; amazement seized
All the host of heaven; back they recoiled afraid
At first, and called me Sin, and for a sign   760
Portentous held me; but, familiar grown,
I pleased, and with attractive graces won
The most averse – thee chiefly, who, full oft
Thyself in me thy perfect image viewing,
Becam'st enamoured; and such joy thou took'st   765
With me in secret that my womb conceived
A growing burden. Meanwhile war arose,
And fields were fought in heaven: wherein remained
(For what could else?) to our almighty foe
Clear victory; to our part loss and rout   770
Through all the empyrean; down they fell,
Driven headlong from the pitch of heaven, down
Into this deep, and in the general fall
I also: at which time this powerful key
Into my hand was given, with charge to keep   775
These gates for ever shut, which none can pass
Without my opening. Pensive here I sat
Alone; but long I sat not, till my womb,
Pregnant by thee, and now excessive grown,
Prodigious motion felt and rueful throes.   780
At last this odious offspring whom thou seest,
Thine own begotten, breaking violent way,
Tore through my entrails, that with fear and pain
Distorted, all my nether shape thus grew
Transformed: but he my inbred enemy   785
Forth issued, brandishing his fatal dart,
Made to destroy: I fled, and cried out "Death";
Hell trembled at the hideous name, and sighed
From all her caves, and back resounded "Death".
I fled, but he pursued (though more, it seems,   790
Inflamed with lust than rage) and swifter far,
Me overtook, his mother, all dismayed,
And, in embraces forcible and foul
Engendering with me, of that rape begot
These yelling monsters, that with ceaseless cry   795
Surround me, as thou saw'st – hourly conceived
And hourly born, with sorrow infinite
To me; for, when they list, into the womb
That bred them they return, and howl, and gnaw
My bowels, their repast; then, bursting forth   800
Afresh, with conscious terrors vex me round,

That rest or intermission none I find.
Before mine eyes in opposition sits
Grim Death, my son and foe, who sets them on,
And me, his parent, would full soon devour   805
For want of other prey, but that he knows
His end with mine involved, and knows that I
Should prove a bitter morsel, and his bane,
Whenever that shall be: so Fate pronounced.
But thou, O father, I forewarn thee, shun   810
His deadly arrow; neither vainly hope
To be invulnerable in those bright arms,
Though tempered heavenly; for that mortal dint,
Save he who reigns above, none can resist.'
    She finished, and the subtle fiend his lore   815
Soon learned, now milder, and thus answered smooth:
'Dear daughter – since thou claim'st me for thy sire,
And my fair son here show'st me, the dear pledge
Of dalliance had with thee in heaven, and joys
Then sweet, now sad to mention, through dire change 820
Befallen us unforeseen, unthought-of – know
I come no enemy, but to set free
From out this dark and dismal house of pain
Both him and thee, and all the heavenly host
Of spirits that, in our just pretences armed,   825
Fell with us from on high; from them I go
This uncouth errand sole, and one for all
Myself expose, with lonely steps to tread
The unfounded deep, and through the void immense
To search, with wandering quest, a place foretold   830
Should be – and, by concurring signs, ere now
Created vast and round – a place of bliss
In the purlieus of heaven; and therein placed
A race of upstart creatures, to supply
Perhaps our vacant room, though more removed,   835
Lest heaven, surcharged with potent multitude,
Might hap to move new broils; be this, or aught
Than this more secret, now designed, I haste
To know; and this once known, shall soon return,
And bring yet to the place where thou and Death   840
Shall dwell at ease, and up and down unseen
Wing silently the buxom air, embalmed

815 lore] lesson.
825 pretences] assertions of claims.
829 unfounded] bottomless.
842 buxom] unresisting.

With odours; there ye shall be fed and filled
Immeasurably: all things shall be your prey.'
   He ceased, for both seemed highly pleased, and Death   845
Grinned horrible a ghastly smile, to hear
His famine should be filled, and blessed his maw
Destined to that good hour; no less rejoiced
His mother bad, and thus bespake her sire:
   'The key of this infernal pit, by due   850
And by command of heaven's all-powerful king,
I keep, by him forbidden to unlock
These adamantine gates; against all force
Death ready stands to interpose his dart,
Fearless to be o'ermatched by living might.   855
But what owe I to his commands above,
Who hates me, and hath hither thrust me down
Into this gloom of Tartarus profound,
To sit in hateful office here confined,
Inhabitant of heaven and heavenly born –   860
Here in perpetual agony and pain,
With terrors and with clamours compassed round
Of mine own brood, that on my bowels feed?
Thou art my father, thou my author, thou
My being gav'st me; whom should I obey   865
But thee, whom follow? Thou wilt bring me soon
To that new world of light and bliss, among
The gods who live at ease, where I shall reign
At thy right hand voluptuous, as beseems
Thy daughter and thy darling, without end.'   870
   Thus saying, from her side the fatal key,
Sad instrument of all our woe, she took;
And, towards the gate rolling her bestial train,
Forthwith the huge portcullis high updrew,
Which, but herself, not all the Stygian powers   875
Could once have moved; then in the key-hole turns
The intricate wards, and every bolt and bar
Of massy iron or solid rock with ease
Unfastens; on a sudden open fly,
With impetuous recoil and jarring sound,   880
The infernal doors, and on their hinges grate
Harsh thunder, that the lowest bottom shook
Of Erebus. She opened, but to shut
Excelled her power: the gates wide open stood,
That with extended wings a bannered host,   885
Under spread ensigns marching, might pass through

883 Erebus] here refers to hell.

With horse and chariots ranked in loose array;
So wide they stood, and like a furnace-mouth
Cast forth redounding smoke and ruddy flame.
Before their eyes in sudden view appear   890
The secrets of the hoary deep – a dark
Illimitable ocean without bound,
Without dimension; where length, breadth, and height,
And time and place, are lost; where eldest Night
And Chaos, ancestors of Nature, hold   895
Eternal anarchy, amidst the noise
Of endless wars, and by confusion stand.
For Hot, Cold, Moist, and Dry, four champions fierce,
Strive here for mastery, and to battle bring
Their embryon atoms: they around the flag   900
Of each his faction, in their several clans,
Light-armed or heavy, sharp, smooth, swift, or slow,
Swarm populous, unnumbered as the sands
Of Barca or Cyrene's torrid soil,
Levied to side with warring winds, and poise   905
Their lighter wings. To whom these most adhere
He rules a moment: Chaos umpire sits,
And by decision more embroils the fray
By which he reigns: next him, high arbiter,
Chance governs all. Into this wild abyss,   910
The womb of Nature, and perhaps her grave,
Of neither sea, nor shore, nor air, nor fire,
But all these in their pregnant causes mixed
Confusedly, and which thus must ever fight,
Unless the almighty maker them ordain   915
His dark materials to create more worlds –
Into this wild abyss the wary fiend
Stood on the brink of hell and looked a while,
Pondering his voyage; for no narrow frith
He had to cross. Nor was his ear less pealed   920
With noises loud and ruinous (to compare
Great things with small) than when Bellona storms
With all her battering engines, bent to raze
Some capital city; or less than if this frame
Of heaven were falling, and these elements   925

891 hoary deep] Job xli. 32.
904] Barca and Cyrene were cities in Cyrenaica, a Roman province in the
    northeast of modern Libya.
905] The atoms are enlisted ('levied') to provide weight for ('poise') and thus
    stabilize the wings.
919 frith] firth.
922 Bellona] Roman goddess of war.

In mutiny had from her axle torn
The steadfast earth. At last his sail-broad vans
He spreads for flight, and, in the surging smoke
Uplifted, spurns the ground; thence many a league,
As in a cloudy chair, ascending rides   930
Audacious, but that seat soon failing, meets
A vast vacuity; all unawares,
Fluttering his pennons vain, plumb-down he drops
Ten thousand fathom deep, and to this hour
Down had been falling, had not by ill chance   935
The strong rebuff of some tumultuous cloud,
Instinct with fire and nitre, hurried him
As many miles aloft; that fury stayed –
Quenched in a boggy Syrtis, neither sea,
Nor good dry land – nigh foundered, on he fares,   940
Treading the crude consistence, half on foot,
Half flying; behoves him now both oar and sail.
As when a griffin through the wilderness
With wingèd course, o'er hill or moory dale,
Pursues the Arimaspian, who by stealth   945
Had from his wakeful custody purloined
The guarded gold; so eagerly the fiend
O'er bog or steep, through strait, rough, dense, or rare,
With head, hands, wings or feet, pursues his way,
And swims, or sinks, or wades, or creeps, or flies;   950
At length a universal hubbub wild
Of stunning sounds, and voices all confused,
Borne through the hollow dark, assaults his ear
With loudest vehemence; thither he plies
Undaunted, to meet there whatever power   955
Or spirit of the nethermost abyss
Might in that noise reside, of whom to ask
Which way the nearest coast of darkness lies
Bordering on light; when straight behold the throne
Of Chaos, and his dark pavilion spread   960
Wide on the wasteful deep; with him enthroned

---

927 vans] fans, i.e. wings.
933 pennons] used in the Latin sense of 'wings'.
937 Instinct] impelled, animated, inflamed.
939] The Syrtes were two sandbanks near Tripoli. Acts xxvii. 17 refers to
    quicksands (from σύρτιν), and in the R.V., Syrtis (from Σύρτιν).
943-7 Griffins were monsters who guarded the gold of Scythia against the one-
    eyed Arimaspians.
948 strait] may mean 'straight', which would contrast with 'rough', as 'dense'
    does with 'rare'.
959-67] Cf. *Aeneid* vi 273-81.

Sat sable-vested Night, eldest of things,
The consort of his reign; and by them stood
Orcus and Ades, and the dreaded name
Of Demogorgon; Rumour next, and Chance,   965
And Tumult and Confusion, all embroiled,
And Discord with a thousand various mouths.
    To whom Satan, turning boldly, thus: 'Ye powers
And spirits of this nethermost abyss,
Chaos and ancient Night, I come no spy   970
With purpose to explore or to disturb
The secrets of your realm, but by constraint
Wandering this darksome desert, as my way
Lies through your spacious empire up to light
Alone and without guide, half lost, I seek   975
What readiest path leads where your gloomy bounds
Confine with heaven; or if some other place,
From your dominion won, the ethereal king
Possesses lately, thither to arrive
I travel this profound; direct my course: 980
Directed, no mean recompense it brings
To your behoof, if I that region lost,
All usurpation thence expelled, reduce
To her original darkness and your sway
(Which is my present journey) and once more   985
Erect the standard there of ancient Night.
Yours be the advantage all, mine the revenge.'
    Thus Satan; and him thus the anarch old,
With faltering speech and visage incomposed,
Answered: 'I know thee, stranger, who thou art –   990
That mighty leading angel, who of late
Made head against heaven's king, though overthrown.
I saw and heard; for such a numerous host
Fled not in silence through the frighted deep,
With ruin upon ruin, rout on rout,   995
Confusion worse confounded; and heaven gates
Poured out by millions her victorious bands,
Pursuing. I upon my frontiers here
Keep residence; if all I can will serve
That little which is left so to defend,   1000

---

964 Orcus, Ades] Both are names for Pluto (Hades), god of the underworld.
965 Demogorgon] an infernal deity mentioned in a scholium on Statius, who
    refers to a mysterious 'name' dreaded by ghosts (*Thebais* iv 514).
988 anarch] Chaos.
989 incomposed] wanting in composure.
990] Mark i. 24.

Encroached on still through our intestine broils
Weakening the sceptre of old Night: first hell,
Your dungeon, stretching far and wide beneath;
Now lately heaven and earth, another world
Hung o'er my realm, linked in a golden chain   1005
To that side heaven from whence your legions fell;
If that way be your walk, you have not far;
So much the nearer danger; go, and speed;
Havoc and spoil and ruin are my gain.'
   He ceased; and Satan stayed not to reply,   1010
But glad that now his sea should find a shore,
With fresh alacrity and force renewed
Springs upward, like a pyramid of fire,
Into the wild expanse, and through the shock
Of fighting elements, on all sides round   1015
Environed, wins his way; harder beset
And more endangered than when Argo passed
Through Bosporus betwixt the jostling rocks,
Or when Ulysses on the larboard shunned
Charybdis, and by the other whirlpool steered.   1020
So he with difficulty and labour hard
Moved on, with difficulty and labour he;
But, he once passed, soon after, when man fell,
Strange alteration! Sin and Death amain,
Following his track – such was the will of heaven –   1025
Paved after him a broad and beaten way
Over the dark abyss, whose boiling gulf
Tamely endured a bridge of wondrous length,
From hell continued, reaching the utmost orb
Of this frail world; by which the spirits perverse   1030
With easy intercourse pass to and fro
To tempt or punish mortals, except whom
God and good angels guard by special grace.
   But now at last the sacred influence
Of light appears, and from the walls of heaven   1035
Shoots far into the bosom of dim Night
A glimmering dawn; here Nature first begins
Her farthest verge, and Chaos to retire,

1001 our] possibly a misprint for 'your'.
1004 heaven] the earth's sky (in 1006, God's heaven).
1005] Homer's golden chain (*Iliad* viii 18-27), a traditional symbol of the order
   and harmony of the universe.
1017-18] The Argo, with Jason and his Argonauts on board, passed through the
   Bosporus, narrowly missing the Symplegades ('jostling rocks').
1019-20] See *Comus* 257-9n., and *Odyssey* xii 234-59.
1026] Matt. vii. 13.

As from her outmost works, a broken foe,
With tumult less and with less hostile din;   1040
That Satan with less toil, and now with ease,
Wafts on the calmer wave by dubious light,
And, like a weather-beaten vessel, holds
Gladly the port, though shrouds and tackle torn;
Or in the emptier waste, resembling air,   1045
Weighs his spread wings, at leisure to behold
Far off the empyreal heaven, extended wide
In circuit, undetermined square or round,
With opal towers and battlements adorned
Of living sapphire, once his native seat;   1050
And, fast by, hanging in a golden chain,
This pendent world, in bigness as a star
Of smallest magnitude close by the moon.
Thither, full fraught with mischievous revenge,
Accursed, and in a cursed hour, he hies.   1055

THE END OF THE SECOND BOOK

1043 holds] remains in.
1048-50] Rev. xxi. 16, 19-21, Cf. *PL* X 381.
1052 pendent world] the created universe.

BOOK III

THE ARGUMENT

God, sitting on his throne, sees Satan flying towards this world, then newly created; shows him to the Son, who sat at his right hand; foretells the success of Satan in perverting mankind; clears his own justice and wisdom from all imputation, having created man free, and able enough to have withstood his tempter; yet declares his purpose of grace towards him, in regard he fell not of his own malice, as did Satan, but by him seduced. The Son of God renders praises to his Father for the manifestation of his gracious purpose towards man: but God again declares that grace cannot be extended towards man without the satisfaction of divine justice; man hath offended the majesty of God by aspiring to Godhead, and therefore, with all his progeny, devoted to death, must die, unless some one can be found sufficient to answer for his offence, and undergo his punishment. The Son of God freely offers himself a ransom for man: the Father accepts him, ordains his incarnation, pronounces his exaltation above all names in heaven and earth; commands all the angels to adore him; they obey, and hymning to their harps in full choir, celebrate the Father and the Son. Meanwhile Satan alights upon the bare convex of this world's outermost orb; where wandering he first finds a place since called the Limbo of Vanity; what persons and things fly up thither: thence comes to the gate of heaven, described ascending by stairs, and the waters above the firmament that flow about it; his passage thence to the orb of the sun: he finds there Uriel, the regent of that orb, but first changes himself into the shape of a meaner angel, and pretending a zealous desire to behold the new creation, and man whom God had placed here, enquires of him the place of his habitation, and is directed: alights first on Mount Niphates.

Hail, holy Light, offspring of heaven first-born
Or of the eternal coeternal beam
May I express thee unblamed? Since God is light,
And never but in unapproachèd light
Dwelt from eternity – dwelt then in thee,   5
Bright effluence of bright essence increate.
Or hear'st thou rather pure ethereal stream,
Whose fountain who shall tell? Before the sun,
Before the heavens thou wert, and at the voice

1 first-born] Col. i. 15.
3 God is light] I John i. 5.
4] I Tim. vi. 16.
6 effluence] emanation.
  increate] uncreated.
7 hear'st thou rather] a Latinism meaning 'would you prefer to be called'.

Of God, as with a mantle didst invest   10
The rising world of waters dark and deep,
Won from the void and formless infinite.
Thee I revisit now with bolder wing,
Escaped the Stygian pool, though long detained
In that obscure sojourn, while in my flight   15
Through utter and through middle darkness borne,
With other notes than to the Orphean lyre
I sung of Chaos and eternal Night,
Taught by the heavenly Muse to venture down
The dark descent, and up to re-ascend,   20
Though hard and rare; thee I revisit safe,
And feel thy sovereign vital lamp; but thou
Revisit'st not these eyes, that roll in vain
To find thy piercing ray, and find no dawn;
So thick a drop serene hath quenched their orbs,   25
Or dim suffusion veiled. Yet not the more
Cease I to wander where the Muses haunt
Clear spring, or shady grove, or sunny hill,
Smit with the love of sacred song; but chief
Thee, Zion, and the flowery brooks beneath,   30
That wash thy hallowed feet, and warbling flow,
Nightly I visit: nor sometimes forget
Those other two equalled with me in fate,
So were I equalled with them in renown,
Blind Thamyris and blind Maeonides,   35
And Tiresias and Phineus, prophets old:
Then feed on thoughts that voluntary move
Harmonious numbers; as the wakeful bird

10 invest] cover, surround.
12–16] The 'void and formless infinite' is chaos, as is 'middle darkness'; the 'Stygian pool' is hell, as is 'utter' (i.e. outer) darkness.
17 Orphean] see *Allegro* 145–50n.
19 heavenly Muse] Urania. See VII 1–39.
25–6 drop serene, dim suffusion] translations of *gutta serena* and *suffusio nigra*, medical terms for diseases of the eye.
26–9] Virgil, *Georgics* ii 475–89.
30 Zion] here represents the Hebrew poetry of the Old Testament. Cf. *PR* IV 347.
35 Thamyris] mythical Thracian bard blinded by the Muses (*Iliad* ii 594–600). Maeonides] Homer's surname.
36 Tiresias] Theban prophet whose blindness, according to Milton's Latin poem *De Idea Platonica*, gave him 'limitless light' *profundun lumen*). Cf. Marvell's 'On *PL*' ll. 43–4 (p. 147).
Phineus] mythical Thracian king who was blinded for revealing the counsels of Zeus to mortals (Hyginus, *Fabulae* xix).
38 numbers] metrical feet, hence 'lines, verses'.
bird] nightingale.

Sings darkling, and, in shadiest covert hid,
Tunes her nocturnal note. Thus with the year   40
Seasons return; but not to me returns
Day, or the sweet approach of even or morn
Or sight of vernal bloom, or summer's rose,
Or flocks, or herds, or human face divine;
But cloud instead and ever-during dark   45
Surrounds me, from the cheerful ways of men
Cut off, and, for the book of knowledge fair,
Presented with a universal blank
Of nature's works, to me expunged and razed,
And wisdom at one entrance quite shut out.   50
So much the rather thou, celestial Light,
Shine inward, and the mind through all her powers
Irradiate; there plant eyes; all mist from thence
Purge and disperse, that I may see and tell
Of things invisible to mortal sight.   55
    Now had the almighty Father from above,
From the pure empyrean where he sits
High throned above all height, bent down his eye,
His own works and their works at once to view:
About him all the sanctities of heaven   60
Stood thick as stars, and from his sight received
Beatitude past utterance; on his right
The radiant image of his glory sat,
His only Son; on earth he first beheld
Our two first parents, yet the only two   65
Of mankind, in the happy garden placed,
Reaping immortal fruits of joy and love,
Uninterrupted joy, unrivalled love,
In blissful solitude; he then surveyed
Hell and the gulf between, and Satan there   70
Coasting the wall of heaven on this side night,
In the dun air sublime, and ready now
To stoop with wearied wings, and willing feet,
On the bare outside of this world, that seemed
Firm land imbosomed without firmament,   75
Uncertain which, in ocean or in air.
Him God beholding from his prospect high,

39 darkling] in the dark.
60 sanctities] a metonymy for 'angels'.
61 his sight] the sight of him.
72 sublime] means 'aloft', and refers to Satan's flight.
73 stoop] 'swoop down', a term from falconry.
74 bare outside] see ll.416–19n.

Wherein past, present, future, he beholds,
Thus to his only Son foreseeing spake:
  'Only-begotten Son, seest thou what rage   80
Transports our adversary, whom no bounds
Prescribed, no bars of hell, nor all the chains
Heaped on him there, nor yet the main abyss
Wide interrupt, can hold; so bent he seems
On desperate revenge, that shall redound   85
Upon his own rebellious head. And now
Through all restraint broke loose he wings his way
Not far off heaven, in the precincts of light,
Directly towards the new-created world,
And man there placed, with purpose to assay   90
If him by force he can destroy, or, worse,
By some false guile pervert: and shall pervert;
For man will hearken to his glozing lies,
And easily transgress the sole command,
Sole pledge of his obedience: so will fall   95
He and his faithless progeny: whose fault?
Whose but his own? Ingrate, he had of me
All he could have; I made him just and right,
Sufficient to have stood, though free to fall.
Such I created all the ethereal powers   100
And spirits, both them who stood and them who failed:
Freely they stood who stood, and fell who fell.
Not free, what proof could they have given sincere
Of true allegiance, constant faith, or love,
Where only what they needs must do appeared,   105
Not what they would? What praise could they receive,
What pleasure I, from such obedience paid,
When will and reason (reason also is choice),
Useless and vain, of freedom both despoiled,
Made passive both, had served necessity,   110
Not me? They therefore as to right belonged
So were created, nor can justly accuse
Their maker, or their making, or their fate,
As if predestination overruled
Their will, disposed by absolute decree   115
Or high foreknowledge; they themselves decreed
Their own revolt, not I: if I foreknew,
Foreknowledge had no influence on their fault,
Which had no less proved certain unforeknown.
So without least impulse or shadow of fate,   120
Or aught by me immutably foreseen,
They trespass, authors to themselves in all,
Both what they judge and what they choose; for so

I formed them free, and free they must remain
Till they enthral themselves: I else must change   125
Their nature, and revoke the high decree
Unchangeable, eternal, which ordained
Their freedom; they themselves ordained their fall.
The first sort by their own suggestion fell,
Self-tempted, self-depraved: man falls, deceived   130
By the other first: man, therefore, shall find grace,
The other, none; in mercy and justice both,
Through heaven and earth, so shall my glory excel;
But mercy, first and last, shall brightest shine.'
    Thus while God spake ambrosial fragrance filled   135
All heaven, and in the blessed spirits elect
Sense of new joy ineffable diffused:
Beyond compare the Son of God was seen
Most glorious; in him all his Father shone
Substantially expressed, and in his face   140
Divine compassion visibly appeared,
Love without end, and without measure grace;
Which uttering, thus he to his Father spake:
    'O Father, gracious was that word which closed
Thy sovereign sentence, that man should find grace;   145
For which both heaven and earth shall high extol
Thy praises, with the innumerable sound
Of hymns and sacred songs, wherewith thy throne
Encompassed shall resound thee ever blessed.
For, should man finally be lost – should man,   150
Thy creature late so loved, thy youngest son,
Fall circumvented thus by fraud, though joined
With his own folly? That be from thee far,
That far be from thee, Father, who art judge
Of all things made, and judgest only right.   155
Or shall the adversary thus obtain
His end, and frustrate thine? Shall he fulfil
His malice, and thy goodness bring to naught
Or proud return, though to his heavier doom
Yet with revenge accomplished, and to hell   160
Draw after him the whole race of mankind,
By him corrupted? Or wilt thou thyself

---

129 first sort] the rebellious angels.
136 spirits elect] the good angels. I Tim. v. 21.
139–40 Heb. 1. i. 3.
153–4] Gen. xviii. 25.
156 adversary] See I 82n.
158 naught] means both 'nothing' and 'evil' (cf. 'naughty').

Abolish thy creation, and unmake,
For him, what for thy glory thou hast made?
So should thy goodness and thy greatness both   165
Be questioned and blasphemed without defence.'
    To whom the great creator thus replied:
'O Son, in whom my soul hath chief delight,
Son of my bosom, Son who art alone
My word, my wisdom, and effectual might,   170
All hast thou spoken as my thoughts are, all
As my eternal purpose hath decreed:
Man shall not quite be lost, but saved who will,
Yet not of will in him, but grace in me
Freely vouchsafed; once more I will renew   175
His lapsèd powers, though forfeit, and enthralled
By sin to foul exorbitant desires:
Upheld by me, yet once more he shall stand
On even ground against his mortal foe –
By me upheld, that he may know how frail   180
His fallen condition is, and to me owe
All his deliverance, and to none but me.
Some I have chosen of peculiar grace,
Elect above the rest; so is my will:
The rest shall hear me call, and oft be warned   185
Their sinful state, and to appease betimes
The incensèd Deity, while offered grace
Invites; for I will clear their senses dark
What may suffice, and soften stony hearts
To pray, repent, and bring obedience due.   190
To prayer, repentance, and obedience due,
Though but endeavoured with sincere intent,
Mine ear shall not be slow, mine eye not shut.
And I will place within them as a guide
My umpire conscience; whom if they will hear,   195
Light after light well used they shall attain,
And to the end persisting safe arrive.
This my long sufferance, and my day of grace,
They who neglect and scorn shall never taste;
But hard be hardened, blind be blinded more,   200
That they may stumble on, and deeper fall;
And none but such from mercy I exclude.
But yet all is not done; man disobeying,

168–9] *Aeneid* i 664, Matt. iii. 17, John i. 18.
180–1] Psalm xxxix. 4.
183–5] Matt. xxii. 14.
189] Ezek. xxxvi. 26.

Disloyal, breaks his fealty, and sins
Against the high supremacy of heaven, 205
Affecting Godhead, and so losing all,
To expiate his treason hath naught left,
But to destruction sacred and devote,
He with his whole posterity must die –
Die he or justice must; unless for him 210
Some other, able, and as willing, pay
The rigid satisfaction, death for death.
Say heavenly powers, where shall we find such love?
Which of ye will be mortal, to redeem
Man's mortal crime, and just, the unjust to save? 215
Dwells in all heaven charity so dear?'
    He asked, but all the heavenly choir stood mute,
And silence was in heaven: on man's behalf
Patron or intercessor none appeared –
Much less that durst upon his own head draw 220
The deadly forfeiture, and ransom set.
And now without redemption all mankind
Must have been lost, adjudged to death and hell
By doom severe, had not the Son of God,
In whom the fullness dwells of love divine, 225
His dearest mediation thus renewed:
    'Father, thy word is passed, man shall find grace;
And shall Grace not find means, that finds her way,
The speediest of thy wingèd messengers,
To visit all thy creatures, and to all 230
Comes unprevented, unimplored, unsought?
Happy for man, so coming; he her aid
Can never seek, once dead in sins and lost –
Atonement for himself, or offering meet,
Indebted and undone, hath none to bring; 235
Behold me, then: me for him, life for life,
I offer; on me let thine anger fall;
Account me man: I for his sake will leave
Thy bosom, and this glory next to thee

---

206 Affecting] seeking.
208 sacred] primarily 'dedicated', but also 'accursed'.
    devote] doomed.
215] I Pet. iii. 18.
216 charity] the 'love' of Rom. v. 8 (ἀγάπη, translated into Latin as *caritas*).
218] Rev. viii. 1.
225] Col. ii. 9.
231 unprevented] unanticipated (i.e. not achieved by prayer). On grace preced-
    ing prayer see XI 3n. Contrast Milton's translation of Psalm lxxxviii. 13
    (ll.55–6).

Freely put off, and for him lastly die   240
Well pleased; on me let Death wreak all his rage;
Under his gloomy power I shall not long
Lie vanquished; thou hast given me to possess
Life in myself for ever; by thee I live;
Though now to Death I yield, and am his due,   245
All that of me can die, yet that debt paid,
Thou wilt not leave me in the loathsome grave
His prey, nor suffer my unspotted soul
For ever with corruption there to dwell;
But I shall rise victorious, and subdue   250
My vanquisher, spoiled of his vaunted spoil;
Death his death's wound shall then receive, and stoop
Inglorious, of his mortal sting disarmed.
I through the ample air in triumph high
Shall lead hell captive maugre hell, and show   255
The powers of darkness bound. Thou, at the sight
Pleased, out of heaven shall look down and smile,
While, by thee raised, I ruin all my foes –
Death last, and with his carcass glut the grave;
Then, with the multitude of my redeemed,   260
Shall enter heaven, long absent, and return,
Father, to see thy face, wherein no cloud
Of anger shall remain, but peace assured
And reconcilement; wrath shall be no more
Thenceforth, but in thy presence joy entire.'   265
     His words here ended; but his meek aspéct
Silent yet spake, and breathed immortal love
To mortal men, above which only shone
Filial obedience: as a sacrifice
Glad to be offered, he attends the will   270
Of his great Father. Admiration seized
All heaven, what this might mean, and whither tend,
Wondering; but soon the almighty thus replied:
     'O thou in heaven and earth the only peace
Found out for mankind under wrath, O thou   275
My sole complacence! Well thou know'st how dear
To me are all my works; nor man the least,
Though last created, that for him I spare
Thee from my bosom and right hand, to save,

247-9] Psalm xvi. 10.
252-3] I Cor. xv. 55-6.
255] Psalm lxviii. 18, Eph. iv. 8. 'Maugre' means 'notwithstanding the power
    of'.
259] I Cor. xv. 26.
276 complacence] source of pleasure and satisfaction.

By losing thee a while, the whole race lost.   280
Thou, therefore, whom thou only canst redeem,
Their nature also to thy nature join;
And be thyself man among men on earth,
Made flesh, when time shall be, of virgin seed,
By wondrous birth; be thou in Adam's room   285
The head of all mankind, though Adam's son.
As in him perish all men, so in thee,
As from a second root, shall be restored
As many as are restored; without thee, none.
His crime makes guilty all his sons; thy merit   290
Imputed, shall absolve them who renounce
Their own both righteous and unrighteous deeds,
And live in thee transplanted, and from thee
Receive new life. So man, as is most just,
Shall satisfy for man, be judged and die,   295
And dying rise, and rising with him raise
His brethren, ransomed with his own dear life.
So heavenly love shall outdo hellish hate,
Giving to death, and dying to redeem,
So dearly to redeem what hellish hate
So easily destroyed, and still destroys   300
In those who, when they may, accept not grace.
Nor shalt thou, by descending to assume
Man's nature, lessen or degrade thine own.
Because thou hast, though throned in highest bliss   305
Equal to God, and equally enjoying
God-life fruition, quitted all to save
A world from utter loss, and hast been found
By merit more than birthright Son of God –
Found worthiest to be so by being good,   310
Far more than great or high; because in thee
Love hath abounded more than glory abounds;
Therefore thy humiliation shall exalt
With thee thy manhood also to this throne:
Here shalt thou sit incarnate, here shalt reign   315
Both God and man, Son both of God and man,
Anointed universal king; all power

287–9] I Cor. xv. 22.
290–1 merit/Imputed] refers to the theological doctrine whereby the sins of
  mankind are imputed to Christ, and his righteousness or merits are
  imputed to mankind. See Romans iv. 3–8, and cf. *PL* XII 294–5, 408–9.
293 transplanted] refers to the theological doctrine whereby God the Father is
  said to 'plant' or 'engraft' believers in Christ, thus rendering them fit for
  their eventual union with the body of Christ. Cf. XII 7n.
299 Giving] submitting.
317–18] Matt. xxviii. 18.

I give thee; reign for ever, and assume
Thy merits; under thee, as head supreme,
Thrones, princedoms, powers, dominions, I reduce: 320
All knees to thee shall bow of them that bide
In heaven, or earth, or under earth in hell;
When thou, attended gloriously from heaven,
Shalt in the sky appear, and from thee send
The summoning archangels to proclaim   325
Thy dread tribunal, forthwith from all winds
The living, and forthwith the cited dead
Of all past ages, to the general doom
Shall hasten; such a peal shall rouse their sleep.
Then all thy saints assembled, thou shalt judge   330
Bad men and angels; thy arraigned shall sink
Beneath thy sentence; hell, her numbers full,
Thenceforth shall be for ever shut. Meanwhile
The world shall burn, and from her ashes spring
New heaven and earth, wherein the just shall dwell,   335
And after all their tribulations long,
See golden days, fruitful of golden deeds,
With joy and love triumphing, and fair truth.
Then thou thy regal sceptre shalt lay by,
For regal sceptre then no more shall need;   340
God shall be all in all. But all ye gods,
Adore him who, to compass all this, dies;
Adore the Son, and honour him as me.'
      No sooner had the almighty ceased but – all
The multitude of angels, with a shout   345
Loud as from numbers without number, sweet
As from blessed voices, uttering joy – heaven rung
With jubilee, and loud hosannas filled
The eternal regions; lowly reverent
Towards either throne they bow, and to the ground   350
With solemn adoration down they cast
Their crowns, inwove with amarant and gold –
Immortal amarant, a flower which once

320] See Col. i. 16 (where Milton's 'princedoms' are called 'principalities').
321–2] Phil. ii. 10.
323–4] Matt. xxiv. 30–1.
327–9] I Cor. xv. 51–2.
334–5] II Pet. iii. 12–13.
343] John v. 23.
352–61] Amarant ('amaranthus' in *Lycidas* 149) is a flower that was an ancient
      symbol of immortality. In I Pet. i. 4 and v. 4 the crown of glory 'that fadeth
      not away' is said in the Greek to be ἀμαράντινον, i.e. unfading, imperishable
      (cf. l. 360).

In Paradise, fast by the tree of life,
Began to bloom, but soon for man's offence   355
To heaven removed where first it grew, there grows
And flowers aloft, shading the fount of life,
And where the river of bliss through midst of heaven
Rolls o'er Elysian flowers her amber stream;
With these, that never fade, the spirits elect   360
Bind their resplendent locks, inwreathed with beams;
Now in loose garlands thick thrown off, the bright
Pavement, that like a sea of jasper shone,
Impurpled with celestial roses smiled.
Then, crowned again, their golden harps they took –   365
Harps ever tuned, that glittering by their side
Like quivers hung; and with preamble sweet
Of charming symphony they introduce
Their sacred song, and waken raptures high:
No voice exempt, no voice but well could join   370
Melodious part; such concord is in heaven.
    'Thee, Father', first they sung, 'omnipotent,
Immutable, immortal, infinite,
Eternal king; thee, author of all being,
Fountain of light, thyself invisible   375
Amidst the glorious brightness where thou sitt'st
Throned inaccessible, but when thou shad'st
The full blaze of thy beams, and through a cloud
Drawn round about thee like a radiant shrine
Dark with excessive bright thy skirts appear,   380
Yet dazzle heaven, that brightest seraphim
Approach not, but with both wings veil their eyes.
Thee next they sang, of all creation first,
Begotten Son, divine similitude,
In whose conspicuous countenance, without cloud   385
Made visible, the almighty Father shines,
Whom else no creature can behold: on thee
Impressed the effulgence of his glory abides;
Transfused on thee his ample spirit rests.
He heaven of heavens, and all the powers therein,   390
By thee created, and by thee threw down
The aspiring dominations; thou that day
Thy Father's dreadful thunder didst not spare,
Nor stop thy flaming chariot-wheels, that shook

370 exempt] excluded from participation.
375–9] I Tim. vi. 16.
381–2] Isa. vi. 2.
383] Col. i. 15–17; Rev. iii. 14.

Heaven's everlasting frame, while o'er the necks   395
Thou drov'st of warring angels disarrayed.
Back from pursuit, thy powers with loud acclaim
Thee only extolled, Son of thy Father's might,
To execute fierce vengeance on his foes,
Not so on man: him, through their malice fallen,   400
Father of mercy and grace, thou didst not doom
So strictly, but much more to pity incline;
No sooner did thy dear and only Son
Perceive thee purposed not to doom frail man
So strictly, but much more to pity inclined   405
He to appease thy wrath, and end the strife
Of mercy and justice in thy face discerned,
Regardless of the bliss wherein he sat
Second to thee, offered himself to die
For man's offence. O unexampled love,   410
Love nowhere to be found less than divine!
Hail, Son of God, saviour of men; thy name
Shall be the copious matter of my song
Henceforth, and never shall my harp thy praise
Forget, nor from thy Father's praise disjoin.'   415
    Thus they in heaven, above the starry sphere,
Their happy hours in joy and hymning spent.
Meanwhile, upon the firm opacous globe
Of this round world, whose first convex divides
The luminous inferior orbs, enclosed   420
From Chaos and the inroad of darkness old,
Satan alighted walks; a globe far off
It seemed, now seems a boundless continent,
Dark, waste, and wild, under the frown of Night
Starless exposed, and ever-threatening storms   425
Of Chaos blustering round, inclement sky,
Save on that side which from the wall of heaven,
Though distant far, some small reflection gains
Of glimmering air less vexed with tempest loud;
Here walked the fiend at large in spacious field.   430
As when a vulture, on Imaus bred,
Whose snowy ridge the roving Tartar bounds,
Dislodging from a region scarce of prey,
To gorge the flesh of lambs or yeanling kids

416-19] The 'starry sphere' is the sphere of the fixed stars; the opaque
('opacous') globe is the created universe; the 'round world' is Earth; the
'first convex' (i.e. first sphere) is the *primum mobile*, the 'bare outside of
this world' of l. 74. Cf. ll. 481-3n.
431 Imaus] mountain range extending from the Himalayas to the Arctic Ocean.

On hills where flocks are fed, flies toward the springs　　435
Of Ganges or Hydaspes, Indian streams,
But in his way lights on the barren plains
Of Sericana, where Chineses drive
With sails and wind their cany wagons light;
So, on this windy sea of land, the fiend　　　　　　　440
Walked up and down alone, bent on his prey:
Alone, for other creature in this place,
Living or lifeless, to be found was none,
None yet, but store hereafter from the earth
Up hither like aerial vapours flew　　　　　　　　　445
Of all things transitory and vain, when sin
With vanity had filled the works of men –
Both all things vain, and all who in vain things
Built their fond hopes of glory or lasting fame,
Or happiness in this or the other life.　　　　　　450
All who have their reward on earth, the fruits
Of painful superstition and blind zeal,
Naught seeking but the praise of men, here find
Fit retribution, empty as their deeds;
All the unaccomplished works of nature's hand,　　455
Abortive, monstrous, or unkindly mixed,
Dissolved on earth, fleet hither, and in vain,
Till final dissolution, wander here –
Not in the neighbouring moon, as some have dreamed;
Those argent fields more likely habitants,　　　　460
Translated saints, or middle spirits hold,
Betwixt the angelical and human kind;
Hither of ill-joined sons and daughters born
First from the ancient world those Giants came,
With many a vain exploit, though then renowned;　　465
The builders next of Babel on the plain
Of Sennaär, and still with vain design

---

436 Hydaspes] modern Jhelum, in Pakistan.
438 Sericana] Cathay, here apparently not distinguished from China (but cf. XI 388, 90).
452 painful] painstaking, laborious.
456 unkindly] contrary to the usual course of nature.
459 some] Ariosto. Milton's Paradise of Fools (ll.444–97) is loosely modelled on a lunar limbo described in *Orlando Furioso* xxxiv.
461 Translated saints] 'Translated' is the term used in Heb. xi. 5 for the conveyance of Enoch to heaven without death (Gen. v. 24); Elijah was similarly honoured (II Kings ii. 1–18).
463–5] Gen. vi. 2–4; cf. *PL* V 447–8, XI 621–2.
466–7] Gen. xi. 1–9. Sennaär is the LXX and Vulgate form of 'Shinar' (verse 2). Cf. XII 38–62.

New Babels, had they wherewithal, would build:
Others came single; he who to be deemed
A god, leaped fondly into Aetna flames,   470
Empedocles; and he who to enjoy
Plato's Elysium, leaped into the sea,
Cleombrotus; and many more, too long,
Embryos and idiots, eremites and friars,
White, black and grey, with all their trumpery.   475
Here pilgrims roam, that strayed so far to seek
In Golgotha him dead who lives in heaven;
And they who, to be sure of Paradise,
Dying put on the weeds of Dominic,
Or in Franciscan think to pass disguised.   480
They pass the planets seven, and pass the fixed,
And that crystalline sphere whose balance weighs
The trepidation talked, and that first moved;
And now Saint Peter at heaven's wicket seems
To wait them with his keys, and now at foot   485
Of heaven's ascent they lift their feet, when lo
A violent cross wind from either coast
Blows them transverse ten thousand leagues awry,
Into the devious air; then might ye see
Cowls, hoods and habits, with their wearers, tossed   490
And fluttered into rags; then relics, beads,
Indulgences, dispenses, pardons, bulls,
The sport of winds: all these, upwhirled aloft,

469-71] There are conflicting accounts of the death of the philosopher and
    statesman Empedocles; according to one tradition he committed suicide to
    hide his own mortality.
471-3] Cleombrotus was so eager to enjoy the immortality described by Plato
    in *Phaedo* that he drowned himself.
474] In Catholic theology a limbo is provided for those who die in original sin,
    but are guiltless of personal sin. 'Embryos and idiots' were consigned to
    this *limbus infantum*.
474-5] The satire is directed against four orders of mendicant friars: Augusti-
    nian Hermits ('eremites'), Carmelites (White Friars), Dominicans (Black
    Friars), and Franciscans (Grey Friars).
477 Golgotha] The Hebrew name for Calvary, where Jesus was crucified.
481-3] Medieval Ptolemaic astronomy assumed the existence of ten spheres;
    seven were planetary spheres (including the sun), the eighth was the sphere
    of the fixed stars (the 'starry sphere' of l. 416), the ninth was the
    'crystalline sphere', and the tenth was the *primum mobile* (see *Fair Infant*
    39n). The 'trepidation' (i.e. libration, oscillation) of the eighth and ninth
    spheres was held to be responsible for the precession of the equinoxes.
484-5] Matt. xvi. 19. Cf. *Lycidas* 108-31.
492 dispenses] dispensations.

Fly o'er the backside of the world far off
Into a limbo large and broad, since called   495
The Paradise of Fools, to few unknown
Long after, now unpeopled and untrod;
All this dark globe the fiend found as he passed,
And long he wandered, till at last a gleam
Of dawning light turned thitherward in haste   500
His travelled steps; far distant he descries,
Ascending by degrees magnificent
Up to the wall of heaven, a structure high;
At top whereof, but far more rich, appeared
The work as of a kingly palace gate,   505
With frontispiece of diamond and gold
Embellished; thick with sparkling orient gems
The portal shone, inimitable on earth
By model, or by shading pencil drawn.
The stairs were such as whereon Jacob saw   510
Angels ascending and descending, bands
Of guardians bright, when he from Esau fled
To Padan-Aram, in the field of Luz
Dreaming by night under the open sky,
And waking cried 'This is the gate of heaven.'   515
Each stair mysteriously was meant, nor stood
There always, but drawn up to heaven sometimes
Viewless; and underneath a bright sea flowed
Of jasper, or of liquid pearl, whereon
Who after came from earth sailing arrived   520
Wafted by angels, or flew o'er the lake
Rapt in a chariot drawn by fiery steeds.
The stairs were then let down, whether to dare
The fiend by easy ascent, or aggravate
His sad exclusion from the doors of bliss: 525
Direct against which opened from beneath,
Just o'er the blissful seat of Paradise,
A passage down to the earth – a passage wide,
Wider by far than that of after-times
Over Mount Zion, and, though that were large,   530

501 travelled] means both 'experienced in travel' and 'wearied'.
502 degrees] steps.
510–15] Gen. xxviii. John i. 51.
518 Viewless] invisible.
    sea] described in 'The Argument' (p. 201) as 'the waters above the
    firmament'.
521 Wafted by angels] refers to Lazarus (Luke xvi. 22).
522] describes Elijah (II Kings ii. 11). Cf. *PR* II 16–17. 'Rapt' means 'carried
    away'.

Over the Promised Land to God so dear,
By which, to visit oft those happy tribes,
On high behests his angels to and fro
Passed frequent, and his eye with choice regard
From Paneas, the fount of Jordan's flood,   535
To Beërsaba, where the Holy Land
Borders on Egypt and the Arabian shore;
So wide the opening seemed, where bounds were set
To darkness, such as bound the ocean wave.
Satan from hence, now on the lower stair,   540
That scaled by steps of gold to heaven gate,
Looks down with wonder at the sudden view
Of all this world at once. As when a scout,
Through dark and desert ways with peril gone
All night, at last by break of cheerful dawn   545
Obtains the brow of some high-climbing hill,
Which to his eye discovers unaware
The goodly prospect of some foreign land
First seen, or some renowned metropolis
With glistering spires and pinnacles adorned,   550
Which now the rising sun gilds with his beams;
Such wonder seized, though after heaven seen,
The spirit malign, but much more envy seized,
At sight of all this world beheld so fair.
Round he surveys – and well might, where he stood   555
So high above the circling canopy
Of night's extended shade – from eastern point
Of Libra to the fleecy star that bears
Andromeda far off Atlantic seas
Beyond the horizon; then from pole to pole   560
He views his breadth, and without longer pause,
Down right into the world's first region throws
His flight precipitant, and winds with ease
Through the pure marble air his oblique way
Amongst innumerable stars, that shone   565
Stars distant, but nigh-hand seemed other worlds;
Or other worlds they seemed, or happy isles,
Like those Hesperian gardens famed of old,

535–6] The fountain Leddan, the largest source of the Jordan, is on the western
    side of the city of Dan, which in late Greek is called *Paneas* (modern
    Baniyas, in Syria). The formula 'from Dan even to Beer-sheba' is common
    in the O.T., and refers to the extreme northern and southern points of
    Israel; Beërsaba is the Vulgate and LXX form.
558 fleecy star] Aries, the Ram.
564 marble] smooth as marble.
568] See *Comus* 393–5n.

Fortunate fields, and groves, and flowery vales;
Thrice happy isles – but who dwelt happy there   570
He stayed not to inquire: above them all
The golden sun, in splendour likest heaven,
Allured his eye; thither his course he bends,
Through the calm firmament – but up or down,
By centre or eccentric, hard to tell,   575
Or longitude – where the great luminary,
Aloof the vulgar constellations thick,
That from his lordly eye keep distance due,
Dispenses light from far; they, as they move
Their starry dance in numbers that compute   580
Days, months, and years, towards his all-cheering lamp
Turn swift their various motions, or are turned
By his magnetic beam, that gently warms
The universe, and to each inward part
With gentle penetration, though unseen,   585
Shoots invisible virtue even to the deep;
So wondrously was set his station bright.
There lands the fiend, a spot like which perhaps
Astronomer in the sun's lucent orb
Through his glazed optic tube yet never saw.   590
The place he found beyond expression bright,
Compared with aught on earth, metal or stone –
Not all parts like, but all alike informed
With radiant light, as glowing iron with fire.
If metal, part seemed gold, part silver clear;   595
If stone, carbuncle most or chrysolite,
Ruby or topaz, to the twelve that shone
In Aaron's breast-plate, and a stone besides,
Imagined rather oft than elsewhere seen –
That stone, or like to that, which here below   600

---

575 centre] centric (orbit). A centric orbit has the earth or sun at its centre; an
   eccentric orbit does not. In the Ptolemaic system eccentric orbits were used
   (along with epicycles; see VIII 84n.) to account for irregularities in
   planetary motion. Ll. 574-6 thus accommodate the possibility of either a
   Ptolemaic or a Copernican universe.
576 longitude] distance as measured by degrees of longitude along the ecliptic.
577 Aloof] apart from.
   vulgar] used for the calculation of distance.
588-90 Sun-spots had been observed by Galileo in 1610, and by Fabricius in
   1611.
596-8] Exod. xxviii. 17-20. Chrysolite appears as the first stone in the fourth
   row in the LXX and Vulgate.
600-1] The 'philosophers' stone' was supposed by alchemists to possess the
   property of changing other metals into gold or silver.

Philosophers in vain so long have sought;
In vain, though by their powerful art they bind
Volatile Hermes, and call up unbound
In various shapes old Proteus from the sea,
Drained through a limbeck to his native form.   605
What wonder then if fields and regions here
Breathe forth elixir pure, and rivers run
Potable gold, when with one virtuous touch
The arch-chemic sun, so far from us remote,
Produces, with terrestrial humour mixed,   610
Here in the dark so many precious things
Of colour glorious and effect so rare?
Here matter new to gaze the devil met
Undazzled; far and wide his eye commands;
For sight no obstacle found here, nor shade,   615
But all sunshine, as when his beams at noon
Culminate from the equator, as they now
Shot upward still direct, whence no way round
Shadow from body opaque can fall; and the air,
Nowhere so clear, sharpened his visual ray   620
To objects distant far, whereby he soon
Saw within ken a glorious angel stand,
The same whom John saw also in the sun;
His back was turned, but not his brightness hid;
Of beaming sunny rays a golden tiar   625
Circled his head, nor less his locks behind
Illustrious on his shoulders fledge with wings
Lay waving round: on some great charge employed
He seemed, or fixed in cogitation deep.

602-3 bind ... Hermes] solidify mercury.
604 Proteus] Greek sea-god who had the power to assume any form he wished,
    hence an appropriate metaphor for the alchemical transmutation of matter.
605 limbeck] alembic, an apparatus used to distil mercury.
606 here] in the sun.
607 elixir] a substance such as the philosophers' stone which would change
    metals into gold.
608 Potable] drinkable.
    virtuous] life-giving.
609 arch-chemic] chief of alchemists, so called because its rays were said to
    penetrate the surface of the earth and produce precious stones. Cf. *PL* V
    300-2, VI 477-81.
610 humour] moisture.
618 still direct] Before the fall occasioned the 'changes in the heavens'
    described in *PL* X 668-91, the sun's ecliptic coincided with the earth's
    equator, and 'direct' beams were therefore a daily occurrence.
623] Rev. xix. 17.
627 Illustrious] lustrous, shining.

Glad was the spirit impure, as now in hope　　　　　630
To find who might direct his wandering flight
To Paradise, the happy seat of man,
His journey's end, and our beginning woe.
But first he casts to change his proper shape,
Which else might work him danger or delay:　　　　　635
And now a stripling cherub he appears,
Not of the prime, yet such as in his face
Youth smiled celestial, and to every limb
Suitable grace diffused, so well he feigned;
Under a coronet his flowing hair　　　　　640
In curls on either cheek played; wings he wore
Of many a coloured plume sprinkled with gold,
His habit fit for speed succinct, and held
Before his decent steps a silver wand.
He drew not nigh unheard; the angel bright,　　　　　645
Ere he drew nigh, his radiant visage turned,
Admonished by his ear, and straight was known
The archangel Uriel – one of the seven
Who in God's presence, nearest to his throne,
Stand ready at command, and are his eyes　　　　　650
That run through all the heavens, or down to the earth
Bear his swift errands over moist and dry,
O'er sea and land; him Satan thus accosts:
　'Uriel, for thou of those seven spirits that stand
In sight of God's high throne, gloriously bright,　　　　　655
The first art wont his great authentic will
Interpreter through highest heaven to bring,
Where all his sons thy embassy attend,
And here art likeliest by supreme decree
Like honour to obtain, and as his eye　　　　　660
To visit oft this new Creation round –
Unspeakable desire to see and know
All these his wondrous works, but chiefly man,
His chief delight and favour, him for whom
All these his works so wondrous he ordained,　　　　　665
Hath brought me from the choirs of cherubim
Alone thus wandering. Brightest seraph, tell
In which of all these shining orbs hath man

---

634 casts] decides.
643 succinct] modifies 'habit', and means 'close-fitting, scant'.
648 Uriel] The name means in Hebrew 'flame (or light) of God', but in the O.T.
　　it is never used of an angel. Milton probably had access to the tradition
　　embodied in the pseudepigraphical Ethiopic Book of Enoch (xx. 2), where
　　Uriel is described as 'the angel who is over the world and Tartarus'.
648-9] Rev. i. 4.

His fixèd seat – or fixèd seat hath none,
But all these shining orbs his choice to dwell –   670
That I may find him, and with secret gaze
Or open admiration him behold
On whom the great creator hath bestowed
Worlds, and on whom hath all these graces poured;
That both in him and all things, as is meet,   675
The universal maker we may praise;
Who justly hath driven out his rebel foes
To deepest hell, and, to repair that loss,
Created this new happy race of men
To serve him better: wise are all his ways.'   680
    So spake the false dissembler unperceived;
For neither man nor angel can discern
Hypocrisy – the only evil that walks
Invisible, except to God alone,
By his permissive will, through heaven and earth;   685
And oft, though wisdom wake, suspicion sleeps
At wisdom's gate, and to simplicity
Resigns her charge, while godness thinks no ill
Where no ill seems: which now for once beguiled
Uriel, though regent of the sun, and held   690
The sharpest-sighted spirit of all in heaven;
Who to the fraudulent impostor foul,
In his uprightness, answer thus returned:
    'Fair angel, thy desire, which tends to know
The works of God, thereby to glorify   695
The great work-master, leads to no excess
That reaches blame, but rather merits praise
The more it seems excess, that led thee hither
From thy empyreal mansion thus alone,
To witness with thine eyes what some perhaps,   700
Contented with report, hear only in heaven:
For wonderful indeed are all his works,
Pleasant to know, and worthiest to be all
Had in remembrance always with delight;
But what created mind can comprehend   705
Their number, or the wisdom infinite
That brought them forth, but hid their causes deep?
I saw when, at his word, the formless mass,
This world's material mould, came to a heap:
Confusion heard his voice, and wild uproar   710

671-2] Echoes Herod's words in Matt. ii. 8.
706-7] Prov. iii. 19.
709 mould] substance.

Stood ruled, stood vast infinitude confined;
Till, at his second bidding, darkness fled,
Light shone, and order from disorder sprung;
Swift to their several quarters hasted then
The cumbrous elements – earth, flood, air, fire;　　715
And this ethereal quintessence of heaven
Flew upward, spirited with various forms,
That rolled orbicular, and turned to stars
Numberless, as thou seest, and how they move:
Each had his place appointed, each his course;　　720
The rest in circuit walls this universe.
Look downward on that globe, whose hither side
With light from hence, though but reflected, shines:
That place is earth, the seat of man; that light
His day, which else, as the other hemisphere,　　725
Night would invade; but there the neighbouring moon
(So call that opposite fair star) her aid
Timely interposes, and her monthly round
Still ending, still renewing, through mid-heaven,
With borrowed light her countenance triform　　730
Hence fills and empties, to enlighten the earth,
And in her pale dominion checks the night.
That spot to which I point is Paradise,
Adam's abode; those lofty shades his bower.
Thy way thou canst not miss; me mine requires.'　　735
　　Thus said, he turned; and Satan, bowing low,
As to superior spirits is wont in heaven,
Where honour due and reverence none neglects,
Took leave, and toward the coast of earth beneath,
Down from the ecliptic, sped with hoped success,　　740
Throws his steep flight in many an airy wheel,
Nor stayed till on Niphates' top he lights.

THE END OF THE THIRD BOOK

---

716 quintessence] the 'fifth essence', the substance of which heavenly bodies
　　were composed, was 'ether'. Cf. *PL* VII 243-4.
730 triform] Diana was thought to be triform for several reasons, among which
　　was conformity to the three phases of the moon.
742 Niphates] mountain on the border of Armenia and Assyria.

BOOK IV

THE ARGUMENT

Satan, now in prospect of Eden, and nigh the place where he must now attempt the bold enterprise which he undertook alone against God and man, falls into many doubts with himself and many passions – fear, envy, and despair; but at length confirms himself in evil; journeys on to Paradise, whose outward prospect and situation is described; overleaps the bounds; sits, in the shape of a cormorant, on the tree of life, as highest in the garden, to look about him. The garden described; Satan's first sight of Adam and Eve; his wonder at their excellent form and happy state, but with resolution to work their fall; overhears their discourse; thence gathers that the tree of knowledge was forbidden them to eat of under penalty of death, and thereon intends to found his temptation by seducing them to transgress; then leaves them a while, to know further of their state by some other means. Meanwhile Uriel, descending on a sunbeam, warns Gabriel, who had in charge the gate of Paradise, that some evil spirit had escaped the deep, and passed at noon by his sphere, in the shape of a good angel, down to Paradise, discovered after by his furious gestures in the mount. Gabriel promises to find him ere morning. Night coming on, Adam and Eve discourse of going to their rest: their bower described; their evening worship. Gabriel, drawing forth his bands of night-watch to walk the round of Paradise, appoints two strong angels to Adam's bower, lest the evil spirit should be there doing some harm to Adam or Eve sleeping: there they find him at the ear of Eve, tempting her in a dream, and bring him, though unwilling, to Gabriel; by whom questioned, he scornfully answers; prepares resistance; but hindered by a sign from heaven, flies out of Paradise.

O for that warning voice, which he who saw
The Apocalypse heard cry in heaven aloud,
Then when the dragon, put to second rout,
Came furious down to be revenged on men,
'Woe to the inhabitants on Earth!' that now,   5
While time was, our first parents had been warned
The coming of their secret foe, and scaped,
Haply so scaped, his mortal snare; for now
Satan, now first inflamed with rage, came down,
The tempter, ere the accuser, of mankind,   10
To wreak on innocent frail man his loss
Of that first battle, and his flight to hell;
Yet not rejoicing in his speed, though bold

1-12] On the 'warning voice' which John heard see Rev. xii. 3-12.

Far off and fearless, nor with cause to boast,
Begins his dire attempt; which, nigh the birth   15
Now rolling, boils in his tumultuous breast,
And like a devilish engine back recoils
Upon himself; horror and doubt distract
His troubled thoughts, and from the bottom stir
The hell within him; for within him hell   20
He brings, and round about him, nor from hell
One step, no more than from himself, can fly
By change of place; now conscience wakes despair
That slumbered, wakes the bitter memory
Of what he was, what is, and what must be   25
Worse; of worse deeds worse sufferings must ensue.
Sometimes towards Eden, which now in his view
Lay pleasant, his grieved look he fixes sad;
Sometimes towards heaven and the full-blazing sun,
Which now sat high in his meridan tower: 30
Then, much revolving, thus in sighs began:
   'O thou that, with surpassing glory crowned,
Look'st from thy sole dominion like the God
Of this new world – at whose sight all the stars
Hide their diminished heads – to thee I call,   35
But with no friendly voice, and add thy name,
O sun, to tell thee how I hate thy beams
That bring to my remembrance from what state
I fell, how glorious once above thy sphere,
Till pride and worse ambition threw me down,   40
Warring in heaven against heaven's matchless king;
Ah, wherefore? He deserved no such return
From me, whom he created what I was
In that bright eminence, and with his good
Upbraided none; nor was his service hard.   45
What could be less than to afford him praise,
The easiest recompense, and pay him thanks,
How due! Yet all his good proved ill in me,
And wrought but malice; lifted up so high,
I sdeigned subjection, and thought one step higher   50
Would set me highest, and in a moment quit
The debt immense of endless gratitude,

17 engine] The primary meaning is 'cannon', and the secondary 'plot'.
2–8] 'Eden' means 'pleasure, delight' in Hebrew.
31 revolving] deliberating, meditating.
37] John iii. 20.
38–9] Rev. ii. 5.
50 sdeigned] disdained.

So burdensome, still paying, still to owe;
Forgetful what from him I still received,
And understood not that a grateful mind   55
By owing owes not, but still pays, at once
Indebted and discharged – what burden then?
Oh, had his powerful destiny ordained
Me some inferior angel, I had stood
Then happy; no unbounded hope had raised   60
Ambition. Yet why not? Some other power
As great might have aspired, and me, though mean,
Drawn to his part; but other powers as great
Fell not, but stand unshaken, from within
Or from without to all temptations armed.   65
Hadst thou the same free will and power to stand?
Thou hadst; whom hast thou then, or what, to accuse,
But heaven's free love dealt equally to all?
Be then his love accursed, since love or hate
To me alike it deals eternal woe.   70
Nay, cursed be thou; since against his thy will
Chose freely what it now so justly rues.
Me miserable! Which way shall I fly
Infinite wrath and infinite despair?
Which way I fly is hell; myself am hell;   75
And, in the lowest deep, a lower deep
Still threatening to devour me opens wide,
To which the hell I suffer seems a heaven.
O, then, at last relent; is there no place
Left for repentance, none for pardon left?   80
None left but by submission; and that word
Disdain forbids me, and my dread of shame
Among the spirits beneath, whom I seduced
With other promises and other vaunts
Than to submit, boasting I could subdue   85
The omnipotent. Ay me, they little know
How dearly I abide that boast so vain,
Under what torments inwardly I groan;
While they adore me on the throne of hell,
With diadem and sceptre high advanced,   90
The lower still I fall, only supreme
In misery: such joy ambition finds.
But say I could repent, and could obtain,
By act of grace my former state; how soon
Would height recall high thoughts, how soon unsay   95

53 still] continually.
66, 67, 71 thou] Satan addresses himself.
79–80] Heb. xii. 17.

What feigned submission swore; ease would recant
Vows made in pain, as violent and void;
For never can true reconcilement grow
Where wounds of deadly hate have pierced so deep;
Which would but lead me to a worse relapse   100
And heavier fall: so should I purchase dear
Short intermission, bought with double smart.
This knows my punisher; therefore as far
From granting he, as I from begging, peace;
All hope excluded thus, behold, instead   105
Of us, outcast, exiled, his new delight,
Mankind, created, and for him this world.
So farewell hope, and, with hope, farewell fear,
Farwell remorse; all good to me is lost;
Evil, be thou my good: by thee at least   110
Divided empire with heaven's king I hold,
By thee, and more than half perhaps will reign;
As man ere long, and this new world, shall know.'
    Thus while he spake, each passion dimmed his face,
Thrice changed with pale – ire, envy, and despair;   115
Which marred his borrowed visage, and betrayed
Him counterfeit, if any eye beheld:
For heavenly minds from such distempers foul
Are ever clear. Whereof he soon aware
Each perturbation smoothed with outward calm,   120
Artificer of fraud; and was the first
That practised falsehood under saintly show,
Deep malice to conceal, couched with revenge:
Yet not enough had practised to deceive
Uriel, once warned; whose eye pursued him down   125
The way he went, and on the Assyrian mount
Saw him disfigured, more than could befall
Spirit of happy sort: his gestures fierce
He marked and mad demeanour, then alone,
As he supposed, all unobserved, unseen.   130
So on he fares, and to the border comes
Of Eden, where delicious Paradise,
Now nearer, crowns with her enclosure green,
As with a rural mound, the champaign head
Of a steep wilderness, whose hairy sides   135
With thicket overgrown, grotesque and wild,

110] Isa. v. 20.
115 pale] pallor.
123 couched] hidden.
126 Assyrian mount] Niphates (III 742).
134 champaign] free from woods and enclosures.

Access denied; and overhead up-grew
Insuperable height of loftiest shade,
Cedar, and pine, and fir, and branching palm,
A sylvan scene, and as the ranks ascend   140
Shade above shade, a woody theatre
Of stateliest view. Yet higher than their tops
The verdurous wall of Paradise up-sprung;
Which to our general sire gave prospect large
Into his nether empire neighbouring round.   145
And higher than that wall a circling row
Of goodliest trees, loaded with fairest fruit,
Blossoms and fruits at once of golden hue,
Appeared, with gay enamelled colours mixed;
On which the sun more glad impressed his beams   150
Than in fair evening cloud, or humid bow,
When God hath showered the earth: so lovely seemed
That landscape; and of pure now purer air
Meets his approach, and to the heart inspires
Vernal delight and joy, able to drive   155
All sadness but despair; now gentle gales,
Fanning their odoriferous wings, dispense
Native perfumes, and whisper whence they stole
Those balmy spoils. As when to them who sail
Beyond the Cape of Hope, and now are past   160
Mozàmbique, off at sea north-east winds blow
Sabean odours from the spicy shore
Of Araby the Blest, with such delay
Well pleased they slack their course, and many a league
Cheered with the grateful smell old Ocean smiles;   165
So entertained those odorous sweets the fiend
Who came their bane, though with them better pleased
Than Asmodëus with the fishy fume
That drove him, though enamoured, from the spouse
Of Tobit's son, and with a vengeance sent   170
From Media post to Egypt, there fast bound.
     Now to the ascent of that steep savage hill

149 enamelled] beautified with various colours.
153 of] expresses transformation from one condition to another.
163 Araby the Blest] the *Arabia Felix* of classical antiquity: Saba (hence
  'Sabean'), i.e. Sheba, modern Yemen.
166-71] In the apocryphal Book of Tobit, Asmodeus (Asmadai in *PL* VI 365,
  and Asmodai in *PR* II 151) is the evil spirit who kills Sara's seven
  husbands, and is exorcized by Tobias ('Tobit's son'), who on the advice of
  the angel Raphael burns the heart and liver of a fish, the smell of which
  drives the spirit 'into the utmost parts of Egypt, and the angel bound him'
  (Tobit viii. 3). In the Greek version of Tobit Asmodeus is merely an evil
  spirit (τὸ πονηρὸν οαιμόνιον), but Milton probably knew that in the Aramaic
  and Hebrew versions he is 'King of the Shedhim (i.e. demons)'.

Satan had journeyed on, pensive and slow;
But further way found none, so thick entwined,
As one continued brake, the undergrowth   175
Of shrubs and tangling bushes had perplexed
All path of man or beast that passed that way;
One gate there only was, and that looked east
On the other side: which when the arch-felon saw,
Due entrance he disdained, and, in contempt,   180
At one slight bound high overleaped all bound
Of hill or highest wall, and sheer within
Lights on his feet. As when a prowling wolf,
Whom hunger drives to seek new haunt for prey,
Watching where shepherds pen their flocks at eve,   185
In hurdled cotes amid the field secure,
Leaps o'er the fence with ease into the fold;
Or as a thief, bent to unhoard the cash
Of some rich burgher, whose substantial doors,
Cross-barred and bolted fast, fear no assault,   190
In at the window climbs, or o'er the tiles;
So clomb this first grand thief into God's fold:
So since into his church lewd hirelings climb.
Thence up he flew, and on the tree of life,
The middle tree and highest there that grew,   195
Sat like a cormorant; yet not true life
Thereby regained, but sat devising death
To them who lived; nor on the virtue thought
Of that life-giving plant, but only used
For prospect, what well used had been the pledge   200
Of immortality. So little knows
Any, but God alone, to value right
The good before him, but perverts best things
To worst abuse, or to their meanest use.
Beneath him, with new wonder, now he views,   205
To all delight of human sense exposed,
In narrow room nature's whole wealth; yea, more –
A heaven on earth: for blissful Paradise
Of God the garden was, by him in the east
Of Eden planted; Eden stretched her line   210
From Auran eastward to the royal towers
Of great Seleucia, built by Grecian kings,

176 had perplexed] would have entangled.
193 lewd] evil, unprincipled.
211 Auran] the Vulgate form of Hauran (Ezek. xlvii. 16, 18), a tract of land east
    of the Jordan.
212] Seleucus Nicator, Alexander's general, built nine cities called Seleucia, one
    of which, on the Tigris, was called 'The Great' to distinguish it from others
    of the same name. Cf. PR III 291.

Or where the sons of Eden long before
Dwelt in Telassar; in this pleasant soil
His far more pleasant garden God ordained;   215
Out of the fertile ground he caused to grow
All trees of noblest kind for sight, smell, taste;
And all amid them stood the tree of life,
High eminent, blooming ambrosial fruit
Of vegetable gold; and next to life,   220
Our death, the tree of knowledge, grew fast by –
Knowledge of good, bought dear by knowing ill.
Southward through Eden went a river large,
Nor changed his course, but through the shaggy hill
Passed underneath ingulfed; for God had thrown   225
That mountain, as his garden-mould, high raised
Upon the rapid current, which through veins
Of porous earth with kindly thirst up-drawn,
Rose a fresh fountain, and with many a rill
Watered the garden; thence united fell   230
Down the steep glade, and met the nether flood,
Which from his darksome passage now appears,
And now, divided into four main streams,
Runs diverse, wandering many a famous realm
And country whereof here needs no account;   235
But rather to tell how, if art could tell
How, from that sapphire fount the crispèd brooks,
Rolling on orient pearl and sands of gold,
With mazy error under pendant shades
Ran nectar, visiting each plant, and fed   240
Flowers worthy of Paradise, which not nice art
In beds and curious knots, but nature boon
Poured forth profuse on hill and dale and plain,
Both where the morning sun first warmly smote
The open field, and where the unpierced shade   245
Embrowned the noontide bowers; thus was this place,
A happy rural seat of various view:
Groves whose rich trees wept odorous gums and balm;
Others whose fruit, burnished with golden rind,

---

214 Telassar] II Kings xix. 12; Isa. xxxvii. 12.
219 blooming] causing to flourish.
223 river] identified as the Tigris in *PL* IX 71-3.
229 fountain] The Vulgate version of Gen. ii. 6 has a fountain instead of mist;
     Sed fons ascendebat e terra.
239 error] used in the Latin sense of 'wandering'.
242 knots] alludes to the dying fashion for formal geometrical garden designs.
     bon] bountiful.
246 Embrowned] darkened.

Hung amiable – Hesperian fables true,   250
If true, here only – and of delicious taste;
Betwixt them lawns, or level downs, and flocks
Grazing the tender herb, were interposed,
Or palmy hillock; or the flowery lap
Of some irriguous valley spread her store,   255
Flowers of all hue, and without thorn the rose.
Another side, umbrageous grots and caves
Of cool recess, o'er which the mantling vine
Lays forth her purple grape, and gently creeps
Luxuriant; meanwhile murmuring waters fall   260
Down the slope hills dispersed, or in a lake,
That to the fringèd bank with myrtle crowned
Her crystal mirror holds, unite their streams.
The birds their choir apply; airs, vernal airs,
Breathing the smell of field and grove, attune   265
The trembling leaves, while universal Pan,
Knit with the Graces and the Hours in dance,
Led on the eternal Spring. Not that fair field
Of Enna, where Proserpine gathering flowers,
Herself a fairer flower, by gloomy Dis   270
Was gathered – which cost Ceres all that pain
To seek her through the world – nor that sweet grove
Of Daphne, by Orontes and the inspired
Castalian spring, might with this Paradise
Of Eden strive; nor that Nyseian isle,   275
Girt with the river Triton, where old Cham,

250-1] See *Comus* 393-5n.
255 irriguous] well-watered.
256 without thorn the rose] a common patristic inference from Gen. iii. 18.
266 universal Pan] here means universal nature, but cf. *Nativity* 89n.
267 Graces, Hours] See *Allegro* 12-16n.
268-72] Proserpina, daughter of Ceres, was carried off by Dis (Pluto) while gathering flowers (near Enna, according to *Metamorphoses* v 385-95). Proserpina was never allowed to leave the underworld permanently, because she had eaten six seeds from the pomegranate of Jove, which in the Renaissance was identified with the fruit which Eve ate.
272-4] Daphne is here a grove near Antioch, beside the river Orontes; in antiquity it had an oracle of Apollo (hence 'inspired') and a stream named Castalia after the spring on Parnassus. Here the nymph Daphne, daughter of the river-god Peneus, was turned into a laurel (see *Comus* 661-2) to protect her from the ravages of Apollo. Cf. *PR* II 187.
275-9] Cham is the Vulgate name for Ham, the son of Noah, who was commonly identified with Ammon, Libyc Jove (called Libyc Hammon in *Nativity* 203), the Egyptian god. According to Diodorus Siculus (*Library* iii. 67-70) the Libyan King Ammon (who was identified with the god Ammon) became the lover of the nymph Amalthea, who gave birth to Bacchus. Ammon hid his lover and their child on Nysa, an island in the 'river Triton' near modern Tunis, in order to protect them from the wrath of his wife Rhea.

Whom Gentiles Ammon call and Libyan Jove,
Hid Amalthea and her florid son,
Young Bacchus, from his stepdame Rhea's eye;
Nor, where Abassin kings their issue guard,   280
Mount Amara – though this by some supposed
True Paradise – under the Ethiop line
By Nilus' head, enclosed with shining rock,
A whole day's journey high, but wide remote
From this Assyrian garden, where the fiend   285
Saw undelighted all delight, all kind
Of living creatures, new to sight and strange.
Two of far nobler shape, erect and tall,
God-like erect, with native honour clad
In naked majesty, seemed lords of all,   290
And worthy seemed; for in their looks divine
The image of their glorious maker shone,
Truth, wisdom, sanctitude severe and pure –
Severe, but in true filial freedom placed,
Whence true authority in men: though both   295
Not equal, as their sex not equal seemed;
For contemplation he and valour formed,
For softness she and sweet attractive grace;
He for God only, she for God in him;
His fair large front and eye sublime declared   300
Absolute rule; and hyacinthine locks
Round from his parted forelock manly hung
Clustering, but not beneath his shoulders broad:
She as a veil down to the slender waist,
Her unadornèd golden tresses wore   305
Dishevelled, but in wanton ringlets waved
As the vine curls her tendrils – which implied
Subjection, but required with gentle sway,
And by her yielded, by him best received
Yielded, with coy submission, modest pride,   310
And sweet reluctant amorous delay.
Nor those mysterious parts were then concealed;
Then was not guilty shame, dishonest shame

280-5] The sons ('issue') of Abyssinian ('Abassin') kings were raised in seclusion
    in palaces on 'Mount Amara', on the equator ('Ethiop line').
300 front] forehead.
    sublime] means both 'exalted, lofty' and 'raised up'.
301-5] See I Cor. xi. 7-15 (and A.V. marginal note to v. 10). Hyacinthine may
    allude to the hair of Odysseus (*Odyssey* vi. 230-1) or to Hyacinth, the boy
    whom Apollo loved (see *Fair Infant* 23-6n.).
310 coy] modest, shy, quiet.
313 dishonest] unchaste, lewd.

Of nature's works, honour dishonourable,
Sin-bred, how have ye troubled all mankind   315
With shows instead, mere shows of seeming pure,
And banished from man's life his happiest life,
Simplicity and spotless innocence.
So passed they naked on, nor shunned the sight
Of God or angel, for they thought no ill: 320
So hand in hand they passed, the liveliest pair
That ever since in love's embraces met –
Adam the goodliest man of men since born
His sons; the fairest of her daughters Eve.
Under a tuft of shade that on a green   325
Stood whispering soft, by a fresh fountain-side,
They sat them down, and after no more toil
Of their sweet gardening labour than sufficed
To recommend cool Zephyr, and made ease
More easy, wholesome thirst and appetite   330
More grateful, to their supper-fruits they fell –
Nectarine fruits, which the compliant boughs
Yielded them, sidelong as they sat recline
On the soft downy bank damasked with flowers:
The savoury pulp they chew, and in the rind,   335
Still as they thirsted, scoop the brimming stream;
Nor gentle purpose, nor endearing smiles
Wanted, nor youthful dalliance, as beseems
Fair couple linked in happy nuptial league,
Alone as they. About them frisking played   340
All beasts of the earth, since wild, and of all chase
In wood or wilderness, forest or den;
Sporting the lion ramped, and in his paw
Dandled the kid; bears, tigers, ounces, pards,
Gambolled before them; the unwieldy elephant,   345
To make them mirth, used all his might, and wreathed
His lithe proboscis; close the serpent sly,
Insinuating, wove with Gordian twine
His braided train, and of his fatal guile
Gave proof unheeded; others on the grass   350

321] The clasping of hands is a traditional symbol of the pledging of faith. Cf.
    IV 488–9, 689, 739, IX 385–6, 1037, XII 648.
329 Zephyr] the west wind.
332 Nectarine] as sweet as nectar, the drink of the gods.
337 purpose] conversation.
341 chase] habitat of wild animals.
344 ounces] See *Comus* 71n.
    pards] The name was used of both panthers and leopards.
348 Insinuating] penetrating by sinuous windings.

Couched, and, now filled with pasture, gazing sat,
Or bedward ruminating; for the sun,
Declined, was hasting now with prone career
To the Ocean Isles, and in the ascending scale
Of heaven the stars that usher evening rose: 355
When Satan, still in gaze as first he stood,
Scarce thus at length failed speech recovered sad:
     'O hell! What do mine eyes with grief behold?
Into our room of bliss thus high advanced
Creatures of other mould – earth-born perhaps,   360
Not spirits, yet to heavenly spirits bright
Little inferior – whom my thoughts pursue
With wonder, and could love; so lively shines
In them divine resemblance, and such grace   364
The hand that formed them on their shape hath poured.
Ah gentle pair, ye little think how nigh
Your change approaches, when all these delights
Will vanish, and deliver ye to woe –
More woe, the more your taste is now of joy:
Happy, but for so happy ill secured   370
Long to continue, and this high seat, your heaven,
Ill fenced for heaven to keep out such a foe
As now is entered; yet no purposed foe
To you, whom I could pity thus forlorn,
Though I unpitied; league with you I seek,   375
And mutual amity, so strait, so close,
That I with you must dwell, or you with me,
Henceforth; my dwelling haply may not please,
Like this fair Paradise, your sense; yet such
Accept your maker's work; he gave it me,   380
Which I as freely give; hell shall unfold,
To entertain you two, her widest gates,
And send forth all her kings; there will be room,
Not like these narrow limits, to receive
Your numerous offspring; if no better place,   385
Thank you who puts me loath to this revenge
On you, who wrong me not, for him who wronged.
And should I at your harmless innocence
Melt, as I do, yet public reason just –
Honour and empire with revenge enlarged   390
By conquering this new world – compels me now
To do what else, though damned, I should abhor.'

354 Ocean Isles] The Azores.
361–2] Psalm viii. 5; Heb. ii. 7.
380–1] Matt. x. 8.

   So spake the fiend, and with necessity,
The tyrant's plea, excused his devilish deeds.
Then from his lofty stand on that high tree   395
Down he alights among the sportful herd
Of those four-footed kinds, himself now one,
Now other, as their shape served best his end
Nearer to view his prey, and unespied,
To mark what of their state he more might learn   400
By word or action marked; about them round
A lion now he stalks with fiery glare;
Then as a tiger, who by chance hath spied
In some purlieu two gentle fawns at play,
Straight couches close; then rising changes oft   405
His couchant watch, as one who chose his ground,
Whence rushing he might surest seize them both
Griped in each paw: when Adam, first of men,
To first of women, Eve, thus moving speech,
Turned him all ear to hear new utterance flow: 410
   'Sole partner and sole part of all these joys,
Dearer thyself than all, needs must the power
That made us, and for us this ample world,
Be infinitely good, and of his good
As liberal and free as infinite;   415
That raised us from the dust, and placed us here
In all this happiness, who at his hand
Have nothing merited, nor can perform
Aught whereof he hath need; he who requires
From us no other service than to keep   420
This one, this easy charge – of all the trees
In Paradise that bear delicious fruit
So various, not to taste that only tree
Of knowledge, planted by the tree of life;
So near grows death to life, whate'er death is –   425
Some dreadful thing no doubt; for well thou know'st
God hath pronounced it death to taste that tree:
The only sign of our obedience left
Among so many signs of power and rule
Conferred upon us, and dominion given   430
Over all other creatures that possess
Earth, air, and sea. Then let us not think hard
One easy prohibition, who enjoy

404 purlieu] tract of land on the edge of a forest.
418 him all ear] ambiguous: 'him' may be Adam or Satan, and 'all ear' can
    apply to Adam or Eve or Satan.
411] The first 'sole' means 'only', the second 'unique, unrivalled'.

Free leave so large to all things else, and choice
Unlimited of manifold delights;   435
But let us ever praise him, and extol
His bounty, following our delightful task,
To prune these growing plants, and tend these flowers;
Which, were it toilsome, yet with thee were sweet.'
 To whom thus Eve replied: 'O thou for whom   440
And from whom I was formed flesh of thy flesh,
And without whom am to no end, my guide
And head, what thou hast said is just and right.
For we to him indeed all praises owe,
And daily thanks – I chiefly, who enjoy   445
So far the happier lot, enjoying thee
Pre-eminent by so much odds, while thou
Like consort to thyself canst nowhere find.
That day I oft remember, when from sleep
I first awaked, and found myself reposed,   450
Under a shade on flowers, much wondering where
And what I was, whence thither brought, and how.
Not distant far from thence a murmuring sound
Of waters issued from a cave, and spread
Into a liquid plain, then stood unmoved,   455
Pure as the expanse of heaven; I thither went
With unexperienced thought, and laid me down
On the green bank, to look into the clear
Smooth lake, that to me seemed another sky.
As I bent down to look, just opposite   460
A shape within the watery gleam appeared,
Bending to look on me; I started back,
It started back, but pleased I soon returned,
Pleased it returned as soon with answering looks
Of sympathy and love; there I had fixed   465
Mine eyes till now, and pined with vain desire,
Had not a voice thus warned me: "What thou seest,
What there thou seest, fair creature, is thyself:
With thee it came and goes: but follow me,
And I will bring thee where no shadow stays   470
Thy coming, and thy soft embraces – he
Whose image thou art; him thou shalt enjoy
Inseparably thine; to him shalt bear

443 head] I Cor. xi. 3.
447 odds] construed as singular in the seventeenth century, and means 'the
 amount by which one thing exceeds or excels another'.
460–6] Alludes to Ovid's story of Narcissus. See *Comus* 230n.
470 stays] waits for.

Multitudes like thyself, and thence be called
Mother of human race"; what could I do,   475
But follow straight, invisibly thus led?
Till I espied thee, fair indeed and tall,
Under a platan; yet methought less fair,
Less winning soft, less amiably mild,
Than that smooth watery image; back I turned;   480
Thou, following, cried'st aloud, "Return, fair Eve;
Whom fliest thou? Whom thou fliest, of him thou art,
His flesh, his bone; to give thee being I lent
Out of my side to thee, nearest my heart,
Substantial life, to have thee by my side   485
Henceforth an individual solace dear:
Part of my soul I seek thee, and thee claim
My other half"; with that thy gentle hand
Seized mine: I yielded, and from that time see
How beauty is excelled by manly grace   490
And wisdom, which alone is truly fair.'
    So spake our general mother, and with eyes
Of conjugal attraction unreproved,
And meek surrender, half-embracing leaned
On our first father; half her swelling breast   495
Naked met his under the flowing gold
Of her loose tresses hid; he in delight
Both of her beauty and submissive charms,
Smiled with superior love, as Jupiter
On Juno smiles when he impregns the clouds   500
That shed May flowers, and pressed her matron lip
With kisses pure; aside the devil turned
For envy, yet with jealous leer malign
Eyed them askance, and to himself thus plained: 504
    'Sight hateful, sight tormenting! Thus these two,
Imparadised in one another's arms,
The happier Eden, shall enjoy their fill
Of bliss on bliss, while I to hell am thrust,
Where neither joy nor love, but fierce desire,
Among our other torments not the least,   510
Still unfulfilled, with pain of longing pines;
Yet let me not forget what I have gained
From their own mouths; all is not theirs, it seems:
One fatal tree there stands, of knowledge called,
Forbidden them to taste: knowledge forbidden?   515

478 platan] plane tree.
486 individual] inseparable. Cf. *Time* 12.
499-501] *Iliad* xiv 246-51; Virgil, *Georgics* ii 325-7.

Suspicious, reasonless: Why should their Lord
Envy them that? Can it be sin to know,
Can it be death? And do they only stand
By ignorance, is that their happy state,
The proof of their obedience and their faith?   520
O fair foundation laid whereon to build
Their ruin! Hence I will excite their minds
With more desire to know, and to reject
Envious commands, invented with design
To keep them low, whom knowledge might exalt   525
Equal with gods; aspiring to be such,
They taste and die: what likelier can ensue?
But first with narrow search I must walk round
This garden, and no corner leave unspied;
A chance but chance may lead where I may meet   530
Some wandering spirit of heaven, by fountain-side,
Or in thick shade retired, from him to draw
What further would be learned. Live while ye may,
Yet happy pair; enjoy, till I return,
Short pleasures; for long woes are to succeed.'   535
    So saying, his proud step he scornful turned,
But with sly circumspection, and began
Through wood, through waste, o'er hill, o'er dale, his roam.
Meanwhile in utmost longitude, where heaven
With earth and ocean meets, the setting sun   540
Slowly descended, and with right aspect
Against the eastern gate of Paradise
Levelled his evening rays; it was a rock
Of alabaster, piled up to the clouds,
Conspicuous far, winding with one ascent   545
Accessible from earth, one entrance high;
The rest was craggy cliff, that overhung
Still as it rose, impossible to climb.
Betwixt these rocky pillars Gabriel sat,
Chief of the angelic guards, awaiting night;   550
About him exercised heroic games
The unarmed youth of heaven; but nigh at hand
Celestial armoury, shields, helms, and spears,
Hung high with diamond flaming and with gold.

539 utmost longitude] the extreme west.
541 with right aspect] directly.
549 Gabriel] means 'man of God' or 'strength of God' in Hebrew. Gabriel is an
   archangel, and his traditional function in Christian (and Muslim) thought is
   to reveal God. In Muslim and Cabbalistic traditions (though not in the
   Bible) he is a warrior (cf. l. 576). Milton seems to have had access to the
   tradition embodied in the Book of Enoch (xx. 7) that Gabriel was
   responsible for Paradise and the cherubim.

Thither came Uriel, gliding through the even   555
On a sunbeam, swift as a shooting star
In autumn thwarts the night, when vapours fired
Impress the air, and shows the mariner
From what point of his compass to beware
Impetuous winds; he thus began in haste: 560
   'Gabriel, to thee thy course by lot hath given
Charge and strict watch that to this happy place
No evil thing approach or enter in;
This day at height of noon came to my sphere
A spirit, zealous, as he seemed, to know   565
More of the almighty's works, and chiefly man,
God's latest image; I described his way
Bent all on speed, and marked his airy gait,
But in the mount that lies from Eden north,
Where he first lighted, soon discerned his looks   570
Alien from heaven, with passions foul obscured;
Mine eye pursued him still, but under shade
Lost sight of him; one of the banished crew,
I fear, hath ventured from the deep, to raise
New troubles; him thy care must be to find.'   575
   To whom the winged warrior thus returned:
'Uriel, no wonder if thy perfect sight,
Amid the sun's bright circle where thou sitt'st,
See far and wide; in at this gate none pass
The vigilance here placed, but such as come   580
Well known from heaven; and since meridian hour
No creature thence; if spirit of other sort,
So minded, have o'erleaped these earthy bounds
On purpose, hard thou know'st it to exclude
Spiritual substance with corporeal bar.   585
But if within the circuit of these walks,
In whatsoever shape, he lurk of whom
Thou tell'st, by morrow dawning I shall know.'
   So promised he; and Uriel to his charge
Returned on that bright beam, whose point now raised
Bore him slope downward to the sun, now fallen   591
Beneath the Azores; whether the prime orb,

557 thwarts] traverses.
561 by lot] like the porters of the temple. I Chron. xxvi. 13.
567 God's latest image] His first image was the Son (III 63).
     described] descried.
568 gait] journey.
580 vigilance] guard.
592-7] Ptolemaic and Copernican cosmologies are presented as alternatives;
     hence the 'prime orb' may be the sun of the first sphere. 'Voluble' means
     'capable of rotation on its axis'.

Incredible how swift, had thither rolled
Diurnal, or this less volúble earth,
By shorter flight to the east, had left him there   595
Arraying with reflected purple and gold
The clouds that on his western throne attend;
Now came still evening on, and twilight grey
Had in her sober livery all things clad;
Silence accompanied; for beast and bird,   600
They to their grassy couch, these to their nests
Were slunk, all but the wakeful nightingale:
She all night long her amorous descant sung;
Silence was pleased; now glowed the firmament
With living sapphires; Hesperus, that led   605
The starry host, rode brightest, till the moon,
Rising in clouded majesty, at length
Apparent queen, unveiled her peerless light,
And o'er the dark her silver mantle threw;
     When Adam thus to Eve: 'Fair consort, the hour   610
Of night, and all things now retired to rest,
Mind us of like repose; since God hath set
Labour and rest, as day and night, to men
Successive, and the timely dew of sleep,
Now falling with soft slumbrous weight, inclines   615
Our eye-lids; other creatures all day long
Rove idle, unemployed, and less need rest;
Man hath his daily work of body or mind
Appointed, which declares his dignity,
And the regard of heaven on all his ways;   620
While other animals unactive range,
And of their doings God takes no account.
To-morrow, ere fresh morning streak the east
With first approach of light, we must be risen,
And at our pleasant labour, to reform   625
Yon flowery arbours, yonder alleys green,
Our walk at noon, with branches overgrown,
That mock our scant manuring, and require
More hands than ours to lop their wanton growth;
Those blossoms also, and those dropping gums,   630
That lie bestrewn, unsightly and unsmooth,
Ask riddance, if we mean to tread with ease;
Meanwhile, as nature wills, night bids us rest.'
     To whom thus Eve, with perfect beauty adorned:
'My author and disposer, what thou bidd'st   635

608 Apparent] manifest.
628 manuring] cultivating.

Unargued I obey: so God ordains:
God is thy law, thou mine: to know no more
Is woman's happiest knowledge, and her praise.
With thee conversing, I forget all time,
All seasons, and their change; all please alike.   640
Sweet is the breath of morn, her rising sweet,
With charm of earliest birds; pleasant the sun,
When first on this delightful land he spreads
His orient beams, on herb, tree, fruit, and flower,
Glistering with dew; fragrant the fertile earth   645
After soft showers; and sweet the coming-on
Of grateful evening mild; then silent night,
With this her solemn bird, and this fair moon,
And these the gems of heaven, her starry train:
But neither breath of morn, when she ascends   650
With charm of earliest birds, nor rising sun
On this delightful land, nor herb, fruit, flower,
Glistering with dew, nor fragrance after showers,
Nor grateful evening mild, nor silent night,
With this her solemn bird, nor walk by moon,   655
Or glittering starlight, without thee is sweet.
But wherefore all night long shine these, for whom
This glorious sight, when sleep hath shut all eyes?'
    To whom our general ancestor replied:
'Daughter of God and man, accomplished Eve,   660
Those have their course to finish round the earth
By morrow evening, and from land to land
In order, though to nations yet unborn,
Ministering light prepared, they set and rise;
Lest total darkness should by night regain   665
Her old possession, and extinguish life
In nature and all things; which these soft fires
Not only enlighten, but with kindly heat ·
Of various influence foment and warm,
Temper or nourish, or in part shed down   670
Their stellar virtue on all kinds that grow
On earth, made hereby apter to receive
Perfection from the sun's more potent ray.
These, then, though unbeheld in deep of night,   674
Shine not in vain; nor think, though men were none,
That heaven would want spectators, God want praise;
Millions of spiritual creatures walk the earth

639 conversing] consorting.
640 seasons] times of day.
642 charm] song.

Unseen, both when we wake, and when we sleep:
All these with ceaseless praise his works behold
Both day and night; how often from the steep   680
Of echoing hill or thicket, have we heard
Celestial voices to the midnight air,
Sole, or responsive each to other's note,
Singing their great creator; oft in bands
While they keep watch, or nightly rounding walk,   685
With heavenly touch of instrumental sounds
In full harmonic number joined, their songs
Divide the night, and lift our thoughts to heaven.'
   Thus talking, hand in hand alone they passed
On to their blissful bower; it was a place   690
Chosen by the sovereign planter, when he framed
All things to man's delightful use; the roof
Of thickest covert was inwoven shade,
Laurel and myrtle, and what higher grew
Of firm and fragrant leaf; on either side   695
Acanthus, and each odorous bushy shrub,
Fenced up the verdant wall; each beauteous flower,
Iris all hues, roses, and jessamine,
Reared high their flourished heads between, and wrought
Mosaic; under foot the violet,   700
Crocus, and hyacinth, with rich inlay
Broidered the ground, more coloured than with stone
Of costliest emblem; other creature here,
Beast, bird, insect, or worm, durst enter none;
Such was their awe of man. In shadier bower   705
More sacred and sequestered, though but feigned,
Pan or Sylvanus never slept, nor nymph
Nor Faunus haunted. Here, in close recess,
With flowers, garlands, and sweet-smelling herbs,
Espousèd Eve decked her first nuptial bed.   710
And heavenly choirs the hymenean sung,
What day the genial angel to our sire

---

688 Divide] means both 'divide into watches' and 'execute florid variations' (cf.
   Passion 4n.).
691 planter] 'God planted a garden' (Gen. ii. 8); God is also a planter in the
   sense of the founder of a colony.
699 flourished] adorned with flowers.
703 emblem] inlay.
707–8] Pan, Sylvanus, and Faunus are often not clearly distinguished from one
   another, but are commonly mentioned together. Cf. *Comus* 268, *PR* II
   190–1.
711 hymenean] wedding hymn; Hymen was the god of marriage. Cf. *PL* XI
   590–1.
712 genial] presiding over marriage and generation.

Brought her, in naked beauty more adorned,
More lovely than Pandora, whom the gods
Endowed with all their gifts; and, O too like   715
In sad event, when to the unwiser son
Of Japhet brought by Hermes, she ensnared
Mankind with her fair looks, to be avenged
On him who had stole Jove's authentic fire.
    Thus at their shady lodge arrived, both stood,   720
Both turned, and under open sky adored
The God that made both sky, air, earth and heaven,
Which they beheld, the moon's resplendent globe,
And starry pole: 'Thou also madest the night,
Maker omnipotent; and thou the day,   725
Which we in our appointed work employed,
Have finished, happy in our mutual help
And mutual love, the crown of all our bliss
Ordained by thee; and this delicious place,
For us too large, where thy abundance wants   730
Partakers, and uncropped falls to the ground.
But thou hast promised from us two a race
To fill the earth, who shall with us extol
Thy goodness infinite, both when we wake,
And when we seek, as now, thy gift of sleep.'   735
    This said unanimous, and other rites
Observing none, but adoration pure,
Which God likes best, into their inmost bower
Handed they went; and, eased the putting-off
These troublesome disguises which we wear,   740
Straight side by side were laid; nor turned, I ween,
Adam from his fair spouse, nor Eve the rites
Mysterious of connubial love refused:
Whatever hypocrites austerely talk
Of purity, and place, and innocence,   745
Defaming as impure what God declares
Pure, and commands to some, leaves free to all.
Our maker bids increase; who bids abstain
But our destroyer, foe to God and man?

714-19] Prometheus ('fore-thought') and Epimetheus ('after-thought') were
    the two sons of the Titan Japhet. Prometheus 'stole Jove's authentic [i.e.
    original] fire', and the gods took their revenge by having Hermes (see
    Comus 637n.) present Pandora ('all ... gifts') to Epimetheus ('the unwiser
    son'), who opened Pandora's box of gifts and thus released all life's ills upon
    the world.
724-5] Psalm lxxiv. 16. 'Pole' means 'sky'.
735 gift of sleep] Psalm cxxvii. 2; *Iliad* ix 712-13; *Aeneid* ii 268-9.
741 ween] surmise.
744-9] I Tim. iv. 1-3.

Hail, wedded love, mysterious law, true source   750
Of human offspring, sole propriety
In Paradise of all things common else.
By thee adulterous lust was driven from men
Among the bestial herds to range; by thee,
Founded in reason, loyal, just, and pure   755
Relations dear, and all the charities
Of father, son, and brother, first were known.
Far be it that I should write thee sin or blame,
Or think thee unbefitting holiest place,
Perpetual fountain of domestic sweets,   760
Whose bed is undefiled and chaste pronounced,
Present, or past, as saints and patriarchs used.
Here Love his golden shafts employs, here lights
His constant lamp, and waves his purple wings,
Reigns here and revels; not in the bought smile   765
Of harlots – loveless, joyless, unendeared,
Casual fruition; nor in court amours,
Mixed dance, or wanton mask, or midnight ball,
Or serenade, which the starved lover sings
To his proud fair, best quitted with disdain.   770
These, lulled by nightingales, embracing slept,
And on their naked limbs the flowery roof
Showered roses, which the morn repaired. Sleep on,
Blest pair; and O yet happiest if ye seek
No happier state, and know to know no more.   775
     Now had night measured with her shadowy cone
Half-way up-hill this vast sublunar vault,
And from their ivory port the cherubim
Forth issuing at the accustomed hour, stood armed
To their night-watches in warlike parade;   780

---

751 propriety] ownership, proprietorship.
756 charities] love, natural affections.
761] Heb. xiii. 4.
763 Cupid's sharp 'golden shafts' kindled love; his blunt leaden shafts put love
  to flight (*Metamorphoses* i 468–71).
769–70] Alludes to the ancient *paraklausithuron*, a serenade sung by a lover
  standing in the cold at his mistress' locked door. 'Starved' means both
  'benumbed with cold' and 'starved for love'.
773 repaired] replaced.
776–7] Because the earth is smaller than the sun, the earth's shadow is cone-
  shaped. When the axis of the cone is halfway between the horizon and the
  zenith ('Half-way up-hill'), the time in Paradise is nine o'clock.
778 ivory port] In classical literature false dreams pass through an ivory gate,
  so it is appropriate that cherubim about to interrupt a false dream do
  likewise (*Odyssey* xix 592 ff., *Aeneid* vi 893 f.).

When Gabriel to his next in power thus spake:
   'Uzziel, half these draw off, and coast the south
With strictest watch; these other wheel the north:
Our circuit meets full west.' As flame they part,
Half wheeling to the shield, half to the spear.   785
From these, two strong and subtle spirits he called
That near him stood, and gave them thus in charge:
   'Ithuriel and Zephon, with winged speed
Search through this garden; leave unsearched no nook;
But chiefly where those two fair creatures lodge,   790
Now laid perhaps asleep, secure of harm.
This evening from the sun's decline arrived
Who tells of some infernal spirit seen
Hitherward bent (who could have thought?) escaped
The bars of hell, on errand bad no doubt: 795
Such, where ye find, seize fast, and hither bring.'
   So saying, on he led his radiant files,
Dazzling the moon; these to the bower direct
In search of whom they sought; him there they found
Squat like a toad, close at the ear of Eve,   800
Assaying by his devilish art to reach
The organs of her fancy, and with them forge
Illusions as he list, phantasms and dreams;
Or if, inspiring venom, he might taint
The animal spirits, that from pure blood arise   805
Like gentle breaths from rivers pure, thence raise,
At least distempered, discontented thoughts,
Vain hopes, vain aims, inordinate desires,
Blown up with high conceits engendering pride.
Him thus intent Ithuriel with his spear   810
Touched lightly; for no falsehood can endure
Touch of celestial temper, but returns
Of force to its own likeness; up he starts,

782 Uzziel] means in Hebrew 'my strength is God'. The word is never used as an
    angel's name in the Bible, but according to a rabbinical tradition Uzziel
    was one of the seven angels in front of the throne of God.
785] 'shield' is left, 'spear' is right in classical military parlance.
788 Ithuriel] means in Hebrew 'discovery of God'. The name does not occur in
    the Bible.
    Zephon] means in Hebrew 'searcher'. The name is not used as an angel's
    name in the Bible.
793 Who] one who.
805] In Renaissance physiology 'spirits' were fluids permeating the blood and
    chief organs of the body; they were distinguished as animal, natural, and
    vital. Animal spirits (from *anima*, soul) were seated in the brain, and
    controlled sensation and voluntary motion.

Discovered and surprised. As when a spark
Lights on a heap of nitrous powder, laid   815
Fit for the tun, some magazine to store
Against a rumoured war, the smutty grain,
With sudden blaze diffused, inflames the air;
So started up, in his own shape, the fiend.
Back stepped those two fair angels, half amazed   820
So sudden to behold the grisly king;
Yet thus, unmoved with fear, accost him soon:
　'Which of those rebel spirits adjudged to hell
Com'st thou, escaped thy prison, and, transformed,
Why satt'st thou like an enemy in wait,   825
Here watching at the head of these that sleep?'
　'Know ye not, then,' said Satan, filled with scorn,
'Know ye not me? Ye knew me once no mate
For you, there sitting where ye durst not soar;
Not to know me argues yourselves unknown.   830
The lowest of your throng; or if ye know,
Why ask ye, and superfluous begin
Your message, like to end as much in vain?'
　To whom thus Zephon, answering scorn with scorn:
'Think not, revolted spirit, thy shape the same,   835
Or undiminished brightness, to be known
As when thou stood'st in heaven upright and pure;
That glory then, when thou no more wast good,
Departed from thee, and thou resemblest now
Thy sin and place of doom obscure and foul.   840
But come, for thou, be sure, shalt give account
To him who sent us, whose charge is to keep
This place inviolable, and these from harm.'
　So spake the cherub; and his grave rebuke,
Severe in youthful beauty, added grace   845
Invincible; abashed the devil stood,
And felt how awful goodness is, and saw
Virtue in her shape how lovely – saw, and pined
His loss; but chiefly to find here observed
His lustre visibly impaired; yet seemed   850
Undaunted. 'If I must contend,' said he,
'Best with the best – the sender, not the sent;
Or all at once: more glory will be won,
Or less be lost.' 'Thy fear,' said Zephon bold,
'Will save us trial what the least can do   855
Single against thee wicked, and thence weak.'

840 obscure] dark.
847 awful] awe-inspiring.

The fiend replied not, overcome with rage;
But, like a proud steed reined, went haughty on,
Champing his iron curb; to strive or fly
He held it vain; awe from above had quelled   860
His heart, not else dismayed. Now drew they nigh
The western point, where those half-rounding guards
Just met, and, closing, stood in squadron joined,
Awaiting next command. To whom their chief,
Gabriel, from the front thus called aloud: 865
   'O friends, I hear the tread of nimble feet
Hasting this way, and now by glimpse discern
Ithuriel and Zephon through the shade;
And with them comes a third, of regal port,
But faded splendour wan, who by his gait   870
And fierce demeanour seems the prince of hell –
Not likely to part hence without contest;
Stand firm, for in his look defiance lours.'
   He scarce had ended, when those two approached,
And brief related whom they brought, where found,   875
How busied, in what form and posture couched.
To whom, with stern regard, thus Gabriel spake:
   'Why hast thou, Satan, broke the bounds prescribed
To thy transgressions, and disturbed the charge
Of others, who approve not to transgress   880
By thy example, but have power and right
To question thy bold entrance on this place;
Employed, it seems, to violate sleep, and those
Whose dwelling God hath planted here in bliss?'
   To whom thus Satan, with contemptuous brow: 885
'Gabriel, thou hadst in heaven the esteem of wise,
And such I held thee; but this question asked
Puts me in doubt. Lives there who loves his pain?
Who would not, finding way, break loose from hell,
Though thither doomed? Thou wouldst thyself, no doubt,
And boldly venture to whatever place   891
Farthest from pain, where thou mightst hope to change
Torment with ease, and soonest recompense
Dole with delight, which in this place I sought;
To thee no reason, who know'st only good,   895
But evil hast not tried; and wilt object
His will who bound us? Let him surer bar

---

869 port] bearing.
879 transgressions] means both 'sins' and (etymologically) 'the action of
    passing over or beyond (a boundary)'.
896 object] adduce as an objection.

His iron gates, if he intends our stay
In that dark durance; thus much what was asked.
The rest is true, they found me where they say;   900
But that implies not violence or harm.'
    Thus he in scorn. The warlike angel moved,
Disdainfully half smiling, thus replied:
'O loss of one in heaven to judge of wise,
Since Satan fell, whom folly overthrew,   905
And now returns him from his prison scaped,
Gravely in doubt whether to hold them wise
Or not who ask what boldness brought him hither
Unlicensed from his bounds in hell prescribed;
So wise he judges it to fly from pain   910
However, and to scape his punishment.
So judge thou still, presumptuous, till the wrath,
Which thou incurr'st by flying, meet thy flight
Sevenfold, and scourge that wisdom back to hell,
Which taught thee yet no better that no pain   915
Can equal anger infinite provoked.
But wherefore thou alone? Wherefore with thee
Came not all hell broke loose? Is pain to them
Less pain, less to be fled, or thou than they
Less hardy to endure? Courageous chief,   920
The first in flight from pain, hadst thou alleged
To thy deserted host this cause of flight,
Thou surely hadst not come sole fugitive.'
    To which the fiend thus answered, frowning stern:
'Not that I less endure, or shrink from pain,   925
Insulting angel; well thou know'st I stood
Thy fiercest, when in battle to thy aid
The blasting volleyed thunder made all speed
And seconded thy else not dreaded spear.
But still thy words at random, as before,   930
Argue thy inexperience what behoves,
From hard assays and ill successes past,
A faithful leader – not to hazard all
Through ways of danger by himself untried;
I, therefore, I alone, first undertook   935
To wing the desolate abyss, and spy
This new-created world, whereof in hell
Fame is not silent, here in hope to find
Better abode, and my afflicted powers

899 durance] imprisonment, constraint.
911 However] howsoever.
926 stood] withstood.

To settle here on earth, or in mid air;   940
Though for possession put to try once more
What thou and thy gay legions dare against;
Whose easier business were to serve their Lord
High up in heaven, with songs to hymn his throne,
And practised distances to cringe, not fight.'   945
    To whom the warrior-angel soon replied:
'To say and straight unsay, pretending first
Wise to fly pain, professing next the spy,
Argues no leader, but a liar traced,
Satan; and couldst thou "faithful" add? O name;   950
O sacred name of faithfulness profaned!
Faithful to whom? To thy rebellious crew?
Army of fiends, fit body to fit head;
Was this your discipline and faith engaged,
Your military obedience, to dissolve   955
Allegiance to the acknowledged power supreme?
And thou, sly hypocrite, who now wouldst seem
Patron of liberty, who more than thou
Once fawned, and cringed, and servilely adored
Heaven's awful monarch? Wherefore, but in hope   960
To dispossess him, and thyself to reign?
But mark what I areed thee now – avaunt;
Fly thither whence thou fledd'st; if from this hour
Within these hallowed limits thou appear,
Back to the infernal pit I drag thee chained,   965
And seal thee so as henceforth not to scorn
The facile gates of hell too slightly barred.'
    So threatened he; but Satan to no threats
Gave heed, but waxing more in rage, replied:
'Then, when I am thy captive, talk of chains,   970
Proud limitary cherub, but ere then
Far heavier load thyself expect to feel
From my prevailing arm, though heaven's king
Ride on thy wings, and thou with thy compeers,
Used to the yoke, draw'st his triumphant wheels   975
In progress through the road of heaven star-paved.'
    While thus he spake, the angelic squadron bright

940 mid air] See *Fair Infant* 16n.
942 gay] brilliantly good (here used ironically).
962 areed] advise.
965–7] Rev. xx. 1–3.
971] A 'limitary' is a guard at a boundary. On Gabriel's responsibility for the
    cherubim see 549n.
976 road of heaven] the Milky Way. Cf. VII 577–81.
977–1015] Cf. *Aeneid* xii 661–952.

Turned fiery red, sharpening in moonèd horns
Their phalanx, and began to hem him round
With ported spears, as thick as when a field   980
Of Ceres ripe for harvest waving bends
Her bearded grove of ears which way the wind
Sways them; the careful ploughman doubting stands
Lest on the threshing-floor his hopeful sheaves
Prove chaff. On the other side, Satan, alarmed,   985
Collecting all his might, dilated stood,
Like Tenerife or Atlas, unremoved:
His stature reached the sky, and on his crest
Sat Horror plumed; nor wanted in his grasp
What seemed both spear and shield; now dreadful deeds
Might have ensued, nor only Paradise,   991
In this commotion, but the starry cope
Of heaven perhaps, or all the elements
At least, had gone to wrack, disturbed and torn
With violence of this conflict, had not soon   995
The eternal, to prevent such horrid fray,
Hung forth in heaven his golden scales, yet seen
Betwixt Astrea and the Scorpion sign,
Wherein all things created first he weighed,
The pendulous round earth with balanced air   1000
In counterpoise, now ponders all events,
Battles and realms; in these he put two weights,
The sequel each of parting and of fight:
The latter quick up flew, and kicked the beam;
Which Gabriel spying thus bespake the fiend: 1005
    'Satan, I know thy strength, and thou know'st mine,
Neither our own, but given; what folly then
To boast what arms can do, since thine no more

---

987 moonèd horns] crescent formation.
980-5] *Iliad* ii 147-50; Virgil, *Georgics* i 226.
980 ported] held diagonally across and close to the body, so that the blade is
    opposite the middle of the left shoulder.
981 Ceres] corn (Ceres is the goddess of agriculture).
983 careful] anxious, full of care.
987 Tenerife] mountain on Canary Island of same name.
    Atlas] alludes to the Titan (see II 306n.) and to 'Mount Atlas' (see XI
    40sn.).
992 cope] vault.
997-8] The constellation Libra (the Scales) is between Scorpio and Virgo (here
    called Astrea because in the Golden Age she lived on earth; see *Nativity*
    141n.).
999-1001 a common Old Testament metaphor (e.g. Isa. xl. 12); 'ponders' means
    both 'weighs' and 'considers' (see I Sam. ii. 3).

Than heaven permits, nor mine, though doubled now
To trample thee as mire; for proof look up,   1010
And read thy lot in yon celestial sign,
Where thou art weighed, and shown how light, how weak
If thou resist.' The fiend looked up, and knew
His mounted scale aloft: nor more, but fled
Murmuring, and with him fled the shades of night.   1015

THE END OF THE FOURTH BOOK

1010] Isa. x. 6.
1012] Dan. v. 27.

BOOK V

THE ARGUMENT

Morning approached, Eve relates to Adam her troublesome dream;
he likes it not, yet comforts her; they come forth to their day
labours: their morning hymn at the door of their bower. God, to
render man inexcusable, sends Raphael to admonish him of his
obedience, of his free estate, of his enemy near at hand, who he is,
and why his enemy, and whatever else may avail Adam to know.
Raphael comes down to Paradise; his appearance described; his
coming discerned by Adam afar off, sitting at the door of his
bower; he goes out to meet him, brings him to his lodge, entertains
him with the choicest fruits of Paradise, got together by Eve; their
discourse at table. Raphael performs his message, minds Adam of
his state and of his enemy; relates, at Adam's request, who that
enemy is, and how he came to be so, beginning from his first revolt
in heaven, and the occasion thereof; how he drew his legions after
him to the parts of the north, and there incited them to rebel with
him, persuading all but only Abdiel, a seraph, who in argument
dissuades and opposes him, then forsakes him.

Now Morn, her rosy steps in the eastern clime
Advancing, sowed the earth with orient pearl,
When Adam waked, so customed; for his sleep
Was airy light, from pure digestion bred,
And temperate vapours bland, which the only sound   5
Of leaves and fuming rills, Aurora's fan,
Lightly dispersed, and the shrill matin song
Of birds on every bough; so much the more
His wonder was to find unwakened Eve,
With tresses discomposed, and glowing cheek,   10
As through unquiet rest; he on his side
Leaning half raised, with looks of cordial love
Hung over her enamoured, and beheld
Beauty which, whether waking or asleep,
Shot forth peculiar graces; then with voice   15
Mild as when Zephyrus on Flora breathes,
Her hand soft touching, whispered thus: 'Awake,

---

1 rosy steps] Imitates the description in Homer and Hesiod of the dawn (Eos,
Aurora) as 'rosy-fingered' (ῥοδοδάκτυλος).

2] *Metamorphoses* xiii 621-2.

16] Zephyrus, the west wind, 'breathes the spring' (*L'Allegro* 18) and thus
produces flowers, of which Flora was the goddess.

17-25] Cf. the aubade in Song of Solomon ii. 10-13. Satan's serenade (38-41)
parodies the same passage.

My fairest, my espoused, my latest found,
Heaven's last, best gift, my ever-new delight;
Awake, the morning shines, and the fresh field   20
Calls us; we lose the prime to mark how spring
Our tended plants, how blows the citron grove,
What drops the myrrh, and what the balmy reed,
How nature paints her colours, how the bee
Sits on the bloom extracting liquid sweet.'   25
   Such whispering waked her, but with startled eye
On Adam; whom embracing, thus she spake:
   'O sole in whom my thoughts find all repose,
My glory, my perfection, glad I see
Thy face, and morn returned; for I this night –   30
Such night till this I never passed – have dreamed,
If dreamed, not as I oft am wont, of thee,
Works of day past, or morrow's next design,
But of offence and trouble, which my mind
Knew never till this irksome night; methought   35
Close at mine ear one called me forth to walk
With gentle voice; I thought it thine; it said,
"Why sleep'st thou, Eve? Now is the pleasant time,
The cool, the silent, save where silence yields
To the night-warbling bird, that now awake   40
Tunes sweetest his love-laboured song; now reigns
Full-orbed the moon, and with more pleasing light,
Shadowy sets off the face of things – in vain,
If none regard; heaven wakes with all his eyes,
Whom to behold but thee, nature's desire,   45
In whose sight all things joy, with ravishment
Attracted by thy beauty still to gaze?"
I rose as at thy call, but found thee not:
To find thee I directed then my walk;
And on, methought, alone I passed through ways   50
That brought me on a sudden to the tree
Of interdicted knowledge; fair it seemed,
Much fairer to my fancy than by day;
And as I wondering looked, beside it stood
One shaped and winged like one of those from heaven   55
By us oft seen: his dewy locks distilled
Ambrosia; on that tree he also gazed;
And, "O fair plant," said he, "with fruit surcharged,
Deigns none to ease thy load and taste thy sweet,
Nor God nor man? Is knowledge so despised?   60
Or envy, or what reserve forbids to taste?

56-7 dewy ... Ambrosia] *Aeneid* i 403-4.

Forbid who will, none shall from me withhold
Longer thy offered good, why else set here?''
This said, he paused not, but with venturous arm
He plucked, he tasted; me damp horror chilled   65
At such bold words vouched with a deed so bold;
But he thus, overjoyed: "O fruit divine,
Sweet of thyself, but much more sweet thus cropped,
Forbidden here, it seems, as only fit
For gods, yet able to make gods of men;   70
And why not gods of men, since good, the more
Communicated, more abundant grows,
The author not impaired, but honoured more?
Here, happy creature, fair angelic Eve,
Partake thou also: happy though thou art,   75
Happier thou may'st be, worthier canst not be;
Taste this, and be henceforth among the gods
Thyself a goddess, not to earth confined,
But sometimes in the air, as we; sometimes
Ascend to heaven, by merit thine, and see   80
What life the gods live there, and such live thou.''
So saying, he drew nigh, and to me held,
Even to my mouth of that same fruit held part
Which he had plucked: the pleasant savoury smell
So quickened appetite that I, methought,   85
Could not but taste. Forthwith up to the clouds
With him I flew, and underneath beheld
The earth outstretched immense, a prospect wide
And various; wondering at my flight and change
To this high exaltation, suddenly   90
My guide was gone, and I, methought, sunk down,
And fell asleep; but O how glad I waked
To find this but a dream!' Thus Eve her night
Related, and thus Adam answered sad:
    'Best image of myself and dearer half,   95
The trouble of thy thoughts this night in sleep
Affects me equally; nor can I like
This uncouth dream – of evil sprung, I fear;
Yet evil whence? In thee can harbour none,
Created pure. But know that in the soul   100
Are many lesser faculties that serve
Reason as chief; among these Fancy next
Her office holds; of all external things,

---

84 savoury] means both 'gratifying to the sense of smell' and 'spiritually
    delightful or edifying'.
94 sad] gravely, seriously.

Which the five watchful senses represent,
She forms imaginations, airy shapes,   105
Which Reason, joining or disjoining, frames
All what we affirm or what deny, and call
Our knowledge or opinion; then retires
Into her private cell when nature rests.
Oft, in her absence, mimic Fancy wakes   110
To imitate her; but, misjoining shapes,
Wild work produces oft, and most in dreams,
Ill matching words and deeds long past or late.
Some such resemblances methinks I find
Of our last evening's talk in this thy dream,   115
But with addition strange; yet be not sad.
Evil into the mind of god or man
May come and go, so unapproved, and leave
No spot or blame behind; which gives me hope
That what in sleep thou did'st abhor to dream   120
Waking thou never wilt consent to do.
Be not disheartened then, nor cloud those looks,
That wont to be more cheerful and serene
Than when fair morning first smiles on the world;
And let us to our fresh employments rise   125
Among the groves, the fountains, and the flowers,
That open now their choicest bosomed smells,
Reserved from night, and kept for thee in store.'
    So cheered he his fair spouse; and she was cheered,
But silently a gentle tear let fall   130
From either eye, and wiped them with her hair:
Two other precious drops that ready stood,
Each in their crystal sluice, he, ere they fell,
Kissed as the gracious signs of sweet remorse
And pious awe, that feared to have offended.   135
    So all was cleared, and to the field they haste.
But first, from under shady arborous roof
Soon as they forth were come to open sight
Of day-spring, and the sun – who, scarce uprisen,
With wheels yet hovering o'er the ocean brim,   140
Shot parallel to the earth his dewy ray,
Discovering in wide landscape all the east
Of Paradise and Eden's happy plains –
Lowly they bowed, adoring, and began
Their orisons, each morning duly paid   145

117 God] means 'angel', but may also mean 'God'.
130-1] Luke vii. 38.
145 orisons] prayers.

In various style; for neither various style
Nor holy rapture wanted they to praise
Their maker, in fit strains pronounced, or sung
Unmeditated; such prompt eloquence
Flowed from their lips, in prose or numerous verse,   150
More tuneable than needed lute or harp
To add more sweetness; and they thus began:
    'These are thy glorious works, parent of good,
Almighty, thine this universal frame,
Thus wondrous fair: thyself how wondrous then!   155
Unspeakable, who sitt'st above these heavens
To us invisible, or dimly seen
In these thy lowest works; yet these declare
Thy goodness beyond thought, and power divine;
Speake ye who best can tell, ye sons of light,   160
Angels – for ye behold him, and with songs
And choral symphonies, day without night,
Circle his throne rejoicing – ye in heaven;
On earth join, all ye creatures, to extol
Him first, him last, him midst, and without end.   165
Fairest of stars, last in the train of night,
If better thou belong not to the dawn,
Sure pledge of day, that crown'st the smiling morn
With thy bright circlet, praise him in thy sphere
While day arises, that sweet hour of prime.   170
Thou sun, of this great world both eye and soul,
Acknowledge him thy greater; sound his praise
In thy eternal course, both when thou climb'st,
And when high noon hast gained, and when thou fall'st.
Moon, that now meet'st the orient sun, now fliest   175
With the fixed stars, fixed in their orb that flies;
And ye five other wandering fires that move

150 numerous] measured, rhythmic.
153–208] This hymn is based on Psalm cxlvii, and on The Song of the Three
    Holy Children (35–66), a LXX addition to the Book of Daniel. This
    apocryphal passage later became the Canticle *Benedicite*, which appears in
    the Book of Common Prayer.
165] Rev. xxii. 13.
166 Fairest of stars] Hesperus (IV 605) here re-appears as Phosphorous, or
    Lucifer.
177 five other wandering fires] Four of the planets are Mercury, Mars, Jupiter,
    and Saturn; the fifth may be Venus, or if 'other' excludes Venus (which
    appeared in l. 166), the earth may be intended (cf. VIII 128–9). 'Wandering
    fires' approximates the Greek phrase for planets, ἀστέρες πλανῆται (wander-
    ing stars).

In mystic dance, not without song, resound
His praise who out of darkness called up light.
Air, and ye elements, the eldest birth   180
Of nature's womb, that in quaternion run
Perpetual circle, multiform, and mix
And nourish all things, let your ceaseless change
Vary to our great maker still new praise.
Ye mists and exhalations, that now rise   185
From hill or streaming lake, dusky or grey,
Till the sun paint your fleecy skirts with gold,
In honour to the world's great author rise;
Whether to deck with clouds the uncoloured sky,
Of wet the thirsty earth with falling showers,   190
Rising or falling, still advance his praise.
His praise, ye winds, that from four quarters blow,
Breathe soft or loud; and wave your tops, ye pines,
With every plant, in sign of worship wave.
Fountains, and ye that warble, as ye flow,   195
Melodious murmurs, warbling tune his praise.
Join voices, all ye living souls; ye birds,
That, singing, up to heaven-gate ascend,
Bear on your wings and in your notes his praise;
Ye that in waters glide, and ye that walk   200
The earth, and stately tread, or lowly creep,
Witness if I be silent, morn or even,
To hill or valley, fountain, or fresh shade,
Made vocal by my song, and taught his praise.
Hail universal Lord, be bounteous still   205
To give us only good; and if the night
Have gathered aught of evil, or concealed,
Disperse it, as now light dispels the dark.'
    So prayed they innocent, and to their thoughts
Firm peace recovered soon, and wonted calm.   210
On to their morning's rural work they haste,
Among sweet dews and flowers, where any row
Of fruit-trees, over-woody, reached too far
Their pampered boughs, and needed hands to check
Fruitless embraces: or they led the vine   215
To wed her elm; she, spoused, about him twines
Her marriageable arms, and with her brings
Her dower, the adopted clusters, to adorn
His barren leaves. Them thus employed beheld

181-2] On the cycle of the group of four ('quaternion') elements see ll. 414-26.
215-19] A traditional idea, both in antiquity (e.g. Virgil, *Georgics* i 2, Horace,
    Odes II. xv. 4, IV. v. 30) and the Renaissance. Cf. *PL* IX 217.

With pity heaven's high king, and to him called   220
Raphael, the sociable spirit, that deigned
To travel with Tobias, and secured
His marriage with the seven-times-wedded maid.
    'Raphael,' said he, 'thou hear'st what stir on earth
Satan, from hell scaped through the darksome gulf,   225
Hath raised in Paradise, and how disturbed
This night the human pair; how he designs
In them at once to ruin all mankind.
Go, therefore; half this day, as friend with friend,
Converse with Adam, in what bower or shade   230
Thou find'st him from the heat of noon retired
To respite his day-labour with repast
Or with repose; and such discourse bring on
As may advise him of his happy state –
Happiness in his power left free to will,   235
Left to his own free will, his will though free
Yet mutable; whence warn him to beware
He swerve not, too secure: tell him withal
His danger, and from whom; what enemy,
Late fallen himself from heaven, is plotting now   240
The fall of others from like state of bliss;
By violence, no, for that shall be withstood;
But by deceit and lies; this let him know,
Lest wilfully transgressing he pretend
Surprisal, unadmonished, unforewarned.'   245
    So spake the eternal Father, and fulfilled
All justice. Nor delayed the wingèd saint
After his charge received; but from among
Thousand celestial ardours, where he stood
Veiled with his gorgeous wings, upspringing light,   250
Flew through the midst of heaven; the angelic choirs
On each hand parting, to his speed gave way
Through all the empyreal road, till, at the gate
Of heaven arrived, the gate self-opened wide,
On golden hinges turning, as by work   255
Divine the sovereign architect had framed.
From hence – no cloud or, to obstruct his sight,
Star interposed, however small – he sees,

224 Raphael] The name means 'God heals' in Hebrew; it does not occur in the
    canonical Scriptures, but the angel Raphael appears in both the apocryphal
    Book of Tobit and the pseudepigraphical Book of Enoch. On his functions
    see Tobit xii. 15; on the service rendered to Tobias (ll. 222-3) see IV
    166-71n.
249 ardours] flames; the word may indicate seraphim (cf. 'fiery seraphim', II
    512; the word 'seraph' derives from the Hebrew verbal root meaning 'to
    burn') or angels in general (Psalm civ. 4).

Not unconform to other shining globes,
Earth, and the garden of God with cedars crowned   260
Above all hills; as when by night the glass
Of Galileo, less assured, observes
Imagined lands and regions in the moon;
Or pilot from amidst the Cyclades
Delos or Samos first appearing kens   265
A cloudy spot. Down thither prone in flight
He speeds, and through the vast ethereal sky
Sails between worlds and worlds, with steady wing
Now on the polar winds; then with quick fan
Winnows the buxom air, till within soar   270
Of towering eagles, to all the fowls he seems
A phoenix, gazed by all, as that sole bird,
When, to enshrine his relics in the sun's
Bright temple, to Egyptian Thebes he flies.
At once on the eastern cliff of Paradise   275
He lights, and to his proper shape returns,
A seraph winged; six wings he wore, to shade
His lineaments divine: the pair that clad
Each shoulder broad came mantling o'er his breast
With regal ornament; the middle pair   280
Girt like a starry zone his waist, and round
Skirted his loins and thighs with downy gold
And colours dipped in heaven; the third his feet
Shadowed from either heel with feathered mail,
Sky-tinctured grain. Like Maia's son he stood,   285
And shook his plumes, that heavenly fragrance filled
The circuit wide. Straight knew him all the bands
Of angels under watch, and to his state
And to his message high in honour rise;
For on some message high they guessed him bound.   290
Their glittering tents he passed, and now is come

261-3] Cf. I 288-91n.
264-5] Delos is a tiny island regarded in antiquity as the centre of the Cyclades,
    the islands of the south Aegean. Samos is an island off the coast of western
    Asia Minor.
266-70] Cf. the descent of Mercury in *Aeneid* iv 238-58.
270 buxom] unresisting.
272-4] The phoenix is a mythical bird which every 500 years was consumed by
    fire in its own nest, whereupon a new phoenix would rise from the ashes and
    fly to Heliopolis, the city of the sun, to deposit 'his relics' in the temple.
    The names Thebes and Heliopolis were used interchangeably in the
    Renaissance. 'Egyptian' distinguishes this city from Boeotian Thebes.
    Cf. *SA* 1699-1707.
277-85] Isa. vi. 2.
285 Maia's son] Mercury. Cf. 266-70n.

Into the blissful field, through groves of myrrh,
And flowering odours, cassia, nard, and balm,
A wilderness of sweets; for nature here
Wantoned as in her prime, and played at will   295
Her virgin fancies, pouring forth more sweet,
Wild above rule or art; enormous bliss.
Him through the spicy forest onward come,
Adam discerned, as in the door he sat
Of his cool bower, while now the mounted sun   300
Shot down direct his fervid rays to warm
Earth's inmost womb, more warmth than Adam needs;
And Eve within, due at her hour, prepared
For dinner savoury fruits, of taste to please
True appetite, and not disrelish thirst   305
Of nectarous draughts between, from milky stream,
Berry or grape: to whom thus Adam called:
    'Haste hither, Eve, and, worth thy sight, behold
Eastward among those trees what glorious shape
Comes this way moving; seems another morn   310
Risen on mid-noon; some great behest from heaven
To us perhaps he brings, and will vouchsafe
This day to be our guest. But go with speed,
And what thy stores contain bring forth, and pour
Abundance fit to honour and receive   315
Our heavenly stranger; well we may afford
Our givers their own gifts, and large bestow
From large bestowed, where nature multiplies
Her fertile growth, and by disburdening grows
More fruitful; which instructs us not to spare.'   320
    To whom thus Eve: 'Adam, earth's hallowed mould,
Of God inspired, small store will serve where store,
All seasons, ripe for use hangs on the stalk;
Save what, by frugal storing, firmness gains
To nourish, and superfluous moist consumes;   325
But I will haste, and from each bough and brake,
Each plant and juiciest gourd, will pluck such choice
To entertain our angel guest, as he
Beholding shall confess that here on earth
God hath dispensed his bounties as in heaven.'   330

---

293 cassia, nard] Exod. xxx. 24; Mark xiv. 3. Cf. *Comus* 991.
297 enormous] deviating from ordinary rule, unusual.
299ff.] The scene in which Adam and Eve entertain Raphael is modelled on the
    scene in Gen. xviii in which Abraham and Sarah receive a theophanic
    visitation.
300-2] Cf. III 609n.

   So saying, with dispatchful looks in haste
She turns, on hospitable thoughts intent
What choice to choose for delicacy best,
What order so contrived as not to mix
Tastes, not well joined, inelegant, but bring   335
Taste after taste upheld with kindliest change:
Bestirs her then, and from each tender stalk
Whatever Earth all-bearing mother yields
In India east or west, or middle shore
In Pontus or the Punic coast, or where   340
Alcinöus reigned, fruit of all kinds, in coat
Rough or smooth rined, or bearded husk, or shell,
She gathers, tribute large, and on the board
Heaps with unsparing hand; for drink the grape
She crushes, inoffensive must, and meaths   345
From many a berry, and from sweet kernels pressed
She tempers dulcet creams – nor these to hold
Wants her fit vessels pure; then strews the ground
With rose and odours from the shrub unfumed.
   Meanwhile our primitive great sire, to meet   350
His godlike guest, walks forth, without more train
Accompanied than with his own complete
Perfections; in himself was all his state,
More solemn than the tedious pomp that waits
On princes, when their rich retinue long   355
Of horses led and grooms besmeared with gold
Dazzles the crowd and sets them all agape.
Nearer his presence, Adam, though not awed,
Yet with submiss approach and reverence meek,
As to a superior nature, bowing low,   360
   Thus said: 'Native of heaven – for other place
None can than heaven such glorious shape contain –
Since by descending from the thrones above,
Those happy places thou hast deigned a while
To want, and honour these, vouchsafe with us,   365
Two only, who yet by sovereign gift possess

338 Earth all-bearing mother] translates the classical Greek title παμμήτωρ γῆ,
   the classical Latin *Magna Mater* (cf. VII 281n.) and the post-classical
   Omniparens.
339–41] 'middle shore' includes the Black Sea (indicated by Pontus, a district
   on the south coast) and the Mediterranean (indicated by the Punic, or
   Carthaginian coast). Alcinöus was the king of the Phaeacians on the
   mythical island of Scheria. On the Garden of Alcinöus cf. *PL* IX 441, and
   Odyssey vii 112–32.
345 must] unfermented wine.
   meaths] mead, here non-alcoholic.
349 unfumed] not burned for incense.

This spacious ground, in yonder shady bower
To rest, and what the garden choicest bears
To sit and taste, till this meridian heat
Be over, and the sun more cool decline.'   370
    Whom thus the angelic virtue answered mild:
'Adam, I therefore came; nor art thou such
Created, or such place hast here to dwell,
As may not oft invite, though spirits of heaven,
To visit thee; lead on then, where thy bower   375
O'ershades; for these mid-hours, till evening rise,
I have at will.' So to the sylvan lodge
They came, that like Pomona's arbour smiled,
With flowerets decked and fragrant smells; but Eve,
Undecked, save with herself, more lovely fair   380
Than wood-nymph, or the fairest goddess feigned
Of three that in Mount Ida naked strove,
Stood to entertain her guest from heaven; no veil
She needed, virtue-proof; no thought infirm
Altered her cheek. On whom the Angel 'Hail'   385
Bestowed – the holy salutation used
Long after to blest Mary, second Eve:
    'Hail mother of mankind, whose fruitful womb
Shall fill the world more numerous with thy sons
Than with these various fruits the trees of God   390
Have heaped this table.' Raised of grassy turf
Their table was, and mossy seats had round,
And on her ample square, from side to side,
All autumn piled, though spring and autumn here
Danced hand-in-hand. A while discourse they hold –   395
No fear lest dinner cool – when thus began
Our author: 'Heavenly stranger, please to taste
These bounties, which our nourisher, from whom
All perfect good, unmeasured-out, descends,
To us for food and for delight hath caused   400

371] Raphael is an archangel, not a virtue, so the phrase may imitate Homeric
      diction and mean 'the virtuous angel'. Cf. VI 355.
372 therefore] for that reason.
378 Pomona] Roman goddess of fruit trees, in Renaissance art often portrayed
      with a pruning-knife in her hand. Cf. IX 393.
381-2] Alludes to the judgement of Paris (on Mount Ida, now Kaz Dag, near
      Troy), who chose Venus over Juno and Minerva as the most beautiful
      goddess. On Eve as Venus see VIII 46-7n., 60-3n.
385-7] Luke i. 28. Cf. X 183n., XI 158-60, XII 379, *PR* II 67-8.
394-5] In a late tradition the Horae came to represent the four seasons, two of
      which are here represented as dancing hand-in-hand. On the simultaneity
      of spring and autumn in Paradise see IV 148.
397 author] ancestor.

The earth to yield: unsavoury food, perhaps,
To spiritual natures; only this I know,
That one celestial Father gives to all.'
   To whom the angel: 'Therefore, what he gives
(Whose praise be ever sung) to man, in part   405
Spiritual, may of purest spirits be found
No ingrateful food: and food alike those pure
Intelligential substances require
As doth your rational; and both contain
Within them every lower faculty   410
Of sense, whereby they hear, see, smell, touch, taste,
Tasting concoct, digest, assimilate,
And corporeal to incorporeal turn.
For know, whatever was created needs
To be sustained and fed; of elements   415
The grosser feeds the purer: earth the sea;
Earth and the sea feed air; the air those fires
Ethereal, and, as lowest, first the moon;
Whence in her visage round those spots, unpurged
Vapours not yet into her substance turned.   420
Nor doth the moon no nourishment exhale
From her moist continent to higher orbs.
The sun, that light imparts to all, receives
From all his alimental recompense
In humid exhalations, and at even   425
Sups with the ocean; though in heaven the trees
Of life ambrosial fruitage bear, and vines
Yield nectar – though from off the boughs each morn
We brush mellifluous dews and find the ground
Covered with pearly grain – yet God hath here   430
Varied his bounty so with new delights
As may compare with heaven; and to taste
Think not I shall be nice.' So down they sat,
And to their viands fell, nor seemingly

407–13] Milton's affirmation of the corporeity of angels is clarified by his
   description of 'first matter' in ll. 473–6. Broadly speaking, Milton's position
   aligns him with Platonic, Patristic, and Protestant views, and against the
   Aristotelian, Scholastic, and Counter-Reformation position.
433 nice] fastidious, difficult to please.
434–8] 'Seemingly' is almost a technical term, for it refers to the Docetist view
   (from δοκεῖν, to seem) that the earthly bodies of spiritual beings (especially
   Christ, but also the angels) were apparent rather than real. Milton's view
   that Raphael physically ate is resolutely Protestant, for in Tobit, which
   Catholics accepted as canonical and Protestants usually rejected from the
   canon, Raphael claims that his eating was illusory ('ye did see a vision'
   Tobit xii. 19). Milton's use of 'transubstantiate' as a digestive term is
   consonant with the anti-Catholic emphasis of the passage.

The angel, nor in mist – the common gloss   435
Of theologians – but with keen dispatch
Of real hunger, and concoctive heat
To transubstantiate: what redounds transpires
Through spirits with ease; nor wonder, if by fire
Of sooty coal the empiric alchemist   440
Can turn, or holds it possible to turn,
Metals of drossiest ore to perfect gold,
As from the mine. Meanwhile at table Eve
Ministered naked, and their flowing cups
With pleasant liquors crowned: O innocence   445
Deserving Paradise! If ever, then,
Then had the sons of God excuse to have been
Enamoured at that sight. But in those hearts
Love unlibidinous reigned, nor jealousy
Was understood, the injured lover's hell.   450
     Thus when with meats and drinks they had sufficed,
Not burdened nature, sudden mind arose
In Adam not to let the occasion pass,
Given him by this great conference, to know
Of things above his world, and of their being   455
Who dwell in heaven, whose excellence he saw
Transcend his own so far, whose radiant forms,
Divine effulgence, whose high power so far
Exceeded human; and his wary speech
Thus to the empyreal minister he framed: 460
     'Inhabitant with God, now know I well
Thy favour, in his honour done to man,
Under whose lowly roof thou hast vouchsafed
To enter, and these earthly fruits to taste,
Food not of angels, yet accepted so   465
As that more willingly thou could'st not seem
At heaven's high feasts to have fed: yet what compare?'
     To whom the wingèd hierarch replied:
'O Adam, one almighty is, from whom
All things proceed, and up to him return,   470
If not depraved from good, created all
Such to perfection; one first matter all,
Endued with various forms, various degrees
Of substance, and in things that live, of life;
But more refined, more spirituous and pure,   475
As nearer to him placed or nearer tending
Each in their several active spheres assigned,
Till body up to spirit work, in bounds
Proportioned to each kind. So from the root
Springs lighter the green stalk, from thence the leaves   480

More airy, last the bright consummate flower
Spirits odórous breathes; flowers and their fruit,
Man's nourishment, by gradual scale sublimed,
To vital spirits aspire, to animal,
To intellectual; give both life and sense,   485
Fancy and understanding; whence the soul
Reason receives, and reason is her being,
Discursive, or intuitive: discourse
Is oftest yours, the latter most is ours,
Differing but in degree, of kind the same.   490
Wonder not then, what God for you saw good
If I refuse not, but convert, as you,
To proper substance; time may come when men
With angels may participate, and find
No inconvenient diet, nor too light fare;   495
And from these corporal nutriments perhaps
Your bodies may at last turn all to spirit,
Improved by tract of time, and winged ascend
Ethereal, as we, or may at choice
Here or in heavenly paradises dwell,   500
If ye be found obedient, and retain
Unalterably firm his love entire
Whose progeny you are. Meanwhile enjoy
Your fill, what happiness this happy state
Can comprehend, incapable of more.'   505
    To whom the patriarch of mankind replied:
'O favourable spirit, propitious guest,
Well hast thou taught the way that might direct
Our knowledge, and the scale of nature set
From centre to circumference, whereon   510
In contemplation of created things,
By steps we may ascend to God. But say,
What meant that caution joined, "If ye be found
Obedient?" Can we want obedience, then,
To him, or possibly his love desert,   515
Who formed us from the dust, and placed us here
Full to the utmost measure of what bliss
Human desires can seek or apprehend?'
    To whom the angel: 'Son of heaven and earth,

484] On 'spirits' and 'animal' spirits see IV 805n. The 'vital spirits' were seated
    in the heart, and sustained life.
501] Isa. i. 19–20.
503 Whose progeny you are] Alludes to Paul's use of the phrase in Acts xvii. 28;
    Paul was quoting the phrase from Aratus' astronomical poem *Phaenomena*;
    cf. *Areopagitica* p. 586, note on 'sentences'.

Attend: that thou art happy, owe to God;   520
That thou continuest such, owe to thyself,
That is, to thy obedience; therein stand.
This was that caution given thee; be advised.
God made thee perfect, not immutable;
And good he made thee, but to persevere   . 525
He left it in thy power – ordained thy will
By nature free, not over-ruled by fate
Inextricable, or strict necessity;
Our voluntary service he requires,
Not our necessitated; such with him   530
Finds no acceptance, nor can find, for how
Can hearts not free be tried whether they serve
Willing or no, who will but what they must
By destiny, and can no other choose?
Myself, and all the angelic host, that stand   535
In sight of God enthroned, our happy state
Hold, as you yours, while our obedience holds;
On other surety none: freely we serve,
Because we freely love, as in our will
To love or not; in this we stand or fall;   540
And some are fallen, to disobedience fallen,
And so from heaven to deepest hell; O fall
From what high state of bliss into what woe!'
    To whom our great progenitor: 'Thy words
Attentive, and with more delighted ear,   545
Divine instructor, I have heard, than when
Cherubic songs by night from neighbouring hills
Aërial music send; nor knew I not
To be, both will and deed, created free;
Yet that we never shall forget to love   550
Our maker, and obey him whose command
Single is yet so just, my constant thoughts
Assured me, and still assure; though what thou tell'st
Hath passed in heaven some doubt within me move,
But more desire to hear, if thou consent,   555
The full relation, which must needs be strange,
Worthy of sacred silence to be heard;
And we have yet large day, for scarce the sun
Hath finished half his journey, and scarce begins
His other half in the great zone of heaven.'   560
    Thus Adam made request, and Raphael,
After short pause assenting, thus began:
    'High matter thou enjoin'st me, O prime of men –

557 Worthy of sacred silence] Horace, *Odes* II. xiii. 29.

Sad task and hard; for how shall I relate
To human sense the invisible exploits   565
Of warring spirits? How, without remorse,
The ruin of so many, glorious once
And perfect while they stood? How, last, unfold
The secrets of another world, perhaps
Not lawful to reveal? Yet for thy good   570
This is dispensed; and what surmounts the reach
Of human sense I shall delineate so,
By likening spiritual to corporal forms,
As may express them best – though what if earth
Be but the shadow of heaven, and things therein   575
Each to other like more than on earth is thought?
    'As yet this world was not, and Chaos wild
Reigned where these heavens now roll, where earth
            now rests
Upon her centre poised, when on a day
(For time, though in eternity, applied   580
To motion, measures all things durable
By present, past, and future), on such day
As heaven's great year brings forth, the empyreal host
Of angels, by imperial summons called,
Innumerable before the almighty's throne   585
Forthwith from all the ends of heaven appeared
Under their hierarchs in orders bright;
Ten thousand thousand ensigns high advanced,
Standards and gonfalons, 'twixt van and rear
Stream in the air, and for distinction serve   590
Of hierarchies, of orders, and degrees;
Or in their glittering tissues bear emblazed
Holy memorials, acts of zeal and love
Recorded eminent. Thus when in orbs
Of circuit inexpressible they stood,   595
Orb within orb, the Father infinite,
By whom in bliss embosomed sat the Son,
Amidst, as from a flaming mount, whose top

566 remorse] sorrow, pity, compassion.
571 dispensed] permitted.
580-2] Aristotle's description of time as the measure of motion (first used by
    Milton in *Hobson* II 7) is here used to discredit the Platonic and Aristotelian
    notion that time and motion cannot exist in eternity, i.e. without reference
    to the created world.
583] The 'great year' or Platonic year was the period (about 36,000 years,
    according to Plato) after which all the heavenly bodies were supposed to
    return to their original positions.
589] gonfalons] banners.

Brightness had made invisible, thus spake:
  '"Hear, all ye angels, progeny of light,   600
Thrones, dominations, princedoms, virtues, powers,
Hear my decree, which unrevoked shall stand.
This day I have begot whom I declare
My only Son, and on this holy hill
Him have anointed, whom ye now behold   605
At my right hand; your head I him appoint,
And by myself have sworn to him shall bow
All knees in heaven, and shall confess him Lord;
Under his great vicegerent reign abide,
United as one individual soul,   610
For ever happy; him who disobeys
Me disobeys, breaks union, and that day,
Cast out from God and blessed vision, falls
Into utter darkness, deep engulfed, his place
Ordained without redemption, without end."   615
  'So spake the Omnipotent, and with his words
All seemed well pleased; all seemed, but were not all.
That day, as other solemn days, they spent
In song and dance about the sacred hill –
Mystical dance, which yonder starry sphere   620
Of planets, and of fixed, in all her wheels
Resembles nearest; mazes intricate,
Eccentric, intervolved, yet regular
Then most when most irregular they seem;
And in their motions harmony divine   625
So smooths her charming tones that God's own ear
Listens delighted. Evening now approached
(For we have also our evening and our morn –
We ours for change delectable, not need),
Forthwith from dance to sweet repast they turn   630
Desirous: all in circles as they stood,
Tables are set, and on a sudden piled
With angels' food; and rubied nectar flows
In pearl, in diamond, and massy gold,
Fruit of delicious vines, the growth of heaven.   635
On flowes reposed, and with fresh flowerets crowned,
They eat, they drink, and in communion sweet

601] Col. i. 16.
603-6] See Heb. i.5, and Milton's translation of Psalm ii. 6-9 (ll. 11-21).
607-8] Isa. xlv. 23; Phil. ii. 9-11.
610 individual] cf. *Time* 12n.
613 blessed vision] cf. I 684n.
614 utter] outer.
618 solemn days] days marked by the celebration of special observances or
    rites.

Quaff immortality and joy, secure
Of surfeit where full measure only bounds
Excess, before the all-bounteous king, who showered   640
With copious hand, rejoicing in their joy.
Now when ambrosial night, with clouds exhaled
From that high mount of God, whence light and shade
Spring both, the face of brightest heaven had changed
To grateful twilight (for night comes not there   645
In darker veil), and roseate dews disposed
All but the unsleeping eyes of God to rest,
Wide over all the plain, and wider far
Than all this globous earth in plain outspread
(Such are the courts of God), the angelic throng,   650
Dispersed in bands and files, their camp extend
By living streams among the trees of life –
Pavilions numberless and sudden reared,
Celestial tabernacles, where they slept,   654
Fanned with cool winds; save those who, in their course,
Melodious hymns about the sovereign throne
Alternate all night long; but not so waked
Satan – so call him now; his former name
Is heard no more in heaven; he, of the first,
If not the first archangel, great in power,   660
In favour and pre-eminence, yet fraught
With envy against the Son of God, that day
Honoured by his great Father, and proclaimed
Messiah, king anointed, could not bear,   664
Through pride, that sight, and thought himself impaired.
Deep malice thence conceiving and disdain,
Soon as midnight brought on the dusky hour
Friendliest to sleep and silence, he resolved
With all his legions to dislodge, and leave
Unworshipped, unobeyed, the throne supreme,   670
Contemptuous, and, his next subordinate
Awakening, thus to him in secret spake:
    ' "Sleep'st thou, companion dear, what sleep can close
Thy eyelids? And rememberest what decree,
Of yesterday, so late hath passed the lips   675

645–6] Rev. xxi. 25.
647] Psalm cxxi. 4.
658 former name] According to a medieval tradition Satan's former name was
    Lucifer. Cf. VII 131–3.
664 Messiah, king anointed] Messiah means 'anointed' in Hebrew.
669 dislodge] a military term meaning 'to leave a place of encampment'.
671 subordinate] presumably Beëlzebub, who is not named in Book V.
673] Alludes to Iliad ii. 23; cf. Aeneid iv 267, 560.

Of heaven's almighty? Thou to me thy thoughts
Wast wont, I mine to thee was wont to impart;
Both waking we were one; how, then, can now
Thy sleep dissent? New laws thou seest imposed;
New laws from him who reigns new minds may raise   680
In us who serve – new counsels, to debate
What doubtful may ensue; more in this place
To utter is not safe. Assemble thou
Of all those myriads which we lead the chief;
Tell them that, by command, ere yet dim night   685
Her shadowy cloud withdraws, I am to haste,
And all who under me their banners wave,
Homeward with flying march where we possess
The quarters of the north, there to prepare
Fit entertainment to receive our king,   690
The great Messiah, and his new commands,
Who speedily through all the hierarchies
Intends to pass triumphant, and give laws."
   'So spake the false archangel, and infused
Bad influence into the unwary breast   695
Of his associate; he together calls,
Or several one by one, the regent powers,
Under him regent; tells, as he was taught,
That, the most high commanding, now ere night,
Now ere dim night had disencumbered heaven,   700
The great hierarchal standard was to move;
Tells the suggested cause, and casts between
Ambiguous words and jealousies, to sound
Or taint integrity; but all obeyed
The wonted signal, and superior voice   705
Of their great potentate; for great indeed
His name, and high was his degree in heaven:
His countenance, as the morning star that guides
The starry flock, allured them, and with lies
Drew after him the third part of heaven's host;   710
Meanwhile, the eternal eye, whose sight discerns
Abstrusest thoughts, from forth his holy mount,
And from within the golden lamps that burn
Nightly before him, saw without their light
Rebellion rising – saw in whom, how spread   715

---

689 north] the traditional home of Satan; cf. Isa. xiv. 13.
697 several] separately.
708-9] Satan imitates ('with lies') Christ as 'morning star'; both identifications
      are Biblical (Isa. xiv. 12; Rev. xxii. 16) Cf. *PR* I 294.
713] Rev. iv. 5.

Among the sons of morn, what multitudes
Were banded to oppose his high decree;
And, smiling, to his only Son thus said:
   ' "Son, thou in whom my glory I behold
In full resplendence, heir of all my might,   720
Nearly it now concerns us to be sure
Of our omnipotence, and with what arms
We mean to hold what anciently we claim
Of deity or empire: such a foe
Is rising, who intends to erect his throne   725
Equal to ours, throughout the spacious north;
Nor so content, hath in his thought to try
In battle what our power is or our right.
Let us advise, and to this hazard draw
With speed what force is left, and all employ   730
In our defence, lest unawares we lose
This our high place, our sanctuary, our hill."
   'To whom the Son, with calm aspéct and clear
Lightning divine, ineffable, serene
Made answer: "Mighty Father, thou thy foes   735
Justly hast in derision, and secure
Laugh'st at their vain designs and tumults vain –
Matter to me of glory, whom their hate
Illustrates, when they see all regal power
Given me to quell their pride, and in event   740
Know whether I be dextrous to subdue
Thy rebels, or be found the worst in heaven."
   'So spake the Son; but Satan with his powers
Far was advanced on winged speed, an host
Innumerable as the stars of night,   745
Or stars of morning, dew-drops which the sun
Impearls on every leaf and every flower.
Regions they passed, the mighty regencies
Of seraphim and potentates and thrones
In their triple degrees – regions to which   750
All thy dominion, Adam, is no more
Than what this garden is to all the earth
And all the sea, from one entire globose
Stretched into longitude; which having passed,

734 Lightning] Cf. Matt. xxvii. 3.
736 in derision] Cf. Milton's translation of Psalm ii. 4 (ll. 8–9).
739 Illustrates] renders illustrious.
750 triple degrees] In a tradition originating in the scheme of Dionysius the Pseudo-Areopagite, the nine orders of angels were divided into three groups of three.
754 into longitude] flat.

At length into the limits of the north   755
They came, and Satan to his royal seat
High on a hill, far blazing, as a mount
Raised on a mount, with pyramids and towers
From diamond quarries hewn and rocks of gold –
The palace of great Lucifer (so call   760
That structure, in the dialect of men
Interpreted) which not long after, he
Affecting all equality with God,
In imitation of that mount whereon
Messiah was declared in sight of heaven,   765
The Mountain of the Congregation called;
For thither he assembled all his train,
Pretending so commanded to consult
About the great reception of their king
Thither to come, and with calumnious art   770
Of counterfeited truth thus held their ears:
    ' "Thrones, dominations, princedoms, virtues, powers –
If these magnific titles yet remain
Not merely titular, since by decree
Another now hath to himself engrossed   775
All power, and us eclipsed under the name
Of king anointed; for whom all this haste
Of midnight march, and hurried meeting here,
This only to consult, how we may best,
With what may be devised of honours new,   780
Receive him coming to receive from us
Knee-tribute yet unpaid, prostration vile,
Too much to one, but double, how endured –
To one and to his image now proclaimed?
But what if better counsels might erect   785
Our minds, and teach us to cast off this yoke?
Will ye submit your necks, and choose to bend
The supple knee? Ye will not, if I trust
To know ye right, or if ye know yourselves
Natives and sons of heaven possessed before   790
By none, and, if not equal all, yet free,
Equally free; for orders and degrees
Jar not with liberty, but well consist.
Who can in reason, then, or right, assume
Monarchy over such as live by right   795
His equals – if in power and splendour less,
In freedom equal? Or can introduce
Law and edict on us, who without law
Err not, much less for this to be our lord,
And look for adoration, to the abuse   800

Of those imperial titles which assert
Our being ordained to govern, not to serve?"
    'Thus far his bold discourse without control
Had audience, when, among the seraphim,
Abdiel, than whom none with more zeal adored   805
The Deity, and divine commands obeyed,
Stood up, and in a flame of zeal severe
The current of his fury thus opposed:
    '"O argument blasphémous, false, and proud –
Words which no ear ever to hear in heaven   810
Expected; least of all from thee, ingrate,
In place thyself so high above thy peers.
Canst thou with impious obloquy condemn
The just decree of God, pronounced and sworn,
That to his only Son, by right endued   815
With regal sceptre, every soul in heaven
Shall bend the knee, and in that honour due
Confess him rightful king? Unjust, thou say'st,
Flatly unjust, to bind with laws the free,
And equal over equals to let reign,   820
One over all with unsucceeded power.
Shalt thou give law to God, shalt thou dispute
With him the points of liberty, who made
Thee what thou art, and formed the powers of heaven
Such as he pleased, and circumscribed their being?   825
Yet, by experience taught, we know how good,
And of our good and of our dignity
How provident, he is – how far from thought
To make us less; bent rather to exalt
Our happy state, under one head more near   830
United. But – to grant it thee unjust
That equal over equals monarch reign –
Thyself, though great and glorious, dost thou count,
Or all angelic nature joined in one,
Equal to him, begotten Son, by whom   835
As by his word, the mighty Father made
All things, even thee, and all the spirits of heaven
By him created in their bright degrees,
Crowned them with glory, and to their glory named

805 Abdiel] The name means in Hebrew 'servant of God'; in the Bible it is used
    only as a human name.
821 unsucceeded] having no successor, everlasting.
822–5] See Rom. ix. 20 and A.V. marginal note, where 'disputest with God' is
    listed as an alternative reading.
835–40] Col. i. 16–17.

Thrones, dominations, princedoms, virtues, powers? –
Essential powers; nor by his reign obscured,   841
But more illustrious made, since he the head
One of our number thus reduced becomes,
His laws our laws, all honour to him done
Returns our own. Cease then this impious rage,   845
And tempt not these; but hasten to appease
The incensèd Father and the incensèd Son
While pardon may be found, in time besought."
   'So spake the fervent angel, but his zeal
None seconded, as out of season judged,   850
Or singular and rash; whereat rejoiced
The apostate, and, more haughty, thus replied:
   ' "That we were formed, then, say'st thou? And the
        work
Of secondary hands, by task transferred   855
From Father to his Son? Strange point and new!
Doctrine which we would know whence learned; who saw
When this creation was? Remember'st thou
Thy making, while the maker gave thee being?
We know no time when we were not as now;
Know none before us, self-begot, self-raised   860
By our own quickening power when fatal course
Had circled his full orb, the birth mature
Of this our native heaven, ethereal sons.
Our puissance is our own; our own right hand
Shall teach us highest deeds, by proof to try   865
Who is our equal; then thou shalt behold
Whether by supplication we intend
Address, and to begirt the almighty throne
Beseeching or besieging. This report,
These tidings, carry to the anointed king;   870
And fly, ere evil intercept thy flight."
   'He said, and, as the sound of waters deep,
Hoarse murmur echoed to his words applause
Through the infinite host; nor less for that
The flaming seraph, fearless, though alone,   875
Encompassed round with foes, thus answered bold:
   ' "O alienate from God, O spirit accursed,
Forsaken of all good; I see thy fall
Determined, and thy hapless crew involved
In this perfidious fraud, contagion spread
Both of thy crime and punishment; henceforth   880

864–5] Psalm xlv. 4.
872] Ezek. i. 24; Rev. xix. 6.

No more be troubled how to quit the yoke
Of God's Messiah; those indulgent laws
Will not be now vouchsafed; other decrees
Against thee are gone forth without recall;   885
That golden sceptre which thou didst reject
Is now an iron rod to bruise and break
Thy disobedience. Well thou didst advise;
Yet not for thy advice or threats I fly
These wicked tents devoted, lest the wrath   890
Impendent, raging into sudden flame,
Distinguish not: for soon expect to feel
His thunder on thy head, devouring fire.
Then who created thee lamenting learn,
When who can uncreate thee thou shalt know.''   895
    'So spake the seraph Abdiel, faithful found;
Among the faithless faithful only he;
Among innumerable false unmoved,
Unshaken, unseduced, unterrified,
His loyalty he kept, his love, his zeal;   900
Nor number nor example with him wrought
To swerve from truth, or change his constant mind,
Though single. From amidst them forth he passed,
Long way through hostile scorn, which he sustained
Superior, nor of violence feared aught;   905
And with retorted scorn his back he turned
On those proud towers, to swift destruction doomed.'

THE END OF THE FIFTH BOOK

886–7] Cf. II 327–8 and 327n.
890 wicked tents] See Num. xvi. 26 and Milton's translation of Psalm lxxxiv. 10
    (ll. 37–40).
    devoted] consigned to destruction, doomed.
906 retorted] thrown back. In the phrase 'he turned' Milton recapitulates the
    root-meaning of retort, which is 'to turn or twist'.
907] II Pet. ii. 1.

BOOK VI

THE ARGUMENT

Raphael continues to relate how Michael and Gabriel were sent forth to battle against Satan and his angels. The first fight described: Satan and his powers retire under night; he calls a council; invents devilish engines, which, in the second day's fight, put Michael and his angels to some disorder; but they at length, pulling up mountains, overwhelmed both the force and machines of Satan. Yet, the tumult not so ending, God, on the third day, sends Messiah his Son, for whom he had reserved the glory of that victory; he, in the power of his Father, coming to the place, and causing all his legions to stand still on either side, with his chariot and thunder driving into the midst of his enemies pursued them, unable to resist, towards the wall of heaven; which opening, they leap down with horror and confusion into the place of punishment prepared for them in the deep. Messiah returns with triumph to his Father.

'All night the dreadless angel, unpursued,
Through heaven's wide champaign held his way, till Morn,
Waked by the circling Hours, with rosy hand
Unbarred the gates of light. There is a cave
Within the Mount of God, fast by his throne, 5
Where Light and Darkness in perpetual round
Lodge and dislodge by turns – which makes through heaven
Grateful vicissitude, like day and night;
Light issues forth, and at the other door
Obsequious Darkness enters, till her hour 10
To veil the heaven, though darkness there might well
Seem twilight here; and now went forth the Morn
Such as in highest heaven, arrayed in gold
Empyreal; from before her vanished night,
Shot through with orient beams; when all the plain 15
Covered with thick embattled squadrons bright,
Chariots, and flaming arms, and fiery steeds,
Reflecting blaze on blaze, first met his view;
War he perceived, war in procinct, and found
Already known what he for news had thought 20

---

1 angel] Abdiel.
2–4] *Metamorphoses* ii 112–14. On 'rosy hand' cf. V 1n.
4–7] Hesiod, *Theogony* 736–57.
19 in procinct] prepared, in readiness.

To have reported; gladly then he mixed
Among those friendly powers, who him received
With joy and acclamations loud, that one,
That of so many myriads fallen yet one,
Returned not lost; on to the sacred hill   25
They led him, high applauded, and present
Before the seat supreme; from whence a voice,
From midst a golden cloud, thus mild was heard:
  ' "Servant of God, well done; well hast thou fought
The better fight, who single hast maintained   30
Against revolted multitudes the cause
Of truth, in word mightier than they in arms,
And for the testimony of truth hast borne
Universal reproach, far worse to bear
Than violence; for this was all thy care –   35
To stand approved in sight of God, though worlds
Judged thee perverse; the easier conquest now
Remains thee – aided by this host of friends,
Back on thy foes more glorious to return
Than scorned thou didst depart, and to subdue   40
By force who reason for their law refuse –
Right reason for their law, and for their king
Messiah, who by right of merit reigns.
Go, Michael, of celestial armies prince,
And thou, in military prowess next,   45
Gabriel; lead forth to battle these my sons
Invincible; lead forth my armed saints,
By thousands and by millions ranged for fight,
Equal in number to that godless crew
Rebellious; them with fire and hostile arms   50
Fearless assault, and to the brow of heaven
Pursuing, drive them out from God and bliss
Into their place of punishment, the gulf
Of Tartarus, which ready opens wide
His fiery chaos to receive their fall."   55
  'So spake the sovereign voice, and clouds began

29–30] Matt. xxv. 21, II Tim. iv. 7. On 'Servant of God' cf. V 805n.
33–4] Psalm lxix. 7.
42 Right reason] a theological term, inherited from the Scholastic (and ultima-
    tely Stoic) idea of *recto ratio*, which describes the faculty implanted in man
    that manifests itself both as conscience and as an ability to distinguish
    truth from falsehood.
44 Michael] The archangel Michael (Hebrew 'who is like God?') was tradition-
    ally regarded as 'prince of angels' (l.281), though Protestants often dis-
    sented from this tradition. On Michael's role in the war in heaven see Rev.
    xii. (cf. Dan. xii. 1).
56–60] Cf. *Nativity* 158–9n.

To darken all the hill, and smoke to roll
In dusky wreaths reluctant flames, the sign
Of wrath awaked; nor with less dread the loud
Ethereal trumpet from on high gan blow;   60
At which command the powers militant
That stood for heaven, in mighty quadrate joined
Of union irresistible, moved on
In silence their bright legions to the sound
Of instrumental harmony, that breathed   65
Heroic ardour to adventurous deeds
Under their godlike leaders, in the cause
Of God and his Messiah. On they move,
Indissolubly firm; nor obvious hill,
Nor straitening vale, nor wood, nor stream, divides   70
Their perfect ranks; for high above the ground
Their march was, and the passive air upbore
Their nimble tread; as when the total kind
Of birds, in orderly array on wing,
Came summoned over Eden to receive   75
Their names of thee; so over many a tract
Of heaven they marched, and many a province wide,
Tenfold the length of this terrene; at last,
Far in the horizon, to the north, appeared
From skirt to skirt a fiery region, stretched   80
In battailous aspect; and, nearer view,
Bristled with upright beams innumerable
Of rigid spears, and helmets thronged, and shields
Various, with boastful argument portrayed,
The banded powers of Satan hasting on   85
With furious expedition; for they weened
That self-same day, by fight or by surprise,
To win the Mount of God, and on his throne
To set the envier of his state, the proud
Aspirer; but their thoughts proved fond and vain   90
In the mid-way; though strange to us it seemed
At first that angel should with angel war,
And in fierce hosting meet, who wont to meet
So oft in festivals of joy and love

58 reluctant] means both 'struggling, writhing' (cf. X 515) and 'unwilling,
    averse'.
60 gan] began to.
62 quadrate] square or rectangle.
69 obvious] lying in the way.
73–6] Gen. ii. 20, *Iliad* ii 459–63, *Aeneid* vii 699–701.
78 terrene] earth.
93 hosting] hostile encounter.

Unanimous, as sons of one great sire,   95
Hymning the eternal Father; but the shout
Of battle now began, and rushing sound
Of onset ended soon each milder thought.
High in the midst, exalted as a god,
The apostate in his sun-bright chariot sat,   100
Idol of majesty divine, enclosed
With flaming cherubim and golden shields;
Then lighted from his gorgeous throne – for now
'Twixt host and host but narrow space was left,
A dreadful interval, and front to front   105
Presented stood, in terrible array
Of hideous length; before the cloudy van,
On the rough edge of battle ere it joined,
Satan with vast and haughty strides advanced,
Came towering, armed in adamant and gold;   110
Abdiel that sight endured not, where he stood
Among the mightiest, bent on highest deeds,
And thus his own undaunted heart explores:
    ' "O heaven! That such resemblance of the highest
Should yet remain, where faith and realty   115
Remain not; wherefore should not strength and might
There fail where virtue fails, or weakest prove
Where boldest, though to sight unconquerable?
His puissance, trusting in the almighty's aid,
I mean to try, whose reason I have tried   120
Unsound and false; nor is it aught but just
That he who in debate of truth hath won
Should win in arms, in both disputes alike
Victor; though brutish that contést and foul,
When reason hath to deal with force, yet so   125
Most reason is that reason overcome." '
    'So pondering, and from his armed peers
Forth stepping opposite, half-way he met
His daring foe, at this prevention more
Incensed, and thus securely him defied: 130
    ' "Proud, art thou met? Thy hope was to have reached
The height of thy aspiring unopposed –
The throne of God unguarded, and his side
Abandoned at the terror of thy power
Or potent tongue; fool, not to think how vain   135

108 edge] cf. I 276n.
115 realty] sincerity, honesty.
120 tried] proved by trial.
129 prevention] stopping another person in the execution of his designs.

Against the omnipotent to rise in arms;
Who out of smallest things could without end
Have raised incessant armies to defeat
Thy folly; or with solitary hand,
Reaching beyond all limit, at one blow,   140
Unaided could have finished thee, and whelmed
Thy legions under darkness; but thou seest
All are not of thy train; there be who faith
Prefer, and piety to God, though then
To thee not visible when I alone   145
Seemed in thy world erroneous to dissent
From all: my sect thou seest; now learn too late
How few sometimes may know when thousands err."
     'Whom the grand foe, with scornful eye askance,
Thus answered: "Ill for thee, but in wished hour   150
Of my revenge, first sought for, thou return'st
From flight, seditious angel, to receive
Thy merited reward, the first assay
Of this right hand provoked, since first that tongue,
Inspired with contradiction, durst oppose   155
A third part of the gods, in synod met
Their deities to assert: who, while they feel
Vigour divine within them, can allow
Omnipotence to none. But well thou com'st
Before thy fellows, ambitious to win   160
From me some plume, that thy success may show
Destruction to the rest; this pause between
(Unanswered lest thou boast) to let thee know;
At first I thought that liberty and heaven
To heavenly souls had been all one; but now   165
I see that most through sloth had rather serve,
Ministering spirits, trained up in feast and song:
Such hast thou armed, the minstrelsy of heaven –
Servility with freedom to contend,
As both their deeds compared this day shall prove."   170
     'To whom in brief thus Abdiel stern replied:
"Apostate, still thou err'st, nor end wilt find
Of erring, from the path of truth remote;
Unjustly thou deprav'st it with the name
Of servitude, to serve whom God ordains,   175
Or nature: God and nature bid the same,

137-9] Matt. iii. 9.
148 my sect] the primary meaning is 'those of my party', but the phrase
     probably glances at the Royalists' derisive use of the word to describe
     various dissenting groups.

When he who rules is worthiest, and excels
Them whom he governs. This is servitude –
To serve the unwise, or him who hath rebelled
Against his worthier, as thine now serve thee,   180
Thyself not free, but to thyself enthralled;
Yet lewdly dar'st our ministering upbraid.
Reign thou in hell, thy kingdom; let me serve
In heaven God ever blest, and his divine
Behests obey, worthiest to be obeyed.   185
Yet chains in hell, not realms, expect: meanwhile,
From me returned, as erst thou saidst, from flight,
This greeting on thy impious crest receive.''
     'So saying, a noble stroke he lifted high,
Which hung not, but so swift with tempest fell   190
On the proud crest of Satan that no sight,
Nor motion of swift thought, less could his shield,
Such ruin intercept; ten paces huge
He back recoiled; the tenth on bended knee
His massy spear upstayed: as if on earth   195
Winds under ground, or waters forcing way
Sidelong had pushed a mountain from his seat,
Half-sunk with all his pines. Amazement seized
The rebel thrones, but greater rage, to see
Thus foiled their mightiest; ours joy filled, and shout,   200
Presage of victory, and fierce desire
Of battle: whereat Michaël bid sound
The archangel trumpet; through the vast of heaven
It sounded, and the faithful armies rung
Hosanna to the highest; nor stood at gaze   205
The adverse legions, nor less hideous joined
The horrid shock; now storming fury rose,
And clamour such as heard in heaven till now
Was never; arms on armour clashing brayed
Horrible discord, and the madding wheels   210
Of brazen chariots raged; dire was the noise
Of conflict; overhead the dismal hiss
Of fiery darts in flaming volleys flew,
And, flying, vaulted either host with fire.
So under fiery cope together rushed
Both battles main with ruinous assault   215

182 lewdly] means both 'foolishly' and 'wickedly'.
209 brayed] made the harsh jarring sound of thunder (not of an animal).
210 madding] frenzied.
216 battles main] the main bodies of the armies, as distinct from the van (l. 107)
    or the wings.

And inextinguishable rage; all heaven
Resounded; and had earth been then, all earth
Had to her centre shook. What wonder, when
Millions of fierce encountering angels fought   220
On either side, the least of whom could wield
These elements, and arm him with the force
Of all their regions? How much more of power
Army against army numberless to raise
Dreadful combustion warring, and disturb,   225
Though not destroy, their happy native seat;
Had not the eternal king omnipotent
From his strong hold of heaven high overruled
And limited their might, though numbered such
As each divided legion might have seemed   230
A numerous host, in strength each armed hand
A legion; led in fight, yet leader seemed
Each warrior single as in chief; expert
When to advance, or stand, or turn the sway
Of battle, open when, and when to close   235
The ridges of grim war; no thought of flight,
None of retreat, no unbecoming deed
That argued fear; each on himself relied
As only in his arm the moment lay
Of victory; deeds of eternal fame   240
Were done, but infinite; for wide was spread
That war, and various: sometimes on firm ground
A standing fight; then, soaring on main wing,
Tormented all the air; all air seemed then
Conflicting fire; long time in even scale   245
The battle hung; till Satan, who that day
Prodigious power had shown, and met in arms
No equal, ranging through the dire attack
Of fighting seraphim confused, at length
Saw where the sword of Michael smote, and felled   250
Squadrons at once: with huge two-handed sway
Brandished aloft, the horrid edge came down
Wide-wasting; such destruction to withstand
He hasted, and opposed the rocky orb
Of tenfold adamant, his ample shield   255
A vast cirumference; at his approach

225 combustion] commotion, tumult.
229 numbered such] so numerous.
236 ridges of ... war] probably imitates an Homeric phrase (πολέμοιο γέφυραι),
     the precise meaning of which is uncertain: it refers either to the ground that
     divides two lines of battle or to the passage that links them.

The great archangel from his warlike toil
Surceased, and glad as hoping here to end
Intestine war in heaven, the arch-foe subdued,
Or captive dragged in chains, with hostile frown   260
And visage all inflamed, first thus began:
  ' "Author of evil, unknown till thy revolt,
Unnamed in heaven, now plenteous as thou seest
These acts of hateful strife – hateful to all,
Though heaviest, by just measure, on thyself   265
And thy adherents – how hast thou disturbed
Heaven's blessed peace, and into nature brought
Misery, uncreated till the crime
Of thy rebellion! How hast thou instilled
Thy malice into thousands, once upright   270
And faithful, now proved false. But think not here
To trouble holy rest; heaven casts thee out
From all her confines. Heaven, the seat of bliss,
Brooks not the works of violence and war.
Hence then, and evil go with thee along,   275
Thy offspring, to the place of evil, hell –
Thou and thy wicked crew; there mingle broils,
Ere this avenging sword begin thy doom,
Or some more sudden vengeance, winged from God,
Precipitate thee with augmented pain." '   280
  'So spake the prince of angels; to whom thus
The adversary: "Nor think thou with wind
Of airy threats to awe whom yet with deeds
Thou canst not. Hast thou turned the least of these
To flight – or if to fall, but that they rise   285
Unvanquished – easier to transact with me
That thou shouldst hope, imperious, and with threats
To chase me hence? Err not that so shall end
The strife which thou call'st evil, but we style
The strife of glory; which we mean to win,   290
Or turn this heaven itself into the hell
Thou fablest; here, however, to dwell free,
If not to reign; meanwhile, thy utmost force –
And join him named Almighty to thy aid –
I fly not, but have sought thee far and nigh."   295
  'They ended parle, and both addressed for fight
Unspeakable; for who, though with the tongue
Of angels, can relate, or to what things;

259] Intestine war] civil war.
282 adversary] See I 82n.
296 parle] discussion between enemies under a truce.

Liken on earth conspicuous, that may lift
Human imagination to such height   300
Of godlike power? For likest gods they seemed,
Stood they or moved, in stature, motion, arms,
Fit to decide the empire of great heaven.
Now waved their fiery swords, and in the air
Made horrid circles; two broad suns their shields   305
Blazed opposite, while Expectation stood
In horror; from each hand with speed retired,
Where erst was thickest fight, the angelic throng,
And left large field, unsafe within the wind
Of such commotion: such as – to set forth   310
Great things by small – if, nature's concord broke,
Among the constellations war were sprung,
Two planets, rushing from aspéct malign
Of fiercest opposition, in mid sky
Should combat, and their jarring spheres confound   315
Together both, with next to almighty arm
Uplifted imminent, one stroke they aimed
That might determine, and not need repeat
As not of power, at once; nor odds appeared
In might or swift prevention; but the sword   320
Of Michael from the armoury of God
Was given him tempered so, that neither keen
Nor solid might resist that edge: it met
The sword of Satan with steep force to smite
Descending, and in half cut sheer; nor stayed,   325
But, with swift wheel reverse, deep entering, shared
All his right side; then Satan first knew pain,
And writhed him to and fro convolved; so sore
The griding sword with discontinuous wound
Passed through him; but the ethereal substance closed,
Not long divisible, and from the gash   331
A stream of nectarous humour issuing flowed
Sanguine, such as celestial spirits may bleed,

313 aspéct] the relative positions of the heavenly bodies. Renaissance astro-
      logers distinguished five positions, two of which (including 'opposition',
      l. 314) were deemed 'malign'. Cf. X 658-9.
320 prevention] anticipation.
321] Jer. i. 25.
326 shared] cut into parts.
329 griding] piercing, wounding.
      discontinuous] producing a separation of the tissues of the body; gaping.
332-3] 'Sanguine' means 'blood-red', but also modifies 'humour', and thus
      refers (in the physiological theory of the 'cardinal humours') to Satan's loss
      of confidence of success. Sanguine humour is 'nectarous' because it is
      produced by the digestion of food and drink, and the angelic drink is nectar
      (V 633).

And all his armour stained, erewhile so bright.
Forthwith, on all sides, to his aid was run   335
By angels many and strong, who interposed
Defence, while others bore him on their shields
Back to his chariot where it stood retired
From off the files of war: there they him laid
Gnashing for anguish, and despite, and shame   340
To find himself not matchless, and his pride
Humbled by such rebuke, so far beneath
His confidence to equal God in power.
Yet soon he healed; for spirits, that live throughout
Vital in every part – not, as frail man,   345
In entrails, heart or head, liver or reins –
Cannot but by annihilating die;
Nor in their liquid texture mortal wound
Receive, no more than can the fluid air:
All heart they live, all head, all eye, all ear,   350
All intellect, all sense; and as they please
They limb themselves, and colour, shape, or size
Assume, as likes them best, condense or rare.
    'Meanwhile, in other parts, like deeds deserved
Memorial, where the might of Gabriel fought,   355
And with fierce ensigns pierced the deep array
Of Moloch, furious king, who him defied,
And at his chariot wheels to drag him bound
Threatened, nor from the holy one of heaven
Refrained his tongue blasphémous, but anon,   360
Down cloven to the waist, with shattered arms
And uncouth pain fled bellowing. On each wing
Uriel and Raphaël his vaunting foe,
Though huge and in a rock of diamond armed,
Vanquished – Adramelech and Asmadai,   365
Two potent thrones, that to be less than gods
Disdained, but meaner thoughts learned in their flight,
Mangled with ghastly wounds through plate and mail;
Nor stood unmindful Abdiel to annoy
The atheist crew, but with redoubled blow   370

346 reins] kidneys.
355 might of] imitates Homeric diction, and means 'mighty'.
357 king] See I 392n.
359–60] II Kings xix. 22.
363 vaunting] means both 'vain-glorious' and 'in the van (i.e. front) of the
    army'.
365 Vanquished] The grammatical object of 'vanquished' is 'foe'. Uriel's foe is
    Adramelech, a god of Assyrian origin brought to Samaria from Sepharvaim
    (II Kings xvii. 31); Raphael's foe is Asmadai (see IV 166–71n.).
370 atheist] impious.

Ariel, and Arioch, and the violence
Of Ramiel, scorched and blasted, overthrew.
I might relate of thousands, and their names
Eternize here on earth; but those elect
Angels, contented with their fame in heaven,   375
Seek not the praise of men: the other sort,
In might though wondrous and in acts of war,
Nor of renown less eager, yet by doom
Cancelled from heaven and sacred memory,
Nameless in dark oblivion let them dwell   380
For strength from truth divided, and from just,
Illaudable, naught merits but dispraise
And ignominy, yet to glory aspires,
Vain-glorious, and through infamy seeks fame:
Therefore eternal silence be their doom.   385
   'And now, their mightiest quelled, the battle swerved,
With many an inroad gored; deformèd rout
Entered, and foul disorder; all the ground
With shivered armour strown, and on a heap
Chariot and charioteer lay overturned,   390
And fiery foaming steeds; what stood recoiled,
O'er-wearied, through the faint Satanic host,
Defensive scarce, or with pale fear surprised –
Then first with fear surprised and sense of pain –
Fled ignominious, to such evil brought   395
By sin of disobedience, till that hour
Not liable to fear, or flight, or pain.
Far otherwise the inviolable saints
In cubic phalanx firm advanced entire,
Invulnerable, impenetrably armed;   400
Such high advantages their innocence
Gave them above their foes – not to have sinned,
Not to have disobeyed; in fight they stood
Unwearied, unobnoxious to be pained   404
By wound, though from their place by violence moved.
   'Now night her course began, and over heaven
Inducing darkness, grateful truce imposed,
And silence on the odious din of war;

371] Ariel means 'lion of God' in Hebrew, and in the O.T. is used as a human
      name and a name for Jerusalem; in a later tradition he was thought to be an
      angel or an evil demon. Arioch means 'like a Lion' and in the O.T. is used of
      various kings; in a later tradition he was identified with the spirit of
      revenge.
372] Ramiel means 'thunder of God' in Hebrew, and in the Book of Enoch
      refers to a fallen angel.
393 Defensive scarce] scarcely capable of defence.
404 unobnoxious] not liable.

Under her cloudy covert both retired,
Victor and vanquished; on the foughten field   410
Michaël and his angels, prevalent
Encamping, placed in guard their watches round,
Cherubic waving fires: on the other part,
Satan with his rebellious disappeared,
Far in the dark dislodged, and void of rest,   415
His potentates to council called by night,
And in the midst thus undismayed began:
   '"O now in danger tried, now known in arms
Not to be overpowered, companions dear,
Found worthy not of liberty alone –   420
Too mean pretence – but, what we more affect,
Honour, dominion, glory, and renown;
Who have sustained one day in doubtful fight
(And, if one day, why not eternal days?)
What heaven's lord had powerfullest to send   425
Against us from about his throne, and judged
Sufficient to subdue us to his will,
But proves not so: then fallible, it seems,
Of future we may deem him, though till now
Omniscient thought. True is, less firmly armed,   430
Some disadvantage we endured, and pain –
Till now not known, but, known, as soon contemned;
Since now we find this our empyreal form
Incapable of mortal injury,
Imperishable, and though pierced with wound,   435
Soon closing, and by native vigour healed.
Of evil, then, so small, as easy think
The remedy: perhaps more valid arms,
Weapons more violent, when next we meet
May serve to better us and worse our foes,   440
Or equal what between us made the odds,
In nature none; if other hidden cause
Left them superior, while we can preserve
Unhurt our minds, and understanding sound,
Due search and consultation will disclose."   445
   'He sat; and in the assembly next upstood
Nisroch, of principalities the prime.
As one he stood escaped from cruel fight
Sore toiled, his riven arms to havoc hewn,

410 foughten field] battlefield.
411 prevalent] prevailing, victorious.
429 Of] in.
447 Nisroch] The Hebrew name for an Assyrian god (II Kings xix. 37).

And, cloudy in aspéct, thus answering spake: 450
  '"Deliverer from new lords, leader to free
Enjoyment of our rights as gods; yet hard
For gods, and too unequal work, we find
Against unequal arms to fight in pain,
Against unpained, impassive; from which evil   455
Ruin must needs ensue; for what avails
Valour or strength, though matchless, quelled with pain,
Which all subdues, and makes remiss the hands
Of mightiest? Sense of pleasure we may well
Spare out of life perhaps, and not repine,   460
But live content – which is the calmest life;
But pain is perfect misery, the worst
Of evils, and, excessive, overturns
All patience. He who therefore can invent
With what more forcible we may offend   465
Our yet unwounded enemies, or arm
Ourselves with like defence, to me deserves
No less than for deliverance what we owe."
  'Whereto with look composed Satan replied:
"Not uninvented that, which thou aright   470
Believ'st so main to our success, I bring;
Which of us who beholds the bright surfáce
Of this ethereous mould whereon we stand –
This continent of spacious heaven, adorned
With plant, fruit, flower ambrosial, gems and gold   475
Whose eye so superficially surveys
These things as not to mind from whence they grow
Deep under ground: materials dark and crude,
Of spiritous and fiery spume, till touched
With heaven's ray, and tempered, they shoot forth   480
So beauteous, opening to the ambient light?
These in their dark nativity the deep
Shall yield us, pregnant with infernal flame;
Which, into hollow engines long and round
Thick-rammed, at the other bore with touch of fire   485
Dilated and infuriate, shall send forth
From far, with thundering noise, among our foes
Such implements of mischief as shall dash
To pieces and o'erwhelm whatever stands
Adverse, that they shall fear we have disarmed   490
The thunderer of his only dreaded bolt.
Nor long shall be our labour; yet ere dawn

471 main] highly important.
485 other bore] the touch-hole.

Effect shall end our wish. Meanwhile revive;
Abandon fear; to strength and counsel joined
Think nothing hard, much less to be despaired."   495
    'He ended, and his words their drooping cheer
Enlightened, and their languished hope revived.
The invention all admired, and each how he
To be the inventor missed; so easy it seemed
Once found, which yet unfound most would have thought
Impossible; yet haply of thy race,   501
In future days, if malice should abound,
Some one, intent on mischief, or inspired
With devilish machination, might devise
Like instrument to plague the sons of men   505
For sin, on war and mutual slaughter bent.
Forthwith from council to the work they flew;
None arguing stood; innumerable hands
Were ready; in a moment up they turned
Wide the celestial soil, and saw beneath   510
The originals of nature in their crude
Conception; sulphurous and nitrous foam
They found, they mingled, and with subtle art
Concocted and adusted, they reduced
To blackest grain, and into store conveyed;   515
Part hidden veins digged up (nor hath this earth
Entrails unlike) of mineral and stone,
Whereof to found their engines and their balls
Of missive ruin; part incentive reed
Provide, pernicious with one touch to fire.   520
So all ere day-spring, under conscious night,
Secret they finished, and in order set,
With silent circumspection, unespied.
    'Now, when fair morn orient in heaven appeared,
Up rose the victor angels, and to arms   525
The matin trumpet sung; in arms they stood
Of golden panoply, refulgent host,
Soon banded; others from the dawning hills
Looked round, and scouts each coast light-armèd scour,
Each quarter, to descry the distant foe,   530
Where lodged, or whither fled, or if for fight,

---

514 Concocted] maturated (i.e. purified) by heating (an alchemical term).
    adjusted] dried up with heat (cf. XII 635).
518 found] cast, mould.
519 incentive] kindling.
520 pernicious] means both 'rapid' (from *pernix*) and 'destructive' (from
    perniciosus).
521 conscious] possessing a guilty knowledge.

In motion or in halt; him soon they met
Under spread ensigns moving nigh, in slow
But firm battalion: back with speediest sail
Zophiel, of cherubim the swiftest wing,   535
Came flying, and in mid air aloud thus cried:
    ' "Arm, warriors, arm for fight – the foe at hand,
Whom fled we thought, will save us long pursuit
This day; fear not his flight; so thick a cloud
He comes, and settled in his face I see   540
Sad resolution and secure; let each
His adamantine coat gird well, and each
Fit well his helm, gripe fast his orbed shield,
Borne even or high; for this day will pour down,
If I conjecture aught, no drizzling shower,   545
But rattling storm of arrows barbed with fire."
    'So warned he them, aware themselves, and soon
In order, quit of all impediment;
Instant without disturb they took alarm,
And onward move embattled: when behold   550
Not distant far, with heavy pace the foe
Approaching gross and huge, in hollow cube
Training his devilish enginery, impaled
On every side with shadowing squadrons deep,
To hide the fraud. At interview both stood   555
A while, but suddenly at head appeared
Satan, and thus was heard commanding loud:
    ' "Vanguard, to right and left the front unfold,
That all may see who hate us how we seek
Peace and composure, and with open breast   560
Stand ready to receive them, if they like
Our overture, and turn not back perverse:
But that I doubt; however, witness heaven;
Heaven, witness thou anon, while we discharge

---

535 Zophiel] The name means 'spy of God'; it does not occur in the Bible.
541 Sad] grave, serious.
549 took alarm] took up arms.
553 Training] hauling.
555 At interview] within mutual view.
560 composure] settlement.
560–7] As Raphael observes (l. 568), the lines contain 'ambiguous words':
    'breast' means 'heart' (as the seat of affections) and, as a military term, 'the
    broad even front of a moving company'; 'overture' means 'opening of
    negotiations with a view to a settlement', and 'orifice', i.e. the mouths of
    the cannons (l. 577); 'touch' plays on the technical meaning of 'touch-
    powder', i.e. the priming powder for the cannons (the same pun occurs in ll.
    479, 485, 520, 584); the puns on 'discharge' and 'loud' are obvious.

Freely our part; ye who appointed stand   565
Do as you have in charge, and briefly touch
What we propound, and loud that all may hear.''
    'So scoffing in ambiguous words, he scarce
Had ended, when to right and left the front
Divided, and to either flank retired;   570
Which to our eyes discovered, new and strange,
A triple mounted row of pillars laid
On wheels (for like to pillars most they seemed,
Or hollowed bodies made of oak or fir,
With branches lopped, in wood or mountain felled),   575
Brass, iron, stony mould, had not their mouths
With hideous orifice gaped on us wide,
Portending hollow truce; at each, behind,
A seraph stood, and in his hand a reed
Stood waving tipped with fire; while we, suspense,   580
Collected stood within our thoughts amused,
Not long, for sudden all at once their reeds
Put forth, and to a narrow vent applied
With nicest touch. Immediate in a flame,
But soon obscured with smoke, all heaven appeared,   585
From those deep-throated engines belched, whose roar
Embowelled with outrageous noise the air,
And all her entrails tore, disgorging foul
Their devilish glut, chained thunderbolts and hail
Of iron globes; which on the victor host   590
Levelled, with such impetuous fury smote,
That whom they hit none on their feet might stand
Though standing else as rocks, but down they fell
By thousands, angel on archangel rolled,
The sooner for their arms; unarmed, they might   595
Have easily, as spirits, evaded swift
By quick contraction or remove; but now
Foul dissipation followed, and forced rout;
Nor served it to relax their serried files.
What should they do? If on they rushed, repulse   600
Repeated, and indecent overthrow
Doubled, would render them yet more despised,
And to their foes a laughter – for in view
Stood ranked of seraphim another row,
In posture to displode their second tire   605

581 amused] put in a muse, absorbed.
587 Embowelled] 'disembowelled', or possibly 'filled the bowels of'.
598 dissipation] scattering, dispersal.
605] means 'in position to fire their second volley'.

Of thunder; back defeated to return
They worse abhorred. Satan beheld their plight,
And to his mates thus in derision called:
    ' "O friends, why come not on these victors proud?
Erewhile they fierce were coming, and when we,   610
To entertain them fair with open front
And breast (what could we more?) propounded terms
Of composition, straight they changed their minds,
Flew off, and into strange vagaries fell,
As they would dance, yet for a dance they seemed   615
Somewhat extravagant and wild, perhaps
For joy of offered peace; but I suppose,
If our proposals once again were heard,
We should compel them to a quick result."
    'To whom thus Belial, in like gamesome mood;   620
"Leader, the terms we sent were terms of weight,
Of hard contents, and full of force urged home,
Such as we might perceive amused them all,
And stumbled many; who receives them right
Had need from head to foot well understand;   625
Not understood, this gift they have besides –
They show us when our foes walk not upright."
    'So they among themselves in pleasant vein
Stood scoffing, heightened in their thoughts beyond
All doubt of victory; eternal might   630
To match with their inventions they presumed
So easy, and of his thunder made a scorn,
And all his host derided, while they stood
A while in trouble; but they stood not long;
Rage prompted them at length, and found them arms   635
Against such hellish mischief fit to oppose.
Forthwith (behold the excellence, the power,
Which God hath in his mighty angels placed)
Their arms away they threw, and to the hills
(For earth hath his variety from heaven   640
Of pleasure situate in hill and dale)
Light as the lightning-glimpse they ran, they flew;
From their foundations, loosening to and fro,
They plucked the seated hills with all their load,

611–12] 'Breast' repeats the pun of l. 560, and 'front' introduces a parallel play
    on the meanings 'the face as expressive of emotion' (here candour) and 'the
    foremost line of an army'.
613 composition] truce.
625 understand] means both 'comprehend' and 'be supported'.
635] *Aeneid* i 150.

Rocks, waters, woods, and, by the shaggy tops   645
Uplifting, bore them in their hands; amaze,
Be sure, and terror, seized the rebel host,
When coming towards them so dread they saw
The bottom of the mountains upward turned,
Till on those cursed engines' triple row   650
They saw them whelmed, and all their confidence
Under the weight of mountains buried deep;
Themselves invaded next, and on their heads
Main promontories flung, which in the air
Came shadowing, and oppressed whole legions armed;   655
Their armour helped their harm, crushed in and bruised,
Into their substance pent – which wrought them pain
Implacable, and many a dolorous groan,
Long struggling underneath, ere they could wind
Out of such prison, though spirits of purest light,   660
Purest at first, now gross by sinning grown.
The rest, in imitation, to like arms
Betook them, and the neighbouring hills uptore;
So hills amid the air encountered hills,
Hurled to and fro with jaculation dire,   665
That underground they fought in dismal shade:
Infernal noise; war seemed a civil game
To this uproar; horrid confusion heaped
Upon confusion rose; and now all heaven
Had gone to wrack, with ruin overspread,   670
Had not the almighty Father, where he sits
Shrined in his sanctuary of heaven secure,
Consulting on the sum of things, foreseen
This tumult, and permitted all, advised,
That his great purpose he might so fulfil,   675
To honour his anointed Son, avenged
Upon his enemies, and to declare
All power on him transferred; whence to his Son,
The assessor of his throne, he thus began:
    '"Effulgence of my glory, Son beloved,   680
Son in whose face invisible is beheld
Visibly, what by deity I am,
And in whose hand what by decree I do,

646 amaze] panic.
654 Main] entire, solid.
665 jaculation] hurling.
674 advised] advisedly.
679 assessor] 'one who sits beside', hence sharing his rank and dignity.
681-2] Col. i. 15.

Second omnipotence; two days are passed,
Two days, as we compute the days of heaven,   685
Since Michael and his powers went forth to tame
These disobedient; sore hath been their fight,
As likeliest was when two such foes met armed:
For to themselves I left them; and thou know'st
Equal in their creation they were formed,   690
Save what sin hath impaired – which yet hath wrought
Insensibly, for I suspend their doom:
Whence in perpetual fight they needs must last
Endless, and no solution will be found:
War wearied hath performed what war can do,   695
And to disordered rage let loose the reins,
With mountains, as with weapons, armed, which
          makes
Wild work in heaven, and dangerous to the main.
Two days are therefore passed; the third is thine:
For thee I have ordained it, and thus far   700
Have suffered, that the glory may be thine
Of ending this great war, since none but thou
Can end it. Into thee such virtue and grace
Immense I have transfused, that all may know
In heaven and hell thy power above compare,   705
And this perverse commotion governed thus,
To manifest thee worthiest to be heir
Of all things – to be heir, and to be king
By sacred unction, thy deserved right.
Go then, thou mightiest, in thy Father's might;   710
Ascend my chariot; guide the rapid wheels
That shake heaven's basis; bring forth all my war;
My bow and thunder, my almighty arms,
Gird on, and sword upon thy puissant thigh;
Pursue these sons of darkness, drive them out   715
From all heaven's bounds into the utter deep;
There let them learn, as likes them, to despise
God, and Messiah his anointed king."
     'He said, and on his Son with rays direct
Shone full; he all his Father full expressed   720
Ineffably into his face received;
And thus the filial Godhead answering spake:
     ' "O Father, O supreme of heavenly thrones,

692 Insensibly] imperceptibly.
698 main] entirety, i.e. the universe.
701 suffered] allowed.
709 unction] anointing (cf. III 317, V 605).

First, highest, holiest, best, thou always seek'st
To glorify thy Son; I always thee,   725
As is most just; this I my glory account,
My exaltation, and my whole delight,
That thou in me, well pleased, declar'st thy will
Fulfilled, which to fulfil is all my bliss.
Sceptre and power, thy giving, I assume,   730
And gladlier shall resign when in the end
Thou shalt be all in all, and I in thee
For ever, and in me all whom thou lov'st;
But whom thou hat'st I hate, and can put on
Thy terrors, as I put thy mildness on,   735
Image of thee in all things: and shall soon,
Armed with thy might, rid heaven of these rebelled,
To their prepared ill mansion driven down,
To chains of darkness and the undying worm,
That from thy just obedience could revolt,   740
Whom to obey, is happiness entire.
Then shall thy saints, ummixed, and from the impure
Far separate, circling thy holy mount,
Unfeignèd halleluiahs to thee sing,
Hymns of high praise, and I among them chief."   745
     'So said, he, o'er his sceptre bowing, rose
From the right hand of glory where he sat;
And the third sacred morn began to shine,
Dawning through heaven; forth rushed with whirlwind
     sound
The chariot of paternal deity,   750
Flashing thick flames, wheel within wheel; undrawn,
Itself instinct with spirit, but convoyed
By four cherubic shapes; four faces each
Had wondrous; as with stars, their bodies all
And wings were set with eyes; with eyes the wheels   755
Of beryl, and careering fires between;
Over their heads a crystal firmament,
Whereon a sapphire throne, inlaid with pure
Amber and colours of the showery arch.
He, in celestial panoply all armed   760
Of radiant Urim, work divinely wrought,
Ascended; at his right hand Victory

734] Psalm cxxxix. 21.
749–59] The imagery is based on Ezek. i. and x. Cf *Penseroso* 53 and *Passion*
    36–40n.
752 instinct] impelled, moved.
761 Urim] Exod. xxviii. 30. See *PR* III 13–15n.

Sat eagle-winged; beside him hung his bow,
And quiver, with three-bolted thunder stored;
And from about him fierce effusion rolled   765
Of smoke and bickering flame and sparkles dire;
Attended with ten thousand thousand saints,
He onward came; far off his coming shone;
And twenty thousand (I their number heard)
Chariots of God, half on each hand, were seen;   770
He on the wings of cherub rode sublime
On the crystalline sky, in sapphire throned –
Illustrious far and wide, but by his own
First seen; them unexpected joy surprised
When the great ensign of Messiah blazed   775
Aloft, by angels borne, his sign in heaven;
Under whose conduct Michael soon reduced
His army, circumfused on either wing,
Under their head embodied all in one.
Before him power divine his way prepared;   780
At his command the uprooted hills retired
Each to his place; they heard his voice, and went
Obsequious; heaven his wonted face renewed,
And with fresh flowerets hill and valley smiled.

'This saw his hapless foes, but stood obdured,   785
And to rebellious fight rallied their powers,
Insensate, hope conceiving from despair.
In heavenly spirits could such perverseness dwell?
But to convince the proud what signs avail,
Or wonders move the obdurate to relent?   790
They, hardened more by what might most reclaim,
Grieving to see his glory, at the sight
Took envy, and, aspiring to his height,
Stood re-embattled fierce, by force or fraud
Weening to prosper, and at length prevail   795
Against God and Messiah, or to fall

763-4] The eagle is the imperial bird of Jove, and the thunderbolt his weapon
    and the weapon of God in the O.T.
766 bickering] flashing, gleaming.
767] Rev. v. 11.
769-70] Psalm lxviii. 17.
771] Psalm xviii. 10; II Sam. xxii. 11.
773 Ilustrious] lustrous, shining.
776] Matt. xxiv. 30.
777 reduced] led back.
785 obdured] hardened in wickedness.
788] imitates *Aeneid* i 11.
789-91, 801] Exod. xiv. 4, 8, 13.

In universal ruin last; and now
To final battle drew, disdaining flight,
Or faint retreat: when the great Son of God
To all his host on either hand thus spake: 800
    ' "Stand still in bright array, ye saints; here stand,
Ye angels armed; this day from battle rest;
Faithful hath been your warfare, and of God
Accepted, fearless in his righteous cause;
And as ye have received, so have ye done,   805
Invincibly; but of this cursed crew
The punishment to other hand belongs;
Vengeance is his, or whose he sole appoints;
Number to this day's work is not ordained,
Nor multitude; stand only and behold   810
God's indignation on these godless poured
By me; not you, but me, they have despised,
Yet envied; against me is all their rage,
Because the Father, to whom in heaven supreme
Kingdom and power and glory appertains,   815
Hath honoured me according to his will.
Therefore to me their doom he hath assigned,
That they may have their wish, to try with me
In battle which the stronger proves – they all,
Or I alone against them; since by strength   820
They measure all, of other excellence
Not emulous, nor care who them excels;
Nor other strife with them do I vouchsafe."
    'So spake the Son, and into terror changed
His countenance, too severe to be beheld,   825
And full of wrath bent on his enemies.
At once the four spread out their starry wings
With dreadful shade contiguous, and the orbs
Of his fierce chariot rolled, as with the sound
Of torrent floods, or of a numerous host.   830
He on his impious foes right onward drove,
Gloomy as night; under his burning wheels
The steadfast empyrean shook throughout,
All but the throne itself of God. Full soon
Among them he arrived, in his right hand   835

808] a Biblical commonplace (e.g. Deut. xxxii. 35).
815] the concluding doxology of the Lord's Prayer (Matt. vi. 13), which was not
    part of the English liturgy until it was incorporated in the 1662 Book of
    Common Prayer.
827–32] See 749–59n.
833] II Sam. xxii. 8.

Grasping ten thousand thunders, which he sent
Before him, such as in their souls infixed
Plagues. They, astonished, all resistance lost,
All courage; down their idle weapons dropped;
O'er shields, and helms, and helmed heads he rode   840
Of thrones and mighty seraphim prostráte,
That wished the mountains now might be again
Thrown on them, as a shelter from his ire.
Nor less on either side tempestuous fell
His arrows, from the fourfold-visaged four,   845
Distinct with eyes, and from the living wheels,
Distinct alike with multitude of eyes;
One spirit in them ruled, and every eye
Glared lightning, and shot forth pernicious fire
Among the accursed, that withered all their strength,   850
And of their wonted vigour left them drained,
Exhausted, spiritless, afflicted, fallen.
Yet half his strength he put not forth, but checked
His thunder in mid-volley; for he meant
Not to destroy, but root them out of heaven;   855
The overthrown he raised, and as a herd
Of goats or timorous flock together thronged,
Drove them before him thunderstruck, pursued
With terrors and with furies to the bounds
And crystal wall of heaven, which, opening wide,   860
Rolled inward, and a spacious gap disclosed
Into the wasteful deep; the monstrous sight
Strook them with horror backward; but far worse
Urged them behind: headlong themselves they threw
Down from the verge of heaven: eternal wrath   865
Burnt after them to the bottomless pit.
   'Hell heard the unsufferable noise; hell saw
Heaven ruining from heaven, and would have fled
Affrighted; but strict fate had cast too deep
Her dark foundations, and too fast had bound.   870
Nine days they fell; confounded Chaos roared,
And felt tenfold confusion in their fall
Through his wild anarchy; so huge a rout
Encumbered him with ruin; hell at last,
Yawning, received them whole, and on them closed –   875
Hell, their fit habitation, fraught with fire

838 Plagues] used in the Greek and Latin sense of 'blows, strokes, wounds'.
845-6] Ezek. x. 9-14. 'Distinct' means 'adorned'.
868 ruining] falling headlong.
874-5] Isa. v. 14.

Unquenchable, the house of woe and pain.
Disburdened heaven rejoiced, and soon repaired
Her mural breach, returning whence it rolled.
Sole victor, from the expulsion of his foes　　　880
Messiah his triumphal chariot turned;
To meet him all his saints, who silent stood
Eye-witnesses of his almighty acts,
With jubilee advanced; and as they went,
Shaded with branching palm, each order bright　　　885
Sung triumph, and him sung victorious king,
Son, heir, and Lord, to him dominion given,
Worthiest to reign; he celebrated rode,
Triumphant through mid heaven, into the courts
And temple of his mighty Father throned　　　890
On high; who into glory him received,
Where now he sits at the right hand of bliss.
　'Thus, measuring things in heaven by things on earth,
At thy request, and that thou may'st beware
By what is past, to thee I have revealed　　　895
What might have else to human race been hid –
The discord which befell, and war in heaven
Among the angelic powers, and the deep fall
Of those too high aspiring who rebelled
With Satan: he who envies now thy state,　　　900
Who now is plotting how he may seduce
Thee also from obedience, that with him
Bereaved of happiness, thou may'st partake
His punishment, eternal misery;
Which would be all his solace and revenge,　　　905
As a despite done against the most high,
Thee once to gain companion of his woe.
But listen not to his temptations; warn
Thy weaker; let it profit thee to have heard,
By terrible example, the reward　　　910
Of disobedience; firm they might have stood,
Yet fell; remember, and fear to transgress.'

THE END OF THE SIXTH BOOK

909 weaker] i.e. weaker vessel (I Pet. iii. 7).

BOOK VII

THE ARGUMENT

Raphael, at the request of Adam, relates how and wherefore this world was first created: that God, after the expelling of Satan and his angels out of heaven, declared his pleasure to create another world, and other creatures to dwell therein; sends his Son with glory, and attendance of angels, to perform the work of creation in six days: the angels celebrate with hymns the performance thereof, and his reascension into heaven.

Descend from heaven, Urania, by that name
If rightly thou art called, whose voice divine
Following, above the Olympian hill I soar,
Above the flight of Pegasean wing.
The meaning, not the name, I call; for thou   5
Nor of the Muses nine, nor on the top
Of old Olympus dwell'st; but, heavenly-born,
Before the hills appeared or fountain flowed,
Thou with eternal wisdom didst converse,
Wisdom thy sister, and with her didst play   10
In presence of the almighty Father, pleased
With thy celestial song. Up led by thee,
Into the heaven of heavens I have presumed,
An earthly guest, and drawn empyreal air,
Thy tempering; with like safety guided down,   15
Return me to my native element;
Lest, from this flying steed unreined (as once
Bellerophon, though from a lower clime)

1 Urania] In early antiquity Urania ('heavenly one') was the name of one of the nine muses, and in late Roman times she was identified specifically as the muse of astronomy. In the Renaissance she was transformed by Pontanus and Du Bartas into the muse of Christian poetry.

3 Olympian hill] Mount Olympus, the home of the gods on the border of Macedonia and Thessaly.

4] Pegasus, the winged horse, created with his hoof Hippocrene (literally 'horse-spring'), the Muses' spring on Mount Helicon.

8-12] See Prov. viii. 22-31. Milton's 'play' reflects the Vulgate (*ludens*) rather than the A.V. ('rejoicing') or the LXX (εὐφραινόμην, rejoicing). Cf. the apocryphal Wisdom of Solomon vii-viii.

17-20] Bellerophon tried to ride Pegasus to heaven, and was toppled from his mount by Jove, whereupon he fell on to the 'Aleian field', Homer's 'plain of wandering'. 'Clime' means both 'region' and 'climb'; 'erroneous' refers to both physical and moral wandering.

Dismounted, on the Aleian field I fall,
Erroneous there to wander and forlorn.   20
Half yet remains unsung, but narrower bound
Within the visible diurnal sphere;
Standing on earth, not rapt above the pole,
More safe I sing with mortal voice, unchanged
To hoarse or mute, though fallen on evil days,   25
On evil days though fallen, and evil tongues,
In darkness, and with dangers compassed round,
And solitude; yet not alone, while thou
Visit'st my slumbers nightly, or when morn
Purples the east; still govern thou my song,   30
Urania, and fit audience find, though few.
But drive far off the barbarous dissonance
Of Bacchus and his revellers, the race
Of that wild rout that tore the Thracian bard
In Rhodope, where woods and rocks had ears   35
To rapture, till the savage clamour drowned
Both harp and voice; nor could the Muse defend
Her son. So fail not thou who thee implores;
For thou art heavenly, she an empty dream.

   Say, Goddess, what ensued when Raphael,
The affable archangel, had forewarned   40
Adam by dire example to beware
Apostasy, by what befell in heaven
To those apostates, lest the like befall
In Paradise to Adam or his race,
Charged not to touch the interdicted tree,   45
If they transgress, and slight that sole command,
So easily obeyed amid the choice
Of all tastes else to please their appetite,
Though wandering. He with his consorted Eve
The story heard attentive, and was filled   50
With admiration and deep muse, to hear
Of things so high and strange – things to their thought
So unimaginable as hate in heaven,
And war so near the peace of God in bliss,   55

22 diurnal sphere] the firmament, which appears to revolve daily around the
   earth.
23 rapt above the pole] carried away in spirit above the celestial pole.
24–8] The lines refer to the 'dangers' of Milton's situation after the Restoration,
   when those who had served in Cromwell's government became liable to
   persecution.
32–8] Cf. *Lycidas* 58–63n. Rhodope is a mountain range on the border of Thrace
   and Macedonia.
52 admiration] wonder, astonishment.

With such confusion; but the evil, soon
Driven back, redounded as a flood on those
From whom it sprung, impossible to mix
With blessedness. Whence Adam soon repealed
The doubts that in his heart arose; and now   60
Led on, yet sinless, with desire to know
What nearer might concern him – how this world
Of heaven and earth conspicuous first began;
When, and whereof, created; for what cause;
What within Eden, or without, was done   65
Before his memory – as one whose drouth,
Yet scarce allayed, still eyes the current stream,
Whose liquid murmur heard new thirst excites,
Proceeded thus to ask his heavenly guest:
    'Great things, and full of wonder in our ears,   70
Far differing from this world, thou hast revealed,
Divine interpreter, by favour sent
Down from the empyrean to forewarn
Us timely of what might else have been our loss,
Unknown, which human knowledge could not reach;   75
For which to the infinitely good we owe
Immortal thanks, and his admonishment
Receive with solemn purpose to observe
Immutably his sovereign will, the end
Of what we are. But, since thou hast vouchsafed   80
Gently, for our instruction, to impart
Things above earthly thought, which yet concerned
Our knowing, as to highest wisdom seemed,
Deign to descend now lower, and relate
What may no less perhaps avail us known –   85
How first began this heaven which we behold
Distant so high, with moving fires adorned
Innumerable; and this which yields or fills
All space, the ambient air, wide interfused,
Embracing round this florid earth; what cause   90
Moved the creator, in his holy rest
Through all eternity, so late to build
In chaos; and the work begun, how soon
Absolved: if unforbid thou may'st unfold

59 repealed] abandoned.
63 conspicuous] visible.
67 current] flowing.
72 Divine interpreter] a comparison of Raphael to Mercury, messenger of the
    gods (*'interpres divum'*, *Aeneid* iv 378).
83 seemed] seemed fitting, appropriate.
94 Absolved] completed.

What we not to explore the secrets ask
Of his eternal empire, but the more　　　　　　95
To magnify his works the more we know.
And the great light of day yet wants to run
Much of his race, though steep; suspense in heaven
Held by thy voice, thy potent voice he hears,
And longer will delay, to hear thee tell　　　　100
His generation, and the rising birth
Of nature from the unapparent deep:
Of if the star of evening and the moon
Haste to thy audience, night with her will bring　　105
Silence, and sleep listening to thee will watch;
Or we can bid his absence till thy song
End, and dismiss thee ere the morning shine.'
　　Thus Adam his illustrious guest besought;
And thus the godlike angel answered mild:　　　110
　'This also thy request, with caution asked,
Obtain; though to recount almighty works
What words or tongue of seraph can suffice,
Or heart of man suffice to comprehend?
Yet what thou canst attain, which best may serve　　115
To glorify the maker, and infer
Thee also happier, shall not be withheld
Thy hearing; such commission from above
I have received, to answer thy desire
Of knowledge within bounds; beyond abstain　　　120
To ask, nor let thine own inventions hope
Things not revealed, which the invisible king,
Only omniscient, hath suppressed in night,
To none communicable in earth or heaven;
Enough is left beside to search and know;　　　125
But knowledge is as food, and needs no less
Her temperance over appetitie, to know
In measure what the mind may well contain;
Oppresses else with surfeit, and soon turns
Wisdom to folly, as nourishment to wind.　　　130
　'Know then that, after Lucifer from heaven
(So call him, brighter once amidst the host
Of angels than that star the stars among)
Fell with his flaming legions through the deep

97] Job xxxvi. 24.
103 unapparent deep] invisible chaos.
106 watch] stay awake (cf. I 332).
116 infer] cause to be, render.
131 Lucifer] See V 658n.

Into his place, and the great Son returned   135
Victorious with his saints, the omnipotent
Eternal Father from his throne beheld
Their multitude, and to his Son thus spake:
    ' "At least our envious foe hath failed, who thought
All like himself rebellious; by whose aid   140
This inaccessible high strength, the seat
Of deity supreme, us dispossessed,
He trusted to have seized, and into fraud
Drew many whom their place knows here no more;
Yet far the greater part have kept, I see,   145
Their station; heaven, yet populous, retains
Number sufficient to possess her realms,
Though wide, and this high temple to frequent
With ministeries due and solemn rites;
But, lest his heart exalt him in the harm   150
Already done, to have dispeopled heaven –
My damage fondly deemed – I can repair
That detriment, if such it be to lose
Self-lost, and in a moment will create
Another world; out of one man a race   155
Of men innumerable, there to dwell,
Not here, till by degrees of merit raised,
They open to themselves at length the way
Up hither, under long obedience tried,
And earth be changed to heaven, and heaven to earth,
One kingdom, joy and union without end.   161
Meanwhile inhabit lax, ye powers of heaven;
And thou, my Word, begotten Son, by thee
This I perform; speak thou, and be it done;
My overshadowing spirit and might with thee   165
I send along; ride forth, and bid the deep
Within appointed bounds be heaven and earth;
Boundless the deep, because I am who fill
Infinitude; nor vacuous the space,
Though I, uncircumscribed, myself retire,   170
And put not forth my goodness, which is free
To act or not; necessity and chance
Approach not me, and what I will is fate."

---

143 fraud] Milton's occasional use of the word in a passive sense (meaning 'in
    the state of being defrauded or deceived') may imitate the Latin *fraus*; the
    usage is unique to Milton. Cf. *PL* IX 643, *PR* I 372.
144] Job vii. 10.
162 inhabit lax] 'Lax' means 'so as to have ample room'. The phrase is a
    Latinism, and imitates *Habitare laxe et magnifice voluit* (Cicero, *De domo sua*
    xliv. 115).

'So spake the almighty, and to what he spake
His Word, the filial Godhead, gave effect.   175
Immediate are the acts of God, more swift
Than time or motion, but to human ears
Cannot without process of speech be told,
So told as earthly notion can receive.
Great triumph and rejoicing was in heaven   180
When such was heard declared the almighty's will;
Glory they sung to the most high, good-will
To future men, and in their dwellings peace –
Glory to him whose just avenging ire
Had driven out the ungodly from his sight   185
And the habitations of the just; to him
Glory and praise whose wisdom had ordained
Good out of evil to create – instead
Of spirits malign, a better race to bring
Into their vacant room, and thence diffuse   190
His good to worlds and ages infinite.
  'So sang the hierarchies; meanwhile the Son
On his great expedition now appeared,
Girt with omnipotence, with radiance crowned
Of majesty divine, sapience and love   195
Immense; and all his Father in him shone.
About his chariot numberless were poured
Cherub and seraph, potentates and thrones,
And virtues, winged spirits, and chariots winged
From the armoury of God, where stand of old   200
Myriads, between two brazen mountains lodged
Against a solemn day, harnessed at hand,
Celestial equipage; and now came forth
Spontaneous, for within them spirit lived,
Attendant on their Lord: heaven opened wide   205
Her ever-during gates, harmonious sound
On golden hinges moving, to let forth
The king of glory, in his powerful Word
And Spirit coming to create new worlds.
On heavenly ground they stood, and from the shore   210
They viewed the vast immeasurable abyss,
Outrageous as a sea, dark, wasteful, wild,
Up from the bottom turned by furious winds
And surging waves, as mountains to assault

182-3 Luke ii. 14.
201] Zech. vi. 1.
204] Ezek. i. 20.
205-9] Psalm xxiv. 7.

Heaven's height, and with the centre mix the pole.   215
  ' "Silence, ye troubled waves, and thou deep, peace,"
Said then the omnific Word: "Your discord end;"
Nor stayed, but, on the wings of cherubim
Uplifted, in paternal glory rode
Far into chaos and the world unborn;   220
For chaos heard his voice; him all his train
Followed in bright procession to behold
Creation and the wonders of his might.
Then stayed the fervid wheels, and in his hand
He took the golden compasses, prepared   225
In God's eternal store, to circumscribe
This universe, and all created things;
One foot he centred, and the other turned
Round through the vast profundity obscure,
And said, "Thus far extend, thus far thy bounds;   230
This be thy just circumference, O world."
Thus God the heaven created, thus the earth,
Matter unformed and void; darkness profound
Covered the abyss; but on the watery calm
His brooding wings the spirit of God outspread,   235
And vital virtue infused, and vital warmth,
Throughout the fluid mass, but downward purged
The black tartareous cold infernal dregs,
Adverse to life; then founded, then conglobed,
Like things to like, the rest to several place   240
Disparted, and between spun out the air,
And earth, self-balanced, on her centre hung.
  ' "Let there be light," said God, and forthwith light
Ethereal, first of things, quintessence pure,
Sprung from the deep, and from her native east   245
To journey through the airy gloom began,
Sphered in a radiant cloud – for yet the sun
Was not; she in a cloudy tabernacle
Sojourned the while. God saw the light was good;
And light from darkness by the hemisphere   250

217 omnific] all-creating.
224 fervid] burning. Cf. VI 832.
225] Prov. viii. 27; Dante, *Paradiso* xix. 40–2.
236] 'Virtue' is divine power and influence; 'Vital warmth' alludes to the *primus calor* which figures in Renaissance Neoplatonist accounts of the creation.
239] 'Founded' means 'moulded, cast'; 'conglobed' means 'formed into a ball'.
243–4] See III 716n.
247–9] Milton recapitulates the traditional solution to the problem that light was created on the first day, but the sun, moon and stars on the fourth. On the 'tabernacle' see Psalm xix. 4.

Divided: light the day, and darkness night,
He named. Thus was the first day even and morn;
Nor passed uncelebrated, nor unsung
By the celestial choirs, when orient light
Exhaling first from darkness they beheld,   255
Birth-day of heaven and earth; with joy and shout
The hollow universal orb they filled,
And touched their golden harps, and hymning praised
God and his works; creator him they sung,
Both when first evening was, and when first morn.   260
    'Again God said, "Let there be firmament
Amid the waters, and let it divide
The waters from the waters"; and God made
The firmament, expanse of liquid, pure,
Transparent, elemental air diffused   265
In circuit to the uttermost convex
Of this great round – partition firm and sure,
The waters underneath from those above
Dividing; for as earth, so he the world
Built on circumfluous waters calm, in wide   270
Crystalline ocean, and the loud misrule
Of chaos far removed, lest fierce extremes
Contiguous might distemper the whole frame:
And heaven he named the firmament; so even
And morning chorus sung the second day.   275
    'The earth was formed, but in the womb as yet
Of waters, embryon immature, involved,
Appeared not; over all the face of earth
Main ocean flowed, not idle, but with warm
Prolific humous softening all her globe,   280
Fermented the great mother to conceive,
Satiate with genial moisture; when God said,
"Be gathered now, ye waters under heaven,
Into one place, and let dry land appear."
Immediately the mountains huge appear   285
Emergent, and their broad bare backs upheave
Into the clouds; their tops ascend the sky;
So high as heaved the tumid hills, so low

---

264 expanse] Cf. A.V. and R.V. marginal notes to Gen. i. 6, and *PL* VII 340.
267, 269 round, world] the universe.
277 involved] enveloped.
279–82] Renaissance Neoplatonists assumed the existence of a *primus humor*
   (cf. 236n.), which was a generative ('genial') moisture.
281 great mother] in antiquity Cybele was honoured as Magna Mater. Cf. V
   338n. and *Arcades* 21n.
283–306] Psalm civ. 6–10.

Down sunk a hollow bottom broad and deep,
Capacious bed of waters; thither they   290
Hasted with glad precipitance, uprolled
As drops on dust conglobing from the dry:
Part rise in crystal wall, or ridge direct,
For haste; such flight the great command impressed
On the swift floods; as armies at the call   295
Of trumpet (for of armies thou hast heard)
Troop to their standard, so the watery throng,
Wave rolling after wave, where way they found —
If steep, with torrent rapture, if through plain,
Soft-ebbing; nor withstood them rock or hill;   300
But they, or underground, or circuit wide
With serpent error wandering, found their way,
And on the washy ooze deep channels wore:
Easy, ere God had bid the ground be dry,
All but within those banks where rivers now   305
Stream, and perpetual draw their humid train.
The dry land earth, and the great receptacle
Of congregated waters he called seas;
And saw that it was good, and said, "Let the earth
Put forth the verdant grass, herb yielding seed,   310
And fruit-tree yielding fruit after her kind,
Whose seed is in herself upon the earth."
He scarce had said when the bare earth, till then
Desert and bare, unsightly, unadorned,
Brought forth the tender grass, whose verdure clad   315
Her universal face with pleasant green;
Then herbs of every leaf, that sudden flowered,
Opening their various colours, and made gay
Her bosom, smelling sweet; and these scarce blown,
Forth flourished thick the clustering vine, forth crept 320
The swelling gourd, up stood the corny reed
Embattled in her field: and the humble shrub,
And bush with frizzled hair implicit: last
Rose, as in dance, the stately trees, and spread
Their branches hung with copious fruit, or gemmed   325

302 error] the primary (Latinate) sense is 'winding course', but the juxtaposi-
    tion of the word with 'serpent' brings out the secondary sense, and thus
    connects the phrase with the fall.
308 congregated waters] cf. *congregationesque aquarum*, the Vulgate rendering
    of Gen. i. 10.
317–19] Cf. the apocryphal II Esdras vi. 44.
322 humble] low-growing.
323 implicit] entangled.
325 gemmed] budded (a Latinism).

Their blossoms; with high woods the hills were crowned,
With tufts the valleys and each fountain-side,
With borders long the rivers, that earth now
Seemed like to heaven, a seat where gods might dwell,
Or wander with delight, and love to haunt   330
Her sacred shades; though God had yet not rained
Upon the earth, and man to till the ground
None was, but from the earth a dewy mist
Went up and watered all the ground, and each
Plant of the field, which ere it was in the earth   335
God made, and every herb before it grew
On the green stem; God saw that it was good;
So even and morn recorded the third day.
     'Again the almighty spake, "Let there be lights
High in the expanse of heaven, to divide   340
The day from night; and let them be for signs,
For seasons, and for days, and circling years;
And let them be for lights, as I ordain
Their office in the firmament of heaven,
To give light on the earth;" and it was so.   345
And God made two great lights, great for their use
To man, the greater to have rule by day,
The less by night, altern; and made the stars,
And set them in the firmament of heaven
To illuminate the earth, and rule the day   350
In their vicissitude, and rule the night,
And light from darkness to divide. God saw,
Surveying his great work, that it was good:
For, of celestial bodies, first the sun
A mighty sphere he framed, unlightsome first,   355
Though of ethereal mould; then formed the moon
Globose, and every magnitude of stars,
And sowed with stars the heaven thick as a field;
Of light by far the greater part he took,
Transplanted from her cloudy shrine, and placed   360
In the sun's orb, made porous to receive
And drink the liquid light, firm to retain
Her gathered beams, great palace now of light.
Hither, as to their fountain, other stars
Repairing in their golden urns draw light.   365
And hence the morning planet gilds her horns;
By tincture or reflection they augment

366] Venus has 'horns' when near to the conjunction, like the moon (cf. Milton's
translation of Psalm cxxxvi. 9, l. 34).
367 tincture] an infusion of a quality.

Their small peculiar, though, from human sight
So far remote, with diminution seen.
First in his east the glorious lamp was seen,   370
Regent of day, and all the horizon round
Invested with bright rays, jocund to run
His longitude through heaven's high road; the grey
Dawn, and the Pleiades before him danced,
Shedding sweet influence; less bright the moon,   375
But opposite in levelled west, was set,
His mirror, with full face borrowing her light
From him, for other light she needed none
In that aspect, and still that distance keeps
Till night; then in the east her turn she shines,   380
Revolved on heaven's great axle, and her reign
With thousand lesser lights dividual holds,
With thousand thousand stars, that then appeared
Spangling the hemisphere; then first adorned
With their bright luminaries, that set and rose,   385
Glad evening and glad morn crowned the fourth day.
   'And God said, "Let the waters generate
Reptile with spawn abundant, living soul;
And let fowl fly above the earth, with wings
Displayed on the open firmament of heaven."   390
And God created the great whales, and each
Soul living, each that crept, which plenteously
The waters generated by their kinds,
And every bird of wing after his kind,
And saw that it was good, and blessed them, saying,   395
"Be fruitful, multiply, and in the seas,
And lakes and running streams the waters fill;
And let the fowl be multiplied on the earth."
Forthwith the sounds and seas, each creek and bay,
With fry innumerable swarm, and shoals   400
Of fish that with their fins and shining scales
Glide under the green wave in sculls that oft
Bank the mid-sea; part, single or with mate,
Graze the sea-weed, their pasture, and through groves
Of coral stray, or sporting with quick glance   405
Show to the sun their waved coats dropped with gold,

368 Their small peculiar] i.e. the small amount of light inherent in them.
373 longitude] course.
376] Job xxxviii. 31.
382 dividual] divided.
402 sculls] schools.
406 dropped] speckled.

Or in their pearly shells at ease, attend
Moist nutriment, or under rocks their food
In jointed armour watch; on smooth the seal
And bended dolphins play: part, huge of bulk,   410
Wallowing unwieldy, enormous in their gait,
Tempest the ocean; there leviathan,
Hugest of living creatures, on the deep
Stretched like a promontory, sleeps or swims,
And seems a moving land, and at his gills   415
Draws in, and at his trunk spouts out, a sea.
Meanwhile the tepid caves, and fens, and shores,
Their brood as numerous hatch from the egg, that soon,
Bursting with kindly rupture, forth disclosed
Their callow young; but feathered soon and fledge   420
They summed their pens, and soaring the air sublime,
With clang despised the ground, under a cloud
In prospect; there the eagle and the stork
On cliffs and cedar-tops their eyries build;
Part loosely wing the region; part, more wise,   425
In common, ranged in figure, wedge their way,
Intelligent of seasons, and set forth
Their airy caravan, high over seas
Flying, and over lands, with mutual wing
Easing their flight: so steers the prudent crane   430
Her annual voyage, borne on winds: the air
Floats as they pass, fanned with unnumbered plumes;
From branch to branch the smaller birds with song
Solaced the woods, and spread their painted wings,
Till even; nor then the solemn nightingale   435
Ceased warbling, but all night tuned her soft lays;
Others, on silver lakes and rivers, bathed
Their downy breast; the swan, with archèd neck
Between her white wings mantling proudly, rows
Her state with oary feet; yet oft they quit   440
The dank, and, rising on stiff pennons, tower
The mid aerial sky; others on ground
Walked firm – the crested cock, whose clarion sounds

---

409 smooth] smooth sea.
412–15] Cf. I 200–8n.
419 kindly] pertaining to nature or birth.
421 summed their pens] brought their feathers to full growth. Cf. *PR* I 14.
422 despised] looked down upon.
429–30 mutual ... flight] Birds flying in a 'wedge' were thought to rest their beaks on those in front.
432 floats] undulates.
439 mantling] forming a mantle.

The silent hours, and the other, whose gay train
Adorns him, coloured with the florid hue   445
Of rainbows and starry eyes. The waters thus
With fish replenished, and the air with fowl,
Evening and morn solemnised the fifth day.
   'The sixth, and of creation last, arose
With evening harps and matin; when God said,   450
"Let the earth bring forth soul living in her kind,
Cattle, and creeping things, and beast of the earth,
Each in their kind." The earth obeyed, and, straight
Opening her fertile womb, teemed at a birth
Innumerous living creatures, perfect forms,   455
Limbed and full-grown; out of the ground up rose,
As from his lair, the wild beast, where he wons
In forest wild, in thicket, brake, or den –
Among the trees in pairs they rose, they walked;
The cattle in the fields and meadows green: 460
Those rare and solitary, these in flocks
Pasturing at once and in broad herds, upsprung.
The grassy clods now calved; now half appeared
The tawny lion pawing to get free
His hinder parts – then springs, as broke from bonds,   465
And rampant shakes his brinded mane; the ounce,
The libbard, and the tiger, as the mole
Rising, the crumbled earth above them threw
In hillocks; the swift stag from underground
Bore up his branching head; scarce from his mould   470
Behemoth, biggest born of earth, upheaved
His vastness; fleeced the flocks and bleating rose,
As plants; ambiguous between sea and land,
The river-horse and scaly crocodile.
At once came forth whatever creeps the ground,   475
Insect or worm; those waved their limber fans
For wings, and smallest lineaments exact
In all the liveries decked of summer's pride,
With spots of gold and purple, azure and green;
These as a line their long dimension drew,   480
Streaking the ground with sinuous trace; not all
Minims of nature; some of serpent kind,

444 other] the peacock.
457 wons] lives.
466 ounce] See *Comus* 71n.
467 libbard] leopard.
471 Behemoth] tentatively identified as the elephant in the A.V. marginal note
     to Job xl. 15.
474 river-horse] translates the Greek 'hippopotamus'.
482 Minims of nature] the smallest forms of animal life.

Wondrous in length and corpulence, involved
Their snaky folds, and added wings. First crept
The parsimonious emmet, provident
Of future, in small room large heart enclosed – 485
Pattern of just equality perhaps
Hereafter – joined in her popular tribes
Of commonalty; swarming next appeared
The female bee, that feeds her husband drone
Deliciously, and builds her waxen cells 490
With honey stored; the rest are numberless,
And thou their natures know'st, and gav'st them names,
Needless to thee repeated; nor unknown
The serpent, subtlest beast of all the field,
Of huge extent sometimes, with brazen eyes, 495
And hairy mane terrific, though to thee
Not noxious, but obedient at thy call.
  'Now heaven in all her glory shone, and rolled
Her motions, as the great first mover's hand
First wheeled their course; earth, in her rich attire 500
Consummate, lovely smiled; air, water, earth,
By fowl, fish, beast, was flown, was swum, was walked,
Frequent; and of the sixth day yet remained;
There wanted yet the master-work, the end
Of all yet done – a creature who not prone 505
And brute as other creatures, but endued
With sanctity of reason, might erect
His stature, and upright with front serene
Govern the rest, self-knowing, and from thence
Magnanimous to correspond with heaven, 510
But grateful to acknowledge whence his good
Descends; thither with heart and voice and eyes
Directed in devotion, to adore
And worship God supreme, who made him chief 515
Of all his works; therefore the omnipotent
Eternal Father (for where is not he

483 corpulence] bulk.
   involved] coiled.
484] Isa. xxx. 6.
485 emmet] ant.
490] Worker bees were thought to be female, and drones male.
497 terrific] terrifying.
504 Frequent] abundantly.
509 front] face.
511 Magnanimous] An Aristotelian term meaning 'greatsouledness' or 'high-
   mindedness'; when blended with Christian ideas by scholastic philosophers
   it came to mean 'fortitude' or 'lofty courage'.

Present?) thus to his Son audibly spake:
"Let us make now man in our image, man
In our similitude, and let them rule   520
Over the fish and fowl of sea and air,
Beast of the field, and over all the earth,
And every creeping thing that creeps the ground."
This said, he formed thee, Adam, thee O man,
Dust of the ground, and in thy nostrils breathed   525
The breath of life; in his own image he
Created thee, in the image of God
Express, and thou becam'st a living soul.
Male he created thee, but thy consort
Female, for race; then blessed mankind, and said,   530
"Be fruitful, multiply, and fill the earth;
Subdue it, and throughout dominion hold
Over fish of the sea, and fowl of the air,
And every living thing that moves on the earth."
Wherever thus created – for no place   535
Is yet distinct by name – thence, as thou know'st,
He brought thee into this delicious grove,
This garden, planted with the trees of God,
Delectable both to behold and taste,
And freely all their pleasant fruit for food   540
Gave thee: all sorts are here that all the earth yields,
Variety without end; but of the tree
Which tasted works knowledge of good and evil
Thou may'st not; in the day thou eat'st, thou diest.
Death is the penalty imposed; beware,   545
And govern well thy appetite, lest Sin
Surprise thee, and her black attendant Death.
      'Here finished he, and all that he had made
Viewed, and behold all was entirely good;
So even and morn accomplished the sixth day;   550
Yet not till the creator from his work
Desisting, though unwearied, up returned,
Up to the heaven of heavens, his high abode,
Thence to behold this new-created world,
The addition of his empire, how it showed   555
In prospect from his throne, how good, how fair,
Answering his great idea. Up he rode,

519–20] See the Vulgate rendering of Gen. i. 26. Expositors of this verse usually
    distinguished between the *Imago Dei*, which was obscured but not lost at
    the fall, and the *Similitudo Dei*, which was destroyed by original sin but
    could be restored by God (traditionally through baptism). For Milton's
    view, see XI 511-25.

557 idea] The term is used in the Platonic sense of 'ideal form'.

Followed with acclamation, and the sound
Symphonious of ten thousand harps, that tuned
Angelic harmonies; the earth, the air   560
Resounded (thou remember'st, for thou heard'st),
The heavens and all the constellations rung,
The planets in their stations listening stood,
While the bright pomp ascended jubilant.
"Open, ye everlasting gates," they sung;   565
"Open, ye heavens, your living doors; let in
The great creator, from his work returned
Magnificent, his six days' work, a world;
Open, and henceforth oft; for God will deign
To visit oft the dwellings of just men   570
Delighted, and with frequent intercourse
Thither will send his winged messengers
On errands of supernal grace." So sung
The glorious train ascending; he through heaven,
That opened wide her blazing portals, led   575
To God's eternal house direct the way –
A broad and ample road, whose dust is gold,
And pavement stars, as stars to thee appear
Seen in the galaxy, that milky way
Which nightly as a circling zone thou seest   580
Powdered with stars. And now on earth the seventh
Evening arose in Eden – for the sun
Was set, and twilight from the east came on,
Forerunning night, when at the holy mount
Of heaven's high-seated top, the imperial throne   585
Of Godhead, fixed for ever firm and sure,
The filial power arrived, and sat him down
With his great Father (for he also went
Invisible, yet stayed: such privilege
Hath omnipresence) and the work ordained,   590
Author and end of all things, and, from work
Now resting, blessed and hallowed the seventh day,
As resting on that day from all his work,
But not in silence holy kept: the harp
Had work, and rested not; the solemn pipe   595

---

563 station] an astronomical term which refers to the apparent standing still of
    a planet at its apogee and perigee, here applied to the position of the
    planets at creation.
564 pomp] triumphal procession.
565-7] Psalm xxiv. 7-9.
577-9] On the Milky Way as a road to the house of Jove see *Metamorphoses* i
    168-71.

And dulcimer, all organs of sweet stop,
All sounds on fret by string or golden wire,
Tempered soft tunings, intermixed with voice
Choral or unison; of incense clouds,
Fuming from golden censers, hid the mount.   600
Creation and the six days' acts they sung:
"Great are thy works, Jehovah, infinite
Thy power; what thought can measure thee, or tongue
Relate thee – greater now in thy return
Than from the giant angels; thee that day   605
Thy thunders magnified; but to create
Is greater than created to destroy.
Who can impair thee, mighty king, or bound
Thy empire? Easily the proud attempt
Of spirits apostate, and their counsels vain,   610
Thou hast repelled, while impiously they thought
Thee to diminish, and from thee withdraw
The number of thy worshippers. Who seeks
To lessen thee, against his purpose serves
To manifest the more thy might; his evil   615
Thou usest, and from thence creat'st more good.
Witness this new-made world, another heaven
From heaven-gate not far, founded in view
On the clear hyaline, the glassy sea;
Of amplitude almost immense, with stars   620
Numerous, and every star perhaps a world
Of destined habitation – but thou know'st
Their seasons; among these the seat of men,
Earth, with her nether ocean circumfused,
Their pleasant dwelling-place. Thrice happy men,   625
And sons of men, whom God hath thus advanced,
Created in his image, there to dwell
And worship him, and in reward to rule
Over his works, on earth, in sea, or air,
And multiply a race of worshippers   630

---

596 dulcimer] not the stringed instrument, but the bagpipe of Dan. iii. 5, 15,
    translated in the A.V. as 'dulcimer'.
599–600] Rev. viii. 3–5.
605 giant angels] a comparison of Satan and his followers to the giants who in
    classical mythology rebelled against Jove.
619 hyaline] the 'sea of glass like unto crystal' (θάλασσα ὑαλίνη) of Rev. iv. 6, xv.
    2, and the waters above the firmament of *PL* III 518–19, VII 268–71.
620 immense] immeasurable.
624 nether ocean] i.e. the ocean of the earth, as opposed to the waters above the
    firmament.

Holy and just; thrice happy, if they know
Their happiness, and persevere upright.''
  'So sung they, and the empyrean rung
With halleluiahs; thus was Sabbath kept.
And thy request think now fulfilled, that asked   635
How first this world and face of things began,
And what before thy memory was done
From the beginning, that posterity,
Informed by thee, might know; if else thou seek'st
Aught, not surpassing human measure, say.'   640

THE END OF THE SEVENTH BOOK

631-2] Virgil, *Georgics* ii 458-60.
632 persevere] a technical theological term referring to steady continuance in
    the faith and life proper to the attainment of eternal life.
634 halleluiahs] See II 243n.

BOOK VIII

THE ARGUMENT

Adam enquires concerning celestial motions; is doubtfully ans-
wered, and exhorted to search rather things more worthy of
knowledge; Adam assents, and still desirous to detain Raphael,
relates to him what he remembered since his own creation – his
placing in Paradise; his talk with God concerning solitude and fit
society; his first meeting and nuptials with Eve; his discourse with
the angel thereupon; who, after admonitions repeated, departs.

The angel ended, and in Adam's ear
So charming left his voice that he a while
Thought him still speaking, still stood fixed to hear;
Then, as new-waked, thus gratefully replied:
   'What thanks sufficient, or what recompense   5
Equal, have I to render thee, divine
Historian, who thus largely hast allayed
The thirst I had of knowledge, and vouchsafed
This friendly condescension, to relate
Things else by me unsearchable – now heard   10
With wonder, but delight, and, as is due,
With glory áttributed to the high
Creator? Something yet of doubt remains,
Which only thy solution can resolve.
When I behold this goodly frame, this world   15
Of heaven and earth consisting, and compute
Their magnitudes – this earth a spot, a grain,
An atom, with the firmament compared
And all her numbered stars, that seem to roll
Spaces incomprehensible (for such   20
Their distance argues, and their swift return
Diurnal) merely to officiate light
Round this opacous earth, this punctual spot,
One day and night, in all their vast survey
Useless besides – reasoning, I oft admire   25
How nature, wise and frugal, could commit

---

2 charming] In Milton's time the word was still strongly felt as a metaphor, and
    meant 'acting upon as with a charm'.
14 solution] explanation, answer.
19 numbered] numerous.
22 officiate] supply.
23 punctual] like a point, minute.

Such disproportions, with superfluous hand
So many nobler bodies to create,
Greater so manifold, to this one use,
For aught appears, and on their orbs impose   30
Such restless revolution day by day
Repeated, while the sedentary earth,
That better might with far less compass move,
Served by more noble than herself, attains
Her end without least motion, and receives,   35
As tribute, such a sumless journey brought
Of incorporeal speed, her warmth and light:
Speed, to describe whose swiftness number fails.'
     So spake our sire, and by his countenance seemed
Entering on studious thoughts abstruse; which Eve   40
Perceiving, where she sat retired in sight,
With lowliness majestic from her seat,
And grace that won who saw to wish her stay,
Rose, and went forth among her fruits and flowers,
To visit how they prospered, bud and bloom,   45
Her nursery; they at her coming sprung,
And, touched by her fair tendance, gladlier grew.
Yet went she not as not with such discourse
Delighted, or not capable her ear
Of what was high; such pleasure she reserved,   50
Adam relating, she sole auditress;
Her husband the relater she preferred
Before the angel, and of him to ask
Chose rather; he, she knew, would intermix
Grateful digressions, and solve high dispute   55
With conjugal caresses: from his lip
Not words alone pleased her. O when meet now
Such pairs, in love and mutual honour joined?
With goddess-like demeanour forth she went,
Not unattended; for on her as queen   60
A pomp of winning Graces waited still,
And from about her shot darts of desire
Into all eyes, to wish her still in sight.
And Raphael now to Adam's doubt proposed

36 sumless] incalculable.
45 visit] examine.
46–7] The response of the fruit and flowers constitutes a comparison of Eve to
Venus, who was in early antiquity an Italic goddess of vegetation, the
guardian of gardens.
60–3] Another comparison of Eve to Venus, here as the goddess of love on
whom the Graces (see *L'Allegro* 12–16n.) attended. Cf. V 381–2. 'Pomp'
means 'train'.

Benevolent and facile thus replied: 65
    'To ask or search I blame thee not, for heaven
Is as the book of God before thee set,
Wherein to read his wondrous works, and learn
His seasons, hours, or days, or months, or years;
This to attain, whether heaven move or earth   70
Imports not, if thou reckon right: the rest
From man or angel the great architect
Did wisely to conceal, and not divulge
His secrets, to be scanned by them who ought
Rather admire; or if they list to try   75
Conjecture, he his fabric of the heavens
Hath left to their disputes – perhaps to move
His laughter at their quaint opinions wide
Hereafter, when they come to model heaven,
And calculate the stars; how they will wield   80
The mighty frame; how build, unbuild, contrive
To save appearances; how gird the sphere
With centric and eccentric scribbled o'er,
Cycle and epicycle, orb in orb;
Already by thy reasoning this I guess,   85
Who art to lead thy offspring, and supposest
That bodies bright and greater should not serve
The less not bright, nor heaven such journeys run,
Earth sitting still, when she alone receives
The benefit; consider, first, that great   90
Or bright infers not excellence; the earth,
Though, in comparison of heaven, so small,
Nor glistering, may of solid good contain
More plenty than the sun that barren shines,
Whose virtue on itself works no effect,   95
But in the fruitful earth; there first received,
His beams, unactive else, their vigour find.
Yet not to earth are those bright luminaries
Officious, but to thee, earth's habitant.
And, for the heaven's wide circuit, let it speak   100
The maker's high magnificence, who built
So spacious, and his line stretched out so far,
That man may know he dwells not in his own –

---

65 facile] mild, courteous, fluent.
78 wide] wide of the mark, mistaken.
82 To save appearances] a scholastic term (originally Greek) referring to the
    construction of hypotheses which satisfactorily explain the observed facts.
83-4] See III 575n.
99 Officious] attentive.
102] Job xxxviii. 5.

An edifice too large for him to fill,
Lodged in a small partition, and the rest   105
Ordained for uses to his Lord best known.
The swiftness of those circles attribute,
Though numberless, to his omnipotence,
That to corporeal substances could add
Speed almost spiritual; me thou think'st not slow,   100
Who since the morning-hour set out from heaven
Where God resides, and ere mid-day arrived
In Eden – distance inexpressible
By numbers that have name. But this I urge,
Admitting motion in the heavens, to show   115
Invalid that which thee to doubt it moved;
Not that I so affirm, though so it seem
To thee who hast thy dwelling here on earth.
God, to remove his ways from human sense,
Placed heaven from earth so far, that earthly sight,   120
If it presume, might err in things too high,
And no advantage gain. What if the sun
Be centre to the world, and other stars,
By his attractive virtue and their own
Incited, dance about him various rounds?   125
Their wandering course now high, now low, then hid,
Progressive, retrograde, or standing still,
In six thou seest; and what if, seventh to these,
The planet earth, so steadfast though she seem,
Insensibly three different motions move?   130
Which else to several spheres thou must ascribe,
Moved contrary with thwart obliquities,
Or save the sun his labour, and that swift

126 wandering] See V 177n.
127] Kepler showed that the stations (see VII 563n.) and retrogressions
    (apparent movements from east to west) of the planets were necessary
    consequences of the revolution of the planets (including the earth) around
    the sun in elliptical orbits.
128-9] The six planets are the moon, Mercury, Venus, Mars, Jupiter, and
    Saturn. In Ptolemaic astronomy the seventh planet is the sun; in Coperni-
    can astronomy, the earth.
130] Two of the motions are the daily rotation of the earth, and its annual
    revolution around the sun. If Raphael is speaking proleptically of the
    postlapsarian universe, the third motion would be the alteration in the
    plane of the earth's equator which causes its axis to describe a cone in
    space, a phenomenon to which Copernicus attributed the precession of the
    seasons (cf. III 481-3n.). If, as seems more likely, he is speaking of the
    prelapsarian universe, then the third motion would probably be Coperni-
    cus' notion of the progressive (but fluctuating) motion of the earth's
    apse-line.
132] i.e. moving in contrary directions on inclined ecliptic planes.

Nocturnal and diurnal rhomb supposed,
Invisible else above all stars, the wheel   135
Of day and night; which needs not thy belief,
If earth, industrious of herself, fetch day,
Travelling east, and with her part averse
From the sun's beam meet night, her other part
Still luminous by his ray. What if that light,   140
Sent from her through the wide transpicuous air,
To the terrestrial moon be as a star,
Enlightening her by day, as she by night
This earth – reciprocal, if land be there,
Fields and inhabitants? Her spots thou seest   145
As clouds, and clouds may rain, and rain produce
Fruits in her softened soil, for some to eat
Allotted there; and other suns perhaps
With their attendant moons, thou wilt descry,
Communicating male and female light –   150
Which two great sexes animate the world,
Stored in each orb perhaps with some that live.
For such vast room in nature unpossessed
By living soul, desert and desolate,
Only to shine, yet scarce to contribute   155
Each orb a glimpse of light, conveyed so far
Down to this habitable, which returns
Light back to them, is obvious to dispute.
But whether thus these things, or whether not –
Whether the sun, predominant in heaven,   160
Rise on the earth, or earth rise on the sun;
He from the east his flaming road begin,
Or she from west her silent course advance
With inoffensive pace that spinning sleeps
On her soft axle, while she paces even,   165
And bears thee soft with the smooth air along –
Solicit not thy thoughts with matters hid;

---

134 rhomb] the *primum mobile* (see *Fair Infant* 39n.).
141 transpicuous] pervious to vision.
150 male and female] original and reflected.
157 this habitable] imitates ἡ οἰκουμένη (sc. γῆ), the inhabited (world), a term used by the Greeks to designate the Greek world, as opposed to barbarian lands.
164 inoffensive] means both 'unoffending' and (etymologically) 'free from hindrance'.
166] Copernican cosmology assumed an atmosphere which moved with the earth to account for the absence of high winds caused by the rotation of the earth.
167 Solicit] disturb, disquiet.

Leave them to God above; him serve and fear;
Of other creatures as him pleases best,
Wherever placed, let him dispose; joy thou   170
In what he gives to thee, this Paradise
And thy fair Eve; heaven is for thee too high
To know what passes there; be lowly wise;
Think only what concerns thee and thy being;
Dream not of other worlds, what creatures there   175
Live, in what state, condition, or degree —
Contented that thus far hath been revealed
Not of earth only, but of highest heaven.'
    To whom thus Adam, cleared of doubt, replied:
'How fully hast thou satisfied me, pure   180
Intelligence of heaven, angel serene,
And, freed from intricacies, taught to live
The easiest way, nor with perplexing thoughts
To interrupt the sweet of life, from which
God hath bid dwell far off all anxious cares,   185
And not molest us, unless we ourselves
Seek them with wandering thoughts, and notions vain.
But apt the mind or fancy is to rove
Unchecked, and of her roving is no end,
Till warned, or by experience taught, she learn   190
That not to know at large of things remote
From use, obscure and subtle, but to know
That which before us lies in daily life,
Is the prime wisdom: what is more is fume,
Or emptiness, or fond impertinence,   195
And renders us in things that most concern
Unpractised, unprepared, and still to seek.
Therefore from this high pitch let us descend
A lower flight, and speak of things at hand
Useful; whence, haply, mention may arise   200
Of something not unseasonable to ask,
By sufferance, and thy wonted favour, deigned.
Thee I have heard relating what was done
Ere my remembrance; now hear me relate
My story, which perhaps thou hast not heard;   205
And day is yet not spent; till then thou seest
How subtly to detain thee I devise,
Inviting thee to hear while I relate —
Fond, were it not in hope of thy reply;
For while I sit with thee, I seem in heaven,   210

168] Eccles. xii. 13.
195 fond impertinence] foolish irrelevance.
197 to seek] deficient.

And sweeter thy discourse is to my ear
Than fruits of palm-tree, pleasantest to thirst
And hunger both, from labour, at the hour
Of sweet repast; they satiate, and soon fill,
Though pleasant; but thy words, with grace divine   215
Imbued, bring to their sweetness no satiety.'
 To whom thus Raphael answered, heavenly meek:
'Nor are thy lips ungraceful, sire of men,
Nor tongue ineloquent; for God on thee
Abundantly his gifts hath also poured,   220
Inward and outward both, his image fair:
Speaking or mute, all comeliness and grace
Attends thee, and each word, each motion, forms.
Nor less think we in heaven of thee on earth
Than of our fellow-servant, and enquire   225
Gladly into the ways of God with man;
For God, we see, hath honoured thee, and set
On man his equal love; say therefore on;
For I that day was absent, as befell,
Bound on a voyage uncouth and obscure,   230
Far on excursion toward the gates of hell,
Squared in full legion (such command we had)
To see that none thence issued forth a spy
Or enemy, while God was in his work,
Lest he incensed at such eruption bold,   235
Destruction with creation might have mixed.
Not that they durst without his leave attempt;
But us he sends upon his high behests
For state, as sovereign king, and to inure
Our prompt obedience. Fast we found, fast shut,   240
The dismal gates, and barricadoed strong,
But, long ere our approaching, heard within
Noise, other than the sound of dance or song –
Torment, and loud lament, and furious rage.
Glad we returned up to the coasts of light   245
Ere Sabbath-evening; so we had in charge.
But thy relation now; for I attend,
Pleased with thy words no less than thou with mine.'
 So spake the godlike power, and thus our sire:
'For man to tell how human life began   250
Is hard; for who himself beginning knew?
Desire with thee still longer to converse

225] Rev. xxii. 8-9.
230 uncouth] strange, unfamiliar.
239 state] dignified observance of ceremony.
242-4] *Aeneid* vi 557-9.

Induced me. As new-waked from soundest sleep,
Soft on the flowery herb I found me laid,
In balmy sweat, which with his beams the sun   255
Soon dried, and on the reeking moisture fed.
Straight toward heaven my wondering eyes I turned,
And gazed a while the ample sky, till, raised
By quick instinctive motion, up I sprung,
As thitherward endeavouring, and upright   260
Stood on my feet; about me round I saw
Hill, dale, and shady woods, and sunny plains.
And liquid lapse of murmuring streams; by these,
Creatures that lived and moved, and walked or flew,
Birds on the branches warbling; all things smiled;   265
With fragrance and with joy my heart o'erflowed.
Myself I then perused, and limb by limb
Surveyed, and sometimes went, and sometimes ran
With supple joints, as lively vigour led;
But who I was, or where, or from what cause,   270
Knew not; to speak I tried, and forthwith spake;
My tongue obeyed, and readily could name
What'er I saw. "Thou sun," said I, "fair light,
And thou enlightened earth, so fresh and gay,
Ye hills and dales, ye rivers, woods, and plains,   275
And ye that live and move, fair creatures, tell,
Tell, if ye saw, how came I thus, how here.
Not of myself; by some great maker then,
In goodness and in power pre-eminent;
Tell me, how may I know him, how adore,   280
From whom I have that thus I move and live,
And feel that I am happier than I know."
While thus I called, and strayed I knew not whither,
From where I first drew air, and first beheld
This happy light, when answer none returned,   285
On a green shady bank, profuse of flowers,
Pensive I sat me down; there gentle sleep
First found me, and with soft oppression seized
My drowsed sense, untroubled, though I thought
I then was passing to my former state   290
Insensible, and forthwith to dissolve:
When suddenly stood at my head a dream,

256 reeking] steaming.
263 lapse] flow.
268 went] walked.
281] Acts xvii. 28.
292] Imitates *Iliad* 20, where Oneiros, god of dreams, stands at the bedside of
     Agamemnon.

Whose inward apparition gently moved
My fancy to believe I yet had being,
And lived; one came, methought, of shape divine,   295
And said, "Thy mansion wants thee, Adam; rise,
First man, of men innumerable ordained
First father; called by thee, I come thy guide
To the garden of bliss, thy seat prepared."
So saying, by the hand he took me, raised,   300
And over fields and waters, as in air
Smooth sliding without step, last led me up
A woody mountain, whose high top was plain,
A circuit wide, enclosed, with goodliest trees
Planted, with walks and bowers, that what I saw   305
Of earth before scarce pleasant seemed. Each tree
Loaden with fairest fruit, that hung to the eye
Tempting, stirred in me sudden appetite
To pluck and eat; whereat I waked, and found
Before mine eyes all real, as the dream   310
Had lively shadowed; here had new begun
My wandering, had not he who was my guide
Up hither from among the trees appeared,
Presence divine. Rejoicing, but with awe,
In adoration at his feet I fell   315
Submiss; he reared me, and, "Whom thou sought'st I am,"
Said mildly, "author of all this thou seest
Above, or round about thee, or beneath.
This Paradise I give thee; count it thine
To till and keep, and of the fruit to eat;   320
Of every tree that in the garden grows
Eat freely with glad heart; fear here no dearth;
But of the tree whose operation brings
Knowledge of good and ill, which I have set
The pledge of thy obedience and thy faith,   325
Amid the garden by the tree of life –
Remember what I warn thee – shun to taste,
And shun the bitter consequence: for know,
The day thou eat'st thereof, my sole command
Transgressed, inevitably thou shalt die,   330

---

320 till and keep] The A.V. makes 'dressing' the garden a prelapsarian
    obligation (Gen. ii. 15) and 'tilling' a postlapsarian obligation (Gen. iii. 23).
    In the Hebrew, Greek (LXX) and Latin (Vulgate) versions, however, the
    same word is used in both verses.
330–1 inevitably ... mortal] a traditional interpretation of Gen. ii. 17, overcom-
    ing the difficulty that Adam did not die on the day that he ate the fruit by
    interpreting death as inevitable mortality. Cf. X 49–52, 210–11.

From that day mortal, and this happy state
Shalt loose, expelled from hence into a world
Of woe and sorrow.'' Sternly he pronounced
The rigid interdiction, which resounds
Yet dreadful in mine ear, though in my choice   335
Not to incur; but soon his clear aspéct
Returned, and gracious purpose thus renewed:
"Not only these fair bounds, but all the earth
To thee and to thy race I give; as lords
Possess it, and all things that therein live,   340
Or live in sea or air, beast, fish, and fowl.
In sign whereof, each bird and beast behold
After their kinds; I bring them to receive
From thee their names, and pay thee fealty
With low subjection; understand the same   345
Of fish within their watery residence,
Not hither summoned, since they cannot change
Their element to draw the thinner air.''
As thus he spake, each bird and beast behold
Approaching two and two – these cowering low   350
With blandishment; each bird stooped on his wing.
I named them as they passed, and understood
Their nature; with such knowledge God endued
My sudden apprehension; but in these
I found not what methought I wanted still,   355
And to the heavenly vision thus presumed:
    ' "O by what name – for thou above all these,
Above mankind, or aught than mankind higher,
Surpassest far my naming – how may I
Adore thee, author of this universe,   360
And all this good to man, for whose well-being
So amply, and with hands so liberal,
Thou hast provided all things? but with me
I see not who partakes. In solitude
What happiness, who can enjoy alone,   365
Or, all enjoying, what contentment find?''
Thus I, presumptuous; and the vision bright,
As with a smile more brightened, thus replied:
    ' "What call'st thou solitude? Is not the earth
With various living creatures, and the air,   370
Replenished, and all these at thy command

332 loose] means both 'dissolve, violate' and 'lose'.
337 purpose] discourse.
371 Replenished] fully and abundantly stocked.

To come and play before thee? Know'st thou not
Their language and their ways? They also know,
And reason not contemptibly; with these
Find pastime, and bear rule; thy realm is large."   375
So spake the universal Lord, and seemed
So ordering. I with leave of speech implored,
And humble deprecation, thus replied:
  ' "Let not my words offend thee, heavenly power;
My maker, be propitious while I speak.   380
Hast thou not made me here thy substitute,
And these inferior far beneath me set?
Among unequals what society
Can sort, what harmony or true delight?
Which must be mutual, in proportion due   385
Given and received; but, in disparity,
The one intense, the other still remiss,
Cannot well suit with either, but soon prove
Tedious alike; of fellowship I speak
Such as I seek, fit to participate   390
All rational delight, wherein the brute
Cannot be human consort; they rejoice
Each with their kind, lion with lioness;
So fitly them in pairs thou hast combined:
Much less can bird with beast, or fish with fowl,   395
So well converse, nor with the ox the ape;
Worse, then, can man with beast, and least of all."
  'Whereto the almighty answered, not displeased:
"A nice and subtle happiness, I see,
Thou to thyself proposest, in the choice   400
Of thy associates, Adam, and wilt taste
No pleasure, though in pleasure, solitary.
What think'st thou, then, of me, and this my state?
Seem I to thee sufficiently possessed
Of happiness, or not, who am alone   405
From all eternity? For none I know
Second to me or like, equal much less.
How have I, then, with whom to hold converse,
Save with the creatures which I made, and those
To me inferior infinite descents   410

379-80] Gen. xviii. 30.
384-9] an extended musical metaphor. 'Intense' means 'taut' (etymologically),
    and 'remiss' means 'diminished in tension'; the human string is thus higher
    in pitch than the animal string.
396 converse] associate familiarly, consort.
402 in pleasure] plays on 'pleasure' as the literal meaning of 'Eden' in Hebrew.
406-7] Cf. Horace, *Odes* I. xii. 17-18.

Beneath what other creatures are to thee?"
  'He ceased, I lowly answered: "To attain
The height and depth of thy eternal ways
All human thoughts come short, supreme of things;
Thou in thyself art perfect, and in thee   415
Is no deficience found; not so is man,
But in degree – the cause of his desire
By conversation with his like to help
Or solace his defects. No need that thou
Should'st propagate, already infinite,   420
And through all numbers absolute, though one;
But man by number is to manifest
His single imperfection, and beget
Like of his like, his image multiplied,
In unity defective, which requires   425
Collateral love and dearest amity.
Thou in thy secrecy although alone,
Best with thyself accompanied, seek'st not
Social communication – yet, so pleased,
Canst raise thy creature to what height thou wilt   430
Of union or communion, deified;
I by conversing cannot these erect
From prone, nor in their ways complacence find."
Thus I emboldened spake, and freedom used
Permissive, and acceptance found; which gained   435
This answer from the gracious voice divine:
  ' "Thus far to try thee, Adam, I was pleased,
And find thee knowing not of beasts alone,
Which thou hast rightly named, but of thyself –
Expressing well the spirit within thee free,   440
My image, not imparted to the brute,
Whose fellowship, therefore, unmeet for thee,
Good reason was thou freely shouldst dislike;
And be so minded still; I, ere thou spak'st,
Knew it not good for man to be alone,   445
And no such company as then thou saw'st
Intended thee – for trial only brought,
To see how thou could'st judge of fit and meet;

415–20] Aristotle, *Eudemian Ethics* 1244b, 1245b.
421] 'Numbers' carries the Latin sense of 'parts' as well as its modern sense;
    'absolute' means 'complete, perfect'.
427–8 Imitates Cicero's famous phrase, *Numquam minus solum, quam cum solus*
    ('never less alone than when alone'). *De Officiis* III. i. 1. Cf. *PL* IX 249, *PR* I
    301–2.
433 complacence] See III 276n.
435 permissive] acting under permission.

What next I bring shall please thee, be assured,
Thy likeness, thy fit help, thy other self,   450
Thy wish exactly to thy heart's desire.''
  'He ended, or I heard no more; for now
My earthly, by his heavenly overpowered,
Which it had long stood under, strained to the height
In that celestial colloquy sublime,   455
As with an object that excels the sense,
Dazzled and spent, sunk down, and sought repair
Of sleep, which instantly fell on me, called
By nature as in aid, and closed mine eyes.
Mine eyes he closed, but open left the cell   460
Of fancy, my internal sight, by which,
Abstract as in a trance, methought I saw,
Though sleeping, where I lay, and saw the shape
Still glorious before whom awake I stood;
Who, stooping, opened my left side, and took   465
From thence a rib, with cordial spirits warm,
And life-blood streaming fresh; wide was the wound,
But suddenly with flesh filled up and healed;
The rib he formed and fashioned with his hands;
Under his forming hands a creature grew,   470
Man-like, but different sex, so lovely fair
That what seemed fair in all the world seemed now
Mean, or in her summed up, in her contained
And in her looks, which from that time infused
Sweetness into my heart unfelt before   475
And into all things from her air inspired
The spirit of love and amorous delight.
She disappeared, and left me dark; I waked
To find her, or for ever to deplore
Her loss, and other pleasures all abjure: 480
When, out of hope, behold her not far off,
Such as I saw her in my dream, adorned
With what all earth and heaven could bestow
To make her amiable; on she came,

---

450 other self] translates the Greek ἕτερος αὐτός and the Latin *alter ego*, both of
    which are used of very intimate friends. Cf. l. 495, and X 128.
453 earthly, heavenly] i.e. nature.
462 Abstract] withdrawn.
    as in a trance] Milton follows the LXX version of Gen. ii. 21 (ἔκστασιν, the
    word translated in Acts x. 10, xxii. 17 as 'trance'); in the A.V. and Vulgate
    Adam falls into a 'deep sleep'.
466 cordial spirits] the 'vital spirits' of V 484; 'cordial' means 'of the heart'.
476 her air inspired] means both 'her manner and appearance inspired' and 'her
    breath breathed'.

Led by her heavenly maker, though unseen   485
And guided by his voice, nor uninformed
Of nuptial sanctity and marriage rites;
Grace was in all her steps, heaven in her eye,
In every gesture dignity and love.
I, overjoyed, could not forbear aloud: 490
  ' "This turn hath made amends; thou hast fulfilled
Thy words, creator bounteous and benign,
Giver of all things fair – but fairest this
Of all thy gifts – nor enviest. I now see
Bone of my bone, flesh of my flesh, my self   495
Before me; woman is her name, of man
Extracted; for this cause he shall forgo
Father and mother, and to his wife adhere,
And they shall be one flesh, one heart, one soul."
  'She heard me thus, and, though divinely brought,
Yet innocence and virgin modesty,   501
Her virtue and the conscience of her worth,
That would be wooed, and not unsought be won,
Not obvious, not obtrusive, but retired,
The more desirable – or, to say all,   505
Nature herself, though pure of sinful thought –
Wrought in her so, that seeing me, she turned;
I followed her; she what was honour knew,
And with obsequious majesty approved
My pleaded reason. To the nuptial bower   510
I led her blushing like the morn; all heaven,
And happy constellations, on that hour
Shed their selectest influence; the earth
Gave sign of gratulation, and each hill;
Joyous the birds; fresh gales and gentle airs   515
Whispered it to the woods, and from their wings
Flung rose, flung odours from the spicy shrub,
Disporting, till the amorous bird of night
Sung spousal, and bid haste the evening star
On his hill-top to light the bridal lamp.   520
  'Thus have I told thee all my state, and brought
My story to the sum of earthly bliss
Which I enjoy, and must confess to find

490 aloud] i.e. saying aloud.
502 conscience] inward knowledge, consciousness.
504 obvious] open to influence.
508 honour] Heb. xiii. 4.
509 obsequious] obedient, dutiful, prompt to serve.
518 bird] the nightingale.
519 evening star] Hesperus. Cf. XI 588-9.

In all things else delight indeed, but such
As, used or not, works in the mind no change,   525
Nor vehement desire – these delicacies
I mean of taste, sight, smell, herbs, fruits, and flowers,
Walks, and the melody of birds: but here,
Far otherwise, transported I behold,
Transported touch: here passion first I felt,   530
Commotion strange, in all enjoyments else
Superior and unmoved, here only weak
Against the charm of beauty's powerful glance.
Or nature failed in me, and left some part
Not proof enough such object to sustain,   535
Or, from my side subducting, took perhaps
More than enough – at least on her bestowed
Too much of ornament, in outward show
Elaborate, of inward less exact.
For well I understand in the prime end   540
Of nature her inferior, in the mind
And inward faculties, which most excel;
In outward also her resembling less
His image who made both, and less expressing
The character of that dominion given   545
O'er other creatures; yet when I approach
Her loveliness, so absolute she seems
And in herself complete, so well to know
Her own, that what she wills to do or say
Seems wisest, virtuousest, discreetest, best;   550
All higher knowledge in her presence falls
Degraded; wisdom in discourse with her
Looses, discountenanced, and like folly shows;
Authority and reason on her wait,
As one intended first, not after made   555
Occasionally; and to consummate all,
Greatness of mind and nobleness their seat
Build in her loveliest, and create an awe
About her, as a guard angelic placed.'
    To whom the angel, with contracted brow: 560
'Accuse not nature, she hath done her part;
Do thou but thine, and be not diffident

536 subducting] taking away.
547 absolute] See l. 421n.
553 Looses] means both 'dissolves' and 'loses'; cf. l. 332.
556 Occasionally] incidentally, i.e. on the occasion of Adam's request for a
    companion.
557 Greatness of mind] magnanimity. See VII 511n.

Of wisdom; she deserts thee not, if thou
Dismiss not her, when most thou need'st her nigh,
By attributing overmuch to things   565
Less excellent, as thou thyself perceiv'st.
For, what admir'st thou, what transports thee so,
An outside? Fair, no doubt, and worthy well
Thy cherishing, thy honouring, and thy love,
Not thy subjection; weigh with her thyself;   570
Then value; oft-times nothing profits more
Than self-esteem, grounded on just and right
Well managed; of that skill the more thou know'st,
The more she will acknowledge thee her head,
And to realities yield all her shows –   575
Made so adorn for thy delight the more,
So awful, that with honour thou may'st love
Thy mate, who sees when thou art seen least wise.
But if the sense of touch whereby mankind
Is propagated seem such dear delight   580
Beyond all other, think the same vouchsafed
To cattle and each beast; which would not be
To them made common and divulged, if aught
Therein enjoyed were worthy to subdue
The soul of man, or passion in him move.   585
What higher in her society thou find'st
Attractive, human, rational, love still:
In loving thou dost well; in passion not,
Wherein true love consists not; love refines
The thoughts, and heart enlarges – hath his seat   590
In reason, and is judicious, is the scale
By which to heavenly love thou may'st ascend,
Not sunk in carnal pleasure; for which cause
Among the beasts no mate for thee was found.'
     To whom thus, half-abashed, Adam replied: 595
'Neither her outside formed so fair, nor aught
In procreation, common to all kinds
(Though higher of the genial bed by far,
And with mysterious reverence, I deem),
So much delights me as those graceful acts,   600
Those thousand decencies, that daily flow
From all her words and actions, mixed with love
And sweet compliance, which declare unfeigned
Union of mind, or in us both one soul –

574 head] I Cor. xi. 3.
577 awful] awe-inspiring.
598 genial] see IV 712n.

Harmony to behold in wedded pair   605
More grateful than harmonious sound to the ear.
Yet these subject not; I to thee disclose
What inward thence I feel, not therefore foiled,
Who meet with various subjects, from the sense
Variously representing, yet, still free,   610
Approve the best, and follow what I approve.
To love thou blam'st me not – for love, thou say'st,
Leads up to heaven, is both the way and guide;
Bear with me, then, if lawful what I ask:
Love not the heavenly spirits, and how their love   615
Express they – by looks only, or do they mix
Irradiance, virtual or immediate touch?'
    To whom the angel, with a smile that glowed
Celestial rosy-red, love's proper hue,
Answered: 'Let it suffice thee that thou know'st   620
Us happy, and without love no happiness.
Whatever pure thou in the body enjoy'st
(And pure thou wert created) we enjoy
In eminence, and obstacle find none
Of membrane, joint, or limb, exclusive bars;   625
Easier than air with air, if spirits embrace,
Total they mix, union of pure with pure
Desiring, nor restrained conveyance need
As flesh to mix with flesh, or soul with soul.
But I can now no more: the parting sun   630
Beyond the earth's green cape and verdant isles
Hesperean sets, my signal to depart.
Be strong, live happy, and love, but first of all
Him whom to love is to obey, and keep
His great command; take heed lest passion sway   635
Thy judgement to do aught which else free will
Would not admit; thine and of all thy sons
The weal or woe in thee is placed; beware.
I in thy persevering shall rejoice,
And all the blest; stand fast; to stand or fall   640
Free in thine own arbitrament it lies.
Perfect within, no outward aid require;
And all temptation to transgress repel.'

608 foiled] overcome.
510-11] *Metamorphoses* vii 20-1.
631 green cape] Cape Verde.
    verdant isles] the Cape Verde Islands.
632 Hesperean sets] i.e. sets in the west.
634-5] I John v. 3.
639 persevering] See VII 632n.

So saying, he arose; whom Adam thus
Followed with benediction: 'Since to part,   645
Go, heavenly guest, ethereal messenger,
Sent from whose sovereign goodness I adore.
Gentle to me and affable hath been
Thy condescension, and shall be honoured ever
With graceful memory; thou to mankind   650
Be good and friendly still, and oft return.'
   So parted they, the angel up to heaven
From the thick shade, and Adam to his bower.

THE END OF THE EIGHTH BOOK

647 whose] him whose.

BOOK IX

THE ARGUMENT

Satan, having compassed the earth, with meditated guile returns
as a mist by night into Paradise; enters into the serpent sleeping.
Adam and Eve in the morning go forth to their labours, which Eve
proposes to divide in several places, each labouring apart: Adam
consents not, alleging the danger lest that enemy of whom they
were forewarned should attempt her found alone; Eve, loath to be
thought not circumspect or firm enough, urges her going apart, the
rather desirous to make trial of her strength; Adam at last yields;
the serpent finds her alone: his subtle approach, first gazing, then
speaking, with much flattery extolling Eve above all other
creatures. Eve, wondering to hear the serpent speak, asks how he
attained to human speech and such understanding not till now; the
serpent answers that by tasting of a certain tree in the garden he
attained both to speech and reason, till then void of both; Eve
requires him to bring her to that tree, and finds it to be the tree of
knowledge forbidden: the serpent, now grown bolder, with many
wiles and arguments induces her at length to eat; she, pleased with
the taste, deliberates a while whether to impart thereof to Adam or
not; at last brings him of the fruit; relates what persuaded her to
eat thereof; Adam, at first amazed, but perceiving her lost,
resolves, through vehemence of love, to perish with her, and
extenuating the trespass, eats also of the fruit; the effects thereof
in them both; they seek to cover their nakedness; then fall to
variance and accusation of one another.

No more of talk where God or angel guest
With man, as with his friend, familiar used
To sit indulgent, and with him partake
Rural repast, permitting him the while
Venial discourse unblamed; I now must change   5
Those notes to tragic – foul distrust, and breach
Disloyal, on the part of man, revolt
And disobedience; on the part of heaven,
Now alienated, distance and distaste,
Anger and just rebuke, and judgement given,   10
That brought into this world a world of woe,
Sin and her shadow Death, and Misery,
Death's harbinger; sad task, yet argument
Not less but more heroic than the wrath

---

2 familiar] The primary meaning is 'as in a family', but the word also evokes the
   phrase 'familiar (i.e. guardian) angel'.
5 Venial] permissible, blameless.
14-16] 'The wrath/Of stern Achilles' is the subject announced at the beginning
   of the *Iliad*; 'his foe' is Hector.

Of stern Achilles on his foe pursued   15
Thrice fugitive about Troy wall; or rage
Of Turnus for Lavinia disespoused;
Or Neptune's ire, or Juno's, that so long
Perplexed the Greek, and Cytherea's son:
In answerable style I can obtain   20
Of my celestial patroness, who deigns
Her nightly visitation unimplored,
And dictates to me slumbering, or inspires
Easy my unpremeditated verse,
Since first this subject for heroic song   25
Pleased me, long choosing and beginning late,
Not sedulous by nature to indite
Wars, hitherto the only argument
Heroic deemed, chief mastery to dissect
With long and tedious havoc fabled knights   30
In battles feigned – the better fortitude
Of patience and heroic martyrdom
Unsung – or to describe races and games,
Or tilting furniture, emblazoned shields,
Impreses quaint, caparisons and steeds,   35
Bases and tinsel trappings, gorgeous knights
At joust and tournament; then marshalled feast
Served up in hall with sewers and seneschals:
The skill of artifice or office mean,
Not that which justly gives heroic name   40
To person or to poem. Me, of these
Nor skilled nor studious, higher argument
Remains, sufficient of itself to raise
That name, unless an age too late, or cold
Climate, or years, damp my intended wing   45
Depressed; and much they may if all be mine,
Not hers who brings it nightly to my ear.
     The sun was sunk, and after him the star

17] In the *Aeneid* Turnus is the suitor of Lavinia; he is killed by Aeneas, who
     marries Lavinia himself.
18–19] In the *Odyssey* 'Neptune's ire' is directed against Odysseus ('the Greek')
     who had blinded Neptune's son, the Cyclops Polyphemus; in the *Aeneid*
     Juno's ire is directed against Aeneas, 'Cytherea's (i.e. Venus') son', who is so
     described because Juno's ire was prompted by Paris' judgement in favour
     of Venus (See V 381–2n.). 'Perplexed' means 'tormented'.
21 celestial patroness] Urania. See VII 1n.
34–8] Alludes to the characteristic preoccupations of romance epic. 'Tilting
     furniture' is armour; 'impreses' are emblems or devices, usually with a
     motto; 'caparisons' are the armour of horses; 'bases' are the cloth housings
     of horses; 'sewers' are waiters, and 'senseschals' are stewards.

Of Hesperus, whose office is to bring
Twilight upon the earth, short arbiter   50
'Twixt day and night, and now from end to end
Night's hemisphere had veiled the horizon round,
When Satan, who late fled before the threats
Of Gabriel out of Eden, now improved
In meditated fraud and malice, bent   55
On man's destruction, maugre what might hap
Of heavier on himself, fearless returned.
By night he fled, and at midnight returned
From compassing the earth – cautious of day
Since Uriel, regent of the sun, descried   60
His entrance, and forewarned the cherubim
That kept their watch; thence, full of anguish, driven,
The space of seven continued nights he rode
With darkness – thrice the equinoctial line
He circled, four times crossed the car of Night   65
From pole to pole, traversing each colure –
On the eighth returned, and on the coast averse
From entrance or cherubic watch by stealth
Found unsuspected way. There was a place –
Now not, though Sin, not Time, first wrought the change –
Where Tigris, at the foot of Paradise,   71
Into a gulf shot under ground, till part
Rose up a fountain by the tree of life;
In with the river sunk, and with it rose
Satan, involved in rising mist, then sought   75
Where to lie hid; sea he had searched and land
From Eden over Pontus, and the Pool
Maeotis, up beyond the river Ob;
Downward as far antarctic; and in length

---

54 improved] increased or augmented (in evil).
56 maugre] in spite of.
63–6] For the first three nights Satan circles the earth at the equator, which
    before the fall was on the same plane as the ecliptic. For the next four
    nights he follows the lines of the colures, i.e. the two great circles
    intersecting rectangularly at the poles, one passing through the equinoctial
    points of the ecliptic, and the other the solstitial points. It is difficult to
    understand how Satan could have stayed in continual darkness, for before
    the fall both poles were in perpetual light (cf. X, 680–7), and even after the
    fall one is always light.
73 fountain] See IV 229n.
75 involved] enveloped.
76–8] Satan travels northwards past Pontus (Pontus Euxinus, the Black Sea),
    'the Pool/Maeotis' (Palus Maeotis, the Sea of Asov), and 'the river Ob',
    which flows into Obskaya Guba and thence into the Arctic Ocean.

West from Orontes to the ocean barred   80
At Darien, thence to the land where flows
Ganges and Indus; thus the orb he roamed
With narrow search, and with inspection deep
Considered every creature, which of all
Most opportune might serve his wiles, and found   85
The serpent subtlest beast of all the field.
Him, after long debate, irresolute
Of thoughts revolved, his final sentence chose
Fit vessel, fittest imp of fraud, in whom
To enter, and his dark suggestions hide   90
From sharpest sight; for in the wily snake
Whatever sleights none would suspicious mark,
As from his wit and native subtlety
Proceeding, which, in other beasts observed,
Doubt might beget of diabolic power   95
Active within beyond the sense of brute.
Thus he resolved, but first from inward grief
His bursting passion into plaints thus poured:
    'O earth, how like to heaven, if not preferred
More justly, seat worthier of gods, as built   100
With second thought, reforming what was old!
For what god, after better, worse would build?
Terrestrial heaven, danced round by other heavens,
That shine, yet bear their bright officious lamps,
Light above light, for thee alone, as seems,   105
In thee concentring all their precious beams
Of sacred influence; as God in heaven
Is centre, yet extends to all, so thou
Centring receiv'st from all those orbs; in thee,
Not in themselves, all their known virtue appears,   110
Productive in herb, plant, and nobler birth
Of creatures animate with gradual life
Of growth, sense, reason, all summed up in man.
With what delight could I have walked thee round,
If I could joy in aught – sweet interchange   115
Of hill and valley, rivers, woods, and plains,
Now land, now sea, and shores with forest crowned,
Rocks, dens, and caves; but I in none of these

80-2] Satan travels westwards past the Orontes River, in Turkey and Syria (see
    IV 272-4n.) to the Pacific Ocean, which is 'barred' (see Job xxxviii. 8-11)
    by Darien (a district in Panama), and thence to India.
89 imp] child.
95 Doubt] suspicion.
112 gradual] arranged in grades (cf. V 483).

Find place or refuge; and the more I see
Pleasures about me, so much more I feel   120
Torment within me, as from the hateful siege
Of contraries; all good to me becomes
Bane, and in heaven much worse would be my state.
But neither here seek I, no, nor in heaven,
To dwell, unless by mastering heaven's supreme;   125
Nor hope to be myself less miserable
By what I seek, but others to make such
As I, though thereby worse to me redound;
For only in destroying I find ease
To my relentless thoughts; and him destroyed,   130
Or won to what may work his utter loss,
For whom all this was made, all this will soon
Follow, as to him linked in weal or woe:
In woe then, that destruction wide may range;
To me shall be the glory sole among   135
The infernal powers, in one day to have marred
What he, almighty styled, six nights and days
Continued making, and who knows how long
Before had been contriving, though perhaps
Not longer than since I in one night freed   140
From servitude inglorious well-nigh half
The angelic name, and thinner left the throng
Of his adorers; he, to be avenged,
And to repair his numbers thus impaired –
Whether such virtue, spent of old, now failed   145
More angels to create – if they at least
Are his created – or to spite us more,
Determined to advance into our room
A creature formed of earth, and him endow,
Exalted from so base original,   150
With heavenly spoils, our spoils; what he decreed
He effected; man he made, and for him built
Magnificent this world, and earth his seat,
Him lord pronounced, and, O indignity!
Subjected to his service angel wings   155
And flaming ministers, to watch and tend
Their earthy charge; of these the vigilance
I dread, and to elude, thus wrapped in mist
Of midnight vapour, glide obscure, and pry
In every bush and brake, where hap may find   160
The serpent sleeping, in whose mazy folds
To hide me, and the dark intent I bring.

155-7] Psalms civ. 4, xci. 11, Heb. i. 14.

O foul descent! That I, who erst contended
With gods to sit the highest, am now constrained
Into a beast, and mixed with bestial slime,   165
This essence to incarnate and imbrute,
That to the height of deity aspired;
But what will not ambition and revenge
Descend to? Who aspires must down as low
As high he soared, obnoxious, first or last,   170
To basest things. Revenge, at first though sweet,
Bitter ere long back on itself recoils;
Let it; I reck not, so it light well aimed,
Since higher I fall short, on him who next
Provokes my envy, this new favourite   175
Of heaven, this man of clay, son of despite,
Whom, us the more to spite, his maker raised
From dust: spite then with spite is best repaid.'
    So saying, through each thicket, dank or dry,
Like a black mist low creeping, he held on   180
His midnight search, where soonest he might find
The serpent; him fast sleeping soon he found
In labyrinth of many a sound self-rolled,
His head the midst, well stored with subtle wiles:
Not yet in horrid shade or dismal den,   185
Nor nocent yet, but on the grassy herb,
Fearless, unfeared, he slept; in at his mouth
The devil entered, and his brutal sense,
In heart or head, possessing soon inspired
With act intelligential; but his sleep   190
Disturbed not, waiting close the approach of morn.
    Now, whenas sacred light began to dawn
In Eden on the humid flowers, that breathed
Their morning incense, when all things that breathe
From the earth's great altar send up silent praise   195
To the creator, and his nostrils fill
With grateful smell, forth came the human pair,
And joined their vocal worship to the choir
Of creatures wanting voice; that done, partake
The season, prime for sweetest scents and airs;   200
Then commune how that day they best may ply

170 obnoxious] exposed, liable (to an influence).
185 horrid] means both 'shaggy, rough' and 'causing horror'.
186 nocent] means both 'guilty' and 'harmful'.
188 brutal] pertaining to animals.
195-7] Gen. viii. 21.
200 season] i.e. early morning.

Their growing work – for much their work outgrew
The hands' dispatch of two, gardening so wide.
And Eve first to her husband thus began:
   'Adam, well may we labour still to dress   205
This garden, still to tend plant, herb, and flower,
Our pleasant task enjoined; but, till more hands
Aid us, the work under our labour grows,
Luxurious by restraint: what we by day
Lop overgrown, or prune, or prop, or bind,   210
One night or two with wanton growth derides,
Tending to wild. Thou, therefore, now advise,
Or hear what to my mind first thoughts present;
Let us divide our labours – thou where choice
Leads thee, or where most needs, whether to wind   215
The woodbine round this arbour, or direct
The clasping ivy where to climb, while I
In yonder spring of roses intermixed
With myrtle find what to redress till noon;
For, while so near each other thus all day   220
Our task we choose, what wonder if so near
Looks intervene and smiles, or objects new
Casual discourse draw on, which intermits
Our day's work, brought to little, though begun
Early, and the hour of supper comes unearned.'   225
   To whom mild answer Adam thus returned:
'Sole Eve, associate sole, to me beyond
Compare above all living creatures dear,
Well hast thou motioned, well thy thoughts employed
How we might best fulfil the work which here   230
God hath assigned us, nor of me shalt pass
Unpraised; for nothing lovelier can be found
In woman than to study household good,
And good works in her husband to promote.
Yet not so strictly hath our Lord imposed   235
Labour as to debar us when we need
Refreshment, whether food or talk between,
Food of the mind, or this sweet intercourse
Of looks and smiles; for smiles from reason flow
To brute denied, and are of love the food –   240
Love, not the lowest end of human life.

217 where to climb] i.e. on the elm. See V 215-19n.
218 spring] a plantation of young trees.
219 redress] set upright again, direct to the right course.
229 motioned] offered a plan.
233] Prov. xxxi. 27.

For not to irksome toil, but to delight,
He made us, and delight to reason joined.
These paths and bowers doubt not but our joint hands
Will keep from wilderness with ease, as wide   245
As we need walk, till younger hands ere long
Assist us; but, if much converse perhaps
Thee satiate, to short absence I could yield;
For solitude sometimes is best society,
And short retirement urges sweet return.   250
But other doubt possesses me, lest harm
Befall thee, severed from me; for thou know'st
What hath been warned us – what malicious foe,
Envying our happiness, and of his own
Despairing, seeks to work us woe and shame   255
By sly assault, and somewhere nigh at hand
Watches, no doubt, with greedy hope to find
His wish and best advantage, us asunder,
Hopeless to circumvent us joined, where each
To other speedy aid might lend at need;   260
Whether is first design be to withdraw
Our fealty from God, or to disturb
Conjugal love – than which perhaps no bliss
Enjoyed by us excites his envy more –
Or this, or worse, leave not the faithful side   265
That gave thee being, still shades thee and protects.
The wife, where danger or dishonour lurks,
Safest and seemliest by her husband stays,
Who guards her, or with her the worst endures.'
          To whom the virgin majesty of Eve,   270
As one who loves, and some unkindness meets,
With sweet austere composure thus replied:
          'Offspring of heaven and earth, and all earth's lord,
That such an enemy we have, who seeks
Our ruin, both by thee informed I learn,   275
And from the parting angel overheard,
As in a shady nook I stood behind,
Just then returned at shut of evening flowers.
But that thou shouldst my firmness therefore doubt
To God or thee, because we have a foe   280
May tempt it, I expected not to hear.
His violence thou fear'st not, being such
As we, not capable of death or pain,

249] Cf. VIII 427-8n.
265 Or] whether.
270 virgin] innocent, chaste.

Can either not receive, or can repel.
His fraud is, then, thy fear; which plain infers   285
Thy equal fear that my firm faith and love
Can by his fraud be shaken or seduced:
Thoughts, which how found they harbour in thy breast,
Adam, misthought of her to thee so dear?'
　　To whom, with healing words, Adam replied: 290
'Daughter of God and man, immortal Eve –
For such thou art, from sin and blame entire –
Not diffident of thee do I dissuade
Thy absence from my sight, but to avoid
The attempt itself, intended by our foe.   295
For he who tempts, though in vain, at least asperses
The tempted with dishonour foul, supposed
Not incorruptible of faith, not proof
Against temptation; thou thyself with scorn
And anger wouldst resent the offered wrong,   300
Though ineffectual found; misdeem not then,
If such affront I labour to avert
From thee alone, which on us both at once
The enemy, though bold, will hardly dare;
Or daring, first on me the assault shall light.   305
Nor thou his malice and false guile contemn –
Subtle he needs must be who could seduce
Angels – nor think superfluous others' aid.
I from the influence of thy looks receive
Access in every virtue – in thy sight   310
More wise, more watchful, stronger, if need were
Of outward strength; while shame, thou looking on,
Shame to be overcome or overreached,
Would utmost vigour raise, and raised unite.
Why shouldst not thou like sense within thee feel   315
When I am present, and thy trial choose
With me, best witness of thy virtue tried?'
　　So spake domestic Adam in his care
And matrimonial love; but Eve, who thought
Less áttributed to her faith sincere,   320
Thus her reply with accent sweet renewed –
　　'If this be our condition, thus to dwell

292 entire] free from reproach, blameless.
293 diffident] distrustful (cf. VIII 562).
296 asperses] injuriously and falsely bespatters.
310 Access] increase.
320 Less] too little (by analogy to the Latin comparative *minor*).
　　sincere] pure. The Protestant catch-phrase *fides sincera* derives from the
　　use of the word in I Pet. ii. 2.

In narrow circuit straitened by a foe,
Subtle or violent, we not endued
Single with like defence wherever met,
How are we happy, still in fear of harm?   325
But harm precedes not sin: only our foe
Tempting affronts us with his foul esteem
Of our integrity: his foul esteem
Sticks no dishonour on our front, but turns
Foul on himself; when wherefore shunned or feared   330
By us, who rather double honour gain
From his surmise proved false, find peace within,
Favour from heaven, our witness, from the event?
And what is faith, love, virtue, unassayed
Alone, without exterior help sustained?   335
Let us not then suspect our happy state
Left so imperfect by the maker wise
As not secure to single or combined;
Frail is our happiness, if this be so,
And Eden were no Eden, thus exposed.'   340
    To whom thus Adam fervently replied:
'O woman, best are all things as the will
Of God ordained them; his creating hand
Nothing imperfect or deficient left
Of all that he created – much less man,   345
Or aught that might his happy state secure,
Secure from outward force; within himself
The danger lies, yet lies within his power;
Against his will he can receive no harm.
But God left free the will, for what obeys   350
Reason is free; and reason he made right,
But bid her well beware, and still erect,
Lest by some fair appearing good surprised,
She dictate false, and misinform the will
To do what God expressly hath forbid.   355
Not then mistrust, but tender love enjoins
That I should mind thee oft; and mind thou me.
Firm we subsist, yet possible to swerve,
Since reason not impossibly may meet
Some specious object by the foe suborned,   360
And fall into deception unaware,

---

328 affronts] means both 'insults' and, as Eve's use of 'front' in l. 330 indicates,
    'sets face to face'.
341 no Eden] i.e. no pleasure. See IV 27–8n.
352 reason ... right] See VI 42n.
353 still erect] unceasingly alert (with a suggestion of 'directed upwards').

Not keeping strictest watch, as she was warned.
Seek not temptation, then, which to avoid
Were better, and most likely if from me   365
Thou sever not: trial will come unsought.
Wouldst thou approve thy constancy, approve
First thy obedience; the other who can know,
Not seeing thee attempted, who attest?
But if thou think trial unsought may find   370
Us both securer than thus warned thou seem'st,
Go; for thy stay, not free, absents thee more;
Go in thy native innocence; rely
On what thou hast of virtue; summon all;
For God towards thee hath done his part: do thine.'   375
    So spake the patriarch of mankind; but Eve
Persisted; yet submiss, though last, replied:
    'With thy permission, then, and thus forewarned,
Chiefly by what thy own last reasoning words
Touched only, that our trial, when least sought,   380
May find us both perhaps far less prepared,
The willinger I go, nor much expect
A foe so proud will first the weaker seek;
So bent, the more shall shame him his repulse.'
    Thus saying, from her husband's hand her hand   385
Soft she withdrew, and like a wood-nymph light,
Oread or dryad, or of Delia's train,
Betook her to the groves, but Delia's self
In gait surpassed and goddess-like deport,
Though not as she with bow and quiver armed,   390
But with such gardening tools as art, yet rude,
Guiltless of fire had formed, or angels brought.
To Pales, or Pomona, thus adorned,
Likest she seemed – Pomana when she fled
Vertumnus – or to Ceres in her prime,   395

---

367 approve] prove.
371 securer] more overconfident.
385–6] Cf. IV 321n.; 'light' means both 'swift, agile' and 'unsteady, susceptible
to slight pressure'.
387] Oreads are mountain nymphs, the favourite companions of Diana (*Aeneid* i
500), and dryads are nymphs of forests and groves; both are mortal
(*Metamorphoses* viii 771). Delia is Diana, who is so called after her
birthplace, Delos.
393] Pales was the Roman goddess of flocks and shepherds; on Pomona see V
378n.
395 Vertumnus] a Roman deity associated with the changing seasons and the
effect of the seasons on vegetation; he assumed a series of disguises, and was
thus able to seduce Pomona (*Metamorphoses* xiv 623–771).

Yet virgin of Proserpina from Jove.
Her long with ardent look his eye pursued
Delighted, but desiring more her stay.
Oft he to her his charge of quick return
Repeated; she to him as oft engaged   400
To be returned by noon amid the bower,
And all things in best order to invite
Noontide repast, or afternoon's repose.
O much deceived, much failing, hapless Eve,
Of thy presumed return! Event perverse!   405
Thou never from that hour in Paradise
Found'st either sweet repast or sound repose;
Such ambush, hid among sweet flowers and shades,
Waited, with hellish rancour imminent,
To intercept thy way, or send thee back   410
Despoiled of innocence, of faith, of bliss.
For now, and since first break of dawn, the fiend,
Mere serpent in appearance, forth was come,
And on his quest where likeliest he might find
The only two of mankind, but in them   415
The whole included race, his purposed prey.
In bower and field he sought, where any tuft
Of grove or garden-plot more pleasant lay,
Their tendance or plantation for delight;
By fountain or by shady rivulet   420
He sought them both, but wished his hap might find
Eve separate; he wished, but not with hope
Of what so seldom chanced, when to his wish,
Beyond his hope, Eve separate he spies,
Veiled in a cloud of fragrance, where she stood,   425
Half-spied, so thick the roses bushing round
About her glowed, oft stooping to support
Each flower of tender stalk, whose head, though gay
Carnation, purple, azure, or specked with gold,
Hung drooping unsustained; them she upstays   430
Gently with myrtle band, mindless the while
Herself, though fairest unsupported flower,
From her best prop so far, and storm so nigh.
Nearer he drew, and many a walk traversed
Of stateliest covert, cedar, pine, or palm;   435
Then voluble and bold, now hid, now seen
Among thick-woven arborets, and flowers

395-6] See IV 268-72n.
421 hap] fortune, chance.
436 voluble] moving rapidly with an undulating movement.
437 arborets] little trees, shrubs.

Embordered on each bank, the hand of Eve:
Spot more delicious than those gardens feigned
Or of revived Adonis, or renowned   440
Alcinous, host of old Laertes' son,
Or that, not mystic, where the sapient king
Held dalliance with his fair Egyptian spouse.
Much he the place admired, the person more.
As one who long in populous city pent,   445
Where houses thick and sewers annoy the air,
Forth issuing on a summer's morn, to breathe
Among the pleasant villages and farms
Adjoined, from each thing met conceives delight –
The smell of grain, or tedded grass, or kine,   450
Or dairy, each rural sight, each rural sound –
If chance with nymph-like step fair virgin pass,
What pleasing seemed, for her now pleases more,
She most, and in her look sums all delight:
Such pleasure took the serpent to behold   455
This flowery plat, the sweet recess of Eve
Thus early, thus alone; her heavenly form
Angelic, but more soft and feminine,
Her graceful innocence, her every air
Of gesture or least action, overawed   460
His malice, and with rapine sweet bereaved
His fierceness of the fierce intent it brought.
That space the evil one abstracted stood
From his own evil, and for the time remained
Stupidly good, of enmity disarmed,   465
Of guile, of hate, of envy, of revenge;
But the hot hell that always in him burns,
Though in mid heaven, soon ended his delight
And tortures him now more, the more he sees
Of pleasure not for him ordained; then soon   470
Fierce hate he recollects, and all his thoughts

438 hand] handiwork.
440] See *Comus* 996-1011n.
441] See V 339-41n. Laertes' son is Odysseus.
442-3] Solomon married a daughter of the Pharaoh (I Kings iii. 1); on the
    garden see Song of Solomon, passim. Solomon is 'sapient' in Kings and
    Chronicles, but Milton also exploits the Latin sense of wisdom (*sapientia*) as
    a kind of taste. (cf. ll. 1017-20).
46 annoy] affect injuriously.
450 tedded] spread out for drying.
    kine] cows.
453 for] because of.
456 plat] patch of ground.

Of mischief, gratulating, thus excites:
　'Thoughts, whither have ye led me? With what sweet
Compulsion thus transported to forget
What hither brought us? Hate, not love, nor hope　　475
Of Paradise for hell, hope here to taste
Of pleasure, but all pleasure to destroy,
Save what is in destroying; other joy
To me is lost. Then let me not let pass
Occasion which now smiles; behold alone　　480
The woman, opportune to all attempts –
Her husband, for I view far round, not nigh,
Whose higher intellectual more I shun,
And strength, of courage haughty, and of limb
Heroic built, though of terrestrial mould;　　485
Foe not informidable, exempt from wound –
I not; so much hath hell debased, and pain
Enfeebled me, to what I was in heaven.
She fair, divinely fair, fit love for gods,
Not terrible, though terror be in love,　　490
And beauty, not approached by stronger hate,
Hate stronger under show of love well feigned –
The way which to her ruin now I tend.'
　So spake the enemy of mankind, enclosed
In serpent, inmate bad, and toward Eve　　495
Addressed his way – not with indented wave,
Prone on the ground, as since, but on his rear,
Circular base of rising folds, that towered
Fold above fold, a surging maze; his head
Crested aloft, and carbuncle his eyes;　　500
With burnished neck of verdant gold, erect
Amidst his circling spires, that on the grass
Floated redundant; pleasing was his shape
And lovely; never since of serpent kind
Lovelier – not those that in Illyria changed　　505
Hermione and Cadmus, or the god

472 gratulating] manifesting joy (in meeting Eve).
481 opportune] conveniently exposed.
491 not] if not.
496 indented] having a zigzag course.
503 redundant] in swelling waves.
505-6] Cadmus, son of the King of Tyre, went in his old age to Illyria (an ancient kingdom which corresponds to modern Albania), where he and his wife Harmonia (Hermione) were turned into serpents (*Metamorphoses* iv 563-603).
506-7] Epidaurus was the sanctuary of Aesculapius (the god of healing), who turned himself into a serpent to travel to Rome to deal with a plague (*Metamorphoses* xv 622-744).

In Epidaurus; nor to which transformed
Ammonian Jove, or Capitoline, was seen,
He with Olympias, this with her who bore
Scipio, the height of Rome. With tract oblique   510
At first, as one who sought access but feared
To interrupt, sidelong he works his way.
As when a ship, by skilful steersman wrought
Nigh river's mouth, or foreland, where the wind
Veers oft, as oft so steers, and shifts her sail,   515
So varied he, and of his tortuous train
Curled many a wanton wreath in sight of Eve,
To lure her eye; she, busied, heard the sound
Of rustling leaves, but minded not, as used
To such disport before her through the field   520
From every beast, more duteous at her call
Than at Circean call the herd disguised.
He bolder now, uncalled before her stood,
But as in gaze admiring; oft he bowed
His turret crest and sleek enamelled neck,   525
Fawning, and licked the ground whereon she trod.
His gentle dumb expression turned at length
The eye of Eve to mark his play; he, glad
Of her attention gained, with serpent tongue
Organic, or impulse of vocal air,   530
His fraudulent temptation thus began:
    'Wonder not, sovereign mistress – if perhaps
Thou canst who are sole wonder – much less arm
Thy looks, the heaven of mildness, with disdain,
Displeased that I approach thee thus, and gaze   535
Insatiate, I thus single, nor have feared

507-9] Ammonian Jove (see IV 275-9n.) assumed the form of a serpent and
    became the father of Alexander the Great, whose mother was Olympias.
    Cf. *PR* III 84.
508-10] The Capitol is the hill in Rome on which stood the Temple of Jupiter
    (hence Capitoline). In antiquity many parallels were drawn between the
    lives of Scipio Africanus and Alexander, and Scipio was accordingly said to
    have been the son of Jupiter Capitolinus, who took the form of a serpent.
510 tract] track, course.
510-14] The initial letters of these lines may be a deliberate acrostic:
    S-A-T-A-N.
522] The 'herd disguised' are those who had been turned into wolves and lions
    by Circe. Homer compares them to dogs fawning on their master (*Odyssey* x
    212-19).
525 enamelled] Cf. IV 149n.
530 Organic] like an organ or instrument.
    impulse] the primary meaning is 'application of sudden force', but the word
    also carries the secondary meaning of 'a suggestion coming from an evil
    spirit'.

Thy awful brow, more awful thus retired.
Fairest resemblance of thy maker fair,
Thee all things living gaze on, all things thine
By gift, and thy celestial beauty adore,   540
With ravishment beheld – there best beheld
Where universally admired; but here
In this enclosure wild, these beasts among,
Beholders rude, and shallow to discern
Half what in thee is fair, one man except,   545
Who sees thee (and what is one?) who shouldst be seen
A goddess among gods, adored and served
By angels numberless, thy daily train?'
So glozed the tempter, and his proem tuned.
Into the heart of Eve his words made way,   550
Though at the voice much marvelling; at length,
Not unamazed, she thus in answer spake:
    'What may this mean? Language of man pronounced
By tongue of brute, and human sense expressed?
The first at least of these I thought denied   555
To beasts, whom God on their creation-day
Created mute to all articulate sound;
The latter I demur, for in their looks
Much reason, and in their actions, oft appears.
Thee, serpent, subtlest beast of all the field   560
I knew, but not with human voice endued;
Redouble then this miracle, and say,
How cam'st thou speakable of mute, and how
To me so friendly grown above the rest
Of brutal kind that daily are in sight: 565
Say, for such wonder claims attention due.'
    To whom the guileful tempter thus replied:
'Empress of this fair world, resplendent Eve,
Easy to me it is to tell thee all
What thou command'st, and right thou shouldst be
        obeyed;
I was at first as other beasts that graze   571
The trodden herb, of abject thoughts and low,
As was my food, nor aught but food discerned
Or sex, and apprehended nothing high:
Till on a day, roving the field, I chanced   575
A goodly tree far distant to behold,
Loaden with fruit of fairest colours mixed,
Ruddy and gold; I nearer drew to gaze,
When from the boughs a savoury odour blown,

549 proem] prelude.
558 demur] to hesitate about.
579 savoury] Cf. V 84n.

Grateful to appetite, more pleased my sense   580
Than smell of sweetest fennel, or the teats
Of ewe or goat dropping with milk at even,
Unsucked of lamb or kid, that tend their play.
To satisfy the sharp desire I had
Of tasting those fair apples, I resolved   585
Not to defer; hunger and thirst at once,
Powerful persuaders, quickened at the scent
Of that alluring fruit, urged me so keen.
About the mossy trunk I wound me soon,
For, high from ground, the branches would require   590
Thy utmost reach, or Adam's: round the tree
All other beasts that saw, with like desire
Longing and envying stood, but could not reach.
Amid the tree now got, where plenty hung
Tempting so nigh, to pluck and eat my fill   595
I spared not, for such pleasure till that hour
At feed or fountain never had I found.
Sated at length, ere long I might perceive
Strange alteration in me, to degree
Of reason in my inward powers, and speech   600
Wanted not long, though to this shape retained.
Thenceforth to speculations high or deep
I turned my thoughts, and with capacious mind
Considered all things visible in heaven,
Or earth, or middle, all things fair and good;   605
But all that fair and good in thy divine
Semblance and in thy beauty's heavenly ray,
United I beheld – no fair to thine
Equivalent or second; which compelled
Me thus, though importune perhaps, to come   610
And gaze, and worship thee of right declared
Sovereign of creatures, universal dame.'
     So talked the spirited sly snake; and Eve,
Yet more amazed, unwary thus replied:
     'Serpent, thy overpraising leaves in doubt   615
The virtue of that fruit, in thee first proved;
But say, where grows the tree? From hence how far?

581-3] Serpents were believed to sharpen their sight with fennel, and to suck
     milk from animals. Fennel was also a common emblem of pride.
605 middle] i.e. between heaven and earth.
609] Horace. *Odes* I. xii. 18.
612 universal dame] mistress of the universe.
613 spirited] means both 'lively' and 'possessed by a spirit'.
614 amazed] means 'bewildered', but also refers to the agent of bewilderment,
     the serpent's 'maze' (l. 499).

For many are the trees of God that grow
In Paradise, and various, yet unknown
To us; in such abundance lies our choice   620
As leaves a greater store of fruit untouched,
Still hanging incorruptible, till men
Grow up to their provision, and more hands
Help to disburden nature of her birth.'
     To whom the wily adder, blithe and glad: 625
'Empress, the way is ready, and not long –
Beyond a row of myrtles, on a flat,
Fast by a fountain, one small thicket past
Of blowing myrrh and balm; if thou accept
My conduct, I can bring thee thither soon.'   630
     'Lead, then,' said Eve. He leading swiftly rolled
In tangles, and made intricate seem straight,
To mischief swift. Hope elevates, and joy
Brightens his crest; as when a wandering fire,
Compact of unctuous vapour, which the night   635
Condenses, and the cold environs round,
Kindled through agitation to a flame –
Which oft, they say, some evil spirit attends –
Hovering and blazing with delusive light,
Misleads the amazed night-wanderer from his way   640
To bogs and mires, and oft through pond or pool,
There swallowed up and lost, from succour far;
So glistered the dire snake, and into fraud
Led Eve, our credulous mother, to the tree
Of prohibition, root of all our woe;   645
Which when she saw, thus to her guide she spake:
     'Serpent, we might have spared our coming hither,
Fruitless to me, though fruit be here to excess,
The credit of whose virtue rest with thee –
Wondrous indeed, if cause of such effects.   650
But of this tree we may not taste nor touch;
God so commanded, and left that command
Sole daughter of his voice: the rest, we live
Law to ourselves; our reason is our law.'
     To whom the tempter guilefully replied: 655
'Indeed? Hath God then said that of the fruit
Of all these garden-trees ye shall not eat,
Yet lords declared of all in earth or air?'

629 blowing] blooming.
635 Compact] composed.
643 fraud] Cf. VII 143n.
654 Rom. ii. 14.

    To whom thus Eve, yet sinless: 'Of the fruit
Of each tree in the garden we may eat;   660
But of the fruit of this fair free, amidst
The garden, God hath said, "Ye shall not eat
Thereof, nor shall ye touch it, lest ye die." '
She scarce had said, though brief, when now more bold
The tempter, but with show of zeal and love   665
To man, and indignation at his wrong,
New part puts on, and as to passion moved,
Fluctuates disturbed, yet comely, and in act
Raised, as of some great matter to begin.
As when of old some orator renowned   670
In Athens or free Rome, where eloquence
Flourished, since mute, to some great cause addressed,
Stood in himself collected, while each part,
Motion, each act, won audience ere the tongue
Sometimes in height began, as no delay   675
Of preface brooking through his zeal of right:
So standing, moving, or to height upgrown,
The tempter, all impassioned, thus began:
    'O sacred, wise, and wisdom-giving plant,
Mother of science, now I feel thy power   680
Within me clear, not only to discern
Things in their causes, but to trace the ways
Of highest agents, deemed however wise.
Queen of this universe, do not believe
Those rigid threats of death; ye shall not die;   685
How should ye? By the fruit? It gives you life
To knowledge. By the threatener? Look on me,
Me who have touched and tasted, yet both live,
And life more perfect have attained than fate
Meant me, by venturing higher than my lot.   690
Shall that be shut to man which to the beast
Is open? Or will God incense his ire
For such a petty trespass, and not praise
Rather your dauntless virtue, whom the pain
Of death denounced, whatever thing death be,   695
Deterred not from achieving what might lead
To happier life, knowledge of good and evil?
Of good, how just! Of evil – if what is evil
Be real, why not known, since easier shunned?
God therefore cannot hurt ye, and be just;   700
Not just, not God; not feared then, nor obeyed;

680 science] knowledge.
687 To] as well as.

Your fear itself of death removes the fear.
Why then was this forbid? Why but to awe,
Why but to keep ye low and ignorant,
His worshippers? He knows that in the day   705
Ye eat thereof your eyes that seem so clear,
Yet are but dim, shall perfectly be then
Opened and cleared, and ye shall be as gods,
Knowing both good and evil, as they know.
That ye should be as gods, since I as man,   710
Internal man, is but proportion meet —
I, of brute, human; ye, of human, gods.
So ye shall die perhaps, by putting off
Human, to put on gods — death to be wished,
Though threatened, which no worse than this can bring.
And what are gods, that man may not become   716
As they, participating godlike food?
The gods are first, and that advantage use
On our belief, that all from them proceeds;
I question it, for this fair earth I see,   720
Warmed by the sun, producing every kind,
Them nothing; if they all things, who enclosed
Knowledge of good and evil in this tree,
That whoso eats thereof forthwith attains
Wisdom without their leave? And wherein lies   725
The offence, that man should thus attain to know?
What can your knowledge hurt him, or this tree
Impart against his will, if all be his?
Or is it envy? And can envy dwell
In heavenly breasts? These, these and many more   730
Causes import your need of this fair fruit.
Goddess humane, reach then, and freely taste.'
     He ended, and his words, replete with guile,
Into her heart too easy entrance won;
Fixed on the fruit she gazed, which to behold   735
Might tempt alone; and in her ears the sound
Yet rung of his persuasive words, impregned
With reason, to her seeming, and with truth;
Meanwhile the hour of noon drew on, and waked
An eager appetite, raised by the smell   740
So savoury of that fruit, which with desire,

713-14] parodies a common N.T. metaphor (e.g. Eph. iv. 22-4, Col. iii. 1-10).
717 participating] partaking of.
722 they all] i.e. they produce all.
731 import] involve as a consequence.
732 humane] means both 'human' and 'gracious'.

Inclinable now grown to touch or taste,
Solicited her longing eye; yet first,
Pausing a while, thus to herself she mused:
    'Great are thy virtues, doubtless, best of fruits   745
Though kept from man, and worthy to be admired,
Whose taste, too long forborne, at first assay
Gave elocution to the mute, and taught
The tongue not made for speech to speak thy praise;
Thy praise he also who forbids thy use   750
Conceals not from us, naming thee the tree
Of knowledge, knowledge both of good and evil;
Forbids us then to taste; but his forbidding
Commends thee more, while it infers the good
By thee communicated, and our want;   755
For good unknown sure is not had, or had
And yet unknown, is as not had at all.
In plain, then, what forbids he but to know?
Forbids us good, forbids us to be wise!
Such prohibitions bind not. But, if death   760
Bind us with after-bands, what profits then
Our inward freedom? In the day we eat
Of this fair fruit, our doom is we shall die.
How dies the serpent? He hath eaten, and lives,
And knows, and speaks, and reasons, and discerns,   765
Irrational till then. For us alone
Was death invented? Or to us denied
This intellectual food, for beasts reserved?
For beasts it seems; yet that one beast which first
Hath tasted envies not, but brings with joy   770
The good befallen him, author unsuspect,
Friendly to man, far from deceit or guile.
What fear I, then? Rather, what know to fear
Under this ignorance of good and evil,
Of God or death, of law or penalty?   775
Here grows the cure of all, this fruit divine,
Fair to the eye, inviting to the taste,
Of virtue to make wise; what hinders, then,
To reach, and feed at once both body and mind?'
    So saying, her rash hand in evil hour   780
Forth reaching to the fruit, she plucked, she ate;
Earth felt the wound, and nature from her seat,
Sighing through all her works, gave signs of woe
That all was lost. Back to the thicket slunk

758 In plain] plainly.
771² author unsuspect] authority not subject to suspicion.

The guilty serpent, and well might, for Eve,   785
Intent now only on her taste, naught else
Regarded; such delight till then, as seemed,
In fruit she never tasted, whether true,
Or fancied so through expectation high
Of knowledge; nor was godhead from her thought.   790
Greedily she engorged without restraint,
And knew not eating death; satiate at length,
And heightened as with wine, jocund and boon,
Thus to herself she pleasingly began:
      'O sovereign, virtuous, precious of all trees   795
In Paradise, of operation blest
To sapience, hitherto obscured, infamed,
And thy fair fruit let hang, as to no end
Created; but henceforth my early care,
Not without song, each morning, and due praise,   800
Shall tend thee, and the fertile burden ease
Of thy full branches, offered free to all;
Till dieted by thee I grow mature
In knowledge, as the gods who all things know;
Though others envy what they cannot give –   805
For had the gift been theirs, it had not here
Thus grown. Experience, next to thee I owe,
Best guide: not following thee, I had remained
In ignorance; thou open'st wisdom's way,
And giv'st access, though secret she retire.   810
And I perhaps am secret: heaven is high –
High, and remote to see from thence distinct
Each thing on earth; and other care perhaps
May have diverted from continual watch
Our great forbidder, safe with all his spies   815
About him. But to Adam in what sort
Shall I appear? Shall I to him make known
As yet my change, and give him to partake
Full happiness with me, or rather not,
But keep the odds of knowledge in my power   820
Without copartner? So to add what wants
In female sex, the more to draw his love,
And render me more equal, and perhaps –

792 eating] i.e. that she was eating. The phrase imitates a Greek construction in
      which the verb 'to know' is followed by a participle (in the nominative)
      without repetition of subject.
795 virtuous, precious] most virtuous, most precious; in Greek and Latin the
      positive can stand for the superlative.
811–13] Job xxii. 13–14, Psalms x. 11, xciv. 7.
815 safe] unlikely to intervene, not at present dangerous.

A thing not undesirable – sometime
Superior; for, inferior, who is free?   825
This may be well; but what if God have seen,
And death ensue? Then I shall be no more;
And Adam, wedded to another Eve,
Shall live with her enjoying, I extinct;
A death to think. Confirmed, then, I resolve   830
Adam shall share with me in bliss or woe;
So dear I love him that with him all deaths
I could endure, without him live no life.'
    So saying, from the tree her step she turned,
But first low reverence done, as to the power   835
That dwelt within, whose presence had infused
Into the plant sciential sap, derived
From nectar, drink of gods. Adam the while,
Waiting desirous her return, had wove
Of choicest flowers a garland to adorn   840
Her tresses, and her rural labours crown,
As reapers oft are wont their harvest queen.
Great joy he promised to his thoughts, and new
Solace in her return, so long delayed;
Yet oft his heart, divine of something ill,   845
Misgave him; he the faltering measure felt,
And forth to meet her went, the way she took
That morn when first they parted; by the tree
Of knowledge he must pass; there he her met,
Scarce from the tree returning; in her hand   850
A bough of fairest fruit, that downy smiled,
New gathered, and ambrosial smell diffused.
To him she hasted; in her face excuse
Came prologue, and apology to prompt,
Which with bland words at will, she thus addressed: 855
    'Hast thou not wondered, Adam, at my stay?
Thee I have missed, and thought it long, deprived
Thy presence – agony of love till now
Not felt, nor shall be twice; for never more
Mean I to try, what rash untried I sought,   860
The pain of absence from thy sight. But strange
Hath been the cause, and wonderful to hear;

832-3] Horace, *Odes* III. ix. 24.
837 sciential] infused with knowledge.
838-41] Cf. *Iliad* xxii 437 ff.
845 divine] diviner.
846 measure] i.e. his heartbeat.
854 apology] defence (not an expression of regret).

This tree is not, as we are told, a tree
Of danger tasted, nor to evil unknown
Opening the way, but of divine effect   865
To open eyes, and make them gods who taste;
And hath been tasted such; the serpent wise,
Or not restrained as we, or not obeying,
Hath eaten of the fruit, and is become
Not dead, as we are threatened, but thenceforth   870
Endued with human voice and human sense,
Reasoning to admiration, and with me
Persuasively hath so prevailed that I
Have also tasted, and have also found
The effects to correspond – opener mine eyes,   875
Dim erst, dilated spirits, ampler heart,
And growing up to godhead; which for thee
Chiefly I sought, without thee can despise.
For bliss, as thou hast part, to me is bliss;
Tedious, unshared with thee, and odious soon.   880
Thou therefore also taste, that equal lot
May join us, equal joy, as equal love;
Lest thou not tasting, different degree
Disjoin us, and I then too late renounce
Deity for thee, when fate will not permit.'   885
    Thus Eve with countenance blithe her story
        told;
But in her cheek distemper flushing glowed.
On the other side, Adam, soon as he heard
The fatal trespass done by Eve, amazed,
Astonied stood and blank, while horror chill   890
Ran through his veins, and all his joints relaxed.
From his slack hand the garland wreathed for Eve
Down dropped, and all the faded roses shed;
Speechless he stood and paie, till thus at length
First to himself he inward silence broke: 895
    'O fairest of creation, last and best
Of all God's works, creature in whom excelled
Whatever can to sight or thought be formed,
Holy, divine, good, amiable, or sweet!
How art thou lost, how on a sudden lost,   900

864 tasted] if tasted.
887 distemper] an imbalance of the humours, or (possibly) intoxication
    (cf. l. 793).
890 Astonied] dazed, dismayed.
    blank] means both 'speechless' and 'pale' (cf. l. 894).
892-3] Cf. Statius, Thebaid vii. 148-50.

Defaced, deflowered, and now to death devote?
Rather, how hast thou yielded to transgress
The strict forbiddance, how to violate
The sacred fruit forbidden? Some cursed fraud
Of enemy hath beguiled thee, yet unknown,   905
And me with thee hath ruined; for with thee
Certain my resolution is to die;
How can I live without thee, how forgo
Thy sweet converse, and love so dearly joined,
To live again in these wild woods forlorn?   910
Should God create another Eve, and I
Another rib afford, yet loss of thee
Would never from my heart; no, no, I feel
The link of nature draw me: flesh of flesh,
Bone of my bone thou art, and from thy state   915
Mine never shall be parted, bliss or woe.'
    So having said, as one from sad dismay
Recomforted, and after thoughts disturbed
Submitting to what seemed remediless,
Thus in calm mood his words to Eve he turned: 920
    'Bold deed thou hast presumed, adventurous Eve,
And peril great provoked, who thus hast dared
Had it been only coveting to eye
That sacred food, sacred to abstinence;
Much more to taste it, under ban to touch.   925
But past who can recall, or done undo?
Not God omnipotent, nor fate; yet so
Perhaps thou shalt not die; perhaps the fact
Is not so heinous now – foretasted fruit,
Profaned first by the serpent, by him first   930
Made common and unhallowed ere our taste,
Nor yet on him found deadly; he yet lives –
Lives, as thou saidst, and gains to live, as man,
Higher degree of life: inducement strong
To us, as likely tasting to attain   935
Proportional ascent, which cannot be
But to be gods, or angels, demi-gods.
Nor can I think that God, creator wise,
Though threatening, will in earnest so destroy
Us, his prime creatures, dignified so high,   940
Set over all his works; which in our fall,
For us created, needs with us must fail,
Dependent made; so God shall uncreate,

901 devote] doomed.
928 fact] evil deed.

Be frustrate, do, undo, and labour loose –
Not well conceived of God, who though his power   945
Creation could repeat, yet would be loath
Us to abolish, lest the adversary
Triumph and say: "Fickle their state whom God
Most favours; who can please him long? Me first
He ruined, now mankind; whom will he next?" –   950
Matter of scorn not to be given the foe;
However, I with thee have fixed my lot,
Certain to undergo like doom; if death
Consort with thee, death is to me as life;
So forcible within my heart I feel   955
The bond of nature draw me to my own –
My own in thee, for what thou art is mine;
Our state cannot be severed; we are one,
One flesh; to lose thee were to lose myself.'
    So Adam; and thus Eve to him replied: 960
'O glorious trial of exceeding love,
Illustrious evidence, example high!
Engaging me to emulate; but, short
Of thy perfection, how shall I attain,
Adam, from whose dear side I boast me sprung,   965
And gladly of our union hear thee speak,
One heart, one soul in both? Whereof good proof
This day affords, declaring thee resolved,
Rather than death, or aught than death more dread,
Shall separate us, linked in love so dear,   970
To undergo with me one guilt, one crime,
If any be, of tasting this fair fruit;
Whose virtue – for of good still good proceeds,
Direct, or by occasion – hath presented
This happy trial of thy love, which else   975
So eminently never had been known.
Were it I thought death menaced would ensue
This my attempt, I would sustain alone
The worst, and not persuade thee – rather die
Deserted than oblige thee with a fact   980
Pernicious to thy peace, chiefly assured

944 labour loose] means either 'undo labour already performed' or 'lose labour'.
947–8] Deut. xxxii. 27; on 'adversary' see I 82n.
953 Certain] resolved.
976 eminently] According to a scholastic tradition which survived in Reforma-
    tion theology God was said to possess the excellencies of human character –
    in this case love – not 'formally', as animals possess them, but 'eminently',
    i.e. in a higher sense. Eve's use of the word is thus blasphemous.
980 oblige] make subject to a penalty.

Remarkably so late of thy so true,
So faithful, love unequalled; but I feel
Far otherwise the event – not death, but life
Augmented, opened eyes, new hopes, new joys,   985
Taste so divine that what of sweet before
Hath touched my sense flat seems to this and
        harsh.
On my experience, Adam, freely taste,
And fear of death deliver to the winds.'
        So saying, she embraced him, and for joy   990
Tenderly wept, much won that he his love
Had so ennobled, as of choice to incur
Divine displeasure for her sake, or death.
In recompense (for such compliance bad
Such recompense best merits), from the bough   995
She gave him of that fair enticing fruit
With liberal hand; he scrupled not to eat,
Against his better knowledge, not deceived,
But fondly overcome with female charm.
Earth trembled from her entrails, as again   1000
In pangs, and nature gave a second groan;
Sky loured, and muttering thunder, some sad drops
Wept at completing of the mortal sin
Original; while Adam took no thought,
Eating his fill, nor Eve to iterate   1005
Her former trespass feared, the more to soothe
Him with her loved society; that now,
As with new wine intoxicated both,
They swim in mirth, and fancy that they feel
Divinity within them breeding wings   1010
Wherewith to scorn the earth; but that false fruit
Far other operation first displayed,
Carnal desire inflaming; he on Eve
Began to cast lascivious eyes, she him
As wantonly repaid; in lust they burn,   1015
Till Adam thus 'gan Eve to dalliance move:
        'Eve, now I see thou art exact of taste
And elegant – of sapience no small part;
Since to each meaning savour we apply,

984 event] outcome, consequence.
998–9] I Tim. ii. 14.
1003–4] Original sin is the theological doctrine according to which the sin of
        Adam was transmitted to all his descendants.
1017–20] Cf. 442–3n. for the play on 'sapience'. 'Savour' refers to both taste
        and perception (cf. V 84n.).

And palate call judicious; I the praise   1020
Yield thee, so well this day thou hast purveyed.
Much pleasure we have lost, while we abstained
From this delightful fruit, nor known till now
True relish, tasting; if such pleasure be
In things to us forbidden, it might be wished   1025
For this one tree had been forbidden ten.
But come; so well refreshed, now let us play,
As meet is, after such delicious fare;
For never did thy beauty since the day
I saw thee first and wedded thee, adorned   1030
With all perfections, so inflame my sense
With ardour to enjoy thee, fairer now
Than ever – bounty of this virtuous tree.'
     So said he, and forbore not glance or toy
Of amorous intent, well understood   1035
Of Eve, whose eye darted contagious fire.
Her hand he seized, and to a shady bank
Thick overhead with verdant roof embowered
He led her, nothing loath; flowers were the couch,
Pansies, and violets, and asphodel,   1040
And hyacinth – earth's freshest, softest lap.
There they their fill of love and love's disport
Took largely, of their mutual guilt the seal,
The solace of their sin, till dewy sleep
Oppressed them, wearied with their amorous play.   1045
     Soon as the force of that fallacious fruit,
That with exhilarating vapour bland
About their spirits had played, and inmost powers
Made err, was now exhaled, and grosser sleep,
Bred of unkindly fumes, with conscious dreams   1050
Encumbered, now had left them, up they rose
As from unrest, and each the other viewing,
Soon found their eyes how opened, and their minds
How darkened; innocence, that as a veil
Had shadowed them from knowing ill, was gone;   1055
Just confidence, and native righteousness
And honour, from about them, naked left
To guilty shame: he covered, but his robe

1029-33] Cf. *Iliad* iii 442 ff., xiv 292 ff.
1034 toy] caressing.
1037] Cf. IV 321n.
1042-4] Prov. vii., esp. v. 18.
1050 unkindly fumes] unnatural vapours. Cf. V 5.
     conscious] Cf. VI 521n.

Uncovered more; so rose the Danite strong,
Herculean Samson, from the harlot-lap   1060
Of Philistean Dalila, and waked
Shorn of his strength; they destitute and bare
Of all their virtue; silent, and in face
Confounded, long they sat, as stricken mute,
Till Adam, though not less than Eve abashed,   1065
At length gave utterance to these words constrained:
    'O Eve, in evil hour thou didst give ear
To that false worm, of whomsoever taught
To counterfeit man's voice – true in our fall,
False in our promised rising; since our eyes   1070
Opened we find indeed, and find we know
Both good and evil, good lost and evil got:
Bad fruit of knowledge, if this be to know,
Which leaves us naked thus, of honour void,
Of innocence, of faith, of purity,   1075
Our wonted ornaments now soiled and stained,
And in our faces evident the signs
Of foul concupiscence; whence evil store,
Even shame, the last of evils; of the first
Be sure then. How shall I behold the face   1080
Henceforth of God or angel, erst with joy
And rapture so oft beheld? Those heavenly shapes
Will dazzle now this earthly with their blaze
Insufferably bright. O might I here
In solitude live savage, in some glade   1085
Obscured, where highest woods, impenetrable
To star or sunlight, spread their umbrage broad,
And brown as evening; cover me, ye pines;
Ye cedars, with innumerable boughs
Hide me, where I may never see them more.   1090
But let us now, as in bad plight, devise
What best may, for the present, serve to hide
The parts of each from other that seem most
To shame obnoxious, and unseemliest seen –   1094
Some tree, whose broad smooth leaves together sewed,
And girded on our loins, may cover round
Those middle parts, that this new comer, shame,
There sit not, and reproach us as unclean.'
    So counselled he, and both together went

1059–62] Judges xvi. Samson is a Danite because his father Manoah was 'of the
    family of the Danites' (Judges xiii. 2); on Dalila as Philistine see *SA* 216n.
1090 them] the 'shapes' of l. 1082.
1094 obnoxious] liable (Cf. *SA* 106).

Into the thickest wood; there soon they choose   1100
The fig-tree – not that kind for fruit renowned,
But such as at this day to Indians known,
In Malabar or Decan spreads her arms
Branching so broad and long that in the ground
The bended twigs take root, and daughters grow   1105
About the mother tree, a pillared shade
High overarched, and echoing walks between:
There oft the Indian herdsman, shunning heat,
Shelters in cool, and tends his pasturing herds
At loop-holes cut through thickest shade; those leaves
They gathered, broad as Amazonian targe,   1111
And with what skill they had together sewed,
To gird their waist – vain covering, if to hide
Their guilt and dreaded shame; O how unlike
To that first naked glory! Such of late   1115
Columbus found the American, so girt
With feathered cincture, naked else and wild,
Among the trees on isles and woody shores.
Thus fenced, and as they thought, their shame in part
Covered, but not at rest or ease of mind,   1120
They sat them down to weep; nor only tears
Rained at their eyes, but high winds worse within
Began to rise, high passions – anger, hate,
Mistrust, suspicion, discord – and shook sore
Their inward state of mind, calm region once   1125
And full of peace, now tossed and turbulent:
For understanding ruled not, and the will
Heard not her lore, both in subjection now
To sensual appetite, who from beneath
Usurping over sovereign reason, claimed   1130
Superior sway; from thus distempered breast
Adam, estranged in look and altered style,
Speech intermitted thus to Eve renewed:
    'Would thou hadst hearkened to my words, and stayed
With me, as I besought thee, when that strange   1135
Desire of wandering, this unhappy morn,
I know not whence possessed thee; we had then
Remained still happy – not, as now, despoiled

1102] refers to the banyan, or Indian fig tree (*ficus religiosa*).
1103 Malabar] (modern Kerala) is on the south-west coast of India; Decan is the
    Indian peninsula.
1111 Amazonian targe] the crescent-shaped shield of the Amazons, a mythical
    race of warrior women.
1121] Psalm cxxxvii. 1.

Of all our good, shamed, naked, miserable.
Let none henceforth seek needless cause to approve   1140
The faith they owe; when earnestly they seek
Such proof, conclude they then begin to fail.'
      To whom, soon moved with touch of blame, thus Eve:
'What words have passed thy lips, Adam severe?
Imput'st thou that to my default, or will   1145
Of wandering, as thou call'st it, which who knows
But might as ill have happened thou being by,
Or to thyself perhaps? Hadst thou been there,
Or here the attempt, thou couldst not have discerned
Fraud in the serpent, speaking as he spake;   1150
No ground of enmity between us known,
Why he should mean me ill or seek to harm;
Was I to have never parted from thy side?
As good have grown there still a lifeless rib.
Being as I am, why didst not thou the head   1155
Command me absolutely not to go,
Going into such danger, as thou saidst?
Too facile then, thou didst not much gainsay,
Nay didst permit, approve, and fair dismiss.
Hadst thou been firm and fixed in thy dissent,   1160
Neither had I transgressed, nor thou with me.'
      To whom, then first incensed, Adam replied:
'Is this the love, is this the recompense
Of mine to thee, ingrateful Eve, expressed
Immutable when thou wert lost, not I –   1165
Who might have lived, and joyed immortal bliss,
Yet willingly chose rather death with thee?
And am I now upbraided as the cause
Of thy transgressing? Not enough severe,
It seems, in thy restraint; what could I more?   1170
I warned thee, I admonished thee, foretold
The danger, and the lurking enemy
That lay in wait; beyond this had been force,
And force upon free will hath here no place.
But confidence then bore thee on, secure   1175
Either to meet no danger, or to find
Matter of glorious trial; and perhaps

1140 approve] prove.
1141 owe] means both 'owe' and 'own'.
1144] *Iliad* xiv 83.
1155 head] I Cor. xi. 3.
1175 confidence, secure] both words mean 'overconfident'.
1177 Matter] pretext, occasion.

I also erred in overmuch admiring
What seemed in thee so perfect that I thought
No evil durst attempt thee; but I rue   1180
That error now, which is become my crime,
And thou the accuser. Thus it shall befall
Him who to worth in women overtrusting,
Lets her will rule: restraint she will not brook,
And left to herself, if evil thence ensue,   1185
She first his weak indulgence will accuse.'
    Thus they in mutual accusation spent
The fruitless hours, but neither self-condemning;
And of their vain contest appeared no end.

THE END OF THE NINTH BOOK

BOOK X

THE ARGUMENT

Man's transgression known, the guardian angels forsake Paradise, and return up to heaven to approve their vigilance, and are approved; God declaring that the entrance of Satan could not be by them prevented. He sends his Son to judge the transgressors; who descends, and gives sentence accordingly; then, in pity, clothes them both, and reascends. Sin and Death sitting till then at the gates of hell, by wondrous sympathy feeling the success of Satan in this new world, and the sin by man there committed, resolve to sit no longer confined in hell, but to follow Satan, their sire, up to the place of man: to make the way easier from hell to this world to and fro, they pave a broad highway or bridge over chaos, according to the track that Satan first made; then, preparing for earth, they meet him, proud of his success, returning to hell; their mutual gratulation. Satan arrives at Pandemonium; in full assembly relates, with boasting, his success against man; instead of applause is entertained with a general hiss by all his audience, transformed, with himself also, suddenly into serpents, according to his doom given in Paradise; then, deluded with a show of the forbidden tree springing up before them, they, greedily reaching to take of the fruit, chew dust and bitter ashes. The proceedings of Sin and Death: God foretells the final victory of his Son over them, and the renewing of all things; but, for the present, commands his angels to make several alterations in the heavens and elements. Adam, more and more perceiving his fallen condition, heavily bewails, rejects the condolement of Eve; she persists, and at length appeases him: then, to evade the curse likely to fall on their offspring, proposes to Adam violent ways which he approves not, but, conceiving better hope, puts her in mind of the late promise made them, that her seed should be revenged on the serpent, and exhorts her, with him, to seek peace of the offended Deity by repentance and supplication.

Meanwhile the heinous and despiteful act
Of Satan done in Paradise, and how
He in the serpent, had perverted Eve,
Her husband she, to taste the fatal fruit,
Was known in heaven; for what can scape the eye   5
Of God all-seeing, or deceive his heart
Omniscient, who, in all things wise and just,
Hindered not Satan to attempt the mind
Of man, with strength entire and free will armed,
Complete to have discovered and repulsed   10
Whatever wiles of foe or seeming friend.

10 Complete] fully equipped or endowed (modifies 'mind').

For still they knew, and ought to have still remembered,
The high injunction not to taste that fruit,
Whoever tempted; which they not obeying
Incurred – what could they less? – the penalty,   15
And, manifold in sin, deserve to fall.
Up into heaven from Paradise in haste
The angelic guards ascended, mute and sad
For man, for of his state by this they knew,
Much wondering how the subtle fiend had stolen   20
Entrance unseen. Soon as the unwelcome news
From earth arrived at heaven-gate, displeased
All were who heard; dim sadness did not spare
That time celestial visages, yet mixed
With pity, violated not their bliss.   25
About the new-arrived, in multitudes,
The ethereal people ran, to hear and know
How all befell; they towards the throne supreme,
Accountable made haste to make appear
With righteous plea, their utmost vigilance,   30
And easily approved; when the most high,
Eternal Father, from his secret cloud
Amidst, in thunder uttered thus his voice:
     'Assembled angels, and ye powers returned
From unsuccessful charge, be not dismayed   35
Nor troubled at these tidings from the earth,
Which your sincerest care could not prevent,
Foretold so lately what would come to pass,
When first this tempter crossed the gulf from hell.
I told ye then he should prevail, and speed   40
On his bad errand – man should be seduced,
And flattered out of all, believing lies
Against his maker; no decree of mine,
Concurring to necessitate his fall,
Or touch with lightest moment of impulse   45
His free will, to her own inclining left
In even scale. But fallen he is; and now
What rests, but that the mortal sentence pass
On his transgression, death denounced that day,
Which he presumes already vain and void,   50

12 still] invariably, always.
19 this] this time.
31 approved] confirmed. Cf. Argument, 'approve their vigilance'.
33] Rev. iv. 5.
40 speed] attain his purpose.
48 rests] remains.
49-52] See VIII 330-1n.

Because not yet inflicted, as he feared,
By some immediate stroke, but soon shall find
Forbearance no acquittance ere day end.
Justice shall not return, as bounty, scorned.
But whom send I to judge them? Whom but thee,   55
Vicegerent Son? To thee I have transferred
All judgement, whether in heaven, or earth, or hell.
Easy it may be seen that I intend
Mercy colleague with justice, sending thee,
Man's friend, his mediator, his designed   60
Both ransom and redeemer voluntary,
And destined man himself to judge man fallen.'
  So spake the Father, and unfolding bright
Toward the right hand his glory, on the Son
Blazed forth unclouded deity; he full   65
Resplendent all his Father manifest
Expressed, and thus divinely answered mild:
  'Father Eternal, thine is to decree;
Mine both in heaven and earth to do thy will
Supreme, that thou in me, thy Son beloved,   70
May'st ever rest well pleased. I go to judge
On earth these thy transgressors; but thou know'st,
Whoever judged, the worst on me must light,
When time shall be; for so I undertook
Before thee, and, not repenting, this obtain   75
Of right, that I may mitigate their doom
On me derived; yet I shall temper so
Justice with mercy as may illustrate most
Them fully satisfied, and thee appease.
Attendance none shall need, nor train, where none   80
Are to behold the judgement but the judged,
Those two; the third best absent is condemned,
Convict by flight, and rebel to all law;
Conviction to the serpent none belongs.'
  Thus saying, from his radiant seat he rose   85
Of high collateral glory; him thrones and powers,
Princedoms, and dominations ministrant,
Accompanied to heaven-gate, from whence
Eden and all the coast in prospect lay.
Down he descended straight; the speed of gods   90
Time counts not, though with swiftest minutes winged.

56–7] John v. 22.
70–1] Matt. iii. 17, xii. 18.
77 derived] diverted.
79 Them] justice and mercy.

Now was the sun in western cadence low
From noon, and gentle airs due at their hour
To fan the earth now waked, and usher in
The evening cool, when he, from wrath more cool,   95
Came, the mild judge and intercessor both,
To sentence man; the voice of God they heard
Now walking in the garden, by soft winds
Brought to their ears, while day declined; they heard,
And from his presence hid themselves among   100
The thickest trees, both man and wife, till God,
Approaching, thus to Adam called aloud:
    'Where art thou, Adam, wont with joy to meet
My coming, seen far off? I miss thee here,
Not pleased, thus entertained with solitude,   105
Where obvious duty erewhile apeared unsought;
Or come I less conspicuous, or what change
Absents thee, or what chance detains? Come forth.'
    He came, and with him Eve, more loath, though first
To offend, discountenanced both, and discomposed;   110
Love was not in their looks, either to God
Or to each other, but apparent guilt,
And shame, and perturbation, and despair,
Anger, and obstinacy, and hate, and guile.
Whence Adam, faltering long, thus answered brief: 115
    'I heard thee in the garden, and of thy voice
Afraid, being naked, hid myself.' To whom
The gracious judge, without revile, replied:
    'My voice thou oft hast heard, and hast not feared,
But still rejoiced; how is it now become   120
So dreadful to thee? That thou art naked, who
Hath told thee? Hast thou eaten of the tree
Whereof I gave thee charge thou shouldst not eat?'
To whom thus Adam, sore beset, replied:
    'O heaven! In evil strait this day I stand   125
Before my judge – either to undergo
Myself the total crime, or to accuse
My other self, the partner of my life,
Whose failing, while her faith to me remains,
I should conceal, and not expose to blame   130

92 cadence] used in the Latin sense of 'falling, sinking down'.
98 soft winds] The A.V. marginal note to Gen. iii. 8 proposes 'wind' instead of
    'cool' and the Vulgate has *aura* (gentle breeze).
106 obvious] coming in the way (i.e. to meet).
112 apparent] evident.
128 other self] see VIII 450n.

By my complaint; but strict necessity
Subdues me, and calamitous constraint,
Lest on my head both sin and punishment,
However insupportable, be all
Devolved; though should I hold my peace, yet thou   135
Wouldst easily detect what I conceal.
This woman, whom thou mad'st to be my help,
And gav'st me as thy perfect gift, so good,
So fit, so acceptable, so divine,
That from her hand I could suspect no ill,   140
And what she did, whatever in itself,
Her doing seemed to justify the deed –
She gave me of the tree, and I did eat.'
To whom the sovereign presence thus replied:
     'Was she thy God, that her thou didst obey   145
Before his voice, or was she made thy guide,
Superior, or but equal, that to her
Thou didst resign thy manhood, and the place
Wherein God set thee above her, made of thee
And for thee, whose perfection far excelled   150
Hers in all real dignity? Adorned
She was indeed, and lovely, to attract
Thy love, not thy subjection; and her gifts
Were such as under government well seemed –
Unseemly to bear rule, which was thy part   155
And person, hadst thou known thyself aright.'
     So having said, he thus to Eve in few:
'Say, woman, what is this which thou hast done?'
     To whom sad Eve, with shame nigh overwhelmed,
Confessing soon, yet not before her judge   160
Bold or loquacious, thus abashed replied:
'The serpent me beguiled, and I did eat.'
     Which when the Lord God heard, without delay
To judgement he proceeded on the accused
Serpent, though brute, unable, to transfer   165
The guilt on him who made him instrument
Of mischief, and polluted from the end
Of his creation – justly then accursed,
As vitiated in nature; more to know
Concerned not man (since he no further knew),   170
Nor altered his offence; yet God at last

149–50] I Cor. xi. 8–9.
151 real] royal.
156 person] rôle.
157 few] few words.

To Satan, first in sin, his doom applied,
Though in mysterious terms, judged as then best;
And on the serpent thus his curse let fall:
     'Because thou hast done this, thou art accursed   175
Above all cattle, each beast of the field;
Upon thy belly grovelling thou shalt go,
And dust shalt eat all the days of thy life.
Between thee and the woman I will put
Enmity, and between thine and her seed;   180
Her seed shall bruise thy head, thou bruise his heel.'
     So spake this oracle – then verified
When Jesus, son of Mary, second Eve,
Saw Satan fall like lightning down from heaven,
Prince of the air; then rising from his grave,   185
Spoiled principalities and powers, triumphed
In open show, and with ascension bright,
Captivity led captive through the air,
The realm itself of Satan, long usurped,
Whom he shall tread at last under our feet,   190
Even he who now foretold his fatal bruise,
And to the woman thus his sentence turned:
     'Thy sorrow I will greatly multiply
By thy conception; children thou shalt bring
In sorrow forth, and to thy husband's will   195
Thine shall submit; he over thee shall rule.'
     On Adam last thus judgement he pronounced:
'Because thou hast hearkened to the voice of thy wife,
And eaten of the tree concerning which
I charged thee, saying "Thou shalt not eat thereof",   200
Cursed is the ground for thy sake; thou in sorrow
Shalt eat thereof all the days of thy life;
Thorns also and thistles it shall bring thee forth
Unbid, and thou shalt eat the herb of the field;
In the sweat of thy face thou shalt eat bread,   205
Till thou return unto the ground; for thou

183 Mary, second Eve] a common Patristic idea, often illustrated in the middle
    ages by the conceit that the Latin form of her name (*Eva*) spelt backwards
    was the first word (*Ave*) of the angel's address to Mary.
184] Luke x. 18.
185] Eph. ii. 2.
186–7] Col. ii. 14–15.
188] Psalm lxviii. 18, Eph. iv. 8.
189–90] Rom. xvi. 20. See the A.V. marginal note, which proposes 'tread'
    instead of 'bruise', presumably reflecting an uneasiness which Milton may
    have shared about the precise meaning of the word translated as 'bruise' in
    Gen. iii. 15.

Out of the ground wast taken: know thy birth,
For dust thou art, and shalt to dust return.'
    So judged he man, both judge and saviour sent,
And the instant stroke of death, denounced that day,   210
Removed far off; then pitying how they stood
Before him naked to the air, that now
Must suffer change, disdained not to begin
Thenceforth the form of servant to assume;
As when he washed his servants' feet, so now,   215
As father of his family, he clad
Their nakedness with skins of beasts, or slain,
Or as the snake, with youthful coat repaid;
And thought not much to clothe his enemies;
Nor he their outward only with the skins   220
Of beasts, but inward nakedness, much more
Opprobrious, with his robe of righteousness
Arraying, covered from his Father's sight.
To him with swift ascent he up returned,
Into his blissful bosom reassumed   225
In glory as of old; to him, appeased,
All, though all-knowing, what had passed with man
Recounted, mixing intercession sweet.
    Meanwhile, ere thus was sinned and judged on earth,
Within the gates of hell sat Sin and Death,   230
In counterview within the gates, that now
Stood open wide, belching outrageous flame
Far into chaos, since the fiend passed through,
Sin opening; who thus now to Death began:
    'O son, why sit we here, each other viewing   235
Idly, while Satan our great author thrives
In other worlds, and happier seat provides
For us, his offspring dear? It cannot be
But that success attends him; if mishap,
Ere this he had returned, with fury driven   240
By his avengers, since no place like this
Can fit his punishment, or their revenge.

210-11] See VIII 330-1n.; 'denounced' means 'proclaimed in the manner of a
    warning'.
214] Phil. ii. 7.
215] John xiii. 5.
216] Heb. ii. 13.
217-18 or ... or] either ... or.
222] Isa. lxi. 10.
232 outrageous] enormous, raging.
235] II Kings vii. 3.
236 author] begetter.

Methinks I feel new strength within me rise,
Wings growing, and dominion given me large
Beyond this deep – whatever draws me on,   245
Or sympathy, or some connatural force,
Powerful at greatest distance to unite
With secret amity things of like kind
By secretest conveyance. Thou, my shade
Inseparable, must with me along;   250
For Death from Sin no power can separate.
But, lest the difficulty of passing back
Stay his return perhaps over this gulf
Impassable, impervious, let us try
Adventurous work – yet to thy power and mine   255
Not unagreeable – to found a path
Over this main from hell to that new world
Where Satan now prevails: a monument
Of merit high to all the infernal host,
Easing their passage hence, for intercourse   260
Or transmigration, as their lot shall lead.
Nor can I miss the way, so strongly drawn
By this new-felt attraction and instinct.'
    Whom thus the meagre shadow answered soon:
'Go whither fate and inclination strong   265
Leads thee; I shall not lag behind, nor err
The way, thou leading: such a scent I draw
Of carnage, prey innumerable, and taste
The savour of death from all things there that live;
Nor shall I to the work thou enterprisest   270
Be wanting, but afford thee equal aid.'
    So saying, with delight he snuffed the smell
Of mortal change on earth. As when a flock
Of ravenous fowl, though many a league remote,
Against the day of battle, to a field   275
Where armies lie encamped come flying, lured
With scent of living carcasses designed
For death the following day in bloody fight;
So scented the grim feature, and upturned
His nostril wide into the murky air,   280
Sagacious of his quarry from so far.
Then both from out hell gates into the waste

257 main] sea (i.e. chaos).
260-1 intercourse/Or transmigration] travel between two places, either both
      ways ('intercourse') or one way ('transmigration').
266 err] mistake.
281 Sagacious] acute in olfactory perception.

Wide anarchy of chaos, damp and dark,
Flew diverse, and with power (their power was great)
Hovering upon the waters, what they met   285
Solid or slimy, as in raging sea
Tossed up and down, together crowded drove,
From each side shoaling, towards the mouth of hell;
As when two polar winds, blowing adverse
Upon the Cronian sea, together drive   290
Mountains of ice, that stop the imagined way
Beyond Petsora eastward to the rich
Cathaian coast. The aggregated soil
Death with his mace petrific, cold and dry,
As with a trident smote, and fixed as firm   295
As Delos, floating once; the rest his look
Bound with Gorgonian rigour not to move,
And with asphaltic slime; broad as the gate,
Deep to the roots of hell the gathered beach
They fastened, and the mole immense wrought on   300
Over the foaming deep high-arched, a bridge
Of length prodigious, joining to the wall
Immovable of this now fenceless world,
Forfeit to Death – from hence a passage broad,
Smooth, easy, inoffensive, down to hell.   305
So, if great things to small may be compared,

288 shoaling] assembling in shoals.
290 Cronian sea] The Arctic Ocean.
291 the imagined way] the north-east passage.
292 Petsora] Pechora, a river in northern Russia.
294 petrific] having the power to petrify.
296 Delos] See V 264–5n. Delos was created as a floating island by Neptune,
    and later anchored by Jove to provide a place for Latona to give birth to
    her twins (see *Sonnet* XII 5–7n.).
297] On Gorgonian see *Comus* 447–52n.; 'rigour' means 'stiffness, hardness'.
298 asphaltic slime] 'Asphaltic' renders the LXX of Gen. xi. 3 (ἄσφαλτος);
    'slime' is the A.V. reading. The Vulgate says *bitumen*, which Milton uses in
    XII 41.
299 gathered beach] assembled ridge of stone.
300 mole] a stone causeway.
302 wall] the 'orb' of II 1029, and the 'firm ... globe' of III 418.
303 fenceless] defenceless.
305 inoffensive] used in the Latin sense of 'free from hindrance, uninterrupted'.
306–11] Xerxes, King of Persia, was the son of Darius, who had built his palace
    in Susa (now Shush, in Iran), a city associated by Aeschylus and Herodotus
    with Memnon (on whom see *Penseroso* 18n.). In 480 BC Xerxes began his
    preparations for a punitive invasion of Greece by building a bridge across
    the Hellespont (the modern Dardanelles); when this bridge was swept away
    by a storm, Xerxes ordered the sea to be scourged.

Xerxes, the liberty of Greece to yoke,
From Susa, his Memnonian palace high,
Came to the sea, and over Hellespont
Bridging his way, Europe with Asia joined,   310
And scourged with many a stroke the indignant waves.
Now had they brought the work by wondrous art
Pontifical – a ridge of pendant rock
Over the vexed abyss, following the track
Of Satan, to the self-same place where he   315
First lighted from his wing and landed safe
From out of chaos – to the outside bare
Of this round world; with pins of adamant
And chains they made all fast, too fast they made
And durable; and now in little space   320
The confines met of empyrean heaven
And of this world, and on the left hand hell,
With long reach interposed; three several ways
In sight to each of these three places led.
And now their way to earth they had descried,   325
To Paradise first tending, when, behold
Satan, in likeness of an angel bright,
Betwixt the Centaur and the Scorpion steering
His zenith, while the sun in Aries rose;
Disguised he came, but those his children dear   330
Their parent soon discerned, though in disguise.
He after Eve seduced, unminded slunk
Into the wood fast by, and changing shape
To observe the sequel, saw his guileful act
By Eve, though all unweeting, seconded   335
Upon her husband – saw their shame that sought
Vain covertures; but, when he saw descend
The Son of God to judge them, terrified
He fled, not hoping to escape, but shun
The present – fearing, guilty, what his wrath   340
Might suddenly inflict; that past, returned
By night, and, listening where the hapless pair
Sat in their sad discourse and various plaint,
Thence gathered his own doom, which understood
Not instant, but of future time, with joy   345
And tidings fraught, to hell he now returned,

---

313 Pontifical] Milton plays on the apparent etymology of the word – *pontem*
   (from *pons*, bridge), *-ficus* (making, from *facere*) – and also utilizes the
   ordinary meaning of 'episcopal' or 'popish'.
328-9] The Centaur (Sagittarius), Scorpion, and Aries (the Ram) are respect-
   ively the ninth, eighth, and first signs of the zodiac.

And at the brink of chaos, near the foot
Of this new wondrous pontifice, unhoped
Met who to meet him came, his offspring dear.
Great joy was at their meeting, and at sight   350
Of that stupendous bridge his joy increased.
Long he admiring stood, till Sin, his fair
Enchanting daughter, thus the silence broke:
   'O parent, these are thy magnific deeds,
Thy trophies, which thou view'st as not thine own;   355
Thou art their author and prime architect;
For I no sooner in my heart divined –
My heart, which by a secret harmony
Still moves with thine, joined in connection sweet –
That thou on earth hadst prospered, which thy looks   360
Now also evidence, but straight I felt –
Though distant from thee worlds between, yet felt –
That I must after thee with this thy son;
Such fatal consequence unites us three;
Hell could no longer hold us in her bounds,   365
Nor this unvoyageable gulf obscure
Detain from following thy illustrious track.
Thou hast achieved our liberty, confined
Within hell gates till now; thou us empowered
To fortify thus far, and overlay   370
With this portentous bridge the dark abyss.
Thine now is all this world; thy virtue hath won
What thy hands builded not; thy wisdom gained,
With odds, what war hath lost, and fully avenged
Our foil in heaven; here thou shalt monarch reign,   375
There didst not; there let him still victor sway,
As battle hath adjudged, from this new world
Retiring, by his own doom alienated,
And henceforth monarchy with thee divide
Of all things, parted by the empyreal bounds,   380
His quadrature, from thy orbicular world,
Or try thee now more dangerous to his throne.'
   Whom thus the prince of darkness answered glad:

347 foot] the end of the slope of the bridge.
348 pontifice] means both 'bridge' and 'priest, bishop, pope'.
364 consequence] the relation of a result to its cause.
375 foil] defeat, disgrace. The etymological sense of 'that which is trampled
     under foot' may be relevant in view of Milton's repeated allusions to Gen.
     iii. 15.
378 doom] judgement, condemnation.
381 quadrature] square. See II 1048-50n.
382 try] demonstrate.

'Fair daughter, and thou son and grandchild both,
High proof ye now have given to be the race   385
Of Satan (for I glory in the name,
Antagonist of heaven's almighty king),
Amply have merited of me, of all
The infernal empire, that so near heaven's door
Triumphal with triumphal act have met,   390
Mine with this glorious work, and made one realm
Hell and this world – one realm, one continent
Of easy thoroughfare. Therefore while I
Descend through darkness, on your road with ease,
To my associate powers, them to acquaint   395
With these successes, and with them rejoice,
You two this way, among these numerous orbs,
All yours, right down to Paradise descend;
There dwell and reign in bliss; thence on the earth
Dominion exercise and in the air,   400
Chiefly on man, sole lord of all declared;
Him first make sure your thrall, and lastly kill.
My substitutes I send ye, and create
Plenipotent on earth, of matchless might
Issuing from me; on your joint vigour now   405
My hold of this new kingdom all depends,
Through Sin to Death exposed by my exploit.
If your joint power prevail, the affairs of hell
No detriment need fear; go, and be strong.'
    So saying, he dismissed them; they with speed   410
Their course through thickest constellations held,
Spreading their bane; the blasted stars looked wan,
And planets, planet-strook, real eclipse
Then suffered. The other way Satan went down
The causey to hell gate; on either side   415
Disparted Chaos overbuilt exclaimed,

386-7] See I 82n.
399-402] Rom. v. 12-21.
409 No detriment] alludes to the charge given when the *decretum ultimum* was passed by the Roman Senate in times of national crisis giving the two consuls dictatorial power: *ne quid respublica detrimenti capiat* ('that the state suffer no harm'); cf. *Areopagitica* p. 597.
    be strong] Deut. xxxi. 7.
412-13] 'Blasted' means 'perniciously breathed upon'; malign planets normally 'blasted', and were not themselves the objects of a blast. Similarly, planets 'struck' ('strook'), and were not themselves stricken by malign influence, and eclipses were normally apparent rather than real.
415 causey] causeway.

And with rebounding surge the bars assailed,
That scorned his indignation; through the gate,
Wide open and unguarded, Satan passed,
And all about found desolate; for those   420
Appointed to sit there had left their charge,
Flown to the upper world; the rest were all
Far to the inland retired, about the walls
Of Pandemonium, city and proud seat
Of Lucifer, so by allusion called   425
Of that bright star to Satan paragoned.
There kept their watch the legions, while the grand
In council sat, solicitous what chance
Might intercept their emperor sent; so he
Departing gave command, and they observed.   430
As when the Tartar from his Russian foe,
By Astracan, over the snowy plains,
Retires, or Bactrian sophy, from the horns
Of Turkish crescent, leaves all waste beyond
The realm of Aladule, in his retreat   435
To Tauris or Casbeen; so these, the late
Heaven-banished host, left desert utmost hell
Many a dark league, reduced in careful watch
Round their metropolis, and now expecting
Each hour their great adventurer from the search   440
Of foreign worlds; he through the midst unmarked,
In show plebeian angel militant
Of lowest order, passed, and from the door
Of that Plutonian hall, invisible
Ascended his high throne, which under state   445
Of richest texture spread, at the upper end
Was placed in regal lustre. Down a while
He sat, and round about him saw, unseen;
At last, as from a cloud, his fulgent head
And shape star-bright appeared, or brighter, clad   450
With what permissive glory since his fall

425-6] Cf. V 658n.
432 Astracan] Astrakhan, a Tartan khanate on the lower Volga.
433 Bactrian sophy] Bactria (modern Afghanistan) was subject to Persia, and
    the Bactrian sophy was the Shah of Persia.
434 crescent] the emblem of the Turkish sultans.
435 realm of Aladule] Armenia, of which Aladule was the last king before the
    Turkish conquest.
436 Tauris, Casbeen] now Tabriz and Kasvin, in Iran; both are former Persian
    capitals.
444 Plutonian] refers to Pluto, god of the underworld.
445 state] canopy.

Was left him, or false glitter; all amazed
At that so sudden blaze, the Stygian throng
Bent their aspéct, and whom they wished beheld,
Their mighty chief returned: loud was the acclaim;   455
Forth rushed in haste the great consulting peers,
Raised from their dark divan, and with like joy
Congratulant approached him, who with hand
Silence, and with these words attention, won:
    'Thrones, dominations, princedoms, virtues, powers,
For in possession such, not only of right,   461
I call ye, and declare ye now, returned
Successful beyond hope, to lead ye forth
Triumphant out of this infernal pit
Abominable, accursed, the house of woe,   465
And dungeon of our tyrant; now possess,
As lords, a spacious world, to our native heaven
Little inferior, by my adventure hard
With peril great achieved. Long were to tell
What I have done, what suffered, with what pain   470
Voyaged the unreal, vast, unbounded deep
Of horrible confusion – over which
By Sin and Death a broad way now is paved,
To expedite your glorious march; but I
Toiled out my uncouth passage, forced to ride   475
The untractable abyss, plunged in the womb
Of unoriginal Night and Chaos wild,
That, jealous of their secrets, fiercely opposed
My journey strange, with clamorous uproar
Protesting fate supreme; thence how I found   480
The new-created world, which fame in heaven
Long had foretold, a fabric wonderful,
Of absolute perfection; therein man
Placed in a paradise, by our exile
Made happy; him by fraud I have seduced   485
From his creator, and the more to increase
Your wonder, with an apple; he, thereat
Offended – worth your laughter – hath given up
Both his beloved man and all his world
To Sin and Death a prey, and so to us,   490
Without our hazard, labour, or alarm,

457 divan] an oriental council of state, especially the Turkish council.
471 unreal] unformed.
475 uncouth] strange, unfamiliar.
477 unoriginal] uncreated.
480 Protesting] appealing to.

To range in, and to dwell, and over man
To rule, as over all he should have ruled.
True is, me also he hath judged; or rather
Me not, but the brute serpent in whose shape   495
Man I deceived; that which to me belongs
Is enmity, which he will put between
Me and mankind: I am to bruise his heel;
His seed – when, is not set – shall bruise my head;
A world who would not purchase with a bruise,   500
Or much more grievous pain? Ye have the account
Of my performance; what remains, ye gods,
But up and enter now into full bliss?'
    So having said, a while he stood, expecting
Their universal shout and high applause   505
To fill his ear; when, contrary, he hears,
On all sides, from innumerable tongues
A dismal universal hiss, the sound
Of public scorn; he wondered, but not long
Had leisure, wondering at himself now more;   510
His visage drawn he felt to sharp and spare,
His arms clung to his ribs, his legs entwining
Each other, till supplanted down he fell,
A monstrous serpent on his belly prone,
Reluctant, but in vain; a greater power   515
Now ruled him, punished in the shape he sinned,
According to his doom; he would have spoke,
But hiss for hiss returned with forked tongue
To forked tongue; for now were all transformed
Alike, to serpents all, as accessories   520
To his bold riot; dreadful was the din
Of hissing through the hall, thick-swarming now
With complicated monsters, head and tail –
Scorpion, and asp, and amphisbaena dire,
Cerastes horned, hydrus, and ellops drear,   525
And dipsas (not so thick swarmed once the soil

506-14] Cf. the transformation of Cadmus (IX 505-6n.), and similar transfor-
    mations described in Lucan, *Pharsalia* ix. 700-33, Dante, *Inferno* xxiv,
    xxv. 'Supplanted' means 'tripped up'.
515 Reluctant] struggling, writhing.
523 complicated] means both 'complex' and 'turned together'.
524 amphisbaena] The name means 'going both ways' in Greek, and refers to a
    serpent with a head at each end.
525 Cerastes] a horned serpent.
    hydrus] a water-snake (not the Hydras of *Comus* 605, nor the Hydras of *PL*
    II 628 and *Sonnet* XV. 7).
    ellops] here refers to a kind of serpent.
526 dipsas] a serpent whose bite caused raging thirst.

Bedropped with blood of Gorgon, or the isle
Ophiusa); but still greatest he the midst,
Now dragon grown, larger than whom the sun
Engendered in the Pythian vale on slime,   530
Huge python; and his power no less he seemed
Above the rest still to retain; they all
Him followed, issuing forth to the open field,
Where all yet left of that revolted rout,
Heaven-fallen, in station stood or just array,   535
Sublime with expectation when to see
In triumph issuing forth their glorious chief;
They saw, but other sight instead – a crowd
Of ugly serpents; horror on them fell,
And horrid sympathy; for what they saw   540
They felt themselves now changing; down their arms,
Down fell both spear and shield; down they as fast,
And the dire hiss renewed, and the dire form
Catched by contagion, like in punishment
As in their crime. Thus was the applause they meant   545
Turned to exploding hiss, triumph to shame
Cast on themselves from their own mouths. There stood
A grove hard by, sprung up with this their change,
His will who reigns above, to aggravate
Their penance, laden with fair fruit, like that   550
Which grew in Paradise, the bait of Eve
Used by the tempter; on that prospect strange
Their earnest eyes they fixed, imagining
For one forbidden tree a multitude
Now risen, to work them further woe or shame;   555
Yet parched with scalding thirst and hunger fierce,
Though to delude them sent, could not abstain,
But on they rolled in heaps, and up the trees
Climbing, sat thicker than the snaky locks
That curled Megaera; greedily they plucked   560
The fruitage fair to sight, like that which grew

526-7] When Perseus was crossing Libya, drops of blood from the head of the
    Gorgon (Medusa) fell on the soil and were changed into snakes, which is
    why Libya is full of deadly serpents (*Metamorphoses* iv 617-20).
528 Ophiusa] in Greek means 'full of serpents'. In antiquity the name was
    applied to at least three different islands.
529-31] The Pythian vale is Delphi, where the serpent that Apollo slew had
    lived. In the Greek of the LXX and the N.T. a python is a possessing spirit
    (e.g. Acts xvi. 16).
536 Sublime] exalted in feeling, elated.
546 exploding] used in the Latin sense of 'hissing (an actor) off the stage'.
560 Megaera] a Fury; see II 596n.

Near that bituminous lake where Sodom flamed;
This, more delusive, not the touch, but taste
Deceived; they, fondly thinking to allay
Their appetite with gust, instead of fruit   565
Chewed bitter ashes, which the offended taste
With spattering noise rejected; oft they assayed,
Hunger and thirst constraining; drugged as oft,
With hatefulest disrelish writhed their jaws
With soot and cinders filled; so oft they fell   570
Into the same illusion, not as man
Whom they triumphed once lapsed. Thus were they
       plagued,
And worn with famine long, and ceaseless hiss,
Till their lost shape, permitted, they resumed –
Yearly enjoined, some say, to undergo   575
This annual humbling certain numbered days,
To dash their pride, and joy for man seduced.
However, some tradition they dispersed
Among the heathen of their purchase got,
And fabled how the serpent, whom they called   580
Ophion, with Eurynome – the wide-
Encroaching Eve perhaps – had first the rule
Of high Olympus, thence by Saturn driven
And Ops, ere yet Dictaean Jove was born.
       Meanwhile in Paradise the hellish pair   585
Too soon arrived – Sin, there in power before
Once actual, now in body, and to dwell
Habitual habitant; behind her Death,
Close following pace for pace, not mounted yet
On his pale horse; to whom Sin thus began: 590

562] The Dead Sea ('bituminous lake') is associated with Sodom in the
apocryphal II Esdras v. 7. In a popular tradition originating in Josephus
(*Bellum Judaicum* IV viii. 4) the fruit growing on the site of Sodom was said
to contain ashes from the fire which destroyed the city. (Gen. xix. 24, Deut.
xxxii. 32).

565 gust] gusto.

568 drugged] nauseated.

579 purchase] booty.

581] The name Ophion derives from the Greek word 'serpent', and refers to a
Titan, the husband of Eurynome (which means 'wide-ruling' in Greek);
they ruled Olympus (see VII 3n.) until they were overthrown by Saturn
and Rhea (Ops), whose son Jove was associated with Mount Dicte, in Crete.
Dictaean was one of Jove's epithets. Cf. I 509-21n. Ophion was tradition-
ally associated with Satan.

587 actual] Actual sin is a technical theological term for a sin which is the
outcome of a free personal act of the individual will, and is therefore to be
contrasted with original sin (see IX 1003-4n.). On sin 'in body' see 816n.

590 pale horse] Rev. vi. 8.

'Second of Satan sprung, all-conquering Death,
What think'st thou of our empire now? Though earned
With travail difficult, not better far
Than still at hell's dark threshold to have sat watch,
Unnamed, undreaded, and thyself half-starved?'   595
    Whom thus the Sin-born monster answered soon:
'To me, who with eternal famine pine,
Alike is hell, or Paradise, or heaven –
There best where most with ravin I may meet:
Which here, though plenteous, all too little seems   600
To stuff this maw, this vast unhidebound corpse.'
    To whom the incestuous mother thus replied:
'Thou therefore on these herbs, and fruits, and flowers,
Feed first, on each beast next, and fish, and fowl –
No homely morsels; and whatever thing   605
The scythe of time mows down, devour unspared,
Till I, in man residing through the race,
His thoughts, his looks, words, actions, all infect,
And season him thy last and sweetest prey.'
    This said, they both betook them several ways,   610
Both to destroy, or unimmortal make
All kinds, and for destruction to mature
Sooner or later; which the almighty seeing,
From his transcendent seat the saints among,
To those bright orders uttered thus his voice: 615
    'See with what heat these dogs of hell advance
To waste and havoc yonder world, which I
So fair and good created, and had still
Kept in that state, had not the folly of man
Let in these wasteful furies, who impute   620
Folly to me – so doth the prince of hell
And his adherents – that with so much ease
I suffer them to enter and possess
A place so heavenly, and conniving seem
To gratify my scornful enemies,   625
That laugh, as if, transported with some fit
Of passion, I to them had quitted all,
At random yielded up to their misrule;
And know not that I called and drew them thither,
My hell-hounds, to lick up the draff and filth   630
Which man's polluting sin with taint hath shed
On what was pure; till crammed and gorged, nigh burst

599 ravin] prey
601 unhidebound] having loose skin.
624 conniving] remaining inactive.

With sucked and glutted offal, at one sling
Of thy victorious arm, well-pleasing Son,
Both Sin and Death, and yawning grave, at last   635
Through chaos hurled, obstruct the mouth of hell
For ever, and seal up his ravenous jaws.
Then heaven and earth, renewed, shall be made pure
To sanctity that shall receive no stain:
Till then the curse pronounced on both precedes.'   640
  He ended, and the heavenly audience loud
Sung Halleluiah, as the sound of seas,
Through multitude that sung: 'Just are thy ways,
Righteous are thy decrees on all thy works;
Who can extenuate thee? Next, to the Son,   645
Destined restorer of mankind, by whom
New heaven and earth shall to the ages rise,
Or down from heaven descend.' Such was their song,
While the creator, calling forth by name
His mighty angels, gave them several charge,   650
As sorted best with present things. The sun
Had first his precept so to move, so shine,
As might affect the earth with cold and heat
Scarce tolerable, and from the north to call
Decrepit winter, from the south to bring   655
Solstitial summer's heat. To the blank moon
Her office they prescribed; to the other five
Their planetary motions and aspécts,
In sextile, square, and trine, and opposite,
Of noxious efficacy, and when to join   660
In synod unbenign; and taught the fixed
Their influence malignant when to shower –
Which of them, rising with the sun or falling,
Should prove tempestuous; to the winds they set
Their corners, when with bluster to confound   665
Sea, air, and shore; the thunder when to roll

633] I Sam. xxv. 29.
638-9] II Pet. iii. 7-13.
641-3] Rev. xix. 6.
643-4] Rev. xv. 3, xvi. 7.
645 extenuate] disparage.
648] Rev. xxi. 2.
656 blank] white, pale.
657] See V 177n.
659 Sextile, square, trine, and opposite are 'aspects' (see VI 313n.) of 60, 90,
    120, and 180 degrees respectively.
661 synod] conjunction, the fifth 'position' (often not called an aspect) of the
    heavenly bodies. Cf. *PR* IV 385n.

With terror through the dark aerial hall.
Some say he bid his angels turn askance
The poles of earth twice ten degrees and more
From the sun's axle; they with labour pushed   670
Oblique the centric globe: some say the sun
Was bid turn reins from the equinoctial road
Like distant breadth – to Taurus with the seven
Atlantic Sisters, and the Spartan Twins,
Up to the Tropic Crab; thence down amain   675
By Leo and the Virgin and the Scales,
As deep as Capricorn, to bring in change
Of seasons to each clime; else had the spring
Perpetual smiled on earth with verdant flowers,
Equal in days and nights, except to those   680
Beyond the polar circles; to them day
Had unbenighted shone, while the low sun,
To recompense his distance, in their sight
Had rounded still the horizon, and not known
Or east or west – which had forbid the snow   685
From cold Estotiland, and south as far
Beneath Magellan. At that tasted fruit,
The sun, as from Thyestean banquet, turned
His course intended; else how had the world
Inhabited, though sinless, more than now   690
Avoided pinching cold and scorching heat?

668 Some] Those who advocate the Copernican model, according to which the
   axis of the earth ('centric globe') is tilted.
671 some] Those who advocate the Ptolemaic model, according to which the
   plane of the sun's orbit is tilted.
673–8] The sun travels through the signs of the zodiac. Before the fall it is in
   Aries, the first sign (l. 329); it now travels to the second sign, Taurus (in
   which are the Pleiades, 'the seven Atlantic Sisters'), the third sign, Gemini
   ('the Spartan Twins'), and the fourth sign, Cancer ('the Tropic Crab').
   Cancer represents the furthest retreat of the sun (i.e. the summer solstice),
   after which the sun descends quickly ('thence down amain') to the fifth
   sign, Leo (the Lion), the sixth, Virgo ('the Virgin'), the seventh, Libra ('the
   Scales'), and continues on this route through Scorpio and Sagittarius 'as
   deep as Capricorn' (the Goat), the tenth sign (i.e. the winter solstice). This
   journey brings the seasons to each region ('clime').
686 Estotiland] the name referred vaguely to the coast of modern Labrador, or
   to an island off its coast.
687 Magellan] either Argentina or the Straits of Magellan.
688 Thyestean banquet] Thyestes, the son of Pelops, suffered from the curse
   that weighed on 'Pelops' line' (see *Penseroso* 99n.). His brother Atreus
   (whose wife Thyestes had seduced) killed one of Thyestes' sons and served
   him to Thyestes as food. According to Seneca, the sun changed course to
   avoid seeing the banquet (*Thyestes* 776–8).

These change in the heavens, though slow, produced
Like change on sea and land – sideral blast,
Vapour, and mist, and exhalation hot,
Corrupt and pestilent; now from the north   695
Of Norumbega, and the Samoed shore,
Bursting their brazen dungeon, armed with ice,
And snow, and hail, and stormy gust and flaw,
Boreas and Caecius and Argeste loud
And Thrascias rend the woods, and seas upturn;   700
With adverse blast upturns them from the south
Notus and Afer, black with thunderous clouds
From Serraliona; thwart of these, as fierce
Forth rush the Levant and the ponent winds,
Eurus and Zephir, with their lateral noise,   705
Sirocco and Libeccio; thus began
Outrage from lifeless things; but Discord first,
Daughter of Sin, among the irrational
Death introduced through fierce antipathy;
Beast now with beast 'gan war, and fowl with fowl,   710
And fish with fish; to graze the herb all leaving
Devoured each other; nor stood much in awe
Of man, but fled him, or with countenance grim
Glared on him passing; these were from without
The growing miseries, which Adam saw   715
Already in part, though hid in gloomiest shade,
To sorrow abandoned, but worse felt within,
And in a troubled sea of passion tossed,
Thus to disburden sought with sad complaint:
     'O miserable of happy! Is this the end   720
Of this new glorious world, and me so late
The glory of that glory? who now, become
Accursed of blessed, hide me from the face

693 sideral] from the stars.
696 Norumbega] New England and the maritime provinces of Canada.
    Samoed] north-eastern Siberia.
697 dungeon] Aeolus imprisoned the winds in a cave on Aeolia, a floating island
    near Sicily.
699–706] Milton is naming the winds in a plan based on the anemology of
    antiquity (Aristotle, *Meteorologica* ii 4–6, *Problemata* xxvi, and Theophras-
    tus, *De Ventis*), in which the horizon is divided into twelve sections of 30
    degrees each and winds blow in opposition to each other. Boreas, the north
    wind, opposes Afer (from Sierra Leone, then a Portuguese possession on the
    west coast of Africa) and Notus, the south wind; Thrascias (NW by 30°)
    opposes Sirocco (SE by 30°); Argestes (NW by 60°) opposes Eurus (SE by
    60°); Zephir (a 'ponent', i.e. western wind) opposes Levant (E); Libeccio
    (SW by 60°) opposes Caecius (NE by 60°).
718] Isa. lvii. 20 may be the ultimate source of this commonplace.

Of God, whom to behold was then my height
Of happiness; yet well, if here would end   725
The misery; I deserved it, and would bear
My own deservings; but this will not serve:
All that I eat or drink, or shall beget,
Is propagated curse. O voice, once heard
Delightfully, "Increase and multiply;"   730
Now death to hear! For what can I increase
Or multiply, but curses on my head?
Who of all ages to succeed, but feeling
The evil on him brought by me, will curse
My head? "Ill fare our ancestor impure;   735
For this we may thank Adam;" but his thanks
Shall be the execration; so besides
Mine own that bide upon me, all from me
Shall with a fierce reflux on me redound –
On me, as on their natural centre, light;   740
Heavy, though in their place. O fleeting joys
Of Paradise, dear bought with lasting woes!
Did I request thee, maker, from my clay
To mould me man? Did I solicit thee
From darkness to promote me, or here place   745
In this delicious garden? As my will
Concurred not to my being, it were but right
And equal to reduce me to my dust,
Desirous to resign and render back
All I received, unable to perform   750
Thy terms too hard, by which I was to hold
The good I sought not. To the loss of that,
Sufficient penalty, why hast thou added
The sense of endless woes? Inexplicable
Thy justice seems; yet, to say truth, too late   755
I thus contest; then should have been refused
Those terms, whatever, when they were proposed;
Thou didst accept them: wilt thou enjoy the good,
Then cavil the conditions? And though God
Made thee without thy leave, what if thy son   760
Prove disobedient, and reproved, retort,
"Wherefore didst thou beget me? I sought it not;"
Wouldst thou admit for his contempt of thee
That proud excuse? Yet him not thy election,

738 own] own curses.
740 light] plays on the meanings 'alight' and 'not heavy'.
743-4] Isa. xiv. 9.
748 equal] used in the Latin sense of 'fair, equitable, just'.
762] Isa. xiv. 10.

But natural necessity, begot.   765
God made thee of choice his own, and of his own
To serve him; thy reward was of his grace;
Thy punishment, then, justly is at his will.
Be it so, for I submit; his doom is fair,
That dust I am, and shall to dust return;   770
O welcome hour, whenever! Why delays
His hand to execute what his decree
Fixed on this day? Why do I overlive,
Why am I mocked with death, and lengthened out
To deathless pain? How gladly would I meet   775
Mortality, my sentence, and be earth
Insensible; how glad would lay me down
As in my mother's lap! There I should rest,
And sleep secure; his dreadful voice no more
Would thunder in my ears; no fear of worse   780
To me and to my offspring would torment me
With cruel expectation. Yet one doubt
Pursues me still – lest all I cannot die;
Lest that pure breath of life, the spirit of man
Which God inspired, cannot together perish   785
With this corporeal clod; then in the grave,
Or in some other dismal place, who knows
But I shall die a living death? O thought
Horrid, if true! Yet why? It was but breath
Of life that sinned: what dies but what had life   790
And sin? The body properly hath neither.
All of me, then, shall die: let this appease
The doubt, since human reach no further knows.
For though the Lord of all be infinite,
Is his wrath also? Be it, man is not so,   795
But mortal doomed. How can he exercise
Wrath without end on man, whom death must end?
Can he make deathless death? That were to make
Strange contradiction, which to God himself
Impossible is held, as argument   800
Of weakness, not of power. Will he draw out,
For anger's sake, finite to infinite
In punished man, to satisfy his rigour

792] Adam temporarily advocates the mortalist heresy, according to which
    both the spiritual and corporeal elements in man die at the same time (and
    are later resurrected together).
803-4] Satisfaction is a technical theological term for the payment of a penalty
    due to God on account of sin. Protestant theologians inherited Anselm's
    doctrine that Christ's death was a sufficient vicarious satisfaction for the
    sins of the world (cf. XII 419).

Satisfied never? That were to extend
His sentence beyond dust and nature's law;   805
By which all causes else according still
To the reception of their matter act,
Not to the extent of their own sphere. But say
That death be not one stroke, as I supposed,
Bereaving sense, but endless misery   810
From this day onward, which I feel begun
Both in me and without me, and so last
To perpetuity – ay me, that fear
Comes thundering back with dreadful revolution
On my defenceless head; both death and I   815
Am found eternal, and incorporate both:
Nor I on my part single; in me all
Posterity stands cursed; fair patrimony
That I must leave ye, sons; O were I able
To waste it all myself, and leave ye none!   820
So disinherited, how would ye bless
Me, now your curse! Ah, why should all mankind,
For one man's fault, thus guiltless be condemned,
If guiltless? But from me what can proceed
But all corrupt – both mind and will depraved   825
Not to do only, but to will the same
With me? How can they, then, acquitted stand
In sight of God? Him after all disputes,
Forced I absolve; all my evasions vain
And reasonings, though through mazes, lead me still   830
But to my own conviction: first and last
On me, me only, as the source and spring
Of all corruption, all the blame lights due;
So might the wrath. Fond wish! Couldst thou support
That burden, heavier than the earth to bear –   835
Than all the world much heavier, though divided
With that bad woman? Thus, what thou desir'st,
And what thou fear'st, alike destroys all hope
Of refuge, and concludes thee miserable
Beyond all past example and futúre –   840
To Satan only like, both crime and doom.
O Conscience! Into what abyss of fears
And horrors hast thou driven me; out of which

804–8] Adam appeals to a scholastic axiom, according to which *omne efficiens
    agit secundum vires recipientis, non suas* (every cause acts according to the
    powers of its recipient, not its own powers).
816] incorporate] refers to Paul's doctrine of the 'body of sin' (*corpus peccati*;
    Rom. vi. 6).

I find no way, from deep to deeper plunged!'
　Thus Adam to himself lamented loud   845
Through the still night – not now, as ere man fell,
Wholesome and cool and mild, but with black air
Accompanied, with damps and dreadful gloom;
Which to his evil conscience represented
All things with double terror; on the ground   850
Outstretched he lay, on the cold ground, and oft
Cursed his creation; death as oft accused
Of tardy execution, since denounced
The day of his offence. 'Why comes not death,'
Said he, 'with one thrice-acceptable stroke   855
To end me? Shall truth fail to keep her word,
Justice divine not hasten to be just?
But death comes not at call, justice divine
Mends not her slowest pace for prayers or cries.
O woods, O fountains, hillocks, dales, and bowers,   860
With other echo late I taught your shades
To answer, and resound far other song.'
Whom thus afflicted when sad Eve beheld,
Desolate where she sat, approaching nigh,
Soft words to his fierce passion she assayed;   865
But her, with stern regard, he thus repelled:
　'Out of my sight, thou serpent! That name best
Befits thee, with him leagued, thyself as false
And hateful: nothing wants, but that thy shape
Like his, and colour serpentine, may show   870
Thy inward fraud, to warn all creatures from thee
Henceforth, lest that too heavenly form, pretended
To hellish falsehood, snare them. But for thee
I had persisted happy, had not thy pride
And wandering vanity, when least was safe,   875
Rejected my forewarning, and disdained
Not to be trusted – longing to be seen,
Though by the devil himself; him overweening
To overreach; but with the serpent meeting,
Fooled and beguiled; by him thou, I by thee,   880
To trust thee from my side, imagined wise,
Constant, mature, proof against all assaults,
And understood not all was but a show,
Rather than solid virtue, all but a rib

867] According to a patristic tradition which drew on Philo, the Hebrew word
　　for Eve means 'serpent'.
872 pretended] held in front as a covering.
884–8] Eve was traditionally thought to have been formed from a bent (hence
　　morally defective) supernumerary rib. Sinister means 'left' (the original
　　Latin sense) as well as 'corrupt, evil'.

Crooked by nature – bent, as now appears,   885
More to the part sinister – from me drawn;
Well if thrown out, as supernumerary
To my just number found. O why did God,
Creator wise, that peopled highest heaven
With spirits masculine, create at last   890
This novelty on earth, this fair defect
Of nature, and not fill the world at once
With men as angels, without feminine;
Or find some other way to generate
Mankind? This mischief had not then befallen,   895
And more that shall befall – innumerable
Disturbances on earth through female snares,
And strait conjunction with this sex; for either
He never shall find out fit mate, but such
As some misfortune brings him, or mistake;   900
Or whom he wishes most shall seldom gain,
Through her perverseness, but shall see her gained
By a far worse, or if she love, withheld
By parents; or his happiest choice too late
Shall meet, already linked and wedlock-bound   905
To a fell adversary, his hate or shame:
Which infinite calamity shall cause
To human life, and household peace confound.'
      He added not, and from her turned; but Eve,
Not so repulsed, with tears that ceased not flowing,   910
And tresses all disordered, at his feet
Fell humble, and embracing them, besought
His peace, and thus proceeded in her plaint:
      'Forsake me not thus, Adam, witness heaven
What love sincere and reverence in my heart   915
I bear thee, and unweeting have offended,
Unhappily deceived; thy suppliant
I beg, and clasp thy knees; bereave me not
Whereon I live, thy gentle looks, thy aid,
Thy counsel in this uttermost distress,   920
My only strength and stay; forlorn of thee,
Whither shall I betake me, where subsist?
While yet we live, scarce one short hour perhaps,
Between us two let there be peace, both joining,
As joined in injuries, one enmity   925
Against a foe by doom express assigned us,
That cruel serpent; on me exercise not
Thy hatred for this misery befallen –

888–95] Cf. Euripides, *Hippolytus* 616–19.

On me already lost, me than thyself
More miserable; both have sinned, but thou   930
Against God only, I against God and thee,
And to the place of judgement will return,
There with my cries importune heaven, that all
The sentence, from thy head removed, may light
On me, sole cause to thee of all this woe,   935
Me, me only, just object of his ire.'
    She ended, weeping; and her lowly plight,
Immovable till peace obtained from fault
Acknowledged and deplored, in Adam wrought
Commiseration; soon his heart relented   940
Towards her, his life so late, and sole delight,
Now at his feet submissive in distress –
Creature so fair his reconcilement seeking,
His counsel whom she had displeased, his aid;
As one disarmed, his anger all he lost,   945
And thus with peaceful words upraised her soon:
    'Unwary, and too desirous, as before
So now, of what thou know'st not, who desir'st
The punishment all on thyself; alas,
Bear thine own first, ill able to sustain   950
His full wrath whose thou feel'st as yet least part,
And my displeasure bear'st so ill. If prayers
Could alter high decrees, I to that place
Would speed before thee, and be louder heard,
That on my head all might be visited,   955
Thy frailty and infirmer sex forgiven,
To me committed, and by me exposed.
But rise; let us no more contend, nor blame
Each other, blamed enough elsewhere, but strive
In offices of love how we may lighten   960
Each other's burden in our share of woe;
Since this day's death denounced, if aught I see,
Will prove no sudden, but a slow-paced evil,
A long day's dying, to augment our pain,
And to our seed (O hapless seed!) derived.'   965
    To whom thus Eve, recovering heart, replied:
'Adam, by sad experiment I know
How little weight my words with thee can find,
Found so erroneous, thence by just event
Found so unfortunate; nevertheless,   970

930-1] Psalm li. 4.
959 elsewhere] probably heaven, but possibly 'the place of judgement' (l. 932).
969 event] outcome, consequence.

Restored by thee, vile as I am, to place
Of new acceptance, hopeful to regain
Thy love, the sole contentment of my heart,
Living or dying from thee I will not hide
What thoughts in my unquiet breast are risen,   975
Tending to some relief of our extremes,
Or end, though sharp and sad, yet tolerable,
As in our evils, and of easier choice.
If care of our descent perplex us most
Which must be born to certain woe, devoured   980
By death at last – and miserable it is
To be to others cause of misery,
Our own begotten, and of our loins to bring
Into this cursed world a woeful race,
That after wretched life must be at last   985
Food for so foul a monster – in thy power
It lies, yet ere conception, to prevent
The race unblest, to being yet unbegot.
Childless thou art; childless remain; so death
Shall be deceived his glut, and with us two   990
Be forced to satisfy his ravenous maw.
But if thou judge it hard and difficult,
Conversing, looking, loving, to abstain
From love's due rites, nuptial embraces sweet,
And with desire to languish without hope   995
Before the present object languishing
With like desire – which would be misery
And torment less than none of what we dread –
Then both ourselves and seed at once to free
From what we fear for both, let us make short;   1000
Let us seek death, or, he not found, supply
With our own hands his office on ourselves;
Why stand we longer shivering under fears
That show no end but death, and have the power,
Of many ways to die the shortest choosing,   1005
Destruction with destruction to destroy?'
    She ended here, or vehement despair
Broke off the rest; so much of death her thoughts
Had entertained as dyed her cheeks with pale.
But Adam, with such counsel nothing swayed,   1010
To better hopes his more attentive mind

979 our descent perplex] our descendants torment.
989 so death] in early editions, printed at beginning of next line.
995] Cf. Dante, *Inferno* iv. 42.
996 object] Eve.

Labouring had raised, and thus to Eve replied:
  'Eve, thy contempt of life and pleasure seems
To argue in thee something more sublime
And excellent than what thy mind contemns: 1015
But self-destruction therefore sought refutes
That excellence thought in thee, and implies
Not thy contempt, but anguish and regret
For loss of life and pleasure overloved.
Or if thou covet death, as utmost end   1020
Of misery, so thinking to evade
The penalty pronounced, doubt not but God
Hath wiselier armed his vengeful ire than so
To be forestalled; much more I fear lest death
So snatched will not exempt us from the pain   1025
We are by doom to pay; rather such acts
Of contumacy will provoke the highest
To make death in us live; then let us seek
Some safer resolution – which methinks
I have in view, calling to mind with heed   1030
Part of our sentence, that thy seed shall bruise
The serpent's head; piteous amends, unless
Be meant whom I conjecture, our grand foe,
Satan, who in the serpent hath contrived
Against us this deceit; to crush his head   1035
Would be revenge indeed – which will be lost
By death brought on ourselves, or childless days
Resolved as thou proposest; so our foe
Shall scape his punishment ordained, and we
Instead shall double ours upon our heads.   1040
No more be mentioned, then, of violence
Against ourselves, and wilful barrenness
That cuts us off from hope, and savours only
Rancour and pride, impatience and despite,
Reluctance against God and his just yoke   1045
Laid on our necks. Remember with what mild
And gracious temper he both heard and judged,
Without wrath or reviling; we expected
Immediate dissolution, which we thought
Was meant by death that day, when lo, to thee   1050
Pains only in child-bearing were foretold,
And bringing forth, soon recompensed with joy,
Fruit of thy womb; on me the curse aslope

1045 Reluctance] resistance, opposition.
1052] John xvi. 21.
1053] Luke i. 42.

Glanced on the ground: with labour I must earn
My bread; what harm? Idleness had been worse;   1055
My labour will sustain me; and lest cold
Or heat should injure us, his timely care
Hath, unbesought, provided, and his hands
Clothed us unworthy, pitying while he judged;
How much more, if we pray him, will his ear   1060
Be open, and his heart to pity incline,
And teach us further by what means to shun
The inclement seasons, rain, ice, hail, and snow,
Which now the sky with various face begins
To show us in this mountain, while the winds   1065
Blow moist and keen, shattering the graceful locks
Of these fair spreading trees; which bids us seek
Some better shroud, some better warmth to cherish
Our limbs benumbed – ere this diurnal star
Leave cold the night, how we his gathered beams   1070
Reflected may with matter sere foment,
Or by collision of two bodies grind
The air attrite to fire; as late the clouds
Justling, or pushed with winds, rude in their shock,
Tine the slant lightning, whose thwart flame, driven down,
Kindles the gummy bark of fir or pine,   1076
And sends a comfortable heat from far,
Which might supply the sun; such fire to use,
And what may else be remedy or cure
To evils which our own misdeeds have wrought,   1080
He will instruct us praying, and of grace
Beseeching him; so as we need not fear
To pass commodiously this life, sustained
By him with many comforts, till we end
In dust, our final rest and native home.   1085
What better can we do than to the place
Repairing where he judged us, prostrate fall
Before him reverent, and there confess

1068 shroud] shelter. Cf. *Comus* 147.
1069 diurnal star] the sun.
1071 foment] means 'cherish with heat, warm' (cf. IV 669) and also draws on
     the Latin *fomentum*, which could mean 'kindling-wood'; 'sere' means 'dry'.
1073 attrite] means 'worn or ground down by friction', but inasmuch as the
     word may be thought to reflect Adam's state of mind, it may carry some of
     its usual theological sense (originally Scholastic, and later Protestant) of
     'having a sorrow for sin which proceeds from a sense of fear rather than (as
     does contrition, l. 1103) from the love of God'.
1075 Tine] kindle.
1078 supply] serve as a substitute for.

Humbly our faults, and pardon beg, with tears
Watering the ground, and with our sighs the air   1090
Frequenting, sent from hearts contrite, in sign
Of sorrow unfeigned and humiliation meek?
Undoubtedly he will relent, and turn
From his displeasure, in whose look serene,
When angry most he seemed and most severe,   1095
What else but favour, grace, and mercy shone?'
  So spake our father penitent, nor Eve
Felt less remorse; they forthwith to the place
Repairing where he judged them, prostrate fell
Before him reverent, and both confessed   1100
Humbly their faults, and pardon begged, with tears
Watering the ground, and with their sighs the air
Frequenting, sent from hearts contrite, in sign
Of sorrow unfeigned and humiliation meek.

THE END OF THE TENTH BOOK

1090-1] Dante, *Inferno* iv. 25-7 (cf. l. 995n.). 'Frequenting' means 'filling'.

BOOK XI

THE ARGUMENT

The Son of God presents to his Father the prayers of our first
parents now repenting, and intercedes for them; God accepts
them, but declares that they must no longer abide in Paradise;
sends Michael with a band of cherubim to dispossess them but first
to reveal to Adam future things: Michael's coming down. Adam
shows to Eve certain ominous signs: he discerns Michael's
approach; goes out to meet him: the angel denounces their
departure. Eve's lamentation. Adam pleads, but submits; the
angel leads him up to a high hill; sets before him in vision what
shall happen till the flood.

Thus they in lowliest plight repentant stood
Praying; for from the mercy-seat above
Prevenient grace descending had removed
The stony from their hearts, and made new flesh
Regenerate grow instead, that sighs now breathed   5
Unutterable, which the spirit of prayer
Inspired, and winged for heaven with speedier flight
Than loudest oratory; ye their port
Not of mean suitors; nor important less
Seemed their petition, than when the ancient pair   10
In fables old, less ancient yet than these,
Deucalion and chaste Pyrrha to restore
The race of mankind drowned, before the shrine
Of Themis stood devout. To heaven their prayers
Flew up, nor missed the way, by envious winds   15
Blown vagabond or frustrate: in they passed

2 mercy-seat] Exod. xxv. 17-22.
3 Prevenient grace] An ancient technical theological term (*gratia praeveniens*)
    for the kind of grace that precedes the free determination of the will. Cf. III
    231n.
3-5] Ezek. xi. 19.
5-7] Rom. viii. 26.
8 port] bearing (cf. IV 869).
10-14] Deucalion (the son of Prometheus) and Pyrrha built a small boat and so
    became the sole survivors when Zeus destroyed mankind with a universal
    flood. When the waters receded the ship landed on Mount Parnassus, and
    Deucalion and Pyrrha consulted the Delphic oracle (which was dedicated
    to Themis, i.e. Justitia, before it became Apollo's) about repopulating the
    earth (*Metamorphoses* i. 313-437).
15-16 nor ... frustrate] Alludes to Milton's 'Paradise of Fools' (III 444-97, esp.
    487-9).

Dimensionless through heavenly doors; then clad
With incense, where the golden altar fumed,
By their great intercessor, came in sight
Before the Father's throne; them the glad Son   20
Presenting thus to intercede began:
    'See, Father, what first-fruits on earth are sprung
From thy implanted grace in man – these sighs
And prayers, which in this golden censer, mixed
With incense, I thy priest before thee bring;   25
Fruits of more pleasing savour, from thy seed
Sown with contrition in his heart, than those
Which, his own hand manuring, all the trees
Of Paradise could have produced, ere fallen
From innocence. Now therefore bend thine ear   30
To supplication; hear his sighs, though mute;
Unskilful with what words to pray, let me
Interpret for him, me his advocate
And propitiation; all his words on me,
Good or not good, engraft; my merit those   35
Shall perfect, and for these my death shall pay.
Accept me, and in me from these receive
The smell of peace toward mankind; let him live,
Before thee reconciled, at least his days
Numbered, though sad, till death, his doom (which I   40
To mitigate thus plead, not to reverse),
To better life shall yield him, where with me
All my redeemed may dwell in joy and bliss,
Made one with me, as I with thee am one.'
    To whom the Father, without cloud, serene: 45
'All thy request for man, accepted Son,
Obtain; all thy request was my decree;
But longer in that Paradise to dwell
The law I gave to nature him forbids;
Those pure immortal elements, that know   50
No gross, no unharmonious mixture foul,
Eject him, tainted now, and purge him off
As a distemper, gross, to air as gross,
And mortal food, as may dispose him best
For dissolution wrought by sin, that first   55
Distempered all things, and of incorrupt
Corrupted. I at first with two fair gifts

18, 24] Rev. viii. 3.
33–4] I John ii. 1–2.
35 engraft] Rom. xi. 16–24. See III 293n.
44] John xvii. 11, 21–3.

Created him endowed – with happiness
And immortality; that fondly lost,
This other served but to eternize woe,   60
Till I provided death; so death becomes
His final remedy, and after life
Tried in sharp tribulation, and refined
By faith and faithful works, to second life,
Waked in the renovation of the just,   65
Resigns him up with heaven and earth renewed.
But let us call to synod all the blest
Through heaven's wide bounds; from them I will not hide
My judgements – how with mankind I proceed,
As how with peccant angels late they saw,   70
And in their state, though firm, stood more confirmed.'
    He ended, and the Son gave signal high
To the bright minister that watched; he blew
His trumpet, heard in Oreb since perhaps
When God descended, and perhaps once more   75
To sound at general doom. The angelic blast
Filled all the regions: from their blissful bowers
Of amarantine shade, fountain or spring,
By the waters of life, where'er they sat
In fellowships of joy, the sons of light   80
Hasted, resorting to the summons high,
And took their seats, till from his throne supreme
The almighty thus pronounced his sovereign will:
    'O sons, like one of us man is become
To know both good and evil, since his taste   85
Of that defended fruit; but let him boast
His knowledge of good lost and evil got,
Happier had it sufficed him to have known
Good by itself and evil not at all.
He sorrows now, repents, and prays contrite –   90
My motions in him; longer than they move,
His heart I know how variable and vain,
Self-left. Lest therefore his now bolder hand

59 fondly] foolishly.
65 renovation] renewal of the body at the resurrection.
66] II Pet. iii. 13.
70 peccant] sinning.
74 Oreb] See I 7–8n.
78 amarantine] See III 352–61n.
86 defended] forbidden.
91 motions] stirring of the soul, inward promptings. Cf. *PR* I 290, *SA* 1382.
93 Self-left] left to itself.

Reach also of the tree of life, and eat,
And live for ever, dream at least to live   95
For ever, to remove him I decree,
And send him from the garden forth, to till
The ground whence he was taken, fitter soil.
Michael, this my behest have thou in charge:
Take to thee from among the cherubim   100
Thy choice of flaming warriors, lest the fiend,
Or in behalf of man, or to invade
Vacant possession, some new trouble raise;
Haste thee, and from the Paradise of God
Without remorse drive out the sinful pair,   105
From hallowed ground the unholy, and denounce
To them and to their progeny, from thence
Perpetual banishment. Yet lest they faint
At the sad sentence rigorously urged –
For I behold them softened, and with tears   110
Bewailing their excess – all terror hide.
If patiently thy bidding they obey,
Dismiss them not disconsolate; reveal
To Adam what shall come in future days,
As I shall thee enlighten; intermix   115
My covenant in the woman's seed renewed;
So send them forth, though sorrowing, yet in peace;
And on the east side of the garden place,
Where entrance up from Eden easiest climbs,
Cherubic watch, and of a sword the flame   120
Wide-waving, all approach far off to fright,
And guard all passage to the tree of life;
Lest Paradise a receptacle prove
To spirits foul, and all my trees their prey,
With whose stolen fruit man once more to delude.'   125
    He ceased, and the archangelic power prepared
For swift descent; with him the cohort bright
Of watchful cherubim; four faces each
Had, like a double Janus; all their shape
Spangled with eyes more numerous than those   130

99 Michael] See VI 44n.
102 in behalf of] with regard to.
106 denounce] See X 210-11n.
111 excess] Cf. *Circumcision* 24n.
128] See VI 753 ('four faces each') and VI 749-59n.
129 double Janus] Janus, the god of gates and of the course of the year, was
    described and depicted in late antiquity as *quadrifrons* (four-faced).

Of Argus, and more wakeful than to drowse,
Charmed with Arcadian pipe, the pastoral reed
Of Hermes, or his opiate rod. Meanwhile,
To resalute the world with sacred light,
Leucothea waked, and with fresh dews embalmed   135
The earth, when Adam and first matron Eve
Had ended now their orisons, and found
Strength added from above, new hope to spring
Out of despair, joy, but with fear yet linked;
Which thus to Eve his welcome words renewed: 140
  'Eve, easily may faith admit that all
The good which we enjoy from heaven descends;
But that from us aught should ascend to heaven
So prevalent as to concern the mind
Of God high-blest, or to incline his will,   145
Hard to belief may seem; yet this will prayer,
Or one short sigh of human breath, upborne
Even to the seat of God. For since I sought
By prayer the offended Deity to appease,
Kneeled and before him humbled all my heart,   150
Methought I saw him placable and mild,
Bending his ear; persuasion in me grew
That I was heard with favour; peace returned
Home to my breast, and to my memory
His promise that thy seed shall bruise our foe;   155
Which, then not minded in dismay, yet now
Assures me that the bitterness of death
Is past, and we shall live. Whence hail to thee,
Eve rightly called, mother of all mankind,
Mother of all things living, since by thee   160
Man is to live, and all things live for man.'
  To whom thus Eve with sad demeanour meek:
'Ill-worthy I such title should belong
To me transgressor, who for thee ordained

131-3] Argus, the son of Arestor, was a giant with one hundred eyes, of which
   only one pair slept at a time. Juno ordered him to guard Io, whom Jove had
   turned into a heifer. Hermes (Mercury) charmed Argus to sleep with his
   pipe of reeds ('pastoral reed') and his sleep-producing wand ('opiate rod'),
   and then slew him (*Metamorphoses* i 568-779).
135] Leucothea (see *Comus* 875n.) was identified by the Romans with Mater
   Matuta, a goddess of dawn.
142] James i. 17.
144 prevalent] powerful.
157-8] I Sam. xv. 32.
158] Cf. V. 385-7n.

A help, became thy snare; to me reproach   165
Rather belongs, distrust and all dispraise;
But infinite in pardon was my judge,
That I, who first brought death on all, am graced
The source of life; next favourable thou,
Who highly thus to entitle me vouchsaf'st,   170
Far other name deserving. But the field
To labour calls us now with sweat imposed,
Though after sleepless night; for see the morn,
All unconcerned with our unrest, begins
Her rosy progress smiling; let us forth,   175
I never from thy side henceforth to stray,
Where'er our day's work lies, though now enjoined
Laborious, till day droop; while here we dwell,
What can be toilsome in these pleasant walks?
Here let us live, though in fallen state, content.'   180
   So spake, so wished, much-humbled Eve, but fate
Subscribed not; nature first gave signs, impressed
On bird, beast, air – air suddenly eclipsed,
After short blush of morn; nigh in her sight
The bird of Jove, stooped from his airy tower,   185
Two birds of gayest plume before him drove;
Down from a hill the beast that reigns in woods,
First hunter then, pursued a gentle brace,
Goodliest of all the forest, hart and hind;
Direct to the eastern gate was bent their flight.   190
Adam observed, and with his eye the chase
Pursuing, not unmoved to Eve thus spake:
   'O Eve, some further change awaits us nigh,
Which heaven by these mute signs in nature shows,
Forerunners of his purpose, or to warn   195
Us, haply too secure of our discharge
From penalty because from death released
Some days: how long, and what till then our life,
Who knows, or more than this, that we are dust,
And thither must return, and be no more?   200
Why else this double object in our sight,
Of flight pursued in the air and o'er the ground
One way the self-same hour? Why in the east
Darkness ere day's mid-course, and morning light
More orient in yon western cloud, that draws   205

180] Phil. iv. 11.
185 bird of Jove, stooped] the eagle, having swooped.
187 beast] lion.
204 Isa. xvi. 3.

O'er the blue firmament a radiant white,
And slow descends, with something heavenly fraught?'
　He erred not, for by this the heavenly bands
Down from a sky of jasper lighted now
In Paradise, and on a hill made halt –　　　　　　　210
A glorious apparition, had not doubt
And carnal fear that day dimmed Adam's eye.
Not that more glorious, when the angels met
Jacob in Mahanaim, where he saw
The field pavilioned with his guardians bright;　　215
Nor that which on the flaming mount appeared
In Dothan, covered with a camp of fire,
Against the Syrian king, who to surprise
One man, assassin-like, had levied war,
War unproclaimed. The princely hierarch　　　220
In their bright stand there left his powers to seize
Possession of the garden; he alone,
To find where Adam sheltered, took his way,
Not unperceived of Adam, who to Eve,
While the great visitant approached, thus spake:　225
　'Eve, now expect great tidings, which perhaps
Of us will soon determine, or impose
New laws to be observed; for I descry
From yonder blazing cloud that veils the hill,
One of the heavenly host, and by his gait,　　　230
None of the meanest – some great potentate
Or of the thrones above, such majesty
Invests him coming; yet not terrible,
That I should fear, nor sociably mild,
As Raphael, that I should much confide,　　　　235
But solemn and sublime; whom, not to offend,
With reverence I must meet, and thou retire.'
　He ended; and the archangel soon drew nigh,
Not in his shape celestial, but as man
Clad to meet man; over his lucid arms　　　　　240
A military vest of purple flowed,

209] Rev. xxi. 11.
213-15] Gen. xxxii. 1-2 *Mahanaim* means 'two camps' in Hebrew (cf. LXX,
　παρεμβολαί, and Vulgate, *id est, Castra*), Milton's 'field pavilioned'.
216-20] II Kings vi. 13-18. 'One man' is Elisha, for the capture of whom 'the
　Syrian king' besieged Dothan.
　assassin] then felt as a metaphor, with reference to the Assassins (literally
　'hashish-eaters'), a Shi'te sect feared for its practice of murdering enemies
　by stealth.
227 determine] cause to end.

Livelier than Meliboean, or the grain
Of Sarra, worn by kings and heroes old
In time of truce; Iris had dipped the woof;
His starry helm unbuckled showed him prime   245
In manhood where youth ended; by his side,
As in glistering zodiac, hung the sword,
Satan's dire dread, and in his hand the spear.
Adam bowed low; he, kingly, from his state
Inclined not, but his coming thus declared: 250
    'Adam, heaven's high behest no preface needs;
Sufficient that thy prayers are heard, and Death,
Then due by sentence when thou didst transgress,
Defeated of his seizure many days,
Given thee of grace, wherein thou may'st repent,   255
And one bad act with many deeds well done
May'st cover; well may then thy Lord, appeased,
Redeem thee quite from Death's rapacious claim;
But longer in this Paradise to dwell
Permits not; to remove thee I am come,   260
And send thee from the garden forth to till
The ground whence thou wast taken, fitter soil.'
He added not, for Adam, at the news
Heart-strook, with chilling gripe of sorrow stood,
That all his senses bound; Eve, who unseen   265
Yet all had heard, with audible lament
Discovered soon the place of her retire:
    'O unexpected stroke, worse than of Death!
Must I leave thee, Paradise? Thus leave
Thee, native soil, these happy walks and shades,   270
Fit haunt of gods, where I had hope to spend,
Quiet, though sad, the respite of that day
That must be mortal to us both? O flowers,
That never will in other climate grow,
My early visitation, and my last   275
At even, which I bred up with tender hand
From the first opening bud, and gave ye names,
Who now shall rear ye to the sun, or rank

---

242 Meliboean] Meliboea, in Thessaly, was famous in antiquity for its purple
    dye.
243 Sarra] Tyre, which was also famous for its dye.
244] See *Comus* 83n.
247] Cf. VI 250, 320-23.
249 state] stateliness of bearing.
264 gripe] spasm.
267 discovered] revealed.

Your tribes, and water from the ambrosial fount?
Thee lastly nuptial bower, by me adorned   280
With what to sight or smell was sweet, from thee
How shall I part, and whither wander down
Into a lower world, to this obscure
And wild? How shall we breathe in other air
Less pure, accustomed to immortal fruits?'   285
      Whom thus the angel interrupted mild:
'Lament not, Eve, but patiently resign
What justly thou hast lost; nor set thy heart,
Thus over-fond, on that which is not thine;
Thy going is not lonely; with thee goes   290
Thy husband; him to follow thou art bound;
Where he abides, think there thy native soil.'
      Adam, by this from the cold sudden damp
Recovering, and his scattered spirits returned,
To Michael thus his humble words addressed: 295
      'Celestial, whether among the thrones, or named
Of them the highest – for such of shape may seem
Prince above princes – gently hast thou told
Thy message, which might else in telling wound,
And in performing end us; what besides   300
Of sorrow and dejection and despair,
Our frailty can sustain, thy tidings bring –
Departure from this happy place, our sweet
Recess, and only consolation left
Familiar to our eyes; all places else   305
Inhospitable appear, and desolate,
Nor knowing us, nor known; and if by prayer
Incessant I could hope to change the will
Of him who all things can, I would not cease
To weary him with my assiduous cries;   310
But prayer against his absolute decree
No more avails than breath against the wind,
Blown stifling back on him that breathes it forth:
Therefore to his great bidding I submit.
This most afflicts me – that, departing hence,   315
As from his face I shall be hid, deprived
His blessed countenance; here I could frequent,
With worship, place by place where he vouchsafed

283 to] compared with.
293 damp] dazed or stupefied condition (i.e. the bound senses of l. 265).
298] Dan. x. 13, and A.V. marginal note.
309 can] knows.
316] Gen. iv. 14.

Presence divine, and to my sons relate,
"On this mount he appeared; under this tree   320
Stood visible; among these pines his voice
I heard; here with him at this fountain talked;"
So many grateful altars I would rear
Of grassy turf, and pile up every stone
Of lustre from the brook, in memory   325
Or monument to ages, and thereon
Offer sweet-smelling gums, and fruits, and flowers;
In yonder nether world where shall I seek
His bright appearances, or footstep trace?
For though I fled him angry, yet recalled   330
To life prolonged and promised race, I now
Gladly behold though but his utmost skirts
Of glory, and far off his steps adore.'
     To whom thus Michael, with regard benign:
'Adam, thou know'st heaven his, and all the earth,   335
Not this rock only; his omnipresence fills
Land, sea, and air, and every kind that lives,
Fomented by his virtual power and warmed;
All the earth he gave thee to possess and rule,
No despicable gift; surmise not then   340
His presence to these narrow bounds confined
Of Paradise or Eden; this had been
Perhaps thy capital seat, from whence had spread
All generations, and had hither come,
From all the ends of the earth, to celebrate   345
And reverence thee their great progenitor.
But this pre-eminence thou hast lost, brought down
To dwell on even ground now with thy sons:
Yet doubt not but in valley and in plain
God is as here, and will be found alike   350
Present, and of his presence many a sign
Still following thee, still compassing thee round
With goodness and paternal love, his face
Express, and of his steps the track divine.
Which that thou may'st believe, and be confirmed   355
Ere thou from hence depart, know I am sent
To show thee what shall come in future days
To thee and to thy offspring; good with bad
Expect to hear, supernal grace contending
With sinfulness of men – thereby to learn   360
True patience, and to temper joy with fear
And pious sorrow, equally inured

338 virtual] effective, potent, powerful.

By moderation either state to bear,
Prosperous or adverse: so shalt thou lead
Safest thy life, and best prepared endure   365
Thy mortal passage when it comes. Ascend
This hill; let Eve (for I have drenched her eyes)
Here sleep below while thou to foresight wak'st,
As once thou slept'st while she to life was formed.'
  To whom thus Adam gratefully replied: 370
'Ascend; I follow thee, safe guide, the path
Thou lead'st me, and to the hand of heaven submit,
However chastening – to the evil turn
My obvious breast, arming to overcome
By suffering, and earn rest from labour won,   375
If so I may attain.' So both ascend
In the visions of God; it was a hill,
Of Paradise the highest, from whose top
The hemisphere of earth in clearest ken
Stretched out to the amplest reach of prospect lay.   380
Not higher that hill, nor wider looking round,
Whereon for different cause the tempter set
Our second Adam in the wilderness,
To show him all earth's kingdoms and their glory.
His eye might there command wherever stood   385
City of old or modern fame, the seat
Of mightiest empire, from the destined walls
Of Cambalu, seat of Cathaian khan,
And Samarkand by Oxus, Temir's throne,
To Paquin, of Sinaean kings, and thence   390
To Agra and Lahore of Great Mogul,
Down to the golden Chersonese, or where

374 obvious] exposed.
377] Ezek. xl. 2.
381–4] Cf. *PR* III 251 ff.
388 Cambalu] capital of Cathay, and seat of the khan.
389 Samarkand] Samarkand, in modern Uzbekistan, about 150 miles from the
    Oxus River (now Amu-Darya), was the seat of Temir Lang, Marlowe's
    Tamburlaine.
390] Peking (Paquin) was the seat of the Chinese (Sinaean) kings; here China is
    clearly distinguished from Cathay (l. 388). Contrast III 438n.
391] Agra, in Uttar Pradesh (northern India), and Lahore, in the Punjab
    (Pakistan), are both former Mogul capitals. 'Great Mogul' was the usual
    European designation for the emperor of Delhi, which after 1526 was the
    capital of a huge Mogul empire.
392 colden Chersonese] *Aurea Chersonesus*, so called because of its fabled
    wealth, was rather vaguely identified with the area east of India, possibly
    the Malay Peninsula. Cf. *PR* IV 74.

The Persian in Ecbatan sat, or since
In Hispahan, or where the Russian czar
In Moscow, or the Sultan in Bizance,   395
Turkestan-born; nor could his eye not ken
The empire of Negus to his utmost port
Ercoco, and the less maritime kings,
Mombaza, and Quiloa, and Melind,
And Sofala – thought Ophir – to the realm   400
Of Congo, and Angola farthest south,
Or thence from Niger flood to Atlas mount,
The kingdoms of Almansor, Fez and Sus,
Marocco, and Algiers, and Tremisen;
On Europe thence, and where Rome was to sway   405
The world: in spirit perhaps he also saw
Rich Mexico, the seat of Montezume,
And Cuzco in Peru, the richer seat
Of Atabalipa, and yet unspoiled

393] Ecbatan, now Hamadan, a Median city which was the summer capital of
Persian kings.
394] Hispahan, now Isfahan, replaced Kasvin (X 436n.) as the Persian capital
in the sixteenth century.
395–6] Bizance (Byzantium, later Constantinople and now Istanbul) was after
1453 the seat of the Turkish Sultans, who belonged to a tribe that had
originally come from Turkestan, in central Asia. The form 'Bizance' derives
from the English bezant, a coin first struck in Byzantium.
397 Negus] the Amharic term for the title of the supreme ruler of Abyssinia
(now Ethiopia).
398] Ercoco (modern Arkiks) is a port on the Red Sea near Massawa.
399] Mombaza (Mombasa, in Kenya), Quiloa (Kilwa Kisiwani, in Tanzania),
and Melind (Malindi, in Kenya) were all Muslim colonies on the coast of
East Africa.
400] Sofala, a port south of the Zambezi (in modern Mozambique), was
sometimes identified with Ophir, which is mentioned many times in the
O.T. as the source of Solomon's gold.
402] The Niger River in modern Guinea and Mali, and the Atlas mountains in
Morocco.
403 Almansor] The Arabic regnal title 'al-Mansur' ('the Victorious') was
applied to many rulers, in this case to the twelfth-century Almohad emir
Abu-Yusuf Ya'qub al-Mansur, the only 'al-Mansur' described in the
accounts of North Africa (all based on Leo Africanus) available to Milton.
Fez] part of the sultanate of Fez and Morocco.
Sus] a province of southern Morocco, once an independent kingdom.
404] On Marocco, see I 583–4n. Tremisen, now Tlemcen, in Algeria, was once an
independent sultanate.
407 Montezume] Montezuma II, last ruler of the Aztec empire, in Mexico, was
defeated by Cortés.
408–9] Cuzco, the Inca capital (in modern Peru), was the seat of Atahuallpa
('Atabalipa'), who was defeated by Pizarro.

Guiana, whose great city Geryon's sons   410
Call El Dorado; but to nobler sights
Michael from Adam's eyes the film removed,
Which that false fruit that promised clearer sight
Had bred; then purged with euphrasy and rue
The visual nerve, for he had much to see,   415
And from the well of life three drops instilled.
So deep the power of these ingredients pierced,
Even to the inmost seat of mental sight,
That Adam, now enforced to close his eyes,
Sunk down, and all his spirits became entranced;   420
But him the gentle angel by the hand
Soon raised, and his attention thus recalled:
    'Adam, now ope thine eyes, and first behold
The effects which thy original crime hath wrought
In some to spring from thee, who never touched   425
The excepted tree, nor with the snake conspired,
Nor sinned thy sin, yet from that sin derive
Corruption to bring forth more violent deeds.'
    His eyes he opened, and beheld a field,
Part arable and tilth, whereon were sheaves   430
New-reaped, the other part sheep-walks and folds;
I' the midst an altar as the landmark stood,
Rustic, of grassy sward; thither anon
A sweaty reaper from his tillage brought
First-fruits, the green ear and the yellow sheaf,   435
Unculled, as came to hand; a shepherd next,
More meek, came with the firstlings of his flock,
Choicest and best; then sacrificing, laid
The inwards and their fat, with incense strewed,

410–11] Manoa, the mythical golden city of Guiana, was called El Dorado by
the Spanish, who are here (following Spenser, *Faerie Queene* V. x. 8–10)
called Geryon's sons. Geryon was a three-headed monster who ruled
Erythea, a mythical island vaguely situated to the west of Europe. On 21
July 1667, about a month before *PL* was published, Guiana was ceded (in
the Peace of Breda) by the English to the Dutch (in exchange for New
York), so 'yet unspoiled' would have been seen as (and conceivably could
have been) a topical reference.

412] Cf. *Iliad* v 127, *Aeneid* ii 604–5.

414 euphrasy] a medicinal plant (eyebright) and (etymologically, from
εὐφρασία) 'good cheer'.
    rue] a medicinal plant, and (in a common play on the word) 'pity,
compassion'; Shakespeare twice calls it 'herb of grace'.

416] Psalm xxxvi. 9.

427–60] For the story of Cain and Abel see Gen. iv.

436 Unculled] not selected.

On the cleft wood, and all due rites performed.   440
His offering soon propitious fire from heaven
Consumed, with nimble glance and grateful steam;
The other's not, for his was not sincere:
Whereat he inly raged, and as they talked,
Smote him into the midriff with a stone   445
That beat out life; he fell, and deadly pale,
Groaned out his soul, with gushing blood effused.
Much at that sight was Adam in his heart
Dismayed, and thus in haste to the angel cried:
    'O teacher, some great mischief hath befallen   450
To that meek man, who well had sacrificed;
Is piety thus and pure devotion paid?'
    To whom Michael thus, he also moved, replied:
'These two are brethren, Adam, and to come
Out of thy loins; the unjust the just hath slain,   455
For envy that his brother's offering found
From heaven acceptance; but the bloody fact
Will be avenged, and the other's faith approved
Lose no reward, though here thou see him die,
Rolling in dust and gore.' To which our sire: 460
    'Alas, both for the deed and for the cause!
But have I now seen death? Is this the way
I must return to native dust? O sight
Of terror, foul and ugly to behold;
Horrid to think, how horrible to feel!'   465
    To whom thus Michael: 'Death thou hast seen
In his first shape on man; but many shapes
Of Death, and many are the ways that lead
To his grim cave – all dismal, yet to sense
More terrible at the entrance than within.   470
Some, as thou saw'st, by violent stroke shall die,
By fire, flood, famine; by intemperance more
In meats and drinks, which on the earth shall bring
Diseases dire, of which a monstrous crew
Before thee shall appear, that thou may'st know   475
What misery the inabstinence of Eve
Shall bring on men.' Immediately a place
Before his eyes appeared, sad, noisome, dark;
A lazar-house it seemed, wherein were laid
Numbers of all diseased – all maladies   480

---

457 fact] evil deed.
458–60] Heb. xi. 4.
468–70] The details are those of the classical underworld (see *Metamorphoses* iv
    432–45, and the famous description in *Aeneid* vi).

Of ghastly spasm, or racking torture, qualms
Of heart-sick agony, all feverous kinds,
Convulsions, epilepsies, fierce catarrhs,
Intestine stone and ulcer, colic pangs,
Demoniac frenzy, moping melancholy,   485
And moon-struck madness, pining atrophy,
Marasmus, and wide-wasting pestilence,
Dropsies and asthmas, and joint-racking rheums.
Dire was the tossing, deep the groans; Despair
Tended the sick, busiest from couch to couch;   490
And over them triumphant Death his dart
Shook, but delayed to strike, though oft invoked
With vows, as their chief good and final hope.
Sight so deform what heart of rock could long
Dry-eyed behold? Adam could not, but wept,   495
Though not of woman born: compassion quelled
His best of man, and gave him up to tears
A space, till firmer thoughts restrained excess,
And, scarce recovering words, his plaint renewed:
    'O miserable mankind, to what fall   500
Degraded, to what wretched state reserved!
Better end here unborn. Why is life given
To be thus wrested from us? Rather why
Obtruded on us thus? Who, if we knew
What we receive, would either not accept   505
Life offered, or soon beg to lay it down,
Glad to be so dismissed in peace. Can thus
The image of God in man, created once
So goodly and erect, though faulty since,
To such unsightly sufferings be debased   510
Under inhuman pains? Why should not man,
Retaining still divine similitude
In part, from such deformities be free,
And for his maker's image sake exempt?'
    'Their maker's image,' answered Michael, 'then   515
Forsook them, when themselves they vilified
To serve ungoverned appetite, and took
His image whom they served – a brutish vice,
Inductive mainly to the sin of Eve.

486 moon-struck madness] lunacy, i.e. intermittent insanity caused by the
    changes of the moon (*luna*).
487 Marasmus] wasting away of the body.
504-6] Adam's response is Stoical (cf. Seneca, *Ad Marciam: De Consolatione*
    xxii. 3).
511-25] See VII 519-20n.
519 Inductive] inducing, leading on.

Therefore so abject is their punishment,   520
Disfiguring not God's likeness, but their own;
Or if his likeness, by themselves defaced
While they pervert pure nature's healthful rules
To loathsome sickness – worthily, since they
God's image did not reverence in themselves.'   525
    'I yield it just,' said Adam, 'and submit.
But is there yet no other way, besides
These painful passages, how we may come
To death, and mix with our connatural dust?'
    'There is,' said Michael, 'if thou well observe   530
The rule of "not too much", by temperance taught
In what thou eat'st and drink'st, seeking from thence
Due nourishment, not gluttonous delight,
Till many years over thy head return;
So may'st thou live, till like ripe fruit thou drop   535
Into thy mother's lap, or be with ease
Gathered, not harshly plucked, for death mature:
This is old age; but then thou must outlive
Thy youth, thy strength, thy beauty, which will change
To withered, weak, and grey; thy senses then,   540
Obtuse, all taste of pleasure must forgo
To what thou hast; and for the air of youth,
Hopeful and cheerful, in thy blood will reign
A melancholy damp of cold and dry,
To weigh thy spirits down, and last consume   545
The balm of life.' To whom our ancestor:
    'Henceforth I fly not death, nor would prolong
Life much – bent rather how I may be quit,
Fairest and easiest, of this cumbrous charge,
Which I must keep till my appointed day   550
Of rendering up, and patiently attend
My dissolution.' Michael replied:
    'Nor love thy life, nor hate; but what thou liv'st
Live well; how long or short permit to heaven;
And now prepare thee for another sight.'   555
    He looked, and saw a spacious plain, whereon
Were tents of various hue: by some were herds
Of cattle grazing: others whence the sound
Of instruments that made melodious chime

531 not too much] Alludes to the ancient aphorism μηδὲν ἄγαν (or *ne quid nimis*), nothing in excess.
535-7] The ultimate source of the comparison is Cicero's essay *De Senectute* 19.
553-4] A classical commonplace (e.g. Horace, *Odes*, I. ix. 9, Martial, *Epigrams* X. xlvii. 13, Seneca, *Epistles* lxv. 18).

Was heard, of harp and organ, and who moved   560
Their stops and chords was seen: his volant touch
Instinct through all proportions low and high
Fled and pursued transverse the resonant fugue.
In other part stood one who, at the forge
Labouring, two massy clods of iron and brass   565
Had melted (whether found where casual fire
Had wasted woods, on mountain or in vale,
Down to the veins of earth, thence gliding hot
To some cave's mouth, or whether washed by stream
From underground); the liquid ore he drained   570
Into fit moulds prepared; from which he formed
First his own tools, then what might else be wrought
Fusile or graven in metal. After these,
But on the hither side, a different sort   574
From the high neighbouring hills, which was their seat,
Down to the plain descended: by their guise
Just men they seemed, and all their study bent
To worship God aright, and know his works
Not hid, nor those things last which might preserve
Freedom and peace to men; they on the plain   580
Long had not walked when from the tents behold
A bevy of fair women, richly gay
In gems and wanton dress; to the harp they sung
Soft amorous ditties, and in dance came on;
The men, though grave, eyed them, and let their eyes   585
Rove without rein, till, in the amorous net
Fast caught, they liked, and each his liking chose;
And now of love they treat, till the evening star,
Love's harbinger, appeared; then all in heat,
They light the nuptial torch, and bid invoke   590
Hymen, then first to marriage rites invoked:

560 who] Jubal, 'the father of all such as handle the harp and organ', Gen. iv. 21.
561 volant] moving rapidly and lightly.
562 Instinct] impelled, animated.
    proportions] melodies, harmony.
564 one] Tubal-cain, 'an instructor of every artificer in brass and iron', Gen. iv. 22.
566 casual] accidental (used of unfortunate events).
573 Fusile] formed by melting or casting.
574–627] Gen. vi. 2–4, the substance of which is recapitulated in ll. 621–2; cf. III 463–5, V 447–8.
578–9] According to an ancient tradition (e.g. Josephus, *Antiquities* I. ii. 3) the descendants of Seth discovered astronomy, the study of God's 'works/Not hid'.
588 evening star] Hesperus, which is also 'love's harbinger' in VIII 519–20.
590–1 invoke/Hymen] See IV 711n.

With feast and music all the tents resound.
Such happy interview, and fair event
Of love and youth not lost, songs, garlands, flowers,
And charming symphonies, attached the heart   595
Of Adam, soon inclined to admit delight,
The bent of nature; which he thus expressed:
    'True opener of mine eyes, prime angel blest,
Much better seems this vision, and more hope
Of peaceful days portends, than those two past: 600
Those were of hate and death, or pain much worse;
Here nature seems fulfilled in all her ends.'
    To whom thus Michael: 'Judge not what is best
By pleasure, though to nature seeming meet,
Created, as thou art, to nobler end,   605
Holy and pure, conformity divine.
Those tents thou saw'st so pleasant were the tents
Of wickedness, wherein shall dwell his race
Who slew his brother: studious they appear
Of arts that polish life; inventors rare;   610
Unmindful of their maker, though his spirit
Taught them; but they his gifts acknowledge none.
Yet they a beauteous offspring shall beget;
For that fair female troop thou saw'st, that seemed
Of goddesses, so blithe, so smooth, so gay,   615
Yet empty of all good wherein consists
Woman's domestic honour and chief praise;
Bred only and completed to the taste
Of lustful appetence, to sing, to dance,
To dress, and troll the tongue, and roll the eye;   620
To these that sober race of men, whose lives
Religious titled them the sons of God,
Shall yield up all their virtue, all their fame,
Ignobly, to the trains and to the smiles
Of these fair atheists, and now swim in joy   625
(Erelong to swim at large) and laugh; for which
The world erelong a world of tears must weep.'

607-8] Psalm lxxxiv. 10. Cain's descendant Jabal 'was the father of such as
    dwell in tents' (Gen. iv. 20).
609-12] The children of Cain were believed to have invented the arts (Gen. iv.
    16-22).
619 appetence] desire, appetite.
620 troll] wag.
621-2] See 574-627n. Milton dissents from the common patristic idea that the
    'sons of God' were fallen angels, and aligns himself with those (such as
    Augustine) who identified them with the descendants of Seth.
624 trains] deceits, snares.

To whom thus Adam, of short joy bereft:
'O pity and shame, that they who to live well
Entered so fair, should turn aside to tread   630
Paths indirect, or in the midway faint!
But still I see the tenor of man's woe
Holds on the same, from woman to begin.'
  'From man's effeminate slackness it begins,'
Said the angel, 'who should better hold his place   635
By wisdom, and superior gifts received.
But now prepare thee for another scene.'
  He looked, and saw wide territory spread
Before him – towns, and rural works between,
Cities of men with lofty gates and towers,   640
Concourse in arms, fierce faces threatening war,
Giants of mighty bone and bold emprise;
Part wield their arms, part curb the foaming steed,
Single or in array of battle ranged
Both horse and foot, nor idly mustering stood;   645
One way a band select from forage drives
A herd of beeves, fair oxen and fair kine,
From a fat meadow-ground, or fleecy flock,
Ewes and their bleating lambs, over the plain,
Their booty; scarce with life the shepherds fly,   650
But call in aid, which makes a bloody fray:
With cruel tournament the squadrons join;
Where cattle pastured late, now scattered lies
With carcasses and arms the ensanguined field
Deserted; others to a city strong   655
Lay siege, encamped, by battery, scale, and mine,
Assaulting; others from the wall defend
With dart and javelin, stones and sulphurous fire;
On each hand slaughter and gigantic deeds.
In other part the sceptred heralds call   660
To council in the city-gates: anon
Grey-headed men and grave, with warriors mixed,
Assemble, and harangues are heard; but soon
In factious opposition, till at last
Of middle age one rising, eminent   665

632–3] In sixteenth- and seventeenth-century etymology 'woman' was said to
  mean 'woe of man'.
638–73] Imitates the scenes depicted on the shields of Achilles (*Iliad* xviii
  478–540) and Aeneas (*Aeneid* viii 626–728).
641 Concourse] hostile encounter.
642 emprise] chivalric prowess.
656 scale] ladder.
665 one] Enoch (Gen. v. 21–4, Heb. xi. 5, Jude 14–15).

In wise deport, spake much of right and wrong,
Of justice, of religion, truth, and peace,
And judgement from above: him old and young
Exploded, and had seized with violent hands,
Had not a cloud descending snatched him thence,   670
Unseen amid the throng; so violence
Proceeded, and oppression, and sword-law,
Through all the plain, and refuge none was found.
Adam was all in tears, and to his guide
Lamenting turned full sad: 'O what are these,   675
Death's ministers, not men, who thus deal death
Inhumanly to men, and multiply
Ten thousandfold the sin of him who slew
His brother; for of whom such massacre
Make they but of their brethren, men of men?   680
But who was that just man, whom had not heaven
Rescued, had in his righteousness been lost?'
     To whom thus Michael: 'These are the product
Of those ill-mated marriages thou saw'st   684
Where good with bad were matched; who of themselves
Abhor to join, and by imprudence mixed,
Produce prodigious births of body or mind.
Such were these giants, men of high renown;
For in those days might only shall be admired,
And valour and heroic virtue called;   690
To overcome in battle, and subdue
Nations, and bring home spoils with infinite
Manslaughter, shall be held the highest pitch
Of human glory, and for glory done,
Of triumph, to be styled great conquerors,   695
Patrons of mankind, gods, and sons of gods –
Destroyers rightlier called, and plagues of men.
Thus fame shall be achieved, renown on earth,
And what most merits fame in silence hid.
But he, the seventh from thee, whom thou beheld'st   700
The only righteous in a world perverse,
And therefore hated, therefore so beset
With foes, for daring single to be just,
And utter odious truth, that God would come

---

669 Exploded] See X 546n.
670-1] Milton probably had access to the tradition embodied in the pseudepi-
     graphical Ethiopic Book of Enoch (xiv. 8-9) that the translation of Enoch
     (see III 461n.) was initiated by an invitation extended by the clouds.
688-9] Gen. vi. 4.
700 seventh from thee] Jude 14; Gen. v. 3-18.

To judge them with his saints – him the most high,   705
Rapt in a balmy cloud, with winged steeds,
Did, as thou saw'st, receive, to walk with God
High in salvation and the climes of bliss,
Exempt from death, to show thee what reward
Awaits the good, the rest what punishment;   710
Which now direct thine eyes and soon behold.'
   He looked, and saw the face of things quite changed;
The brazen throat of war had ceased to roar;
All now was turned to jollity and game,
To luxury and riot, feast and dance,   715
Marrying or prostituting, as befell,
Rape or adultery, where passing fair
Allured them; thence from cups to civil broils.
At length a reverend sire among them came,
And of their doings great dislike declared,   720
And testified against their ways; he oft
Frequented their assemblies, whereso met,
Triumphs or festivals, and to them preached
Conversion and repentance, as to souls
In a prison, under judgements imminent;   725
But all in vain; which when he saw, he ceased
Contending, and removed his tents far off;
Then from the mountain hewing timber tall,
Began to build a vessel of huge bulk,
Measured by cubit, length, and breadth, and height,   730
Smeared round with pitch, and in the side a door
Contrived, and of provisions laid in large
For man and beast: when lo a wonder strange!
Of every beast, and bird, and insect small,
Came sevens and pairs, and entered in, as taught   735
Their order; last the sire and his three sons,

706] A conflation of the tradition described in 670-1n. with the description of
    the translation of Elijah (II Kings ii. 11).
707 walk with God] Gen. v. 24.
714-18] Luke xvii. 26-7; 'luxury' means 'lust'.
717 passing fair] 'Fair' means 'beautiful woman', and 'passing' plays on the
    senses 'passing by' and 'exceedingly'.
719-53] Gen. vi. 5-vii. 24; Heb. xi. 7.
719 reverend sire] Noah.
723-5] I Pet. iii. 18-21.
734] Insects were added to the Biblical passenger-list by those Renaissance
    commentators on Genesis who had rejected the traditional belief that
    insects arose spontaneously from putrefaction and instead believed with
    Milton that insects were generated in the same way as other animals (cf. IV
    704, VII 476).

With their four wives; and God made fast the door.
Meanwhile the south-wind rose, and with black wings
Wide-hovering, all the clouds together drove
From under heaven; the hills to their supply   740
Vapour, and exhalation dusk and moist,
Sent up amain; and now the thickened sky
Like a dark ceiling stood: down rushed the rain
Impetuous, and continued till the earth
No more was seen; the floating vessel swum   745
Uplifted, and secure with beaked prow
Rode tilting o'er the waves; all dwellings else
Flood overwhelmed, and them with all their pomp
Deep under water rolled; sea covered sea,
Sea without shore: and in their palaces,   750
Where luxury late reigned, sea-monsters whelped
And stabled: of mankind, so numerous late,
All left in one small bottom swum embarked.
How didst thou grieve then, Adam, to behold
The end of all thy offspring, end so sad,   755
Depopulation; thee another flood,
Of tears and sorrow a flood thee also drowned,
And sunk thee as thy sons; till gently reared
By the angel, on thy feet thou stood'st at last,
Though comfortless, as when a father mourns   760
His children, all in view destroyed at once,
And scarce to the angel utter'dst thus thy plaint:
   'O visions ill foreseen! Better had I
Lived ignorant of future – so had borne
My part of evil only, each day's lot   765
Enough to bear; those now that were dispensed
The burden of many ages on me light
At once, by my foreknowledge gaining birth
Abortive, to torment me, ere their being,
With thought that they must be. Let no man seek   770
Henceforth to be foretold what shall befall
Him or his children – evil, he may be sure,
Which neither his foreknowing can prevent,
And he the future evil shall no less
In apprehension than in substance feel   775
Grievous to bear; but that care now is past;

738-53] Many of the details are drawn from Ovid's account of the universal
   flood in *Metamorphoses* i 253-347. Cf. ll. 10-14n.
753 bottom] boat.
765-6] Matt. vi. 34.
773-4 neither ... And] Imitates the Latin construction '*neque ... et*'.

Man is not whom to warn; those few escaped,
Famine and anguish will at last consume,
Wandering that watery desert; I had hope,
When violence was ceased and war on earth,   780
All would have then gone well, peace would have crowned
With length of happy days, the race of man;
But I was far deceived, for now I see
Peace to corrupt no less than war to waste.
How comes it thus? Unfold, celestial guide,   785
And whether here the race of man will end.'
    To whom thus Michael: 'Those whom last thou saw'st
In triumph and luxurious wealth, are they
First seen in acts of prowess eminent
And great exploits, but of true virtue void;   790
Who having spilt much blood, and done much waste,
Subduing nations, and achieved thereby
Fame in the world, high titles, and rich prey,
Shall change their course to pleasure, ease, and sloth,
Surfeit, and lust, till wantonness and pride   795
Raise out of friendship hostile deeds in peace.
The conquered also, and enslaved by war,
Shall, with their freedom lost, all virtue lose,
And fear of God – from whom their piety feigned
In sharp contest of battle found no aid   800
Against invaders; therefore, cooled in zeal,
Thenceforth shall practise how to live secure,
Worldly or dissolute, on what their lords
Shall leave them to enjoy; for the earth shall bear
More than enough, that temperance may be tried;   805
So all shall turn degenerate, all depraved,
Justice and temperance, truth and faith, forgot;
One man except, the only son of light
In a dark age, against example good,
Against allurement, custom, and a world   810
Offended; fearless of reproach and scorn,
Or violence, he of their wicked ways
Shall them admonish, and before them set
The paths of righteousness, how much more safe
And full of peace, denouncing wrath to come   815
On their impenitence, and shall return
Of them derided, but of God observed
The one just man alive: by his command
Shall build a wondrous ark, as thou beheld'st,

787–807] Milton's description is designed to embrace the seventeenth century
    as well as the time of the flood.

To save himself and household from amidst   820
A world devote to universal rack.
No sooner he, with them of man and beast
Select for life, shall in the ark be lodged
And sheltered round, but all the cataracts
Of heaven set open on the earth shall pour   825
Rain day and night; all fountains of the deep,
Broke up, shall heave the ocean to usurp
Beyond all bounds, till inundation rise
Above the highest hills; then shall this mount
Of Paradise by might of waves be moved   830
Out of his place, pushed by the horned flood,
With all his verdure spoiled, and trees adrift,
Down the great river to the opening gulf,
And there take root, an island salt and bare,
The haunt of seals, and orcs, and sea-mews' clang –   835
To teach thee that God attributes to place
No sanctity, if none be thither brought
By men who there frequent or therein dwell.
And now what further shall ensue behold.'
    He looked, and saw the ark hull on the flood,   840
Which now abated; for the clouds were fled,
Driven by a keen north-wind, that blowing dry,
Wrinkled the face of deluge, as decayed;
And the clear sun on his wide watery glass
Gazed hot, and of the fresh wave largely drew,   845
As after thirst; which made their flowing shrink
From standing lake to tripping ebb, that stole
With soft foot towards the deep, who now had stopped
His sluices, as the heaven his windows shut.
The ark no more now floats, but seems on ground,   850

---

821 devote] doomed.

824-7] Gen. vii. 11. 'Cataracts' transliterates the LXX (καταρράκται) or the
    Vulgate *cataractae*); the Greek term probably and the Latin term certainly
    mean 'flood-gates', which is the A.V. marginal reading. The A.V. 'windows'
    translates the Hebrew word for 'lattices, windows' (cf. Isa. lx. 8, where the
    same Hebrew word is used).

833] The 'great river' is probably the Euphrates (Gen. xv. 18), and the 'gulf' the
    Persian Gulf.

834 salt] i.e. barren (a common O.T. usage).

835 orcs] whales, ferocious sea-monsters.
    sea-mews] gulls.

840 hull] drift.

842 north-wind] Gen. viii. 1; *Metamorphoses* i 328.

848-9] Gen. viii. 2.

850-4] Gen. viii. 4-5; *Metamorphoses* i. 343-5.

Fast on the top of some high mountain fixed.
And now the tops of hills as rocks appear;
With clamour thence the rapid currents drive
Towards the retreating sea their furious tide.
Forthwith from out the ark a raven flies,   855
And after him, the surer messenger,
A dove sent forth once and again to spy
Green tree or ground whereon his foot may light;
The second time returning, in his bill
An olive-leaf he brings, pacific sign;   860
Anon dry ground appears, and from his ark
The ancient sire descends, with all his train;
Then with uplifted hands, and eyes devout,
Grateful to heaven, over his head beholds
A dewy cloud, and in the cloud a bow   865
Conspicuous with three listed colours gay,
Betokening peace from God, and covenant new.
Whereat the heart of Adam, erst so sad,
Greatly rejoiced, and thus his joy broke forth:
     'O thou, who future things canst represent   870
As present, heavenly instructor, I revive
At this last sight, assured that man shall live,
With all the creatures, and their seed preserve.
Far less I now lament for one whole world
Of wicked sons destroyed, than I rejoice   875
For one man found so perfect, and so just,
That God vouchsafes to raise another world
From him, and all his anger to forget.
But say, what mean those coloured streaks in heaven,
Distended as the brow of God appeased?   880
Or serve they as a flowery verge to bind
The fluid skirts of that same watery cloud,
Lest it again dissolve and shower the earth?'
     To whom the archangel: 'Dextrously thou aim'st;
So willingly doth God remit his ire: 885
Though late repenting him of man depraved,
Grieved at his heart, when looking down he saw
The whole earth filled with violence, and all flesh
Corrupting each their way; yet those removed,
Such grace shall one just man find in his sight   890
That he relents, not to blot out mankind,

865–701] Gen. ix. 8–17.
866] The three colours (red, yellow, blue) are arranged in bands ('listed').
886–90] Gen. vi. 6–12.

And makes a covenant never to destroy
The earth again by flood, nor let the sea
Surpass his bounds, nor rain to drown the world
With man therein or beast; but when he brings   895
Over the earth a cloud, will therein set
His triple-coloured bow, whereon to look
And call to mind his covenant; day and night,
Seed-time and harvest, heat and hoary frost,
Shall hold their course, till fire purge all things new,   900
Both heaven and earth, wherein the just shall dwell.'

THE END OF THE ELEVENTH BOOK

898–901] Gen. viii. 22; II Pet. iii. 6–13.

BOOK XII

THE ARGUMENT

The angel Michael continues, from the flood, to relate what shall
succeed; then, in the mention of Abraham, comes by degrees to
explain who that seed of the woman shall be which was promised
Adam and Eve in the fall: his incarnation, death, resurrection, and
ascension; the state of the Church till his second coming. Adam,
greatly satisfied and recomforted by these relations and promises,
descends the hill with Michael; wakens Eve, who all this while had
slept, but with gentle dreams composed to quietness of mind and
submission. Michael in either hand leads them out of Paradise, the
fiery sword waving behind them, and the cherubim taking their
stations to guard the place.

As one who in his journey baits at noon,
Though bent on speed, so here the archangel paused
Betwixt the world destroyed and world restored,
If Adam aught perhaps might interpose;
Then, with transition sweet, new speech resumes: 5
    'Thus thou hast seen one world begin and end,
And man as from a second stock proceed.
Much thou hast yet to see, but I perceive
Thy mortal sight to fail; objects divine
Must needs impair and weary human sense;   10
Henceforth what is to come I will relate;
Thou therefore give due audience, and attend.
    'This second source of men, while yet but few,
And while the dread of judgement past remains
Fresh in their minds, fearing the Deity,   15
With some regard to what is just and right
Shall lead their lives, and multiply apace,
Labouring the soil, and reaping plenteous crop,
Corn, wine, and oil; and from the herd or flock
Oft sacrificing bullock, lamb, or kid,   20
With large wine-offerings poured, and sacred feast,
Shall spend their days in joy unblamed, and dwell
Long time in peace, by families and tribes,
Under paternal rule: till one shall rise,

---

1 baits] used of travellers who stop at an inn.
7 second stock] literally Noah, and typologically Christ, in whom believers were
    said to be 'engrafted'. Cf. III 293n.
18-21] Deut. xiv. 23-6.
24-37] On Nimrod see Gen. x. 8-10.

Of proud, ambitious heart, who not content   25
With fair equality, fraternal state,
Will arrogate dominion undeserved
Over his brethren, and quite dispossess
Concord and law of nature from the earth –
Hunting (and men, not beasts, shall be his game)   30
With war and hostile snare such as refuse
Subjection to his empire tyrannous;
A mighty hunter thence he shall be styled
Before the Lord, as in despite of heaven,
Or from heaven claiming second sovereignty,   35
And from rebellion shall derive his name,
Though of rebellion others he accuse.
He with a crew, whom like ambition joins
With him or under him to tyrannize,
Marching from Eden towards the west, shall find   40
The plain, wherein a black bituminous gurge
Boils out from under ground, the mouth of hell;
Of brick, and of that stuff, they cast to build
A city and tower, whose top may reach to heaven;
And get themselves a name, lest far dispersed   45
In foreign lands, their memory be lost –
Regardless whether good or evil fame.
But God, who oft descends to visit men
Unseen, and through their habitations walks,
To mark their doings, them beholding soon,   50
Comes down to see their city, ere the tower
Obstruct heaven-towers, and in derision sets
Upon their tongues a various spirit, to raze
Quite out their native language, and instead
To sow a jangling noise of words unknown;   55
Forthwith a hideous gabble rises loud
Among the builders; each to other calls,
Not understood – till, hoarse and all in rage,
As mocked they storm; great laughter was in heaven,
And looking down to see the hubbub strange   60
And hear the din; thus was the building left

36] The popular derivation of Nimrod from *marad*, to rebel, rests on a false
etymology.
38–62] On the Tower of Babel see Gen. xi. 1–9 and cf. *PL* III 466–8. Although
Nimrod is associated with Babel in Gen. x. 10, the tradition that he built
the tower seems to have been initiated by Josephus (*Antiquities* I iv. 2,
vi. 2).
41 bituminous] see X 298n.
gurge] whirlpool.
43 cast] resolve.
53 various] causing difference or dissimilarity.

Ridiculous, and the work Confusion named.'
   Whereto thus Adam, fatherly displeased:
'O execrable son, so to aspire
Above his brethren, to himself assuming   65
Authority usurped, from God not given;
He gave us only over beast, fish, fowl,
Dominion absolute; that right we hold
By his donation: but man over men
He made not lord – such title to himself   70
Reserving, human left from human free.
But this usurper his encroachment proud
Stays not on man; to God his tower intends
Siege and defiance. Wretched man! What food
Will he convey up thither, to sustain   75
Himself and his rash army, where thin air
Above the clouds will pine his entrails gross,
And famish him of breath, if not of bread?'
   To whom thus Michael: 'Justly thou abhorr'st
That son, who on the quiet state of men   80
Such trouble brought, affecting to subdue
Rational liberty; yet know withal,
Since thy original lapse, true liberty
Is lost, which always with right reason dwells
Twinned, and from her hath no dividual being;   85
Reason in man obscured, or not obeyed,
Immediately inordinate desires
And upstart passions catch the government
From reason, and to servitude reduce
Man, till then free. Therefore, since he permits   90
Within himself unworthy powers to reign
Over free reason, God in judgement just,
Subjects him from without to violent lords,
Who oft as undeservedly enthral
His outward freedom; tyranny must be,   95
Though to the tyrant thereby no excuse.
Yet sometimes nations will decline so low
From virtue, which is reason, that no wrong,
But justice and some fatal curse annexed,
Deprives them of their outward liberty,   100
Their inward lost: witness the irreverent son

---

62 Confusion] See Gen. xi. 9, A.V. marginal note. The Hebrew text contains a
   play on the words 'confound' (*balal*) and *Babel* (Babylon). Cf. l. 343.
84 right reason] see VI 42n.
85 dividual] separate, distinct, particular.
101–4] On Ham and Canaan see Gen. ix. 22–7.

Of him who built the ark, who for the shame
Done to his father, heard this heavy curse,
"Servant of servants", on his vicious race.
Thus will this latter, as the former world,   105
Still tend from bad to worse, till God at last,
Wearied with their iniquities, withdraw
His presence from among them, and avert
His holy eyes, resolving from thenceforth
To leave them to their own polluted ways,   110
And one peculiar nation to select
From all the rest, of whom to be invoked –
A nation from one faithful man to spring;
Him on this side Euphrates yet residing,
Bred up in idol-worship – O that men   115
(Canst thou believe?) should be so stupid grown,
While yet the patriarch lived who scaped the flood,
As to forsake the living God, and fall
To worship their own work in wood and stone
For gods! Yet him God the most high vouchsafes   120
To call by wisdom from his father's house,
His kindred, and false gods, into a land
Which he will show him, and from him will raise
A mighty nation, and upon him shower
His benediction so that in his seed   125
All nations shall be blest; he straight obeys,
Not knowing to what land, yet firm believes;
I see him, but thou canst not, with what faith
He leaves his gods, his friends, and native soil,
Ur of Chaldaea, passing now the ford   130
To Haran – after him a cumbrous train
Of herds and flocks, and numerous servitude –

111-13] Among the several kinds of election distinguished by Protestant
   theologians were the general, or national election of the Jews (who are thus
   called 'peculiar', i.e. specially chosen) and the election of an individual
   (such as Abraham, or the apostles) to a particular office. Neither of these
   should be confused with the individual election to salvation (a doctrine
   related to predestination). Cf. 'race elect', l. 214.
113-64] On Abraham see Gen. xi. 27-xxv. 10.
114-15] Joshua xxiv. 2.
117] Gen. ix. 28.
120-30] Gen. xii. 1-3, Gal. iii. 6-18, Acts vii. 2-7, Heb. xi. 8.
130-1] Haran is a city of north-western Mesopotamia (now Turkey). Line 114
   suggests that Milton thought Ur was east of the Euphrates (cf. Acts vii. 2),
   so the 'ford/To Haran' cannot be across the Euphrates, but must rather be
   across one of the tributaries coming from the north-east (cf. PR III 257).
132 servitude] slaves and servants.

Not wandering poor, but trusting all his wealth
With God, who called him, in a land unknown.
Canaan he now attains; I see his tents   135
Pitched about Sechem, and the neighbouring plain
Of Moreh; there by promise he receives
Gift to his progeny of all that land,
From Hamath northward to the desert south
(Things by their names I call, though yet unnamed),   140
From Hermon east to the great western sea;
Mount Hermon, yonder sea, each place behold
In prospect, as I point them: on the shore,
Mount Carmel; here, the double-founted stream,
Jordan, true limit eastward; but his sons   145
Shall dwell to Senir, that long ridge of hills.
This ponder, that all nations of the earth
Shall in his seed be blessed; by that seed
Is meant thy great deliverer, who shall bruise
The serpent's head; whereof to thee anon   150
Plainlier shall be revealed. This patriarch blest,
Whom "faithful Abraham" due time shall call,
A son, and of his son a grandchild leaves,
Like him in faith, in wisdom, and renown;
The grandchild, with twelve sons increased, departs   155
From Canaan to a land hereafter called
Egypt, divided by the river Nile;
See where it flows, disgorging at seven mouths
Into the sea; to sojourn in that land
He comes, invited by a younger son   160

135-7] Gen. xii. 5-6.
139 Hamath] a city and ancient kingdom on the Orontes (now Hama, in Syria).
141] Mount Hermon, on the border of Lebanon and Syria, was the highest
    mountain of Palestine. In the Hebrew of the O.T. the Mediterranean is
    variously called the 'Hinder (i.e. western) Sea' (e.g. Zech. xiv. 8), the 'Great
    Sea' (e.g. Num. xxxiv. 6), or simply 'The Sea' (e.g. Num. xxxiv. 5).
144-5] Mount Carmel is a promontory near Haifa. The belief that the Jordan is
    'double-founted' is at least as old as Jerome, who argued that the springs
    'Jor' and 'Dan' ran together into a river appropriately called 'Jordan'. In
    fact the Hebrew word for Jordan is not related to 'Dan'.
146] Senir was the Amorite name for Mount Hermon (Deut. iii. 9), which was
    commonly represented on seventeenth-century maps as a range of hills.
147-8] Gen. xxii. 18.
152] In Gen. xvii. 5 Abram's name is changed to Abraham, and the termination
    -raham is connected with the Hebrew word for multitude to make the name
    mean 'father of a multitude' (see A.V. marginal note).
153] The son is Isaac, the grandchild Jacob.
155-64] Gen. xxxix-i. The 'younger son' is Joseph.

In time of dearth – a son whose worthy deeds
Raise him to be the second in that realm
Of Pharaoh; there he dies, and leaves his race
Growing into a nation, and now grown
Suspected to a sequent king, who seeks   165
To stop their overgrowth, as inmate guests
Too numerous; whence of guests he makes them slaves
Inhospitably, and kills their infant males:
Till by two brethren (those two brethren call
Moses and Aaron) sent from God to claim   170
His people from enthralment, they return
With glory and spoil, back to their Promised Land.
But first the lawless tyrant, who denies
To know their God, or message to regard,
Must be compelled by signs and judgements dire: 175
To blood unshed the rivers must be turned;
Frogs, lice, and flies must all his palace fill
With loathed intrusion, and fill all the land;
His cattle must of rot and murrain die;
Botches and blains must all his flesh emboss,   180
And all his people; thunder mixed with hail,
Hail mixed with fire, must rend the Egyptian sky,
And wheel on the earth, devouring where it rolls;
What it devours not, herb, or fruit, or grain,
A darksome cloud of locusts swarming down   185
Must eat, and on the ground leave nothing green;
Darkness must overshadow all his bounds,
Palpable darkness, and blot out three days;
Last, with one midnight-stroke, all the first-born
Of Egypt must lie dead. Thus with ten wounds   190
The river-dragon tamed at length submits
To let his sojourners depart, and oft
Humbles his stubborn heart, but still as ice
More hardened after thaw; till in his rage,
Pursuing whom he late dismissed, the sea   195
Swallows him with his host, but them lets pass,

164-8] Exod. i. The king is named as Busiris in I 307 (see I 306-11n.).
169-90] Exod. iii-xii.
173 denies] refuses.
179 murrain] cattle plague.
180 Botches, blains] boils, blisters.
184-8] Cf. I 338-43. The darkness is palpable in Eox. x. 21, where the Vulgate
    reading is *palpari queant*.
191] Pharaoh is identified with the crocodile ('river-dragon') in Ezek. xxix. 3.
194-214] Exod. xiv. 5-31.

As on dry land, between two crystal walls,
Awed by the rod of Moses so to stand
Divided till his rescued gain their shore:
Such wondrous power God to his saint will lend,　　200
Though present in his angel, who shall go
Before them in a cloud, and pillar of fire –
By day a cloud, by night a pillar of fire –
To guide them in their journey, and remove
Behind them, while the obdurate king pursues;　　205
All night he will pursue, but his approach
Darkness defends between till morning-watch;
Then through the fiery pillar and the cloud
God looking forth will trouble all his host,
And craze their chariot-wheels: when, by command,　　210
Moses once more his potent rod extends
Over the sea; the sea his rod obeys;
On their embattled ranks the waves return,
And overwhelm their war; the race elect
Safe towards Canaan, from the shore, advance　　215
Through the wild desert – not the readiest way,
Lest, entering on the Canaanite alarmed,
War terrify them inexpert, and fear
Return them back to Egypt, choosing rather
Inglorious life with servitude; for life　　220
To noble and ignoble is more sweet
Untrained in arms, where rashness leads not on.
This also shall they gain by their delay
In the wide wilderness: there they shall found
Their government, and their great senate choose　　225
Through the twelve tribes, to rule by laws ordained;
God, from the mount of Sinai, whose grey top
Shall tremble, he descending, will himself,
In thunder, lightning, and loud trumpets' sound,
Ordain them laws – part, such as appertain　　230
To civil justice; part, religious rites

200–4] Exod. xiii. 21–2.
207 defends] repels.
210 craze] shatter (cf. I 311).
214 war] army.
214–20] Exod. xiii. 17–18. On 'race elect' see ll. 111–13n.
224–6] Exod. xxiv. 1–11; Num. xi. 16–25.
225 Senate] See Acts v. 21; the Greek word which is there translated 'senate' (γερουσία) is sometimes used in the LXX to mean 'Sanhedrin' (συνέδριον), which is the word translated as 'council' in the same passage. It therefore seems likely that Milton saw this senate as the beginning of the Sanhedrin.
227–30] Exod. xix. 16–20.

Of sacrifice, informing them, by types
And shadows, of that destined seed to bruise
The serpent, by what means he shall achieve
Mankind's deliverance. But the voice of God   235
To mortal ear is dreadful: they beseech
That Moses might report to them his will,
And terror cease; he grants what they besought,
Instructed that to God is no access
Without mediator, whose high office now   240
Moses in figure bears, to introduce
One greater, of whose day he shall foretell,
And all the prophets, in their age, the times
Of great Messiah shall sing. Thus laws and rites
Established, such delight hath God in men   245
Obedient to his will that he vouchsafes
Among them to set up his tabernacle –
The holy one with mortal men to dwell;
By his prescript a sanctuary is framed
Of cedar, overlaid with gold; therein   250
An ark, and in the ark his testimony,
The records of his covenant; over these
A mercy-seat of gold, between the wings
Of two bright cherubim; before him burn
Seven lamps, as in a zodiac representing   255
The heavenly fires; over the tent a cloud
Shall rest by day, a fiery gleam by night,
Save when they journey; and at length they come,
Conducted by his angel, to the land
Promised to Abraham and his seed; the rest   260
Were long to tell – how many battles fought,
How many kings destroyed, and kingdoms won;
Or how the sun shall in mid-heaven stand still
A day entire, and night's due course adjourn,
Man's voice commanding, "Sun, in Gibeon stand,   265
And thou, Moon, in the vale of Aialon,
Till Israel overcome" – so call the third
From Abraham, son of Isaac, and from him
His whole descent, who thus shall Canaan win.'
        Here Adam interposed: 'O sent from heaven,   270
Enlightener of my darkness, gracious things

232-4] Heb. viii. 3-5.
235-8] Exod. xx. 18-20.
238-44] Deut. xviii. 15-19; Acts iii. 22, vii. 37.
245-56] Exod. xxv, xxvi, xxxvii; Heb. ix.
256-8] Exod. xl. 34-8.
263-7] Joshua x. 12-13. 'Israel' is Jacob (Gen. xxxii. 28).

Thou hast revealed, those chiefly which concern
Just Abraham and his seed; now first I find
Mine eyes true opening, and my heart much eased,
Erewhile perplexed with thoughts what would become 275
Of me and all mankind; but now I see
His day, in whom all nations shall be blest –
Favour unmerited by me, who sought
Forbidden knowledge by forbidden means.
This yet I apprehend not – why to those   280
Among whom God will deign to dwell on earth
So many and so various laws are given;
So many laws argue so many sins
Among them; how can God with such reside?'
     To whom thus Michael: 'Doubt not but that sin   285
Will reign among them, as of thee begot;
And therefore was law given them, to evince
Their natural pravity, by stirring up
Sin against law to fight, that when they see
Law can discover sin, but not remove,   290
Save by those shadowy expiations weak,
The blood of bulls and goats, they may conclude
Some blood more precious must be paid for man,
Just for unjust, that in such righteousness,
To them by faith imputed, they may find   295
Justification towards God, and peace
Of conscience, which the law by ceremonies
Cannot appease, nor man the moral part
Perform, and not performing cannot live.
So law appears imperfect, and but given   300
With purpose to resign them, in full time,
Up to a better covenant, disciplined
From shadowy types to truth, from flesh to spirit,
From imposition of strict laws to free
Acceptance of large grace, from servile fear   305
To filial, works of law to works of faith.
And therefore shall not Moses, though of God
Highly beloved, being but the minister
Of law, his people into Canaan lead;

276-7 see/His day] John viii. 56.
285-306] A characteristically Protestant statement of the relation of the
     Mosaic law of the O.T. covenant to the 'better covenant' of 'righteousness
     ... by faith imputed'. The doctrine is broadly based on the epistles to the
     Romans, Hebrews, and Galatians.
288 pravity] depravity.
294-5 See III 290-1n.
307-9] Deut. xxxiv.

But Joshua, whom the Gentiles Jesus call,   310
His name and office bearing who shall quell
The adversary serpent, and bring back
Through the world's wilderness long-wandered man
Safe to eternal paradise of rest.
Meanwhile they, in their earthly Canaan placed,   315
Long time shall dwell and prosper, but when sins
National interrupt their public peace,
Provoking God to raise them enemies –
From whom as oft he saves them penitent,
By judges first, then under kings; of whom   320
The second, both for piety renowned
And puissant deeds, a promise shall receive
Irrevocable, that his regal throne
For ever shall endure; the like shall sing
All prophecy – that of the royal stock   325
Of David (so I name this king) shall rise
A son, the woman's seed to thee foretold,
Foretold to Abraham as in whom shall trust
All nations, and to kings foretold of kings
The last, for of his reign shall be no end.   330
But first a long succession must ensue;
And his next son, for wealth and wisdom famed,
The clouded ark of God, till then in tents
Wandering, shall in a glorious temple enshrine.
Such follow him as shall be registered   335
Part good, part bad; of bad the longer scroll:
Whose foul idolatries and other faults,
Heaped to the popular sum, will so incense
God, as to leave them, and expose their land,
Their city, his temple, and his holy ark,   340
With all his sacred things, a scorn and prey
To that proud city whose high walls thou saw'st
Left in confusion, Babylon thence called.

310] 'Jesus' is the Greek form of the Hebrew 'Joshua', who is so called in the
    LXX and N.T. (e.g. Heb. iv. 8).
321-4] On the promise which David ('The second') received see II Sam. vii. 16.
325-7] A common O.T. prophecy (e.g. Psalm lxxxix. 36-7), applied to Jesus in
    the N.T. (e.g. Luke i. 32).
330] a characteristic theme of Messianic prophecies (e.g. Dan. vii. 14, Luke i.
    33).
332-4] On the Temple of Solomon ('next son') see I Kings v.-ix. 9, II Chronicles
    ii-v.
343] See l. 62n.

There in captivity he lets them dwell
The space of seventy years; then brings them back,   345
Remembering mercy, and his covenant sworn
To David, stablished as the days of heaven.
Returned from Babylon by leave of kings,
Their lords, whom God disposed, the house of God
They first re-edify, and for a while   350
In mean estate live moderate, till grown
In wealth and multitude, factious they grow;
But first among the priests dissension springs –
Men who attend the altar, and should most
Endeavour peace: their strife pollution brings   355
Upon the temple itself; at last they seize
The sceptre, and regard not David's sons;
Then lose it to a stranger, that the true
Anointed king Messiah might be born
Barred of his right; yet at his birth a star   360
Unseen before in heaven proclaims him come,
And guides the eastern sages, who enquire
His place, to offer incense, myrrh, and gold:
His place of birth a solemn angel tells
To simple shepherds, keeping watch by night;   365
They gladly thither haste, and by a choir
Of squadroned angels hear his carol sung.
A virgin is his mother, but his sire
The power of the most high; he shall ascend
The throne hereditary, and bound his reign   370
With earth's wide bounds, his glory with the heavens.'
    He ceased, discerning Adam with such joy
Surcharged as had like grief been dewed in tears,
Without the vent of words; which these he breathed:
    'O prophet of glad tidings, finisher   375

344-7] Refers to the Babylonian Captivity. Under Nebuchadnezzar Jews were
   deported to Babylon in 597 and 586 BC (II Kings xxiv. 14-16; xxv. 11);
   they were allowed to return after the Persian King Cyrus captured Babylon
   in 538 BC (Ezra ii). On the estimate of 'seventy years' see Jer. xxv. 12.
348-50] Ezra, Neh. i-vi. The kings are Cyrus, Artaxerxes, and Darius.
353-8] See the apocryphal II Macc. iii-vi. 'They' (l. 356) are the Hasmonaean
   dynasty, one of whom, Aristobulus I, seized civil power and became the
   first person to assume the title 'King of the Jews'. The 'stranger' is
   Antipater, who in 47 BC was appointed by Julius Caesar procurator of
   Judea, as a reward for services rendered against Pompey; he was the father
   of Herod the Great.
360-9] Matt. ii, Luke ii.
369-71] Psalm ii. 8; *Aeneid* i 278-9, 287.
373 Surcharged] overwhelmed.

Of utmost hope! Now clear I understand
What oft my steadiest thoughts have searched in vain –
Why our great expectation should be called
The seed of woman; virgin mother, hail;
High in the love of heaven, yet from my loins   380
Thou shalt proceed, and from thy womb the Son
Of God most high; so God with man unites.
Needs must the serpent now his capital bruise
Expect with mortal pain; say where and when
Their fight, what stroke shall bruise the victor's heel.'   385
    To whom thus Michael: 'Dream not of their fight
As of a duel, or the local wounds
Of head or heel; not therefore joins the Son
Manhood to Godhead, with more strength to foil
Thy enemy; nor so is overcome   390
Satan, whose fall from heaven, a deadlier bruise,
Disabled not to give thee thy death's wound;
Which he who comes thy saviour shall recure,
Not by destroying Satan, but his works
In thee and in thy seed; nor can this be,   395
But by fulfilling that which thou didst want,
Obedience to the law of God, imposed
On penalty of death, and suffering death,
The penalty to thy transgression due,
And due to theirs which out of thine will grow: 400
So only can high justice rest appaid.
The law of God exact he shall fulfil
Both by obedience and by love, though love
Alone fulfil the law; thy punishment
He shall endure, by coming in the flesh   405
To a reproachful life and cursed death,
Proclaiming life to all who shall believe
In his redemption, and that his obedience
Imputed becomes theirs by faith – his merits
To save them, not their own, though legal, works.   410
For this he shall live hated, be blasphemed,

379–82] Luke i. 28–35.
383 capital] means both 'on the head' and 'fatal'.
393 recure] heal, make whole.
394–5] I John iii. 8.
396 want] lack.
401 appaid] satisfied.
403–4] Rom. xiii. 10.
408–9] See III 290–1n.
410 legal] in accordance with the Mosaic law.

Seized on by force, judged, and to death condemned
A shameful and accursed, nailed to the cross
By his own nation, slain for bringing life;
But to the cross he nails thy enemies –   415
The law that is against thee, and the sins
Of all mankind, with him there crucified,
Never to hurt them more who rightly trust
In this his satisfaction; so he dies,
But soon revives; Death over him no power   420
Shall long usurp; ere the third dawning light
Return, the stars of morn shall see him rise
Out of his grave, fresh as the dawning light,
Thy ransom paid, which man from Death redeems –
His death for man, as many as offered life   425
Neglect not, and the benefit embrace
By faith not void of works; this godlike act
Annuls thy doom, the death thou shouldst have died,
In sin for ever lost from life; this act
Shall bruise the head of Satan, crush his strength,   430
Defeating Sin and Death, his two main arms,
And fix far deeper in his head their stings
Than temporal death shall bruise the victor's heel,
Or theirs whom he redeems – a death like sleep,
A gentle wafting to immortal life.   435
Nor after resurrection shall he stay
Longer on earth than certain times to appear
To his disciples – men who in his life
Still followed him; to them shall leave in charge
To teach all nations what of him they learned   440
And his salvation, them who shall believe
Baptizing in the profluent stream – the sign
Of washing them from guilt of sin to life
Pure, and in mind prepared, if so befall,
For death like that which the redeemer died.   445
All nations they shall teach; for from that day
Not only to the sons of Abraham's loins
Salvation shall be preached, but to the sons

415-17] Col. ii. 14.
419 satisfaction] See X 803-4n.
441-5] Milton concurred with many Protestants in asserting that baptism was
    for 'them who shall believe' rather than for infants, in asserting that one
    should be baptized in running ('profluent') water rather than in a font, and
    in emphasizing that baptism is a 'sign' in the face of Counter-Reformation
    assertions (at the Council of Trent) that it is more than a sign. 'Washing'
    renders the original meaning (in Greek) of the word 'baptize'.

Of Abraham's faith wherever through the world;
So in his seed all nations shall be blest.   450
Then to the heaven of heavens he shall ascend
With victory, triumphing through the air
Over his foes and thine; there shall surprise
The serpent, prince of air, and drag in chains
Through all his realm, and there confounded leave;   455
Then enter into glory, and resume
His seat at God's right hand, exalted high
Above all names in heaven; and thence shall come,
When this world's dissolution shall be ripe,
With glory and power, to judge both quick and dead –   460
To judge the unfaithful dead, but to reward
His faithful, and receive them into bliss,
Whether in heaven or earth; for then the earth
Shall all be paradise, far happier place
Than this of Eden, and far happier days.'   465
     So spake the archangel Michaël; then paused,
As at the world's great period; and our sire,
Replete with joy and wonder, thus replied:
     'O goodness infinite, goodness immense,
That all this good of evil shall produce,   470
And evil turn to good – more wonderful
Than that which by creation first brought forth
Light out of darkness! Full of doubt I stand,
Whether I should repent me now of sin
By me done and occasioned, or rejoice   475
Much more that much more good thereof shall spring –
To God more glory, more good-will to men
From God – and over wrath grace shall abound.
But say, if our deliverer up to heaven
Must reascend, what will betide the few,   480
His faithful, left among the unfaithful herd,
The enemies of truth? Who then shall guide
His people, who defend? Will they not deal
Worse with his followers than with him they dealt?'
     'Be sure they will,' said the angel; 'but from heaven   485

453–5] Rev. xx. 1–3, Eph. ii. 2.
460 judge ... dead] this common N.T. phrase (e.g. II Tim. iv. 1) also occurs in
    the Apostles' Creed.
469–78] Adam recapitulates the traditional paradox of the 'fortunate fall' (*felix culpa*) and the traditional assertion that man's salvation is 'more wonderful' than God's act of creation.
478] Rom. v. 20.

He to his own a Comforter will send,
The promise of the Father, who shall dwell,
His Spirit within them, and the law of faith
Working through love upon their hearts shall write,
To guide them in all truth, and also arm   490
With spiritual armour, able to resist
Satan's assaults, and quench his fiery darts –
What man can do against them not afraid,
Though to the death; against such cruelties
With inward consolations recompensed,   495
And oft supported so as shall amaze
Their proudest persecutors; for the Spirit,
Poured first on his apostles, whom he sends
To evangelize the nations, then on all
Baptized, shall them with wondrous gifts endue   500
To speak all tongues, and do all miracles,
As did their Lord before them. Thus they win
Great numbers of each nation to receive
With joy the tidings brought from heaven: at length,
Their ministry performed, and race well run,   505
Their doctrine and their story written left,
They die: but in their room, as they forewarn,
Wolves shall succeed for teachers, grievous wolves,
Who all the sacred mysteries of heaven
To their own vile advantages shall turn   510
Of lucre and ambition, and the truth
With superstitions and traditions taint,
Left only in those written records pure,
Though not but by the Spirit understood.
Then shall they seek to avail themselves of names,   515
Places, and titles, and with these to join
Secular power, though feigning still to act
By spiritual; to themselves appropriating
The Spirit of God, promised alike and given
To all believers; and from that pretence,   520

---

486 Comforter] The Holy Spirit (John xv. 26).
488-9] Gal. v. 6, Hebrews viii. 10.
491-2] Eph. vi. 11-17.
493] Psalm lvi. 11.
497-502] Acts ii.
505 race well run] a N.T. metaphor (e.g. Hebrews xii. 1).
508] Cf. Acts xx. 29, *Sonnet* XVI 14, *Lycidas* 113-31.
511-14] a characteristically Protestant assertion of the right of the believer to
    interpret Scripture guided solely by the Holy Spirit without reference to
    any authority or tradition.

Spiritual laws by carnal power shall force
On every conscience – laws which none shall find
Left them enrolled, or what the Spirit within
Shall on the heart engrave. What will they then
But force the spirit of grace itself, and bind   525
His consort, liberty? What but unbuild
His living temples, built by faith to stand –
Their own faith, not another's? For on earth
Who against faith and conscience can be heard
Infallible? Yet many will presume: 530
Whence heavy persecution shall arise
On all who in the worship persevere
Of spirit and truth; the rest, far greater part,
Will deem in outward rites and specious forms
Religion satisfied; truth shall retire   535
Bestuck with slanderous darts, and works of faith
Rarely be found; so shall the world go on,
To good malignant, to bad men benign,
Under her own weight groaning, till the day
Appear of respiration to the just   540
And vengeance to the wicked, at return
Of him so lately promised to thy aid,
The woman's seed – obscurely then foretold,
Now amplier known thy Saviour and thy Lord;
Last in the clouds from heaven to be revealed   545
In glory of the Father, to dissolve
Satan with his perverted world; then raise
From the conflagrant mass, purged and refined,
New heavens, new earth, ages of endless date
Founded in righteousness and peace and love,   550
To bring forth fruits, joy and eternal bliss.'
  He ended; and thus Adam last replied:
'How soon hath thy prediction, seer blest,
Measured this transient world, the race of time,
Till time stand fixed; beyond is all abyss –   555
Eternity, whose end no eye can reach.
Greatly instructed I shall hence depart,

525-6] II Cor. iii. 17.
527] I Cor. iii. 17.
532-3] John iv. 23-4.
539] Rom. viii. 22.
540] See Acts iii. 19, where the phrase καιροὶ ἀναψύξεως, translated quite
     correctly as 'times of refreshing' in the A.V., could also be translated 'times
     of respiration' (i.e. respite).
545-6] Matt. xxiv. 30.

Greatly in peace of thought, and have my fill
Of knowledge, what this vessel can contain;
Beyond which was my folly to aspire.   560
Henceforth I learn that to obey is best,
And love with fear the only God, to walk
As in his presence, ever to observe
His providence, and on him sole depend,
Merciful over all his works, with good   565
Still overcoming evil, and by small
Accomplishing great things – by things deemed weak
Subverting worldly-strong, and wordly-wise
By simply meek; that suffering for truth's sake
Is fortitude to highest victory,   570
And to the faithful death the gate of life –
Taught this by his example whom I now
Acknowledge my Redeemer ever blest.'
　　To whom thus also the angel last replied:
'This having learned, thou hast attained the sum   575
Of wisdom; hope no higher, though all the stars
Thou knew'st by name, and all the ethereal powers,
All secrets of the deep, all nature's works,
Or works of God in heaven, air, earth, or sea;
And all the riches of this world enjoy'dst,   580
And all the rule, one empire; only add
Deeds to thy knowledge answerable, add faith,
Add virtue, patience, temperance, add love,
By name to come called Charity, the soul
Of all the rest: then wilt thou not be loath   585
To leave this Paradise, but shalt possess
A paradise within thee, happier far.
Let us descend now, therefore, from this top
Of speculation; for the hour precise
Exacts our parting hence; and see, the guards,   590
By me encamped on yonder hill, expect
Their motion, at whose front a flaming sword,
In signal of remove, waves fiercely round;
We may no longer stay; go, waken Eve;

565] Psalm cxlv. 9.
566] Rom. xii. 21.
567-8] I Cor. i. 27.
581-7] II Pet. i. 5-7, I Cor. xiii, *PL* III 216n.
588-9 top/Of speculation] The primary meaning is 'place which affords
　　an extensive view', and the secondary sense is 'limit of theological
　　speculation'.
591-2 expect/Their motion] await their order to move.
593 remove] departure.

Her also I with gentle dreams have calmed,   595
Portending good, and all her spirits composed
To meek submission: thou at season fit
Let her with thee partake what thou hast heard –
Chiefly what may concern her faith to know,
The great deliverance by her seed to come   600
(For by the woman's seed) on all mankind –
That ye may live, which will be many days,
Both in one faith unanimous; though sad
With cause for evils past, yet much more cheered
With meditation on the happy end.'   605
     He ended, and they both descend the hill;
Descended, Adam to the bower where Eve
Lay sleeping ran before, but found her waked;
And thus with words not sad she him received:
     'Whence thou return'st and whither went'st I know;
For God is also in sleep, and dreams advise,   611
Which he hath sent propitious, some great good
Presaging, since, with sorrow and heart's distress
Wearied, I fell asleep; but now lead on;
In me is no delay; with thee to go   615
Is to stay here; without thee here to stay
Is to go hence unwilling; thou to me
Art all things under heaven, all places thou,
Who for my wilful crime art banished hence.
This further consolation yet secure   620
I carry hence: though all by me is lost,
Such favour I unworthy am vouchsafed,
By me the promised seed shall all restore.'
     So spake our mother Eve, and Adam heard
Well pleased, but answered not; for now too nigh   625
The archangel stood, and from the other hill
To their fixed station, all in bright array,
The cherubim descended, on the ground
Gliding meteorous, as evening mist
Risen from a river o'er the marish glides,   630
And gathers ground fast at the labourer's heel
Homeward returning. High in front advanced,
The brandished sword of God before them blazed,
Fierce as a comet; which with torrid heat,

602] Gen. v. 5.
630 marish] marsh.
634–6] According to an ancient tradition the 'flaming sword' of Gen. iii. 24 was
     the heat of the tropics (hence 'Libyan'). On 'adust' see VI 514n.

And vapour as the Libyan air adust,   635
Began to parch that temperate clime; whereat
In either hand the hastening angel caught
Our lingering parents, and to the eastern gate
Led them direct, and down the cliff as fast
To the subjected plain – then disappeared.   640
They looking back, all the eastern side beheld
Of Paradise, so late their happy seat,
Waved over by that flaming brand; the gate
With dreadful faces thronged and fiery arms;   644
Some natural tears they dropped, but wiped them soon,
The world was all before them, where to choose
Their place of rest, and providence their guide;
They hand in hand with wandering steps and slow,
Through Eden took their solitary way.

THE END OF THE TWELFTH BOOK

640 subjected] subjacent, situated at a lower level.
648] Cf. IV 321n.

PARADISE REGAIN'D.

A

POEM

In IV *BOOKS*.

To which is added

SAMSON AGONISTES.

The Author

John Milton.

PARADISE REGAINED

BOOK I

I who erewhile the happy garden sung,
By one man's disobedience lost, now sing
Recovered Paradise to all mankind,
By one man's firm obedience fully tried
Through all temptation, and the tempter foiled   5
In all his wiles, defeated and repulsed,
And Eden raised in the waste wilderness.
   Thou spirit, who led'st this glorious eremite
Into the desert, his victorious field
Against the spiritual foe, and brought'st him thence   10
By proof the undoubted Son of God, inspire,
As thou art wont, my prompted song, else mute,
And bear through height or depth of nature's bounds,
With prosperous wing full summed, to tell of deeds
Above heroic, though in secret done,   15
And unrecorded left through many an age,
Worthy to have not remained so long unsung.
   Now had the great proclaimer, with a voice
More awful than the sound of trumpet, cried
Repentance, and heaven's kingdom nigh at hand   20
To all baptised; to his great baptism flocked
With awe the regions round, and with them came
From Nazareth the son of Joseph deemed
To the flood Jordan – came as then obscure,
Unmarked, unknown; but him the Baptist soon   25
Descried, divinely warned, and witness bore

Paradise Regained. The poem was written between 1665 and 1670, but the
   precise period of composition is not known. In the notes which follow there
   is no attempt to list allusions to the two Biblical accounts of the temptation
   in Matthew iv. 1–11 and Luke iv. 1–13.
1–2 Cf. *Aeneid* i 1–4.
2–4] Rom. v. 19.
7] Isa. li. 3.
8 eremite] used in the Greek sense of 'desert-dweller' (ἐημίτης).
14] See *PL* VII 421n.
18–32] See Matt. iii, Mark i. 2–11, Luke iii. 1–22, John i. 6–34.
19] Isa. lviii. 1.

As to his worthier, and would have resigned
To him his heavenly office, nor was long
His witness unconfirmed; on him baptised
Heaven opened, and in likeness of a dove   30
The Spirit descended, while the Father's voice
From heaven pronounced him his beloved Son.
That heard the Adversary, who roving still
About the world, at that assembly famed
Would not be last, and with the voice divine   35
Nigh thunder-struck, the exalted man to whom
Such high attest was given, a while surveyed
With wonder; then, with envy fraught and rage,
Flies to his place, nor rests, but in mid air
To council summons all his mighty peers,   40
Within thick clouds and dark tenfold involved,
A gloomy consistory; and them amidst,
With looks aghast and sad, he thus bespake:
    'O ancient powers of air and this wide world
(For much more willingly I mention air,   45
This our old conquest, than remember hell,
Our hated habitation), well ye know
How many ages, as the years of men,
This universe we have possessed, and ruled
In manner at our will the affairs of earth,   50
Since Adam and his facile consort Eve
Lost Paradise, deceived by me, though since
With dread attending when that fatal wound
Shall be inflicted by the seed of Eve
Upon my head; long the decrees of heaven   55
Delay, for longest time to him is short;
And now, too soon for us, the circling hours
This dreaded time have compassed, wherein we
Must bide the stroke of that long-threatened wound
(At least, if so we can, and by the head   60
Broken be not intended all our power

---

33 Adversary] Satan. See *PL* I 82n.
33–4] Job i. 7.
39 mid air] See *Fair Infant* 16n.
42 consistory] means 'council', and is here used with ironic reference to the
    ecclesiastical sense of an assembly of cardinals convoked by the Pope and,
    in the Anglican church, a bishop's court.
44–5] Eph. ii. 2.
48 as] i.e. as reckoned according to.
51 facile] easily led.
53 attending when] awaiting (me) until.
53–5] Gen. iii. 15.

To be infringed, our freedom and our being
In this fair empire won of earth and air)
For this ill news I bring: the woman's seed,
Destined to this, is late of woman born;   65
His birth to our just fear gave no small cause,
But his growth now to youth's full flower, displaying
All virtue, grace and wisdom to achieve
Things highest, greatest, multiplies my fear.
Before him a great prophet, to proclaim   70
His coming, is sent harbinger, who all
Invites, and in the consecrated stream
Pretends to wash off sin, and fit them so
Purified to receive him pure, or rather
To do him honour as their king; all come,   75
And he himself among them was baptised –
Not thence to be more pure, but to receive
The testimony of heaven, that who he is
Thenceforth the nations may not doubt; I saw
The prophet do him reverence; on him, rising   80
Out of the water, heaven above the clouds
Unfold her crystal doors; thence on his head
A perfect dove descend (whate'er it meant),
And out of heaven the sovereign voice I heard,
"This is my Son beloved, in him am pleased."   85
His mother, then, is mortal, but his sire
He who obtains the monarchy of heaven;
And what will he not do to advance his Son?
His first-begot we know, and sore have felt,
When his fierce thunder drove us to the deep;   90
Who this is we must learn, for man he seems
In all his lineaments, though in his face
The glimpses of his Father's glory shine.
Ye see our danger on the utmost edge
Of hazard, which admits no long debate,   95
But must with something sudden be opposed
(Not force, but well-couched fraud, well-woven snares),
Ere in the head of nations he appear,
Their king, their leader, and supreme on earth.
I, when no other durst, sole undertook   100
The dismal expedition to find out

62 infringed] shattered, broken.
73 Pretends] professes.
74] I John iii. 3.
87 obtains] used in the Latin sense of 'holds'.
97 couched] means both 'hidden' and 'expressed in words'.

And ruin Adam, and the exploit performed
Successfully: a calmer voyage now
Will waft me; and the way found prosperous once
Induces best to hope of like success.'   105
    He ended, and his words impression left
Of much amazement to the infernal crew,
Distracted and surprised with deep dismay
At these sad tidings; but no time was then
For long indulgence to their fears or grief: 110
Unanimous they all commit the care
And management of this main enterprise
To him, their great dictator, whose attempt
At first against mankind so well had thrived
In Adam's overthrow, and led their march   115
From hell's deep-vaulted den to dwell in light,
Regents, and potentates, and kings, yea gods,
Of many a pleasant realm and province wide.
So to the coast of Jordan he directs
His easy steps, girded with snaky wiles,   120
Where he might likeliest find this new-declared,
This man of men, attested Son of God,
Temptation and all guile on him to try;
So to subvert whom he suspected raised
To end his reign on earth so long enjoyed: 125
But, contrary, unweeting he fulfilled
The purposed counsel, pre-ordained and fixed,
Of the Most High, who in full frequence bright
Of angels, thus to Gabriel smiling spake:
    'Gabriel, this day by proof thou shalt behold,   130
Thou and all angels conversant on earth
With man or men's affairs, how I begin
To verify that solemn message late,
On which I sent thee to the virgin pure
In Galilee, that she should bear a son,   135
Great in renown, and called the Son of God;
Then told'st her, doubting how these things could be

112 main] highly important.
113 dictator] In the seventeenth century the word was used with reference to
    the institution of the dictatorship in early Republican Rome, when a
    'dictator' was a magistrate invested with absolute but temporary power in
    times of military (and later domestic) crisis.
117 gods] According to a patristic tradition (embodied in *PL* I 356–522) the
    fallen angels became pagan gods.
128 frequence] assembly.
129–40] Gabriel (on whom see *PL* IV 549n.) here appears as the angel of the
    annunciation. See Luke i. 26–55.

To her a virgin, that on her should come
The Holy Ghost, and the power of the Highest
O'ershadow her; this man, born and now upgrown,   140
To show him worthy of his birth divine
And high prediction, henceforth I expose
To Satan; let him tempt, and now assay
His utmost subtlety, because he boasts
And vaunts of his great cunning to the throng   145
Of his apostasy; he might have learnt
Less overweening, since he failed in Job,
Whose constant perseverance overcame
Whate'er his cruel malice could invent.
He now shall know I can produce a man,   150
Of female seed, far abler to resist
All his solicitations, and at length
All his vast force, and drive him back to hell —
Winning by conquest what the first man lost
By fallacy surprised. But first I mean   155
To exercise him in the wilderness;
There he shall first lay down the rudiments
Of his great warfare, ere I send him forth
To conquer Sin and Death, the two grand foes,
By humiliation and strong sufferance: 160
His weakness shall o'ercome Satanic strength,
And all the world, and mass of sinful flesh;
That all the angels and ethereal powers —
They now, and men hereafter — may discern
From what consummate virtue I have chose   165
This perfect man, by merit called my Son,
To earn salvation for the sons of men.'
    So spake the eternal Father, and all heaven
Admiring stood a space; then into hymns
Burst forth, and in celestial measures moved,   170
Circling the throne and singing, while the hand
Sung with the voice, and this the argument:
    'Victory and triumph to the Son of God,
Now entering his great duel, not of arms,
But to vanquish by wisdom hellish wiles!   175
The Father knows the Son; therefore secure

147–9] Job i–ii. Cf. I 368–70, 424–6, III 64–8, 95. The comparison of Jesus to
    Job can be traced to Gregory's *Moralia in Job*.
157–8] Cf. *Aeneid* xi 156–7.
161] I Cor. i. 27.
171 hand] i.e. the hand which plays a musical instrument.
176] John x. 15.

Ventures his filial virtue, though untried,
Against whate'er may tempt, whate'er seduce,
Allure, or terrify, or undermine.
Be frustrate, all ye stratagems of hell,   180
And, devilish machinations, come to nought!'
    So they in heaven their odes and vigils tuned;
Meanwhile the Son of God, who yet some days
Lodged in Bethabara, where John baptised,
Musing and much revolving in his breast   185
How best the mighty work he might begin
Of Saviour to mankind, and which way first
Publish his godlike office now mature,
One day forth walked alone, the Spirit leading
And his deep thoughts, the better to converse   190
With solitude, till, far from track of men,
Thought following thought, and step by step led on,
He entered now the bordering desert wild,
And, with dark shades and rocks environed round,
His holy meditations thus pursued: 195
    'O what a multitude of thoughts at once
Awakened in me swarm, while I consider
What from within I feel myself, and hear
What from without comes often to my ears,
Ill sorting with my present state compared.   200
When I was yet a child, no childish play
To me was pleasing; all my mind was set
Serious to learn and know, and thence to do,
What might be public good; myself I thought
Born to that end, born to promote all truth,   205
All righteous things; therefore, above my years,
The Law of God I read, and found it sweet;
Made it my whole delight, and in it grew
To such perfection that, ere yet my age
Had measured twice six years, at our great feast   210
I went into the Temple, there to hear
The teachers of our Law, and to propose
What might improve my knowledge or their own;
And was admired by all, yet this not all
To which my spirit aspired; victorious deeds   215

182 vigils] prayers sung at a nocturnal service.
184 Bethabara] John i. 28.
204–5] John xviii. 37.
206–7] Cf. *Aeneid* ix 311.
207–8] Cf. Milton's translation of Psalm i. 2 (l.5).
209–14] Luke ii. 46–50. The 'feast' is Passover; 'admired' means 'marvelled at'.

Flamed in my heart, heroic acts – one while
To rescue Israel from the Roman yoke,
Then to subdue and quell, o'er all the earth,
Brute violence and proud tyrannic power,
Till truth were freed, and equity restored: 220
Yet held it more humane, more heavenly, first
By winning words to conquer willing hearts,
And make persuasion do the work of fear;
At least to try, and teach the erring soul,
Not wilfully misdoing, but unaware   225
Misled; the stubborn only to subdue.
These growing thoughts my mother soon perceiving,
By words at times cast forth, inly rejoiced,
And said to me apart, "High are thy thoughts,
O Son, but nourish them, and let them soar   230
To what height sacred virtue and true worth
Can raise them, though above example high;
By matchless deeds express thy matchless sire.
For know, thou art no son of mortal man;
Though men esteem thee low of parentage,   235
Thy Father is the eternal King who rules
All heaven and earth, angels and sons of men;
A messenger from God foretold thy birth
Conceived in me a virgin; he foretold
Thou shouldst be great, and sit on David's throne,   240
And of thy kingdom there should be no end.
At thy nativity a glorious choir
Of angels, in the fields of Bethlehem, sung
To shepherds watching at their folds by night,
And told them the Messiah now was born,   245
Where they might see him; and to thee they came,
Directed to the manger where thou lay'st,
For in the inn was left no better room;
A star, not seen before, in heaven appearing,
Guided the wise men thither from the east,   250
To honour thee with incense, myrrh, and gold;
By whose bright course led on they found the place,
Affirming it thy star, new-graven in heaven,
By which they knew thee King of Israel born.
Just Simeon and prophetic Anna, warned   255
By vision, found thee in the Temple, and spake,
Before the altar and the vested priest,
Like things of thee to all that present stood."

238–54] Matt. i–ii, Luke i–ii.
255–8] Luke ii. 25–38.

This having heard, straight I again revolved
The Law and Prophets, searching what was writ   260
Concerning the Messiah, to our scribes
Known partly, and soon found of whom they spake
I am – this chiefly, that my way must lie
Through many a hard assay, even to the death,
Ere I the promised kingdom can attain,   265
Or work redemption for mankind, whose sins'
Full weight must be transferred upon my head.
Yet, neither thus disheartened or dismayed,
The time prefixed I waited; when behold
The Baptist (of whose birth I oft had heard,   270
Not knew by sight) now come, who was to come
Before Messiah, and his way prepare.
I, as all others, to his baptism came,
Which I believed was from above; but he
Straight knew me, and with loudest voice proclaimed 275
Me him (for it was shown him so from heaven)
Me him whose harbinger he was; and first
Refused on me his baptism to confer,
As much his greater, and was hardly won;
But as I rose out of the laving stream,   280
Heaven opened her eternal doors, from whence
The Spirit descended on me like a dove;
And last, the sum of all, my Father's voice,
Audibly heard from heaven, pronounced me his,
Me his beloved Son, in whom alone   285
He was well pleased; by which I knew the time
Now full, that I no more should live obscure,
But openly begin, as best becomes
The authority which I derived from heaven.
And now by some strong motion I am led   290
Into this wilderness; to what intent
I learn not yet, perhaps I need not know;
For what concerns my knowledge God reveals.'
    So spake our morning star, then in his rise,
And, looking round, on every side beheld   295
A pathless desert, dusk with horrid shades;

259 revolved] searched through, studied.
266–7] Isa. iii. 6.
270–89] See ll. 18–32n.
279 hardly won] with difficulty persuaded.
281 eternal doors] Psalm xxiv. 7 (*portae aeternales* Vulgate).
286–7] Gal. iv. 4.
290 motion] See *PL* XI 91n.
294 morning star] Rev. xxii. 16.
296 horrid] bristling.

The way he came not having marked, return
Was difficult, by human steps untrod;
And he still on was led, but with such thoughts
Accompanied of things past and to come   300
Lodged in his breast, as well might recommend
Such solitude before choicest society.
    Full forty days he passed – whether on hill
Sometimes, anon in shady vale, each night
Under the covert of some ancient oak   305
Or cedar, to defend him from the dew,
Or harboured in one cave, is not revealed;
Nor tasted human food, nor hunger felt,
Till those days ended, hungered then at last
Among wild beasts; they at his sight grew mild, 310
Nor sleeping him nor waking harmed; his walk
The fiery serpent fled and noxious worm;
The lion and fierce tiger glared aloof.
But now an aged man in rural weeds,
Following, as seemed, the quest of some stray ewe, 315
Or withered sticks to gather, which might serve
Against a winter's day, when winds blow keen,
To warm him wet returned from field at eve,
He saw approach; who first with curious eye
Perused him, then with words thus uttered spake: 320
    'Sir, what ill chance hath brought thee to this place,
So far from path or road of men, who pass
In troop or caravan? For single none
Durst ever, who returned, and dropped not here
His carcass, pined with hunger and with drouth.   325
I ask the rather, and the more admire,
For that to me thou seem'st the man whom late
Our new baptising prophet at the ford
Of Jordan honoured so, and called thee Son
Of God; I saw and heard, for we sometimes   330
Who dwell this wild, constrained by want, come forth
To town or village nigh (nighest is far),
Where aught we hear, and curious are to hear,
What happens new; fame also finds us out.'

301–2] See *PL* VIII 427–8n.
310–13] Mark i. 13. The docility of the animals derives from various O.T.
    prophecies (e.g. Isa. xi. 6–9). One of the eight Hebrew words used for
    'serpent' in the Old Testament is *saraph*, 'fiery serpent' (e.g. Num. xxi. 6–
    8). 'Worm' is used in a general sense: in Micah vii. 17, on which l. 312 is
    based, the A.V. marginal note to 'worms' is 'creeping things'.
334 fame . . . out] i.e. news (Latin *fama*, report) also reaches us.

To whom the Son of God: 'Who brought me hither   335
Will bring me hence; no other guide I seek.'
   'By miracle he may,' replied the swain;
'What other way I see not; for we here
Live on tough roots and stubs, to thirst inured
More than the camel, and to drink go far –   340
Men to much misery and hardship born;
But, if thou be the Son of God, command
That out of these hard stones be made thee bread;
So shalt thou save thyself, and us relieve
With food, whereof we wretched seldom taste.'   345
   He ended, and the Son of God replied:
'Think'st thou such force in bread? Is it not written
(For I discern thee other than thou seem'st)
Man lives not by bread only, but each word
Proceeding from the mouth of God, who fed   350
Our fathers here with manna? In the mount
Moses was forty days, nor eat nor drank;
And forty days Elijah without food
Wandered this barren waste; the same I now.
Why dost thou, then, suggest to me distrust,   355
Knowing who I am, as I know who thou art?'
   Whom thus answered the arch-fiend, now undisguised:
' 'Tis true, I am that spirit unfortunate
Who, leagued with millions more in rash revolt,
Kept not my happy station, but was driven   360
With them from bliss to the bottomless deep –
Yet to that hideous place not so confined
By rigour unconniving but that oft,
Leaving my dolorous prison, I enjoy
Large liberty to round this globe of earth,   365
Or range in the air; nor from the heaven of heavens
Hath he excluded my resort sometimes.
I came, among the sons of God, when he
Gave up into my hands Uzzean Job,
To prove him, and illustrate his high worth;   370
And when to all his angels he proposed

339 stubs] stumps.
349–50] Jesus' answer (Matt. iv. 4, Luke iv. 4) is a quotation from Deut. viii. 3.
351–2] Exod. xxiv. 18, xxxiv. 28, Deut. ix. 9.
353–4] I Kings xix. 8.
363 unconniving] refers to God's eye, which never closes (cf. Latin *inconivus*).
371–6] I Kings xxii. 20–38; II Chron. xviii. 19–34. The identification of this
    'lying spirit' with Satan is suggested in the cross-reference to Job i. 6 in the
    A.V. marginal note to II Chronicles xviii. 20. On 'fraud' see *PL* VII 143n.

To draw the proud king Ahab into fraud,
That he might fall in Ramoth, they demurring,
I undertook that office, and the tongues
Of all his flattering prophets glibbed with lies   375
To his destruction, as I had in charge:
For what he bids I do; though I have lost
Much lustre to my native brightness, lost
To be beloved of God, I have not lost
To love, at least contemplate and admire,   380
What I see excellent in good, or fair,
Or virtuous; I should so have lost all sense.
What can be then less in me than desire
To see thee and approach thee, whom I know
Declared the Son of God, to hear attent   385
Thy wisdom, and behold thy godlike deeds?
Men generally think me much a foe
To all mankind: why should I? They to me
Never did wrong or violence; by them
I lost not what I lost, rather by them   390
I gained what I have gained, and with them dwell
Copartner in these regions of the world,
If not disposer – lend them oft my aid,
Oft my advice by presages and signs,
And answers, oracles, portents and dreams,   395
Whereby they may direct their future life.
Envy, they say, excites me, thus to gain
Companions of my misery and woe.
At first it may be; but, long since with woe
Nearer acquainted, now I feel by proof   400
That fellowship in pain divides not smart,
Nor lightens aught each man's peculiar load.
Small consolation, then, were man adjoined;
This wounds me most (what can it less?) that man,
Man fallen, shall be restored, I never more.'   405
        To whom our Saviour sternly thus replied:
'Deservedly thou griev'st, composed of lies
From the beginning, and in lies wilt end;
Who boast'st release from hell, and leave to come
Into the heaven of heavens; thou com'st indeed,   410
As a poor miserable captive thrall
Comes to the place where he before had sat
Among the prime in splendour, now deposed,
Ejected, emptied, gazed, unpitied, shunned,

393–6] According to a patristic tradition fallen angels were responsible for the
        oracular pronouncements of classical antiquity.
414 emptied] See *Circumcision* 20n.

A spectacle of ruin, or of scorn,   415
To all the host of heaven; the happy place
Imparts to thee no happiness, no joy –
Rather inflames thy torment, representing
Lost bliss, to thee no more communicable;
So never more in hell than when in heaven.   420
But thou art serviceable to heaven's King.
Wilt thou impute to obedience what thy fear
Extorts, or pleasure to do ill excites?
What but thy malice moved thee to misdeem
Of righteous Job, then cruelly to afflict him   425
With all inflictions? But his patience won.
The other service was thy chosen task,
To be a liar in four hundred mouths;
For lying is thy sustenance, thy food.
Yet thou pretend'st to truth; all oracles   430
By thee are given, and what confessed more true
Among the nations? That hath been thy craft,
By mixing somewhat true to vent more lies.
But what have been thy answers, what but dark,
Ambiguous, and with double sense deluding,   435
Which they who asked have seldom understood,
And, not well understood, as good not known?
Who ever by consulting at thy shrine,
Returned the wiser, or the more instruct
To fly or follow what concerned him most,   440
And run not sooner to his fatal snare?
For God hath justly given the nations up
To thy delusions; justly, since they fell
Idolatrous; but, when his purpose is
Among them to declare his providence,   445
To thee not known, whence hast thou then thy truth,
But from him, or his angels president
In every province, who, themselves disdaining
To approach thy temples, give thee in command
What, to the smallest tittle, thou shalt say   450
To thy adorers? Thou, with trembling fear,
Or like a fawning parasite, obey'st;
Then to thyself ascrib'st the truth foretold.
But this thy glory shall be soon retrenched;
Nor more shalt thou by oracling abuse   455
The Gentiles; henceforth oracles are ceased,

428] I Kings xxii. 6.
447 president] presiding.
454 retrenched] cut short.
456] Cf. *Nativity* 173; Micah v. 12.

And thou no more with pomp and sacrifice
Shall be enquired at Delphos or elsewhere –
At least in vain, for they shall find thee mute.
God hath now sent his living oracle   460
Into the world, to teach his final will,
And sends his spirit of truth henceforth to dwell
In pious hearts, an inward oracle
To all truth requisite for men to know.'
    So spake our Saviour; but the subtle fiend,   465
Though inly stung with anger and disdain,
Dissembled, and this answer smooth returned:
    'Sharply thou hast insisted on rebuke,
And urged me hard with doings which not will,
But misery, hath wrested from me; where   470
Easily canst thou find one miserable,
And not enforced oft-times to part from truth,
If it may stand him more in stead to lie,
Say and unsay, feign, flatter, or abure?
But thou art placed above me, thou art Lord;   475
From thee I can and must submiss, endure
Check or reproof, and glad to scape so quit.
Hard are the ways of truth, and rough to walk,
Smooth on the tongue discoursed, pleasing to the ear,
And tunable as sylvan pipe or song;   480
What wonder, then, if I delight to hear
Her dictates from thy mouth? Most men admire
Virtue who follow not her lore: permit me
To hear thee when I come (since no man comes),
And talk at least, though I despair to attain.   485
Thy Father, who is holy, wise, and pure,
Suffers the hypocrite or atheous priest
To tread his sacred courts, and minister
About his altar, handling holy things,
Praying or vowing, and vouchsafed his voice   490
To Balaam reprobate, a prophet yet
Inspired; disdain not such access to me.'
    To whom our Saviour, with unaltered brow:
'Thy coming hither, though I know thy scope,
I bid not, or forbid; do as thou find'st   495

462] John xvi. 13.
477 quit] discharged.
486–90] Satan assumes with Scholastic and Counter-Reformation theologians
    that the sacraments confer grace *ex opere operato*, through the act per-
    formed, regardless of the subjective attitude of the minister (or the
    recipient).

Permission from above; thou canst not more.'
  He added not; and Satan, bowing low
His grey dissimulation, disappeared,
Into thin air diffused: for now began
Night with her sullen wing to double-shade   500
The desert; fowls in their clay nests were couched;
And now wild beasts came forth the woods to roam.

THE END OF THE FIRST BOOK

500 sullen] of a dark and dull colour.

BOOK II

Meanwhile the new-baptised, who yet remained
At Jordan with the Baptist, and had seen
Him whom they heard so late expressly called
Jesus Messiah, Son of God declared,
And on that high authority had believed,   5
And with him talked, and with him lodged – I mean
Andrew and Simon, famous after known,
With others, though in Holy Writ not named –
Now missing him, their joy so lately found,
So lately found and so abruptly gone,   10
Began to doubt, and doubted many days,
And, as the days increased, increased their doubt;
Sometimes they thought he might be only shown,
And for a time caught up to God, as once
Moses was in the mount and missing long;   15
And the great Thisbite, who on fiery wheels
Rode up to heaven, yet once again to come.
Therefore, as those young prophets then with care
Sought lost Elijah, so in each place these
Nigh to Bethabara – in Jericho   20
The city of palms, Aenon, and Salem old,
Machaerus, and each town or city walled
On this side the broad lake Genezaret,

1–7] John i. 35–41. *Messiah* is the Hebrew term which was translated into the
    Greek of the LXX and the New Testatment as χριστός, Christ. Both words
    mean 'the anointed one'.
15] Exod. xxxii. 1.
16–17] Elijah is called 'the Tishbite' in I Kings xvii. 1; the precise meaning of
    the term is not known, but see ll. 312–14n. On his second coming see Mal.
    iv. 5. See *PL* III 522n.
18–19] II Kings ii. 15–17.
20–4] On Bethabara see John i. 28; on Jericho as 'city of palms' see Deut. xxxiv.
    3. On Aenon and Salem see John iii. 23; Salem is 'old' in deference to a
    patristic tradition which identified the 'Salim' of John the Baptist with the
    Salem of Melchizedek (Gen. xiv. 18, Heb. vii. 1–2). Machaerus was a
    fortress overlooking the Dead Sea from the east; John the Baptist was
    imprisoned and executed there. Genezaret is the name of the Sea of Galilee
    in I Macc. xi. 67, Luke v. 1, and in Josephus. Perea is the name given by
    Josephus to the district described in rabbinical literature and the N.T. as
    'beyond Jordan' (see Matt. xi. 1).

Or in Perea – but returned in vain.
Then on the bank of Jordan, by a creek,   25
Where winds with reeds and osiers whispering play,
Plain fishermen (no greater men them call)
Close in a cottage low together got,
Their unexpected loss and plaints outbreathed:
    'Alas, from what high hope to what relapse   30
Unlooked-for are we fallen! Our eyes beheld
Messiah certainly now come, so long
Expected of our fathers; we have heard
His words, his wisdom full of grace and truth:
"Now, now, for sure, deliverance is at hand;   35
The kingdom shall to Israel be restored":
Thus we rejoiced, but soon our joy is turned
Into perplexity and new amaze:
For whither is he gone, what accident
Hath rapt him from us? Will he now retire   40
After appearance, and again prolong
Our expectation? God of Israel,
Send thy Messiah forth, the time is come;
Behold the kings of the earth, how they oppress
Thy chosen, to what height their power unjust   45
They have exalted, and behind them cast
All fear of thee; arise, and vindicate
Thy glory; free thy people from their yoke!
But let us wait; thus far he hath performed –
Sent his Anointed, and to us revealed him,   50
By his great prophet pointed at and shown
In public, and with him we have conversed;
Let us be glad of this, and all our fears
Lay on his providence; he will not fail,
Nor will withdraw him now, nor will recall –   55
Mock us with his blest sight, then snatch him hence:
Soon we shall see our hope, our joy, return.'
    Thus they out of their plaints new hope resume
To find whom at the first they found unsought;
But to his mother Mary, when she saw   60
Others returned from baptism, not her son,
Nor left at Jordan, tidings of him none;
Within her breast though calm, her breast though pure,

34] John i. 14.
36] Acts i. 6.
40 rapt] carried away.
44] Psalm ii. 2.
50 Anointed] See ll. 1–7n.

Motherly cares and fears got head, and raised
Some troubled thoughts, which she in sighs thus clad: 65
  'Oh, what avails me now that honour high,
To have conceived of God, or that salute,
"Hail, highly favoured, among women blest!"
While I to sorrows am no less advanced,
And fears as eminent above the lot   70
Of other women, by the birth I bore;
In such a season born, when scarce a shed
Could be obtained to shelter him or me
From the bleak air; a stable was our warmth,
A manger his; yet soon enforced to fly   75
Thence into Egypt, till the murderous king
Were dead, who sought his life, and missing filled
With infant blood the streets of Bethlehem;
From Egypt home returned, in Nazareth
Hath been our dwelling many years; his life   80
Private, unactive, calm, contemplative,
Little suspicious to any king; but now,
Full grown to man, acknowledged, as I hear,
By John the Baptist, and in public shown,
Son owned from heaven by his Father's voice,   85
I looked for some great change. To honour? No,
But trouble, as old Simeon plain foretold,
That to the fall and rising he should be
Of many in Israel, and to a sign
Spoken against – that through my very soul   90
A sword shall pierce; this is my favoured lot,
My exaltation to afflictions high;
Afflicted I may be, it seems, and blest;
I will not argue that, nor will repine.
But where delays he now? Some great intent   95
Conceals him; when twelve years he scarce had seen,
I lost him, but so found, as well I saw
He could not lose himself, but went about
His Father's business; what he meant I mused –
Since understand; much more his absence now   100
Thus long to some great purpose he obscures.
But I to wait with patience am inured;
My heart hath been a storehouse long of things

67–8] Cf. *PL* V 385–7n.
87–91] Luke ii. 34–5; cf. I 255–8.
92 exaltation] Miriam, the Hebrew form of Mary, is of uncertain etymology,
    but was sometimes believed to mean 'exaltation'.
96–9] Luke ii. 42–51.
103–4] Luke ii. 19.

And sayings laid up, portending strange events.'
   Thus Mary, pondering oft, and oft to mind   105
Recalling what remarkably had passed
Since first her salutation heard, with thoughts
Meekly composed awaited the fulfilling:
The while her son, tracing the desert wild,
Sole, but with holiest meditations fed,   110
Into himself descended, and at once
All his great work to come before him set –
How to begin, how to accomplish best
His end of being on earth, and mission high:
For Satan, with sly preface to return,   115
Had left him vacant, and with speed was gone
Up to the middle region of thick air,
Where all his potentates in council sat.
There, without sign of boast, or sign of joy,
Solicitous and blank, he thus began: 120
   'Prince, heaven's ancient sons, ethereal thrones –
Demonian spirits now, from the element
Each of his reign allotted, rightlier called,
Powers of fire, air, water, and earth beneath
(So may we hold our place and these mild seats   125
Without new trouble!) – such an enemy
Is risen to invade us, who no less
Threatens than our expulsion down to hell.
I, as I undertook, and with the vote
Consenting in full frequence was empowered,   130
Have found him, viewed him, tasted him; but find
Far other labour to be undergone
Than when I dealt with Adam, first of men,
Though Adam by his wife's allurement fell
However to this man inferior far –   135
If he be man by mother's side at least,
With more than human gifts from heaven adorned,
Perfections absolute, graces divine,
And amplitude of mind to greatest deeds;
Therefore I am returned, lest confidence   140

---

115 preface] used in the etymological sense of 'something said before', with
    reference to I 483–5.
116 vacant] unoccupied.
117] See *Fair Infant* 16n.
120 blank] disconcerted, resourceless.
130 frequence] assembly.
131 tasted] experienced, examined.
139 amplitude of mind] magnanimity; see *PL* VII 511n.

Of my success with Eve in Paradise
Deceive ye to persuasion over-sure
Of like succeeding here; I summon all
Rather to be in readiness with hand
Or counsel to assist, lest I, who erst   145
Thought none my equal, now be overmatched.'
    So spake the old serpent, doubting, and from all
With clamour was assured their utmost aid
At his command; when from amidst them rose
Belial, the dissolutest spirit that fell,   150
The sensualest, and after Asmodai
The fleshliest incubus, and thus advised:
    'Set women in his eye and in his walk,
Among daughters of men the fairest found;
Many are in each region passing fair   155
As the noon sky; more like to goddesses
Than mortal creatures, graceful and discreet,
Expert in amorous arts, enchanting tongues
Persuasive, virgin majesty with mild
And sweet allayed, yet terrible to approach,   160
Skilled to retire, and in retiring draw
Hearts after them tangled in amorous nets.
Such object hath the power to soften and tame
Severest temper, smooth the rugged'st brow,
Enerve, and with voluptuous hope dissolve,   165
Draw out with credulous desire, and lead
At will the manliest, resolutest breast,
As the magnetic hardest iron draws.
Women, when nothing else, beguiled the heart
Of wisest Solomon, and made him build,   170
And made him bow, to the gods of his wives.'
    To whom quick answer Satan thus returned:
'Belial, in much uneven scale thou weigh'st
All others by thyself; because of old
Thou thyself dot'st on womankind, admiring   175
Their shape, their colour, and attractive grace,
None are, thou think'st, but taken with such toys.
Before the flood, thou, with thy lusty crew,
False titled sons of God, roaming the earth,

---

147 old serpent] Rev. xii. 9, xx. 2.
150 Belial] Cf. *PL* I 490–505, II 109–17, and I 490n.
151 Asmodai] See *PL* VI 166–71n.
152 incubus] an evil spirit that had sexual intercourse with women while they
    slept.
169–71] I Kings xi. 1–8.

Cast wanton eyes on the daughters of men,   180
And coupled with them, and begot a race.
Have we not seen, or by relation heard,
In courts and regal chambers how thou lurk'st,
In wood or grove, by mossy fountain-side,
In valley or green meadow, to waylay   185
Some beauty rare, Callisto, Clymene,
Daphne, or Semele, Antiopa,
Or Amymone, Syrinx, many more,
Too long – then lay'st thy scapes on names adored,
Apollo, Neptune, Jupiter, or Pan,   190
Satyr, or Faun, or Sylvan? But these haunts
Delight not all; among the sons of men
How many have with a smile made small account
Of beauty and her lures, easily scorned
All her assaults, on worthier things intent!   195
Remember that Pellean conqueror,
A youth, how all the beauties of the East
He slightly viewed, and slightly overpassed;
How he surnamed of Africa dismissed,
In his prime youth, the fair Iberian maid.   200
For Solomon, he lived at east, and, full
Of honour, wealth, high fare, aimed not beyond
Higher design than to enjoy his state;
Thence to the bait of women lay exposed.
But he whom we attempt is wiser far   205
Than Solomon, of more exalted mind,
Made and set wholly on the accomplishment
Of greatest things; what woman will you find,
Though of this age the wonder and the fame,
On whom his leisure will vouchsafe an eye   210

178–81] Gen. vi. 1–4. Cf. *PL* III 463–5, V 447–8, XI 574–627.
186–8] Callisto, one of the 'nymphs of Diana's train' (l. 355), was the mother by
    Zeus of Arcas (see *Comus* 341n.); Clymene, an oceanid, was the mother
    by Helius of Phaethon; on Daphne see *PL* IV 272–4n.; Semele was
    consumed by the fire of Jove, by whom she was the mother of Bacchus, who
    was born posthumously from the thigh of Jove; Antiopa was the mother by
    Zeus of Amphion and Zethus; Amymone was the mother by Poseidon of
    Nauphius; Syrinx was pursued by Pan and changed into a reed.
191 haunts] habits.
196–8] The 'Pellean conqueror' is Alexander the Great (born at Pella, in
    Macedonia), who in 333 BC (at the age of twenty-three) captured and
    treated honourably the wife and daughters of Darius.
199–200] In 210 BC Scipio Africanus, aged twenty-four, restored a beautiful
    Spanish captive to her lover after the fall of New Carthage.
205–6] Matt. xii. 42.

Of fond desire? Or should she, confident,
As sitting queen adored on beauty's throne,
Descend with all her winning charms begirt
To enamour, as the zone of Venus once
Wrought that effect on Jove, so fables tell;   215
How would one look from his majestic brow,
Seated as on the top of virtue's hill,
Discountenance her despised, and put to rout
All her array; her female pride deject,
Or turn to reverent awe! For beauty stands   220
In the admiration only of weak minds
Led captive; cease to admire, and all her plumes
Fall flat, and shrink into a trivial toy,
At every sudden slighting quite abashed;
Therefore with manlier objects we must try   225
His constancy – with such as have more show
Of worth, of honour, glory, and popular praise
(Rocks whereon greatest men have oftest wrecked);
Or that which only seems to satisfy
Lawful desires of nature, not beyond;   230
And now I know he hungers, where no food
Is to be found, in the wide wilderness;
The rest commit to me; I shall let pass
No advantage, and his strength as oft assay.'
    He ceased, and heard their grant in loud acclaim;   235
Then forthwith to him takes a chosen band
Of spirits likest to himself in guile,
To be at hand and at his beck appear,
If cause were to unfold some active scene
Of various persons, each to know his part;   240
Then to the desert takes with these his flight;
Where still, from shade to shade, the Son of God,
After forty days' fasting, had remained,
Now hungering first, and to himself thus said: 244
    'Where will this end? Four times ten days I have passed
Wandering this woody maze, and human food
Nor tasted, nor had appetite; that fast
To virtue I impute not, or count part
Of what I suffer here; if nature need not,
Or God support nature without repast,   250
Though needing, what praise is it to endure?
But now I feel I hunger, which declares

214–15] *Iliad* xiv 214 ff.
223–3] Alludes to Ovid's remark about the peacock (*Ars Amatoria* i. 627–8).
236–7] Matt. xii. 45.

Nature hath need of what she asks; yet God
Can satisfy that need some other way,
Though hunger still remain: so it remain   255
Without this body's wasting, I content me,
And from the sting of famine fear no harm,
Nor mind it, fed with better thoughts, that feed
Me hungering more to do my Father's will.'
 It was the hour of night, when thus the Son   260
Communed in silent walk, then laid him down
Under the hospitable cover nigh
Of trees thick interwoven; there he slept,
And dreamed, as appetite is wont to dream,
Of meats and drinks, nature's refreshment sweet;   265
Him thought he by the brook of Cherith stood,
And saw the ravens with their horny beaks
Food to Elijah bringing even and morn –
Though ravenous, taught to abstain from what they
  brought;
He saw the prophet also, how he fled   270
Into the desert, and how there he slept
Under a juniper – then how, awaked,
He found his supper on the coals prepared,
And by the angel was bid rise and eat,
And eat the second time after repose,   275
The strength whereof sufficed him forty days;
Sometimes that with Elijah he partook,
Or as a guest with Daniel at his pulse.
Thus wore out night; and now the herald lark
Left his ground-nest, high towering to descry   280
The Morn's approach, and greet her with his song;
As lightly from his grassy couch up rose
Our Saviour, and found all was but a dream;
Fasting he went to sleep, and fasting waked.
Up to a hill anon his steps he reared,   285
From whose high top to ken the prospect round,
If cottage were in view, sheep-cote, or herd;
But cottage, herd, or sheep-cote, none he saw –
Only in a bottom saw a pleasant grove,
With chant of tuneful birds resounding loud;   290
Thither he bent his way, determined there
To rest at noon, and entered soon the shade,

259] John iv. 34.
266–9] I Kings xvii. 3–7; 'ravenous' is a pun.
270–6] I Kings xix. 3–8.
278] Dan. i. 8–19.

High-roofed, and walks beneath, and alleys brown,
That opened in the midst a woody scene;
Nature's own work it seemed (Nature taught Art),   295
And, to a superstitious eye, the haunt
Of wood-gods and wood-nymphs; he viewed it round,
When suddenly a man before him stood,
Not rustic as before, but seemlier clad,
As one in city, or court, or palace bred,   300
And with fair speech these words to him addressed:
    'With granted leave officious I return,
But much more wonder that the Son of God
In this wild solitude so long should bide,
Of all things destitute, and, well I know   305
Not without hunger. Others of some note,
As story tells, have trod this wilderness:
The fugitive bond-woman, with her son,
Outcast Nebaioth, yet found he relief
By a providing angel; all the race   310
Of Israel here had famished, had not God
Rained from heaven manna; and that prophet bold,
Native of Thebez, wandering here was fed
Twice by a voice inviting him to eat.
Of thee these forty days none hath regard,   315
Forty and more deserted here indeed.'
To whom thus Jesus: 'What conclud'st thou hence?
They all had need; I, as thou seest, have none.'
    'How hath thou hunger then?' Satan replied;
'Tell me, if food were now before thee set,   320
Wouldst thou not eat?' 'Thereafter as I like
The giver,' answered Jesus. 'Why should that
Cause thy refusal?' said the subtle fiend.
'Hast thou not right to all created things?
Owe not all creatures, by just right, to thee   325
Duty and service, nor to stay till bid,
But tender all their power? Nor mention I
Meats by the law unclean, or offered first

302 officious] Satan uses the word in the sense 'eager to serve or please' (cf.
    Latin *officiosus*), but by the seventeenth century the word had also come to
    mean 'unduly forward in proffering services'.
308–10] Gen. xxi. 9–21. Ismael is here called by the name of his eldest son
    Nebaioth (Gen. xxv. 13).
310–12] Exod. xvi. 35.
312–14] I Kings xix. 3–8. Thebez is Milton's conjectural identification of the
    place signified by the word 'Thisbite' (l. 16).
327–8 nor ... unclean] a falsehood. See l. 345n.
328–9 or ... idols] Acts xv. 29, I Cor. viii. 4–13, x. 25–31.

To idols – those young Daniel could refuse;
Nor proffered by an enemy – though who   330
Would scruple that, with want oppressed? Behold
Nature ashamed, or, better to express,
Troubled, that thou shouldst hunger, hath purveyed
From all the elements her choicest store,
To treat thee as beseems, and as her Lord   335
With honour; only deign to sit and eat.'
    He spake no dream; for as his words had end,
Our Saviour, lifting up his eyes, beheld
In ample space under the broadest shade,
A table richly spread in regal mode,   340
With dishes piled and meats of noblest sort
And savour – beasts of chase, or fowl of game,
In pastry built, or from the spit, or boiled,
Grisamber-steamed; all fish, from sea or shore,
Freshet or purling brook, of shell or fin,   345
And exquisitest name, for which was drained
Pontus, and Lucrine bay, and Afric coast,
Alas how simple, to these cates compared,
Was that crude apple that diverted Eve!
And at a stately sideboard, by the wine   350
That fragrant smell diffused, in order stood
Tall stripling youths rich-clad, of fairer hue
Than Ganymede or Hylas; distant more,
Under the trees now tripped, now solemn stood,
Nymphs of Diana's train, and Naiades   355
With fruits and flowers from Amalthea's horn,
And ladies of the Hesperides, that seemed
Fairer than feigned of old, or fabled since
Of fairy damsels met in forest wide

329 those . . . refuse] Dan. i. 8.
344 Grisamber] ambergris, a morbid secretion in the intestines of the sperm-whale, used in cookery to impart a sweet odour to food.
345 shell] The Mosaic dietary laws forbid as 'an abomination' all fish without fins or scales (Lev. xi. 9–12).
347] Pontus, i.e. Pontus Euxinus, the Black Sea, was famous in antiquity for its fish; Lucrine bay, a salt-water lagoon in Campania, for its shellfish.
353] Ganymede was the cupbearer of Jove, and Hylas was the page of Hercules.
355 Naiades] river and fountain nymphs.
356] 'Amalthea's horn' is the Greek phrase (κέρας Ἀμαλθείας) equivalent to the Latin *cornu copiae*, the horn of plenty. Milton seems to allude specifically to the horn of Achelous, which the Naiades filled with fruit and flowers (*Metamorphoses* ix 87–8.
357] See *Comus* 393–5n.

By knights of Logres, or of Lyonesse,   360
Lancelot, or Pelleas, or Pellenore;
And all the while harmonious airs were heard
Of chiming strings or charming pipes; and winds
Of gentlest gale Arabian odours fanned
From their soft wings, and Flora's earliest smells.   365
Such was the splendour; and the tempter now
His invitation earnestly renewed:
    'What doubts the Son of God to sit and eat?
These are not fruits forbidden; no interdict
Defends the touching of these viands pure;   370
Their taste no knowledge works, at least of evil,
But life preserves, destroys life's enemy,
Hunger, with sweet restorative delight.
All these are spirits of air, and woods, and springs,
Thy gentle ministers, who come to pay   375
Thee homage, and acknowledge thee their Lord;
What doubt'st thou, Son of God? Sit down and eat.'
    To whom thus Jesus temperately replied:
'Said'st thou not that to all things I had right?
And who withholds my power that right to use?   380
Shall I receive by gift what of my own,
When and where likes me best, I can command?
I can at will, doubt not, as soon as thou,
Command a table in this wilderness,
And call swift flights of angels ministrant,   385
Arrayed in glory, on my cup to attend:
Why shouldst thou, then, obtrude this diligence
In vain, where no acceptance it can find?
And with my hunger what hast thou to do?
Thy pompous delicacies I contemn,   390
And count thy specious gifts no gifts, but guiles.'
    To whom thus answered Satan, malcontent:
'That I have also power to give thou seest;
If of that power I bring thee voluntary

360] Logres is the area of England east of the Severn and south of the Humber.
    Lyonesse is a mythical country (associated with Arthur), once located
    between Land's End and the Scilly Isles, and now covered by the sea.
361] In Malory both Lancelot and Pelleas have amorous adventures. Pellenore
    may be an allusion to Pellenore's son Percival, whose experience of a
    banquet and sexual temptation bears some resemblance to that of Milton's
    Jesus (*Morte d'Arthur* xiv. 9).
365] Flora] Roman goddess of flowers.
368] What doubts] Why hesitates.
370] Defends] forbids.
384] Psalm lxxviii. 19.

What I might have bestowed on whom I pleased,   395
And rather opportunely in this place
Chose to impart to thy apparent need,
Why shouldst thou not accept it? But I see
What I can do or offer is suspect;
Of these things others quickly will dispose,   400
Whose pains have earned the far-fet spoil.' With that
Both table and provision vanished quite,
With sound of harpies' wings and talons heard,
Only the importune tempter still remained,
And with these words his temptation pursued: 405
    'By hunger, that each other creature tames,
Thou art not to be harmed, therefore not moved;
Thy temperance, invincible besides,
For no allurement yields to appetite;
And all thy heart is set on high designs,   410
High actions. But wherewith to be achieved?
Great acts require great means of enterprise;
Thou art unknown, unfriended, low of birth,
A carpenter thy father known, thyself
Bred up in poverty and straits at home,   415
Lost in a desert here and hunger-bit;
Which way, or from what hope, dost thou aspire
To greatness? Whence authority deriv'st?
What followers, what retinue canst thou gain,
Or at thy heels the dizzy multitude,   420
Longer than thou canst feed them on thy cost?
Money brings honour, friends, conquest, and realms;
What raised Antipater the Edomite,
And his son Herod placed on Judah's throne
(Thy throne) but gold, that got him puissant friends? 425
Therefore, if at great things thou wouldst arrive,
Get riches first, get wealth, and treasure heap –
Not difficult, if thou hearken to me,
Riches are mine, fortune is in my hand;
They whom I favour thrive in wealth amain,   430
While virtue, valour, wisdom, sit in want.'
    To whom thus Jesus patiently replied:
'Yet wealth without these three is impotent
To gain dominion, or to keep it gained.

401 fet] fetched.
403 harpies] See *Comus* 605n.
414] Matt. xiii. 55.
423–5] See *PL* XII 353–8n.
429] Hag. ii. 8.

Witness those ancient empires of the earth,   435
In height of all their flowing wealth dissolved;
But men endued with these have oft attained,
In lowest poverty, to highest deeds –
Gideon, and Jephtha, and the shepherd lad
Whose offspring on the throne of Judah sat   440
So many ages, and shall yet regain
That seat, and reign in Israel without end.
Among the heathen (for throughout the world
To me is not unknown what hath been done
Worthy of memorial) canst thou not remember   445
Quintius, Fabricius, Curius, Regulus?
For I esteem those names of men so poor,
Who could do mighty things, and could contemn
Riches, though offered from the hand of kings.
And what in me seems wanting but that I   450
May also in this poverty as soon
Accomplish what they did, perhaps and more?
Extol not riches, then, the toil of fools,
The wise man's cumbrance, if not snare; more apt
To slacken virtue and abate her edge   455
Than prompt her to do aught may merit praise.
What if with like aversion I reject
Riches and realms! Yet not for that a crown,
Golden in show, is but a wreath of thorns,
Brings dangers, troubles, cares, and sleepless nights,   460
To him who wears the regal diadem,
When on his shoulders each man's burden lies;
For therein stands the office of a king,
His honour, virtue, merit, and chief praise,
That for the public all this weight he bears.   465
Yet he who reigns within himself, and rules
Passions, desires, and fears, is more a king –

439] On Gideon see Judges vi–viii; on Jephtha see Judges xi–xii; on David, 'the
shepherd lad', see Psalm lxxviii. 70–1, Ezek. xxxiv. 23–4.
441–2] Luke i. 32–3.
446] Lucius Quinctius Cincinnatus was a farmer who in 458 BC was appointed
dictator and defeated the Aequi. Gaius Fabricius Luscinus, consul in 282
and 278 BC, was famous for his poverty, austerity, and incorruptibility.
Manius Curius Dentatus was a Roman plebeian hero, famous for his
humble birth, incorruptibility, and frugality. Marcus Atilius Regulus, a
hero of the First Punic War (255 BC), was according to legend tortured to
death in Carthage (see Horace, *Odes* III. v).
453 toil] trap, snare.
458 for that] because.
466–7] Prov. xvi. 32.

Which every wise and virtuous man attains;
And who attains not, ill aspires to rule
Cities of men, or headstrong multitudes,   470
Subject himself to anarchy within,
Or lawless passions in him, which he serves.
But to guide nations in the way of truth
By saving doctrine, and from error lead
To know, and, knowing, worship God aright,   475
Is yet more kingly; this attracts the soul,
Governs the inner man, the nobler part;
That other o'er the body only reigns,
And oft by force – which to a generous mind
So reigning can be no sincere delight.   480
Besides, to give a kingdom hath been thought
Greater and nobler done, and to lay down
Far more magnanimous, than to assume.
Riches are needless, then, both for themselves,
And for thy reason why they should be sought   485
To gain a sceptre, oftest better missed.'

THE END OF THE SECOND BOOK

481–3] Seneca, *Thyestes* 529. Milton may have in mind the abdications of
    Diocletian (in AD 305), the Emperor Charles V (1555), and Christina of
    Sweden (1654). On 'magnanimous' see *PL* VII 511n.

BOOK III

So spake the Son of God; and Satan stood
A while as mute, confounded what to say,
What to reply, confuted and convinced
Of his weak arguing and fallacious drift;
At length, collecting all his serpent wiles, 5
With soothing words renewed, him thus accosts:
  'I see thou know'st what is of use to know,
What best to say canst say, to do canst do;
Thy actions to thy words accord; thy words
To thy large heart give utterance due; thy heart 10
Contains of good, wise, just, the perfect shape.
Should kings and nations from thy mouth consult,
Thy counsel would be as the oracle
Urim and Thummim, those oraculous gems
On Aaron's breast, or tongue of seers old 15
Infallible; or wert thou sought to deeds
That might require the array of war, thy skill
Of conduct would be such that all the world
Could not sustain thy prowess, or subsist
In battle, though against thy few in arms. 20
These godlike virtues wherefore dost thou hide?
Affecting private life, or more obscure
In savage wilderness, wherefore deprive
All earth her wonder at thy acts, thyself
The fame and glory – glory, the reward 25
That sole excites to high attempts the flame
Of most erected spirits, most tempered pure
Ethereal, who all pleasures else despise,
All treasures and all gain esteem as dross,
And dignities and powers, all but the highest? 30

13–15] The precise meaning of Urim and Thummim is not known. The
vocalization of the words indicates that Massoretic scholars connected
Urim with light, and Thummim with perfection, or innocence. The plural
form is probably not intended to indicate plurality (as the R.V. marginal
note to Exod. xxviii. 30 would have it) but is rather an intensive plural.
Urim and Thummim are associated with the breastplate of Aaron in Exod.
xxviii. 30 and Lev. viii. 8. They are most clearly oracular in the LXX text
of I Sam. xiv. 41–2, part of which may be translated 'And Saul said, "if the
guilt be in me or in Jonathan my son, give Urim, O Lord God of Israel; but
if you say it is in my people Israel, give Thummin"'.
22 Affecting] seeking.
27 erected] exalted.

Thy years are ripe, and over-ripe: the son
Of Macedonian Philip had ere these
Won Asia, and the throne of Cyrus held   ·
At his dispose; young Scipio had brought down
The Carthaginian pride; young Pompey quelled   35
The Pontic king, and in tríumph had rode.
Yet years, and to ripe years judgement mature,
Quench not the thirst of glory, but augment.
Great Julius, whom now all the world admires,
The more he grew in years, the more inflamed   40
With glory, wept that he had lived so long
Inglorious: but thou yet are not too late.'
　　To whom our Saviour calmly thus replied:
'Thou neither dost persuade me to seek wealth
For empire's sake, nor empire to affect   45
For glory's sake, by all thy argument.
For what is glory but the blaze of fame,
The people's praise, if always praise unmixed?
And what the people but a herd confused,
A miscellaneous rabble, who extol   50
Things vulgar, and well weighed, scarce worth the praise?
They praise and they admire they know not what,
And know not whom, but as one leads the other;
And what delight to be by such extolled,
To live upon their tongues, and be their talk?   55
Of whom to be dispraised were no small praise –
His lot who dares be singularly good.
The intelligent among them and the wise
Are few, and glory scarce of few is raised.
This is true glory and renown – when God,   60
Looking on the earth, with approbation marks

31–4] Jesus was 'about thirty' at his baptism (Luke iii. 23). Philip of Macedon's
　　son was Alexander the Great, who in 334 BC (aged twenty-two) crossed the
　　Hellespont and 'won Asia', and in 330 assumed the throne of the empire
　　which Cyrus had founded.

34–5] Scipio was sent to Spain as proconsul in 210 BC, aged twenty-four, and
　　eight years later defeated the Carthaginians in the battle of Zama, thus
　　ending the Second Punic War.

35–6] Pompey defeated Mithridates VI, King of Pontus, in 66 BC (when he was
　　forty) and in 61 BC returned to Italy to celebrate the most magnificent
　　triumph that Rome had ever witnessed. Pompey had been granted a
　　triumph in 81 BC (though he was merely an *eques*, and not legally qualified
　　for one) and another in 71 BC. Even if Satan is referring to this earliest
　　triumph, he certainly misrepresents Pompey's age during the Mithridatic
　　War.

39–42] According to Plutarch, in 68 BC Caesar (aged thirty) read the history of
　　Alexander's campaigns, and wept because Alexander, at his age, was the
　　king of so many people, whereas Caesar had yet to achieve a brilliant
　　success (*Life of Caesar* xi. 3).

The just man, and divulges him through heaven
To all his angels, who with true applause
Recount his praises; thus he did to Job,
When, to extend his fame through heaven and earth,   65
As thou to thy reproach may'st well remember,
He asked thee, "Hast thou seen my servant Job?"
Famous he was in heaven; on earth less known,
Where glory is false glory, attributed
To things not glorious, men not worthy of fame.   70
They err who count it glorious to subdue
By conquest far and wide, to overrun
Large countries, and in field great battles win,
Great cities by assault; what do these worthies
But rob and spoil, burn, slaughter, and enslave   75
Peaceable nations, neighbouring or remote,
Made captive, yet deserving freedom more
Than those their conquerors, who leave behind
Nothing but ruin wheresoe'er they rove,
And all the flourishing works of peace destroy,   80
Then swell with pride, and must be titled gods,
Great benefactors of mankind, deliverers,
Worshipped with temple, priest, and sacrifice?
One is the son of Jove, of Mars the other;
Till conqueror Death discover them scarce men,   85
Rolling in brutish vices, and deformed,
Violent or shameful death their due reward.
But if there be in glory aught of good,
It may by means far different be attained,
Without ambition, war, or violence –   90
By deeds of peace, by wisdom eminent,

---

62 divulges] publicly proclaims.

64–8] Cf. I 147–9n.

81 titled gods] The title *divus* was accorded to deceased Roman emperors, and
from the time of Domitian emperors were regarded as gods during their
lifetime. Antiochus II of Syria had assumed the title ὁ θεός (a god). Cf. Acts
ii. 22, where the voice of Herod Agrippa I is said to be that of a god.

82 benefactors] The title εὐεργέτης (benefactor) was conferred on various
persons by the Greeks, and was enjoyed by two of the Macedonian kings of
Egypt, Ptolemy III and Ptolemy VIII. Cf. Luke xxii. 25, which refers to
the title.

deliverers] The title Σωτήρ (deliverer, saviour) was anciently used of deities,
and in Hellenistic times it was used of kings to imply deification. The most
famous holder of the title was probably Ptolemy I. In the LXX the word is
used of various warriors, and of God; in the N.T. it is often applied to Jesus.

84] The 'son of Jove' is Alexander (see *PL* IX 507–9n.); the son of Mars is
Romulus, first king of Rome and (after his translation to heaven) the god
Quirinus.

91–2] II Pet. i. 6.

By patience, temperance; I mention still
Him whom thy wrongs, with saintly patience borne,
Made famous in a land and times obscure;
Who names not now with honour patient Job?   95
Poor Socrates (who next more memorable?),
By what he taught and suffered for so doing,
For truth's sake suffering death unjust, lives now
Equal in fame to proudest conquerors.
Yet, if for fame and glory aught be done,   100
Aught suffered – if young African for fame
His wasted country freed from Punic rage –
The deed becomes unpraised, the man at least,
And loses, though but verbal, his reward.
Shall I seek glory, then, as vain men seek,   105
Oft not deserved? I seek not mine, but his
Who sent me, and thereby witness whence I am.'
    To whom the tempter, murmuring, thus replied:
'Think not so slight of glory, therein least
Resembling thy great Father: he seeks glory,   110
And for his glory all things made, all things
Orders and governs; nor content in heaven,
By all his angels glorified, requires
Glory from men, from all men, good or bad,
Wise or unwise, no difference, no exemption;   115
Above all sacrifice, or hallowed gift,
Glory he requires, and glory he receives,
Promiscuous from all nations, Jew, or Greek,
Or barbarous, nor exception hath declared;
From us, his foes pronounced, glory he exacts.'   120
    To whom our Saviour fervently replied:
'And reason; since his word all things produced,
Though chiefly not for glory as prime end,
But to show forth his goodness, and impart
His good communicable to every soul   125
Freely; of whom what could he less expect
Than glory and benediction – that is, thanks –
The slightest, easiest, readiest recompense
From them who could return him nothing else,
And, not returning that, would likeliest render   130
Contempt instead, dishonour, obloquy?
Hard recompense, unsuitable return

96–9] According to an ancient tradition the teaching and death of Socrates
    foreshadowed that of Jesus.
101–2] See ll. 34–5n.
106–7] John v. 31–2, vii. 18, viii. 50.
119 barbarous] non-Hellenic.

For so much good, so much beneficence!
But why should man seek glory, who of his own
Hath nothing, and to whom nothing belongs   135
But condemnation, ignominy, and shame –
Who, for so many benefits received,
Turned recreant to God, ingrate and false,
And so of all true good himself despoiled;
Yet, sacrilegious, to himself would take   140
That which to God alone of right belongs?
Yet so much bounty is in God, such grace,
That who advance his glory, not their own,
Them he himself to glory will advance.'
    So spake the Son of God; and here again   145
Satan had not to answer, but stood struck
With guilt of his own sin – for he himself,
Insatiable of glory, had lost all;
Yet of another plea bethought him soon –
    'Of glory, as thou wilt,' said he, 'so deem;   150
Worth or not worth the seeking, let it pass;
But to a kingdom thou art born – ordained
To sit upon thy father David's throne,
By mother's side thy father, though thy right
Be now in powerful hands, that will not part   155
Easily from possession won with arms;
Judea now and all the promised land,
Reduced a province under Roman yoke,
Obeys Tiberius, nor is always ruled
With temperate sway: oft have they violated   160
The Temple, oft the Law, with foul affronts,
Abominations rather, as did once

---

138 recreant] false, apostate.
146 not] nothing.
153] Luke i. 32.
154] The gospels are silent about the ancestry of Mary, but according to
    patristic tradition she was descended from David.
157–60] In AD 6 Judea was annexed to the province of Syria, and was thereafter
    ruled by procurators. Tiberius was Roman emperor from AD 14–37. From
    AD 26–36 the procurator of Judea was Pontius Pilate; Josephus and Philo
    both testify to the intemperance of his rule (*Antiquities* xviii. 3, *Jewish War*
    ii. 8 ff.; *Legatio ad Gaium* xxxviii).
160–3] In 169 BC Antiochus IV had pillaged the temple, and had forced the
    Jews to offer swine on the altar; he later rededicated the temple to
    Olympian Zeus, thus precipitating the Maccabean revolt. In 63 BC Pompey
    had entered the Holy of Holies with several of his officers. When Pontius
    Pilate had arrived in Judea in AD 26 he had offended the Jews by bringing
    images of the emperor into Jerusalem.

Antiochus: and think'st thou to regain
Thy right in sitting still, or thus retiring?
So did not Maccabeus: he indeed   165
Retired unto the desert, but with arms;
And o'er a mighty king so oft prevailed
That by strong hand his family obtained,
Though priests, the crown, and David's throne usurped,
With Modin and her suburbs once content.   170
If kingdom move thee not, let move thee zeal
And duty – zeal and duty are not slow,
But on Occasion's forelock watchful wait.
They themselves rather are occasion best –
Zeal of thy Father's house, duty to free   175
Thy country from her heathen servitude;
So shalt thou best fulfil, best verify,
The prophets old, who sung thy endless reign –
The happier reign the sooner it begins:
Reign then; what canst thou better do the while?'   180
    To whom our Saviour answer thus returned:
'All things are best fulfilled in their due time,
And time there is for all things, Truth hath said;
If of my reign prophetic writ hath told
That it shall never end, so, when begin   185
The Father in his purpose hath decreed –
He in whose hand all times and seasons roll.
What if he hath decreed that I shall first
Be tried in humble state, and things adverse,
By tribulations, injuries, insults,   190
Contempts, and scorns, and snares, and violence
Suffering, abstaining, quietly expecting
Without distrust or doubt, that he may know
What I can suffer, how obey? Who best
Can suffer, best can do; best reign who first   195
Well hath obeyed – just trial ere I merit
My exaltation without change or end.
But what concerns it thee when I begin
My everlasting kingdom, why are thou

165–70] The revolt led by Mattathias and his son Judas Maccabeus began in
     Modin, the location of which has not been established with certainty. See I
     Macc. ii–ix.
173 Occasion] opportunity, the forelock of which was proverbial.
175] Psalm lxix. 9, John ii. 17.
182–3] Eccles. iii. 1.
187] Acts i. 7.
194–6] A classical commonplace, a version of which occurs in Matt. xx. 26–7.

Solicitous, what moves thy inquisition?   200
Know'st thou not that my rising is thy fall,
And my promotion will be thy destruction?'
    To whom the tempter, inly racked, replied:
'Let that come when it comes; all hope is lost
Of my reception into grace; what worse?   205
For where no hope is left is left no fear;
If there be worse, the expectation more
Of worse torments me than the feeling can.
I would be at the worst; worst is my port,
My harbour, and my ultimate repose,   210
The end I would attain, my final good.
My error was my error, and my crime
My crime; whatever, for itself condemned,
And will alike be punished, whether thou
Reign or reign not – though to that gentle brow   215
Willingly I could fly, and hope thy reign,
From that placid aspéct and meek regard,
Rather than aggravate my evil state,
Would stand between me and thy Father's ire
(Whose ire I dread more than the fire of hell)   220
A shelter and a kind of shading cool
Interposition, as a summer's cloud.
If I then to the worst that can be haste,
Why move thy feet so slow to what is best,
Happiest, both to thyself and all the world,   225
That thou, who worthiest art, shouldst be their king?
Perhaps thou linger'st in deep thoughts detained
Of the enterprise so hazardous and high;
No wonder, for though in thee be united
What of perfection can in man be found,   230
Or human nature can receive, consider
Thy life hath yet been private, most part spent
At home, scarce viewed the Galilean towns,
And once a year Jerusalem few days'
Short sojourn; and what thence couldst thou observe? 235
The world thou hast not seen, much less her glory,
Empires, and monarchs, and their radiant courts –
Best school of best experience, quickest in sight
In all things that to greatest actions lead.
The wisest, unexperienced, will be ever   240
Timorous and loath, with novice modesty
(As he who, seeking asses, found a kingdom)

221–2] Isa. xxv. 4–5.
234] Luke ii. 41.
242 he] Saul; I Sam. ix–x. 1.

Irresolute, unhardy, unadventurous;
But I will bring thee where thou soon shalt quit
Those rudiments, and see before thine eyes   245
The monarchies of the earth, their pomp and state –
Sufficient introduction to inform
Thee, of thyself so apt, in regal arts,
And regal mysteries; that thou may'st know
How best their opposition to withstand.'   250
   With that (such power was given him then), he took
The Son of God up to a mountain high.
It was a mountain at whose verdant feet
A spacious plain outstretched in circuit wide
Lay pleasant; from his side two rivers flowed,   255
The one winding, the other straight, and left between
Fair champaign, with less rivers interveined,
Then meeting joined their tribute to the sea;
Fertile of corn the glebe, of oil, and wine,
With herds the pasture thronged, with flocks the hills;   260
Huge cities and high-towered, that well might seem
The seats of mightiest monarchs; and so large
The prospect was that here and there was room
For barren desert, fountainless and dry.
To this high mountain-top the tempter brought   265
Our Saviour, and new train of words began:
   'Well have we speeded, and o'er hill and dale,
Forest and field and flood, temples and towers,
Cut shorter many a league; here thou behold'st
Assyria, and her empire's ancient bounds,   270
Araxes and the Caspian lake; thence on
As far as Indus east, Euphrates west,
And oft beyond; to south the Persian bay,
And, inaccessible, the Arabian drouth;

247 inform] train.
249 mysteries] In Milton's time the word 'mystery' retained the senses of two
    different Latin roots, and meant both 'skill, occupation' (from *ministerium*)
    and 'secret' (from *mysterium*).
255–6] The 'two rivers' are the Euphrates and the Tigris. The Greek word
    Tigris was known in antiquity to derive from the Persian word *tigra*, 'an
    arrow', hence Milton's 'straight'.
257 champaign] Mesopotamia.
271 Araxes] now Aras, a river which rises in eastern Turkey, and forms the
    Soviet–Iranian border as it flows to the Caspian.
274 drouth] desert.

Here, Nineveh, of length within her wall   275
Several days' journey, built by Ninus old,
Of that first golden monarchy the seat,
And seat of Salmanassar, whose success
Israel in long captivity still mourns;
There Babylon, the wonder of all tongues,   280
As ancient, but rebuilt by him who twice
Judah and all thy father David's house
Led captive, and Jerusalem laid waste,
Till Cyrus set them free; Persepolis,
His city, there thou seest, and Bactra there;   285
Ecbatana her structure vast there shows,
And Hecatompylos her hundred gates;
There Susa by Choaspes, amber stream,
The drink of none but kings; of later fame
Built by Emathian or by Parthian hands,   290
The great Seleucia, Nisibis, and there
Artaxata, Teredon, Ctesiphon,
Turning with easy eye, thou may'st behold.
All these the Parthian (now some ages past
By great Arsaces led, who founded first   295
That empire) under his dominion holds,
From the luxurious kings of Antioch won.

275–9] Ninus was the legendary eponymous founder of Nineveh, the Assyrian
    capital on the Tigris. On the 'several days' journey' requisite to walk
    around it see Jonah iii. 3. Shalmaneser (or Salmanasar in II Esdras xiii. 40),
    King of Assyria from 727–722 BC, made Hoshea of Samaria (King of Israel)
    'his servant' (II Kings xvii. 3), and later besieged Samaria, and 'carried
    Israel away into Assyria' (II Kings xvii. 4–6).

280–4] See PL XII 344–7n.; 'wonder of all tongues' refers to such wonders as
    the temple of Bel and the hanging gardens, but also glances at the
    confusion of tongues (PL XII 38–62).

284–9] Persepolis was the summer capital of Persia, and Susa (see PL X 306–
    11n.) the winter residence of the kings on the banks of the Choaspes, which
    according to an ancient tradition was 'the drink of none but kings'. Bactra
    (now Balkh, in Afghanistan) was the capital of the Persian province of
    Bactria (cf. PL X 433n.). On Ecbatana see PL XI 393n. Hecatompylos
    ('hundred-gated') was a royal residence of Parthian kings; its location is not
    known.

290–2] Emathian refers to the Macedonian successors of Alexander, the Seleu-
    cids. On Seleucia see PL IV 212n. Nisibis is modern Nusaybin, in Turkey.
    Artaxata was the ancient capital of Armenia. Teredon was an ancient
    Babylonian city near the confluence of the Tigris and Euphrates. Ctesi-
    phon, on the Tigris near Seleucia, was the winter capital of Parthia.

294–7] The Parthian Empire was founded by Arsaces in 247 BC in the Seleucid
    satrapy of Parthia, south of the Caspian Sea. The Seleucid capital was
    Antioch.

And just in time thou com'st to have a view
Of his great power; for now the Parthian king
In Ctesiphon hath gathered all his host   300
Against the Scythian, whose incursions wild
Have wasted Sogdiana; to her aid
He marches now in haste: see, though from far,
His thousands, in what martial equipage
They issue forth, steel bows and shafts their arms,   305
Of equal dread in flight or in pursuit –
All horsemen, in which fight they most excel;
See how in warlike muster they appear,
In rhombs, and wedges, and half-moons, and wings.'
    He looked, and saw what numbers numberless   310
The city gates outpoured, light-armed troops
In coats of mail and military pride.
In mail their horses clad, yet fleet and strong,
Prancing their riders bore, the flower and choice
Of many provinces from bound to bound –   315
From Arachosia, from Candaor east,
And Margiana, to the Hyrcanian cliffs
Of Caucasus, and dark Iberian dales;
From Atropatia, and the neighbouring plains
Of Adiabene, Media, and the south   320
Of Susiana, to Balsara's haven.
He saw them in their forms of battle ranged,
How quick they wheeled, and flying behind them shot

298–336] Milton's account of a war between the Scythians (an ancient tribe of
  south Russia) and the Parthians does not refer to any specific historical
  event.
302 Sogdiana] an ancient province of the Achaemenian Empire, and the north-
  eastern limit of Alexander's empire. At the time of Jesus it was not a
  Parthian province, but was occupied by the Scythians.
306] Many classical authors testify that Parthian horsemen often shot their
  arrows backwards while in real or pretended flight.
316–21] Arachosia, called White India by the Parthians, was their easternmost
  province: it occupied an area that straddles modern Afghanistan and
  Pakistan. Candaor (now Kendahar, in Afghanistan) was the frontier city of
  the Parthian Empire. Margiana was a province centred on the ancient town
  of Merv (now Mary, Turkmanistan). Hyrcania was a province south-east of
  the Caspian Sea. Iberia (modern Georgia) was a vassal state rather than a
  province, as were Atropatia (now Azerbaijan) and Adiabene (the ancient
  Assyria). Ancient Media was divided into four provinces by the Parthians.
  Susiana (modern Ilam, in south-west Iran) was a rebellious vassal state.
  Balsara (modern Basra) was not founded until AD 636; it was built on the
  joint stream that unites the Tigris and the Euphrates, and at the time of
  Jesus the site was probably part of the Persian Gulf. Jesus has viewed the
  Parthian Empire in a huge semi-circle from east to north to west.

Sharp sleet of arrowy showers against the face
Of their pursuers, and overcame by flight;   325
The field all iron cast a gleaming brown.
Nor wanted clouds of foot, nor, on each horn,
Cuirassiers all in steel for standing fight.
Chariots, or elephants endorsed with towers
Of archers; nor of labouring pioneers   330
A multitude, with spades and axes armed,
To lay hills plain, fell woods, or valleys fill,
Or where plain was raise hill, or overlay
With bridges rivers proud, as with a yoke;
Mules after these, camels and dromedaries,   335
And waggons fraught with útensils of war.
Such forces met not, nor so wide a camp,
When Agrican, with all his northern powers,
Besieged Albracca, as romances tell,
The city of Gallaphrone, from thence to win   340
The fairest of her sex, Angelica,
His daughter, sought by many prowest knights,
Both paynim and the peers of Charlemagne.
Such and so numerous was their chivalry;
At sight whereof the fiend yet more presumed,   345
And to our Saviour thus his words renewed:
    'That thou may'st know I seek not to engage
Thy virtue, and not every way secure
On no slight grounds thy safety, near and mark
To what end I have brought thee hither, and show   350
All this fair sight: thy kingdom, though foretold
By prophet or by angel, unless thou
Endeavour, as thy father David did,
Thou never shalt obtain; prediction still
In all things, and all men, supposes means;   355
Without means used, what it predicts revokes.
But say thou wert possessed of David's throne

---

328 Cuirassiers] horse soldiers wearing cuirasses, i.e. body armour consisting of
    a breastplate and a backplate.
329 endorsed] used in the etymological sense of 'carrying on the back'.
337–43] In Boiardo's *Orlando Innamorato* I. x–xiv, Agrican, the Tartar king,
    besieges with 2,200,000 men Albracca, a city of Gallaphrone, King of
    Cathay, in order to win the latter's daughter, the fair Angelica. At the
    beginning of the poem Angelica had won the heart of the *douzepers* (the
    twelve 'peers of Charlemagne'), including Orlando, and of the pagan
    (paynim) knights. 'Prowest' means 'most gallant'.
353] David's struggle ('endeavour') for the throne is described in I Sam. xvi–II
    Sam. v.

By free consent of all, none opposite,
Samaritan or Jew; how couldst thou hope
Long to enjoy it quiet and secure   360
Between two such enclosing enemies,
Roman and Parthian? Therefore one of these
Thou must make sure thy own: the Parthian first,
By my advice, as nearer, and of late
Found able by invasion to annoy   365
Thy country, and captive lead away her kings,
Antigonus and old Hyrcanus, bound,
Maugre the Roman; it shall be my task
To render thee the Parthian at dispose:
Choose which thou wilt, by conquest or by league.   370
By him thou shalt regain, without him not,
That which alone can truly reinstall thee
In David's royal seat, his true successor –
Deliverance of thy brethren, those ten tribes
Whose offspring in his territory yet serve   375
In Habor, and among the Medes dispersed:
Ten sons of Jacob, two of Joseph, lost
Thus long from Israel, serving, as of old
Their fathers in the land of Egypt served,
This offer sets before thee to deliver.   380
These if from servitude thou shalt restore
To their inheritance, then, nor till then,
Thou on the throne of David in full glory,

358 opposite] opposed.
359] The hostility of the Jews to the Samaritans was proverbial (John iv. 9,
    vii. 48).
361-2] Although the peace between Rome and Parthia established by Augustus
    lasted until AD 58, the Romans had periodically prepared for war during
    the time of Jesus, and enmity between Rome and Parthia had previously
    been well established by the invasions of Sulla, Pompey, Crassus, and
    Antony.
364-8] 'Of late' is an exaggeration, and the captivity of Antigonus is a
    fabrication. Antigonus, the last member of the cadet branch of the
    Hasmonaean dynasty (see *PL* XII 353-8n.), supported the Parthian
    invasion of Judea in 40 BC and was made king. He then mutilated his uncle
    Hyrcanus II (whom Caesar had appointed ethnarch) to render him inelig-
    ible for priestly office, and gave him to the Parthians as a prisoner. Herod
    fled to Rome, where he was appointed King of Judea, and three years later
    re-captured Jerusalem, and deposed and crucified Antigonus. 'Maugre'
    means 'in spite of'.
373-8] David ruled all twelve tribes. After the death of Solomon in 933 BC the
    tribes of Judah and Benjamin attached themselves to Rehoboam, and the
    other ten tribes, including the 'two of Joseph' (Manasseh and Ephraim),
    followed Jeroboam, and in 721 BC were carried away to Assyria, and placed
    'in Halah and in Habor ... and in the cities of the Medes' (II Kings
    xviii. 11).

From Egypt to Euphrates and beyond,
Shalt reign, and Rome or Caesar not need fear.'   385
    To whom our Saviour answered thus, unmoved:
'Much ostentation vain of fleshly arm
And fragile arms, much instrument of war,
Long in preparing, soon to nothing brought,
Before mine eyes thou hast set; and in my ear   390
Vented much policy, and projects deep
Of enemies, of aids, battles, and leagues,
Plausible to the world, to me worth naught.
Means I must use, thou say'st; prediction else
Will unpredict, and fail me of the throne!   395
My time, I told thee (and that time for thee
Were better farthest off), is not yet come;
When that comes, think not thou to find me slack
On my part aught endeavouring, or to need
Thy politic maxims, or that cumbersome   400
Luggage of war there shown me – argument
Of human weakness rather than of strength.
My brethren, as thou call'st them, those ten tribes,
I must deliver, if I mean to reign
David's true heir, and his full sceptre sway   405
To just extent over all Israel's sons!
But whence to thee this zeal? Where was it then
For Israel, or for David, or his throne,
When thou stood'st up his tempter to the pride
Of numbering Israel – which cost the lives   410
Of threescore and ten thousand Israelites
By three days' pestilence? Such was thy zeal
To Israel then, the same that now to me.
As for those captive tribes, themselves were they
Who wrought their own captivity, fell off   415
From God to worship calves, the deities
Of Egypt, Baal next and Ashtaroth,
And all the idolatries of heathen round,
Besides their other worse than heathenish crimes;
Nor in the land of their captivity   420
Humbled themselves, or penitent besought

384] See I Kings iv. 21, where 'the river' is the Euphrates.
396–7] John vii. 6.
409–12] I Chron. xxi. 1–14.
414–19] The 'captive tribes' are the ten tribes in Assyria. Jeroboam erected
    calves of gold at Bethel and Dan in imitation of the gods of Egypt (I Kings
    xii. 28; cf. *PL* I 482–5 and notes). On Baal and Ashtaroth see *Nativity* 197–
    200 and notes, and cf. *PL* I 421–3.

The God of their forefathers, but so died
Impenitent, and left a race behind
Like to themselves, distinguishable scarce
From Gentiles, but by circumcision vain,   425
And God with idols in their worship joined.
Should I of these the liberty regard,
Who, freed, as to their ancient patrimony,
Unhumbled, unrepentant, unreformed,
Headlong would follow, and to their gods perhaps   430
Of Bethel and of Dan? No, let them serve
Their enemies who serve idols with God.
Yet he at length, time to himself best known,
Remembering Abraham, by some wondrous call
May bring them back, repentant and sincere,   435
And at their passing cleave the Assyrian flood,
While to their native land with joy they haste,
As the Red Sea and Jordan once he cleft,
When to the promised land their fathers passed.'
To his due time and providence I leave them.'   440
    So spake Israel's true King, and to the fiend
Made answer meet, that made void all his wiles.
So fares it when with truth falsehood contends.

THE END OF THE THIRD BOOK

425] Rom. ii. 25.
431–2] Jer. v. 19.
436 Assyrian flood] Euphrates; see Isa. xi. 15–16.
438] Exod. xiv. 21–2, Joshua iii. 14–17.

BOOK IV

Perplexed and troubled at his bad success
The tempter stood, nor had what to reply,
Discovered in his fraud, thrown from his hope
So oft, and the persuasive rhetoric
That sleeked his tongue, and won so much on Eve,   5
So little here, nay lost; but Eve was Eve,
This far his over-match, who, self-deceived
And rash, beforehand had no better weighed
The strength he was to cope with, or his own.
But – as a man who had been matchless held   10
In cunning, over-reached where least he thought,
To salve his credit, and for very spite,
Still will be tempting him who foils him still,
And never cease, though to his shame the more;
Or as a swarm of flies in vintage-time,   15
About the wine-press where sweet must is poured,
Beat off, returns as oft with humming sound;
Or surging waves against a solid rock,
Though all to shivers dashed, the assault renew,
Vain battery, and in froth or bubbles end –   20
So Satan, whom repulse upon repulse
Met ever, and to shameful silence brought,
Yet gives not o'er, though desperate of success,
And his vain importunity pursues.
He brought our Saviour to the western side   25
Of that high mountain, whence he might behold
Another plain, long, but in breadth not wide,
Washed by the southern sea, and on the north
To equal length backed with a ridge of hills
That screened the fruits of the earth and seats of men   30
From cold Septentrion blasts; thence in the midst
Divided by a river, of whose banks

1 Perplexed] distressed.
  success] result.
15–17] *Iliad* ii 469–71, xvi 641–3, xvii 570–2.
18–20] *Iliad* xv 618–21, *Aeneid* vii 586–90.
27–33] The long and narrow plain of Lazio (Latium) lies south-west of the
    Apennines ('a ridge of hills'), which protect it from the north wind
    (Septentrion). The river is the Tiber, and the 'imperial city' Rome.

On each side an imperial city stood,
With towers and temples proudly elevate
On seven small hills, with palaces adorned,   35
Porches and theatres, baths, aqueducts,
Statues and trophies, and triumphal arcs,
Gardens and groves, presented to his eyes,
Above the height of mountains interposed –
By what strange parallax, or optic skill   40
Of vision, multiplied through air, or glass
Of telescope, were curious to enquire.
And now the tempter thus his silence broke:
    'The city which thou seest no other deem
Than great and glorious Rome, queen of the earth   45
So far renowned, and with the spoils enriched
Of nations; there the Capitol thou seest,
Above the rest lifting his stately head
On the Tarpeian rock, her citadel
Impregnable; and there Mount Palatine,   50
The imperial palace, compass huge, and high
The structure, skill of noblest architects,
With gilded battlements, conspicuous far,
Turrets and terraces, and glittering spires.
Many a fair edifice besides, more like   55
Houses of gods (so well I have disposed
My airy microscope) thou may'st behold
Outside and inside both, pillars and roofs,
Carved work, the hand of famed artificers
In cedar, marble, ivory, or gold.   60
Thence to the gates cast round thine eye, and see
What conflux issuing forth, or entering in:
Praetors, proconsuls to their provinces

40 parallax] difference of the apparent position of an object caused by an actual
    change of position of the point of observation.
47 Capitol] one of the 'seven small hills'.
49] The 'Tarpeian rock' is the steep cliff that surrounds much of the Capitoline
    hill. The citadel (*arx*) was on the northern summit of the hill, and the
    Temple of Jupiter on the southern summit.
50–4] The Palatine is another of Rome's seven hills. Milton's description of the
    'imperial palace' (presumably the Domus Tiberiana, on the west corner of
    the hill) is speculative: its location makes terraces possible, but Roman
    buildings did not have turrets and spires.
59 hand] handiwork.
63] Under Tiberius the election of the praetors (who then numbered about 14)
    was transferred to the Senate, who appointed them as civil magistrates.
    They sometimes acted as provincial governors. Under the emperors a
    proconsul was the governor of a senatorial province.

Hasting, or on return, in robes of state;
Lictors and rods, the ensigns of their power;   65
Legions and cohorts, turms of horse and wings;
Or embassies from regions far remote,
In various habits, on the Appian road,
Or on the Aemilian – some from farthest south,
Syene, and where the shadow both way falls,   70
Meroë, Nilotic isle, and, more to west,
The realm of Bocchus to the Blackmoor sea;
From the Asian kings (and Parthian among these),
From India and the golden Chersoness,
And utmost Indian isle Taprobane,   75
Dusk faces with white silken turbans wreathed;
From Gallia, Gades, and the British west;
Germans, and Scythians, and Sarmatians north
Beyond Danubius to the Tauric pool.
All nations now to Rome obedience pay –   80
To Rome's great emperor, whose wide domain,
In ample territory, wealth and power,
Civility of manners, arts and arms,
And long renown, thou justly may'st prefer
Before the Parthian; these two thrones except,   85

65] Lictors were officers attending upon magistrates; they carried bundles of rods (*fasces*) before the magistrates as an emblem of their power.
66] There were ten cohorts in a legion, and a legion under the Empire numbered about six thousand men. 'Turms' were troops of about thirty horsemen.
68–9] The chief Roman road to south Italy was the Via Appia, which ended at Brindisi. The Via Aemelia ran from Rimini to Piacenza.
69–79] Syene (modern Aswan, in Egypt) was the southernmost limit of the Roman Empire. The Island of Meroë is the region bounded on three sides by the Nile, the Atbara, and the Blue Nile; as it lies between the Tropic of Cancer and the Equator, shadows fall to the south in summer and the north in winter. Bocchus was the king of ancient Mauretania (modern Morocco and coastal Algeria, not modern Mauritania) at the time of the Jugurthine War (111–106 BC); the 'Blackmoor sea' is the portion of the Mediterranean off the coast of Mauretania. On 'golden Chersoness' see *PL* XI 392n. The Taprobane described by ancient writers was identified in Milton's time with either Ceylon or Sumatra. Gallia (Gaul) encompassed modern France and Belgium, and parts of Holland, Germany, and Switzerland. Gades was the Latin name for Cadiz. As Britain had not yet been conquered in the reign of Tiberius, 'the British West' is probably Brittany, which was part of the imperial province of Lugudunensis. The Scythians were a south Russian tribe who by the time of Tiberius had been displaced by the Sarmatians, a related tribe. Until Dacia was invaded in AD 101, the Danube (Danubius) was the north-east frontier of the Empire. The Tauric pool is the Sea of Azov, on the shores of which was the Bosporan Kingdom, the ruler of which had been given his royal title by Tiberius.

The rest are barbarous, and scarce worth the sight,
Shared among petty kings too far removed;
These having shown thee, I have shown thee all
The kingdoms of the world, and all their glory.
This emperor hath no son, and now is old,   90
Old and lascivious, and from Rome retired
To Capreae, an island small but strong
On the Campanian shore, with purpose there
His horrid lusts in private to enjoy;
Committing to a wicked favourite   95
All public cares, and yet of him suspicious;
Hated of all, and hating; with what ease,
Endued with regal virtues as thou art,
Appearing, and beginning noble deeds,
Might'st thou expel this monster from his throne,   100
Now made a sty, and, in his place ascending,
A victor-people free from servile yoke!
And with my help thou may'st; to me the power
Is given, and by that right I give it thee.
Aim therefore at no less than all the world;   105
Aim at the highest; without the highest attained,
Will be for thee no sitting, or not long,
On David's throne, be prophesied what will.'
     To whom the Son of God, unmoved, replied:
'Nor doth this grandeur and majestic show   110
Of luxury, though called magnificence,
More than of arms before, allure mine eye,
Much less my mind; though thou should'st add to tell
Their sumptuous gluttonies, and gorgeous feasts
On citron tables or Atlantic stone   115
(For I have also heard, perhaps have read),
Their wines of Setia, Cales, and Falerne,
Chios and Crete, and how they quaff in gold,
Crystal, and myrrhine cups, embossed with gems

90–7] The emperor is Tiberius (42 BC–AD 37), whose sons – Drusus, Germanius
(an adopted son), and an infant – were all dead by AD 23. He returned to
Capri (Capreae) in AD 26. His 'wicked favourite' was Sejanus, who after
being denounced by Tiberius was executed in AD 31. Stories of Tiberius'
vice on Capri (recounted by Seutonius and Tacitus) lack serious evidence.
He was indeed hated by the Romans, who welcomed the news of his death.
103–4] Luke iv. 6.
115] Citron is the wood of the highly-prized citrus tree; Atlantic means 'from
the Atlas mountains'.
117–18] Wines from these three Italian districts (all south of Rome) and two
Greek islands were all mentioned by Roman writers.
119] Ancient writers describe 'myrrhine cups' and bowls (*murrina vasa*), but
the identity and provenance of myrrha were (and are) disputed.

And studs of pearl – to me should'st tell, who thirst   120
And hunger still; then embassies thou show'st
From nations far and nigh; what honour that,
But tedious waste of time, to sit and hear
So many hollow compliments and lies,
Outlandish flatteries! Then proceed'st to talk   125
Of the emperor, how easily subdued,
How gloriously; I shall, thou say'st, expel
A brutish monster: what if I withal
Expel a devil who first made him such?
Let his tormentor, Conscience, find him out;   130
For him I was not sent, nor yet to free
That people, victor once, now vile and base,
Deservedly made vassal – who, once just,
Frugal, and mild, and temperate, conquered well,
But govern ill the nations under yoke,   135
Peeling their provinces, exhausted all
By lust and rapine; first ambitious grown
Of triumph, that insulting vanity;
Then cruel, by their sports to blood inured
Of fighting beasts, and men to beasts exposed;   140
Luxurious by their wealth, and greedier still,
And from the daily scene effeminate.
What wise and valiant man would seek to free
These, thus degenerate, by themselves enslaved,
Or could of inward slaves make outward free?   145
Know therefore when my season comes to sit
On David's throne, it shall be like a tree
Spreading and overshadowing all the earth,
Or as a stone that shall to pieces dash
All monarchies besides throughout the world –   150
And of my kingdom there shall be no end;
Means there shall be to this, but what the means
Is not for thee to know, nor me to tell.'
    To whom the tempter, impudent, replied:
'I see all offers made by me how slight   155
Thou valuest, because offered, and reject'st;
Nothing will please the difficult and nice,
Or nothing more than still to contradict;

---

136 Peeling] plundering.
142 scene] stage performance, play.
147–8] Dan. iv. 10–12.
149–50] Dan. ii. 31–5.
151] Luke i. 33.
157 nice] fastidious, difficult to please.

On the other side I know also thou that I
On what I offer set as high esteem,   160
Nor what I part with mean to give for naught;
All these, which in a moment thou behold'st,
The kingdoms of the world, to thee I give –
For, given to me, I give to whom I please –
No trifle; yet with this reserve, not else,   165
On this condition, if thou wilt fall down,
And worship me as thy superior lord –
Easily done – and hold them all of me;
For what can less so great a gift deserve?'
   Whom thus our Saviour answered with disdain: 170
'I never liked thy talk, thy offers less,
Now both abhor, since thou hast dared to utter
The abominable terms, impious condition;
But I endure the time, till which expired
Thou hast permission on me. It is written,   175
The first of all commandments, "Thou shalt worship
The Lord thy God, and only him shalt serve";
And dar'st thou to the Son of God propound
To worship thee, accursed, now more accursed
For this attempt, bolder than that on Eve,   180
And more blasphémous? Which expect to rue.
The kingdoms of the world to thee were given,
Permitted rather, and by thee usurped;
Other donation none thou canst produce;
If given, by whom but by the King of kings,   185
God over all supreme? If given to thee,
By thee how fairly is the giver now
Repaid! But gratitude in thee is lost
Long since. Wert thou so void of fear or shame
As offer them to me, the Son of God –   190
To me my own, on such abhorred pact,
That I fall down and worship thee as God?
Get thee behind me; plain thou now appear'st
That Evil One, Satan for ever damned.'
   To whom the fiend with fear abashed replied: 195
'Be not so sore offended, Son of God –
Though sons of God both angels are and men –
If I to try whether in higher sort
Than these thou bear'st that title, have proposed
What both from men and angels I receive,   200
Tetrarchs of fire, air, flood, and on the earth,

201 Tetrarchs] Rulers of fourth parts (like Herod Antipas and his brother
    Philip, Luke iii. 1).

Nations besides from all the quartered winds –
God of this world invoked, and world beneath.
Who then thou art, whose coming is foretold
To me most fatal, me it most concerns.   205
The trial hath endamaged thee no way,
Rather more honour left and more esteem;
Me naught advantaged, missing what I aimed.
Therefore let pass, as they are transitory,
The kingdoms of this world; I shall no more   210
Advise thee; gain them as thou canst, or not.
And thou thyself seem'st otherwise inclined
Than to a worldly crown, addicted more
To contemplation and profound dispute;
As by that early action may be judged,   215
When, slipping from thy mother's eye, thou went'st
Alone into the Temple, there wast found
Among the gravest rabbis disputant
On points and questions fitting Moses' chair,
Teaching, not taught; the childhood shows the man,   220
As morning shows the day. Be famous, then,
By wisdom; as thy empire must extend,
So let extend thy mind o'er all the world
In knowledge: all things in it comprehend;
All knowledge is not couched in Moses' law,   225
The Pentateuch, or what the prophets wrote;
The Gentiles also know, and write, and teach
To admiration, led by nature's light;
And with the Gentiles much thou must converse,
Ruling them by persuasion, as thou mean'st;   230
Without their learning, how wilt thou with them,
Or they with thee, hold conversation meet?
How wilt thou reason with them, how refute
Their idolisms, traditions, paradoxes?
Error by his own arms is best evinced.   235
Look once more, ere we leave this specular mount,
Westward, much nearer by south-west; behold
Where on the Aegean shore a city stands,
Built nobly, pure the air and light the soil –

203] II Cor. iv. 4.
215–20] Luke ii. 41–50. On 'Moses' chair', from which the Law was expounded,
    see Exod. xviii. 13–16 and Matt. xxiii. 2.
226 Pentateuch] the first five books of the O.T.
228 To admiration] admirably.
235 evinced] overcome.
236 specular] cf. *PL* XII 588–9n.

Athens, the eye of Greece, mother of arts   240
And eloquence, native to famous wits
Or hospitable, in her sweet recess,
City or suburban, studious walks and shades;
See there the olive-grove of Academe,
Plato's retirement, where the Attic bird   245
Trills her thick-warbled notes the summer long;
There, flowery hill, Hymettus, with the sound
Of bees' industrious murmur, oft invites
To studious musing; there Ilissus rolls
His whispering stream; within the walls then view   250
The schools of ancient sages – his who bred
Great Alexander to subdue the world,
Lyceum there; and painted Stoa next:
There thou shalt hear and learn the secret power
Of harmony, in tones and numbers hit   255
By voice or hand, and various-measured verse,
Aeolian charms and Dorian lyric odes,
And his who gave them breath, but higher sung,
Blind Melesigenes, thence Homer called,
Whose poem Phoebus challenged for his own.   260
Thence what the lofty grave tragedians taught

240] Athens and Sparta had been described in antiquity as the eyes of Greece; here 'eye' means 'the seat of intelligence or light'.

244–6] Plato established his school in the Academy, a wooded park in a suburb of Athens. Nearby was Colonus, which according to Sophocles, who was born there, was the home of many nightingales (*Oedipus at Colonus* 671).

247–50] Hymettus is a range of hills south-east of Athens; Hymettus honey was famed for its pale colour and sweet flavour. Bees were said to have fed the infant Plato with honey. Plato's *Phaedrus* is set beside the Ilissus, a small river which rises in Hymettus.

250–3] Alexander's tutor was Aristotle, who founded his school, the Lyceum, in a park north-east of Athens (not 'within the walls'). The *Stoa Poikile* ('painted Stoa') was a covered colonnade on the north side of the Athenian market-place; Zeno and his followers taught in this stoa, and so were called Stoics.

257] The lyric poems of Sappho and Alcaeus are written in the Aeolian dialect (Lesbos, where both were born, belonged to the Aeolians), and are here called 'charms' in imitation of Latin *carmen* (song). Pindar wrote in the Dorian dialect.

259] Melesigenes is an Homeric epithet commonly used in the ancient lives of Homer; it affirms that he was born near the river Meles (near Smyrna, modern Izmir); 'thence' refers to 'Blind', for according to an ancient popular etymology Homer (ὅμηρος) was the Cumean word for 'blind'.

260] See the epigram in *Greek Anthology* ix. 455, in which Apollo/Phoebus claims authorship of Homer's poems.

In chorus or iambic, teachers best
Of moral prudence, with delight received
In brief sententious precepts, while they treat
Of fate, and chance, and change in human life,   265
High actions and high passions best describing;
Thence to the famous orators repair,
Those ancient whose resistless eloquence
Wielded at will that fierce democraty,
Shook the Arsenal, and fulmined over Greece   270
To Macedon and Artaxerxes' throne;
To sage philosophy next lend thine ear,
From heaven descended to the low-roofed house
Of Socrates – see there his tenement –
Whom, well inspired, the oracle pronounced   275
Wisest of men; from whose mouth issued forth
Mellifluous streams that watered all the schools
Of Academics old and new, with those
Surnamed Peripatetics, and the sect
Epicurean, and the Stoic severe;   280

262] Iambic refers to the metre of the dialogue in Greek tragedy (iambic
trimeter acatalectic); the chorus is written in various metres. Cf. Milton's
preface to *SA*.

264] Probably refers specifically to the style of Euripides, which was said by
Quintilian (X. i. 68) to be *sententiis densus* (dense with philosophical
aphorisms).

270] The naval dockyard at Pireus was called the Arsenal, which Demosthenes
could be said to have shaken when on his advice public funds were directed
from its construction to the war against Philip of Macedon; there was a
large explosion at the *Arsenale* in Venice on 15 September 1569; 'fulmined'
means 'sent forth lightning and thunder' (cf. Aristophanes' comment on
Pericles in *Archarnians* 530–1).

273–4] According to Cicero, Socrates was the first to call philosophy down from
heaven (*Tusculan Disputations* V. iv. 10). He is said to have a small house
(οἰκίδιον) in Aristophanes, *Clouds* 92.

275–6] Plato, *Apology* 21.

276–7] On Socrates as the fountain of philosophy see Quintilian I. x. 13.

278] According to an ancient distinction Academic philosophy had three
phases: Plato founded the Old Academy, Arcesilias the Middle Academy,
and Carneades the New Academy.

279–80] Peripatetics were Aristotelians, so called from the covered walk
(περίπατος) in the buildings which Theophrastus provided for the school.
The 'sect Epicurean' descended from Socrates through his friend Aristip-
pus, whose grandson (also Aristippus) founded the Cyrenaics, the intellec-
tual pioneers of Epicureanism. Similarly, the Stoics descended from
Socrates through his friend Aristhenes, whose Cynic sect influenced Stoic
doctrine. See *Comus* 707–8n.

These here revolve, or, as thou likest, at home,
Till time mature thee to a kingdom's weight;
These rules will render thee a king complete
Within thyself, much more with empire joined.'
　　To whom our Saviour sagely thus replied:　　285
'Think not but that I know these things; or, think
I know them not, not therefore am I short
Of knowing what I ought: he who receives
Light from above, from the fountain of light,
No other doctrine needs, though granted true;　　290
But these are false, or little else but dreams,
Conjectures, fancies, built on nothing firm.
The first and wisest of them all professed
To know this only, that he nothing knew;
The next to fabling fell and smooth conceits;　　295
A third sort doubted all things, though plain sense;
Others in virtue placed felicity,
But virtue joined with riches and long life;
In corporal pleasure he, and careless ease;
The Stoic last in philosophic pride,　　300
By him called virtue; and his virtuous man,
Wise, perfect in himself, and all possessing,
Equal to God, oft shames not to prefer,
As fearing God nor man, contemning all
Wealth, pleasure, pain or torment, death and life –　　305
Which, when he lists, he leaves, or boasts he can;
For all his tedious talk is but vain boast,
Or subtle shifts conviction to evade.
Alas, what can they teach, and not mislead,
Ignorant of themselves, of God much more,　　310
And how the world began, and how man fell,
Degraded by himself, on grace depending?
Much of the soul they talk, but all awry,
And in themselves seek virtue, and to themselves
All glory arrogate, to God give none;　　315
Rather accuse him under usual names,

293–4 first] Socrates. See Plato, *Apology* 21–3.
295 next] Plato.
296 third sort] the Sceptics, founded by Pyrrhon. A form of scepticism was also
　　espoused by Arcesilias and Carneades (l. 278n.).
297–8 Others] Aristotle and the Peripatetics.
299 he] Epicurus, who was reviled by patristic writers because he taught that
　　man is mortal, that the cosmos is a result of accident, that there is no
　　providential god, and that the criterion of the good life is pleasure.
300–9] Cf. *PL* II 564n.

Fortune and Fate, as one regardless quite
Of mortal things. Who, therefore, seeks in these
True wisdom finds her not, or, by delusion
Far worse, her false resemblance only meets,   320
An empty cloud. However, many books,
Wise men have said, are wearisome; who reads
Incessantly, and to his reading brings not
A spirit and judgement equal or superior,
(And what he brings what needs he elsewhere seek?)   325
Uncertain and unsettled still remains,
Deep-versed in books and shallow in himself,
Crude or intoxicate, collecting toys
And trifles for choice matters, worth a sponge,
As children gathering pebbles on the shore.   330
Or, if I would delight my private hours
With music or with poem, where so soon
As in our native language can I find
That solace? All our Law and story strewed
With hymns, our Psalms with artful terms inscribed,   335
Our Hebrew songs and harps, in Babylon
That pleased so well our victor's ear, declare
That rather Greece from us these arts derived –
Ill imitated while they loudest sing
The vices of their deities, and their own,   340
In fable, hymn, or song, so personating
Their gods ridiculous, and themselves past shame.
Remove their swelling epithets, thick-laid
As varnish on a harlot's cheek, the rest,
Thin-sown with aught of profit or delight,   345
Will far be found unworthy to compare
With Zion's songs, to all true tastes excelling,
Where God is praised aright and godlike men,
The Holiest of Holies and his saints –

319–21] Cf. *Passion* 56n.
321–2] Eccles. xii. 12.
328 Crude] unable to digest.
329 worth a sponge] means both 'worth very little' and 'worthy to be
    obliterated'.
334 story] the historical books of the O.T.
335 artful terms] probably refers to the rubrics in the Massoretic and LXX
    texts of the Psalms.
336–7] Psalm cxxxvii. 1–3.
338] The idea that the arts were original to the Jews, who while in bondage had
    passed them on to the Egyptians, who in turn bequeathed them to the
    Greeks, was a Patristic and Renaissance commonplace.
347] Cf. *PL* III 30n.

Such are from God inspired, not such from thee –   350
Unless where moral virtue is expressed
By light of nature, not in all quite lost.
Their orators thou then extoll'st as those
The top of eloquence – statists indeed,
And lovers of their country, as may seem;   355
But herein to our prophets far beneath,
As men divinely taught, and better teaching
The solid rules of civil government,
In their majestic, unaffected style,
Than all the oratory of Greece and Rome.   360
In them is plainest taught, and easiest learnt,
What makes a nation happy, and keeps it so,
What ruins kingdoms, and lays cities flat;
These only, with our Law, best form a king.'
    So spake the Son of God; but Satan, now   365
Quite at a loss, for all his darts were spent,
Thus to our Saviour, with stern brow, replied:
    'Since neither wealth nor honour, arms nor arts,
Kingdom nor empire, pleases thee, nor aught
By me proposed in life contemplative   370
Or active, tended on by glory or fame,
What dost thou in this world? The wilderness
For thee is fittest place: I found thee there,
And thither will return thee; yet remember
What I foretell thee: soon thou shalt have cause   375
To wish thou never hadst rejected, thus
Nicely or cautiously, my offered aid,
Which would have set thee in short time with ease
On David's throne, or throne of all the world,
Now at full age, fulness of time, thy season,   380
When prophecies of thee are best fulfilled.
Now, contrary – if I read aught in heaven,
Or heaven write aught of fate – by what the stars
Voluminous, or single characters
In their conjunction met, give me to spell,   385
Sorrows and labours, opposition, hate,
Attends thee; scorns, reproaches, injuries,

---

351 Unless] refers back to 'unworthy' (l. 346).
354 statists] statesmen.
384] an analogy to a large book ('voluminous') and to single letters ('characters') in the book.
385] Conjunction, the apparent proximity of two heavenly bodies, is an unfavourable sign in astrology. Cf. *PL* X 661n. 'Spell' means 'interpret' (cf. *Penseroso* 170–1).

Violence and stripes, and, lastly, cruel death;
A kingdom they portend thee, but what kingdom,
Real or allegoric, I discern not;   390
Nor when, eternal sure – as without end,
Without beginning; for no date prefixed
Directs me in the starry rubric set.'
    So saying, he took (for still he knew his power
Not yet expired), and to the wilderness   395
Brought back the Son of God, and left him there,
Feigning to disappear. Darkness now rose,
As daylight sunk, and brought in louring Night,
Her shadowy offspring, unsubstantial both,
Privation mere of light and absent day.   400
Our Saviour, meek, and with untroubled mind
After his airy jaunt, though hurried sore,
Hungry and cold, betook him to his rest,
Wherever, under some concourse of shades,
Whose branching arms thick-intertwined might shield 405
From dews and damps of night his sheltered head;
But, sheltered, slept in vain; for at his head
The tempter watched, and soon with ugly dreams
Disturbed his sleep; and either tropic now
Gan thunder, and both ends of heaven; the clouds   410
From many a horrid rift abortive poured
Fierce rain with lightning mixed, water with fire
In ruin reconciled; nor slept the winds
Within their stony caves, but rushed abroad
From the four hinges of the world, and fell   415
On the vexed wilderness, whose tallest pines,
Though rooted deep as high, and sturdiest oaks,
Bowed their stiff necks, loaden with stormy blasts,
Or torn up sheer; ill wast thou shrouded then,
O patient Son of God, yet only stood'st   420
Unshaken; nor yet stayed the terror there:
Infernal ghosts and hellish furies round
Environed thee; some howled, some yelled, some shrieked,

393 rubric] a title or caption written in red letters.
402 jaunt] fatiguing journey.
409–10] 'Either tropic' means north (Cancer) and south (Capricorn); the 'ends
    of heaven' are presumably east and west.
411 abortive] probably means 'unnaturally premature'.
412–13] Cf. Aeschylus, *Agamemnon* 650–1; 'ruin' means both 'falling' and
    'destruction'.
415 hinges] cardinal points (Latin *cardo*, hinge).
419 shrouded] sheltered.

Some bent at thee their fiery darts, while thou
Sat'st unappalled in calm and sinless peace.   425
Thus passed the night so foul, till Morning fair
Came forth with pilgrim steps, in amice grey;
Who with her radiant finger stilled the roar
Of thunder, chased the clouds, and laid the winds,
And grisly spectres, which the fiend had raised   430
To tempt the Son of God with terrors dire.
And now the sun with more effectual beams
Had cheered the face of earth, and dried the wet
From drooping plant, or dropping tree; the birds,
Who all things now behold more fresh and green,   435
After a night of storm so ruinous,
Cleared up their choicest notes in bush and spray,
To gratulate the sweet return of morn;
Nor yet, amidst this joy and brightest morn,
Was absent, after all his mischief done,   440
The prince of darkness; glad would also seem
Of this fair change, and to our Saviour came;
Yet with no new device – they all were spent –
Rather by this his last affront resolved,
Desperate of better course, to vent his rage   445
And mad despite to be so oft repelled.
Him walking on a sunny hill he found,
Backed on the north and west by a thick wood;
Out of the wood he starts in wonted shape,
And in a careless mood thus to him said: 450
    'Fair morning yet betides thee, Son of God,
After a dismal night; I heard the rack,
As earth and sky would mingle; but myself
Was distant; and these flaws, though mortals fear them,
As dangerous to the pillared frame of heaven,   455
Or to the earth's dark basis underneath,
Are to the main as inconsiderable
And harmless, if not wholesome, as a sneeze
To man's less universe, and soon are gone;
Yet, as being ofttimes noxious where they light   460
On man, beast, plant, wasteful and turbulent,

427 amice] an article of costume (variously a cap, hood, or cape) made of, or
    lined with, grey fur.
452 rack] destruction (as in 'rack and ruin').
453] *Aeneid* i 133–4.
454 flaws] squalls.
455] Cf. *Comus* 598n.
457 main] universe.

Like turbulencies in the affairs of men,
Over whose heads they roar, and seem to point,
They oft fore-signify and threaten ill:
This tempest at this desert most was bent;   465
Of men at thee, for only thou here dwell'st.
Did I not tell thee, if thou didst reject
The perfect season offered with my aid
To win thy destined seat, but wilt prolong
All to the push of fate, pursue thy way   470
Of gaining David's throne no man knows when –
For both the when and how is nowhere told –
Thou shalt be what thou art ordained, no doubt;
For angels have proclaimed it, but concealing
The time and means: each act is rightliest done   475
Not when it must, but when it may be best.
If thou observe not this, be sure to find
What I foretold thee – many a hard assay
Of dangers, and adversities, and pains,
Ere thou of Israel's sceptre get fast hold;   480
Whereof the ominous night that closed thee round,
So many terrors, voices, prodigies,
May warn thee, as a sure foregoing sign.'
    So talked he, while the Son of God went on,
And stayed not, but in brief him answered thus: 485
    'Me worse than wet thou find'st not; other harm
Those terrors which thou speak'st of did me none;
I never feared they could, though noising loud
And threatening nigh; what they can do as signs
Betokening or ill-boding I contemn   490
As false portents, not sent from God, but thee;
Who, knowing I shall reign past thy preventing,
Obtrud'st thy offered aid, that I, accepting,
At least might seem to hold all power of thee,
Ambitious Spirit, and would'st be thought my god;   495
And storm'st, refused, thinking to terrify
Me to thy will; desist – thou art discerned,
And toil'st in vain – nor me in vain molest.'
    To whom the fiend, now swoll'n with rage, replied:
'Then hear, O Son of David, virgin-born,   500
For Son of God to me is yet in doubt;
Of the Messiah I have heard foretold
By all the prophets; of thy birth, at length
Announced by Gabriel, with the first I knew,
And of the angelic song in Bethlehem field,   505
On thy birth-night, that sung thee Saviour born.
From that time seldom have I ceased to eye

Thy infancy, thy childhood, and thy youth,
Thy manhood last, though yet in private bred;
Till, at the ford of Jordan, whither all   510
Flocked to the Baptist, I among the rest –
Though not to be baptised – by voice from heaven
Heard thee pronounced the Son of God beloved.
Thenceforth I thought thee worth my nearer view
And narrower scrutiny, that I might learn   515
In what degree or meaning thou art called
The Son of God, which bears no single sense;
The son of God I also am, or was;
And, if I was, I am; relation stands:
All men are sons of God; yet thee I thought   520
In some respect far higher so declared.
Therefore I watched thy footsteps from that hour,
And followed thee still on to this waste wild,
Where, by all best conjectures, I collect
Thou art to be my fatal enemy.   525
Good reason, then, if I beforehand seek
To understand my adversary, who
And what he is; his wisdom, power, intent;
By parle or composition, truce or league,
To win him, or win from him what I can.   530
And opportunity I here have had
To try thee, sift thee, and confess have found thee
Proof against all temptation, as a rock
Of adamant and as a centre, firm
To the utmost of mere man both wise and good,   535
Not more; for honours, riches, kingdoms, glory,
Have been before contemned, and may again:
Therefore, to know what more thou art than man,
Worth naming Son of God by voice from heaven,
Another method I must now begin.'   540
    So saying, he caught him up, and, without wing
Of hippogrif, bore through the air sublime,
Over the wilderness and o'er the plain,
Till underneath them fair Jerusalem,
The holy city, lifted high her towers,   545
And higher yet the glorious Temple reared

518–20] See Job i. 6, and Milton's translation of Psalm lxxxii. 6.
524 collect] infer.
529 composition] truce.
542 hippogrif] a fabulous creature, half horse ('hippo' means 'horse'), half
    griffin. Ariosto's *ippogrifo* carries his heroes on their journeys.
546–8] Milton draws on Josephus (*Jewish War* V. v. 6) for his description of the
    temple that Herod the Great built.

Her pile, far off appearing like a mount
Of alabaster, topped with golden spires:
There, on the highest pinnacle, he set
The Son of God, and added thus in scorn: 550
 'There stand, if thou wilt stand; to stand upright
Will ask thee skill; I to thy Father's house
Have brought thee, and highest placed: highest is best;
Now show thy progeny; if not to stand,
Cast thyself down; safely, if Son of God;   555
For it is written, "He will give command
Concerning thee to his angels; in their hands
They shall uplift thee, lest at any time
Thou chance to dash thy foot against a stone." '
    To whom thus Jesus: 'Also it is written,   560
"Tempt not the Lord thy God";' he said, and stood.
But Satan, smitten with amazement, fell;
As when Earth's son, Antaeus (to compare
Small things with greatest), in Irassa strove
With Jove's Alcides, and, oft foiled, still rose,   565
Receiving from his mother earth new strength,
Fresh from his fall, and fiercer grapple joined,
Throttled at length in the air expired and fell,
So, after many a foil, the Tempter proud,
Renewing fresh assaults, amidst his pride   570
Fell whence he stood to see his victor fall.
And as that Theban monster that proposed
Her riddle, and him, who solved it not, devoured,
That once found out and solved, for grief and spite
Cast herself headlong from the Ismenian steep,   575
So, struck with dread and anguish, fell the fiend,
And to his crew, that sat consulting, brought
Joyless triumphals of his hoped success,
Ruin, and desperation, and dismay,
Who durst so proudly tempt the Son of God.   580

549] The meaning of 'pinnacle' (πτερύγιον, Vulgate *pinnaculum* and *pinna*) in
    Matt. iv. 5 and Luke iv. 9 was (and is) disputed; in Milton's time it was
    variously identified as a parapet, the ridge of the roof, the flat roof, a spire,
    etc.

563-8] Antaeus was a giant who when wrestling renewed his strength by
    touching his mother Gaea (the earth). Hercules was the son of Zeus and
    Alceme (hence 'Jove's'), whose husband Amphitryon was the son of
    Alceaeus (hence 'Alcides'). At Irassa, in Libya, Hercules lifted Antaeus off
    the ground and strangled him.

572-5] The Theban monster is the Sphinx, who leapt to her death from the
    acropolis at Thebes ('Ismenian steep', so called from the river Ismenus)
    after Oedipus answered her riddle.

578 triumphals] tokens of success.

So Satan fell; and straight a fiery globe
Of angels on full sail of wing flew nigh,
Who on their plumy vans received him soft
From his uneasy station, and upbore,
As on a floating couch, through the blithe air;   585
Then, in a flowery valley, set him down
On a green bank, and set before him spread
A table of celestial food, divine
Ambrosial fruits fetched from the tree of life,
And from the fount of life ambrosial drink,   590
That soon refreshed him wearied, and repaired
What hunger, if aught hunger, had impaired,
Or thirst; and, as he fed, angelic choirs
Sung heavenly anthems of his victory
Over temptation and the tempter proud: 595
    'True image of the Father, whether throned
In the bosom of bliss, and light of light
Conceiving, or, remote from heaven, enshrined
In fleshy tabernacle and human form,
Wandering the wilderness – whatever place,   600
Habit, or state, or motion, still expressing
The Son of God, with godlike force endued
Against the attempter of thy Father's throne
And thief of Paradise; him long of old
Thou didst debel, and down from heaven cast   605
With all his army; now thou hast avenged
Supplanted Adam, and, by vanquishing
Temptation, has regained lost Paradise,
And frustrated the conquest fraudulent;
He never more henceforth will dare set foot   610
In Paradise to tempt; his snares are broke:
For, though that seat of earthly bliss be failed,
A fairer Paradise is founded now
For Adam and his chosen sons, whom thou,
A Saviour, art come down to reinstall;   615
Where they shall dwell secure, when time shall be,
Of tempter and temptation without fear.
But thou, infernal serpent, shalt not long
Rule in the clouds; like an autumnal star,

581 globe] used in the Latin sense of a throng.
583 vans] fans, i.e. wings.
589] Gen. ii. 9, Rev. xxii. 2, 14. 'Ambrosial' here means 'heavenly' and
    'fragrant'.
605 debel] vanquish, expel by force of arms.
611] Psalm cxxiv. 7.
619 autumnal star] a meteor or comet. Cf. *PL* II 708–11.

Or lightning, thou shalt fall from heaven, trod down   620
Under his feet; for proof, ere this thou feel'st
Thy wound – yet not thy last and deadliest wound –
By this repulse received, and hold'st in hell
No triumph; in all her gates Abaddon rues
Thy bold attempt; hereafter learn with awe   625
To dread the Son of God: he, all unarmed,
Shall chase thee, with the terror of his voice,
From thy demoniac holds, possession foul –
Thee and thy legions; yelling they shall fly,
And beg to hide them in a herd of swine,   630
Lest he command them down into the deep,
Bound, and to torment sent before their time.
Hail, Son of the Most High, heir of both worlds,
Queller of Satan; on thy glorious work
Now enter, and begin to save mankind.'   635
    Thus they the Son of God, our Saviour meek,
Sung victor, and, from heavenly feast refreshed,
Brought on his way with joy; he, unobserved,
Home to his mother's house private returned.

620–1] Gen. iii. 15, Mal. iv. 3, Luke x. 18, and Rom. xvi. 20 (on which see *PL* X
    189–90n.).
624 Abaddon] In his translation of Psalm lxxxviii. l. 47 Milton translates this
    Hebrew word as 'perdition'. Elsewhere it refers to the destruction asso-
    ciated with Sheol (Job xxvi. 6, Prov. xv. 11, xxvii. 20) and with death (Job
    xxxviii. 22). Cf. Rev. ix. 11.
628] Rev. xviii. 2.
630–2] Matt. viii. 28–33.
636] Matt. xi. 29.

SAMSON
AGONISTES,
A
DRAMATIC POEM.

The Author
John Milton.

Ariſtot. l'oct. Cap. 6.

*Tragœdia eſt imitatio actionis ſeria, &c. Per miſericordiam &
metum perficiens talium affectuum luſtrationem.*

Samson Agonistes. The date of composition is not known. The traditional assumption has been that it was composed between 1666 and 1670, but arguments have been advanced for dates in the 1640s and 1650s. The notes that follow do not attempt to list allusions to the story of Samson as recounted in Judges xiii–xvi.

Title-page] In Milton's time the word *Samson* was popularly (and incorrectly) believed to mean 'there the second time'. *Agonistes*, a transliteration of a Greek word, could refer to a combatant at the national games, a pleader, or an actor; it could also refer to one who struggles for something, or to a champion (of virtue or truth). In the Greek text of Luke xxii. 44 the 'agony' of Jesus is an 'agonia' (ἀγωνία), a mental and spiritual struggle. The idea of the Christian life as a spiritual struggle may originate in Paul's injunction to 'fight the good fight of faith' (I Tim. vi. 12).

The words in Greek are the opening words of Aristotle's definition of tragedy with a Latin translation of those words ('Tragedy is the imitation of a serious action') and of the passage at the end of the definition which deals with catharsis. Milton translates and amplifies this passage in the opening sentence of his preface.

OF THAT SORT OF DRAMATIC POEM
CALLED TRAGEDY

Tragedy, as it was anciently composed, hath been ever held the gravest, moralest, and most profitable of all other poems: therefore said by Aristotle to be of power, by raising pity and fear, or terror, to purge the mind of those and such-like passions – that is, to temper and reduce them to just measure with a kind of delight, stirred up by reading or seeing those passions well imitated. Nor is nature wanting in her own effects to make good his assertion; for so, in physic, things of melancholic hue and quality are used against melancholy, sour against sour, salt to remove salt humours. Hence philosophers and other gravest writers, as Cicero, Plutarch, and others, frequently cite out of tragic poets, both to adorn and illustrate their discourse. The Apostle Paul himself thought it not unworthy to insert a verse of Euripides[1] into the text of Holy Scriptures, I Cor. xv. 33; and Paraeus,[2] commenting on the *Revelation*, divides the whole book, as a tragedy, into acts, distinguished each by a chorus of heavenly harpings and song between. Heretofore men in highest dignity have laboured not a little to be thought able to compose a tragedy. Of that honour Dionysius[3] the elder was no less ambitious than before of his attaining to the tyranny. Augustus[4] Caesar also had begun his *Ajax*, but unable to please his own judgement with what he had begun, left it unfinished. Seneca,[5] the philosopher, is by some thought the author of those tragedies (at least the best of them) that go under that

---

1 Euripides] see *Areopagitica* p. 586, n.11.
2 Paraeus] The German theologian David Paraeus (David Wängler, 1548–1622); Milton refers to chapter 8 of his *In Divinam Apocalypsin* (1618), translated as *On the Divine Apocalypse* in 1644.
3 Dionysius] Dionysius I (c. 430–367 BC), tyrant of Syrace, often contended for the prize of tragedy at Athens, and in the year of his death won first prize at the Athenian Lenaea with his *Ransoming of Hector*.
4 Augustus] The suicide of Ajax was a popular subject for tragedy; on Augustus' attempt see Suetonius II 85.
5 Seneca] The mistaken notion that the Stoic philosopher and the tragedian were separate people originated in a poem by Sidonius Apollinaris, the fifth-century Bishop of Clermont (*Carmina* IX 230–8), and still prevailed in Milton's time.

name. Gregory Nazianzen,[1] a Father of the Church, thought it not unbeseeming the sanctity of his person to write a tragedy, which he entitled *Christ Suffering*. This is mentioned to vindicate tragedy from the small esteem, or rather infamy, which in the account of many it undergoes at this day, with other common interludes; happening through the poet's error or intermixing comic stuff with tragic sadness[2] and gravity, or introducing trivial and vulgar persons, which by all judicious hath been counted absurd, and brought in without discretion, corruptly to gratify the people. And though ancient tragedy use no prologue,[3] yet using sometimes, in case of self-defence or explanation, that which Martial[4] calls an epistle, in behalf of this tragedy, coming forth after the ancient manner, much different from what among us passes for best, thus much beforehand may be epistled – that chorus is here introduced after the Greek manner, not ancient only, but modern, and still in use among the Italians. In the modelling therefore of this poem, with good reason, the ancients and Italians are rather followed, as of much more authority and fame. The measure of verse used in the chorus is of all sorts, called by the Greeks monostrophic, or rather apolelymenon, without regard had to strophe, antistrophe, or epode – which were a kind of stanzas framed only for the music, then used with the chorus that sung; not essential to the poem, and therefore not material; or, being divided into stanzas or pauses, they may be called alloeostropha.[5] Division into act and scene, referring chiefly to the stage (to which this work never was intended) is here omitted.

It suffices if the whole drama be found not produced

---

1 Gregory] Gregory Nazianen (329–389) was long thought to have written *Christus Patiens*, but his authorship is now doubted.

2 sadness] seriousness.

3 prologue] a prefatory speech to the audience, not to be confused with Aristotle's notion of a prologue (πρόλογος), the portion of the play that precedes the first chorus (in SA ll. 1–114).

4 Martial prefaces five of the twelve books of his *Epigrams* with prose epistles. In the preface to Book ii he makes his friend Decianus object to the use of an epistle.

5 The 'strophe' ('turning') was the stanza sung by the Chorus as they moved from right to left across the orchestra; the 'antistrophe' ('counter-turn') was the metrically identical stanza sung in reply as they moved from left to right. The 'epode' was the conclusion of the song, distinct in metre, sung as they stood still. 'Monostrophic' refers to the repetition of a single strophe. 'Apolelymenon' means 'freed', i.e. from stanzaic patterns. 'Alloeostropha' means 'of irregular strophes'.

beyond the fifth act.[1] Of the style and uniformity,[2] and that
commonly called the plot, whether intricate or explicit[3] –
which is nothing indeed but such economy,[4] or disposition
of the fable, as may stand best with verisimilitude and
decorum – they only will best judge who are not unac-
quainted with Aeschylus, Sophocles, and Euripides, the
three tragic poets unequalled yet by any, and the best rule
to all who endeavour to write tragedy. The circumscription
of time wherein the whole drama begins and ends is,
according to ancient rule and best example, within the
space of twenty-four hours.[5]

1 produced ... act] echoes Horace's injunction that plays should not extend
   beyond the fifth act (*neu sit quinto productior actu*).
2 'Style' in Aristotle's *Poetics* (xxii) means diction; 'uniformity' probably refers
   to Aristotle's insistence on consistency of characterization (xv).
3 According to Aristotle's *Poetics* (x) plot is either simple ('explicit') or complex
   ('intricate').
4 economy] management, arrangement, called by Aristotle the 'putting
   together of the incidents' (*Poetics* vi).
5 'Unity of time' in Aristotle's *Poetics* (v) is not a rule, but an observation to the
   effect that tragedy 'tries' to confine itself to one day. Unity of time became a
   precept at the hands of Castelvetro (see *Of Education* p. 566 n.7) and other
   Renaissance theorists. 'Best example' must exclude plays by Aeschylus
   (*Persians, Agamemnon*, and *Eumenides*) Sophocles (*Trachiniae*), and Euri-
   pides (*Suppliants*), for these five plays (and others no longer extant) do not
   observe the unity of time.

SAMSON AGONISTES

THE ARGUMENT

Samson, made captive, blind, and now in the prison at Gaza, there
to labour as in a common workhouse, on a festival day, in the
general cessation from labour, comes forth into the open air, to a
place nigh, somewhat retired, there to sit a while and bemoan his
condition. Where he happens at length to be visited by certain
friends and equals of his tribe, which make the Chorus, who seek to
comfort him what they can; then by his old father, Manoa, who
endeavours the like, and withal tells him his purpose to procure his
liberty by ransom; lastly, that this feast was proclaimed by the
Philistines as a day of thanksgiving for their deliverance from the
hands of Samson – which yet more troubles him. Manoa then
departs to prosecute his endeavour with the Philistian lords for
Samson's redemption; who, in the meanwhile, is visited by other
persons, and lastly, by a public officer to require his coming to the
feast before the lords and people, to play or show his strength in
their presence. He at first refuses, dismissing the public officer with
absolute denial to come; at length persuaded inwardly that this
was from God, he yields to go along with him, who came now the
second time with great threatenings to fetch him; the Chorus yet
remaining on the place, Manoa returns full of joyful hope to
procure ere long his son's deliverance; in the midst of which
discourse an Hebrew comes in haste, confusedly at first, and
afterwards more distinctly, relating the catastrophe[1] – what
Samson had done to the Philistines, and by accident to himself;
wherewith the tragedy ends.

THE PERSONS

SAMSON.	HARAPHA of Gath.
MANOA, the father of	Public Officer.
Samson.	Messenger.
DALILA, his wife.	Chorus of Danites.

The Scene, before the Prison in Gaza.[2]

---

1 Catastrophe ('overturning') is used in the dramatic sense of 'the change which
   produces the conclusion or final event; the dénouement'.
2 Gaza] See *PL* I 464–6n.

Sams. A little onward lend thy guiding hand

1–2] Cf. the opening of Sophocles' *Oedipus at Colonus*, where the blind Oedipus
   is led by his daughter Antigone; and see also Euripides, *Phoenician Women*
   834–5.

To these dark steps, a little further on;
For yonder bank hath choice of sun or shade;
There I am wont to sit, when any chance
Relieves me from my task of servile toil,   5
Daily in the common prison else enjoined me,
Where I, a prisoner chained, scarce freely draw
The air, imprisoned also, close and damp,
Unwholesome draught; but here I feel amends –
The breath of heaven fresh blowing, pure and sweet,   10
With day-spring born; here leave me to respire.
This day a solemn feast the people hold
To Dagon, their sea-idol, and forbid
Laborious works; unwillingly this rest
Their superstition yields me; hence, with leave   15
Retiring from the popular noise, I seek
This unfrequented place, to find some ease –
Ease to the body some, none to the mind
From restless thoughts, that like a deadly swarm
Of hornets armed, no sooner found alone   20
But rush upon me thronging, and present
Times past, what once I was, and what am now.
Oh, wherefore was my birth from heaven foretold
Twice by an angel, who at last, in sight
Of both my parents, all in flames ascended   25
From off the altar where an offering burned,
As in a fiery column charioting
His godlike presence, and from some great act
Or benefit revealed to Abraham's race?
Why was my breeding ordered and prescribed   30
As of a person separate to God,
Designed for great exploits, if I must die
Betrayed, captived, and both my eyes put out,
Made of my enemies the scorn and gaze,
To grind in brazen fetters under task   35
With this heaven-gifted strength? O glorious strength,
Put to the labour of a beast, debased
Lower than bond-slave! Promise was that I
Should Israel from Philistian yoke deliver;
Ask for this great deliverer now, and find him   40
Eyeless in Gaza, at the mill with slaves,

---

11 day-spring] dawn.
  Dagon] See *Nativity* 199n. and cf. *PL* I 457–66.
16 popular] of the populace.
31 person separate to God] renders the literal meaning of 'Nazarite' (l. 318). See
  Num. vi. 1–21, Judges xiii. 5, 7.

Himself in bonds under Philistian yoke;
Yet stay; let me not rashly call in doubt
Divine prediction; what if all foretold
Had been fulfilled but through mine own default?   45
Whom have I to complain of but myself?
Who this high gift of strength committed to me,
In what part lodged, how easily bereft me,
Under the seal of silence could not keep,
But weakly to a woman must reveal it,   50
O'ercome with importunity and tears?
O impotence of mind in body strong!
But what is strength without a double share
Of wisdom? Vast, unwieldy, burdensome,
Proudly secure, yet liable to fall   55
By weakest subtleties; not made to rule,
But to subserve where wisdom bears command.
God, when he gave me strength, to show withal,
How slight the gift was, hung it in my hair.
But peace, I must not quarrel with the will   60
Of highest dispensation, which herein
Haply had ends above my reach to know;
Suffices that to me strength is my bane,
And proves the source of all my miseries –
So many, and so huge, that each apart   65
Would ask a life to wail; but, chief of all,
O loss of sight, of thee I most complain!
Blind among enemies, O worse than chains,
Dungeon, or beggary, or decrepit age!
Light, the prime work of God, to me is extinct,   70
And all her various objects of delight
Annulled, which might in part my grief have eased;
Inferior to the vilest now become
Of man or worm, the vilest here excel me:
They creep, yet see; I, dark in light, exposed   75
To daily fraud, contempt, abuse, and wrong,
Within doors, or without, still as a fool,
In power of others, never in my own –
Scarce half I seem to live, dead more than half.
O dark, dark, dark, amid the blaze of noon,   80
Irrecoverably dark, total eclipse
Without all hope of day!
O first-created beam, and thou great word,
'Let there be light, and light was over all,'

53–6] a classical commonplace (e.g. Horace, *Odes* III. iv. 65).
77 still] invariably.

Why am I thus bereaved thy prime decree? 85
The sun to me is dark
And silent as the moon,
When she deserts the night,
Hid in her vacant interlunar cave.
Since light so necessary is to life, 90
And almost life itself, if it be true
That light is in the soul,
She all in every part, why was the sight
To such a tender ball as the eye confined,
So obvious and so easy to be quenched, 95
And not, as feeling, through all parts diffused,
That she might look at will through every pore?
Then had I not been thus exiled from light,
As in the land of darkness, yet in light,
To live a life half dead, a living death, 100
And buried; but O yet more miserable!
Myself my sepulchre, a moving grave;
Buried, yet not exempt,
By privilege of death and burial,
From worst of other evils, pains, and wrongs; 105
But made hereby obnoxious more
To all the miseries of life,
Life in captivity
Among inhuman foes.
But who are these? For with joint pace I hear 110
The tread of many feet steering this way;
Perhaps my enemies, who come to stare
At my affliction, and perhaps to insult –
Their daily practice to afflict me more.
   Chor. This, this is he; softly a while; 115
Let us not break in upon him;
O change beyond report, thought, or belief!
See how he lies at random, carelessly diffused,
With languished head unpropped,
As one past hope, abandoned, 120
And by himself given over,
In slavish habit, ill-fitted weeds
O'er-worn and soiled;

---

87 silent] not shining (cf. Latin *luna silens*).
89 vacant] at leisure (cf. Latin *vacare*).
92–3] The idea that the soul is 'all in every part' of the body is a patristic and
    Renaissance commonplace.
95 obvious] exposed.
106 obnoxious] exposed to harm.

Or do my eyes misrepresent? Can this be he,
That heroic, that renowned,   125
Irresistible Samson? Whom, unarmed,
No strength of man, or fiercest wild beast, could withstand;
Who tore the lion as the lion tears the kid;
Ran on embattled armies clad in iron,
And, weaponless himself,   130
Made arms ridiculous, useless the forgery
Of brazen shield and spear, the hammered cuirass,
Chalybean-tempered steel, and frock of mail
Adamantean proof;
But safest he who stood aloof,   135
When insupportably his foot advanced,
In scorn of their proud arms and warlike tools,
Spurned them to death by troops. The bold Ascalonite
Fled from his lion ramp; old warriors turned
Their plated backs under his heel,   140
Or grovelling soiled their crested helmets in the dust.
Then with what trivial weapon came to hand,
The jaw of a dead ass, his sword of bone,
A thousand foreskins fell, the flower of Palestine,
In Ramath-lechi, famous to this day: 145
Then by main force pulled up, and on his shoulders bore,
The gates of Azza, post and massy bar,
Up to the hill by Hebron, seat of giants old –
No journey of a sabbath-day, and loaded so –
Like whom the Gentiles feign to bear up heaven.   150
Which shall I first bewail –
Thy bondage or lost sight,

131 forgery] the act of forging metal.
132 cuirass] See *PR* III 328n.
133 Chalybean] The Chalybes were a Black Sea tribe famed in Greek legend as
   the first workers in iron.
136 insupportably] irresistibly.
138] See *PL* I 464–6n.
144 foreskins] uncircumcised Philistines.
145 Ramath-lechi] For the popular etymology see Judges xv. 17; the phrase
   probably means 'the height of the jawbone' (see A.V. and R.V. marginal
   notes).
147] See *PL* I 464–6n.
148] Hebron was anciently called Kirjath-arba (Joshua xiv. 15) i.e. the city of
   Arba. Arba was the father of Anak, whose descendants (the Anakim) were
   giants (Joshua xv. 13–14, Num. xiii. 32–3, Deut. i. 28, ii. 10–21, ix. 1–2).
149] In the Jerusalem Targum the prohibition in Exod. xvi. 29 forbids walking
   more than 2,000 ells (c. 1,200 yards) on the sabbath. See Acts i. 12.
150 whom] Atlas, on whom see *PL* II 306n.

Prison within prison
Inseparably dark?
Thou art become (O worst imprisonment!)   155
The dungeon of thyself; thy soul,
(Which men enjoying sight oft without cause complain)
Imprisoned now indeed,
In real darkness of the body dwells,
Shut up from outward light   160
To incorporate with gloomy night;
For inward light, alas,
Puts forth no visual beam.
O mirror of our fickle state,
Since man on earth, unparalleled!   165
The rarer thy example stands,
By how much from the top of wondrous glory,
Strongest of mortal men,
To lowest pitch of abject fortune thou art fallen.
For him I reckon not in high estate   170
Whom long descent of birth,
Or the sphere of fortune, raises;
But thee, whose strength, while virtue was her mate,
Might have subdued the earth,
Universally crowned with highest praises.   175
    Sams. I hear the sound of words; their sense the air
Dissolves unjointed ere it reach my ear.
    Chor. He speaks: let us draw nigh. Matchless in night,
The glory late of Israel, now the grief;
We come, thy friends and neighbours not unknown,   180
From Eshtaol and Zora's fruitful vale,
To visit or bewail thee; or, if better,
Counsel or consolation we may bring,
Salve to thy sores: apt words have power to swage
The tumours of a troubled mind,   185
And are as balm to festered wounds.
    Sams. Your coming, friends, revives me; for I learn
Now of my own experience, not by talk,
How counterfeit a coin they are who 'friends'
Bear in their superscription (of the most   190
I would be understood); in prosperous days
They swarm, but in adverse withdraw their head,

---

181 Eshtaol, Zora] towns variously allotted to Judah (Joshua xv. 33, where
    they are 'in the valley') and Dan (e.g. Joshua xix. 41); Milton chooses the
    latter. Between the two cities Samson began to be moved by the Spirit of
    the Lord (Judges xiii. 25) and was later buried (Judges xvi. 31).
184 swage] assuage.

Not to be found, though sought. Ye see, O friends,
How many evils have enclosed me round;
Yet that which was the worst now least afflicts me,   195
Blindness; for, had I sight, confused with shame,
How could I once look up, or heave the head,
Who, like a foolish pilot, have shipwrecked
My vessel trusted to me from above,
Gloriously rigged, and for a word, a tear,   200
Fool, have divulged the secret gift of God
To a deceitful woman? Tell me, friends,
Am I not sung and proverbed for a fool
In every street? Do they not say, 'How well
Are come upon him his deserts'? Yet why?   205
Immeasurable strength they might behold
In me; of wisdom nothing more than mean:
This with the other should at least have paired;
These two, proportioned ill, drove me transverse.
　　Chor. Tax not divine disposal; wisest men   210
Have erred, and by bad women been deceived;
And shall again, pretend they ne'er so wise.
Deject not, then, so overmuch thyself,
Who hast of sorrow thy full load besides;
Yet, truth to say, I oft have heard men wonder   215
Why thou should'st wed Philistian women rather
Than of thine own tribe fairer, or as fair,
At least of thy own nation, and as noble.
　　Sams. The first I saw at Timna, and she pleased
Me, not my parents, that I sought to wed   220
The daughter of an infidel: they knew not
That what I motioned was of God; I knew
From intimate impulse, and therefore urged
The marriage on, that, by occasion hence,
I might begin Israel's deliverance –   225
The work to which I was divinely called;
She proving false, the next I took to wife
(O that I never had! Fond wish too late.)
Was in the vale of Sorec, Dálila,
That specious monster, my accomplished snare.   230
I thought it lawful from my former act,
And the same end, still watching to oppress

203] Job xxx. 9 (Vulgate has *proverbium*).
216] The Bible does not state that Dalila was a Philistine, nor that she was
　　married to Samson. There is strong patristic support for Milton's assump-
　　tions, but some exegetical traditions made her an Israelite and Samson's
　　mistress (l. 537). Cf. *PL* IX 1061.

Israel's oppressors; of what now I suffer
She was not the prime cause, but I myself,
Who, vanquished with a peal of words (O weakness!),   235
Gave up my fort of silence to a woman.
    Chor. In seeking just occasion to provoke
The Philistine, thy country's enemy,
Thou never wast remiss, I bear thee witness;
Yet Israel still serves with all his sons.   240
    Sams. That fault I take not on me, but transfer
On Israel's governors and heads of tribes,
Who, seeing those great acts which God had done
Singly by me against their conquerors,
Acknowledged not, or not at all considered,   245
Deliverance offered; I, on the other side,
Used no ambition to commend my deeds;
The deeds themselves, though mute, spoke loud the doer;
But they persisted deaf, and would not seem
To count them things worth notice, till at length   250
Their lords, the Philistines, with gathered powers
Entered Judea, seeking me, who then
Safe to the rock of Etham was retired –
Not flying, but forecasting in what place
To set upon them, what advantaged best;   255
Meanwhile the men of Judah, to prevent
The harass of their land, beset me round;
I willingly on some conditions came
Into their hands, and they as gladly yield me
To the uncircumcised a welcome prey,   260
Bound with two cords; but cords to me were threads
Touched with the flame: on their whole host I flew
Unarmed, and with a trivial weapon felled
Their choicest youth; they only lived who fled.
Had Judah that day joined, or one whole tribe,   265
They had by this possessed the towers of Gath,
And lorded over them whom now they serve;
But what more oft, in nations grown corrupt,
And by their vices brought to servitude,
Than to love bondage more than liberty –   270
Bondage with ease than strenuous liberty –
And to despise, or envy, or suspect,
Whom God hath of his special favour raised
As their deliverer? If he aught begin,

247 ambition] used in the Latin sense of 'canvassing'.
266] 'By this' means 'by this time'; on Gath (here used synecdochically for
     Philistia) see *PL* I 464–6n.

How frequent to desert him, and at last   275
To heap ingratitude on worthiest deeds!
   Chor. Thy words to my remembrance bring
How Succoth and the fort of Penuel
Their great deliverer contemned,
The matchless Gideon, in pursuit   280
Of Madian, and her vanquished kings;
And how ingrateful Ephraim
Had dealt with Jephtha, who by argument,
Not worse than by his shield and spear,
Defended Israel from the Ammonite,   285
Had not his prowess quelled their pride
In that sore battle when so many died
Without reprieve, adjudged to death
For want of well pronouncing *shibboleth*.
   Sams. Of such examples add me to the roll;   290
Me easily indeed mine may neglect,
But God's proposed deliverance not so.
   Chor. Just are the ways of God,
And justifiable to men,
Unless there be who think not God at all;   295
If any be, they walk obscure:
For of such doctrine never was there school,
But the heart of the fool,
And no man therein doctor but himself.
   Yet more there be who doubt his ways not just,   300
As to his own edicts found contradicting;
Then give the reins to wandering thought,
Regardless of his glory's diminution,
Till, by their own perplexities involved,
They ravel more, still less resolved,   305
But never find self-satisfying solution.
   As if they would confine the interminable,
And tie him to his own prescript,
Who made our laws to bind us, not himself,
And hath full right to exempt   310

277–81] Gideon pursued Zebah and Zalmunna, kings of Midian ('Madian' in
    Vulgate and in A.V. Acts vii. 29) and was refused bread for his army by the
    men of Succoth and of Penuel (Judges viii. 1–17).
282–9] See Judges xi and xii. 1–6. Jephtha occupied the fords of the Jordan, and
    any Ephraimite that crossed and tried to deny his nationality was asked to
    pronounce *shibboleth*; the 42,000 Ephraimites who revealed their nationa-
    lity by saying *sibboleth* were executed.
291 mine] my people.
295 think not God] i.e. think that there is no God.
296–8] Psalm xiv. 1, Eccles. ii. 14; 'obscure' means 'in darkness'.

Whomso it pleases him by choice
From national obstriction, without taint
Of sin, or legal debt;
For with his own laws he can best dispense.
    He would not else, who never wanted means,   315
Nor in respect of the enemy just cause,
To set his people free,
Have prompted this heroic Nazarite,
Against his vow of strictest purity,
To seek in marriage that fallacious bride,   320
Unclean, unchaste.
    Down, Reason, then; at least, vain reasonings down;
Though Reason here aver
That moral verdict quits her of unclean:
Unchaste was subsequent; her stain, not his.   325
    But see, here comes thy reverend sire,
With careful step, locks white as down,
Old Manoa: advise
Forthwith how thou ought'st to receive him.
    Sams. Ay me, another inward grief, awaked   330
With mention of that name, renews the assault.
    Man. Brethren and men of Dan – for such ye seem,
Though in this uncouth place – if old respect,
As I suppose, towards your once gloried friend,
My son, now captive, hither hath informed   335
Your younger feet, while mine, cast back with age,
Came lagging after, say if he be here.
    Chor. As signal now in low dejected state
As erst in highest, behold him where he lies.
    Man. O miserable change! Is this the man,   340
That invincible Samson, far renowned,
The dread of Israel's foes, who with a strength
Equivalent to angels' walked their streets,
None offering fight; who, single combatant,

312 obstriction] obligation (coined by Milton from medieval Latin *obstrictio-nem*). In Samson's time Jews were not specifically forbidden to marry Philistines, though social contact with Gentiles was certainly forbidden by N.T. times (John xviii. 28, Acts x. 28). Milton may have had in mind Paul's injunction against marriage with unbelievers (II Cor. vi. 14). See also l. 380n. and ll. 857–61n.
318–19] See l. 31n. There was no Nazaritic vow of celibacy; such a vow is an inference from the strong ascetic element in the abstinence from wine and strong drink (see ll. 541–52).
327 careful] full of grief.
328 advise] ponder.
333 uncouth] strange, unknown.

Duelled their armies ranked in proud array,   345
Himself an army – now unequal match
To save himself against a coward armed
At one spear's length? O ever-failing trust
In mortal strength! And O what not in man
Deceivable and vain? Nay, what thing good   350
Prayed for, but often proves our woe, our bane?
I prayed for children, and thought barrenness
In wedlock a reproach; I gained a son,
And such a son as all men hailed me happy:
Who would be now a father in my stead?   355
O, wherefore did God grant me my request,
And as a blessing with such pomp adorned?
Why are his gifts desirable, to tempt
Our earnest prayers, then, given with solemn hand
As graces, draw a scorpion's tail behind?   360
For this did the angel twice descend? For this
Ordained thy nurture holy, as of a plant
Select and sacred? Glorious for a while,
The miracle of men; then in an hour
Ensnared, assaulted, overcome, led bound,   365
Thy foes' derision, captive, poor and blind,
Into a dungeon thrust, to work with slaves!
Alas, methinks whom God hath chosen once
To worthiest deeds, if he through frailty err,
He should not so o'erwhelm, and as a thrall   370
Subject him to so foul indignities,
Be it but for honour's sake of former deeds.
    Sams. Appoint not heavenly disposition, father.
Nothing of all these evils hath befallen me
But justly; I myself have brought them on;   375
Sole author I, sole cause: if aught seem vile,
As vile hath been my folly, who have profaned
The mystery of God, given me under pledge
Of vow, and have betrayed it to a woman,
A Canaanite, my faithless enemy.   380
This well I knew, nor was at all surprised,
But warned by oft experience: did not she
Of Timna first betray me, and reveal

---

373 Appoint] arraign.
380] The Philistines were immigrants into Canaan from Caphtor (see l. 1713,
    Jer. xlvii. 4, Amos ix. 7), but Milton's use of the term Canaanite to describe
    them may imply an extension of the injunction against marrying members
    of the seven autochthonous nations (Deut. vii. 3) to the current inhabi-
    tants, the Philistines.

The secret wrested from me in her height
Of nuptial love professed, carrying it straight 385
To them who had corrupted her, my spies
And rivals? In this other was there found
More faith? Who, also in her prime of love,
Spousal embraces, vitiated with gold,
Though offered only, by the scent conceived, 390
Her spurious first-born, treason against me?
Thrice she assayed, with flattering prayers and sighs,
And amorous reproaches, to win from me
My capital secret, in what part my strength 394
Lay stored, in what part summed, that she might know;
Thrice I deluded her, and turned to sport
Her importunity, each time perceiving
How openly and with what impudence
She purposed to betray me, and (which was worse
Than undissembled hate) with what contempt 400
She sought to make me traitor to myself;
Yet, the fourth time, when, mustering all her wiles,
With blandished parleys, feminine assaults,
Tongue-batteries, she surceased not day nor night
To storm me, over-watched and wearied out; 405
At times when men seek most repose and rest,
I yielded, and unlocked her all my heart,
Who, with a grain of manhood well resolved,
Might easily have shook off all her snares;
But foul effeminacy held me yoked 410
Her bond-slave: O indignity, O blot
To honour and religion! Servile mind
Rewarded well with servile punishment!
The base degree to which I now am fallen,
These rags, this grinding, is not yet so base 415
As was my former servitude, ignoble,
Unmanly, ignominious, infamous,
True slavery; and that blindness worse than this,
That saw not how degenerately I served.
    Man. I cannot praise thy marriage-choices, son – 420
Rather approved them not; but thou didst plead
Divine impulsion prompting how thou might'st
Find some occasion to infest our foes.
I state not that; this I am sure – our foes
Found soon occasion thereby to make thee 425

394 capital] plays on the meanings 'relating to the head', 'important', and 'fatal'.
405 over-watched] wearied with too much watching.
424 state not] have no opinion on.

Their captive, and their triumph; thou the sooner
Temptation found'st, or over-potent charms,
To violate the sacred trust of silence
Deposited within thee – which to have kept
Tacit was in thy power; true; and thou bear'st   430
Enough, and more, the burden of that fault;
Bitterly hast thou paid, and still art paying,
That rigid score. A worse thing yet remains:
This day the Philistines a popular feast
Here celebrate in Gaza, and proclaim   435
Great pomp, and sacrifice, and praises loud,
To Dagon, as their god who hath delivered
Thee, Samson, bound and blind, into their hands –
Them out of thine, who slew'st them many a slain.
So Dagon shall be magnified, and God,   440
Besides whom is no god, compared with idols,
Disglorified, blasphemed, and had in scorn
By the idolatrous rout amidst their wine;
Which to have come to pass by means of thee,
Samson, of all thy sufferings think the heaviest,   445
Of all reproach the most with shame that ever
Could have befallen thee and thy father's house.
      Sams. Father, I do acknowledge and confess
That I this honour, I this pomp, have brought
To Dagon, and advanced his praises high   450
Among the heathen round – to God have brought
Dishonour, obloquy, and oped the mouths
Of idolists and atheists; have brought scandal
To Israel, diffidence of God, and doubt
In feeble hearts, propense enough before   455
To waver, or fall off and join with idols:
Which is my chief affliction, shame and sorrow,
The anguish of my soul, that suffers not
Mine eye to harbour sleep, or thoughts to rest.
This only hope relieves me, that the strife   460
With me hath end; all the contest is now
'Twixt God and Dagon; Dagon hath presumed,
Me overthrown, to enter lists with God,
His deity comparing and preferring
Before the God of Abraham. He, be sure,   465
Will not connive, or linger, thus provoked,
But will arise, and his great name assert;

439] The second 'them' imitates the Latin dative of disadvantage, and means
    'to their loss'.
466 connive] remain inactive.

Dagon must stoop, and shall ere long receive
Such a discomfit as shall quite despoil him
Of all these boasted trophies won on me,   470
And with confusion blank his worshippers.
    Man. With cause this hope relieves thee: and these
        words
I as a prophecy receive; for God –
Nothing more certain – will not long defer
To vindicate the glory of his name   475
Against all competition, nor will long
Endure it doubtful whether God be Lord
Or Dagon. But for thee what shall be done?
Thou must not in the meanwhile, here forgot,
Lie in this miserable loathsome plight   480
Neglected. I already have made way
To some Philistian lords, with whom to treat
About thy ransom; well they may by this
Have satisfied their utmost of revenge,
By pains and slaveries, worse than death, inflicted   485
On thee, who now no more canst do them harm.
    Sams. Spare that proposal, father; spare the trouble
Of that solicitation; let me here,
As I deserve, pay on my punishment,
And expiate, if possible, my crime,   490
Shameful garrulity. To have revealed
Secrets of men, the secrets of a friend,
How heinous had the fact been, how deserving
Contempt and scorn of all – to be excluded
All friendship, and avoided as a blab,   495
The mark of fool set on his front! But I
God's counsel have not kept, his holy secret
Presumptuously have published, impiously,
Weakly at least and shamefully – a sin
That Gentiles in their parables condemn   500
To their abyss and horrid pains confined.
    Man. Be penitent, and for thy fault contrite,
But act not in thy own affliction, son;
Repent the sin, but, if the punishment
Thou canst avoid, self-preservation bids;   505

---

469 discomfit] defeat.
471 blank] disconcert.
493 fact] evil deed.
496 But I] in 1671 text, printed at beginning of next line.
500–1] Alludes to the myth of Tantalus, who was punished for betraying the
    gods' secrets; on his punishment see *PL* II 614n.

Or the execution leave to high disposal,
And let another hand, not thine, exact
Thy penal forfeit from thyself; perhaps
God will relent, and quit thee all his debt;
Who ever more approves and more accepts   510
(Best pleased with humble and filial submission)
Him who, imploring mercy, sues for life,
Than who, self-rigorous, chooses death as due;
Which argues over-just, and self-displeased
For self-offence more than for God offended.   515
Reject not, then, what offered means who knows
But God hath set before us to return thee
Home to thy country and his sacred house,
Where thou may'st bring thy offerings, to avert
His further ire, with prayers and vows renewed.   520
    Sams. His pardon I implore; but, as for life,
To what end should I seek it? When in strength
All mortals I excelled, and great in hopes,
With youthful courage, and magnanimous thoughts
Of birth from heaven foretold and high exploits,   525
Full of divine instinct, after some proof
Of acts indeed heroic, far beyond
The sons of Anak, famous now and blazed,
Fearless of danger, like a petty god
I walked about, admired of all, and dreaded   530
On hostile ground, none daring my affront.
Then, swoll'n with pride, into the snare I fell
Of fair fallacious looks, venereal trains,
Softened with pleasure and voluptuous life,
At length to lay my head and hallowed pledge   535
Of all my strength in the lascivious lap
Of a deceitful concubine, who shore me,
Like a tame wether, all my precious fleece,
Then turned me out ridiculous, despoiled,
Shaven, and disarmed among my enemies.   540
    Chor. Desire of wine and all delicious drinks,
Which many a famous warrior overturns,
Thou could'st repress; nor did the dancing ruby,
Sparkling out-poured, the flavour or the smell,

---

509 his debt] i.e. the debt due to him.
524 magnanimous] See *PL* VII 511n.
528] See l. 148n.
531 my affront] an encounter with me.
533 venereal trains] snares of sexual desire.
541–52] Cf. l. 31n., ll. 318–19n. On l. 545 cf. Judges ix. 13.

Or taste, that cheers the heart of gods and men,   545
Allure thee from the cool crystalline stream.
   Sams. Wherever fountain or fresh current flowed
Against the eastern ray, translucent, pure
With touch ethereal of heaven's fiery rod,
I drank, from the clear milky juice allaying   550
Thirst, and refreshed; nor envied them the grape
Whose heads that turbulent liquor fills with fumes.
   Chor. O madness, to think use of strongest wines
And strongest drinks our chief support of health,
When God with these forbidden made choice to rear   555
His mighty champion, strong above compare,
Whose drink was only from the liquid brook.
   Sams. But what availed this temperance, not complete
Against another object more enticing?
What boots it at one gate to make defence,   560
And at another to let in the foe,
Effeminately vanquished? By which means,
Now blind, disheartened, shamed, dishonoured, quelled,
To what can I be useful? Wherein serve
My nation, and the work from heaven imposed?   565
But to sit idle on the household hearth,
A burdenous drone; to visitants a gaze,
Or pitied object; these redundant locks,
Robustious to no purpose, clustering down,
Vain monument of strength; till length of years   570
And sedentary numbness craze my limbs
To a contemptible old age obscure.
Here rather let me drudge, and earn my bread,
Till vermin, or the draff of servile food,
Consume me, and oft-invocated death   575
Hasten the welcome end of all my pains.
   Man. Wilt thou then serve the Philistines with that gift
Which was expressly given thee to annoy them?
Better at home lie bed-rid, not only idle,
Inglorious, unemployed, with age outworn.   580
But God, who caused a fountain at thy prayer
From the dry ground to spring, thy thirst to allay

557 liquid] clear.
560 boots] avails, profits.
568 redundant] abounding to excess or fullness.
571 craze] render infirm.
582] The word that Milton transcribes as 'lechi' (l. 145) may in Judges xv. 19
    refer to either the jawbone or the place named after the jawbone. In A.V.
    and Vulgate the water comes from the jaw. Milton's 'dry ground' places
    him in the other tradition, that of the Jonathan Targum, the LXX,
    Josephus, and the A.V. margin.

After the brunt of battle, can as easy
Cause light again within thy eyes to spring,
Wherewith to serve him better than thou hast: 585
And I persuade me so; why else his strength
Miraculous yet remaining in those locks?
His might continues in thee not for naught,
Nor shall his wondrous gifts be frustrate thus.
    Sams. All otherwise to me my thoughts portend –   590
That these dark orbs no more shall treat with light,
Nor the other light of life continue long,
But yield to double darkness nigh at hand;
So much I feel my genial spirits droop,
My hopes all flat: nature within me seems   595
In all her functions weary of herself;
My race of glory run, and race of shame,
And I shall shortly be with them that rest.
    Man. Believe not these suggestions, which proceed
From anguish of the mind, and humours black   600
That mingle with thy fancy. I however
Must not omit a father's timely care
To prosecute the means of thy deliverance
By ransom or how else: meanwhile be calm,
And healing words from these thy friends admit.   605
    Sams. O that torment should not be confined
To the body's wounds and sores,
With maladies innumerable
In heart, head, breast, and reins,
But must secret passage find   610
To the inmost mind,
There exercise all his fierce accidents,
And on her purest spirits prey,
As on entrails, joints, and limbs,
With answerable pains, but more intense,   615
Though void of corporal sense.
    My griefs not only pain me
As a lingering disease,
But, finding no redress, ferment and rage;
Nor less than wounds immedicable   620
Rankle, and fester, and gangrene,
To black mortification.
Thoughts, my tormentors, armed with daily stings,

594 genial] pertaining to genius or natural disposition.
600 humours black] melancholy; see *Education* p. 562, n.4.
609 reins] kidneys.
612 accidents] used in the medical sense of 'symptoms'.

Mangle my apprehensive tenderest parts,
Exasperate, exulcerate, and raise   625
Dire inflammation, which no cooling herb
Or medicinal liquor can assuage,
Nor breath of vernal air from snowy alp.
Sleep hath forsook and given me o'er
To death's benumbing opium as my only cure;   630
Thence faintings, swoonings of despair,
And sense of heaven's desertion.
    I was his nursling once and choice delight,
His destined from the womb,
Promised by heavenly message twice descending.   635
Under his special eye
Abstemious I grew up and thrived amain;
He led me on to mightiest deeds,
Above the nerve of mortal arm,
Against the uncircumcised, our enemies: 640
But now hath cast me off as never known,
And to those cruel enemies,
Whom I by his appointment had provoked,
Left me, all helpless with the irreparable loss
Of sight, reserved alive to be repeated   645
The subject of their cruelty or scorn.
Nor am I in the list of them that hope:
Hopeless are all my evils, all remediless;
This one prayer yet remains, might I be heard,
No long petition – speedy death,   650
The close of all my miseries and the balm.
    Chor. Many are the sayings of the wise,
In ancient and in modern books enrolled,
Extolling patience as the truest fortitude,
And to the bearing well of all calamities,   655
All chances incident to man's frail life,
Consolatories writ
With studied argument, and much persuasion sought,
Lenient of grief and anxious thought;
But with the afflicted in his pangs their sound   660

---

624 apprehensive] pertaining to sensuous or mental impressions.
625 exulcerate] cause ulcers in.
639 nerve] muscle.
657 Consolatories] *Consolationes* are very common in the literature of antiquity;
    they range from simple letters to philosophical treatises (see e.g. Plutarch,
    Consolatio ad Uxorem). Later Christian consolers (Ambrose, Jerome, Pauli-
    nus of Nova) shifted the emphasis of the consolation from reasoned
    argument (l. 658) to feeling (l. 663).

Little prevails, or rather seems a tune
Harsh, and of dissonant mood from his complaint
Unless he feel within
Some source of consolation from above,
Secret refreshings that repair his strength   665
And fainting spirits uphold.
  God of our fathers, what is man,
That thou towards him with hand so various –
Or might I say contrarious? –
Temper'st thy providence through his short course: 670
Not evenly, as thou rul'st
The angelic orders, and inferior creatures mute,
Irrational and brute?
Nor do I name of men the common rout,
That, wandering loose about,   675
Grow up and perish as the summer fly,
Heads without name, no more remembered;
But such as thou hast solemnly elected,
With gifts and graces eminently adorned,
To some great work, thy glory,   680
And people's safety, which in part they effect;
Yet toward these, thus dignified, thou oft,
Amidst their height of noon,
Changest thy countenance and thy hand, with no regard
Of highest favours past   685
From thee on them, or them to thee of service.
  Nor only dost degrade them, or remit
To life obscured, which were a fair dismission,
But throw'st them lower than thou didst exalt them high –
Unseemly falls in human eye,   690
Too grievous for the trespass or omission;
Oft leav'st them to the hostile sword
Of heathen and profane, their carcasses
To dogs and fowls a prey, or else captived,

667–70] Cf. Psalm viii. 4, Job vii. 17–20, and the speech of the Chorus in Seneca,
    Hippolytus 1123 ff.
678–704] If *SA* was written after the Restoration, these lines may allude to the
    indignities suffered by the Commonwealth leaders at the hands of the
    Restoration government. Ll. 693–4 may be a specific allusion (phrased in
    Homeric language: *Iliad* i 4–5) to the disinterment of the bodies of
    Bradshaw, Cromwell, and Ireton from Westminster Abbey; their bodies
    (and possibly Pride's) were hanged publicly for a day and reburied at
    Tyburn. Lambert and Martin (Parliamentary generals) were imprisoned
    ('captived'), and Vane (on whom see Milton's *Sonnet* XVII) was condemned
    to death by a tribunal which Milton would doubtless have regarded as
    'unjust'.

Or to the unjust tribunals, under change of times, 695
And condemnation of the ingrateful multitude.
If these they scape, perhaps in poverty
With sickness and disease thou bow'st them down,
Painful diseases and deformed,
In crude old age; 700
Though not disordinate, yet causeless suffering
The punishment of dissolute days; in fine,
Just or unjust alike seem miserable,
For oft alike both come to evil end.
 So deal not with this once thy glorious champion, 705
The image of thy strength, and mighty minister.
What do I beg? How hast thou dealt already?
Behold him in this state calamitous, and turn
His labours, for thou canst, to peaceful end.
 But who is this? What thing of sea or land – 710
Female of sex it seems –
That, so bedecked, ornate, and gay,
Comes this way sailing,
Like a stately ship
Of Tarsus, bound for the isles 715
Of Javan or Gadire,
With all her bravery on, and tackle trim,
Sails filled, and streamers waving,
Courted by all the winds that hold them play;
An amber scent of odorous perfume 720
Her harbinger, a damsel train behind?
Some rich Philistian matron she may seem;
And now, at nearer view, no other certain
Than Dalila thy wife. 724
 Sams. My wife, my traitress, let her not come near me.
 Chor. Yet on she moves; now stands and eyes thee fixed,
About to have spoke; but now, with head declined,
Like a fair flower surcharged with dew, she weeps,
And words addressed seem into tears dissolved,
Wetting the borders of her silken veil: 730
But now again she makes address to speak.
 Dal. With doubtful feet and wavering resolution
I came, still dreading thy displeasure, Samson;

702 in fine] in short.
715 Tarsus] 'Ship of Tarshish' is a common O.T. expression for a large and
 strong ship, and Tarshish is a maritime country somewhere far to the west
 of Palestine. Milton's spelling *may* suggest that he identified Tarshish with
 Tarsus, the chief city of ancient Cicilia.
716] Javan is Ionia (see *PL* I 508n.), and Gadire was the Greek name for Cadiz.

Which to have merited, without excuse,
I cannot but acknowledge; yet, if tears   735
May expiate (though the fact more evil drew
In the perverse event than I foresaw),
My penance hath not slackened, though my pardon
No way assured. But conjugal affection,
Prevailing over fear and timorous doubt,   740
Hath led me on, desirous to behold
Once more thy face, and know of thy estate;
If aught in my ability may serve
To lighten what thou suffer'st, and appease
Thy mind with what amends is in my power –   745
Though late, yet in some part to recompense
My rash but more unfortunate misdeed.
      Sams. Out, out, hyena! These are thy wonted arts,
And arts of every woman false like thee –
To break all faith, all vows, deceive, betray;   750
Then, as repentant, to submit, beseech,
And reconcilement move with feigned remorse,
Confess, and promise wonders in her change –
Not truly penitent, but chief to try
Her husband, how far urged his patience bears,   755
His virtue or weakness which way to assail:
Then, with more cautious and instructed skill,
Again transgresses, and again submits;
That wisest and best men, full oft beguiled,
With goodness principled not to reject   760
The penitent, but ever to forgive,
Are drawn to wear out miserable days,
Entangled with a poisonous bosom-snake,
If not by quick destruction soon cut off,
As I by thee, to ages an example.   765
      Dal. Yet hear me, Samson; not that I endeavour
To lessen or extenuate my offence,
But that, on the other side, if it be weighed
By itself, with aggravations not surcharged,
Or else with just allowance counterpoised,   770
I may, if possible, thy pardon find
The easier towards me, or thy hatred less.
First granting, as I do, it was a weakness
In me, but incident to all our sex,

736 fact] evil deed.
748 hyena] The note on Ecclus. xiii. 18 in the Geneva Bible explains that the
    hyena 'counterfaiteth the voyce of men, and so enticeth them out of their
    houses and devoureth them'; cf. Pliny, *Naturalis Historia* viii. 44.

Curiosity, inquisitive, importune   775
Of secrets, then with like infirmity
To publish them – both common female faults –
Was it not weakness also to make known,
For importunity, that is for naught,
Wherein consisted all thy strength and safety?   780
To what I did thou show'dst me first the way.
But I to enemies revealed, and should not.
Nor should'st thou have trusted that to woman's frailty:
Ere I to thee, thou to thyself wast cruel.
Let weakness, then, with weakness come to parle,   785
So near related, or the same of kind;
Thine forgive mine, that men may censure thine
The gentler, if severely thou exact not
More strength from me than in thyself was found.
And what if love, which thou interpret'st hate,   790
The jealousy of love, powerful of sway
In human hearts, nor less in mine towards thee,
Caused what I did? I saw thee mutable
Of fancy; feared lest one day thou would'st leave me,
As her at Timna; sought by all means, therefore,   795
How to endear, and hold thee to me firmest:
No better way I saw than by importuning
To learn thy secrets, get into my power
Thy key of strength and safety; thou wilt say,
'Why, then, revealed?' I was assured by those   800
Who tempted me that nothing was designed
Against thee but safe custody and hold:
That made for me; I knew that liberty
Would draw thee forth to perilous enterprises,
While I at home sat full of cares and fears,   805
Wailing thy absence in my widowed bed;
Here I should still enjoy thee, day and night,
Mine and love's prisoner, not the Philistines',
Whole to myself, unhazarded abroad,
Fearless at home of partners in my love.   810
These reasons in love's law have passed for good,
Though fond and reasonless to some perhaps;
And love hath oft, well meaning, wrought much woe,
Yet always pity or pardon hath obtained.
Be not unlike all others, not austere   815
As thou art strong, inflexible as steel.

800–2] In the A.V. of Judges xvi. 5 the stated motive is affliction, which follows
   Vulgate *affligere*; according to the A.V. marginal note the stated motive is
   only humiliation, which follows LXX ταπείνωσαι.

If thou in strength all mortals dost exceed,
In uncompassionate anger do not so.
   Sams. How cunningly the sorceress displays
Her own transgressions, to upbraid me mine!   820
That malice, not repentance, brought thee hither,
By this appears: I gave, thou say'st, the example,
I led the way – bitter reproach, but true;
I to myself was false ere thou to me:
Such pardon, therefore, as I give my folly   825
Take to thy wicked deed; which when thou seest
Impartial, self-severe, inexorable,
Thou wilt renounce thy seeking, and much rather
Confess it feigned; weakness is thy excuse,
And I believe it – weakness to resist   830
Philistian gold: if weakness may excuse,
What murderer, what traitor, parricide,
Incestuous, sacrilegious, but may plead it?
All wickedness is weakness; that plea, therefore,
With God or man will gain thee no remission.   835
But love constrained thee; call it furious rage
To satisfy thy lust; love seeks to have love;
My love how could'st thou hope, who took'st the way
To raise in me inexpiable hate,
Knowing, as needs I must, by thee betrayed?   840
In vain thou striv'st to cover shame with shame,
Or by evasions thy crime uncover'st more.
   Dal. Since thou determin'st weakness for no plea
In man or woman, though to thy own condemning,
Hear what assaults I had, what snares besides,   845
What sieges girt me round, ere I consented;
Which might have awed the best-resolved of men,
The constantest, to have yielded without blame.
It was not gold, as to my charge thou lay'st,
That wrought with me; thou knowest the magistrates
And princes of my country came in person,   851
Solicited, commanded, threatened, urged,
Adjured by all the bonds of civil duty
And of religion – pressed how just it was,
How honourable, how glorious, to entrap   855
A common enemy, who had destroyed
Such numbers of our nation: and the priest
Was not behind, but ever at my ear,

857–61] The priest is Milton's invention, and is probably meant to emphasize
    the analogy to seventeenth-century views about marriage with unbelievers
    (cf. l. 321n.).

Preaching how meritorious with the gods
It would be to ensnare an irreligious   860
Dishonourer of Dagon; what had I
To oppose against such powerful arguments?
Only my love of thee held long debate,
And combated in silence all these reasons
With hard contest; at length, that grounded maxim,   865
So rife and celebrated in the mouths
Of wisest men – that to the public good
Private respects must yield – with grave authority
Took full possession of me, and prevailed;
Virtue, as I thought, truth, duty, so enjoining.   870
    Sams. I thought where all thy circling wiles would
       end –
In feigned religion, smooth hypocrisy.
But, had thy love, still odiously pretended,
Been, as it ought, sincere, it would have taught thee
Far other reasonings, brought forth other deeds.   875
I, before all the daughters of my tribe
And of my nation, chose thee from among
My enemies, loved thee, as too well thou knew'st,
Too well; unbosomed all my secrets to thee,
Not out of levity, but overpowered   880
By thy request, who could deny thee nothing;
Yet now am judged an enemy. Why, then,
Didst thou at first receive me for thy husband –
Then, as since then, thy country's foe professed?
Being once a wife, for me thou wast to leave   885
Parents and country; nor was I their subject,
Nor under their protection, but my own;
Thou mine, not theirs; if aught against my life
Thy country sought of thee, it sought unjustly,
Against the law of nature, law of nations;   890
No more thy country, but an impious crew
Of men conspiring to uphold their state
By worse than hostile deeds, violating the ends
For which our country is a name so dear;
Not therefore to be obeyed. But zeal moved thee;   895
To please thy gods thou didst it; gods unable
To acquit themselves and prosecute their foes
But by ungodly deeds, the contradiction
Of their own deity, gods cannot be –
Less therefore to be pleased, obeyed, or feared;   900

885–6] Gen. ii. 24.

These false pretexts and varnished colours failing,
Bare in thy guilt, how foul must thou appear!
   Dal. In argument with men a woman ever
Goes by the worse, whatever be her cause.   904
   Sams. For want of words, no doubt, or lack of breath:
Witness when I was worried with thy peals.
   Dal. I was a fool, too rash, and quite mistaken
In what I thought would have succeeded best.
Let me obtain forgiveness of thee, Samson;
Afford me place to show what recompense   910
Towards thee I intend for what I have misdone,
Misguided; only what remains past cure
Bear not too sensibly, nor still insist
To afflict thyself in vain; though sight be lost,
Life yet hath many solaces, enjoyed   915
Where other senses want not their delights –
At home, in leisure and domestic ease,
Exempt from many a care and chance to which
Eyesight exposes, daily, men abroad.
I to the lords will intercede, not doubting   920
Their favourable ear, that I may fetch thee
From forth this loathsome prison-house, to abide
With me, where my redoubled love and care,
With nursing diligence, to me glad office,
May ever tend about thee to old age,   925
With all things grateful cheered, and so supplied
That what by me thou hast lost thou least shalt miss.
   Sams. No, no; of my condition take no care;
It fits not; thou and I long since are twain;
Nor think me so unwary or accursed   930
To bring my feet again into the snare
Where once I have been caught; I know thy trains,
Though dearly to my cost, thy gins, and toils;
Thy fair enchanted cup, and warbling charms,
No more on me have power, their force is nulled,   935
So much of adder's wisdom I have learned,
To fence my ear against thy sorceries.
If in my flower of youth and strength, when all men
Loved, honoured, feared me, thou alone could hate me,
Thy husband, slight me, sell me, and forgo me,   940
How would'st thou use me now, blind, and thereby

---

913 sensibly] acutely, intensely.
926 grateful] agreeable, pleasing to the mind and senses.
934–5] Alludes to the myth of Circe, on which see *Comus* 50n.
936–7] Psalm lviii. 4.

Deceivable, in most things as a child
Helpless, thence easily contemned and scorned,
And last neglected? How would'st thou insult,
When I must live uxorious to thy will   945
In perfect thraldom, how again betray me,
Bearing my words and doings to the lords
To gloss upon, and, censuring, frown or smile?
This jail I count the house of liberty
To thine, whose doors my feet shall never enter.   950
    Dal. Let me approach at least, and touch thy hand.
    Sams. Not for thy life, lest fierce remembrance wake
My sudden rage to tear thee joint by joint.
At distance I forgive thee; go with that;
Bewail thy falsehood, and the pious works   955
It hath brought forth to make thee memorable
Among illustrious women, faithful wives;
Cherish thy hastened widowhood with the gold
Of matrimonial treason: so farewell.
    Dal. I see thou art implacable, more deaf   960
To prayers than winds and seas; yet winds to seas
Are reconciled at length, and sea to shore:
Thy anger, unappeasable, still rages,
Eternal tempest never to be calmed.
Why do I humble thus myself, and, suing   965
For peace, reap nothing but repulse and hate,
Bid go with evil omen, and the brand
Of infamy upon my name denounced?
To mix with thy concernments I desist
Henceforth, nor too much disapprove my own.   970
Fame, if not double-faced, is double-mouthed,
And with contráry blast proclaims most deeds;
On both his wings, one black, the other white,
Bears greatest names in his wild airy flight.
My name, perhaps, among the circumcised   975
In Dan, in Judah, and the bordering tribes,
To all posterity may stand defamed,
With malediction mentioned, and the blot
Of falsehood most unconjugal traduced.
But in my country, where I most desire,   980
In Ecron, Gaza, Asdod, and in Gath,
I shall be named among the famousest
Of women, sung at solemn festivals,
Living and dead recorded, who to save

981] See *PL* I 464–6n.

Her country from a fierce destroyer chose   985
Above the faith of wedlock bands; my tomb
With odours visited and annual flowers;
Not less renowned than in Mount Ephraim
Jael, who, with inhospitable guile,
Smote Sisera sleeping, through the temples nailed.   990
Nor shall I count it heinous to enjoy
The public marks of honour and reward
Conferred upon me for the piety
Which to my country I was judged to have shown.
At this whoever envies or repines,   995
I leave him to his lot, and like my own,
    Chor. She's gone – a manifest serpent by her sting
Discovered in the end, till now concealed.
    Sams. So let her go: God sent her to debase me,
And aggravate my folly, who committed   1000
To such a viper his most sacred trust
Of secrecy, my safety, and my life.
    Chor. Yet beauty, though injurious, hath strange power,
After offence returning, to regain
Love once possessed, nor can be easily   1005
Repulsed, without much inward passion felt,
And secret sting of amorous remorse.
    Sams. Love-quarrels oft in pleasing concord end,
Not wedlock-treachery, endangering life.
    Chor. It is not virtue, wisdom, valour, wit,   1010
Strength, comeliness of shape, or amplest merit
That woman's love can win, or long inherit;
But what it is, hard is to say,
Harder to hit,
(Which way soever men refer it) –   1015
Much like thy riddle, Samson – in one day
Or seven though one should musing sit;

---

987 odours] Jer. xxxiv. 5.
988–90] The killing of Sisera by Jael is described in Judges iv. 4–22, and
    celebrated (in verse) in Judges v. 2–31. 'Mount Ephraim' is here mentioned
    as the home of Deborah, the prophetess who 'judged Israel at that time'
    (Judges iv. 4).
993 piety] used in the sense of Latin *pietas*, the Roman attitude of dutiful
    respect for gods, relatives, and (in this case) homeland.
1000 aggravate] make more grievous and burdensome.
1006 passion] the primary sense is 'suffering', but the word could also refer to a
    sexual impulse (as in *PL* I 454).
1008] Cf. Terence, *Andria* III. iii. 23.
1012 inherit] keep.
1016 riddle] Judges xiv. 8–14.

If any of these, or all, the Timnian bride
Had not so soon preferred
Thy paranymph, worthless to thee compared,   1020
Successor in thy bed,
Nor both so loosely disallied
Their nuptials, nor this last so treacherously
Had shorn the fatal harvest of thy head.
Is it for that such outward ornament   1025
Was lavished on their sex, that inward gifts
Were left for haste unfinished, judgement scant,
Capacity not raised to apprehend
Or value what is best
In choice, but oftest to affect the wrong?   1030
Or was too much of self-love mixed,
Of constancy no root infixed,
That either they love nothing, or not long?
Whate'er it be, to wisest men and best,
Seeming at first all heavenly under virgin veil,   1035
Soft, modest, meek, demure,
Once joined, the contrary she proves – a thorn
Intestine, far within defensive arms
A cleaving mischief, in his way to virtue
Adverse and turbulent; or by her charms   1040
Draws him awry, enslaved
With dotage, and his sense depraved
To folly and shameful deeds, which ruin ends.
What pilot so expert but needs must wreck,
Embarked with such a steers-mate at the helm?   1045
Favoured of heaven who finds
One virtuous, rarely found,
That in domestic good combines:
Happy that house! His way to peace is smooth:
But virtue which breaks through all opposition,   1050
And all temptation can remove,
Most shines and most is ácceptable above.
Therefore God's universal law
Gave to the man despotic power
Over his female in due awe,   1055
Nor from that right to part an hour,
Smile she or lour:

1020] In Greek antiquity 'paranymph' meant 'friend of the bridegroom' (the
    modern 'best man'). Milton follows the Vulgate rendering of Judges xiv. 20
    in interpreting the word 'friend' in this technical sense (Vulgate uses
    pronubus).
1038 Intestine] internal, domestic.
1046-9] Prov. xxxi. 10-28.

So shall he least confusion draw
On his whole life, not swayed
By female usurpation, not dismayed.   1060
   But had we best retire? I see a storm.
   Sams. Fair days have oft contracted wind and rain.
   Chor. But this another kind of tempest brings.
   Sams. Be less abstruse: my riddling days are past.
   Chor. Look now for no enchanting voice, nor fear   1065
The bait of honeyed words; a rougher tongue
Draws hitherward; I know him by his stride,
The giant Harapha of Gath, his look
Haughty, as is his pile high-built and proud.
Comes he in peace? What wind hath blown him hither
I less conjecture than when first I saw   1071
The sumptuous Dalila floating this way:
His habit carries peace, his brow defiance.
   Sams. Or peace or not, alike to me he comes.
   Chor. His fraught we soon shall know: he now arrives.
   Har. I come not, Samson, to condole thy chance,   1076
As these perhaps, yet wish it had not been,
Though for no friendly intent. I am of Gath;
Men call me Harapha, of stock renowned
As Og, or Anak, and the Emims old   1080
That Kiriathaim held; thou know'st me now,
If thou at all art known. Much I have heard
Of thy prodigious might and feats performed,
Incredible to me, in this displeased –
That I was never present on the place   1085
Of those encounters, where we might have tried
Each other's force in camp or listed field;
And now am come to see of whom such noise
Hath walked about, and each limb to survey,

1062 contracted] drawn together.
1068] In the A.V. of II Sam. xxi the Hebrew word *harapha* is treated as a common noun and translated as 'the giant'; the A.V. marginal notes to verses 16, 18, and 20 record the minority view (in which Milton seems to concur) that *harapha* is a proper name (cf. LXX ῥαφά) and that the Philistine champions should be called 'the sons of Rapha' (see ll. 1248–9). *Harapha* means 'to become limp or slack', and is often used in a spiritual or moral sense (e.g. Joshua xviii. 3, Prov. xxiv. 10, Jer. vi. 24).
1075 fraught] freight, the cargo of a ship.
1080–1] On Og see Milton's Psalm 136, 69n. On Anak see *SA* 148n. The Emims were a race of giants (Deut. ii. 10–11) living on the plain of Kiriathaim (Gen. xiv. 5, A.V. marginal note).
1087 camp or listed field] 'Camp' is used in the Latin sense of 'plain, field'; a 'listed field' is one converted into lists for tilting.

If thy appearance answer loud report.   1090
   Sams. The way to know were not to see, but taste.
   Har. Dost thou already single me? I thought
Gyves and the mill had tamed thee. O that fortune
Had brought me to the field where thou art famed
To have wrought such wonders with an ass's jaw;   1095
I should have forced thee soon wish other arms,
Or left thy carcass where the ass lay thrown;
So had the glory of prowess been recovered
To Palestine, won by a Philistine
From the unforeskinned race, of whom thou bear'st   1100
The highest name for valiant acts; that honour,
Certain to have won by mortal duel from thee,
I lose, prevented by thy eyes put out.
   Sams. Boast not of what thou would'st have done, but
     do
What then thou would'st; thou seest it in thy hand.   1105
   Har. To combat with a blind man I disdain,
And thou hast need much washing to be touched.
   Sams. Such usage as your honourable lords
Afford me, assassinated and betrayed;
Who durst not with their whole united powers   1110
In fight withstand me single and unarmed,
Nor in the house with chamber ambushes
Close-banded durst attack me, no, not sleeping,
Till they had hired a woman with their gold,
Breaking her marriage-faith, to circumvent me.   1115
Therefore, without feigned shifts, let be assigned
Some narrow place enclosed, where sight may give thee,
Or rather flight, no great advantage on me;
Then put on all thy gorgeous arms, thy helmet
And brigandine of brass, thy broad habergeon,   1120
Vant-brace and greaves and gauntlet; add thy spear,
A weaver's beam, and seven-times-folded shield:

1093 Gyves] shackles.
1109 assassinated] treacherously wounded.
1113 Close-] secretly.
1120–1] 'Brigandine' is body armour composed of iron rings or small thin iron
    plates sewn on to canvas, linen, or leather; an 'habergeon' is a sleeveless
    coat of mail or scale armour; 'vant-brace' is armour for the forearm, and
    'greaves' are pieces of armour for the leg below the knee.
1122–3] On the comparison of the spear to the weaver's beam see I Sam. xvii. 7,
    II Sam. xxi. 19, I Chron. xx. 5; 'seven-times-folded' alludes to the shield of
    Ajax, which was made with the hides of seven bulls (*Iliad* vii 220). David
    confronted Goliath with a staff (I Sam. xvii. 40, 43).

I only with an oaken staff will meet thee,
And raise such outcries on thy clattered iron,
Which long shall not withhold me from thy head,   1125
That in a little time, while breath remains thee,
Thou oft shalt wish thyself at Gath, to boast
Again in safety what thou would'st have done
To Samson, but shalt never see Gath more.
   Har. Thou durst not thus disparage glorious arms,   1130
Which greatest heroes have in battle worn,
Their ornament and safety, had not spells
And black enchantments, some magician's art,
Armed thee or charmed thee strong, which thou from
      heaven
Feign'dst at thy birth was given thee in thy hair,   1135
Where strength can least abide, though all thy hairs
Were bristles ranged liked those that ridge the back
Of chafed wild boars or ruffled porcupines.
   Sams. I know no spells, use no forbidden arts;
My trust is in the living God, who gave me,   1140
At my nativity, this strength, diffused
No less through all my sinews, joints, and bones,
Than thine, while I preserved these locks unshorn,
The pledge of my unviolated vow.
For proof hereof, if Dagon be thy god,   1145
Go to his temple, invocate his aid
With solemnest devotion, spread before him
How highly it concerns his glory now
To frustrate and dissolve these magic spells,
Which I to be the power of Israel's God   1150
Avow, and challenge Dagon to the test,
Offering to combat thee, his champion bold,
With the utmost of his godhead seconded:
Then thou shalt see, or rather to thy sorrow
Soon feel, whose God is strongest, thine or mine.   1155
   Har. Presume not on thy God: whate'er he be,
Thee he regards not, owns not, hath cut off
Quite from his people, and delivered up
Into thy enemies' hand; permitted them
To put out both thine eyes, and fettered send thee   1160
Into the common prison, there to grind
Among the slaves and asses, thy comrádes,
As good for nothing else, no better service

1139–40] Alludes to the oath taken before the judges by medieval combatants;
    each combatant had to swear that he was not aided by magic, and trusted
    only in God.

With those thy boisterous locks; no worthy match
For valour to assail, nor by the sword   1165
Of noble warrior, so to stain his honour,
But by the barber's razor best subdued.
    Sams. All these indignities, for such they are
From thine, these evils I deserve and more,
Acknowledge them from God inflicted on me   1170
Justly, yet despair not of his final pardon,
Whose ear is ever open, and his eye
Gracious to re-admit the suppliant;
In confidence whereof I once again
Defy thee to the trial of mortal fight   1175
By combat to decide whose god is God,
Thine, or whom I with Israel's sons adore.
    Har. Fair honour that thou dost thy God, in trusting
He will accept thee to defend his cause,
A murderer, a revolter, and a robber.   1180
    Sams. Tongue-doughty giant, how dost thou prove me
      these?
    Har. Is not thy nation subject to our lords?
Their magistrates confessed it when they took thee
As a league-breaker, and delivered bound
Into our hands; for hadst thou not committed   1185
Notorious murder on those thirty men
At Ascalon, who never did thee harm,
Then, like a robber, stripp'dst them of their robes?
The Philistines, when thou hadst broke the league,
Went up with armed powers thee only seeking,   1190
To others did no violence nor spoil.
    Sams. Among the daughters of the Philistines
I chose a wife, which argued me no foe,
And in your city held my nuptial feast;
But your ill-meaning politician lords,   1195
Under pretence of bridal friends and guests,
Appointed to await me thirty spies,
Who, threatening cruel death, constrained the bride
To wring from me, and tell to them, my secret,
That solved the riddle which I had proposed.   1200
When I perceived all set on enmity,
As on my enemies, wherever chanced,
I used hostility, and took their spoil,
To pay my underminers in their coin.

1169 thine] thy people.
1197] The account in Judges says nothing about the 'companions' being spies.
    Milton has drawn on Josephus, *Antiquities* V. viii. 6.
1204 underminers] secret assailants.

My nation was subjected to your lords.   1205
It was the force of conquest; force with force
Is well ejected when the conquered can.
But I, a private person, whom my country
As a league-breaker gave up bound, presumed
Single rebellion, and did hostile acts.   1210
I was not private, but a person raised,
With strength sufficient, and command from heaven,
To free my country; if their servile minds
Me, their deliverer sent, would not receive,
But to their masters gave me up for nought,   1215
The unworthier they; whence to this day they serve.
I was to do my part from heaven assigned,
And had performed it if my known offence
Had not disabled me, not all your force:
These shifts refuted, answer thy appellant,   1220
Thou by his blindness maimed for high attempts,
Who now defies thee thrice to single fight,
As a petty enterprise of small enforce.
    Har. With thee, a man condemned, a slave enrolled,
Due by the law to capital punishment?   1225
To fight with thee no man of arms will deign.
    Sams. Cam'st thou for this, vain boaster, to survey me,
To descant on my strength, and give thy verdict?
Come nearer; part not hence so slight informed;
But take good heed my hand survey not thee.   1230
    Har. O Baäl-zebub! Can my ears unused
Hear these dishonours, and not render death?
    Sams. No man withholds thee; nothing from thy hand
Fear I incurable; bring up thy van;
My heels are fettered, but my fist is free.   1235
    Har. This insolence other kind of answer fits.
    Sams. Go, baffled coward, lest I run upon thee,
Though in these chains, bulk without spirit vast,
And with one buffet lay thy structure low,
Or swing thee in the air, then dash thee down,   1240
To the hazard of thy brains, and shattered sides.
    Har. By Ashtaroth, ere long thou shalt lament
These braveries, in irons loaden on thee.
    Chor. His giantship is gone somewhat crestfallen,

1220 appellant] the challenger in single combat.
1223 enforce] exertion.
1231 Baäl-zebub] See *Nativity* 197n. and *PL* I 81n.
1234 van] vanguard.
1237 baffled] disgraced, dishonoured.
1242 Ashtaroth] See *Nativity* 200n.

Stalking with less unconscionable strides, 1245
And lower looks, but in a sultry chafe.
   Sams. I dread him not, nor all his giant brood,
Though fame divulge him father of five sons,
All of gigantic size, Goliath chief.
   Chor. He will directly to the lords, I fear, 1250
And with malicious counsel stir them up
Some way or other yet further to afflict thee.
   Sams. He must allege some cause, and offered fight
Will not dare mention, lest a question rise
Whether he durst accept the offer or not; 1255
And that he durst not plain enough appeared.
Much more affliction than already felt
They cannot well impose, nor I sustain,
If they intend advantage of my labours,
The work of many hands, which earns my keeping, 1260
With no small profit daily to my owners.
But come what will; my deadliest foe will prove
My speediest friend, by death to ride me hence;
The worst that he can give, to me the best.
Yet so it may fall out, because their end 1265
Is hate, not help to me, it may with mine
Draw their own ruin who attempt the deed.
   Chor. O how comely it is, and how reviving
To the spirits of just men long oppressed,
When God into the hands of their deliverer 1270
Puts invincible might,
To quell the mighty of the earth, the oppressor,
The brute and boisterous force of violent men,
Hardy and industrious to support
Tyrannic power, but raging to pursue 1275
The righteous, and all such as honour truth;
He all their ammunition
And feats of war defeats,
With plain heroic magnitude of mind
And celestial vigour armed; 1280
Their armouries and magazines contemns,
Renders them useless, while

1245 unconscionable] unreasonably excessive.
1248-9] In II Sam. xxi. 15-22 four sons of Rapha (see l. 1068n.) are described, one of whom is named as Goliath. A comparison with I Chron. xx. 5 led the A.V. translators to refer to this giant as 'the brother of Goliath', who thus became a fifth son. Milton may have identified this Goliath with the giant whom David killed (I Sam. xvii).
1279 magnitude of mind] See *PL* VII 511n.

With winged expedition
Swift as the lightning glance he executes
His errand on the wicked, who, surprised,   1285
Lose their defence, distracted and amazed.
　　But patience is more oft the exercise
Of saints, the trial of their fortitude,
Making them each his own deliverer,
And victory over all   1290
That tyranny or fortune can inflict;
Either of these is in thy lot,
Samson, with might endued
Above the sons of men; but sight bereaved
May chance to number thee with those   1295
Whom patience finally must crown
　　This idol's day hath been to thee no day of rest,
Labouring thy mind
More than the working day thy hands;
And yet, perhaps, more trouble is behind;   1300
For I descry this way
Some other tending; in his hand
A sceptre or quaint staff he bears –
Comes on amain, speed in his look.
By his habit I discern him now   1305
A public officer, and now at hand.
His message will be short and voluble.
　　Off. Hebrews, the prisoner Samson here I seek.
　　Chor. His manacles remark him; there he sits.
　　Off. Samson, to thee our lords thus bid me say: 1310
This day to Dagon is a solemn feast,
With sacrifices, triumph, pomp, and games;
Thy strength they know surpassing human rate,
And now some public proof thereof require
To honour this great feast, and great assembly: 1315
Rise, therefore, with all speed, and come along,
Where I will see thee heartened and fresh clad,
To appear as fits before the illustrious lords.
　　Sams. Thou know'st I am an Hebrew; therefore tell them
Our law forbids at their religious rites   1320
My presence; for that cause I cannot come.
　　Off. This answer, be assured, will not content them.

1303 quaint] skilfully made.
1307 voluble] rapid and ready of speech.
1309 remark] mark, distinguish.
1320] Exod. xx. 4–5.

Sams. Have they not sword-players, and every sort
Of gymnic artists, wrestlers, riders, runners,
Jugglers and dancers, antics, mummers, mimics,   1325
But they must pick me out, with shackles tired,
And over-laboured at their public mill,
To make them sport with blind activity?
Do they not seek occasion of new quarrels
On my refusal, to distress me more,   1330
Or make a game of my calamities?
Return the way thou cam'st; I will not come.
   Off. Regard thyself; this will offend them highly.
   Sams. Myself? My conscience, and internal peace.
Can they think me so broken, so debased   1335
With corporal servitude, that my mind ever
Will condescend to such absurd commands?
Although their drudge, to be their fool or jester,
And, in my midst of sorrow and heart-grief,
To show them feats, and play before their god –   1340
The worst of all indignities, yet on me
Joined with supreme contempt? I will not come.
   Off. My message was imposed on me with speed,
Brooks no delay: is this thy resolution?   1344
   Sams. So take it with what speed thy message needs.
   Off. I am sorry what this stoutness will produce.
   Sams. Perhaps thou shalt have cause to sorrow indeed.
   Chor. Consider, Samson; matters now are strained
Up to the height, whether to hold or break.
He's gone, and who knows how he may report   1350
Thy words by adding fuel to the flame?
Expect another message, more imperious,
More lordly thundering than thou well wilt bear.
   Sams. Shall I abuse this consecrated gift
Of strength, again returning with my hair   1355
After my great transgression – so requite
Favour renewed, and add a greater sin
By prostituting holy things to idols,
A Nazarite, in place abominable,
Vaunting my strength in honour to their Dagon?   1360
Besides, how vile, contemptible, ridiculous,
What act more execrably unclean, profane?
   Chor. Yet with this strength thou serv'st the Philistines,
Idolatrous, uncircumcised, unclean.

1325 antics] clowns.
1342 Joined] enjoined.

Sams. Not in their idol-worship, but by labour   1365
Honest and lawful to deserve my food
Of those who have me in their civil power.
    Chor. Where the heart joins not, outward acts defile not.
    Sams. Where outward force constrains, the sentence
        holds:
But who constrains me to the temple of Dagon,   1370
Not dragging? The Philistian lords command:
Commands are no constraints. If I obey them,
I do it freely, venturing to displease
God for the fear of man, and man prefer,
Set God behind; which, in his jealousy,   1375
Shall never, unrepented, find forgiveness.
Yet that he may dispense with me, or thee,
Present in temples at idolatrous rites
For some important cause, thou need'st not doubt.   1379
    Chor. How thou wilt here come off surmounts my reach.
    Sams. Be of good courage; I begin to feel
Some rousing motions in me, which dispose
To something extraordinary my thoughts.
I with this messenger will go along –
Nothing to do, be sure, that may dishonour   1385
Our Law, or stain my vow of Nazarite.
If there be aught of presage in the mind,
This day will be remarkable in my life
By some great act, or of my days the last.
    Chor. In time thou hast resolved: the man returns.   1390
    Off. Samson, this second message from our lords
To thee I am bid say. Art thou our slave,
Our captive, at the public mill our drudge,
And dar'st thou, at our sending and command,
Dispute thy coming? Come without delay;   1395
Or we shall find such engines to assail
And hamper thee, as thou shalt come of force,
Though thou wert firmlier fastened than a rock.
    Sams. I could be well content to try their art,
Which to no few of them would prove pernicious.   1400
Yet, knowing their advantages too many,
Because they shall not trail me through their streets
Like a wild beast, I am content to go.
Masters' commands come with a power resistless
To such as owe them absolute subjection;   1405

1369 sentence] aphorism (i.e. line 1368).
1377 dispense with] grant a relaxation of the strict letter of the law in a special
    case.
1382 motions] See *PL* XI 91n.

And for a life who will not change his purpose?
(So mutable are all the ways of men.)
Yet this be sure, in nothing to comply
Scandalous or forbidden in our Law.
    Off. I praise thy resolution; doff these links: 1410
By this compliance thou wilt win the lords
To favour, and perhaps to set thee free.
    Sams. Brethren, farewell; your company along
I will not wish, lest it perhaps offend them
To see me girt with friends; and how the sight 1415
Of me, as of a common enemy,
So dreaded once, may now exasperate them
I know not. Lords are lordliest in their wine;
And the well-feasted priest then soonest fired
With zeal, if aught religion seem concerned; 1420
No less the people, on their holy-days,
Impetuous, insolent, unquenchable;
Happen what may, of me expect to hear
Nothing dishonourable, impure, unworthy
Our God, our Law, my nation, or myself; 1425
The last of me or no I cannot warrant.
    Chor. Go, and the Holy One
Of Israel be thy guide
To what may serve his glory best, and spread his name
Great among the heathen round; 1430
Send thee the angel of thy birth, to stand
Fast by thy side, who from thy father's field
Rode up in flames after his message told
Of thy conception, and be now a shield
Of fire; that spirit that first rushed on thee 1435
In the camp of Dan,
Be efficacious in thee now at need.
For never was from heaven imparted
Measure of strength so great to mortal seed
As in thy wondrous actions hath been seen. 1440
But wherefore comes old Manoa in such haste
With youthful steps? Much livelier than erewhile
He seems: supposing here to find his son,
Or of him bringing to us some glad news? 1444
    Man. Peace with you, brethren; my inducement hither
Was not at present here to find my son,
By order of the lords new parted hence
To come and play before them at their feast.
I heard all as I came; the city rings,
And numbers thither flock: I had no will, 1450
Lest I should see him forced to things unseemly.

But that which moved my coming now was chiefly
To give ye part with me what hope I have
With good success to work his liberty.
   Chor. That hope would much rejoice us to partake   1455
With thee; say, reverend sire: we thirst to hear.
   Man. I have attempted, one by one, the lords,
Either at home, or through the high street passing,
With supplication prone and father's tears,
To accept of ransom for my son, their prisoner;   1460
Some much averse I found, and wondrous harsh,
Contemptuous, proud, set on revenge and spite;
That part most reverenced Dagon and his priests;
Others more moderate seeming, but their aim
Private reward, for which both god and state   1465
They easily would set to sale; a third
More generous far and civil, who confessed
They had enough revenged, having reduced
Their foe to misery beneath their fears;
The rest was magnanimity to remit,   1470
If some convenient ransom were proposed.
What noise or shout was that? It tore the sky.
   Chor. Doubtless the people shouting to behold
Their once great dread, captive and blind before them,
Or at some proof of strength before them shown.   1475
   Man. His ransom, if my whole inheritance
May compass it, shall willingly be paid
And numbered down: much rather I shall choose
To live the poorest in my tribe, than richest
And he in that calamitous prison left.   1480
No, I am fixed not to part hence without him.
For his redemption all my patrimony,
If need be, I am ready to forgo
And quit; not wanting him, I shall want nothing.
   Chor. Fathers are wont to lay up for their sons;   1485
Thou for thy son art bent to lay out all:
Sons wont to nurse their parents in old age;
Thou in old age car'st how to nurse thy son,
Made older than thy age through eyesight lost.
   Man. It shall be my delight to tend his eyes,   1490
And view him sitting in his house, ennobled
With all those high exploits by him achieved,

1461–71] If *SA* was written after the Restoration, these lines could be a topical
    allusion to the attitudes of various groups aligned with the new govern-
    ment towards Commonwealth figures (such as Milton himself). On 'magna-
    nimity' see *PL* VII 511n.

And on his shoulders waving down those locks
That of a nation armed the strength contained;
And I persuade me God hath not permitted   1495
His strength again to grow up with his hair
Garrisoned round about him like a camp
Of faithful soldiery, were not his purpose
To use him further yet in some great service –
Not to sit idle with so great a gift   1500
Useless, and thence ridiculous, about him.
And, since his strength with eyesight was not lost,
God will restore him eyesight to his strength.
   Chor. Thy hopes are not ill founded, nor seem vain,
Of his delivery, and thy joy thereon   1505
Conceived, agreeable to a father's love;
In both which we, as next, participate.
   Man. I know your friendly minds, and – O, what
     noise!
Mercy of heaven, what hideous noise was that?
Horribly loud, unlike the former shout.   1510
   Chor. Noise call you it, or universal groan,
As if the whole inhabitation perished;
Blood, death, and dreadful deeds are in that noise,
Ruin, destruction at the utmost point.
   Man. Of ruin indeed methought I heard the noise; 1515
O it continues; they have slain my son.
   Chor. Thy son is rather slaying them: that outcry
From slaughter of one foe could not ascend.
   Man. Some dismal accident it needs must be;
What shall we do – stay here, or run and see?   1520
   Chor. Best keep together here, lest, running thither,
We unawares run into danger's mouth.
This evil on the Philistines is fallen:
From whom could else a general cry be heard?
The sufferers then will scarce molest us here;   1525
From other hands we need not much to fear.
What if, his eyesight (for to Israel's God
Nothing is hard) by miracle restored,
He now be dealing dole among his foes,
And over heaps of slaughtered walk his way?   1530
   Man. That were a joy presumptuous to be thought.
   Chor. Yet God hath wrought things as incredible
For his people of old; what hinders now?
   Man. He can, I know, but doubt to think he will;

1529 dole] plays on the meanings 'grief, sorrow' and 'that which is charitably
   doled out'.

Yet hope would fain subscribe, and tempts belief.   1535
A little stay will bring some notice hither.
   Chor. Of good or bad so great, of bad the sooner;
For evil news rides post, while good news baits.
And to our wish I see one hither speeding –
An Hebrew, as I guess, and of our tribe.   1540
   Messenger. O whither shall I run, or which way fly
The sight of this so horrid spectacle,
Which erst my eyes beheld, and yet behold?
For dire imagination still pursues me.
But providence or instinct of nature seems,   1545
Or reason, though disturbed and scarce consulted,
To have guided me aright, I know not how,
To thee first, reverend Manoa, and to these
My countrymen, whom here I knew remaining,
As at some distance from the place of horror,   1550
So in the sad event too much concerned.
   Man. The accident was loud, and here before thee
With rueful cry; yet what it was we hear not,
No preface needs; thou seest we long to know.
   Mess. It would burst forth, but I recover breath,   1555
And sense distract, to know well what I utter.
   Man. Tell us the sum; the circumstance defer.
   Mess. Gaza yet stands, but all her sons are fallen,
All in a moment overwhelmed and fallen.   1559
   Man. Sad, but thou know'st to Israelites not saddest
The desolation of a hostile city.
   Mess. Feed on that first; there may in grief be surfeit.
   Man. Relate by whom.
   Mess. By Samson.
   Man. That still lessens
The sorrow, and converts it nigh to joy.
   Mess. Ah Manoa, I refrain too suddenly   1565
To utter what will come at last too soon,
Lest evil tidings, with too rude irruption
Hitting thy aged ear, should pierce too deep.
   Man. Suspense in news is torture; speak them out.
   Mess. Then take the worst in brief: Samson is dead.   1570
   Man. The worst indeed – O, all my hopes defeated
To free him hence! But Death, who sets all free,
Hath paid his ransom now and full discharge.

1538 baits] used of travellers who stop at an inn.
1567 irruption] bursting in.
1570] Cf. Sophocles, *Electra* 673: 'in brief, Orestes is dead'.

What windy joy this day had I conceived,
Hopeful of his delivery, which now proves   1575
Abortive as the first-born bloom of spring
Nipped with the lagging rear of winter's frost.
Yet, ere I give the reins to grief, say first
How died he; death to life is crown or shame.
All by him fell, thou say'st; by whom fell he?   1580
What glorious hand gave Samson his death's wound?
   Mess. Unwounded of his enemies he fell.
   Man. Wearied with slaughter, then, or how? Explain.
   Mess. By his own hands.
   Man. Self-violence? What cause
Brought him so soon at variance with himself   1585
Among his foes?
   Mess. Inevitable cause –
At once both to destroy and be destroyed;
The edifice, where all were met to see him,
Upon their heads and on his own he pulled.
   Man. O lastly over-strong against thyself!   1590
A dreadful way thou took'st to thy revenge.
More than enough we know; but while things yet
Are in confusion, give us, if thou canst,
Eye-witness of what first or last was done,
Relation more particular and distinct.   1595
   Mess. Occasions drew me early to this city,
And, as the gates I entered with sun-rise,
The morning trumpets festival proclaimed
Through each high street; little I had dispatched,
When all abroad was rumoured that this day   1600
Samson should be brought forth, to show the people
Proof of his mighty strength in feats and games;
I sorrowed at his captive state, but minded
Not to be absent at that spectacle.
The building was a spacious theatre,   1605
Half round on two main pillars vaulted high,
With seats where all the lords, and each degree
Of sort, might sit in order to behold;
The other side was open, where the throng
On banks and scaffolds under sky might stand: 1610

1596 Occasions] affairs, business.
1605 theatre] In the Hebrew, LXX, Vulgate and A.V. of Judges xvi. 27 the
    building is called a house and has 3,000 people on the roof. In Milton's
    account the common people stand outside the building (l. 1659) rather than
    on top of it.
1608 sort] rank.
1610 banks] benches.

I among these aloof obscurely stood.
The feast and noon grew high, and sacrifice
Had filled their hearts with mirth, high cheer, and wine,
When to their sports they turned. Immediately
Was Samson as a public servant brought,   1615
In their state livery clad: before him pipes
And timbrels; on each side went armed guards;
Both horse and foot before him and behind,
Archers and slingers, cataphracts and spears.
At sight of him the people with a shout   1620
Rifted the air, clamouring their god with praise,
Who had made their dreadful enemy their thrall.
He patient, but undaunted, where they led him,
Came to the place; and what was set before him,
Which without help of eye might be assayed,   1625
To heave, pull, draw, or break, he still performed
All with incredible, stupendous force,
None daring to appear antagonist.
At length, for intermission sake, they led him
Between the pillars; he his guide requested   1630
(For so from such as nearer stood we heard),
As over-tired, to let him lean a while
With both his arms on those two massy pillars,
That to the arched roof gave main support.
He unsuspicious led him; which when Samson   1635
Felt in his arms, with head a while inclined,
And eyes fast fixed, he stood, as one who prayed,
Or some great matter in his mind revolved.
At last, with head erect, thus cried aloud:
'Hitherto, Lords, what your commands imposed   1640
I have performed, as reason was, obeying,
Not without wonder or delight beheld.
Now, of my own accord, such other trial
I mean to show you of my strength yet greater
As with amaze shall strike all who behold.'   1645
This uttered, straining all his nerves, he bowed;
As with the force of winds and waters pent
When mountains tremble, those two massy pillars
With horrible convulsion to and fro
He tugged, he shook, till down they came, and drew   1650
The whole roof after them with burst of thunder
Upon the heads of all who sat beneath,

1619 cataphracts] soldiers in full armour; Milton took this sense of the word
        directly from Latin *cataphractus*, Greek κατάφρακτος, 'clad in full armour'.
1647–8] Cf. *PL* I 230–7n.

Lords, ladies, captains, counsellors, or priests,
Their choice nobility and flower, not only
Of this, but each Philistian city round,   1655
Met from all parts to solemnize this feast.
Samson, with these immixed, inevitably
Pulled down the same destruction on himself;
The vulgar only scaped, who stood without.
    Chor. O dearly bought revenge, yet glorious!   1660
Living or dying thou hast fulfilled
The work for which thou wast foretold
To Israel, and now liest victorious
Among thy slain self-killed,
Not willingly, but tangled in the fold   1665
Of dire Necessity, whose law in death conjoined
Thee with thy slaughtered foes, in number more
Than all thy life had slain before.
    Semichor. While their hearts were jocund and sublime,
Drunk with idolatry, drunk with wine   1670
And fat regorged of bulls and goats,
Chanting their idol, and preferring
Before our living Dread, who dwells
In Silo, his bright sanctuary,
Among them he a spirit of frenzy sent,   1675
Who hurt their minds,
And urged them on with mad desire
To call in haste for their destroyer;
They, only set on sport and play,
Unweetingly importuned   1680
Their own destruction to come speedy upon them.
So fond are mortal men,
Fallen into wrath divine,
As their own ruin on themselves to invite,
Insensate left, or to sense reprobate,   1685
And with blindness internal struck.
    Semichor. But he, though blind of sight,
Despised, and thought extinguished quite,
With inward eyes illuminated,
His fiery virtue roused   1690

1659 vulgar] the common people (Latin *vulgus*).
1671 fat] The Mosaic law forbade the eating of animal fat (Lev. iii. 17).
1674] Shiloh (Silo) was the site of the principal Jewish sanctuary at the time of
    the Judges (Judges xviii. 31); 'bright' probably alludes to the presence of
    the *Shekinah*, the glory of God dwelling among men (see John i. 14 for a
    probable N.T. expression of the idea).
1685 sense reprobate] Rom. i. 28.

From under ashes into sudden flame,
And as an evening dragon came,
Assailant on the perched roosts
And nests in order ranged
Of tame villatic fowl; but as an eagle   1695
His cloudless thunder bolted on their heads.
So Virtue, given for lost,
Depressed and overthrown, as seemed,
Like that self-begotten bird,
In the Arabian woods embossed,   1700
That no second knows nor third,
And lay erewhile a holocaust,
From out her ashy womb now teemed,
Revives, reflourishes, then vigorous most
When most unactive deemed;   1705
And, though her body die, her fame survives,
A secular bird, ages of lives.
        Man. Come, come; no time for lamentation now,
Nor much more cause: Samson hath quit himself
Like Samson, and heroicly hath finished   1710
A life heroic, on his enemies
Fully revenged – hath left them years of mourning
And lamentation to the sons of Caphtor
Through all Philistian bounds; to Israel
Honour hath left and freedom, let but them   1715
Find courage to lay hold on this occasion;
To himself and father's house eternal fame;
And, which is best and happiest yet, all this
With God not parted from him, as was feared,
But favouring and assisting to the end.   1720
Nothing is here for tears, nothing to wail
Or knock the breast, no weakness, no contempt
Dispraise, or blame, nothing but well and fair,
And what may quiet us in a death so noble.
Let us go find the body where it lies   1725
Soaked in his enemies' blood, and from the stream
With lavers pure, and cleansing herbs, wash off
The clotted gore. I, with what speed the while

1692 dragon] a huge serpent or snake (cf. *PL* X 529 and Rev. xii. 9).
1695 villatic] used in the sense of Latin *villaticus*, belonging to a *villa*, i.e. a
    country house or farm.
1699–707] Cf. *PL* V 272–4n. 'Embossed' is used of a hunted animal which has
    taken shelter in a wood; 'secular' means 'living for an age'.
1713 Caphtor] See l. 380n.
1727 lavers] water-jugs or basins.

(Gaza is not in plight to say us nay)
Will send for all my kindred, all my friends,   1730
To fetch him hence, and solemnly attend,
With silent obsequy and funeral train,
Home to his father's house; there will I build him
A monument, and plant it round with shade
Of laurel ever green and branching palm,   1735
With all his trophies hung, and acts enrolled
In copious legend, or sweet lyric song;
Thither shall all the valiant youth resort,
And from his memory inflame their breasts
To matchless valour and adventures high;   1740
The virgins also shall, on feastful days,
Visit his tomb with flowers, only bewailing
His lot unfortunate in nuptial choice,
From whence captivity and loss of eyes.
    Chor. All is best, though we oft doubt   1745
What the unsearchable dispose
Of highest Wisdom brings about,
And ever best found in the close.
Oft he seems to hide his face,
But unexpectedly returns,   1750
And to his faithful champion hath in place
Bore witness gloriously; whence Gaza mourns,
And all that band them to resist
His uncontrollable intent;
His servants he, with new acquist   1755
Of true experience from this great event,
With peace and consolation hath dismissed,
And calm of mind, all passion spent.

1745–8] Cf. the final chorus used by Euripides in *Alcestis, Andromache, Bacchae*,
    and *Helena*.
1749] Psalms xxvii. 9, xxx. 7, civ. 29.
1751 in place] in presence, at hand.
1755 acquist] acquisition.

OF EDUCATION. TO MASTER
SAMUEL HARTLIB

MASTER HARTLIB,[1]

I am long since persuaded that to say and do aught worth memory and imitation, no purpose or respect should sooner move us than simply the love of God and of mankind. Nevertheless, to write now the reforming of education, though it be one of the greatest and noblest designs that can be thought on, and for the want whereof this nation perishes, I had not yet at this time been induced but by your earnest entreaties and serious conjurements; as having my mind diverted for the present in the pursuance of some other assertions, the knowledge and the use of which cannot but be a great furtherance both to the enlargement of truth and honest living with much more peace.

Nor should the laws of any private friendship have prevailed with me to divide thus or transpose my former thoughts; but that I see those aims, those actions which have won you with me the esteem of a person sent hither by some good providence from a far country to be the occasion and incitement of great good to this island, and, as I hear, you have obtained the same repute with men of most approved wisdom and some of the highest authority among us; not to mention the learned correspondence which you hold in foreign parts, and the extraordinary pains and diligence which you have used in this matter both here and beyond the seas, either by the definite will of God so ruling, or the peculiar sway of nature, which also is God's working.

Neither can I think that, so reputed and so valued as you are, you would, to the forfeit of your own discerning ability, impose upon me an unfit and over-ponderous argument; but that the satisfaction, which you profess to have received from those incidental discourses which we have wandered into, hath pressed and almost constrained you into a persuasion, that what you require from me in this point I neither ought nor can in conscience defer beyond this time, both of so much need at once, and so much opportunity to try what God hath determined.

I will not resist, therefore, whatever it is either of divine or human obligement that you lay upon me; but will forthwith set down in writing, as you request me, that voluntary idea, which hath long in silence presented itself to me, of a better education, in extent and comprehension far more large, and yet of time far shorter and of attainment far more certain, than hath been yet in practice. Brief I shall endeavour to be; for that which I have to say assuredly this nation hath extreme need should be done sooner than spoken. To tell you, therefore, that I have benefited herein among old renowned authors I shall spare; and to search what many modern Januas and

---

1 Hartlib] See Introduction p. xxii.

Didactics[1] more than ever I shall read have projected, my inclination leads me not. But if you can accept of these few observations which have flowered off, and are, as it were, the burnishing of many contemplative years altogether spent in the search of religious and civil knowledge, and such as pleased you so well in the relating, I here give you them to dispose of.

The end, then, of learning is, to repair the ruins of our first parents by regaining to know God aright, and out of that knowledge to love him, to imitate him, to be like him, as we may the nearest, by possessing our souls of true virtue, which, being united to the heavenly grace of faith, makes up the highest perfection. But because our understanding cannot in this body found itself but on sensible things, nor arrive so clearly to the knowledge of God and things invisible as by orderly conning over the visible and inferior creature, the same method is necessarily to be followed in all discreet teaching.

And seeing every nation affords not experience and tradition enough for all kind of learning, therefore we are chiefly taught the languages of those people who have at any time been most industrious after wisdom; so that language is but the instrument conveying to us things useful to be known. And though a linguist should pride himself to have all the tongues that Babel cleft the world into, yet if he have not studied the solid things in them as well as the words and lexicons, he were nothing so much to be esteemed a learned man as any yeoman or tradesman competently wise in his mother-dialect only.

Hence appear the many mistakes which have made learning generally so unpleasing and so unsuccessful. First, we do amiss to spend seven or eight years merely in scraping together so much miserable Latin and Greek as might be learned otherwise easily and delightfully in one year. And that which casts our proficiency therein so much behind is our time lost in too oft idle vacancies given both to schools and universities; partly in a preposterous[2] exaction, forcing the empty wits of children to compose themes, verses, and orations, which are the acts of ripest judgement, and the final work of a head filled, by long reading and observing, with elegant maxims and copious invention.

These are not matters to be wrung from poor striplings, like blood out of the nose, or the plucking of untimely fruit; besides the ill habit which they get of wretched barbarizing against the Latin and Greek idiom with their untutored Anglicisms, odious to be read, yet not to be avoided without a well-continued and judicious conversing among pure authors, digested, which they scarce taste. Whereas, if after some preparatory grounds of speech by their certain forms got into memory they were led to the praxis[3] hereof in some chosen short book lessoned thoroughly to them, they might then forthwith proceed to learn the substance of good things and arts in due order, which would bring the

---

1 Januas and Didactics] alludes to two books by the Moravian writer on education, Johann Amos Comenius: *Janua Linguarum Reserata* (1631) and *Didactica Magna*. In 1644 the *Didactica* existed only as an unpublished manuscript in Czech, but Hartlib had published abstracts in Latin (1637) and English (1642).
2 preposterous] used in the Latinate sense of 'reversing first and last'.
3 praxis] practice.

whole language quickly into their power. This I take to be the most rational and most profitable way of learning languages, and whereby we may best hope to give account to God of our youth spent herein.

And for the usual method of teaching arts, I deem it to be an old error of universities, not yet well recovered from the scholastic[1] grossness of barbarous ages, that, instead of beginning with arts most easy (and those be such as are most obvious to the sense), they present their young unmatriculated novices at first coming with the most intellective abstractions of logic and metaphysics; so that they, having but newly left those grammatic flats and shallows were they stuck unreasonably to learn a few words with lamentable construction, and now on the sudden transported under another climate,[2] to be tossed and turmoiled with their unballasted wits in fathomless and unquiet deeps of controversy, do, for the most part, grow into hatred and contempt of learning, mocked and deluded all this while with ragged notions and babblements, while they expected worthy and delightful knowledge; till poverty or youthful years call them importunately their several ways, and hasten them, with the sway of friends, either to an ambitious and mercenary, or ignorantly zealous divinity: some allured to the trade of law, grounding their purposes not on the prudent and heavenly contemplation of justice and equity, which was never taught them, but on the promising and pleasing thoughts of litigious terms,[3] fat contentions, and flowing fees. Others betake them to state affairs with souls so unprincipled in virtue and true generous breeding, that flattery, and court shifts,[4] and tyrannous aphorisms appear to them the highest points of wisdom, instilling their barren hearts with a conscientious slavery, if, as I rather think, it be not feigned. Others, lastly, of a more delicious[5] and airy spirit, retire themselves, knowing no better, to the enjoyments of ease and luxury, living out their days in feast and jollity; which, indeed, is the wisest and safest course of all these, unless they were with more integrity undertaken. And these are the errors, and these are the fruits of mis-spending our prime youth at the schools and universities, as we do, either in learning mere words, or such things chiefly as were better unlearnt.

I shall detain you no longer in the demonstration of what we should not do, but straight conduct you to a hillside, where I will point you out the right path of a virtuous and noble education; laborious indeed at the first ascent, but else so smooth, so green, so full of goodly prospect and melodious sounds on every side, that the harp of Orpheus[6] was not more charming. I doubt not but ye shall have more ado to drive our dullest and laziest youth, our stocks and stubs,[7] from

1 scholastic] a contemptuous reference to the scholarly traditions of medieval universities.
2 climate] latitude.
3 terms] periods during which courts of law are in session.
4 court shifts] the intrigues of the royal court.
5 delicious] addicted to sensuous indulgence.
6 Orpheus] mythical Greek singer, associated with learning and culture.
7 stocks and stubs] the stumps and the stubs of broken branches of trees, here abusively applied to students.

the infinite desire of such a happy nurture, than we have now to haul and drag our choicest and hopefullest wits to that asinine feast of sowthistles[1] and brambles which is commonly set before them as all the food and entertainment of their tenderest and most docible[2] age. I call, therefore, a complete and generous[3] education, that which fits a man to perform justly, skilfully, and magnanimously[4] all the offices, both private and public, of peace and war. And how all this may be done between twelve and one-and-twenty, less time than is now bestowed in pure trifling at grammar and sophistry, is to be thus ordered:

First, to find out a spacious house and ground about it fit for an academy, and big enough to lodge one hundred and fifty persons, whereof twenty or thereabout may be attendants, all under the government of one who shall be thought of desert sufficient, and ability either to do all, or wisely to direct and oversee it done. This place should be at once both school and university, not needing a remove to any other house of scholarship, except it be some peculiar college of law or physic,[5] where they mean to be practitioners; but as for those general studies which take up all our time from Lily[6] to the commencing,[7] as they term it, master of art, it should be absolute. After this pattern, as many edifices may be converted to this use as shall be needful in every city throughout this land, which would tend much to the increase of learning and civility[8] everywhere. This number, less or more, thus collected, to the convenience of a foot-company[9] or interchangeably two troops of cavalry, should divide their day's work into three parts as it lies orderly – their studies, their exercise, and their diet.

For their studies: first, they should begin with the chief and necessary rules of some good grammar, either that now used, or any better; and while this is doing, their speech is to be fashioned to a distinct and clear pronunciation, as near as may be to the Italian, especially in the vowels. For we Englishmen, being far northerly, do not open our mouths in the cold air wide enough to grace a southern tongue, but are observed by all other nations to speak exceeding close and inward; so that to smatter Latin with an English mouth is as ill hearing as law French.[10]

1 sowthistles] European weeds with thistle-like leaves.
2 docible] teachable.
3 generous] appropriate to those of high birth.
4 magnanimously] See *PL* VII 511n.
5 physic] medicine.
6 Lily] William Lily, high master of St Paul's School from 1512 to 1522, had contributed to a Latin grammar book which was popularly known as *Lily's Grammar*; it was Milton's textbook when he was a pupil at St Paul's.
7 commencing] the Cambridge term for the taking of a university degree.
8 civility] good citizenship.
9 foot] infantry.
10 law French] Anglo-Norman French had been the language of the English legal system until the sixteenth century; it was rare by 1600 and was to be abolished by Cromwell in 1650 and restored at the Restoration. Legal texts quote the notorious 'fuit assault per prisoner la condemne pur felony que puis son condemnation ject un brickbat a le dit justice que narrowly mist'.

Next, to make them expert in the usefullest points of grammar, and withal to season them and win them early to the love of virtue and true labour, ere any flattering seducement or vain principle seize them wandering, some easy and delightful book of education should be read to them, whereof the Greeks have store, as Cebes,[1] Plutarch,[2] and other Socratic discourses;[3] but in Latin we have none of classic authority extant, except the two or three first books of Quintilian[4] and some select pieces elsewhere.

But here the main skill and groundwork will be to temper them[5] such lectures and explanations upon every opportunity, as may lead and draw them in willing obedience, inflamed with the study of[6] learning and the admiration of virtue, stirred up with high hopes of living to be brave men and worthy patriots, dear to God and famous to all ages: that they may despise and scorn all their childish and ill-taught qualities, to delight in manly and liberal[7] exercises; which he who hath the art and proper eloquence to catch them with, what with mild and effectual persuasions, and what with the intimation of some fear, if need be, but chiefly by his own example, might in a short space gain them to an incredible diligence and courage, infusing into their young breasts such an ingenuous and noble ardour as would not fail to make many of them renowned and matchless men.

At the same time, some other hour of the day might be taught them the rules of arithmetic, and, soon after, the elements of geometry, even playing, as the old manner[8] was. After evening repast till bed-time their thoughts would be best taken up in the easy grounds of religion and the story of Scripture.

The next step would be to the authors of agriculture, Cato,[9] Varro,[10] and Columella,[11] for the matter is most easy; and if the language is difficult, so much the better; it is not a difficulty above their years.

---

1 Cebes] the Πίναξ ('Table') attributed (incorrectly) to Cebes of Thebes (a pupil of Socrates); the author argues that true education extends beyond erudition to encompass development of character. The 'Table' had been read in Greek in English schools in the sixteenth century, but Milton seems to assume that at this stage, Greek authors will be read in Latin translation.

2 Plutarch] The Περὶ παιδῶν ἀγωγῆς ('On the Education of Children'), erroneously attributed to Plutarch, was widely influential in Renaissance Europe.

3 other ... discourses] books in the form of dialogues, such as Plato's *Republic*.

4 Quintilian] Quintilian's *Institutio Oratoria* devotes twelve books to the training of the orator: Book I discusses childhood education; Book II, which contains the famous chapter 'On the Good Teacher', discusses the nature and uses of rhetoric; Book III is an account of the origins and parts of rhetoric.

5 temper them] adapt to their abilities.

6 study of] used in the Latinate sense of 'desire for'; cf. *PL* I 107.

7 liberal] appropriate to a gentleman.

8 old manner] Plato recommended the use of play to teach arithmetic and geometry to children (*Laws* VII 819b–20d).

9 Cato] *De Agri Cultura*, by Cato the Censor, written c. 160 BC; see *Areopagitica* p. 581, n.1.

10 Varro] *Rerum Rusticarum*, by Marcus Terentius Varro, written c. 37 BC.

11 Columella] *De Re Rustica*, by Lucius Junius Columella, written AD 60–5.

And here will be an occasion of inciting and enabling them hereafter to improve the tillage of their country, to recover the bad soil, and to remedy the waste that is made of good; for this was one of Hercules'[1] praises.

Ere half these authors be read (which will soon be with plying hard and daily) they cannot choose but be masters of an ordinary prose: so that it will be then seasonable for them to learn in any modern author the use of the globes and all the maps, first with the old names and then with the new; or they might then be capable to read any compendious method of natural philosophy; and, at the same time, might be entering into the Greek tongue, after the same manner as was before prescribed for the Latin; whereby the difficulties of grammar being soon overcome, all the historical[2] physiology of Aristotle[3] and Theophrastus[4] are open before them and, as I may say, under contribution. The like access will be to Vitruvius,[5] to Seneca's *Natural Questions*,[6] to Mela,[7] Celsus,[8] Pliny,[9] or Solinus.[10] And having thus past the principles of arithmetic, geometry, astronomy, and geography, with a general compact of physics,[11] they may descend[12] in mathematics to the instrumental[13] science of trigonometry, and from

---

1 Hercules] According to Pliny (XVII 50) the use of manure to enrich soil had its origins in the cleaning of the Augean stables by Hercules.

2 historical] used in the classical sense of 'systematic'.

3 Aristotle] refers primarily to *Historia Animalium* (an account of facts about animals), *De Partibus Animalium* ('On the Causes of the Facts about Animals') *De Animalium Generatione* ('On the Generation of Animals'), and the spurious *De Plantis* ('On Plants').

4 Theophrastus] pupil and successor of Aristotle, here mentioned as the author of Περὶ φυτῶν ἱστορίας('Plant Researches', a description and taxonomy of plants) and Περὶ φυτῶν αἰτιῶν ('The Aetiology of Plants', a study of plant physiology).

5 Vitruvius] *De Architectura*, the treatise on architecture and engineering by Marcus Vitruvius Pollio (who practised architecture early in the reign of Augustus), had been rediscovered in the fifteenth century and had quickly become the standard text for the architects of Renaissance Europe.

6 *Natural Questions*] *Naturales Quaestiones* is a popular manual of meteorology and astronomy, written by Seneca after his retirement in AD 162.

7 Mela] *De Situ Orbis*, a Latin treatise which surveys the geography of the known world, was written by Pomponius Mela c. AD 43.

8 Celsus] Early in the first century AD Aulus Cornelius Celsus wrote an encyclopaedia, of which only the eight books on medicine (*De Medicina*) survive in their entirety; the style of Celsus was an important model for Renaissance writing in Latin.

9 Pliny] Pliny the Elder's *Naturalis Historia* (written c. AD 77) is a vast compendium of cosmology, biology (and its medical applications) and mineralogy (and its applications to medicine, art and architecture).

10 Solinus] The *Collectanea Rerum Memorabilium*, written by Gaius Julius Solinus c. AD 200, is a geographical survey of the known world, drawn almost entirely (without acknowledgement) from Pliny and Mela.

11 physics] science.

12 descend] proceed from general principles to specific applications.

13 instrumental] useful.

thence to fortification, architecture, enginery,[1] or navigation. And in natural philosophy they may proceed leisurely from the history of meteors,[2] minerals, plants, and living creatures, as far as anatomy.

Then also in course might be read to them out of some not tedious writer the institution of physic;[3] that they may know the tempers, the humours, the seasons,[4] and how to manage a crudity;[5] which he who can wisely and timely do is not only a great physician to himself and to his friends, but also may at some time or other save an army by this frugal and expenseless means only, and not let the healthy and stout bodies of young men rot away under him for want of this discipline, which is a great pity, and no less a shame to the commander.

To set forward all these proceedings in nature and mathematics, what hinders but that they may procure, as oft as shall be needful, the helpful experiences of hunters, fowlers, fishermen, shepherds, gardeners, apothecaries; and in other sciences, architects, engineers, mariners, anatomists, who, doubtless, would be ready, some for reward and some to favour such a hopeful seminary. And this would give them such a real tincture of natural knowledge[6] as they shall never forget, but daily augment with delight. Then also those poets which are now counted most hard will be both facile and pleasant. Orpheus,[7] Hesiod,[8] Theocritus,[9] Aratus,[10] Nicander,[11]

---

1 enginery] the art of constructing military equipment.
2 history of meteors] systematic study of atmospheric phenomena; the term 'meteors' included airy meteors (winds), aqueous meteors (precipitation), luminous meteors (rainbows, the aurora etc.) and igneous meteors (lightning, shooting stars etc.).
3 institution of physic] elementary instruction in medicine.
4 tempers ... seasons] In ancient medicine each of the four principal bodily fluids ('cardinal humours') was associated with a temperament ('temper'). Thus blood was associated with sanguinity, phlegm (mucus) with a phlegmatic temperament, yellow bile (secreted by the liver) with choler (an irascible and passionate temperament), and black bile (an imaginary fluid) with melancholy. The balance of humours was thought to vary with the seasons.
5 crudity] undigested matter in the stomach.
6 natural knowledge] knowledge of nature.
7 Orpheus] The only scientific poem attributed to the mythical Orpheus was *Lithica* (on precious stones).
8 Hesiod] As the *Theogony* is not a scientific work, Milton is presumably referring to Hesiod's *Works and Days*, which contains practical instruction on agriculture, seafaring and social and religious conduct.
9 Theocritus] The pastoral *Idylls* of Theocritus, written in Greek in the third century BC, describe the life and landscape of ancient rural Italy.
10 ⁰Aratus] refers to the *Phaenomena* (on astronomy) of Aratus of Soli, a Greek poet of the third century BC, and to his *Diosemeia* (on weather signs), which was in Milton's time considered to be a separate poem by the same author, and is now thought to be part of the same poem.
11 Nicander] the *Theriaca* (on venomous animals and the remedies for their bites) and the *Alexipharmaca* (on poisons and their antidotes) of Nicander of Colophon, a Greek poet of the second century BC.

Oppian,[1] Dionysius;[2] and, in Latin, Lucretius,[3] Manilius,[4] and the rural part of Virgil.[5]

By this time years and good general precepts will have furnished them more distinctly with that act of reason which in ethics is called proairesis,[6] that they may with some judgement contemplate upon moral good and evil. Then will be required a special reinforcement of constant and sound indoctrinating to set them right and firm, instructing them more amply in the knowledge of virtue and the hatred of vice, while their young and pliant affections are led through all the moral works of Plato,[7] Xenophon,[8] Cicero,[9] Plutarch,[10] Laertius,[11] and those Locrian remnants;[12] but still to be reduced[13] in their nightward studies, wherewith they close the day's work, under

---

1 Oppian] refers to the *Cynegatica* (on hunting) of Oppian of Cilicia, a Greek poet of the second century AD, and to the *Halieutica* (on fishing), which was in Milton's time attributed to the same poet, but is now thought to be the work of Oppian of Syria (third century AD).

2 Dionysius] the Περιήγησις τῆς οἰκουμένης ('A Guide to the Inhabited World'), a geographical survey by the Greek poet Dionysius 'Periegetes', who probably wrote in the second century AD.

3 Lucretius] the *De Natura Rerum* by Titus Lucretius Carus, a poet and philosopher of the first century BC; Lucretius' poem sets out an atomistic theory of the cosmos (based on Epicurus) with a view to destroying superstitious beliefs about intervention in the world by the gods; cf. *Areopagitica* p. 581.

4 Manilius] the *Astronomica* (on astrology) of Marcus Manilius, who wrote the poem in the early years of the first century AD.

5 rural ... Virgil] the *Eclogues* and *Georgics*.

6 proairesis] a Greek term for moral choice; 'ethics' may refer specifically to Aristotle's *Nichomachean Ethics*, in which 'proairesis' is deemed to be the defining characteristic of moral action.

7 Plato] a vague reference, possibly referring to the early dialogues of Plato, which explore the nature of virtue.

8 Xenophon] probably the recollections of Socrates in *Apology for Socrates, Memorabilia* and *Symposium* and the accounts of Cyrus the elder in *Cyropaedia* and *Anabasis* written by Plato's contemporary Xenophon, the Greek general, historian and philosopher.

9 Cicero] probably *De Officiis* (on conduct) and *De Finibus* (on goodness and morality), both written in 45 and 44 BC.

10 Plutarch] Plutarch's short treatises on moral philosophy, such as *De Virtute Morali* and *De Profectibus in Virtute*.

11 Laertius] Περὶ βίον δογμάτων καὶ ἀποφθεγμάτων τῶν ἐν φιλοσοφία εὐδοκιμησάντων ('On the Lives and Doctrines of Famous Philosophers from Thales to Epicurus') by Diogenes Laertius, a Greek author of the third century AD.

12 Locrian remnants] Περὶ γυχᾶ κόσμω καὶ φύσιος ('On the Soul of the World and its Nature'), a treatise attributed to Timaeus of Locri (the principal speaker in Plato's *Timaeus*) but in fact a paraphrase of *Timaeus* written in the first century AD.

13 reduced] led back.

the determinate sentence of David[1] or Solomon,[2] or the evangels[3] and apostolic Scriptures.[4]

Being perfect in the knowledge of personal duty, they may then begin the study of economics.[5] And either now or before this they may have easily learned at any odd hour the Italian tongue. And soon after, but with wariness and good antidote, it would be wholesome enough to let them taste some choice comedies, Greek, Latin, or Italian; those tragedies also that treat of household matters, as *Trachiniae, Alcestis*,[6] and the like.

The next move must be to the study of politics; to know the beginning, end, and reasons of political societies, that they may not, in a dangerous fit of the commonwealth, be such poor shaken uncertain reeds, of such a tottering conscience as many of our great councillors have lately shown themselves, but steadfast pillars of the state. After this they are to dive into the grounds of law and legal justice, delivered first and with best warrant by Moses,[7] and, as far as human prudence can be trusted, in those extolled remains[8] of Grecian Law-givers, Lycurgus,[9] Solon,[10] Zaleucus,[11] Charondas;[12] and thence to all the Roman edicts[13] and tables,[14] with their Justinian;[15] and so down

1 David] the Psalms, traditionally attributed to King David.

2 Solomon] Proverbs, Canticles, Ecclesiastes and (possibly) the Wisdom of Solomon, all of which were attributed to King Solomon.

3 evangels] the canonical gospels of Matthew, Mark, Luke and John.

4 apostolic Scriptures] the canonical Acts and Epistles and the Book of Revelation.

5 economics] household management.

6 *Trachiniae, Alcestis*] Sophocles' *Trachiniae* and Euripides' *Alcestis* both dramatize the suffering and sacrifice of devoted wives.

7 Moses] refers to the Torah, i.e. the legislation contained in the Pentateuch, which was then attributed to Moses, the 'Lawgiver' of ancient Israel.

8 remains] As the Greek codes of law had not survived, Milton refers to the accounts in later classical writers, chiefly Plutarch, Herodotus and Aristotle (*Politics*).

9 Lycurgus] architect of the Spartan constitution in the eighth century BC (possibly mythical).

10 Solon] Athenian statesman who comprehensively reformed the constitution of Athens early in the sixth century BC; the 'remains' do not include the central modern source, Aristotle's account in Ἀθηναίων πολιτεία ('On the Constitution of Athens'), which was not recovered from the sands of Egypt until 1890.

11 Zaleucus] the Greek lawgiver (seventh century BC) of Locri, in southern Italy, compiler of the first written Greek code of law.

12 Charondas] the Greek lawgiver (sixth century BC) of Catana (now Catania), in Sicily.

13 edicts] refers both to imperial edicts and to the *Edictum Perpetuum*, a codification of the annual edicts of Roman magistrates compiled by the jurist Salvius Julianus in AD 130 on the instructions of the Emperor Hadrian.

14 tables] the Twelve Tables were the first Roman code of law, said to have been framed in 451-450 BC; fragments are quoted by later authors. Cf. *Areopagitica* p. 580.

15 Justinian] the *Institutes, Digest, Code* and '*Novels*', compilations of law prepared at the command of the Emperor Justinian (AD 483-565) and later collectively known as the *Corpus Juris Civilis*; this collection is the principal source of earlier Roman law.

to the Saxon and common laws[1] of England and the statutes.[2].

Sundays also and every evening may now be understandingly spent in the highest matters of theology and church history, ancient and modern: and ere this time at a set hour the Hebrew tongue might have been gained, that the Scriptures may be now read in their own original; whereto it would be no impossibility to add the Chaldee[3] and the Syrian[4] dialect.

When all these employments are well conquered, then will the choice histories,[5] heroic poems,[6] and Attic tragedies[7] of stateliest and most regal argument, with all the famous political orations, offer themselves; which, if they were not only read, but some of them got by memory, and solemnly pronounced with right accent and grace, as might be taught, would endue them even with the spirit and vigour of Demosthenes or Cicero,[8] Euripides or Sophocles.

And now, lastly, will be the time to read with them those organic[9] arts which enable men to discourse and write perspicuously, elegantly, and according to the fitted style of lofty, mean[10] or lowly. Logic, therefore, so much as is useful, is to be referred to this due place, with all her well-couched heads and topics, until it be time to open her contracted palm into a graceful and ornate rhetoric taught out of the rule of Plato,[11] Aristotle,[12] Phalereus,[13] Cicero,[14]

---

1 Saxon ... laws] may refer to the *Lex Saxonum* (c. 800), a collection of ancient Saxon law; alternatively, Milton may be distinguishing between the Anglo-Saxon law of England (which had many local variations) and the law common to the whole kingdom that resulted from the centralized system of justice that developed in the twelfth century; the 'common law' of England is also distinguished from the systems of civil law (based on Roman law) in Europe.

2 statutes] probably an abridgement such as Edmund Wingate's *Exact Abridgement of All Statutes ... from Magna Carta till 1641* (1641).

3 Chaldee] Aramaic, the language of Palestine at the time of Jesus, of a few passages in the Old Testament, and of the Targumim (translations of the Old Testament made when Hebrew ceased to be the language of the Jews).

4 Syrian] Syriac, a branch of Aramaic written in a different alphabet and the language of important translations of the Bible (notably the *Peshitta*) and of Greek patristic works, many of which survive only in Syriac.

5 histories] probably Herodotus and Thucydides (in Greek) and Sallust and Livy (in Latin).

6 heroic poems] *Iliad, Odyssey* and *Aeneid*.

7 Attic tragedies] the tragedies of ancient Athens by Aeschylus, Sophocles and Euripides.

8 Demosthenes or Cicero] the orations of the Athenian orator Demosthenes (384-322 BC), and of Cicero (106-43 BC), the Roman politician and rhetorician.

9 organic] serving as a means to an end.

10 mean] middle.

11 Plato] *Gorgias* and *Phaedrus*.

12 Aristotle] *Ars Rhetorica* ('On the Art of Oratory').

13 Phalereus] Περι ἑρμηνείας ('On Style'), which was in Milton's time attributed to the Athenian orator Demetrius Phalereus (fourth century BC) but is now thought to be by a later author.

14 Cicero] refers to *De Oratore, Brutus* and *Orator* and also to the *Rhetorica ad Herennium*, which Milton thought the work of Cicero.

Hermogenes,[1] Longinus.[2]

To which poetry would be made subsequent, or, indeed, rather precedent, as being less subtle[3] and fine, but more simple, sensuous, and passionate; I mean not here the prosody of a verse which they could not but have hit on before among the rudiments of grammar, but that sublime art which in Aristotle's *Poetics*,[4] in Horace,[5] and the Italian commentaries of Castelvetro,[6] Tasso,[7] Mazzoni,[8] and others, teaches what the laws are of a true epic poem, what of a dramatic, what of a lyric, what decorum is, which is the grand masterpiece to observe. This would make them soon perceive what despicable creatures our common rhymers and playwrights be; and show them what religious, what glorious and magnificent use might be made of poetry, both in divine and human things.

From hence, and not till now, will be the right season of forming them to be able writers and composers in every excellent matter, when they shall be thus fraught with an universal insight into things; or whether they be to speak in parliament or council, honour and attention would be waiting on their lips. There would then appear in pulpits other visages, other gestures, and stuff otherwise wrought, than what we now sit under, ofttimes to as great a trial of our patience as any other that they preach to us.

These are the studies wherein our noble and our gentle[9] youth ought to bestow their time in a disciplinary way from twelve to one-and-twenty, unless they rely more upon their ancestors dead than upon themselves living. In which methodical course it so is supposed they must proceed by the steady pace of learning onward, as at convenient times for memory's sake to retire back into the middle ward,[10] and sometimes into the rear, of what they have been taught, until they

1 Hermogenes] refers to a series of textbooks on rhetoric by Hermogenes of Tarsus (second century AD), the most significant of which is Περὶ ἰδεῶν ('On Style'); these texts were widely read in the Renaissance.
2 Longinus] Περὶ ὕψους (traditionally translated as 'On the Sublime'), which in Milton's time was attributed to Cassius Longinus, the Athenian rhetorician (AD 213-73), but is now thought to be a work of the first century AD.
3 subtle] used with reference to the plain style, which Cicero and Quintilian call *subtile* ('fine' or 'thin') and Milton calls 'lowly'.
4 *Poetics*] The fragment of Aristotle's *Poetics* that survives is mainly concerned with tragedy, but also has sections on the nature of poetry and on epic.
5 Horace] the *Ars Poetica*, which deals largely with epic and drama.
6 Castelvetro] Ludovico Castelvetro's seminal and eccentric commentary on Aristotle's *Poetics* (1570) contains the first formulation of the three dramatic 'unities' (time, place and action).
7 Tasso] Torquato Tasso's *Apologia* (1585), *Discorsi dell'arte poetica* (written c. 1565, published 1587) and *Discorsi del poema eroico* (1594).
8 Mazzoni] The philosopher Giacomo Mazzoni championed Dante in *Discorso composto in difesa della comedia di Dante* (1572) and *Della difesa della comedia di Dante* (1587).
9 gentle] of a lower degree of rank than 'noble'.
10 middle ward] Armies in battle were divided into a fore ward, middle ward and rear ward.

have confirmed and solidly united the whole body of their perfected knowledge, like the last embattling of a Roman legion. Now will be worth the seeing what exercises and recreations may best agree and become those studies.

Their Exercise

The course of study hitherto briefly described is, what I can guess by reading, likest to those ancient and famous schools of Pythagoras,[1] Plato,[2] Isocrates,[3] Aristotle,[4] and such others, out of which were bred such a number of renowned philosophers, orators, historians, poets, and princes all over Greece, Italy, and Asia, besides the flourishing studies of Cyrene[5] and Alexandria.[6] But herein it shall exceed them, and supply a defect as great as that which Plato[7] noted in the commonwealth of Sparta. Whereas that city trained up their youth most for war, and these in their academies and Lyceum all for the gown,[8] this institution of breeding which I here delineate shall be equally good both for peace and war. Therefore, about an hour and a half ere they eat at noon should be allowed them for exercise, and due rest afterwards; but the time for this may be enlarged at pleasure, according as their rising in the morning shall be early. The exercise which I command first is the exact use of their weapon,[9] to guard, and to strike safely with edge or point. This will keep them healthy, nimble, strong, and well in breath; is also the likeliest means to make them grow large and tall, and to inspire them with a gallant and fearless courage; which, being tempered with seasonable lectures and precepts to make them of true fortitude and patience, will turn into a native and heroic valour, and make them hate the cowardice of doing wrong. They must be also practised in all the locks and grips of wrestling, wherein Englishmen are wont to excel, as need may often be in fight to tug, to grapple, and to close. And this, perhaps, will be enough wherein to prove and heat their single strength.

The interim of unsweating themselves regularly, and convenient

1 Pythagoras] The philosopher and mathematician Pythagoras founded a school at Croton (in Italy) c. 531 BC; it was revived in the fourth century at Tarentum.

2 Plato] Plato founded his Academy c. 385 BC in a wood sacred to the god Academus on the outskirts of Athens; it survived until AD 529.

3 Isocrates] The Athenian orator Isocrates opened a school on Chios c. 395 BC, and another in 392 BC in Athens, near the Lyceum, where he taught until at least 339 BC, when he was 97 years old.

4 Aristotle] founded his 'Peripatetic' school (see *PR* IV 279–80n.) in the Lyceum, a park north-east of Athens, in 335 BC.

5 Cyrene] Aristippus founded an Epicurean school in Cyrene (now Shahhat, in Libya); see *PR* IV 279–80n and *Areopatigica* p. 579.

6 Alexandria] The great library founded in Alexandria by Ptolemy I early in the third century BC was the centre of literature in the Hellenistic world.

7 Plato] *Laws* I 626–30, 634–6.

8 gown] the toga, the outer garment of a Roman citizen in time of peace; see *Sonnet* XVII 3n.

9 weapon] sword.

rest before meat, may both with profit and delight be taken up in recreating and composing their travailed spirits with the solemn and divine harmonies of music heard or learned either whilst the skilful organist plies his grave and fancied[1] descant in lofty fugues, or the whole symphony with artful and unimaginable touches adorn and grace the well-studied chords of some choice composer; sometimes the lute or soft organ-stop, waiting on elegant voices either to religious, martial, or civil ditties,[2] which, if wise men and prophets be not extremely out, have a great power over dispositions and manners to smooth and make them gentle from rustic harshness and distempered[3] passions. The like also would not be unexpedient after meat, to assist and cherish nature in her first concoction,[4] and send their minds back to study in good tune and satisfaction.

Where having followed it under vigilant eyes until about two hours before supper, they are, by a sudden alarum or watchword, to be called out on their military motions, under sky or covert, according to the season, as was the Roman wont; first on foot, then, as their age permits, on horseback to all the art of cavalry; that having in sport, but with much exactness and daily muster, served out the rudiments of their soldiership in all the skill of embattling, marching, encamping, fortifying, besieging, and battering, with all the helps of ancient and modern strategems, tactics,[5] and warlike maxims, they may, as it were out of a long war, come forth renowned and perfect commanders in the service of their country.

They would not then, if they were trusted with fair and hopeful armies, suffer them for want of just and wise discipline to shed away from about them like sick feathers, though they be never so oft supplied; they would not suffer their empty and unrecruitable[6] colonels of twenty men in a company to quaff out or convey into secret hoards the wages of a delusive list and miserable remnant; yet in the meanwhile to be overmastered with a score or two of drunkards, the only soldiery left about them, or else to comply with all rapines and violences. No, certainly, if they knew aught of that knowledge which belongs to good men or good governors, they would not suffer these things.

But to return to our own institute. Besides these constant exercises at home, there is another opportunity of gaining experience to be won from pleasure itself abroad: in those vernal seasons of the year, when the air is calm and pleasant, it were an injury and sullenness against nature not to go out and see her riches and partake in her rejoicing with heaven and earth. I should not, therefore, be a persuader to

1 fancied] fanciful.
2 ditties] songs.
3 distempered] of unbalanced temperament (because of an imbalance in the humours).
4 first concoction] the first of the three stages of digestion.
5 stratagems, tactics] Ancient sources would include the *Strategemata* of Sextus Julius Frontinus (c. AD 30–104) and another by the Macedonian rhetorician Polyaenus (prepared for the Parthian War of 162 AD) and a Greek *Tactica* attributed (erroneously) to Aelian (Claudius Aelianus, c. AD 170–235).
6 unrecruitable] unable to secure recruits.

them of studying much then, after two or three years that they have well laid their grounds, but to ride out in companies with prudent and staid guides to all the quarters of the land, learning and observing all places of strength, all commodities of building and of soil for towns and tillage, harbours, and ports for trade. Sometimes taking sea as far as to our navy, to learn there also what they can in the practical knowledge of sailing and sea-fight.

These ways would try all their peculiar gifts of nature, and if there were any secret excellence among them, would fetch it out and give it fair opportunity to advance itself by, which could not but mightily redound to the good of this nation, and bring into fashion again those old admired virtues and excellences, with far more advantage now in this purity of Christian knowledge.

Nor shall we then need the monsieurs of Paris to take our hopeful youth into their slight and prodigal custodies, and send them over back again transformed into mimics, apes, and kickshaws.[1] But if they desire to see other countries at three or four and twenty years of age, not to learn principles, but to enlarge experience and make wise observation, they will by that time be such as shall deserve the regard and honour of all men where they pass, and the society and friendship of those in all places who are best and most eminent. And perhaps then other nations will be glad to visit us for their breeding, or else to imitate us in their own country.

Now, lastly, for their diet there cannot be much to say, save only that it would be best in the same house; for much time else would be lost abroad, and many ill habits got; and that it should be plain, healthful, and moderate, I suppose is out of controversy.

Thus, Mr Hartlib, you have a general view in writing, as your desire was, of that which at several times I had discoursed with you concerning the best and noblest way of education; not beginning, as some have done, from the cradle, which yet might be worth many considerations, if brevity had not been my scope. Many other circumstances also I could have mentioned; but this, to such as have the worth in them to make trial, for light and direction may be enough. Only I believe that this is not a bow for every man to shoot in[2] that counts himself a teacher, but will require sinews almost equal to those which Homer gave Ulysses.[3] Yet I am withal[4] persuaded that it may prove much more easy in the assay[5] than it now seems at distance, and much more illustrious: howbeit not more difficult than I imagine; and that imagination presents me with nothing but very happy and very possible according to best wishes, if God have so decreed, and this age have spirit and capacity enough to apprehend.

1 kickshaws] grotesque persons.
2 in] with.
3 Ulysses] In *Odyssey* XXI Penelope agrees to forsake the home of Odysseus (Ulysses) for any suitor who could string the great bow of Odysseus and shoot an arrow through 12 axes; the suitors all fail, and then the disguised Ulysses accomplishes the task while remaining seated, and then kills the suitors.
4 withal] nevertheless.
5 assay] implementation in order to test merit.

APPENDIX

Extract from 'The Life of Mr John Milton' (1694) by Milton's nephew
Edward Phillips

Soon after his return [from Italy], and visits paid to his father and
other friends, he took him a lodging in St Bride's Churchyard, at the
house of one Russell, a tailor, where he first undertook the education
and instruction of his sister's two sons, the younger whereof had been
wholly committed to his charge and care. And here, by the way, I
judge it not impertinent to mention the many authors both of the
Latin and Greek, which through his excellent judgement and way of
teaching, far above the pedantry of common public schools (where
such authors are scarce ever heard of), were run over within no greater
compass of time than from ten to fifteen or sixteen years of age. Of the
Latin, the four grand authors *De Re Rustica*, Cato, Verro, Columella[1]
and Palladius;[2] Cornelius Celsus,[3] an ancient physician of the Romans;
a great part of Pliny's[4] *Natural History*; Vitruvius[5] his *Architecture*;
Frontinus[6] his *Stratagems*; with the two egregious poets, Lucretius
and Manilius.[7] Of the Greek, Hesiod,[8] a poet equal with Homer;
Aratus[9] his *Phaenomena* and *Diosemeia*; Dionysius[10] *Afer De Situ
Orbis*; Oppian's[11] *Cynegetics* and *Halieutics*; Quintus Calaber[12] his
Poem of the Trojan War continued from Homer; Apollonius Rhodius[13]
his *Argonautics*; and in prose, Plutarch's[14] *Placita Philosophorum* and
Περὶ
Παιδῶν' Ἀγωγης; Geminus's[15] *Astronomy*; Xenophon's[16] *Cyri Institutio*

---

1 Cato ... Columella] See *Education* p. 560.
2 Palladius] Rutilius Taurus Aemilianus Palladius (fourth century AD), author
   of a poem on agriculture (*De Re Rustica*) largely based on Columella.
3 Celsus] See *Education* p. 561.
4 Pliny] See *Education* p. 561.
5 Vitruvius] See *Education* p. 561.
6 Frontinus] See *Education* p. 568, n.5.
7 Lucretius, Manilius] See *Education* p. 563.
8 Hesiod] See *Education* p. 562.
9 Aratus] See *Education* p. 562.
10 Dionysius] See *Education* p. 563.
11 Oppian] See *Education* p. 563.
12 Quintus Calaber] Quintus Smyrnaeus, author (fourth century AD) of a Greek
   continuation of the *Iliad* (the *Posthomerica*) found in Calabria (hence
   'Calaber').
13 Apollonius Rhodius] author (fourth century BC) of the *Argonautica*, the
   great Greek epic of the Alexandrian period.
14 Plutarch] See *Education* p. 560. The *Placito Philosophorum*, a compendium
   of Ionic and Stoic views on the phenomena of the universe and of life, is no
   longer attributed to Plutarch.
15 Geminus] author of Εἰσαγωγὴ εἰς τα φαινόμενα, an introduction to astronomy
   (c. 70 BC).
16 Xenophon] See *Education* p. 563.

and *Anabasis*; Aelian's[1] *Tactics*; and Polyaenus his *Warlike Stratagems*. Thus by teaching, he in some measure increased his own knowledge, having the reading of all these authors as it were by proxy; and all this might possibly have conduced to the preserving of his eyesight, had he not moreover been perpetually busied in his own laborious undertakings of the book or pen.

Nor did the time thus studiously employed in conquering the Greek and Latin tongues hinder the attaining of the chief oriental languages, *viz* the Hebrew, Chaldee and Syriac,[2] as far as to go through the *Pentateuch*, or Five Books of Moses, in Hebrew; to make a good entrance into the *Targum*, or Chaldee Paraphrase; and to understand several chapters of St Matthew in the Syriac Testament; besides an introduction into several arts and sciences by reading Urstisius[3] his *Arithmetic*, Ryff's[4] *Geometry*, Petiscus[5] his *Trigonometry*, Joannes de Sacro Bosco[6] *De Sphaera*; and into the Italian and French tongues, by reading in Giovan Villani's[7] *History of the Transactions between several petty States of Italy*; and in French a great part of Pierre d'Avity,[8] the famous geographer of France in his time. The Sunday's work[9] was, for the most part, the reading each day a chapter of the Greek Testament, and hearing his learned exposition upon the same.

1 Aelian, Polyaenus] See *Education* p. 568, n.5.
2 Hebrew ... Syriac] See *Education* p. 565.
3 Urstisius] *Elementa Arithmeticae* (1579), by Christianus Urstisius.
4 Ryff] *Quaestiones Geometricae* (1600), by Petrus Ryff.
5 Petiscus] *Trigonometria* (1595), by the German mathematician Bartholomaus Pitiscus, who coined the term 'trigonometry'.
6 Sacro Bosco] the Latin name of John Halifax of Holywood, the thirteenth-century author of the Ptolemaic treatise *Tractatus de Sphaera*.
7 Villani] Giovanni Villani (c. 1276–1348), author of a seminal chronicle on medieval Florence (*Croniche Fiorentine*).
8 Pierre d'Avity] *Les Etats, Empires et Principautés du Monde* (1614).
9 Sunday's work] See *Education* p. 565.

AREOPAGITICA;

A
SPEECH

OF

MR. *John Milton,*

For the Liberty of Vnlicenc'd
PRINTING,

To the Parlament of ENGLAND.

This is true Liberty when free born men
Having to advise the public may speak free,
Which he who can, and will, deserv's high praise,
Who neither can nor will, may hold his peace;
What can be juster in a State then this?
                          Euripid. Hicetid.

Areopagitica title-page] 'Areopagitica' is a Greek word meaning 'things pertaining to the Areopagus', the Council of Athens usually known as the *Boule*. Milton's title recalls the *Areopagiticus*, an oration written (but not delivered) by the Athenian orator Isocrates (436–338 BC). By the time of Isocrates the *Boule* had become a court, and Isocrates urged the members of the *Ecclesia* (see below, p. 577, n.3) to reassert the ancient right of the *Boule* to supervise all aspects of Athenian life.

Euripid. Hicetid.] Euripides' *Supplices* ('Hicetid[es]'); see p. 139.

AREOPAGITICA

A SPEECH FOR THE LIBERTY OF UNLICENSED PRINTING, TO THE PARLIAMENT OF ENGLAND
(1644)

They, who to states[1] and governors of the Commonwealth direct their speech, High Court of Parliament, or, wanting[2] such access in a private condition, write that which they foresee may advance the public good; I suppose them, as at the beginning of no mean endeavour, not a little altered[3] and moved inwardly in their minds: some with doubt of what will be the success,[4] others with fear of what will be the censure;[5] some with hope, others with confidence of[6] what they have to speak. And me perhaps each of these dispositions, as the subject[7] was whereon I entered, may have at other times variously affected; and likely might in these foremost expressions now also disclose which of them swayed most, but that the very attempt of this address thus made, and the thought of whom it hath recourse to, hath got the power within me to a passion, far more welcome than incidental to a preface.

Which though I stay not to confess, ere any ask, I shall be blameless, if it be no other than the joy and gratulation which it brings to all who wish and promote their country's liberty; whereof this whole discourse proposed will be a certain testimony, if not a trophy. For this is not the liberty which we can hope, that no grievance ever should arise in the Commonwealth – that let no man in this world expect; but when complaints are freely heard, deeply considered and speedily reformed, then is the utmost bound of civil liberty attained, that wise men look for. To which if I now manifest by the very sound of this which I shall utter, that we are already in good part arrived, and yet from such a steep disadvantage of tyranny and superstition grounded into our principles as was beyond the manhood of a Roman recovery, it will be attributed first, as is most due, to the strong assistance of God our deliverer, next to your faithful guidance and undaunted wisdom, Lords and Commons of England. Neither is it, in God's esteem, the diminution of his glory, when honourable things are spoken of good men and worthy magistrates; which if I now first[8]

---

1 states] rulers.
2 wanting] lacking.
3 altered] disturbed.
4 success] result (either good or bad).
5 censure] verdict, opinion.
5 of] based upon.
7 subject] Milton had already published eight prose works, of which two (the second edition of *Doctrine and Discipline of Divorce* and *Judgement of Martin Bucer*, both published earlier in 1644) had been addressed to Parliament.
8 if I now first] Milton had already praised the Long Parliament in *Apology for Smectymnuus* (1642) and *Doctrine and Discipline* (1643).

should begin to do, after so fair a progress of your laudable deeds, and such a long[1] obligement upon the whole realm to[2] your indefatigable virtues, I might be justly reckoned among the tardiest, and the unwillingest of them that praise ye.

Nevertheless there being three principal things, without which all praising is but courtship[3] and flattery: first, when that only is praised which is solidly worth praise; next, when greatest likelihoods are brought that such things are truly and really in those persons to whom they are ascribed; the other, when he who praises, by showing that such his actual persuasion is of whom he writes, can demonstrate that he flatters not; the former two of these I have heretofore endeavoured, rescuing the employment from him[4] who went about to impair your merits with a trivial and malignant encomium; the latter as belonging chiefly to mine own acquittal, that whom I so extolled I did not flatter, hath been reserved opportunely to this occasion.

For he who freely magnifies what hath been nobly done, and fears not to declare as freely what might be done better, gives ye the best covenant of his fidelity; and that his loyalest affection and his hope waits on your proceedings. His highest praising is not flattery, and his plainest advice is a kind of praising. For though I should affirm and hold by argument, that it would fare better with truth, with learning and the Commonwealth, if one of your published orders, which I should name, were called in; yet at the same time it could not but much redound to the lustre of your mild and equal government, whenas private persons are hereby animated to think ye better pleased with public advice, than other statists[5] have been delighted heretofore with public flattery. And men will then see what difference there is between the magnanimity of a triennial[6] Parliament, and that jealous haughtiness of prelates and cabin counsellors[7] that usurped of late, whenas they shall observe ye in the midst of your victories and successes more gently brooking written exceptions against a voted

1 long] since 3 November 1640, when the Long Parliament had been convened.
2 to] for.
3 courtship] the practice of the arts of a courtier.
4 him] Joseph Hall, Bishop of Norwich and author of *Humble Remonstrance to the High Court of Parliament* (1641), the publication of which had initiated the Smectymnuus controversy (so called from the initials of the five Puritans who had attacked Hall) to which Milton had contributed *Animadversions* (1641) and *Apology for Smectymnuus* and in the course of which Milton had been reviled by Hall in *A Short Answer to the Tedious Vindication of Smectymnuus* (1641); the encomium to Parliament occurs in Hall's *Modest Confutation of a Slanderous and Scurrilous Libel* (1642).
5 statists] statesmen.
6 triennial] In February 1641 the Long Parliament had passed the Triennial Parliaments Act, which stipulated that not more than three years were to elapse between the dissolution of one parliament and the summoning of its successor.
7 cabin counsellors] the king's favourites, who met in his private apartments to conduct business; Charles I established a formal Cabinet Council (as distinct from the Privy Council), later called the Cabinet.

order than other courts, which had produced nothing worth memory but the weak ostentation of wealth, would have endured the least signified dislike at any sudden proclamation.

If I should thus far presume upon the meek demeanour of your civil and gentle greatness, Lords and Commons, as what your published order hath directly said, that to gainsay, I might defend myself with ease, if any should accuse me of being new or insolent, did they but know how much better I find ye esteem it to imitate the old and elegant humanity of Greece, than the barbaric pride of a Hunnish and Norwegian stateliness. And out of those ages, to whose polite wisdom and letters we owe that we are not yet[1] Goths and Jutlanders, I could name him[2] who from his private house wrote that discourse to the Parliament of Athens,[3] that persuades them to change the form of democracy which was then established. Such honour was done in those days to men who professed the study of wisdom and eloquence, not only in their own country, but in other lands, that cities[4] and seigniories[5] heard them gladly, and with great respect, if they had aught in public to admonish the state. Thus did Dion Prusaeus,[6] a stranger and a private orator, counsel the Rhodians against a former edict; and I abound with other like examples, which to set here would be superfluous.

But if from the industry of a life wholly dedicated to studious labours, and those natural endowments haply not the worse for two and fifty degrees of northern latitude, so much must be derogated, as to count me not equal to any of those who had this privilege, I would obtain to be thought not so inferior, as yourselves are superior to the most of them who received their counsel: and how far you excel them, be assured, Lords and Commons, there can no greater testimony appear, than when your prudent spirit acknowledges and obeys the voice of reason from what quarter soever it be heard speaking; and renders ye as willing to repeal any Act of your own setting forth, as any set forth by your predecessors.

If ye be thus resolved, as it were injury to think ye were not, I know not what should withhold me from presenting ye with a fit instance wherein to show both that love of truth which ye eminently profess, and that uprightness of your judgement which is not wont to be partial to yourselves; by judging over again that Order which ye have ordained to regulate Printing:– that no book, pamphlet, or paper shall be henceforth printed, unless the same be first approved and licensed

1 yet] still.

2 him] Isocrates; see note on title-page, p. 574.

3 Parliament of Athens] refers to the *Ecclesia* (the assembly of all adult males), which Isocrates addressed on the subject of the powers of the *Boule* (the Council of the Areopagus).

4 cities] republics (self-governing states).

5 seigniories] states ruled by a lord.

6 Dion Prusaeus] The *Rhodiaca* of the Greek orator Dio Cocceianus (c. AD 40–112, later called Chrysostomos, 'golden-mouthed'), who was born in Prusa (Bithynia), was an attack on the Rhodians for altering the names on their statues to those of men then in power.

by such, or at least one of such, as shall thereto be appointed. For that part which preserves justly every man's copy[1] to himself, or provides for the poor,[2] I touch not, only wish they be not made pretences to abuse and persecute honest and painful[3] men, who offend not in either of these particulars. But that other clause of Licensing Books, which we thought had died with his brother quadragesimal and matrimonial[4] when the prelates expired,[5] I shall now attend with such a homily, as shall lay before ye, first the inventors of it, to be those whom ye will be loath to own; next what is to be thought in general of reading, whatever sort the books be; and that this Order avails nothing to the suppressing of scandalous, seditious, and libellous books, which were mainly intended to be suppressed. Last, that it will be primely to the discouragement of all learning, and the stop of truth, not only by disexercising and blunting our abilities in what we know already, but by hindering and cropping the discovery that might be yet further made both in religious and civil wisdom.

I deny not, but that it is of greatest concernment in the Church and Commonwealth, to have a vigilant eye how books demean themselves as well as men: and thereafter to confine, imprison, and do sharpest justice on them as malefactors. For books are not absolutely dead things, but do contain a potency of life in them to be as active as that soul was whose progeny they are; nay, they do preserve as in a vial the purest efficacy and extraction of that living intellect that bred them. I know they are as lively, and as vigorously productive, as those fabulous dragon's teeth;[6] and being sown up and down, may chance to spring up armed men. And yet, on the other hand, unless wariness be used, as good almost kill a man as kill a good book: who kills a man kills a reasonable creature, God's image; but he who destroys a good book, kills reason itself, kills the image of God, as it were in the eye. Many a man lives a burden to the earth;[7] but a good book is the precious life-blood of a master spirit, embalmed and treasured up on purpose to a life beyond life. 'Tis true, no age can restore a life, whereof perhaps there is no great loss; and revolutions of ages do not oft recover the loss of a rejected truth, for the want of which whole nations fare the worse.

We should be wary therefore what persecutions we raise against the living labours of public men, how we spill[8] that seasoned life of man,

1 copy] copyright.
2 poor] The Order protected the right to print any book assigned to the Company of Stationers 'for their relief and maintenance of their poor'.
3 painful] painstaking.
4 quadragesimal and matrimonial] Archbishops could grant dispensations from the law, last proclaimed in 1631, forbidding the eating of meat during Lent (Quadragesima), and bishops could grant marriage licences, which were dispensations from the obligation to publish marriage banns.
5 prelates expired] Bishops had been excluded from Parliament by the passing of the Bishops' Exclusion Bill in February 1642.
6 dragon's teeth] In Ovid's accounts of Cadmus and Jason (*Metamorphoses* III 101-30 and VII 121-42), armed men spring from the teeth of a slain dragon.
7 burden ... earth] a famous Homeric phrase, ἄχθος ἀρούρης (Latin *pondera terrae*); *Iliad* XVIII 104, *Odyssey* XX 379 etc.
8 spill] destroy.

preserved and stored up in books; since we see a kind of homicide may be thus committed, sometimes a martyrdom, and if it extend to the whole impression, a kind of massacre; whereof the execution ends not in the slaying of an elemental life, but strikes at that ethereal and fifth essence,[1] the breath of reason itself, slays an immortality rather than a life. But lest I should be condemned of introducing licence, while I oppose licensing, I refuse not the pains to be so much historical, as will serve to show what hath been done by ancient and famous commonwealths against this disorder, till the very time that this project of licensing crept out of the Inquisition,[2] was catched up by our prelates, and hath caught some of our presbyters.[3]

In Athens, where books and wits were ever busier than in any other part of Greece, I find but only two sorts of writings which the magistrate cared to take notice of; those either blasphemous and atheistical, or libellous. Thus the books of Protagoras[4] were by the judges of Areopagus commanded to be burnt, and himself banished the territory for a discourse begun with his confessing not to know 'whether there were gods, or whether not.' And against defaming, it was agreed that none should be traduced by name, as was the manner of *Vetus Comoedia*,[5] whereby we may guess how they censured libelling. And this course was quick[6] enough, as Cicero writes, to quell both the desperate wits of other atheists, and the open way of defaming, as the event[7] showed. Of other sects and opinions, though tending to voluptuousness, and the denying of divine providence, they took no heed.

Therefore we do not read that either Epicurus,[8] or that libertine school of Cyrene,[9] or what the Cynic[10] impudence uttered, was ever questioned by the laws. Neither is it recorded that the writings of those old comedians were suppressed, though the acting of them were forbid; and that Plato commended the reading of Aristophanes, the loosest of them all, to his royal scholar Dionysius,[11] is commonly

1 fifth essence] See *PL* III 714-18 and 716n.
2 Inquisition] The first *Index Librorum Prohibitorum* ('List of Prohibited Books') was issued by the Council of the Inquisition in 1557.
3 presbyters] the Presbyterians, who had a majority in Parliament; on 'prelates ... presbyters' cf. 'On the New Forcers' 20.
4 Protagoras] This account of the burning of the books of the sophist Protagoras of Abdera (fifth century BC) derives from Cicero, *De Natura Deorum* I. 23; the 'discourse' that Milton cites is Περὶ θεῶν ('On the Gods').
5 *Vetus Comoedia*] the 'Old Comedy' of Athens in the fifth century BC, of which the only complete plays are those of Aristophanes; 'traducing by name' was restricted by legislation (Scholia on Aristophanes' *Acharnenses* 67).
5 quick] powerful.
7 event] result.
8 Epicurus] See *PR* IV 299n.
9 Cyrene; Milton deemed the Cyrenaics (*Of Education* p. 567, n.5. and *PR* IV 279-80n.) 'libertine' because they taught that pleasures of the senses were the purpose of life.
10 Cynic] See *Comus* 707-8n.; the impudence of the Cynic Diogenes was the subject of many ancient anecdotes, such as his (apocryphal) request to Alexander the Great that he not stand between him and the sun.
11 Dionysius] According to the anonymous Ἀριστοφάνους βίος ('Life of Aristophanes'), Plato recommended that Dionysius II, tyrant of Syracuse, read Aristophanes in order to learn about the constitution of the Athenians.

known, and may be excused, if holy Chrysostom,[1] as is reported, nightly studied so much the same author and had the art to cleanse a scurrilous vehemence into the style of a rousing sermon.

That other leading city of Greece, Lacedaemon,[2] considering that Lycurgus[3] their lawgiver was so addicted to elegant learning, as to have been the first that brought out of Ionia the scattered works of Homer, and sent the poet Thales from Crete to prepare and mollify the Spartan surliness with his smooth songs and odes, the better to plant among them law and civility, it is to be wondered how museless and unbookish they were, minding nought but the feats of war. There needed no licensing of books among them, for they disliked all but their own laconic[4] apothegms, and took a slight occasion to chase Archilochus[5] out of their city, perhaps for composing in a higher strain than their own soldierly ballads and roundels could reach to. Or if it were for his broad verses, they were not therein so cautious but they were as dissolute in their promiscuous conversing;[6] whence Euripides affirms in *Andromache*,[7] that their women were all unchaste. Thus much may give us light after[8] what sort of books were prohibited among the Greeks.

The Romans also, for many ages trained up only to a military roughness resembling most the Lacedaemonian guise, knew of learning little but what their twelve Tables,[9] and the Pontific College with their augurs and flamens[10] taught them in religion and law, so unacquainted with other learning, that when Carneades and Critolaus, with the Stoic Diogenes[11] coming ambassadors to Rome, took

1 Chrysostom] St John Chrysostom (347-407), patriarch of Constantinople.
2 Lacedaemon] Sparta.
3 Lycurgus] According to Plutarch's biography (from which all the anecdotes in this paragraph derive), Lycurgus, the (possibly mythical) law-giver of Sparta, discovered the epics of Homer in Ionia and later sent the poet and musician Thaletas of Gortyn (Crete) to Sparta.
4 laconic] plays on its derivation from 'Laconia', meaning 'Spartan'.
5 Archilochus] Archilochus of Paros, Greek poet of the seventh century BC, whose expulsion from Sparta is variously attributed to the obscenity of his poetry (Valerius Maximus VI 3) or his satirical declaration that he would rather throw away his shield than his life (Plutarch, *Instituta Laconica* 239b), a sentiment opposed to the famous instruction of the Spartan mother to her son that he was to return from battle with his shield or on it.
6 conversing] associations.
7 *Andromache*] *Andromache* 590-3; this prejudice derived from the Spartan practice, much discussed by the Athenians (e.g. Plato, *Laws* 806a and Aristotle, *Politics* II. 9), of nude men and women participating together in athletic exercises; Milton's account departs from Plutarch, who defended the practice.
8 after] regarding.
9 twelve Tables] See *Of Education*, p. 564, n.13.
10 Pontific ... flamens] The *collegium pontificum*, which presided over the religion of ancient Rome, included *flamines* (senior priests) but not augurs (diviners who declared whether or not the gods would approve a proposed action), who had their own *collegium*.
11 Carneades ... Diogenes] In 156-155 BC Athens sent to Rome a delegation of philosophers consisting of Carneades (founder and head of the New Academy), Critolaus of Phaselis (head of the Peripatetic school) and Diogenes of Babylon (head of the Stoic school); see *PR* IV 278n, 279-80n.

thereby occasion to give the city a taste of their philosophy, they were suspected for seducers by no less a man than Cato the Censor,[1] who moved it in the Senate to dismiss them speedily, and to banish all such Attic babblers out of Italy. But Scipio[2] and others of the noblest senators withstood him and his old Sabine[3] austerity; honoured and admired the men; and the censor himself at last, in his old age,[4] fell to the study of what whereof before he was so scrupulous. And yet at the same time, Naevius[5] and Plautus, the first Latin comedians, had filled the city with all the borrowed scenes of Menander and Philemon.[6] Then began to be considered there also what was to be done to libellous books and authors; for Naevius was quickly cast into prison for his unbridled pen, and released by the tribunes upon his recantation; we read also that libels were burnt, and the makers punished by Augustus.[7] The like severity, no doubt, was used, if aught were impiously written against their esteemed gods. Except in these two points, how the world went in books, the magistrate kept no reckoning.

And therefore Lucretius[8] without impeachment versifies his Epicurism[9] to Memmius,[10] and had the honour to be set forth the second time by Cicero,[11] so great a father of the commonwealth; although himself disputes against that opinion in his own writings. Nor was the satirical sharpness or naked plainness of Lucilius, or Catullus, or

---

1 Cato the Censor] Marcus Porcius Cato (234-149 BC), who had been censor of Rome in 184 BC, had long argued that Hellenic culture threatened to destroy Roman values; he vehemently urged the dismissal of the philosophers on the grounds that their views were subversive.

2 Scipio] Scipio the Younger, adoptive grandson of Scipio Africanus (see *PR* III 34-5n, 101-2), was a friend of the Greek historian Polybius and a noted philhellenist and patron of Greek culture.

3 Sabine] an ancient race who lived north-east of Rome, where Cato's father had a farm; here used by Milton to suggest simple and rugged austerity of manner.

4 old age] According to Cicero's *Cato Maior De Senectute* (VIII 26), Cato took up the study of Greek language and literature in old age.

5 Naevius] The playwright and epic poet Gnaeus Naevius was imprisoned c. 240 BC for satirizing the Scipios and the prominent family of the Metelli.

6 Plautus, Menander, Philemon] Plautus' *Stichus, Bacchides, Cistellaria* and *Aulularia* are all adaptations of plays by Menander; Plautus' *Mercator, Trinummus* and (probably) *Mostellaria* are adaptations of plays by Philemon; Menander and Philemon were the leading writers of the 'New Comedy' of the late fourth century BC in Athens.

7 Augustus] According to Tacitus (*Annals* I 72), Augustus revived the laws of libel when provoked by the satires of Cassius Severus, publicly burned his works and sent him into exile.

8 Lucretius] See *Of Education* p. 563, n.3.

9 Epicurism] See *PR* IV 299n.

10 Memmius] Lucretius dedicated *De Rerum Natura* to Gaius Memmius, the patron of Catullus and Cinna.

11 Cicero] Cicero, who was hailed in the Senate as *parens patriae* ('father of his country') for having crushed the conspiracy of Catiline, is said by St Jerome to have edited Lucretius' poem; he attacks Epicureanism in *De Natura Deorum* (I-II), *De Finibus* (I-II) and *Tusculan Disputations* (II-III).

Flaccus,[1] by any order prohibited. And for matters of state, the story of Titus Livius, though it extolled that part which Pompey held, was not therefore suppressed by Octavius[2] Caesar of the other faction. But that Naso[3] was by him banished in his old age, for the wanton poems of his youth, was but a mere covert of state over some secret cause: and besides, the books were neither banished nor called in. From hence we shall meet with little else but tyranny in the Roman empire, that we may not marvel, if not so often bad as good books were silenced. I shall therefore deem to have been large enough, in producing what among the ancients was punishable to write; save only which, all other arguments were free to treat on.

By this time[4] the emperors were become Christians, whose discipline in this point I do not find to have been more severe than what was formerly in practice. The books of those whom they took to be grand heretics were examined, refuted, and condemned in the General Councils;[5] and not till then were prohibited, or burnt, by authority of the emperor. As for the writings of heathen authors, unless they were plain incentives against Christianity, as those of Porphyrius[6] and Proclus,[7] they met with no interdict that can be cited, till about the year 400, in a Carthaginian Council,[8] wherein bishops themselves were

1 Lucilius ... Flaccus] Lucilius was the originator of Roman verse satire; Catullus, the greatest lyric poet of Rome, wrote satires about the personal life of Julius Caesar; Flaccus is the family name of Horace (Quintus Horatius Flaccus), whose Lucilian *Satires* were never directed against his contemporaries.

2 Titus Livius, Pompey, Octavius] The Roman historian Livy (Titus Livius) wrote a history ('story'), now lost, of the war between Pompey and Octavius Caesar (who later became 'Augustus'); the passage in Tacitus on which Milton here draws (*Annals* IV 34-5) is memorably translated by Ben Jonson in *Sejanus* III. i. 407-60.

3 Naso] Ovid (Publius Ovidius Naso) was banished by Augustus in AD 8; in his poems of exile he hints that his banishment may have been occasioned by a youthful poem on the art of seduction (*Ars Amatoria*) and by an indiscretion that (he insists) was not criminal in nature. His books were not banished, but were withdrawn from public libraries.

4 By this time] The first emperor publicly to profess Christianity was Constantine, who ended the persecution of Christians with the so-called 'Edict of Milan' in 313.

5 General Councils] General (as opposed to local or 'particular') Councils were convened to deal with matters of doctrine; by Milton's time there had been 19 General Councils: the first at Nicea in 325 (on Arianism) and the last at Trento (on Protestantism).

6 Porphyrius] The Κατὰ Χριστιανῶν ('Against the Christians') of the Neoplatonist philosopher Porphyry was condemned to be burnt by Constantine (before 325) and Theodosius II (in 448).

7 Proclus] Proclus (c. 412-85), the last great Neoplatonist, and a fervent enemy of Christianity; his Κατὰ Χριστιανῶν ('Against the Christians') seems not to have been banned (though it was later answered by John Philoponus), but he had to flee to Asia Minor for a year because of his views.

8 Carthaginian Council] Milton draws his information from Pietro Sarpi (see below), who probably had in mind the Carthaginian Council of May 419, which produced the collection of canons known as the *Codex Canonum Ecclesia Africanae*, which was available to Sarpi in an edition of 1610 and in Dionysius Exiguus.

forbid to read the books of gentiles,[1] but heresies they might read: while others long before them, on the contrary, scrupled more the books of heretics than of gentiles. And that the primitive[2] Councils and bishops were wont only to declare what books were not commendable, passing[3] no further, but leaving it to each one's conscience to read or to lay by, till after the year 800, is observed already by Padre Paolo,[4] the great unmasker of the Trentine Council.

After which time the Popes of Rome, engrossing what they pleased of political rule into their own hands, extended their dominion over men's eyes, as they had before over their judgements, burning and prohibiting to be read what they fancied not; yet sparing in their censures, and the books not many which they so dealt with: till Martin V,[5] by his bull, not only prohibited, but was the first that excommunicated the reading of heretical books; for about that time Wycliffe[6] and Huss,[7] growing terrible, were they who first drove the Papal Court[8] to a stricter policy of prohibiting. Which course Leo X[9] and his successors followed, until the Council of Trent[10] and the Spanish Inquisition,[11] engendering together, brought forth, or perfected, those

1 gentiles] pagans.
2 primitive] refers to the early church.
3 passing] proceeding.
4 Padre Paolo] Fra Paolo Servita was the religious name of the Venetian polemicist Pietro Sarpi (1552–1623), whose *Istoria del Concilio Tridentino* ('History of the Council of Trent') Milton read in the Italian edition published in London in 1619 under the name of Pietro Soave Polano (an anagram of Paolo Sarpi Veneto); Sarpi's account depicts the Council of Trent (1545–63), 'the Odyssey of our age', as the culmination of the process whereby the papacy usurped the power that rightly belonged to all the clergy.
5 Martin V] elected pope at Council of Constance in 1417, and issued the 'bull' (papal mandate) to which Milton refers in 1418.
6 Wycliffe] John Wycliffe (c. 1329–84), English reformer; in 1415 the Council of Constance condemned Wycliffe for 267 errors, and ordered that his writings be burnt and his bones dug up.
7 Huss] John Huss, the Bohemian reformer, was excommunicated by the antipope John XXIII in February 1411; he travelled to the Council of Constance with a safe-conduct of the Emperor Sigismund, and was there burnt at the stake on 6 July 1415.
8 Papal Court] the Curia, which administers the government of the Catholic Church.
9 Leo X] Giovanni de' Medici, pope from 1513–21; the Lateran Council of 1515 formulated the decree *De Impressione Librorum*, which required that all books be approved by the appropriate ecclesiastical authority prior to publication.
10 Council of Trent] On 8 April 1546 the Council forbade the sale or possession of any anonymous book which had not been previously approved.
11 Spanish Inquisition] an inquisition established by Ferdinand and Isabella in 1479 to persecute the heresies of converts from Judaism and Islam, and later of mystics and Protestants. In 1502 Ferdinand and Isabella established censure of all books as a state institution; all books had to be examined by bishops. After 1527 the Inquisition issued the licence to print, and in 1542 issued the first Spanish 'Index of Prohibited Books'.

catalogues and expurging Indexes,[1] that rake through the entrails of many an old good author, with a violation worse than any could be offered to his tomb. Nor did they stay in matters heretical, but any subject that was not to their palate, they either condemned in a Prohibition, or had it straight into the new Purgatory[2] of an Index.

To fill up the measure of encroachment, their last invention was to ordain that no book, pamphlet, or paper should be printed (as if St Peter had bequeathed them the keys of the press also out of Paradise) unless it were approved and licensed under the hands of two or three glutton friars. For example:

Let the Chancellor Cini be pleased to see if in this present work be contained aught that may withstand the printing.

Vincent Rabatta, Vicar[3] of Florence.

I have seen this present work, and find nothing athwart the Catholic faith and good manners: in witness whereof I have given, etc.

Nicolò Cini, Chancellor of Florence.

Attending[4] the precedent relation, it is allowed that this present work of Davanzati[5] may be printed.

Vincent Rabatta, etc.

It may be printed, July 15.

Friar Simon Mompei d'Amelia, Chancellor of the Holy Office in Florence.

Sure they have a conceit, if he of the bottomless pit had not long since broke prison, that this quadruple exorcism would bar him down. I fear their next design will be to get into their custody the licensing of that which they say* Claudius intended, but went not through with. Vouchsafe to see another of their forms, the Roman stamp:[6]

*Quo veniam daret flatum crepitumque ventris in convivio emittendi. Sueton. in Claudio.

1 catalogues ... Indexes] the *Index Librorum Prohibitorum* ('List of Prohibited Books') and the *Index Expurgatorius* (a list of books that could be read after specified passages had been deleted). Overlapping but not identical indices were issued by the Roman 'Congregation of the Index' and the Holy Office in Madrid, because the Spanish Inquisition was an autonomous institution under royal jurisdiction.

2 Prohibition, Purgatory] plays on *Prohibitorum* and *Expurgatorius*.

3 Vicar] bishop's deputy.

4 Attending] as a consequence of.

5 Davanzati] Milton's four examples are his translations (from Italian) of the permissions on the last page of *Scisma d'Inghilterra* (1638) by Bernardo Davanzati Bostichi; the *Scisma* is in turn a condensed translation of *De Origini ac Progressu Schismatis Anglicani*, by the English Jesuit Nicholas Sanders (1586).

*Quo ... Claudio] Milton's marginal note: Claudius, having heard of a man who endangered his health by trying to restrain his flatulence, is said to have contemplated an edict 'allowing the privilege of breaking wind quietly or noisily at dinner parties' (Suetonius, *Divus Claudius* XXXII).

6 Roman stamp] Milton's two examples are his translations (from Latin) of the permissions at the beginning of *De Duplici Statu Religionis Apud Scotis* (1628) of George Conn, a Scottish Roman Catholic.

Imprimatur,[1] if it seem good to the reverend Master of the Holy Palace.

Belcastro, Vicegerent.

Imprimatur, Friar Nicolo Rodolphi, Master of the Holy Palace.

Sometimes five *Imprimaturs* are seen together dialogue-wise in the piazza of one title-page, complimenting and ducking each to other with their shaven reverences,[2] whether the author, who stands by in perplexity at the foot of his epistle, shall to the press or to the sponge.[3] These are the pretty responsories,[4] these are the dear antiphonies,[5] that so bewitched of late our prelates and their chaplains with the goodly echo they made; and besotted us to the gay imitation of a lordly *Imprimatur*, one from Lambeth House,[6] another from the west end of Paul's;[7] so apishly Romanizing, that the word of command still was set down in Latin; as if the learned grammatical pen that wrote it would cast no ink without Latin; or perhaps, as they thought, because no vulgar tongue[8] was worthy to express the pure conceit[9] of an *Imprimatur*; but rather, as I hope, for that our English, the language of men, ever famous and foremost in the achievements of liberty, will not easily find servile letters enow to spell such a dictatory presumption English.

And thus ye have the inventors and the original of book-licensing ripped up and drawn as lineally as any pedigree. We have it not, that can be heard of, from any ancient state, or polity or church; nor by any statute[10] left us by our ancestors elder or later; nor from the modern custom of any reformed city or Church abroad; but from the most antichristian council and the most tyrannous inquisition that ever enquired. Till then books were ever as freely admitted into the world as any other birth; the issue of the brain was no more stifled than the issue of the womb: no envious Juno[11] sat cross-legged over the nativity of any man's intellectual offspring; but if it proved a monster, who denies but that it was justly burnt, or sunk into the sea? But that a book, in worse condition than a peccant soul, should be to stand before a jury ere it be born to the world, and undergo yet

1 *Imprimatur*] 'let it be printed'.
2 shaven reverences] i.e. bowing their tonsured heads to each other.
3 sponge] used to erase writing.
4 responsories] anthems said or sung by soloist and choir alternately.
5 antiphonies] antiphons: hymns sung by two choirs.
6 Lambeth House] London residence of the Archbishops of Canterbury, since 1658 called Lambeth Palace.
7 Paul's] In the Norman St Paul's Cathedral (destroyed 1666), the palace of the Bishop of London adjoined the north-west corner of the nave. In the Star Chamber Decree of 1643, certain categories of books had to be licensed by either the Archbishop of Canterbury or the Bishop of London.
8 vulgar tongue] vernacular language.
9 conceit] idea.
10 statute] as distinguished from the 'decree' of the Star Chamber.
11 Juno] Juno as goddess of childbirth (Juno Eileithyia) could retard the birth of a child by crossing her legs (e.g. Ovid, *Metamorphoses* IX 281–323, in which Juno and Eileithyia are portrayed as separate goddesses).

in darkness the judgement of Radamanth[1] and his colleagues, ere it can pass the ferry[2] backward into light, was never heard before, till that mysterious iniquity,[3] provoked and troubled at the first entrance of Reformation, sought out new limbos[4] and new hells wherein they might include our books also within the number of their damned. And this was the rare morsel so officiously snatched up, and so ill-favouredly imitated by our inquisiturient[5] bishops, and the attendant minorities[6] their chaplains. That ye like not now these most certain authors of this licensing order, and that all sinister intention was far distant from your thoughts, when ye were importuned the passing it, all men who know the integrity of your actions, and how ye honour truth, will clear ye readily.

But some will say, what though the inventors were bad, the thing for all that may be good. It may so; yet if that thing be no such deep invention, but obvious, and easy for any man to light on, and yet best and wisest commonwealths through all ages and occasions have forborne to use it, and falsest seducers and oppressors of men were the first who took it up, and to no other purpose but to obstruct and hinder the first approach of Reformation; I am of those who believe it will be a harder alchemy than Lullius[7] ever knew, to sublimate any good use out of such an invention. Yet this only is what I request to gain from this reason, that it may be held a dangerous and suspicious fruit, as certainly it deserves, for[8] the tree that bore it, until I can dissect one by one the properties it has. But I have first to finish, as was propounded, what is to be thought in general of reading books, whatever sort they be, and whether be more the benefit or the harm that thence proceeds?

Not to insist upon the examples of Moses,[9] Daniel,[10] and Paul, who were skilful in all the learning of the Egyptians, Chaldeans, and Greeks, which could not probably be without reading their books of all sorts; in Paul especially, who thought it no defilement to insert into Holy Scripture the sentences[11] of three Greek poets, and one of them

1 Radamanth] Rhadamanthys and his 'colleagues' Minos and Aeacus were the judges of the dead in Hades.
2 ferry] The ferry of Charon took the dead in Hades from light to darkness.
3 mysterious iniquity] the papacy, here identified with the whore of Revelation xvii. 1–5.
4 limbos] See *PL* III 474n.
5 inquisiturient] eager to play the inquisitor (Milton's Latinate coinage).
6 minorities] alludes contemptuously to the 'Friars Minor' (Franciscans), so called as a sign of their humility, which was much mocked by Protestants.
7 Lullius] refers to the alchemical treatises attributed to Ramon Llull (c. 1235– c. 1316), the Catalan poet, mystic and missionary.
8 for] on account of.
9 Moses] 'And Moses was learned in all the wisdom of the Egyptians' (Acts vii. 22).
10 °Daniel] Daniel had 'knowledge and skill in all learning and wisdom' (Dan. i. 17).
11 sentences] sayings: 'for we also are his offspring' (Acts xvii. 28, from Aratus, quoted in *PL* V 503); 'the Cretans are always liars, evil beasts, slow bellies' (Titus i. 12, from Epimenides); 'evil communications corrupt good manners' (I Cor. xv. 33, attributed in the preface to *SA* (p. 507) to the tragedian Euripides).

a tragedian; the question was notwithstanding sometimes contro-
verted among the primitive doctors, but with great odds on that side
which affirmed it both lawful and profitable; as was then evidently
perceived, when Julian the Apostate[1] and subtlest enemy to our faith
made a decree forbidding Christians the study of heathen learning:
for, said he, they wound us with our own weapons, and with our own
arts and sciences they overcome us. And indeed the Christians were
put so to their shifts by this crafty means, and so much in danger to
decline into all ignorance, that the two Apollinarii[2] were fain, as a man
may say, to coin all the seven liberal sciences[3] out of the Bible,
reducing it into divers forms of orations, poems, dialogues, even to the
calculating of a new Christian grammar. But, saith the historian
Socrates,[4] the providence of God provided better than the industry of
Apollinarius and his son, by taking away that illiterate law with the
life of him who devised it. So great an injury they then held it to be
deprived of Hellenic learning; and thought it a persecution more
undermining, and secretly decaying the Church, than the open cruelty
of Decius[5] or Diocletian.[6]

And perhaps it was the same politic drift that the devil whipped St
Jerome[7] in a Lenten dream, for reading Cicero; or else it was a
phantasm bred by the fever which had then seized him. For had an
angel been his discipliner, unless it were for dwelling too much upon
Ciceronianisms, and had chastised the reading, not the vanity, it had
been plainly partial; first to correct him for grave Cicero, and not for
scurril Plautus, whom he confesses to have been reading, not long
before; next to correct him only, and let so many more ancient fathers
wax old in those pleasant and florid studies without the lash of such a
tutoring apparition; insomuch that Basil[8] teaches how some good use

1 Julian the Apostate] Roman emperor from 361-3, raised as a Christian but later
repudiated Christianity and reinstituted the pagan cult. He forbade Christians
to teach classical literature and philosophy; there was no decree forbidding
Christians to study the classics, but they could not do so because they would
not attend pagan schools.
2 Apollinarii] The grammarian Apollinarius the Elder rewrote much of the Old
Testament in classical verse forms; his son, the rhetorician Apollinarius after
whom the first great Christological heresy was later named, rewrote much of
the New Testament in Socratic dialogues.
3 seven ... sciences] the *trivium* (grammar, logic, rhetoric) and the *quadrivium*
(arithmetic, geometry, astronomy, music).
4 Socrates] Socrates Scholasticus, fifth-century Constantinopolitan author of the
Ἐκκλησιαστικὴ ἱστορία ('History of the Church'), a continuation of Eusebius
(see p. 588) from 305-439; Milton is quoting III. 16.
5 Decius] emperor 249-51, initiator of the first systematic persecution of
Christians.
6 Diocletian] emperor 284-305, initiator in 303 of a savage persecution that lasted
till 313 (see above p. 582, n.4.).
7 St Jerome] The Biblical scholar Jerome (c. 341-420) recounts the dream in which
he was whipped by an angel (*Epistle* XXII); Milton, following Sarpi, identifies
the flagellator as the devil.
8 Basil] Basil the Great (c. 330-79), Bishop of Caesarea; Milton has remembered the
general sense of Basil's *Ad Adulescentes* ('To the Young', on reading pagan
literature) but *Margites* is not mentioned.

may be made of *Margites*,[1] a sportful poem, not now extant, writ by Homer; and why not then of *Morgante*,[2] an Italian romance much to the same purpose?

But if it be agreed we shall be tried by visions, there is a vision recorded by Eusebius,[3] far ancienter than this tale of Jerome to the nun Eustochium,[4] and, besides, has nothing of a fever in it. Dionysius Alexandrinus[5] was about the year 240 a person of great name in the Church for piety and learning, who had wont to avail himself much against heretics by being conversant in their books; until a certain presbyter laid it scrupulously to his conscience, how he durst venture himself among those defiling volumes. The worthy man, loath to give offence, fell into a new debate with himself what was to be thought, when suddenly a vision sent from God (it is his own epistle that so avers it) confirmed him in these words: 'Read any books whatever come to thy hands, for thou art sufficient both to judge aright, and to examine each matter.' To this revelation he assented the sooner, as he confesses, because it was answerable to that of the Apostle to the Thessalonians, 'Prove all things, hold fast that which is good.'[6] And he might have added another remarkable saying of the same author: 'To the pure, all things are pure';[7] not only meats and drinks, but all kind of knowledge whether of good or evil; the knowledge cannot defile, nor consequently the books, if the will and conscience be not defiled.

For books are as meats and viands are; some of good, some of evil substance; and yet God, in that unapocryphal vision, said without exception, 'Rise, Peter, kill and eat,'[8] leaving the choice to each man's discretion. Wholesome meats to a vitiated stomach differ little or nothing from unwholesome; and best books to a naughty mind are not unappliable to occasions of evil. Bad meats will scarce breed good nourishment in the healthiest concoction;[9] but herein the difference is of bad books, that they to a discreet and judicious reader serve in many respects to discover, to confute, to forewarn, and to illustrate. Whereof what better witness can ye expect I should produce, than one of your own now sitting in Parliament, the chief of learned men reputed in this land, Mr Selden;[10] whose volume of natural and

1 *Margites*] a satirical poem (of which only a small fragment survives) attributed in antiquity to Homer.
2 *Morgante*] the mock-chivalric epic *Morgante Maggiore* (1481) by Luigi Pulci.
3 Eusebius] Bishop of Caesaria (preceding Basil), author of Ἐκκλησιαστικὴ ἱστορία ('History of the Church' to 324); Milton refers to VII. 7.
4 Eustochium] Julia Eustochium, the nun to whom Jerome addressed *Epistle* XXII (on virginity) in 385, had to flee Rome with Jerome because of the offence caused by the letter.
5 Dionysius Alexandrinus] Dionysius the Great, Bishop of Alexandria from 247; the incident is recorded in his third *Epistle* ('On Baptism, to Philemon'), which survives in Eusebius; Milton takes the date from Sarpi.
6 'Prove ... good'] I Thess. v. 21, which Milton boldly substitutes for an apocryphal verse cited by Dionysius.
7 'To ... pure'] Titus i. 15.   8 'Rise ... eat'] Acts x. 13.   9 concoction] digestion.
10 Selden] The historian and lawyer John Selden (1584-1654) was in 1644 Member of Parliament for the University of Oxford; Milton here translates a passage in the preface to Selden's treatise on the national and natural law of the Jews (*De Jure Naturali et Gentium juxta Disciplinam Ebraeorum*, 1640).

national laws proves, not only by great authorities brought together, but by exquisite[1] reasons and theorems almost mathematically demonstrative, that all opinions, yea errors, known, read, and collated, are of main service and assistance toward the speedy attainment of what is truest. I conceive, therefore, that when God did enlarge the universal diet of man's body, saving ever the rules of temperance, he then also, as before, left arbitrary the dieting and repasting of our minds; as wherein every mature man might have to exercise his own leading capacity.

How great a virtue is temperance, how much of moment through the whole life of man! Yet God commits the managing so great a trust, without particular law or prescription, wholly to the demeanour of every grown man. And therefore when he himself tabled the Jews from heaven, that omer,[2] which was every man's daily portion of manna, is computed to have been more than might have well sufficed the heartiest feeder thrice as many meals. For those actions which enter into a man, rather than issue out of him, and therefore defile not,[3] God uses not to captivate under a perpetual childhood of prescription, but trusts him with the gift of reason to be his own chooser; there were but little work left for preaching, if law and compulsion should grow so fast upon those things which heretofore were governed only by exhortation. Solomon informs us, that much reading is a weariness to the flesh;[4] but neither he nor other inspired author tells us that such or such reading is unlawful: yet certainly had God thought good to limit us herein, it had been much more expedient to have told us what was unlawful than what was wearisome. As for the burning of those Ephesian books by St Paul's converts; 'tis replied the books were magic, the Syriac[5] so renders them. It was a private act, a voluntary act, and leaves us to a voluntary imitation: the men in remorse burnt those books which were their own; the magistrate by this example is not appointed;[6] these men practised the books, another might perhaps have read them in some sort usefully.

Good and evil we know in the field of this world grow up together almost inseparably; and the knowledge of good is so involved and interwoven with the knowledge of evil, and in so many cunning resemblances hardly to be discerned, that those confused seeds which were imposed upon Psyche[7] as an incessant labour to cull out, and sort asunder, were not more intermixed. It was from out the rind of one apple tasted, that the knowledge of good and evil, as two twins cleaving together, leaped forth into the world. And perhaps this is

1 exquisite] carefully chosen.
2 omer] a dry measure of about 7 pints (Exodus xvi. 16–36).
3 those . . . not] Matt. xv. 17–20; Mark vii. 15–23.   4 much . . . flesh] Eccles. xii. 12.
5 Syriac] The Greek text of Acts xix. 19 uses a euphemism, but the Syriac text (see *Education*, p. 565, n.4) alludes specifically to magic.
6 appointed] enabled to decide.
7 Psyche] In *The Golden Ass*, a Latin novel written in the late second century AD by Apuleius, Venus mixes together a large quantity of seeds and instructs her daughter-in-law Psyche to sort them before evening; the task is accomplished by some helpful ants.

that doom which Adam fell into of knowing good and evil,[1] that is to say of knowing good by evil. As therefore the state of man now is; what wisdom can there be to choose, what continence to forbear without the knowledge of evil? He that can apprehend and consider vice with all her baits and seeming pleasures, and yet abstain, and yet distinguish, and yet prefer that which is truly better, he is the true warfaring[2] Christian.

I cannot praise a fugitive and cloistered virtue, unexercised and unbreathed, that never sallies out and sees her adversary, but slinks out of the race, where that immortal garland is to be run for, not without dust and heat. Assuredly we bring not innocence into the world, we bring impurity much rather; that which purifies us is trial, and trial is by what is contrary. That virtue therefore which is but a youngling in the contemplation of evil, and knows not the utmost that vice promises to her followers, and rejects it, is but a blank virtue, not a pure; her whiteness is but an excremental[3] whiteness. Which was the reason why our sage and serious poet Spenser, whom I dare be known to think a better teacher than Scotus or Aquinas,[4] describing true temperance under the person of Guyon,[5] brings him in with his palmer through the cave of Mammon, and the bower of earthly bliss, that he might see and know, and yet abstain. Since therefore the knowledge and survey of vice is in this world so necessary to the constituting of human virtue, and the scanning of error to the confirmation of truth, how can we more safely, and with less danger, scout into the regions of sin and falsity than by reading all manner of tractates and hearing all manner of reason? And this is the benefit which may be had of books promiscuously read.

But of the harm that may result hence, three kinds are usually reckoned. First, is feared the infection that may spread; but then all human learning and controversy in religious points must remove out of the world, yea the Bible itself; for that ofttimes relates blasphemy not nicely, it describes the carnal sense of wicked men not unelegantly, it brings in holiest men passionately murmuring against Providence through all the arguments of Epicurus: in other great disputes it answers dubiously and darkly to the common reader. And ask a Talmudist[6] what ails the modesty of his marginal *keri*, that Moses and

---

1 knowing ... evil] Gen. iii. 5, 22.
2 warfaring] 'wayfaring' in the printed text, but corrected by hand to 'warfaring' in the presentation copies.
3 excremental] superficial.
4 Scotus, Aquinas] Differences between the theology of the Franciscan Duns Scotus and the Dominican Thomas Aquinas were the subject of the central theological debate of the late middle ages.
5 Guyon] In Spenser's *Faerie Queene*, the palmer accompanies Guyon to the Bower of Bliss (II. xii), but not to the Cave of Mammon (II. vii. 2; II. viii. 3).
6 Talmudist] a student of the Talmud, the Jewish compilation (written in Aramaic in the early centuries of the Christian era) which embodies the Mishnah (Jewish oral law) and the Gemara (rabbinical commentary on the Mishnah); it exists in two versions known as the Palestinian (or Jerusalem) Talmud and the Babylonian Talmud.

all the prophets cannot persuade him to pronounce the textual *chetiv*.[1] For these causes we all know the Bible itself put by the Papist into the first rank of prohibited books. The ancientest fathers must be next removed, as Clement of Alexandria,[2] and that Eusebian book[3] of Evangelic Preparation, transmitting our ears through a hoard of heathenish obscenities to receive the Gospel. Who finds not that Irenaeus,[4] Epiphanius,[5] Jerome,[6] and others discover more heresies than they well confute, and that oft for heresy which is the truer opinion?

Nor boots it to say for these, and all the heathen writers of greatest infection, if it must be thought so, with whom is bound up the life of human learning, that they writ in an unknown tongue, so long as we are sure those languages are known as well to the worst of men, who are both most able, and most diligent to instil the poison they suck, first into the courts of princes, acquainting them with the choicest delights and criticisms[7] of sin. As perhaps did that Petronius whom Nero called his Arbiter, the master of his revels;[8] and the notorious ribald[9] of Arezzo, dreaded and yet dear to the Italian courtiers. I name not him for posterity's sake, whom Henry VIII named in merriment his Vicar of hell.[10] By which compendious way all the contagion that foreign books can infuse will find a passage to the people far easier and

1 *keri, chetiv*] technical Massoretic terms. As Jews were forbidden to pronounce the tetragrammaton YHWH (Yahweh), for example, this 'textual *chetiv*' was glossed in the margin with an acceptable substitute ('marginal *keri*'), in this case *Adonai*, the Hebrew word for 'Lord'. When the vowels of *Adonai* were imposed on the consonants of YHWH as a reminder of the *keri*, the composite word 'Jehovah' came into existence.

2 Clement of Alexandria] refers to the Προτρεπτικός πρὸς Ἕλληνας ('Exhortation to the Greeks') of the Athenian Titus Flavius Clemens (c. 150–c. 215), a Christian convert who became head of the Catechetical school of Alexandria; the treatise purports to demonstrate the superiority of Christianity to pagan religion and philosophy.

3 Eusebian book] The *Praeparatio Evangelica* of Eusebius (see above, p. 588) is an attack on Greek philosophy which argues that at best (in Plato) such philosophy derived from the Bible (cf. *PR* IV 338).

4 Irenaeus] Bishop of Lyons (c. 130–c. 200), author of *Adversus omnes Haereses*, an attack on Gnosticism (in Greek) that survives in complete form only in a literal Latin translation.

5 Epiphanius] Bishop of Salamis (c. 315–403), author of *Panarion* ('medicine-chest'), commonly known as the 'Refutation of all the Heresies'.

6 Jerome] the polemical writings of Jerome variously attack such heresies as Arianism, Pelagianism and Origenism.

7 criticisms] finer points.

8 Petronius ... revels] The Roman satirist Petronius, author of *Satyricon*, was made *arbiter elegantiarum* ('director of amusements') by the emperor Nero (Tacitus, *Annals* XVI 18); Milton's translation refers to the office of 'Master of the Revels', who was responsible for the censorship of plays from 1545 to 1624, when he was superseded by his official superior, the Lord Chamberlain.

9 ribald] The poet, playwright and letter-writer Pietro Aretino (1492–1556), who preferred to be known as Pietro of Arezzo (his birthplace), was dubbed by Ariosto 'the Scourge of Princes'; he lived on money given to him by senior political figures who feared his biting and richly obscene satire.

10 Vicar of hell] the courtier Sir Francis Bryan (d. 1550), whose nickname (conferred by Thomas Cromwell) was, according to Davanzati (see p. 584), confirmed (in laughter) by Henry VIII when he discovered that Bryan, a member of the Boleyn family, had committed adultery with both Anne Boleyn and her mother.

shorter than an Indian voyage, though it could be sailed either by the north of Cathay eastward, or of Canada[1] westward, while our Spanish licensing gags the English press never so severely.

But, on the other side, that infection which is from books of controversy in religion is more doubtful and dangerous to the learned than to the ignorant; and yet those books must[2] be permitted untouched by the licenser. It will be hard to instance where any ignorant man hath been ever seduced by papistical book in English, unless it were commended and expounded to him by some of that clergy; and indeed all such tractates, whether false or true, are as the prophecy of Isaiah was to the eunuch, not to be understood without a guide.[3] But of our priests and doctors how many have been corrupted by studying the comments of Jesuits and Sorbonists,[4] and how fast they could transfuse that corruption into the people, our experience is both late and sad. It is not forgot, since the acute and distinct Arminius[5] was perverted merely by the perusing of a nameless discourse written at Delft, which at first he took in hand to confute.

Seeing, therefore, that those books, and those in great abundance, which are likeliest to taint both life and doctrine, cannot be suppressed without the fall of learning and of all ability in disputation, and that these books of either sort are most and soonest catching to the learned, from whom to the common people whatever is heretical or dissolute may quickly be conveyed, and that evil manners are as perfectly learnt without books a thousand other ways which cannot be stopped, and evil doctrine not with books can propagate, except a teacher guide, which he might also do without writing, and so beyond prohibiting, I am not able to unfold, how this cautelous[6] enterprise of licensing can be exempted from the number of vain and impossible attempts. And he who were pleasantly disposed could not well avoid to liken it to the exploit of that gallant man who thought to pound up the crows by shutting his park gate.

Besides another inconvenience, if learned men be the first receivers

---

1 Canada] then a small French colony; from 1603-15 Champlain had made repeated attempts to find a route to the East Indies through the St Lawrence River.
2 must] not according to the Licensing Order, which makes no such exemption, but to avoid 'the fall of learning' mentioned in the next paragraph.
3 not ... guide] Acts viii. 27-35.
4 Sorbonists] members of the Theology Faculty of the University of Paris, which from 1554 had its seat at the Sorbonne.
5 Arminius] Milton has simplified the conversion of Arminius. Jacob Arminius (1560-1609), the Dutch theologian, was asked in 1589 to refute both the anonymous ('nameless') *Responsio ad argumenta quaedam Bezae et Calvini ex Tractatu de praedestione* (1589), by the infralapsarian ministers of Delft Arent Cornelisz and Reginald Donteclock, and the views of the conditional predestinarian Dirck Coornhert. In the process he rejected both the supralapsarianism of Beza and Calvin and the infralapsarianism of the ministers of Delft, and was converted to Coornhert's position, which soon became known as Arminianism. Milton was not yet an Arminian, and in 1644 Arminianism was associated with Archbishop Laud, whose judicial execution Parliament was about to arrange.
6 cautelous] deceitful.

out of books and dispreaders[1] both of vice and error, how shall the licensers themselves be confided in, unless we can confer upon them, or they assume to themselves above all others in the land, the grace of infallibility and uncorruptedness? And again, if it be true that a wise man, like a good refiner, can gather gold out of the drossiest volume, and that a fool will be a fool with the best book, yea or without book, there is no reason that we should deprive a wise man of any advantage to his wisdom, while we seek to restrain from a fool, that which being restrained will be no hindrance to his folly. For if there should be so much exactness always used to keep that from him which is unfit for his reading, we should in the judgement of Aristotle not only, but of Solomon and of our Saviour,[2] not vouchsafe him good precepts, and by consequence not willingly admit him to good books; as being certain that a wise man will make better use of an idle[3] pamphlet, than a fool will do of sacred Scripture.

'Tis next alleged we must not expose ourselves to temptations without necessity, and next to that, not employ our time in vain things. To both these objections one answer will serve, out of the grounds already laid, that to all men such books are not temptations, nor vanities, but useful drugs and materials wherewith to temper and compare effective and strong medicines, which man's life cannot want.[4] The rest, as children and childish men, who have not the art to qualify and prepare these working minerals, well may be exhorted to forbear, but hindered forcibly they cannot be by all the licensing that sainted[5] Inquisition could ever yet contrive. Which is what I promised to deliver next, that this Order of licensing conduces nothing to the end for which it was framed; and hath almost prevented[6] me by being clear already while thus much hath been explaining. See the ingenuity of Truth, who, when she gets a free and willing hand, opens herself faster than the pace of method and discourse can overtake her.

It was the task which I began with, to show that no nation, or well-instituted state, if they valued books at all, did ever use this way of licensing; and it might be answered, that this is a piece of prudence lately discovered. To which I return, that as it was a thing slight and obvious to think on, so if it had been difficult to find out, there wanted not among them long since who suggested such a course; which they not following, leave us a pattern of their judgement that it was not the not knowing, but the not approving, which was the cause of their not using it.

Plato, a man of high authority, indeed, but least of all for his commonwealth, in the book of his Laws,[7] which no city ever yet received, fed his fancy by making many edicts to his airy burgomasters,

1 dispreaders] those who spread.
2 Aristotle, Solomon, Saviour] *Ethics* I. iii. 1095a; Prov. xxiii. 9; Matt. vii. 6.
3 idle] useless.
4 want] dispense with.
5 sainted] glances at *Sancta Inquisición* (the Spanish Inquisition).
6 prevented] gone before.
7 Laws] Plato's late dialgue, the *Laws*, examines (as did the *Republic*) the best constitution for a city; on the restrictions on learning and poetry see *Laws* VII 801.

which they who otherwise admire him wish had been rather buried and excused in the genial cups of an Academic night-sitting.[1] By which laws he seems to tolerate no kind of learning but by unalterable decree, consisting most of practical traditions, to the attainment whereof a library of smaller bulk than his own Dialogues would be abundant. And there also enacts, that no poet should so much as read to any private man what he had written, until the judges and law-keepers had seen it, and allowed it. But that Plato meant this law peculiarly to that commonwealth which he had imagined, and to no other, is evident. Why was he not else a lawgiver to himself, but a transgressor, and to be expelled by his own magistrates; both for the wanton epigrams[2] and dialogues which he made, and his perpetual reading of Sophron Mimus[3] and Aristophanes, books of grossest infamy, and also for commending the latter of them, though he were the malicious libeller of his chief friends,[4] to be read by the tyrant Dionysius, who had little need of such trash to spend his time on? But that he knew this licensing of poems had reference and dependence to many other provisos there set down in his fancied republic, which in this world could have no place: and so neither he himself, nor any magistrate, or city ever imitated that course, which, taken apart from those other collateral injunctions, must needs be vain and fruitless. For if they fell upon one kind of strictness, unless their care were equal to regulate all other things of like aptness to corrupt the mind, that single endeavour they knew would be but a fond labour; to shut and fortify one gate against corruption, and be necessitated to leave others round about wide open.

If we think to regulate printing, thereby to rectify manners, we must regulate all recreations and pastimes, all that is delightful to man. No music must be heard, no song be set or sung, but what is grave and Doric.[5] There must be licensing dancers, that no gesture, motion, or deportment be taught our youth but what by their allowance shall be thought honest; for such Plato[6] was provided of; it will ask more than the work of twenty licensers to examine all the lutes, the violins, and the guitars in every house; they must not be suffered to prattle as they do, but must be licensed what they may say. And who shall silence all the airs and madrigals that whisper softness in chambers? The windows also, and the balconies must be thought on; there are shrewd[7] books, with dangerous frontispieces, set to

1 cups ... night-sitting] A 'symposium' was a Greek drinking-party that followed the evening meal; 'Academic' refers to Plato's Academy (*PR* IV 244-6n).

2 wanton epigrams] Plato's homosexual epigrams appear in the *Greek Anthology* and in Diogenes Laertius (III. 23).

3 Sophron Mimus] Sophron of Syracuse, writer of mimes (fifth century BC), who, according to Diogenes Laertius (III. 13) and a fragment of Douris of Samos, was greatly admired by Plato.

4 friends] Aristophanes satirizes philosophers (especially Socrates) in *Clouds*; on Dionysius see p. 579, n.11.

5 Doric] Dorian, a mode of ancient music associated by Plato with courage (*Republic* 393c-399d) and by Aristotle with the golden mean (*Politics* VIII 1339a-1342b).

6 Plato] *Laws* VII. 2.   7 shrewd] wicked.

sale; who shall prohibit them, shall twenty licensers? The villages also must have their visitors to inquire what lectures[1] the bagpipe and the rebeck[2] reads, even to the ballatry and the gamut of every municipal fiddler, for these are the countryman's Arcadias, and his Montemayors.[3]

Next, what more national corruption, for which England hears ill abroad, than household gluttony: who shall be the rectors of our daily rioting? And what shall be done to inhibit the multitudes that frequent those houses where drunkenness is sold and harboured? Our garments also should be referred to the licensing of some more sober workmasters to see them cut into a less wanton garb. Who shall regulate all the mixed conversation[4] of our youth, male and female together, as is the fashion of this country? Who shall still appoint what shall be discoursed, what presumed, and no further? Lastly, who shall forbid and separate all idle resort, all evil company? These things will be, and must be; but how they shall be least hurtful, how least enticing, herein consists the grave and governing wisdom of a state.

To sequester out of the world into Atlantic and Utopian[5] polities which never can be drawn into use, will not mend our condition; but to ordain wisely as in this world of evil, in the midst whereof God hath placed us unavoidably. Nor is it Plato's licensing of books will do this, which necessarily pulls along with it so many other kinds of licensing, as will make us all both ridiculous and weary, and yet frustrate; but those unwritten, or at least unconstraining, laws of virtuous education, religious and civil nurture, which Plato there[6] mentions as the bonds and ligaments of the commonwealth, the pillars and the sustainers of every written statute; these they be which will bear chief sway in such matters as these, when all licensing will be easily eluded. Impunity and remissness, for certain, are the bane of a commonwealth; but here the great art lies, to discern in what the law is to bid restraint and punishment, and in what things persuasion only is to work.

If every action which is good or evil in man at ripe years, were to be under pittance and prescription and compulsion, what were virtue but a name, what praise could be then due to well-doing, what

1 visitors, lectures] 'visitors' was an emotive word, referring to Archbishop Laud's Metropolitan Visitation of his suffragan dioceses in 1634 and of the universities in 1636; the visitors reported on such matters as the orthodoxy of sermons, some of which were 'lectures', sermons given by lecturers, i.e. ordained stipendiary clergy (many of whom were Puritans) appointed by town corporations, parishes or individuals.

2 bagpipe, rebeck] The bagpipe was associated with rural England (not Scotland), as was the rebeck, an early bowed instrument.

3 Arcadias, Montemayors] pastoral romances, with reference to the *Arcadia* of Jacopo Sannazaro (1504) and the *Diana* of Jorge de Montemayor (1559), and their literary descendants such as Lope de Vega (*Arcadia*, 1598), Sir Philip Sidney (*Arcadia*, 1590) and James Shirley (*Arcadia*, 1640).

4 conversation] intimate association.

5 Atlantic, Utopian] the ideal commonwealths designed by Francis Bacon (*New Atlantis*, 1627) and Thomas More (*Utopia*, 1516); the constitution of Atlantis is the chief subject of Plato's unfinished *Critias*.

6 there] *Laws* I 643-4.

gramercy[1] to be sober, just, or continent? Many there be that complain of divine providence for suffering Adam to transgress; foolish tongues! When God gave him reason, he gave him freedom to choose, for reason is but choosing; he had been else a mere artificial Adam, such an Adam as he is in the motions.[2] We ourselves esteem not of that obedience, or love, or gift, which is of force; God therefore left him free, set before him a provoking object, ever almost in his eyes; herein consisted his merit, herein the right of his reward, the praise of his abstinence. Wherefore did he create passions within us, pleasures round about us, but that these rightly tempered are the very ingredients of virtue?

They are not skilful considerers of human things, who imagine to remove sin by removing the matter of sin; for, besides that it is a huge heap increasing under the very act of diminishing, though some part of it may for a time be withdrawn from some persons, it cannot from all, in such a universal thing as books are; and when this is done, yet the sin remains entire. Though ye take from a covetous man all his treasure, he has yet one jewel left, ye cannot bereave him of his covetousness. Banish all objects of lust, shut up all youth into the severest discipline that can be exercised in any hermitage, ye cannot make them chaste, that came not thither so: such great care and wisdom is required to the right managing of this point. Suppose we could expel sin by this means; look how much we thus expel of sin, so much we expel of virtue: for the matter of them both is the same; remove that, and ye remove them both alike. This justifies the high providence of God, who, though he commands us temperance, justice, continence, yet pours out before us, even to a profuseness, all desirable things, and gives us minds that can wander beyond all limit and satiety. Why should we then affect a rigour contrary to the manner of God and of nature, by abridging or scanting those means, which books freely permitted are, both to the trial of virtue and the exercise of truth? It would be better done, to learn that the law must needs be frivolous, which goes to restrain things, uncertainly and yet equally working to good and to evil. And were I the chooser, a dram of well-doing should be preferred before many times as much the forcible hindrance of evil-doing. For God sure esteems the growth and completing of one virtuous person more than the restraint of ten vicious.

And albeit whatever thing we hear or see, sitting, walking, travelling, or conversing, may be fitly called our book, and is of the same effect that writings are; yet grant the thing to be prohibited were only books, it appears that this order hitherto is far insufficient to the end which it intends. Do we not see, not once or oftener, but weekly, that continued court-libel[3] against the Parliament and City, printed, as the wet sheets can witness, and dispersed among us, for all that licensing can do? Yet this is the prime service a man would think,

1 gramercy] thanks. 2 motions] puppet-shows.
3 court-libel] *Mercurius Aulicus* ('Court Mercury'), a weekly Royalist newspaper which had been published in Oxford since 1642 and was (as Milton says) reprinted on secret presses in London.

wherein this Order should give proof of itself. If it were executed, you'll say. But certain, if execution be remiss or blindfold now, and in this particular, what will it be hereafter and in other books? If then the Order shall not be vain and frustrate, behold a new labour, Lords and Commons; ye must repeal and proscribe all scandalous and unlicensed books already printed and divulged; after ye have drawn them up into a list, that all may know which are condemned, and which not; and ordain that no foreign books be delivered out of custody, till they have been read over. This office wil require the whole time of not a few overseers, and those no vulgar[1] men. There be also books which are partly useful and excellent, partly culpable and pernicious; this work will ask as many more officials,[2] to make expurgations and expunctions, that the commonwealth of learning be not damnified.[3] In fine,[4] when the multitude of books increase upon their hands, ye must be fain to catalogue all those printers who are found frequently offending, and forbid the importation of their whole suspected typography. In a word, that this your Order may be exact and not deficient, ye must reform it perfectly according to the model of Trent and Seville,[5] which I know ye abhor to do.

Yet though ye should condescend[6] to this, which God forbid, the Order still would be but fruitless and defective to that end whereto ye meant it. If to prevent sects and schisms, who is so unread or so uncatechized in story,[7] that hath not heard of many sects refusing books as a hindrance, and preserving their doctrine unmixed for many ages, only by unwritten traditions? The Christian faith, for that was once a schism, is not unknown to have spread all over Asia, ere any Gospel or Epistle was seen in writing. If the amendment of manners be aimed at, look into Italy and Spain, whether those places be one scruple the better, the honester, the wiser, the chaster, since all the inquisitional rigour that hath been executed upon books.

Another reason, whereby to make it plain that this Order will miss the end it seeks, consider by the quality which ought to be in every licenser. It cannot be denied but that he who is made judge to sit upon the birth or death of books, whether they may be wafted[8] into this world or not, had need to be a man above the common measure, both studious, learned, and judicious; there may be else no mean mistakes in the censure of what is passable or not; which is also no mean injury. If he be of such worth as behoves him, there cannot be a more tedious and unpleasing journey-work,[9] a greater loss of time levied upon his

1 vulgar] ordinary.
2 officials] The Officials Principal, the presiding officers of the ecclesiastical courts, were hated by Puritans.
3 commonwealth ... damnified] Milton's adaptation of *ne quid respublica detrimenti capiat* (see *PL* X 409n.); 'damnified' means 'harmed'.
4 In fine] finally.
5 Trent, Seville] On Trent, see p. 583, n. 10; Seville was the seat of the first (1481) and most infamous of the tribunals of the Spanish Inquisition.
6 condescend] agree.   7 story] history.
8 wafted] across the river that separates unborn souls from the living world (e.g. Plato, *Phaedo* 113).
9 journey-work] hack-work, drudgery.

head, than to be made the perpetual reader of unchosen books and pamphlets, ofttimes huge volumes. There is no book that is acceptable unless at certain seasons; but to be enjoined the reading of that at all times, and in a hand scarce legible, whereof three pages would not down at any time in the fairest print, is an imposition which I cannot believe how he that values time and his own studies, or is but of a sensible[1] nostril, should be able to endure. In this one thing I crave leave of the present licensers to be pardoned for so thinking; who doubtless took this office up, looking on it through their obedience to the Parliament, whose command perhaps made all things seem easy and unlaborious to them; but that this short trial hath wearied them out already, their own expressions and excuses to them who make so many journeys to solicit their licence are testimony enough. Seeing therefore those who now possess the employment by all evident signs wish themselves well rid of it; and that no man of worth, none that is not a plain unthrift of his own hours is ever likely to succeed them, except he mean to put himself to the salary of a press corrector; we may easily foresee what kind of licensers we are to expect hereafter, either ignorant, imperious, and remiss, or basely pecuniary. This is what I had to show, wherein this Order cannot conduce to that end whereof it bears the intention.

I lastly proceed from the no good it can do, to the manifest hurt it causes, in being first the greatest discouragement and affront that can be offered to learning, and to learned men.

It was the complaint and lamentation of prelates, upon every least breath of a motion to remove pluralities,[2] and distribute more equally church revenues, that then all learning would be for ever dashed and discouraged. But as for that opinion, I never found cause to think that the tenth part of learning stood or fell with the clergy; nor could I ever but hold it for a sordid and unworthy speech of any churchman who had a competency[3] left him. If therefore ye be loath to dishearten heartily and discontent, not the mercenary crew of false pretenders to learning, but the free and ingenuous sort of such as evidently were born to study, and love learning for itself, not for lucre or any other end but the service of God and of truth, and perhaps that lasting fame and perpetuity of praise which God and good men have consented shall be the reward of those whose published labours advance the good of mankind; then know that, so far to distrust the judgement and the honesty of one who hath but a comon repute in learning, and never yet offended, as not to count him fit to print his mind without a tutor and examiner, lest he should drop a schism, or something of corruption, is the greatest displeasure and indignity to a free and knowing spirit that can be put upon him.

What advantage is it to be a man over it is to be a boy at school, if we have only escaped the ferula[4] to come under the fescue[5] of an *Imprimatur*, if serious and elaborate writings, as if they were no more than the theme of a grammar-lad under his pedagogue, must not be

1 sensible] sensitive.   2 pluralities] See *On the New Forcers* 3n.
3 competency] income sufficient to live modestly.
4 ferula] the cane used by schoolmasters for beating boys.
5 fescue] a schoolmaster's pointer.

uttered[1] without the cursory eyes of a temporizing and extemporizing licenser? He who is not trusted with his own actions, his drift not being known to be evil, and standing to the hazard of law and penalty, has no great argument to think himself reputed, in the commonwealth wherein he was born, for other than a fool or a foreigner. When a man writes to the world, he summons up all his reason and deliberation to assist him; he searches, meditates, is industrious, and likely consults and confers with his judicious friends; after all which done he takes himself to be informed in what he writes, as well as any that writ before him; if, in this the most consummate act of his fidelity and ripeness, no years, no industry, no former proof of his abilities can bring him to that state of maturity, as not to be still mistrusted and suspected, unless he carry all his considerate diligence, all his midnight watchings and expense of Palladian oil,[2] to the hasty view of an unleisured licenser, perhaps much his younger, perhaps far his inferior in judgement, perhaps one who never knew the labour of book-writing; and if he be not repulsed or slighted, must appear in print like a puny[3] with his guardian, and his censor's hand on the back of his title to be his bail and surety that he is no idiot or seducer, it cannot be but a dishonour and derogation to the author, to the book, to the privilege and dignity of learning.

And what if the author shall be one so copious of fancy, as to have many things well worth the adding come into his mind after licensing, while the book is yet under the press, which not seldom happens to the best and diligentest writers; and that perhaps a dozen times in one book? The printer dares not go beyond his licensed copy; so often then must the author trudge to his leave-giver, that those his new insertions may be viewed; and many a jaunt will be made, ere that licenser, for it must be the same man, can either be found, or found at leisure; meanwhile either the press must stand still, which is no small damage, or the author lose his accuratest thoughts, and send the book forth worse than he had made it, which to a diligent writer is the greatest melancholy and vexation that can befall.

And how can a man teach with authority, which is the life of teaching, how can he be a doctor in his book as he ought to be, or else had better be silent, whenas all he teaches, all he delivers, is but under the tuition, under the correction of his patriarchal[4] licenser to blot or alter[5] what precisely accords not with the hidebound humour which he calls his judgement? When every acute reader, upon the first sight of a pedantic[6] licence, will be ready with these like words to ding[7] the book a quoit's distance from him: 'I hate a pupil teacher, I endure not an instructor that comes to me under the wardship of an overseeing fist. I know nothing of the licenser, but that I have his own hand[8]

1 uttered] published.
2 Palladian oil] the olive oil given by Pallas Athene, goddess of wisdom, here used to refer to the oil burned by lamps.
3 puny] a minor.
4 patriarchal] glances at Laud's (alleged) ambition to be Patriarch of Britain.
5 alter] Laud was charged (among other things) with wanting to alter books of which the licensers did not approve.
6 pedantic] pertaining to a schoolmaster.
7 ding] throw.   8 hand] signature.

here for his arrogance; who shall warrant me his judgement? 'The State, sir,' replies the stationer,[1] but has a quick return. 'The State shall be my governors, but not my critics; they may be mistaken in the choice of a licenser, as easily as this licenser may be mistaken in an author; this is some common stuff;' and he might add from Sir Francis Bacon, 'That such authorized books are but the language of the times.'[2] For though a licenser should happen to be judicious more than ordinary, which will be a great jeopardy of the next succession, yet his very office and his commission enjoins him to let pass nothing but what is vulgarly received already.

Nay, which is more lamentable, if the work of any deceased author, though never so famous in his lifetime and even to this day, come to their hands for licence to be printed, or reprinted, if there be found in his book one sentence of a venturous edge, uttered in the height of zeal and who knows whether it might not be the dictate of a divine spirit, yet not suiting with every low decrepit humour of their own, though it were Knox[3] himself, the reformer of a kingdom, that spake it, they will not pardon him their dash;[4] the sense of that great man shall to all posterity be lost, for the fearfulness or the presumptuous rashness of a perfunctory licenser. And to what an author this violence hath been lately done, and in what book of greatest consequence to be faithfully published, I could now instance, but shall forbear till a more convenient season.

Yet if these things be not resented seriously and timely by them who have the remedy in their power, but that such iron-moulds[5] as these shall have authority to gnaw out the choicest periods of exquisitest books, and to commit such a treacherous fraud against the orphan remainders of worthiest men after death, the more sorrow will belong to that hapless race of men, whose misfortune it is to have understanding. Henceforth let no man care to learn, or care to be more than worldly-wise; for certainly in higher matters to be ignorant and slothful, to be a common steadfast dunce, will be the only pleasant life, and only in request.

And as it is a particular disesteem of every knowing person alive, and most injurious to the written labours and monuments of the dead, so to me it seems an undervaluing and vilifying of the whole nation. I cannot set so light by all the invention, the art, the wit, the grave and solid judgement which is in England, as that it can be comprehended in any twenty capacities how good soever, much less that it should not pass except their superintendence be over it, except it be sifted and strained with their strainers, that it should be uncurrent without their manual stamp. Truth and understanding are not such wares as to be monopolized[6] and traded in by tickets[7] and statutes and

1 stationer] publisher, bookseller.
2 'That ... times'] quoted from Bacon's *Advertisement Touching the Controversies of the Church of England*, written in 1589 and published as *A Wise and Moderate Discourse concerning Church Affairs* in 1640 or 1641.
3 Knox] John Knox (c. 1505-72), the Scottish reformer.
4 dash] erasing line.   5 iron-moulds] spots of rust.
6 monopolized] The granting of monopolies, both legally (until 1624) and illegally, was one of the most resented features of the reign of Charles.
7 tickets] commercial documents.

standards.[1] We must not think to make a staple[2] commodity of all the knowledge in the land, to mark and license it like our broadcloth and our woolpacks. What is it but a servitude like that imposed by the Philistines,[3] not to be allowed the sharpening of our own axes and coulters,[4] but we must repair from all quarters to twenty licensing forges? Had anyone written and divulged erroneous things and scandalous to honest life, misusing and forfeiting the esteem had of his reason among men, if after conviction this only censure were adjudged him that he should never henceforth write but what were first examined by an appointed officer, whose hand should be annexed to pass his credit for him that now he might be safely read; it could not be apprehended less than a disgraceful punishment. Whence to include the whole nation, and those that never yet thus offended, under such a diffident and suspectful prohibition, may plainly be understood what a disparagement it is. So much the more, whenas debtors[5] and delinquents[6] may walk abroad without a keeper, but unoffensive books must not stir forth without a visible jailer in their title.

Nor is it to the common people less than a reproach; for if we be so jealous over them, as that we dare not trust them with an English pamphlet, what do we but censure them for a giddy, vicious, and ungrounded people; in such a sick and weak state of faith and discretion, as to be able to take nothing down but through the pipe[7] of a licenser? That this is care or love of them, we cannot pretend, whenas, in those popish places where the laity are most hated and despised, the same strictness is used over them. Wisdom we cannot call it, because it stops but one breach of licence, nor that neither; whenas those corruptions which it seeks to prevent, break in faster at other doors which cannot be shut.

And in conclusion, it reflects to the disrepute of our ministers also, of whose labours we should hope better, and of the proficiency which their flock reaps by them, than that after all this light of the Gospel which is, and is to be, and all this continual preaching, they should be still frequented with such an unprincipled, unedified and laic rabble,[8] as that the whiff of every new pamphlet should stagger them out of their catechism and Christian walking. This may have much reason

---

1 standards] weights and measures fixed by law.
2 staple] controlled by a 'staple', a town or body of merchants with exclusive commercial rights over a product.
3 Philistines] Israelites had to go to the Philistines to have their tools sharpened (I Sam. xiii. 19-21).
4 coulter] vertical iron blade fixed in front of the ploughshare.
5 debtors] Members of Parliament and their dependants were protected from incarceration for debt (until 1648), as were those who lived in sanctuaries such as the precincts of dissolved monasteries (on which streets of houses had often been built).
6 delinquents] those who had assisted the king in the Civil War; such delinquents had been made liable to prison and sequestration in March 1643, but in January 1644 pardon had been offered to those who confessed, and they were allowed to compound for their sequestrated estates.
7 pipe] tube for feeding patients too weak to swallow.
8 laic rabble] Laud had been accused of attempting to degrade the role of the laity in the life of the church.

to discourage the ministers when such a low conceit[1] is had of all their exhortations, and the benefiting of their hearers, as that they are not thought fit to be turned loose to three sheets of paper without a licenser; that all the sermons, all the lectures preached, printed, vented in such numbers, and such volumes, as have now well-nigh made all other books unsaleable, should not be armour enough against one single enchiridion,[2] without the castle of St Angelo[3] of an *Imprimatur*.

And lest some should persuade ye, Lords and Commons, that these arguments of learned men's discouragement at this your Order are mere flourishes, and not real, I could recount what I have seen and heard in other countries, where this kind of inquisition tyrannizes; when I have sat among their learned men, for that honour I had, and been counted happy to be born in such a place of philosophic freedom, as they supposed England was, while themselves did nothing but bemoan the servile condition into which learning amongst them was brought; that this was it which had damped the glory of Italian wits; that nothing had been there written now these many years but flattery and fustian. There it was that I found and visited the famous Galileo,[4] grown old a prisoner to the Inquisition, for thinking in astronomy otherwise than the Franciscan and Dominican licensers thought.

And though I knew that England then was groaning loudest under the prelatical yoke, nevertheless I took it as a pledge of future happiness, that other nations were so persuaded of her liberty. Yet was it beyond my hope that those worthies were then breathing in her air, who should be her leaders to such a deliverance, as shall never be forgotten by any revolution of time that this world hath to finish. When that was once begun, it was as little in my fear that, what words of complaint I heard among learned men of other parts uttered against the Inquisition, the same I should hear by as learned men at home uttered in time of Parliament[5] against an order of licensing; and that so generally that when I had disclosed myself a companion of their discontent, I might say, if without envy,[6] that he[7] whom an honest quaestorship had endeared to the Sicilians was not more by them importuned against Verres,[8] than the favourable opinion which I had among many who honour ye, and are known and respected by ye, loaded me with entreaties and persuasions, that I would not despair to

1 conceit] estimation.
2 enchiridion] means both 'manual' and (in Greek) 'dagger'.
3 St Angelo] fortress on the Tiber close to the Vatican; in Milton's time used as the papal prison.
4 Galileo] In 1638 or 1639 Milton had visited Galileo (who had died in 1642) in Il Gioiello, Galileo's house at Arcetri (near Florence), where he had been placed under permanent house arrest by the Inquisition.
5 in ... Parliament] as distinct from the period when Parliament had not been convened, during the 'personal rule' of Charles (1629-40).
6 without envy] without exciting ill feeling (Latin *sine invidia*).
7 he] Cicero, who had been elected *quaestor* (an official in charge of public finance) in 75 BC, and served in western Sicily.
8 Verres] In 70 BC Cicero secured (through the eloquence of his *Verrine Orations*) the conviction of Gaius Verres (proconsul in Sicily from 73-71) for extortion.

lay together that which just reason should bring into my mind, toward the removal of an undeserved thraldom upon learning. That this is not therefore the disburdening of a particular fancy, but the common grievance of all those who had prepared their minds and studies above the vulgar pitch to advance truth in others, and from others to entertain it, thus much may satisfy.

And in their name I shall for neither friend nor foe conceal what the general murmur is; that if it come to inquisitioning again and licensing, and that we are so timorous of ourselves, and so suspicious of all men, as to fear each book and the shaking of every leaf, before we know what the contents are; if some who but of late were little better than silenced from preaching shall come now to silence us from reading, except what they please, it cannot be guessed what is intended by some but a second tyranny over learning: and will soon put it out of controversy, that bishops and presbyters are the same to us, both name and thing. That those evils of prelaty, which before from five to six and twenty sees were distributively charged upon the whole people, will now light wholly upon learning, is not obscure to us: whenas now the pastor of a small unlearned parish on the sudden shall be exalted archbishop over a large diocese of books, and yet not remove, but keep his other cure too, a mystical pluralist. He who but of late cried down the sole ordination of every novice Bachelor of Art, and denied sole jurisdiction over the simplest parishioner, shall now at home in his private chair assume both these over worthiest and excellentest books and ablest authors that write them.

This is not, ye covenants[1] and protestations[2] that we have made! This is not to put down prelaty; this is but to chop[3] an episcopacy; this is but to translate the Palace Metropolitan[4] from one kind of dominion into another; this is but an old canonical sleight of commuting[5] our penance. To startle thus betimes at a mere unlicensed pamphlet will after a while be afraid of every conventicle,[6] and a while after will make a conventicle of every Christian meeting. But I am certain that a state governed by the rules of justice and fortitude, or a church built and founded upon the rock of faith and true knowledge, cannot be so pusillanimous. While things are yet not[7] constituted in religion, that freedom of writing should be restrained by a discipline imitated from the prelates and learnt by them from the Inquisition, to shut us all up again into the breast of a licenser, must needs give cause of doubt and discouragement to all learned and religious men.

1 covenants] the Scottish 'National Covenant' (February 1638) and the 'Solemn League and Covenant' (September 1643).
2 protestations] the Protestation of May 1641, formulated to protect Parliament from the use of force by Charles.
3 chop] exchange.
4 Palace Metropolitan] the Archbishop's palace at Canterbury (Lambeth was not a palace until 1658).
5 commuting] the medieval system of commutation, under which a penance could be replaced by a lesser penance and a payment.
6 conventicle] a religious meeting elsewhere than in a church.
7 yet not] the Westminster Assembly was still formulating its views, and did not submit its 'Confession of Faith' to Parliament until 1646.

Who cannot but discern the fineness of this politic drift, and who are the contrivers; that while bishops were to be bated down,[1] then all presses might be open; it was the people's birthright and privilege in time of Parliament, it was the breaking forth of light? But now, the bishops abrogated and voided out the Church, as if our Reformation sought no more but to make room for others into their seats under another name, the episcopal arts begin to bud again, the cruse of truth must run no more oil,[2] liberty of printing must be enthralled again under a prelatical commission of twenty, the privilege of the people nullified, and, which is worse, the freedom of learning must groan again, and to her old fetters: all this the Parliament yet sitting. Although their own late arguments and defences against the prelates might remember them, that this obstructing violence meets for the most part with an event utterly opposite to the end which it drives at; instead of suppressing sects and schisms, it raises them and invests them with a reputation. 'The punishing of wits enhances their authority,' saith the Viscount St Albans;[3] 'and a forbidden writing is thought to be a certain spark of truth that flies up in the faces of them who seek to tread it out.' This Order, therefore, may prove a nursing-mother to sects, but I shall show how it will be a step-dame to Truth: and first by disenabling us to the maintenance of what is known already.

Well knows he who uses to consider, that our faith and knowledge thrives by exercise, as well as our limbs and complexion. Truth is compared in Scripture[4] to a streaming fountain; if her waters flow not in a perpetual progression, they sicken into a muddy pool of conformity and tradition. A man may be a heretic in the truth; and if he believe things only because his pastor says so, or the Assembly[5] so determines, without knowing other reason, though his belief be true, yet the very truth he holds becomes his heresy.

There is not any burden that some would gladlier post off to another than the charge and care of their religion. There be, who knows not that there be, of Protestants and professors[6] who live and die in as arrant an implicit faith[7] as any lay Papist of Loreto.[8] A wealthy man, addicted to his pleasure and to his profits, finds religion to be a traffic so entangled, and of so many piddling accounts, that of all mysteries[9] he cannot skill to keep a stock going upon that trade. What should

1 bated down] cast down, humbled (aphetic form of 'abated').
2 cruse ... oil] I Kings xvii. 9–15; a 'cruse' is a vessel for holding liquids.
3 Viscount St Albans] Francis Bacon; the quotation is an earlier part of the sentence quoted on p. 600.
4 in Scripture] possibly Prov. xviii. 4.
5 Assembly] the Westminster Assembly.
6 professors] Puritans.
7 implicit faith] refers to a scholastic distinction, much despised by Puritans, between the *fides explicita* ('explicit faith' requiring understanding) expected of the higher clergy and the *fides implicita* ('implicit faith' accepted on the authority of the church) appropriate to the lesser clergy and the laity.
8 Loreto] the site (near Ancona, in Italy) of the Holy House of the Virgin Mary; it was transported by angels from Nazareth to Loreto (via Dalmatia) in 1291.
9 mysteries] occupations.

he do? Fain he would have the name to be religious, fain he would bear
up with his neighbours in that. What does he therefore, but resolves to
give over toiling, and to find himself out some factor, to whose care
and credit he may commit the whole managing of his religious affairs;
some divine of note and estimation that must be. To him he adheres,
resigns the whole warehouse of his religion, with all the locks and keys,
into his custody; and indeed makes the very person of that man his
religion; esteems his associating with him a sufficient evidence and
commendatory of his own piety. So that a man may say his religion is
now no more within himself, but is become a dividual movable,[1] and
goes and comes near him, according as that good man frequents the
house. He entertains him, gives him gifts, feasts him, lodges him; his
religion comes home at night, prays, is liberally supped, and sump-
tuously laid to sleep, rises, is saluted, and after the malmsey, or some
well-spiced brewage, and better breakfasted than he[2] whose morning
appetite would have gladly fed on green figs between Bethany and
Jerusalem, his religion walks abroad at eight, and leaves his kind
entertainer in the shop trading all day without his religion.

Another sort there be who, when they hear that all things shall be
ordered, all things regulated and settled, nothing written but what
passes through the custom-house of certain publicans[3] that have the
tunnaging and poundaging[4] of all free-spoken truth, will straight give
themselves up into your hands, make 'em and cut 'em out what
religion ye please: there be delights, there be recreations and jolly
pastimes that will fetch the day about from sun to sun, and rock the
tedious year as in a delightful dream. What need they torture their
heads with that which others have taken so strictly and so unalterably
into their own purveying? These are the fruits which a dull ease and
cessation of our knowledge will bring forth among the people. How
goodly and how to be wished were such an obedient unanimity as this,
what a fine conformity would it starch us all into! Doubtless a staunch
and solid piece of framework, as any January could freeze together.

Nor much better will be the consequence even among the clergy
themselves. It is no new thing never heard of before, for a parochial
minister, who has his reward and is at his Hercules' pillars[5] in a warm
benefice, to be easily inclinable, if he have nothing else that may rouse
up his studies, to finish his circuit in an English concordance and

---

1 dividual movable] something separable and portable.
2 he] Jesus, who destroyed the fig tree (Matt. xxi. 17-19; Mark xi. 12-14).
3 publicans] tax-collectors.
4 tunnaging, poundaging] tunnage was a tax of three shillings on each 'tun' (barrel)
   of imported wine; poundage was a tax of one shilling per pound sterling on all
   other exports and imports except for staple commodities (see p. 601). From the
   reign of Henry V monarchs had been granted 'tunnage and poundage' for life
   by their first parliaments. Parliament refused to do so on the accession of
   Charles, and relented only when (in 1641) Charles agreed to a bill making it
   illegal for a king to levy such taxes without the consent of Parliament.
5 Hercules' pillars] Calpe (Gibraltar) and Abyla (Apes' Hill), on the Moroccan
   coast) marked the limits of enterprise for the merchants of ancient Greece and
   Rome.

a topic folio,[1] the gatherings and savings of a sober graduateship, a harmony[2] and a catena;[3] treading the constant round of certain common doctrinal heads, attended with the uses, motives, marks, and means; out of which, as out of an alphabet, or sol-fa,[4] by forming and transforming, joining and disjoining variously, a little bookcraft, and two hours' meditation, might furnish him unspeakably to the performance of more than a weekly charge of sermoning; not to reckon up the infinite helps of interlinearies, breviaries, synopses, and other loitering gear.[5] But as for the multitude of sermons ready printed and piled up, on every text that is not difficult, our London trading St Thomas in his vestry, and add to boot St Martin and St Hugh,[6] have not within their hallowed limits more vendible ware of all sorts ready made; so that penury he never need fear of pulpit provision, having where so plenteously to refresh his magazine. But if his rear and flanks be not impaled,[7] if his back door be not secured by the rigid licenser, but that a bold book may now and then issue forth and give the assault to some of his old collections in their trenches, it will concern him then to keep waking, to stand in watch, to set good guards and sentinels about his received opinions, to walk the round and counter-round with his fellow inspectors, fearing lest any of his flock be seduced, who also then would be better instructed, better exercised and disciplined. And God send that the fear of this diligence, which must then be used, do not make us affect the laziness of a licensing church.

For if we be sure we are in the right, and do not hold the truth guiltily, which becomes not, if we ourselves condemn not our own weak and frivolous teaching, and the people for an untaught and irreligious gadding rout, what can be more fair than when a man judicious, learned, and of a conscience, for aught we know, as good as theirs that taught us what we know, shall not privily from house to house, which is more dangerous, but openly by writing publish to the world what his opinion is, what his reasons, and wherefore that which is now thought cannot be sound? Christ urged it as wherewith to justify himself, that he preached in public;[8] yet writing is more public than preaching; and more easy to refutation, if need be, there being so many whose business and profession merely it is to be the champions of truth; which if they neglect, what can be imputed but their sloth, or unability?

---

1 topic folio] commonplace book.
2 harmony] usually a 'harmony of the gospels', designed to reconcile apparently conflicting accounts of the life of Jesus.
3 catena] a 'chain' of extracts from different Biblical commentators bearing on a single subject.
4 sol-fa] musical scale.
5 interlinearies ... gear] texts in ancient languages with interlinear translations, abridgements, synopses and other equipment conducive to sloth.
6 St Thomas ... St Hugh] churches in London near which printed sermons could be bought. There has never been a church dedicated to St Hugh in London, but there may have been a place-name recalling a chapel to St Hugh on the site of the Charterhouse west of Aldersgate, as Hugh of Lincoln was commonly honoured by the Carthusians.
7 impaled] enclosed with stakes.   8 in public] John xviii. 19–20.

Thus much we are hindered and disinured by this course of licensing, toward the true knowledge of what we seem to know. For how much it hurts and hinders the licensers themselves in the calling of their ministry, more than any secular employment, if they will discharge that office as they ought, so that of necessity they must neglect either the one duty or the other, I insist not, because it is a particular, but leave it to their own conscience, how they will decide it there.

There is yet behind of what I proposed to lay open, the incredible loss and detriment that this plot of incensing puts us to; more than if some enemy at sea should stop up all our havens and ports and creeks, it hinders and retards the importation of our richest merchandise, truth; nay, it was first established and put in practice by antichristian malice and mystery on set purpose to extinguish, if it were possible, the light of Reformation, and to settle[1] falsehood; little differing from that policy wherewith the Turk upholds his *Alcoran*,[2] by the prohibiting of printing. 'Tis not denied, but gladly confessed, we are to send our thanks and vows to heaven louder than most of nations, for that great measure of truth which we enjoy, especially in those main points between us and the Pope, with his appurtenances the prelates; but he who thinks we are to pitch our tent here, and have attained the utmost prospect of reformation that the mortal glass wherein we contemplate can show us, till we come to beatific vision,[3] that man by this very opinion declares that he is yet far short of truth.

Trust indeed came once into the world with her divine master, and was a perfect shape most glorious to look on; but when he ascended, and his apostles after him were laid asleep, then straight arose a wicked race of deceivers, who, as that story[4] goes of the Egyptian Typhon with his conspirators, how they dealt with the good Osiris, took the virgin Truth, hewed her lovely form into a thousand pieces, and scattered them to the four winds. From that time ever since, the sad friends of Truth, such as durst appear, imitating the careful search that Isis made for the mangled body of Osiris, went up and down gathering up limb by limb, still as they could find them. We have not yet found them all, Lords and Commons, nor ever shall do, till her master's second coming; he shall bring together every joint and member, and shall mould them into an immortal feature[5] of loveliness and perfection. Suffer not these licensing prohibitions to stand at every place of opportunity, forbidding and disturbing them that continue seeking, that continue to do our obsequies[6] to the torn body of our martyred saint.

1 settle] establish.   2 *Alcoran*] the Koran.   3 beatific vision] See *PL* I 684n.
4 story] The Egyptian god Set (identified by the Greeks with Typhon) and his
    fellow conspirators killed Osiris; Osiris' wife-sister Isis eventually found his
    body, and revived it long enough to make her pregnant. Set subsequently
    discovered the body and tore it into 14 pieces; Isis found 13 of the pieces and
    reassembled them – the missing piece, his penis, had been eaten by a crab.
    Milton's allegorical reading of the story derives in part from Plutarch's 'On Isis
    and Osiris'.
5 feature] shape.   6 obsequies] commemorative rites.

We boast our light; but if we look not wisely on the sun itself, it smites us into darkness. Who can discern those planets that are oft combust,[1] and those stars of brightest magnitude that rise and set with the sun,[2] until the opposite motion[3] of their orbs bring them to such a place in the firmament, where they may be seen evening or morning? The light which we have gained was given us, not to be ever staring on, but by it to discover onward things more remote from our knowledge. It is not the unfrocking of a priest, the unmitring of a bishop, and the removing him from off the presbyterian shoulders, that will make us a happy nation. No, if other things as great in the church, and in the rule of life both economical and political, be not looked into and reformed, we have looked so long upon the blaze that Zwinglius and Calvin[4] have beaconed up to us, that we are stark blind. There be who perpetually complain of schisms and sects, and make it such a calamity that any man dissents from their maxims. 'Tis their own pride and ignorance which causes the disturbing, who neither will hear with meekness, nor can convince; yet all must be suppressed which is not found in their syntagma.[5] They are the troublers, they are the dividers of unity, who neglect and permit not others to unite those dissevered pieces which are yet wanting to the body of Truth. To be still searching what we know not by what we know, still closing up truth to truth as we find it (for all her body is homogeneal and proportional), this is the golden rule[6] in theology as well as in arithmetic, and makes up the best harmony in a church; not the forced and outward union of cold and neutral, and inwardly divided minds.

Lords and Commons of England, consider what nation it is whereof ye are, and whereof ye are the governors; a nation not slow and dull, but of a quick, ingenious and piercing spirit, acute to invent, subtle and sinewy to discourse, but beneath the reach of any point the highest that human capacity can soar to. Therefore the studies of learning in her deepest sciences have been so ancient and so eminent among us, that writers of good antiquity and ablest judgement have been persuaded that even the school of Pythagoras[7] and the Persian wisdom[8] took beginning from the old philosophy of this island. And

1 combust] A planet is said to be 'combust' (burnt) when it approaches the sun and is apparently extinguished by the sun's light.
2 stars . . . sun] refers to the heliacal rising of stars before or after sunset or sunrise.
3 opposite motion] refers to the apparent movements from east to west caused by the disparity between the daily east-west revolution of the *primum mobile* and the slightly slower revolution of the starry firmament, bringing it back to the same relative position at the end of the 'great year' (see *PL* V 583n.).
4 Zwinglius, Calvin] Ulrich Zwingli (1484-1531) and John Calvin (1509-64), leaders of the Reformation in Zürich and Geneva.
5 syntagma] compendium of systematic theology.
6 golden rule] in arithmetic, the rule of proportion, according to which the knowledge of the relative magnitude of two quantities enables one to generate other values in proportion (M:N::P:Q).
7 Pythagoras] The doctrine of metempsychosis was believed to have been taken by Pythagoras from the Druids; in debates about the relative ages of the two universities Pythagoras was popularly said to have taught in the 'School of Pythagoras', a Norman house in the grounds of St John's College, Cambridge.
8 Persian wisdom] Pliny the Younger hints at the possibility that Zoroastrian magic may have derived from Druid magic (*Naturalis Historia* XXX 2).

that wise and civil Roman, Julius Agricola,[1] who governed once here for Caesar, preferred the natural wits of Britain before the laboured studies of the French. Nor is it for nothing that the grave and frugal Transylvanian[2] sends out yearly from as far as the mountainous borders of Russia, and beyond the Hercynian wilderness,[3] not their youth, but their staid men, to learn our language and our theologic arts.

Yet that which is above all this, the favour and the love of heaven, we have great argument to think in a peculiar manner propitious and propending[4] towards us. Why else was this nation chosen before any other, that out of her, as out of Zion,[5] should be proclaimed and sounded forth the first tidings and trumpet of Reformation to all Europe? And had it not been the obstinate perverseness of our prelates against the divine and admirable spirit of Wycliffe to suppress him as a schismatic and innovator, perhaps neither the Bohemian Huss[6] and Jerome,[7] no nor the name of Luther or of Calvin, had been ever known: the glory of reforming all our neighbours had been completely ours. But now, as our obdurate clergy have with violence demeaned[8] the matter, we are become hitherto the latest and backwardest scholars, of whom God offered to have made us the teachers. Now once again by all concurrence of signs, and by the general instinct of holy and devout men, as they daily and solemnly express their thoughts, God is decreeing to begin some new and great period in his church, even to the reforming of Reformation itself: what does he then but reveal himself to his servants, and as his manner is, first to his Englishmen? I say, as his manner is, first to us, though we mark not the method of his counsels, and are unworthy.

Behold now this vast city: a city of refuge,[9] the mansion house of liberty, encompassed and surrounded with his protection; the shop of war hath not there more anvils and hammers waking, to fashion out the plates and instruments[10] of armed justice in defence of beleaguered truth, than there be pens and heads there, sitting by their studious lamps, musing, searching, revolving new notions and ideas wherewith to present, as with their homage and their fealty, the approaching Reformation; others as fast reading, trying all things, assenting to the force of reason and convincement. What could a man require more from a nation so pliant and so prone to seek after knowledge? What

---

1 Julius Agricola] legate of Britain from 78–85 AD under three Caesars (Vespasian, Titus and Domitian); on the comparison of Britons and Gauls see *Agricola* (XXI) by his son-in-law Tacitus.

2 Transylvanian] Transylvania (now absorbed into Romania) was a semi-independent principality which was precariously dominated by anti-Trinitarian Protestants.

3 Hercynian wilderness] the *Hercynia Silva* of classical literature, a vast forest covering much of central and eastern Europe.

4 propending] being favourably inclined.

5 Zion] Jerusalem.

6 Wycliffe, Huss] See notes p. 583.

7 Jerome] Jerome of Prague, Bohemian reformer (disciple of Wycliffe and Huss) who died at the stake in 1416.

8 demeaned] conducted.

9 city of refuge] Numbers xxxv. 11–15.

10 plates and instruments] breastplates and weapons.

wants there to such a towardly and pregnant soil, but wise and faithful labourers, to make a knowing people, a nation of prophets, of sages, and of worthies? We reckon more than five months yet to harvest; there need not be five weeks, had we but eyes to lift up, the fields are white already.[1]

Where there is much desire to learn, there of necessity will be much arguing, much writing, many opinions; for opinion in good men is but knowledge in the making. Under these fantastic terrors of sect and schism, we wrong the earnest and zealous thirst after knowledge and understanding which God hath stirred up in this city. What some lament of, we rather should rejoice at, should rather praise this pious forwardness among men, to reassume the ill-deputed care of their religion into their own hands again. A little generous prudence, a little forbearance of one another, and some grain of charity might win all these diligences to join, and unite in one general and brotherly search after truth; could we but forgo this prelatical tradition of crowding free consciences and Christian liberties into canons and precepts of men. I doubt not, if some great and worthy stranger should come among us, wise to discern the mould and temper of a people, and how to govern it, observing the high hopes and aims, the diligent alacrity of our extended thoughts and reasonings in the pursuance of truth and freedom, but that he would cry out as Pyrrhus[2] did, admiring the Roman docility and courage: if such were my Epirots, I would not despair the greatest design that could be attempted, to make a church or kingdom happy.

Yet these are the men cried out against for schismatics and sectaries; as if, while the temple[3] of the Lord was building, some cutting, some squaring the marble, others hewing the cedars, there should be a sort of irrational men who could not consider there must be many schisms and many dissections made in the quarry and in the timber, ere the house of God can be built. And when every stone is laid artfully together, it cannot be united into a continuity, it can but be contiguous in this world; neither can every piece of the building be of one form; nay rather the perfection consists in this, that, out of many moderate varieties and brotherly dissimilitudes that are not vastly disproportional, arises the goodly and the graceful symmetry that commends the whole pile and structure.

Let us therefore be more considerate builders, more wise in spiritual architecture, when great reformation is expected. For now the time seems come, wherein Moses the great prophet may sit in heaven rejoicing to see that memorable and glorious wish of his fulfilled, when not only our seventy elders, but all the Lord's people, are become prophets. No marvel then though some men, and some good men too perhaps, but young in goodness, as Joshua then was, envy

1 five ... already] an adaptation of John iv. 35, in which the period is four months.
2 Pyrrhus] king of Epirus who after the battle of Heraclea (280 BC in which he defeated the Romans is said to have declared that it would be easy for him to conquer the world if he had Romans as his soldiers, or for the Romans to do so if he were their king (Florus, *Epitome bellorum omnium* I. 18).
3 temple] Solomon's temple (I Kings v–vi).

them.[1] They fret, and out of their own weakness are in agony, lest these divisions and subdivisions will undo us. The adversary again applauds, and waits the hour; 'when they have branched themselves out,' saith he, 'small enough into parties and partitions, then will be our time.' Fool! He sees not the firm root, out of which we all grow, though into branches; nor will beware until he see our small divided maniples[2] cutting through at every angle of his ill-united and unwieldy brigade. And that we are to hope better of all these supposed sects and schisms, and that we shall not need that solicitude, honest perhaps, though over-timorous, of them that vex in this behalf, but shall laugh in the end at those malicious applauders of our differences, I have these reasons to persuade me.

First, when a city shall be as it were besieged and blocked about, her navigable river infested, inroads and incursions round, defiance and battle oft rumoured to be marching up even to her walls and suburb trenches;[3] that then the people, or the greater part, more than at other times, wholly taken up with the study of highest and most important matters to be reformed, should be disputing, reasoning, reading, inventing, discoursing, even to a rarity and admiration,[4] things not before discoursed or written of, argues first a singular goodwill, contentedness and confidence in your prudent foresight and safe government, Lords and Commons; and from thence derives itself to a gallant bravery and well-grounded contempt of their enemies, as if there were no small number of as great spirits among us, as his was, who when Rome was nigh besieged[5] by Hannibal, being in the city, bought that piece of ground at no cheap rate, whereon Hannibal himself encamped his own regiment.

Next, it is a lively and cheerful presage of our happy success and victory. For as in a body, when the blood is fresh, the spirits pure and vigorous, not only to vital but to rational faculties, and those in the acutest and the pertest[6] operations of wit and subtlety, it argues in what good plight and constitution the body is; so when the cheerfulness of the people is so sprightly up, as that it has not only wherewith to guard well its own freedom and safety, but to spare, and to bestow upon the solidèst and sublimest points of controversy and new invention, it betokens us not degenerated, nor drooping to a fatal decay, but casting off the old and wrinkled skin of corruption to outlive these pangs and wax young again, entering the glorious ways of truth and prosperous virtue, destined to become great and honourable in these latter ages. Methinks I see in my mind a noble and

---

1 Moses, all prophets, Joshua] Numbers xi. 27–9.
2 maniples] military units of 120–200 men in the Roman army.
3 suburb trenches] London was threatened in November 1642 (see *Sonnet* VIII, headnote), and the following summer thousands of Londoners dug a twelve-mile circuit of trenches through the suburbs; the victory of the Royalist forces at Lostwithiel on 2 September 1644 had placed Charles in a position to attack London.
4 to ... admiration] to an exceptional and astonishing degree.
5 besieged] in 211 BC; the story is in Livy XXVI 11.
6 pertest] liveliest.

puissant nation rousing herself like a strong man[1] after sleep, and shaking her invincible locks; methinks I see her as an eagle mewing[2] her mighty youth, and kindling her undazzled eyes at the full midday beam; purging and unscaling her long-abused sight at the fountain itself of heavenly radiance; while the whole noise of timorous and flocking birds, with those also that love the twilight, flutter about, amazed at what she means, and in their envious gabble would prognosticate[3] a year of sects and schisms.

What should ye do then? Should ye suppress all this flowery crop of knowledge and new light sprung up and yet springing daily in this city? Should ye set an oligarchy of twenty engrossers over it, to bring a famine upon our minds again, when we shall know nothing but what is measured to us by their bushel? Believe it, Lords and Commons, they who counsel ye to such a suppressing do as good as bid ye suppress yourselves; and I will soon show how. If it be desired to know the immediate cause of all this free writing and free speaking, there cannot be assigned a truer than your own mild and free and humane government; it is the liberty, Lords and Commons, which your own valorous and happy counsels have purchased us, liberty which is the nurse of all great wits; this is that which hath rarefied and enlightened our spirits like the influence[4] of heaven; this is that which hath enfranchised, enlarged and lifted up our apprehensions degrees above themselves.

Ye cannot make us now less capable, less knowing, less eagerly pursuing of the truth, unless ye first make yourselves, that made us so, less the lovers, less the founders of our true liberty. We can grow ignorant again, brutish, formal and slavish, as ye found us; but you then must first become that which ye cannot be, oppressive, arbitrary and tyrannous, as they were from whom ye have freed us. That our hearts are now more capacious, our thoughts more erected to the search and expectation of greatest and exactest things, is the issue of your own virtue propagated in us; ye cannot suppress that, unless ye reinforce an abrogated and merciless law,[5] that fathers may dispatch at will their own children. And who shall then stick closest to ye, and excite others? Not he who takes up arms for coat and conduct,[6] and his four nobles[7] of Danegelt.[8] Although I dispraise not the defence of just

---

1 strong man] Samson (Judges xvi. 6-14).

2 mewing] renew through moulting.

3 prognosticate] would cause a prediction by the augurs (p. 580 n.10). who analysed the signs given by birds.

4 influence] astrological influence of the stars.

5 law] the *patria potestas*, in Roman law the power that a father exercised over his male descendants; in early law it included the right to inflict capital punishment.

6 coat and conduct] an illegal tax imposed by Charles in 1640 for clothing and paying the travelling expenses of new recruits.

7 nobles] noble: a coin worth 6s.8d.

8 Danegelt] originally a tax (exacted between 991 and 1016) to raise money for tribute exacted by the Danes, here used with reference to ship-money, the tax raised by Charles in 1634 and 1635 for the navy, and subsequently declared illegal by the Long Parliament.

immunities, yet love my peace better, if that were all. Give me the liberty to know, to utter, and to argue freely according to conscience, above all liberties.

What would be best advised, then, if it be found hurtful and so unequal[1] to suppress opinions for the newness or the unsuitableness to a customary acceptance, will not be my task to say. I only shall repeat what I have learned from one of your own honourable number, a right noble and pious lord, who, had he not sacrificed his life and fortunes to the church and commonwealth, we had not now missed and bewailed a worthy and undoubted patron of this argument. Ye know him. I am sure; yet I for honour's sake, and may it be eternal to him, shall name him, the Lord Brooke.[2] He writing of episcopacy and by the way treating of sects and schisms, left ye his vote, or rather now the last words of his dying charge, which I know will ever be of dear and honoured regard with ye, so full of meekness and breathing charity, that next to his[3] last testament, who bequeathed love and peace to his disciples, I cannot call to mind where I have read or heard words more mild and peaceful. He there exhorts us to hear with patience and humility those, however they be miscalled, that desire to live purely, in such a use of God's ordinances, as the best guidance of their conscience gives them, and to tolerate them, though in some disconformity to ourselves. The book itself will tell us more at large, being published to the world, and dedicated to the Parliament by him who, both for his life and for his death, deserves that what advice he left be not laid by without perusal.

And now the time in special[4] is, by privilege to write and speak what may help to the further discussing of matters in agitation. The temple of Janus[5] with his two controversal faces might now not unsignificantly be set open. And though all the winds of doctrine were let loose to play upon the earth, so Truth be in the field, we do injuriously by licensing and prohibiting, to misdoubt her strength. Let her and Falsehood grapple; who ever knew Truth put to the worse, in a free and open encounter? Her confuting is the best and surest suppressing. He who hears what praying there is for light and clearer knowledge to be sent down among us, would think of other matters to be constituted beyond the discipline of Geneva,[6] framed and fabricked already to our hands. Yet when the new light which we beg for shines in upon us, there be who envy and oppose, if it come not first in at their

1 unequal] unjust.
2 Brooke] The Parliamentary general Robert Greville, second Lord Brooke, had been killed in the attack on Lichfield Cathedral in March 1643. Milton refers to the conclusion of Brooke's *Discourse Opening the Nature of that Episcopacy which is Exercised in England* (1641).
3 his] Jesus' (John xiv. 21, 27).
4 in special] especially fitting (because Parliament and the Westminster Assembly were in session, and the country at war).
5 Janus] the Roman god of doorways; his two heads faced in opposite directions ('controversal' is Milton's coinage, punning on 'controversial'). The temple of Janus, a gate in the Forum in Rome, was open during war and closed during peace (Livy I 19).
6 discipline of Geneva] Presbyterianism.

casements. What a collusion is this, whenas we are exhorted by the wise man[1] to use diligence, to seek for wisdom as for hidden treasures early and late, that another order shall enjoin us to know nothing but by statute? When a man hath been labouring the hardest labour in the deep mines of knowledge, hath furnished out his findings in all their equipage, drawn forth his reasons as it were a battle[2] ranged, scattered and defeated all objections in his way, calls out his adversary into the plain, offers him the advantage of wind and sun, if he please, only that he may try the matter by dint of argument: for his opponents then to skulk, to lay ambushments, to keep a narrow bridge of licensing where the challenger should pass, though it be valour enough in soldiership, is but weakness and cowardice in the wars of Truth.

For who knows not that Truth is strong, next to the Almighty? She needs no policies, nor stratagems, nor licensings to make her victorious; those are the shifts and the defences that error uses against her power: give her but room, and do not bind her when she sleeps, for then she speaks not true, as the old Proteus[3] did, who spake oracles only when he was caught and bound, but then rather she turns herself into all shapes, except her own, and perhaps tunes her voice according to the time, as Micaiah did before Ahab,[4] until she be adjured into her own likeness. Yet it is not impossible that she may have more shapes than one. What else is all that rank of things indifferent,[5] wherein Truth may be on this side or on the other, without being unlike herself? What but a vain shadow else is the abolition of those ordinances, that handwriting nailed to the cross?[6] What great purchase is this Christian liberty which Paul so often boasts of? His doctrine is, that he who eats or eats not, regards a day or regards it not, may do either to the Lord. How many other things might be tolerated in peace, and left to conscience, had we but charity, and were it not the chief stronghold of our hypocrisy to be ever judging one another?

I fear yet this iron yoke of outward conformity hath left a slavish print upon our necks; the ghost of a linen decency[7] yet haunts us. We stumble and are impatient at the least dividing of one visible congregation from another, though it be not in fundamentals; and through our forwardness to suppress, and our backwardness to recover any enthralled piece of truth out of the grip of custom, we care not to keep truth separated from truth, which is the fiercest rent and disunion of all. We do not see that while we still affect by all means a rigid external formality, we may as soon fall again into a gross

1 wise man] Solomon (Proverbs ii. 4-5).   2 battle] army.
3 Proteus] sea-god who tended Poseidon's seals and was able to assume any shape to avoid prophesying, but if held would answer questions (*Odyssey* IV 385-93, imitated by Virgil, *Georgics* IV 387-452).
4 as . . . Ahab] I Kings xxii. 1-37.
5 things indifferent] translates the technical theological term *adiaphora*, which included doctrines not essential for salvation and various rites and practices.
6 ordinances . . . cross] Col. ii. 14.
7 linen decency] The vestiarian controversy of the previous century had re-emerged as part of the dispute about church-government; Laud enforced, in the name of 'decency', the use of the surplice; Puritans favoured the black 'Geneva gown'.

conforming stupidity, a stark and dead congealment of wood and hay and stubble,[1] forced and frozen together, which is more to the sudden degenerating of a church than many subdichotomies of petty schisms.

Not that I can think well of every light separation, or that all in a church is to be expected gold and silver and precious stones:[2] it is not possible for man to sever the wheat from the tares,[3] the good fish from the other fry; that must be the angels' ministry at the end of mortal things. Yet if all cannot be of one mind – as who looks they should be? – this doubtless is more wholesome, more prudent, and more Christian that many be tolerated, rather than all compelled. I mean not tolerated popery, and open superstition, which, as it extirpates all religions and civil supremacies, so itself should be extirpate, provided first that all charitable and compassionate means be used to win and regain the weak and the misled; that also which is impious or evil absolutely, either against faith or manners,[4] no law can possibly permit, that intends not to unlaw itself, but those neighbouring differences, or rather indifferences, are what I speak of, whether in some point of doctrine or of discipline, which, though they may be many, yet need not interrupt the unity of spirit, if we could but find among us the bond of peace.

In the meantime if any one would write, and bring his helpful hand to the slow-moving reformation which we labour under, if Truth have spoken to him before others, or but seemed at least to speak, who hath so bejesuited us that we should trouble that man with asking licence to do so worthy a deed? And not consider this, that if it come to prohibiting, there is not aught more likely to be prohibited than truth itself; whose first appearance to our eyes, bleared and dimmed with prejudice and custom, is more unsightly and unplausible than many errors, even as the person is of many a great man slight and contemptible to see to. And what do they tell us vainly of new opinions, when this very opinion of theirs, that none must be heard, but whom they like, is the worst and newest opinion of all others; and is the chief cause why sects and schisms do so much abound, and true knowledge is kept at distance from us; besides yet a greater danger which is in it.

For when God shakes a kingdom with strong and healthful commotions to a general reforming, 'tis not untrue that many sectaries and false teachers are then busiest in seducing; but yet more true it is, that God then raises to his own work men of rare abilities, and more than common industry, not only to look back, and revise what hath been taught heretofore, but to gain further and go on some new enlightened steps in the discovery of truth. For such is the order of God's enlightening his church, to dispense and deal out by degrees his beam, so as our earthly eyes may best sustain it.

Neither is God appointed and confined, where and out of what place these his chosen shall be first heard to speak; for he sees not as man sees, chooses not as man chooses, lest we should devote ourselves

1 wood ... stubble] I Cor. iii. 10-13. 2 gold ... stones] I Cor. iii. 10-13.
3 sever ... tares] Matt. xiii. 24-30, 36-43. 4 manners] moral conduct.

again to set places, and assemblies, and outward callings of men; planting our faith one while in the old Convocation house, and another while in the Chapel at Westminster[1] when all the faith and religion that shall be there canonized[2] is not sufficient without plain convincement, and the charity of patient instruction, to supple the least bruise of conscience, to edify the meanest Christian who desires to walk in the spirit, and not in the letter of human trust, for all the number of voices that can be there made; no, though Harry VII himself there, with all his liege tombs about him, should lend them voices from the dead, to swell their number.

And if the men be erroneous who appear to be the leading schismatics, what withholds us but our sloth, our self-will, and distrust in the right cause, that we do not give them gentle meeting and gentle dismissions, that we debate not and examine the matter thoroughly with liberal and frequent audience; if not for their sakes, yet for our own? Seeing no man who hath tasted learning, but will confess the many ways of profiting by those who, not contented with stale receipts, are able to manage, and set forth new positions to the world. And were they but as the dust and cinders of our feet, so long as in that notion they may yet serve to polish and brighten the armoury of Truth, even for that respect they were not utterly to be cast away. But if they be of those whom God hath fitted for the special use of these times with eminent and ample gifts, and those perhaps neither among the priests nor among the Pharisees, and we in the haste of a precipitant zeal shall make no distinction, but resolve to stop their mouths, because we fear they come with new and dangerous opinions, as we commonly forejudge them ere we understand them, no less than woe to us, while, thinking thus to defend the Gospel, we are found the persecutors.

There have been not a few since the beginning of this Parliament, both of the Presbytery and others, who by their unlicensed books, to the contempt of an *Imprimatur*, first broke that triple ice clung about our hearts, and taught the people to see day; I hope that none of those were the persuaders to renew upon us this bondage which they themselves have wrought so much good by contemning. But if neither the check that Moses gave to young Joshua,[3] nor the countermand[4] which our Saviour gave to young John, who was so ready to prohibit those whom he thought unlicensed, be not enough to admonish our

---

1] old ... Westminster] the Convocations of Canterbury and York are the provincial assemblies of the Church of England; the 'old' Convocation house of the province of Canterbury was the chapter-house in Westminster Abbey; the Long Parliament transferred the powers of Convocation to the Westminster Assembly, which met in the Chapel of Henry VII ('Harry VII'), also in Westminster Abbey.

2 shall ... canonized] the Assembly was expected to produce a Confession of Faith, a Directory of Worship, a Catechism and a 'Frame of Discipline or Church-Government'.

3 Moses, Joshua] See p. 611.

4 countermand] Luke ix. 49–50; the youth of John is an inference from the fact that he survived until the reign of Trajan, which started in AD 98 (Eusebius III 23).

elders how unacceptable to God their testy mood of prohibiting is, if neither their own remembrance what evil hath abounded in the church by this let of licensing, and what good they themselves have begun by transgressing it, be not enough, but they will persuade and execute the most Dominican[1] part of the Inquisition over us, and are already with one foot in the stirrup so active at suppressing, it would be no unequal distribution in the first place to suppress the suppressors themselves; whom the change of their condition hath puffed up, more than their late experience of harder times hath made wise.

And as for regulating the press, let no man think to have the honour of advising ye better than yourselves have done in that Order[2] published next before this, 'that no book be printed, unless the printer's and the author's name, or at least the printer's, be registered.' Those which otherwise come forth, if they be found mischievous and libellous, the fire and the executioner,[3] will be the timeliest and the most effectual remedy that man's prevention can use. For this authentic Spanish policy of licensing books, if I have said aught, will prove the most unlicensed book itself within a short while; and was the immediate image of Star Chamber decree[4] to that purpose made in those very times when that Court did the rest of those her pious works, for which she is now fallen[5] from the stars with Lucifer. Whereby ye may guess what kind of state prudence, what love of the people, what care of religion or good manners there was at the contriving, although with singular hypocrisy it pretended to bind books to their good behaviour. And how it got the upper hand of your precedent Order so well constituted before, if we may believe those men whose profession gives them cause to inquire most, it may be doubted there was in it the fraud of some old patentees and monopolizers in the trade of bookselling; who under pretence of the poor in their Company not to be defrauded, and the just retaining of each man his several copy, which God forbid should be gainsaid, brought divers glosing colours to the House, which were indeed but colours, and serving to no end except it be to exercise a superiority over their neighbours; men who do not therefore labour in an honest profession to which learning is indebted, that they should be made other men's vassals. Another end is thought was aimed at by some of them in procuring by petition[6] this Order, that, having power in their hands, malignant books might the easier scape abroad, as the event shows.

1 Dominican] The Dominican friar Tomás de Torquemada presided as Grand Inquisitor over the most savage period of the Spanish Inquisition; under his administration 2,000 heretics were burnt and 17,000 mutilated.
2 Order] Milton quotes from the Order of 29 January 1642.
3 executioner] the official who executed the orders to burn books and mutilate authors and printers.
4 decree] *A Decree of Star Chamber, Concerning Printing*; see Introduction p. xxiii.
5 now fallen] The Court of Star Chamber had been abolished on 5 July 1641; on Lucifer see Isaiah xiv. 12.
6 petition] In April 1643 the Stationers' Company had petitioned Parliament to reinstate the restrictions on publishing that had disappeared with the Star Chamber.

But of these sophisms and elenchs[1] of merchandise I skill not. This I know, that errors in a good government and in a bad are equally almost incident; for what magistrate may not be misinformed, and much the sooner, if liberty of printing be reduced into the power of a few? But to redress willingly and speedily what hath been erred, and in highest authority to esteem a plain advertisement more than others have done a sumptuous bribe, is a virtue (honoured Lords and Commons) answerable to your highest actions, and whereof none can participate but greatest and wisest men.

1 sophisms and elenchs] misleading arguments and false defences.

THE LICENSING ORDER OF
14 JUNE 1643

An Order of the Lords and Commons Assembled in Parliament

Whereas divers good orders have been lately made by both Houses of Parliament, for suppressing the great late abuses and frequent disorders in printing many false, forged, scandalous, seditious, libellous and unlicensed papers, pamphlets, and books, to the great defamation of religion and government – which orders (notwithstanding the diligence of the Company of Stationers to put them in full execution) have taken little or no effect, by reason the bill in preparation, for redress of the said disorders, hath hitherto been retarded through the present distractions, and very many, as well Stationers and Printers, as others of sundry other professions not free of the Stationers' Company, have taken upon them to set up sundry private printing presses in corners, and to print, vend, publish and disperse books, pamphlets and papers, in such multitudes, that no industry could be sufficient to discover or bring to punishment all the several abounding delinquents; and by reason that divers of the Stationers' Company and others being delinquents (contrary to former orders and the constant custom used among the said Company) have taken liberty to print, vend and publish the most profitable vendible copies of books, belonging to the Company and other Stationers, especially of such agents as are employed in putting the said orders in execution, and that by way of revenge for giving information against them to the Houses for their delinquences in printing, to the great prejudice of the said Company of Stationers and Agents, and to their discouragement in this public service.

It is therefore ordered by the Lords and Commons in Parliament that no order or declaration of both, or either House of Parliament shall be printed by any, but by order of one or both the said Houses; nor other book, pamphlet, paper, nor part of any such book, pamphlet, or paper, shall from henceforth be printed, bound, stitched or put to sale by any person or persons whatsoever, unless the same be first approved of and licensed under the hands of such person or persons as both or either of the said Houses shall appoint for the licensing of the same, and entered in the register book of the Company of Stationers, according to ancient custom, and the printer thereof to put his name thereto. And that no person or persons shall hereafter print, or cause to be reprinted any book or books, or part of book of books heretofore allowed of and granted to the said Company of Stationers for their relief and maintenance of their poor, without the licence or consent of the master, wardens and assistants of the said Company; nor any book or books lawfully licensed and entered in the register of the said Company for any particular member thereof, without the licence and consent of the owner or owners thereof; not yet import any such book or books, or part of book or books formerly printed here, from beyond the seas, upon pain of forfeiting the same to the owner or owners of the copies of the said books, and such further punishment as shall be thought fit.

And the master and wardens of the said Company, the gentleman-usher of the House of Peers, the sergeant of the Commons' House and their deputies, together with the persons formerly appointed by the Committee of the House of Commons for Examinations, are hereby authorized and required, from time to time, to make diligent search in all places where they shall think meet for all unlicensed printing presses, and all presses any way employed in the printing of scandalous or unlicensed papers, pamphlets, books, or any copies of books belonging to the said Company, or any member thereof, without their approbation and consents, and to seize and carry away such printing presses' letters, together with the nut, spindle, and other materials of every such irregular printer, which they find so misemployed, unto the common hall of the said Company, there to be defaced and made unserviceable according to ancient custom; and likewise to make diligent search in all suspected printing-houses, warehouses, shops and other places for such scandalous and unlicensed books, papers, pamphlets and all other books, not entered, nor signed with the printer's name as aforesaid, being printed or reprinted by such as have no lawful interest in them, or any way contrary to this Order, and the same to seize and carry away to the said common hall, there to remain till both or either House of Parliament shall dispose thereof; and likewise to apprehend all authors, printers, and other persons whatsoever employed in compiling, printing, stitching, binding, publishing and dispersing of the said scandalous, unlicensed, and unwarrantable papers, books and pamphlets as aforesaid, and all those who shall resist the said parties in searching after them, and to bring them afore either of the Houses or the Committee of Examinations, that so they may receive such further punishments as their offences shall demerit, and not to be released until they have given satisfaction to the parties employed in their apprehension for their pains and charges, and given sufficient caution not to offend in like sort for the future. And all justices of the peace, captains, constables and other officers, are hereby ordered and required to be aiding and assisting to the foresaid persons in the due execution of all and singular the premises, and in the apprehension of all offenders against the same; and in case of opposition to break open doors and locks.

And it is further ordered that this Order be forthwith printed and published, to the end that notice may be taken thereof, and all contemners of it left inexcusable.

FINIS

ABOUT THE EDITOR

GORDON CAMPBELL is Reader in English at the University of Leicester and author of many essays on Renaissance topics in a variety of learned journals. He is the editor of the journal *Renaissance Studies* and *The Year's Work in English Studies*.

This book is set in Old Style. Throughout the first half of
the nineteenth century, modern typefaces were pre-
dominant in all areas of publishing. In 1852, how-
ever, Miller and Richard, who had been in the
forefront of modern face production, set a
new trend when they issued specimens
of a regularized old face which was
named Old Style. Types of this
kind became popular in
the second half of
the nineteenth
century.